Jesse Liberty

SAMS Teach Yourself

C++

in 21 Days

FOURTH EDITION

SAMS

201 West 103rd St., Indianapolis, Indiana, 46290 USA

Sams Teach Yourself C++ in 21 Days, Fourth Edition

Copyright © 2001 by Sams Publishing

International Standard Book Number: 0-672-32072-X

Library of Congress Catalog Card Number: 00-108507

Printed in the United States of America

First Printing: March 2001

04   03   02   01   4   3

Trademarks

Warning and Disclaimer

EXECUTIVE EDITOR
Michael Stephens

ACQUISITIONS EDITOR
Carol Ackerman

DEVELOPMENT EDITOR
Howard Lee Harkness

MANAGING EDITOR
Matt Purcell

PROJECT EDITOR
George E. Nedeff

COPY EDITOR
Kim Cofer

INDEXER
Erika Millen

PROOFREADERS
Benjamin Berg
Candice Hightower

TECHNICAL EDITORS
Howard Lee Harkness
Brett Hall

TEAM COORDINATOR
Vicki Harding

INTERIOR DESIGNER
Gary Adair

COVER DESIGNER
Aren Howell

PAGE LAYOUT
Ayanna Lacey
Heather Hiatt Miller
Stacey Richwine-DeRome

Contents at a Glance

Contents

About the Author

Jesse Liberty is the author of a dozen books on C++, C# and object-oriented analysis and design. He is president of Liberty Associates, Inc. (`http://www.LibertyAssociates.com`), where he provides .net development, contract programming, mentoring, consulting, and training.

Jesse was a distinguished software engineer at AT&T, a software architect for Xerox and LinkNet (PBS), and vice president of Citibank's Development Division. He lives with his wife, Stacey, and his daughters, Robin and Rachel, in the suburbs of Cambridge, Massachusetts. He supports his books on his Web site at `http://www.libertyassociates.com`—click on Books and Resources.

Dedication

This book is dedicated to the living memory of David Levine.

Acknowledgments

A fourth edition is another chance to acknowledge and to thank those folks without whose support and help this book literally would have been impossible. First among them remain Stacey, Robin, and Rachel Liberty.

I must also thank my editors at Sams for being professionals of the highest quality; and I must especially acknowledge and thank Carol Ackerman, George Nedeff, Kim Cofer, Erika Millen, Howard Lee Harkness, Benjamin Berg, and Candice Hightower.

I would like to acknowledge the folks who taught me how to program: Skip Gilbrech and David McCune, and those who taught me C++, including Stephen Zagieboylo. I would like to thank the many readers who helped me find errors and typos in the earlier editions of this book.

Finally, I'd like to thank Mrs. Kalish, who taught my sixth-grade class how to do binary arithmetic in 1965, when neither she nor we knew why.

Tell Us What You Think!

As the reader of this book, *you* are our most important critic and commentator. We value your opinion and want to know what we're doing right, what we could do better, what areas you'd like to see us publish in, and any other words of wisdom you're willing to pass our way.

I welcome your comments. You can fax, e-mail, or write me directly to let me know what you did or didn't like about this book—as well as what we can do to make our books stronger.

Please note that I cannot help you with technical problems related to the topic of this book, and that due to the high volume of mail I receive, I might not be able to reply to every message. You'll find support for this book at `http://www.LibertyAssociates.com`*.*

When you write, please be sure to include this book's title and author as well as your name and phone or fax number. I will carefully review your comments and share them with the author and editors who worked on the book.

Fax: 317-581-4770

E-mail: `Feedback@samspublishing.com`

Mail: Michael Stephens
           Sams Publishing
           201 West 103rd Street
           Indianapolis, IN 46290 USA

Introduction

This book is designed to help you teach yourself how to program with C++. While no one can learn a serious programming language in just three weeks, this book will introduce you to the major concepts of the C++ language. Each of the lessons in this book has been designed so that you can complete it in a single day.

In just 21 chapters, you'll learn about such fundamentals as managing input and output, loops and arrays, object-oriented programming, templates, and creating C++ applications—all in well-structured and easy-to-follow lessons. Lessons provide sample listings—complete with sample output and an analysis of the code—to illustrate the topics of the day.

To help you become more proficient, each lesson ends with a set of common questions and answers, exercises, and a quiz. You can check your progress by examining the quiz and exercise answers provided in Appendix D, "Answers."

Who Should Read This Book

You don't need any previous experience in programming to learn C++ with this book. This book starts from the beginning and teaches you both the language and the concepts involved with programming C++. You'll find the numerous examples of syntax and detailed analysis of code an excellent guide as you begin your journey into C++ programming. Whether you are just beginning or already have some experience programming, you will find that this book's clear organization makes learning C++ fast and easy.

Conventions

Note

These boxes highlight information that can make your C++ programming more efficient and effective.

FAQ

What do FAQs do?

Answer: These Frequently Asked Questions provide greater insight into the use of the language and clarify potential areas of confusion.

Caution   These boxes focus your attention on problems or side effects that can occur in specific situations.

These boxes provide clear definitions of essential terms.

Do	**Don't**
DO use the "Do/Don't" boxes to find a quick summary of a fundamental principle in a lesson.	**DON'T** overlook the useful information offered in these boxes.

This book uses various typefaces to help you distinguish C++ code from regular English. Actual C++ code is typeset in a special monospace font. Placeholders—words or characters temporarily used to represent the real words or characters you would type in code—are typeset in *italic monospace*. New or important terms are typeset in *italic*.

In the listings in this book, each real code line is numbered. If you see an unnumbered line in a listing, you'll know that the unnumbered line is really a continuation of the preceding numbered code line (some code lines are too long for the width of the book). In this case, you should type the two lines as one; do not divide them.

WEEK 1

At a Glance

As you prepare for your first week of learning how to program in C++, you will need a few things: a compiler, an editor, and this book. If you don't have a C++ compiler and an editor, you can still use this book, but you won't get as much out of it as you would if you were to do the exercises.

The best way to learn to program is by writing programs! At the end of each day you will find a workshop containing a quiz and some exercises. Be sure to take the time to answer all the questions, and to evaluate your work as objectively as you can. The later chapters build on the lessons in the earlier chapters, so be sure you fully understand the material before moving on.

A Note to C Programmers

The material in the first five days will be familiar to you. Be sure to skim the material and to do the exercises, to make sure you are fully up to speed before going on to Day 6, "Object-Oriented Programming."

Where You Are Going

The first week covers the material you need to get started with programming in general, and with C++ in particular. On Day 1, "Getting Started," and Day 2, "The Anatomy of a C++ Program," you will be introduced to the basic concepts of programming and program flow. On Day 3, "Variables and Constants," you will learn about variables and constants and how to use data in your programs. On Day 4, "Expressions and Statements," you will learn how programs branch based

1

2

3

4

5

6

7

on the data provided and the conditions encountered when the program is running. On Day 5, "Functions," you will learn what functions are and how to use them, and on Day 6 you will learn about classes and objects. Day 7, "More Program Flow," teaches more about program flow, and by the end of the first week you will be writing real object-oriented programs.

DAY 1

Getting Started

Introduction

Welcome to *Sams Teach Yourself C++ in 21 Days*! Today you will get started on your way to becoming a proficient C++ programmer.

Today you will learn

- Why C++ is the emerging standard in software development.
- The steps to develop a C++ program.
- How to enter, compile, and link your first working C++ program.

A Brief History of C++

Computer languages have undergone dramatic evolution since the first electronic computers were built to assist in artillery trajectory calculations during World War II. Early on, programmers worked with the most primitive computer instructions: machine language. These instructions were represented by long strings of ones and zeros. Soon, assemblers were invented to map machine instructions to human-readable and -manageable mnemonics, such as ADD and MOV.

In time, higher-level languages evolved, such as BASIC and COBOL. These languages let people work with something approximating words and sentences, such as Let I = 100. These instructions were translated back into machine language by interpreters and compilers.

An interpreter translates a program as it reads it, turning the program instructions, or code, directly into actions. A compiler translates the code into an intermediary form. This step is called compiling, and it produces an object file. The compiler then invokes a linker, which turns the object file into an executable program.

Because interpreters read the code as it is written and execute the code on the spot, interpreters are easy for the programmer to work with. Today, most interpreted programs are referred to as scripts, and the interpreter itself is often called a Script Engine.

Some languages, such as Visual Basic, call the interpreter the runtime library. Java calls its runtime interpreter a Virtual Machine (VM), but in this case the VM is provided by the browser (such as Internet Explorer or Netscape).

Compilers introduce the extra steps of compiling the source code (which is readable by humans) into object code (which is readable by machines). This extra step is inconvenient, but compiled programs run very fast because the time-consuming task of translating the source code into machine language is done once (at compile time) and is not required when you execute the program.

Another advantage of many compiled languages such as C++ is that you can distribute the executable program to people who don't have the compiler. With an interpreted language, you must have the interpreter to run the program.

For many years, the principal goal of computer programmers was to write short pieces of code that would execute quickly. The program needed to be small because memory was expensive, and it needed to be fast because processing power was also expensive. As computers have become smaller, cheaper, and faster, and as the cost of memory has fallen, these priorities have changed. Today the cost of a programmer's time far outweighs the cost of most of the computers in use by businesses. Well-written, easy-to-maintain code is at a premium. Easy to maintain means that as business requirements change, the program can be extended and enhanced without great expense.

Note

The word program is used in two ways: to describe individual instructions (or source code) created by the programmer, and to describe an entire piece of executable software. This distinction can cause enormous confusion, so we will try to distinguish between the source code on one hand, and the executable on the other.

Solving Problems

The problems programmers are asked to solve today are totally different from the problems we were solving twenty years ago. In the 1980s, programs were created to manage large amounts of raw data. The people writing the code and the people using the program were all computer professionals. Today, computers are in use by far more people, and most know very little about how computers and programs work. Computers are tools used by people who are more interested in solving their business problems than struggling with the computer.

Ironically, as we make our programs easier for this new audience to use, we make the programs themselves far more sophisticated and complex. Gone are the days when users typed in cryptic commands at esoteric prompts, only to see a stream of raw data. Today's programs use sophisticated "user-friendly interfaces" involving multiple windows, menus, dialog boxes, and the myriad metaphors with which we've all become familiar.

With the development of the Web, computers have entered a new era of market penetration; more people are using computers than ever before, and their expectations are very high. In the few years since the first edition of this book, programs have become larger and more complex, and the need for programming techniques to help manage this complexity has become manifest.

As programming requirements have changed, both languages and the techniques used for writing programs have evolved. Although the complete history is fascinating, this book will focus on the transformation from procedural programming to object-oriented programming.

Procedural, Structured, and Object-Oriented Programming

Until recently, programs were thought of as a series of procedures that acted upon data. A procedure, or function, is a set of specific instructions executed one after the other. The data was quite separate from the procedures, and the trick in programming was to keep track of which functions called which other functions, and what data was changed. To make sense of this potentially confusing situation, structured programming was created.

The principal idea behind structured programming is as simple as the idea of divide and conquer. A computer program can be thought of as consisting of a set of tasks. Any task that is too complex to be described simply is broken down into a set of smaller component tasks, until the tasks are sufficiently small and self-contained enough that they are easily understood.

As an example, computing the average salary of every employee of a company is a rather complex task. You can, however, break it down into the following subtasks:

1. Find out what each person earns.
2. Count how many people you have.
3. Total all the salaries.
4. Divide the total by the number of people you have.

Totaling the salaries can be broken down into the following steps:

1. Get each employee's record.
2. Access the salary.
3. Add the salary to the running total.
4. Get the next employee's record.

In turn, obtaining each employee's record can be broken down into the following:

1. Open the file of employees.
2. Go to the correct record.
3. Read the data from disk.

Structured programming remains an enormously successful approach for dealing with complex problems. By the late 1980s, however, some of the deficiencies of structured programming had become all too clear.

First, a natural desire is to think of data (employee records, for example) and what you can do with that data (sort, edit, and so on) as a single idea. Unfortunately, structured programs separate data structures from the functions that manipulate them, and there is no natural way to link data with functions in structured programming. Structured programming is often called procedural programming because of its focus on procedures (rather than on "objects").

Second, programmers found themselves constantly reinventing new solutions to old problems. This is often called "reinventing the wheel," which is the opposite of reusability. The idea behind reusability is to build components that have known properties, and then to be able to plug them into your program as you need them. This is modeled after the hardware world—when an engineer needs a new transistor, she doesn't usually invent one, she goes to the big bin of transistors and finds one that works the way she needs it to, or perhaps modifies it. No similar option existed for a software engineer.

Object-oriented programming attempts to respond to these programming requirements, providing techniques for managing enormous complexity, achieving reuse of software components, and coupling data with the tasks that manipulate that data.

The essence of object-oriented programming is to model "objects" (that is, things) rather than "data." The objects you model might be onscreen widgets such as buttons and list boxes, or they might be real-world objects such as bicycles, airplanes, cats, and water.

Objects have characteristics (fast, spacious, black, wet) and they have capabilities (accelerate, fly, purr, bubble). It is the job of object-oriented programming to represent these objects in the programming language.

C++ and Object-Oriented Programming

C++ fully supports object-oriented programming, including the three pillars of object-oriented development: encapsulation, inheritance, and polymorphism.

Encapsulation

When an engineer needs to add a resistor to the device she is creating, she doesn't typically build a new one from scratch. She walks over to a bin of resistors, examines the colored bands that indicate the properties, and picks the one she needs. The resistor is a "black box" as far as the engineer is concerned—she doesn't much care how it does its work, as long as it conforms to her specifications. She doesn't need to look inside the box to use it in her design.

The property of being a self-contained unit is called encapsulation. With encapsulation, we can accomplish data hiding. Data hiding is the highly valued characteristic that an object can be used without the user knowing or caring how it works internally. Just as you can use a refrigerator without knowing how the compressor works, you can use a well-designed object without knowing about its internal data members.

Similarly, when the engineer uses the resistor, she need not know anything about the internal state of the resistor. All the properties of the resistor are encapsulated in the resistor object; they are not spread out through the circuitry. It is not necessary to understand how the resistor works to use it effectively. Its data is hidden inside the resistor's casing.

C++ supports encapsulation through the creation of user-defined types, called classes. You'll see how to create classes on Day 6, "Object-Oriented Programming." Once created, a well-defined class acts as a fully encapsulated entity—it is used as a whole unit. The actual inner workings of the class should be hidden. Users of a well-defined class do not need to know how the class works; they just need to know how to use it.

Inheritance and Reuse

When the engineers at Acme Motors want to build a new car, they have two choices: They can start from scratch, or they can modify an existing model. Perhaps their Star model is nearly perfect, but they'd like to add a turbocharger and a six-speed transmission. The chief engineer would prefer not to start from the ground up, but rather to say, "Let's build another Star, but let's add these additional capabilities. We'll call the new model a Quasar." A Quasar is a kind of Star, but a specialized one with new features. (According to NASA, quasars are extremely luminous bodies that emit an astonishing amount of energy.)

C++ supports inheritance. A new type, which is an extension of an existing type, can be declared. This new subclass is said to derive from the existing type and is sometimes called a derived type. The Quasar is derived from the Star and thus inherits all its qualities, but can add to them or modify them as needed. Inheritance and its application in C++ are discussed on Day 12, "Inheritance," and Day 16, "Advanced Inheritance."

Polymorphism

The new Quasar might respond differently than a Star does when you press down on the accelerator. The Quasar might engage fuel injection and a turbocharger, whereas the Star would simply let gasoline into its carburetor. A user, however, does not have to know about these differences. He can just "floor it," and the right thing will happen, depending on which car he's driving.

C++ supports the idea that different objects do "the right thing" through what is called function polymorphism and class polymorphism. Poly means many, and morph means form. Polymorphism refers to the same name taking many forms, and it is discussed on Day 10, "Advanced Functions," and Day 14, "Polymorphism."

How C++ Evolved

As object-oriented analysis, design, and programming began to catch on, Bjarne Stroustrup took the most popular language for commercial software development, C, and extended it to provide the features needed to facilitate object-oriented programming.

Although it is true that C++ is a superset of C and that virtually any legal C program is a legal C++ program, the leap from C to C++ is very significant. C++ benefited from its relationship to C for many years because C programmers could ease into their use of C++. To really get the full benefit of C++, however, many programmers found they had to unlearn much of what they knew and learn a new way of conceptualizing and solving programming problems.

Should I Learn C First?

The question inevitably arises: "Because C++ is a superset of C, should you learn C first?" Stroustrup and most other C++ programmers agree that not only is it unnecessary to learn C first, it may be advantageous not to do so.

C programming is based on structured programming concepts; C++ is based on object-oriented programming. It is a mistake to learn C first because you'll only have to "unlearn" the bad habits of mind fostered by C.

This book does not assume you have any prior programming experience. If you are a C programmer, however, the first few chapters of this book will largely be review. Starting in Day 6, we begin the real work of object-oriented software development.

C++ and Java and C#

C++ is now the overwhelmingly predominant language for the development of commercial software. In recent years, Java has challenged that dominance, but the pendulum swings back, and many of the programmers who left C++ for Java have recently begun to return. In any case, the two languages are so similar that to learn one is to learn 90 percent of the other.

C# is a new language developed by Microsoft for its .Net platform. C# is essentially a subset of C++, and while the languages are different in a few important ways, learning C++ will provide 90 percent of what you need to know about C#. It will be many years before we know if C# will be a serious contender for programmer consideration; even if it is, the work you do on C++ will be an excellent investment.

The ANSI Standard

The Accredited Standards Committee, operating under the procedures of the American National Standards Institute (ANSI), has created an international standard for C++.

The C++ Standard is now also referred to as ISO (International Standards Organization) Standard, the NCITS (National Committee for Information Technology Standards) Standard, the X3 (the old name for NCITS) Standard, and the ANSI/ISO Standard. This book will continue to refer to ANSI standard code because that is the more commonly used term.

Note | ANSI is usually pronounced "antsy" with a silent "t."

The ANSI standard is an attempt to ensure that C++ is portable—ensuring, for example, that ANSI-standard–compliant code you write for Microsoft's compiler will compile without errors using a compiler from any other vendor. Further, because the code in this book is ANSI compliant, it should compile without errors on a Mac, a Windows box, or an Alpha.

For most students of C++, the ANSI standard will be invisible. The standard has been stable for a while, and all the major manufacturers support the ANSI standard. We have endeavored to ensure that all the code in this edition of this book is ANSI compliant.

Preparing to Program

C++, perhaps more than other languages, demands that the programmer design the program before writing it. Trivial problems, such as the ones discussed in the first few chapters of this book, don't require much design. Complex problems, however, such as the ones professional programmers are challenged with every day, do require design, and the more thorough the design, the more likely it is that the program will solve the problems it is designed to solve, on time and on budget. A good design also makes for a program that is relatively bug-free and easy to maintain. It has been estimated that fully 90 percent of the cost of software is the combined cost of debugging and maintenance. To the extent that good design can reduce those costs, it can have a significant impact on the bottom-line cost of the project.

The first question you need to ask when preparing to design any program is, "What is the problem I'm trying to solve?" Every program should have a clear, well-articulated goal, and you'll find that even the simplest programs in this book do so.

The second question every good programmer asks is, "Can this be accomplished without resorting to writing custom software?" Reusing an old program, using pen and paper, or buying software off the shelf is often a better solution to a problem than writing something new. The programmer who can offer these alternatives will never suffer from lack of work; finding less-expensive solutions to today's problems will always generate new opportunities later.

Assuming you understand the problem and it requires writing a new program, you are ready to begin your design.

The process of fully understanding the problem (analysis) and creating a solution (design) is the necessary foundation for writing a world-class commercial application.

Your Development Environment

This book makes the assumption that your compiler has a mode in which you can write directly to the screen, without worrying about a graphical environment, such as the ones in Windows or on the Macintosh. Look for an option such as *console* or *easy window* or check your compiler's documentation.

Your compiler may have its own built-in text editor, or you may be using a commercial text editor or word processor that can produce text files. The important thing is that whatever you write your program in, it must save simple, plain-text files, with no word processing commands embedded in the text. Examples of safe editors include Windows Notepad, the DOS Edit command, Brief, Epsilon, EMACS, and vi. Many commercial word processors, such as WordPerfect, Word, and dozens of others, also offer a method for saving simple text files.

The files you create with your editor are called source files, and for C++ they typically are named with the extension .cpp, .cp, or .c. In this book, we'll name all the source code files with the .cpp extension, but check your compiler for what it needs.

Note

> Most C++ compilers don't care what extension you give your source code, but if you don't specify otherwise, many will use .cpp by default. Be careful, however; some compilers treat .c files as C code and .cpp files as C++ code. Again, please check your documentation.

Do	Don't
DO use a simple text editor to create your source code, or use the built-in editor that comes with your compiler. **DO** save your files with the .c, .cp, or .cpp extension. **DO** check your documentation for specifics about your compiler and linker to ensure that you know how to compile and link your programs.	**DON'T** use a word processor that saves special formatting characters. If you do use a word processor, save the file as ASCII text.

Creating the Program

Although the source code in your file is somewhat cryptic, and anyone who doesn't know C++ will struggle to understand what it is for, it is still in what we call human-readable form. Your source code file is not a program and it can't be executed, or run, as a program can.

Creating an Object File with the Compiler

To turn your source code into a program, you use a compiler. How you invoke your compiler and how you tell it where to find your source code will vary from compiler to compiler; check your documentation.

After your source code is compiled, an object file is produced. This file is often named with the extension .obj. This is still not an executable program, however. To turn this into an executable program, you must run your linker.

Creating an Executable File with the Linker

C++ programs are typically created by linking one or more .obj files with one or more libraries. A library is a collection of linkable files that were supplied with your compiler, that you purchased separately, or that you created and compiled. All C++ compilers come with a library of useful functions (or procedures) and classes that you can include in your program. We'll be talking about functions and classes in great detail in the next few days.

The steps to create an executable file are

1. Create a source code file with a .cpp extension.
2. Compile the source code into a file with the .obj extension.
3. Link your .obj file with any needed libraries to produce an executable program.

The Development Cycle

If every program worked the first time you tried it, that would be the complete development cycle: Write the program, compile the source code, link the program, and run it. Unfortunately, almost every program, no matter how trivial, can and will have errors, or bugs. Some bugs will cause the compile to fail, some will cause the link to fail, and some will show up only when you run the program.

Whatever type of bug you find, you must fix it, and that involves editing your source code, recompiling and relinking, and then rerunning the program. This cycle is represented in Figure 1.1, which diagrams the steps in the development cycle.

FIGURE 1.1

The steps in the development of a C++ program.

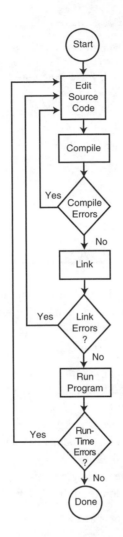

HELLO.cpp—Your First C++ Program

Traditional programming books begin by writing the words "Hello World" to the screen, or a variation on that statement. This time-honored tradition is carried on here.

Type the first program directly into your editor, exactly as shown. After you are certain it is correct, save the file, compile it, link it, and run it. It will print the words Hello World to your screen. Don't worry too much about how it works; this is really just to get you comfortable with the development cycle. Every aspect of this program will be covered over the next couple of days.

Warning

> The following listing contains line numbers on the left. These numbers are
> for reference within the book. They should not be typed into your editor.
> For example, in line 0 of Listing 1.1, you should enter:
>
> `#include <iostream>`

LISTING 1.1   HELLO.cpp, the Hello World Program

```
0:  #include <iostream>
1:
2:  int main()
3:  {
4:    std::cout << "Hello World!\n";
5:    return 0;
6:  }
```

Make certain you enter this exactly as shown. Pay careful attention to the punctuation.
The << in line 4 is the redirection symbol, produced on most keyboards by holding the
Shift key and pressing the comma key twice. Between the letters std and cout on line 4
are two colons (:). Lines 4 and 5 each end with semicolon (;).

Also check to make sure you are following your compiler directions properly. Most compilers will link automatically, but check your documentation. If you get errors, look over
your code carefully and determine how it is different from the above. If you see an error
on line 1, such as cannot find file iostream, check your compiler documentation for
directions on setting up your include path or environment variables. If you receive an
error that there is no prototype for main, add the line int main(); just before line 2. In
that case, you will need to add this line before the beginning of the main function in
every program in this book. Most compilers don't require this, but a few do.

Your finished program will look like this:

```
1: #include <iostream>
2: int main(); // most compilers don't need this line
3: int main()
4: {
5:     std::cout <<"Hello World!\n";
6:     return 0;
7: }
```

Note

It is difficult to read a program to yourself if you don't know how to pronounce the special characters and keywords. You read the first line "Pound include (some say hash-include, others say sharp-include) eye-oh-stream." You read line 5 "ess-tee-dee-see-out 'Hello World'"

Try running `HELLO.exe`; it should write

`Hello World!`

directly to your screen. If so, congratulations! You've just entered, compiled, and run your first C++ program. It may not look like much, but almost every professional C++ programmer started out with this exact program.

Using the Standard Libraries

If you have a very old compiler, the program shown above will not work—the new ANSI standard libraries will not be found. In that case, please change your program to look like this:

```
0:   #include <iostream.h>
1:
2:   int main()
3:   {
4:        cout << "Hello World!\n";
5:        return 0;
6:   }
```

Notice that the library name now ends in `.h` (dot-h) and that we no longer use `std::` in front of `cout` on line 4. This is the old, pre-ANSI style of header files. If your compiler works with this and not with the earlier version, then you have an antiquated compiler. Your compiler will be fine for the early chapters, but when we get to templates and exceptions, your compiler will not work.

Getting Started with Your Compiler

This book is *not* compiler specific. That means that the programs in this book should work with *any* ANSI-compliant C++ compiler on any platform (Windows, Mac, UNIX, Linux, and so on).

That said, the vast majority of programmers are working in the Windows environment, and the vast majority of professional programmers use the Microsoft compilers. I can't show you the details of compiling and linking with every possible compiler, but I can show you how to get started with Visual C++ 6, and that ought to be similar enough to whatever compiler you are using to be a good head start.

Compilers differ, however, so be sure to check your documentation.

Building the Hello World Project

To create and test the Hello World program, follow these steps:

1. Start the compiler.
2. Choose File, New from the menus.
3. Choose Win32 Console Application and enter a project name, such as Example 1, and click OK.
4. Choose An Empty Project from the menu of choices and click OK.
5. Choose File, New from the menus.
6. Choose C++ Source File and name it ex1.
7. Enter the code as indicated previously.
8. Choose Build, Build Example1.exe.
9. Check that you have no build errors.
10. Press Control+F5 to run the program.
11. Press the Spacebar to end the program.

FAQ

I can run the program but it flashes by so quickly I can't read it. What is wrong?

Answer: Check your compiler documentation; there ought to be a way to cause your program to pause after execution. With the Microsoft compilers the trick is to use Control+F5.

With Borland compilers, right-click in the editing window click on Target Expert, change the Platform to Win 3.1 (16), and then recompile/link/run the program. The output window will stay open until you close it.

Finally, with any compiler, you can add the following lines immediately before the return statement (that is, between lines 4 and 5 in Listing 1.1:

```
int x;
std::cin >> x;
```

This will cause the program to pause, waiting for you to enter a value. To end the program, enter a number (for example, 1) and then press Enter.

The meaning of std::cin and std::cout will be discussed in coming days; for now just use it as a magical incantation.

Compile Errors

Compile-time errors can occur for any number of reasons. Usually they are a result of a typo or other inadvertent minor error. Good compilers will not only tell you what you did wrong, they'll point you to the exact place in your code where you made the mistake. The great ones will even suggest a remedy!

You can see this by intentionally putting an error into your program. If HELLO.cpp ran smoothly, edit it now and remove the closing brace on line 7. Your program will now look like Listing 1.2.

LISTING 1.2   Demonstration of Compiler Error

```
0:  #include <iostream>
1:
2:  int main()
3:  {
4:    std::cout << "Hello World!\n";
5:    return 0;
```

Recompile your program and you should see an error that looks similar to the following:

`Hello.cpp(7) : fatal error C1004: unexpected end of file found`

This error tells you the file and line number of the problem and what the problem is (although I admit it is somewhat cryptic).

Sometimes the errors just get you to the general vicinity of the problem. If a compiler could perfectly identify every problem, it would fix the code itself.

Summary

After reading this chapter, you should have a good understanding of how C++ evolved and what problems it was designed to solve. You should feel confident that learning C++ is the right choice for anyone interested in programming in the next decade. C++ provides the tools of object-oriented programming and the performance of a systems-level language, which makes C++ the development language of choice.

Today you learned how to enter, compile, link, and run your first C++ program, and what the normal development cycle is. You also learned a little of what object-oriented programming is all about. You will return to these topics during the next three weeks.

Q&A

Q **What is the difference between a text editor and a word processor?**

A A text editor produces files with plain text in them. No formatting commands or other special symbols are required by a particular word processor. Text files do not have automatic word wrap, bold print, italic, and so forth.

Q **If my compiler has a built-in editor, must I use it?**

A Almost all compilers will compile code produced by any text editor. The advantages of using the built-in text editor, however, might include the capability to quickly move back and forth between the edit and compile steps of the development cycle. Sophisticated compilers include a fully integrated development environment, enabling the programmer to access help files, edit, and compile the code in place, and to resolve compile and link errors without ever leaving the environment.

Q **Can I ignore warning messages from my compiler?**

A Many books hedge on this one, but I'll stake myself to this position: No! Get into the habit, from day one, of treating warning messages as errors. C++ uses the compiler to warn you when you are doing something you may not intend. Heed those warnings and do what is required to make them go away.

Q **What is compile time?**

A Compile time is the time when you run your compiler, in contrast to link time (when you run the linker) or runtime (when running the program). This is just programmer shorthand to identify the three times when errors usually surface.

Workshop

The Workshop provides quiz questions to help you solidify your understanding of the material covered and exercises to provide you with experience in using what you've learned. Try to answer the quiz and exercise questions before checking the answers in Appendix D, and make sure you understand the answers before continuing to the next chapter.

Quiz

1. What is the difference between an interpreter and a compiler?
2. How do you compile the source code with your compiler?
3. What does the linker do?
4. What are the steps in the normal development cycle?

Exercises

1. Look at the following program and try to guess what it does without running it.

```
1: #include <iostream>
2: int main()
3: {
4:    int x = 5;
5:    int y = 7;
6:    std::cout << "\n";
7:    std::cout << x + y << " " << x * y;
8:    std::cout << "\n";
9:    return 0;
10:}
```

2. Type in the program from Exercise 1, and then compile and link it. What does it do? Does it do what you guessed?

3. Type in the following program and compile it. What error do you receive?

```
1: include <iostream>
2: int main()
3: {
4:     std::cout << "Hello World\n";
5:     return 0;
6: }
```

4. Fix the error in the program in Exercise 3 and recompile, link, and run it. What does it do?

DAY 2

The Anatomy of a C++ Program

C++ programs consist of objects, functions, variables, and other component parts. Most of this book is devoted to explaining these parts in depth, but to get a sense of how a program fits together, you must see a complete working program.

Today you will learn

- The parts of a C++ program.
- How the parts work together.
- What a function is and what it does.

A Simple Program

Even the simple program HELLO.cpp from Day 1, "Getting Started," had many interesting parts. This section will review this program in more detail. Listing 2.1 reproduces the original version of HELLO.cpp for your convenience.

LISTING 2.1   HELLO.cpp Demonstrates the Parts of a C++ Program

```
0:  #include <iostream>
1:
2:  int main()
3:  {
4:      std::cout << "Hello World!\n";
5:      return 0;
6:  }
```

OUTPUT   Hello World!

ANALYSIS   On line 0, the file iostream is included into the current file.

Here's how that works: The first character is the # symbol, which is a signal to the pre-processor. Each time you start your compiler, the preprocessor is run. The preprocessor reads through your source code, looking for lines that begin with the pound symbol (#) and acts on those lines before the compiler runs. The preprocessor is discussed in detail on Day 21, "What's Next."

The command include is a preprocessor instruction that says, "What follows is a file-name. Find that file and read it in right here." The angle brackets around the filename tell the preprocessor to look in all the usual places for this file. If your compiler is set up correctly, the angle brackets will cause the preprocessor to look for the file iostream in the directory that holds all the include files for your compiler. The file iostream (Input-Output-Stream) is used by cout, which assists with writing to the screen. The effect of line 0 is to include the file iostream into this program as if you had typed it in yourself. The preprocessor runs before your compiler each time the compiler is invoked. The pre-processor translates any line that begins with a pound symbol (#) into a special command, getting your code file ready for the compiler.

Line 2 begins the actual program with a function named main(). Every C++ program has a main() function. A function is a block of code that performs one or more actions. Usually functions are invoked or called by other functions, but main() is special. When your program starts, main() is called automatically.

main(), like all functions, must state what kind of value it will return. The return value type for main() in HELLO.cpp is int, which means that this function will return an integer to the operating system when it completes. In this case, it returns the integer value 0, as shown on line 5. Returning a value to the operating system is a relatively unimportant and little used feature, but the C++ standard does require that main() be declared as shown.

2

> **Note** Some compilers will let you declare `main()` to return `void`. This is no longer legal C++, and you should not get into bad habits. Have `main()` return `int`, and simply return 0 as the last line in `main()`.

> **Note** Some operating systems enable you to test the value returned by a program. The convention is to return 0 to indicate that the program ended normally.

All functions begin with an opening brace ({) and end with a closing brace (}). The braces for the `main()` function are on lines 3 and 6. Everything between the opening and closing braces is considered a part of the function.

The meat and potatoes of this program is on line 4. (My wife is a vegetarian, and I was tempted to write "the tofu and vegetables," but I thought that was a bit over the top.)

The object `cout` is used to print a message to the screen. We'll cover objects in general on Day 6, "Object-Oriented Programming," and `cout` and its related object `cin` in detail on Day 17, "Streams." These two objects, `cin` and `cout`, are used in C++ to handle input (for example, from the keyboard) and output (for example, to the screen), respectively.

`cout` is an object provided by the standard library. A library is a collection of classes. The standard library is the standard collection that comes with every ANSI-compliant compiler.

You designate to the compiler that the `cout` object you want to use is part of the standard library by using the namespace specifier `std`. Because you might have objects with the same name from more than one vendor, C++ divides the world into "namespaces." A namespace is a way to say "when I say cout, I mean the cout that is part of the standard namespace, not some other namespace." You say that to the compiler by putting the characters `std` followed by two colons before the `cout`. We'll talk about namespaces more in coming days.

Here's how `cout` is used: Type the word `cout`, followed by the output redirection operator (<<). Whatever follows the output redirection operator is written to the screen. If you want a string of characters written, be sure to enclose them in double quotes ("), as shown on line 4.

A text string is a series of printable characters.

The final two characters, \n, tell cout to put a new line after the words Hello World! This special code is explained in detail when cout is discussed on Day 18, "Namespaces."

The main() function ends on line 6 with the closing brace.

A Brief Look at cout

On Day 17 you will see how to use cout to print data to the screen. For now, you can use cout without fully understanding how it works. To print a value to the screen, write the word cout, followed by the insertion operator (<<), which you create by typing the less-than character (<) twice. Even though this is two characters, C++ treats it as one.

Follow the insertion character with your data. Listing 2.2 illustrates how this is used. Type in the example exactly as written, except substitute your own name where you see Jesse Liberty (unless your name *is* Jesse Liberty).

LISTING 2.2   Using cout

```
0:   // Listing 2.2 using std::cout
1:   #include <iostream>
2:   int main()
3:   {
4:       std::cout << "Hello there.\n";
5:       std::cout << "Here is 5: " << 5 << "\n";
6:       std::cout << "The manipulator std::endl ";
7:       std::cout << "writes a new line to the screen.";
8:       std::cout <<  std::endl;
9:       std::cout << "Here is a very big number:\t" << 70000;
10:      std::cout << std::endl;
11:      std::cout << "Here is the sum of 8 and 5:\t";
12:      std::cout << 8+5 << std::endl;
13:      std::cout << "Here's a fraction:\t\t";
14:      std::cout << (float) 5/8 << std::endl;
15:      std::cout << "And a very very big number:\t";
16:      std::cout << (double) 7000 * 7000 << std::endl;
17:      std::cout << "Don't forget to replace Jesse Liberty";
18:      std::cout << "with your name...\n";
19:      std::cout << "Jesse Liberty is a C++ programmer!\n";
20:      return 0;
21:   }
```

OUTPUT

```
Hello there.
Here is 5: 5
The manipulator endl writes a new line to the screen.
Here is a very big number:    70000
Here is the sum of 8 and 5:   13
Here's a fraction:            0.625
And a very very big number:   4.9e+07
Don't forget to replace Jesse Liberty with your name...
Jesse Liberty is a C++ programmer!
```

Note

> Some compilers have a bug that requires that you put parentheses around
> the addition before passing it to cout. Thus, line 11 would change to
>
> ```
> 11: cout << "Here is the sum of 8 and 5:\t" << (8+5) << endl;
> ```

ANALYSIS On line 1, the statement #include <iostream> causes the iostream file to be added to your source code. This is required if you use cout and its related functions.

On line 4 is the simplest use of cout, printing a string or series of characters. The symbol \n is a special formatting character. It tells cout to print a newline character to the screen; it is pronounced "slash-n" or "new line."

Three values are passed to cout on line 5, and each value is separated by the insertion operator. The first value is the string "Here is 5: ". Note the space after the colon. The space is part of the string. Next, the value 5 is passed to the insertion operator and the newline character (always in double quotes or single quotes). This causes the line

```
Here is 5: 5
```

to be printed to the screen. Because no newline character is present after the first string, the next value is printed immediately afterward. This is called concatenating the two values.

On line 6, an informative message is printed, and then the manipulator endl is used. The purpose of endl is to write a new line to the screen. (Other uses for endl are discussed on Day 16.) Note that endl is also provided by the standard library.

Note

> endl stands for *end line* and is end-ell rather than end-one. It is commonly
> pronounced "end-ell."

On line 9, a new formatting character, \t, is introduced. This inserts a tab character and is used on lines 9 to 15 to line up the output. Line 9 shows that not only integers, but long integers as well, can be printed. Line 12 demonstrates that cout will do simple addition. The value of 8+5 is passed to cout, but 13 is printed.

On line 14, the value 5/8 is inserted into cout. The term (float) tells cout that you want this value evaluated as a decimal equivalent, and so a fraction is printed. On line 16 the value 7000 * 7000 is given to cout, and the term (double) is used to tell cout that this is a floating point value. All this will be explained on Day 3, "Variables and Constants," when data types are discussed.

On line 16 you substituted your name, and the output confirmed that you are indeed a C++ programmer. It must be true, because the computer said so!

Using the Standard Namespace

You'll notice that the use of std:: in front of both cout and endl becomes rather distracting after a while. Although using the namespace designation is good form, it is tedious to type. The ANSI standard allows two solutions to this minor problem.

The first is to tell the compiler, at the beginning of the code listing, that you'll be using the standard library cout and endl, as shown in Listing 2.3.

LISTING 2.3   Using the using Keyword

```
 0:  // Listing 2.3 - using the using keyword
 1:  #include <iostream>
 2:  int main()
 3:  {
 4:      using std::cout;
 5:      using std::endl;
 6:
 7:      cout << "Hello there.\n";
 8:      cout << "Here is 5: " << 5 << "\n";
 9:      cout << "The manipulator endl ";
10:      cout << "writes a new line to the screen.";
11:      cout <<  endl;
12:      cout << "Here is a very big number:\t" << 70000;
13:      cout <<  endl;
14:      cout << "Here is the sum of 8 and 5:\t";
15:      cout << 8+5 << endl;
16:      cout << "Here's a fraction:\t\t";
17:      cout << (float) 5/8 << endl;
18:      cout << "And a very very big number:\t";
19:      cout << (double) 7000 * 7000 << endl;
20:      cout << "Don't forget to replace Jesse Liberty";
```

LISTING 2.3 continued

```
21:        cout << "with your name...\n";
22:        cout << "Jesse Liberty is a C++ programmer!\n";
23:        return 0;
24:  }
```

OUTPUT

```
Hello there.
Here is 5: 5
The manipulator endl writes a new line to the screen.
Here is a very big number:     70000
Here is the sum of 8 and 5:    13
Here's a fraction:             0.625
And a very very big number:    4.9e+07
Don't forget to replace Jesse Liberty with your name...
Jesse Liberty is a C++ programmer!
```

ANALYSIS   You will note that the output is identical. The only difference between Listing 2.3 and Listing 2.2 is that on lines 4 and 5 we inform the compiler that we'll be using two objects from the standard library. We do this with the keyword using. Once this has been done, we no longer need to qualify the cout and endl objects.

The second way to avoid the inconvenience of writing std:: in front of cout and endl is to simply tell the compiler that we'll be using the entire namespace standard; that is, any object not otherwise designated can be assumed to be from the standard namespace. In this case, rather than writing using std::cout; we would simply write using namespace std; as shown in Listing 2.4.

LISTING 2.4   Using the namespace Keyword

```
0:   // Listing 2.3 - using namespace std
1:   #include <iostream>
2:   int main()
3:   {
4:       using namespace std;
5:
6:       cout << "Hello there.\n";
7:       cout << "Here is 5: " << 5 << "\n";
8:       cout << "The manipulator endl ";
9:       cout << "writes a new line to the screen.";
10:      cout <<  endl;
11:      cout << "Here is a very big number:\t" << 70000;
12:      cout <<  endl;
13:      cout << "Here is the sum of 8 and 5:\t";
14:      cout << 8+5 << endl;
15:      cout << "Here's a fraction:\t\t";
16:      cout << (float) 5/8 << endl;
```

LISTING 2.4   continued

```
17:        cout << "And a very very big number:\t";
18:        cout << (double) 7000 * 7000 << endl;
19:        cout << "Don't forget to replace Jesse Liberty";
20:        cout << "with your name...\n";
21:        cout << "Jesse Liberty is a C++ programmer!\n";
22:        return 0;
23:    }
```

ANALYSIS   Again the output would be identical to the earlier versions of this program. The advantage to writing using namespace std; is that you do not have to specifically designate the objects you're actually using (for example, cout and endl;). The disadvantage is that you run the risk of inadvertently using objects from the wrong library.

Purists prefer to write std:: in front of each instance of cout or endl. The lazy prefer to write using namespace std; and be done with it. In this book we'll split the difference and most often we'll say which objects we're using, but from time to time we'll try each of the other styles just for fun.

Comments

When you are writing a program, it is always clear and self-evident what you are trying to do. Funny thing, though—a month later, when you return to the program, it can be quite confusing and unclear. I'm not sure how that confusion creeps into your program, but it always does.

To fight the onset of bafflement, and to help others understand your code, you'll want to use comments. Comments are text that is ignored by the compiler, but that may inform the reader of what you are doing at any particular point in your program.

Types of Comments

C++ comments come in two flavors: the double-slash (//) comment, and the slash-star (/*) comment. The double-slash comment, which will be referred to as a C++-style comment, tells the compiler to ignore everything that follows this comment, until the end of the line.

The slash-star comment tells the compiler to ignore everything that follows until it finds a star-slash (*/) comment mark. These marks will be referred to as C-style comments. Every /* must be matched with a closing */.

As you might guess, C-style comments are used in the C language as well, but C++-style comments are not part of the official definition of C.

Many C++ programmers use the C++-style comment most of the time and reserve C-style comments for blocking out large blocks of a program. You can include C++-style comments within a block "commented out" by C-style comments; everything, including the C++-style comments, is ignored between the C-style comment marks.

Using Comments

Some people recommend writing comments at the top of each function, explaining what the function does and what values it returns.

I disagree, and here is why: header comments are forever out-of-date because virtually no one remembers to update the comment when they update the code. Functions should be named so that little ambiguity exists about what they do, and confusing and obscure bits of code should be redesigned and rewritten so as to be self-evident. As often as not, comments are a lazy programmer's excuse for obscurity.

This is not to suggest that comments ought never be used, only that they should not be relied upon to clarify obscure code; instead, fix the code. In short, write your code well, and use comments to supplement understanding.

Listing 2.5 demonstrates the use of comments, showing that they do not affect the processing of the program or its output.

LISTING 2.5   HELP.cpp Demonstrates Comments

```
0:  #include <iostream>
1:
2:  int main()
3:  {
4:      using std::cout;
5:
6:      /* this is a comment
7:      and it extends until the closing
8:      star-slash comment mark */
9:      cout << "Hello World!\n";
10:     // this comment ends at the end of the line
11:     cout << "That comment ended!\n";
12:
13:     // double slash comments can be alone on a line
14:     /* as can slash-star comments */
15:     return 0;
16: }
```

 OUTPUT

```
Hello World!
That comment ended!
```

ANALYSIS   The comments on lines 6–8 are completely ignored by the compiler, as are the comments on lines 10, 13, and 14. The comment on line 10 ended with the end of the line, however, but the comments on lines 6 and 14 required a closing comment mark.

A Final Word of Caution About Comments

Comments that state the obvious are less than useful. In fact, they can be counterproductive because the code may change and the programmer may neglect to update the comment. What is obvious to one person may be obscure to another, however, so judgment is required.

The bottom line is that comments should not say *what* is happening, they should say *why* it is happening.

Functions

Although main() is a function, it is an unusual one. To be useful, a function must be called, or invoked, during the course of your program. main() is invoked by the operating system.

A program is executed line-by-line in the order it appears in your source code until a function is reached. Then the program branches off to execute the function. When the function finishes, it returns control to the line of code immediately following the call to the function.

A good analogy for this is sharpening your pencil. If you are drawing a picture and your pencil point breaks, you might stop drawing, go sharpen the pencil, and then return to what you were doing. When a program needs a service performed, it can call a function to perform the service and then pick up where it left off when the function is finished running. Listing 2.6 demonstrates this idea.

LISTING 2.6   Demonstrating a Call to a Function

```
0:  #include <iostream>
1:
2:  // function Demonstration Function
3:  // prints out a useful message
4:  void DemonstrationFunction()
5:  {
6:      std::cout << "In Demonstration Function\n";
7:  }
8:
9:  // function main - prints out a message, then
```

LISTING 2.6   continued

```
10:    // calls DemonstrationFunction, then prints out
11:    // a second message.
12:    int main()
13:    {
14:        std::cout << "In main\n" ;
15:        DemonstrationFunction();
16:        std::cout << "Back in main\n";
17:        return 0;
18:    }
```

OUTPUT

```
In main
In Demonstration Function
Back in main
```

ANALYSIS The function DemonstrationFunction() is defined on lines 5–7. When it is called, it prints a message to the screen and then returns.

Line 12 is the beginning of the actual program. On line 14, main() prints out a message saying it is in main(). After printing the message, line 15 calls DemonstrationFunction(). This call causes the commands in DemonstrationFunction() to execute. In this case, the entire function consists of the code on line 6, which prints another message. When DemonstrationFunction() completes (line 7), it returns to where it was called from. In this case, the program returns to line 16, where main() prints its final line.

Note

> Note that it made no sense to use the using statement in DemonstrationFunction, as we're only using cout once; therefore I fully designated it by writing std::cout. In main() I might have chosen to use the using statement, but once again I simply designated the namespace, as shown on lines 14 and 16.

Using Functions

Functions either return a value or they return void, meaning they return nothing. A function that adds two integers might return the sum, and thus would be defined to return an integer value. A function that just prints a message has nothing to return and would be declared to return void.

Functions consist of a header and a body. The header consists, in turn, of the return type, the function name, and the parameters to that function. The parameters to a function enable values to be passed into the function. Thus, if the function were to add two numbers, the numbers would be the parameters to the function. Here's a typical function header:

```
int Sum(int a, int b)
```

A parameter is a declaration of what type of value will be passed in; the actual value passed in by the calling function is called the argument. Many programmers use the terms parameters and arguments as synonyms. Others are careful about the technical distinction. This book will use the terms interchangeably.

The body of a function consists of an opening brace, zero or more statements, and a closing brace. The statements constitute the work of the function. A function may return a value, using a return statement. This statement will also cause the function to exit. If you don't put a return statement into your function, it will automatically return void at the end of the function. The value returned must be of the type declared in the function header.

Note

> Functions are covered in more detail on Day 5, "Functions." The types that can be returned from a function are covered in more detail on Day 3, "Variables and Constants." The information provided today is to present you with an overview because functions will be used in almost all your C++ programs.

Listing 2.7 demonstrates a function that takes two integer parameters and returns an integer value. Don't worry about the syntax or the specifics of how to work with integer values (for example, int x) for now; that is covered in detail on Day 3.

LISTING 2.7   FUNC.cpp Demonstrates a Simple Function

```
 0:  #include <iostream>
 1:  int Add (int x, int y)
 2:  {
 3:      std::cout << "In Add(), received " << x << " and " << y << "\n";
 4:      return (x+y);
 5:  }
 6:
 7:  int main()
 8:  {
 9:      using std::cout;
10:      using std::cin;
11:
12:
13:      cout << "I'm in main()!\n";
14:      int a, b, c;
```

LISTING 2.7   continued

```
15:     cout << "Enter two numbers: ";
16:     cin >> a;
17:     cin >> b;
18:     cout << "\nCalling Add()\n";
19:     c=Add(a,b);
20:     cout << "\nBack in main().\n";
21:     cout << "c was set to " << c;
22:     cout << "\nExiting...\n\n";
23:     return 0;
24:  }
```

OUTPUT
```
I'm in main()!
Enter two numbers: 3 5

Calling Add()
In Add(), received 3 and 5

Back in main().
c was set to 8
Exiting...
```

ANALYSIS The function Add() is defined on line 1. It takes two integer parameters and returns an integer value. The program itself begins on line 7. The program prompts the user for two numbers (lines 15–17). The user types each number, separated by a space, and then presses the Enter key. main() passes the two numbers typed in by the user as arguments to the Add() function on line 19.

Processing branches to the Add() function, which starts on line 1. The parameters a and b are printed and then added. The result is returned on line 4, and the function returns.

In lines 16 and 17, the cin object is used to obtain a number for the variables a and b, and cout is used to write the values to the screen. Variables and other aspects of this program are explored in depth in the next few days.

Summary

The difficulty in learning a complex subject, such as programming, is that so much of what you learn depends on everything else there is to learn. This chapter introduced the basic parts of a simple C++ program. It also introduced the development cycle and a number of important new terms.

Q&A

Q What does `#include` do?

A This is a directive to the preprocessor, which runs when you call your compiler. This specific directive causes the file named after the word `include` to be read in, as if it were typed in at that location in your source code.

Q What is the difference between // comments and /* style comments?

A The double-slash comments (`//`) "expire" at the end of the line. Slash-star (`/*`) comments are in effect until a closing comment (`*/`). Remember, not even the end of the function terminates a slash-star comment; you must put in the closing comment mark, or you will get a compile-time error.

Q What differentiates a good comment from a bad comment?

A A good comment tells the reader why this particular code is doing whatever it is doing or explains what a section of code is about to do. A bad comment restates what a particular line of code is doing. Lines of code should be written so that they speak for themselves. Reading the line of code should tell you what it is doing without needing a comment.

Workshop

The Workshop provides quiz questions to help you solidify your understanding of the material covered and exercises to provide you with experience in using what you've learned. Try to answer the quiz and exercise questions before checking the answers in Appendix D, and make sure you understand the answers before continuing to the next chapter.

Quiz

1. What is the difference between the compiler and the preprocessor?
2. Why is the function `main()` special?
3. What are the two types of comments, and how do they differ?
4. Can comments be nested?
5. Can comments be longer than one line?

Exercises

1. Write a program that writes "I love C++" to the screen.
2. Write the smallest program that can be compiled, linked, and run.

3. **BUG BUSTERS:** Enter this program and compile it. Why does it fail? How can you fix it?

```
1: #include <iostream>
2: main()
3: {
4:      std::cout << Is there a bug here?";
5: }
```

4. Fix the bug in Exercise 3 and recompile, link, and run it.

2

DAY 3

Variables and Constants

Programs need a way to store the data they use. Variables and constants offer various ways to represent, store, and manipulate that data.

Today you will learn

- How to declare and define variables and constants.
- How to assign values to variables and manipulate those values.
- How to write the value of a variable to the screen.

What Is a Variable?

In C++ a variable is a place to store information. A variable is a location in your computer's memory in which you can store a value and from which you can later retrieve that value.

Notice that this is temporary storage. When you turn the computer off, these variables are lost. Permanent storage is a different matter. Typically, variables are permanently stored either to a database or to a file on disk. Storing to a file on disk is discussed on Day 16, "Advanced Inheritance."

Data Is Stored in Memory

Your computer's memory can be viewed as a series of cubbyholes. Each cubbyhole is one of many, many such holes all lined up. Each cubbyhole—or memory location—is numbered sequentially. These numbers are known as memory addresses. A variable reserves one or more cubbyholes in which you may store a value.

Your variable's name (for example, myVariable) is a label on one of these cubbyholes so that you can find it easily without knowing its actual memory address. Figure 3.1 is a schematic representation of this idea. As you can see from the figure, myVariable starts at memory address 103. Depending on the size of myVariable, it can take up one or more memory addresses.

FIGURE 3.1

A schematic represen-tation of memory.

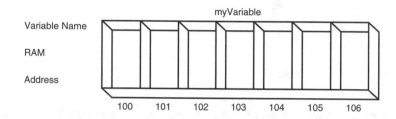

Variable Name

RAM

Address

      100   101   102   103   104   105   106

Note

> *RAM* stands for Random Access Memory. When you run your program, it is loaded into RAM from the disk file. All variables are also created in RAM. When programmers talk about memory, it is usually RAM to which they are referring.

Setting Aside Memory

When you define a variable in C++, you must tell the compiler what kind of variable it is: an integer, a character, and so forth. This information tells the compiler how much room to set aside and what kind of value you want to store in your variable.

Each cubbyhole is one byte large. If the type of variable you create is four bytes in size, it needs four bytes of memory, or four cubbyholes. The type of the variable (for example, integer) tells the compiler how much memory (how many cubbyholes) to set aside for the variable.

There was a time when it was imperative that programmers understood bits and bytes; after all, these are the fundamental units of storage. Computer programs have gotten better at abstracting away these details, but it is still helpful to understand how data is stored. For a quick review of the underlying concepts in binary math, please take a look at Appendix A, "Binary and Hexadecimal."

Note
> If mathematics makes you want to run from the room screaming, then don't bother with Appendix A; you won't really need it. The truth is that programmers no longer need to be mathematicians; though we do need to be comfortable with logic and rational thinking.

Size of Integers

On any one computer, each variable type takes up a single, unchanging amount of room. That is, an integer might be two bytes on one machine and four on another, but on either computer it is always the same, day in and day out.

A char variable (used to hold characters) is most often one byte long.

Note
> There is endless debate about how to pronounce char. Some say it as "car," some say it as "char"(coal), others say it as "care." Clearly, car is correct because that is how *I* say it, but feel free to say it however you like.

A short integer is two bytes on most computers, a long integer is usually four bytes, and an integer (without the keyword short or long) can be two or four bytes. You'd think the language would specify this exactly, but it doesn't. All it says is that a short must be less than or equal to the size of an int, which in turn must be less than or equal to the size of a long.

That said, you're probably working on a computer with a 2-byte short and a 4-byte int, with a 4-byte long.

The size of an integer is determined by the processor (16 bit or 32 bit) and the compiler you use. On modern 32-bit (Pentium) computers using modern compilers (for example, Visual C++ 4 or later), integers are *four* bytes. This book assumes a 4-byte integer, although your mileage may vary.

A character is a single letter, number, or symbol that takes up one byte of memory.

Compile and run Listing 3.1 on your computer and it will tell you the exact size of each of these types.

LISTING 3.1   Determining the Size of Variable Types on Your Computer

```
0:   #include <iostream>
1:
2:   int main()
3:   {
4:       using std::cout;
5:
6:       cout << "The size of an int is:\t\t"
7:          << sizeof(int)    << " bytes.\n";
8:       cout << "The size of a short int is:\t"
9:          << sizeof(short)  << " bytes.\n";
10:      cout << "The size of a long int is:\t"
11:         << sizeof(long)   << " bytes.\n";
12:      cout << "The size of a char is:\t\t"
13:         << sizeof(char)   << " bytes.\n";
14:      cout << "The size of a float is:\t\t"
15:          << sizeof(float)  << " bytes.\n";
16:      cout << "The size of a double is:\t"
17:         << sizeof(double) << " bytes.\n";
18:      cout << "The size of a bool is:\t"
19:         << sizeof(bool)   << " bytes.\n";
20:
21:      return 0;
22:  }
```

OUTPUT

```
The size of an int is:          4 bytes.
The size of a short int is:     2 bytes.
The size of a long int is:      4 bytes.
The size of a char is:          1 bytes.
The size of a float is:         4 bytes.
The size of a double is:        8 bytes.
The size of a bool is:          1 bytes.
```

Note   On your computer, the number of bytes presented might be different.

Most of Listing 3.1 should be pretty familiar. I've split the lines to make them fit for the book, so for example, lines 6 and 7 could really be on a single line. The compiler ignores white space (spaces, tabs, line returns) and so treats these as a single line.

The one new feature in this program is the use of the sizeof() operator in lines 6–19. sizeof() is provided by your compiler, and it tells you the size of the object you pass in as a parameter. On line 7, for example, the keyword int is passed into sizeof(). Using sizeof(), I was able to determine that on my computer an int is equal to a long int, which is four bytes.

signed and unsigned

All integer types come in two varieties: signed and unsigned. The idea here is that
sometimes you need negative numbers and sometimes you don't. Integers (short and
long) without the word "unsigned" are assumed to be signed. signed integers are either
negative or positive. unsigned integers are always positive.

Because you have the same number of bytes for both signed and unsigned integers, the
largest number you can store in an unsigned integer is twice as big as the largest positive
number you can store in a signed integer. An unsigned short integer can handle numbers from 0 to 65,535. Half the numbers represented by a signed short are negative,
thus a signed short can only represent numbers from –32,768 to 32,767. If this is confusing, be sure to read Appendix A.

Fundamental Variable Types

Several other variable types are built into C++. They can be conveniently divided into
integer variables (the type discussed so far), floating-point variables, and character variables.

Floating-point variables have values that can be expressed as fractions—that is, they are
real numbers. Character variables hold a single byte and are used for holding the 256
characters and symbols of the ASCII and extended ASCII character sets.

The ASCII character set is the set of characters standardized for use on computers.
ASCII is an acronym for American Standard Code for Information Interchange. Nearly
every computer operating system supports ASCII, although many support other international character sets as well.

The types of variables used in C++ programs are described in Table 3.1. This table shows
the variable type, how much room this book assumes it takes in memory, and what kinds
of values can be stored in these variables. The values that can be stored are determined
by the size of the variable types, so check your output from Listing 3.1.

TABLE 3.1 Variable Types

Type	Size	Values
bool	1 byte	true or false
unsigned short int	2 bytes	0 to 65,535
short int	2 bytes	–32,768 to 32,767
unsigned long int	4 bytes	0 to 4,294,967,295
long int	4 bytes	–2,147,483,648 to 2,147,483,647
int (16 bit)	2 bytes	–32,768 to 32,767

TABLE 3.1 continued

Type	Size	Values
int (32 bit)	4 bytes	–2,147,483,648 to 2,147,483,647
unsigned int (16 bit)	2 bytes	0 to 65,535
unsigned int (32 bit)	4 bytes	0 to 4,294,967,295
char	1 byte	256 character values
float	4 bytes	1.2e–38 to 3.4e38
double	8 bytes	2.2e–308 to 1.8e308

Note

The sizes of variables might be different from those shown in Table 3.1, depending on the compiler and the computer you are using. If your computer had the same output as was presented in Listing 3.1, Table 3.1 should apply to your compiler. If your output from Listing 3.1 was different, you should consult your compiler's manual for the values that your variable types can hold.

Defining a Variable

You create or define a variable by stating its type, followed by one or more spaces, followed by the variable name and a semicolon. The variable name can be virtually any combination of letters, but it cannot contain spaces. Legal variable names include x, J23qrsnf, and myAge. Good variable names tell you what the variables are for; using good names makes it easier to understand the flow of your program. The following statement defines an integer variable called myAge:

```
int myAge;
```

Note

When you declare a variable, memory is allocated (set aside) for that variable. The *value* of the variable will be whatever happened to be in that memory at that time. You will see in a moment how to assign a new value to that memory.

As a general programming practice, avoid such horrific names as J23qrsnf, and restrict single-letter variable names (such as x or i) to variables that are used only very briefly. Try to use expressive names such as myAge or howMany. Such names are easier to understand three weeks later when you are scratching your head trying to figure out what you meant when you wrote that line of code.

Try this experiment: Guess what these programs do, based on the first few lines of code:

Example 1

```
int main()
{
    unsigned short x;
    unsigned short y;
    unsigned short z;
    z = x * y;
    return 0;
}
```

Example 2

```
int main ()
{
    unsigned short Width;
    unsigned short Length;
    unsigned short Area;
    Area = Width * Length;
    return 0;
}
```

Note
If you compile this program, your compiler will warn that these values are not initialized. You'll see how to solve this problem shortly.

Clearly, the purpose of the second program is easier to guess, and the inconvenience of having to type the longer variable names is more than made up for by how much easier it is to maintain the second program.

Case Sensitivity

C++ is case sensitive. In other words, uppercase and lowercase letters are considered to be different. A variable named age is different from Age, which is different from AGE.

Note
Some compilers allow you to turn case sensitivity off. Don't be tempted to do this; your programs won't work with other compilers, and other C++ programmers will be very confused by your code.

Various conventions exist for how to name variables, and although it doesn't much matter which method you adopt, it is important to be consistent throughout your program because inconsistent naming will confuse other programmers when they read your code.

Many programmers prefer to use all lowercase letters for their variable names. If the name requires two words (for example, my car), two popular conventions are used: my_car or myCar. The latter form is called camel notation because the capitalization looks something like a camel's hump.

Some people find the underscore character (my_car) to be easier to read, but others prefer to avoid the underscore because it is more difficult to type. This book uses camel notation, in which the second and all subsequent words are capitalized: myCar, theQuickBrownFox, and so forth.

Note

Many advanced programmers employ a notation style referred to as Hungarian notation. The idea behind Hungarian notation is to prefix every variable with a set of characters that describes its type. Integer variables might begin with a lowercase letter i, longs might begin with a lowercase l. Other notations indicate constants, globals, pointers, and so forth. Most of this is much more important in C programming and won't be used in this book.

It is called Hungarian notation because the man who invented it, Charles Simonyi of Microsoft, is Hungarian. You can find his original monograph at http://www.strangecreations.com//library/c/naming.txt.

Microsoft has moved away from Hungarian notation recently, and the design recommendations for C# strongly recommend *not* using Hungarian notation. Their reasoning for C# applies equally well to C++.

Keywords

Some words are reserved by C++, and you may not use them as variable names. These are keywords used by the compiler to control your program. Keywords include if, while, for, and main. Your compiler manual should provide a complete list, but generally, any reasonable name for a variable is almost certainly not a keyword. A list of C++ keywords is available in Appendix B.

Do	Don't
DO define a variable by writing the type, then the variable name.	**DON'T** use C++ keywords as variable names.
DO use meaningful variable names.	**DON'T** use unsigned variables for negative numbers.
DO remember that C++ is case sensitive.	
DO understand the number of bytes each variable type consumes in memory and what values can be stored in variables of that type.	

Creating More Than One Variable at a Time

You can create more than one variable of the same type in one statement by writing the type and then the variable names, separated by commas. For example:

```
unsigned int myAge, myWeight;    // two unsigned int variables
long int area, width, length;        // three long integers
```

As you can see, myAge and myWeight are each declared as unsigned integer variables. The second line declares three individual long variables named area, width, and length. The type (long) is assigned to all the variables, so you cannot mix types in one definition statement.

Assigning Values to Your Variables

You assign a value to a variable by using the assignment operator (=). Thus, you would assign 5 to Width by writing

```
unsigned short Width;
Width = 5;
```

 Note long is a shorthand version of long int, and short is a shorthand version of short int.

You can combine these steps and initialize Width when you define it by writing

```
unsigned short Width = 5;
```

Initialization looks very much like assignment, and with integer variables, the difference is minor. Later, when constants are covered, you will see that some values must be initialized because they cannot be assigned to. The essential difference is that initialization takes place at the moment you create the variable.

Just as you can define more than one variable at a time, you can initialize more than one variable at creation. For example:

```
// create two long variables and initialize them
long width = 5, length = 7;
```

This example initializes the long integer variable width to the value 5 and the long integer variable length to the value 7. You can even mix definitions and initializations:

```
int myAge = 39, yourAge, hisAge = 40;
```

This example creates three type int variables, and it initializes the first and third.

Listing 3.2 shows a complete program, ready to compile, that computes the area of a rectangle and writes the answer to the screen.

LISTING 3.2   A Demonstration of the Use of Variables

```
0:   // Demonstration of variables
1:   #include <iostream>
2:
3:   int main()
4:   {
5:      using std::cout;
6:      using std::endl;
7:
8:      unsigned short int Width = 5, Length;
9:      Length = 10;
10:
11:     // create  an unsigned short and initialize with result
12:     // of multiplying Width by Length
13:     unsigned short int Area  = (Width * Length);
14:
15:     cout << "Width:" << Width << "\n";
16:     cout << "Length: "  << Length << endl;
17:     cout << "Area: " << Area << endl;
18:     return 0;
19:  }
```

```
Width:5
Length: 10
Area: 50
```

Line 1 includes the required `include` statement for the `iostream`'s library so that `cout` will work. Line 3 begins the program. Lines 5 and 6 define `cout` and `endl` as being part of the standard (`std`) namespace.

On line 8, `Width` is defined as an `unsigned short` integer, and its value is initialized to 5. Another `unsigned short` integer, `Length`, is also defined, but it is not initialized. On line 9, the value 10 is assigned to `Length`.

On line 13, an `unsigned short` integer, `Area`, is defined, and it is initialized with the value obtained by multiplying `Width` times `Length`. On lines 15–17, the values of the variables are printed to the screen. Note that the special word `endl` creates a new line.

typedef

It can become tedious, repetitious, and, most important, error-prone to keep writing `unsigned short int`. C++ enables you to create an alias for this phrase by using the keyword `typedef`, which stands for type definition.

In effect, you are creating a synonym, and it is important to distinguish this from creating a new type (which you will do on Day 6, "Object-Oriented Programming"). `typedef` is used by writing the keyword `typedef`, followed by the existing type, then the new name, and ending with a semicolon. For example,

```
typedef unsigned short int USHORT;
```

creates the new name `USHORT` that you can use anywhere you might have written `unsigned short int`. Listing 3.3 is a replay of Listing 3.2, using the type definition `USHORT` rather than `unsigned short int`.

LISTING 3.3   A Demonstration of `typedef`

```
 0:  // ****************
 1:  // Demonstrates typedef keyword
 2:  #include <iostream>
 3:
 4:  typedef unsigned short int USHORT;    //typedef defined
 5:
 6:  int main()
 7:  {
 8:
 9:      using std::cout;
10:      using std::endl;
11:
12:      USHORT  Width = 5;
13:      USHORT Length;
```

LISTING 3.3 continued

```
14:      Length = 10;
15:      USHORT Area  = Width * Length;
16:      cout << "Width:" << Width << "\n";
17:      cout << "Length: "  << Length << endl;
18:      cout << "Area: " << Area <<endl;
19:      return 0;
20:  }
```

OUTPUT
Width:5
Length: 10
Area: 50

Note   * indicates multiplication.

ANALYSIS   On line 4, USHORT is typedefined (some programmers say "typedef'ed") as a synonym for unsigned short int. The program is very much like Listing 3.2, and the output is the same.

When to Use short and When to Use long

One source of confusion for new C++ programmers is when to declare a variable to be type long and when to declare it to be type short. The rule, when understood, is fairly straightforward: If any chance exists that the value you'll want to put into your variable will be too big for its type, use a larger type.

As shown in Table 3.1, unsigned short integers, assuming that they are two bytes, can hold a value only up to 65,535. signed short integers split their values between positive and negative numbers, and thus their maximum value is only half that of the unsigned.

Although unsigned long integers can hold an extremely large number (4,294,967,295), that is still quite finite. If you need a larger number, you'll have to go to float or double, and then you lose some precision. Floats and doubles can hold extremely large numbers, but only the first 7 or 9 digits are significant on most computers. That means that the number is rounded off after that many digits.

Shorter variables use up less memory. These days, memory is cheap and life is short. Feel free to use int, which will probably be four bytes on your machine.

Wrapping Around an **unsigned** Integer

That unsigned long integers have a limit to the values they can hold is only rarely a problem, but what happens if you do run out of room?

When an unsigned integer reaches its maximum value, it wraps around and starts over, much as a car odometer might. Listing 3.4 shows what happens if you try to put too large a value into a short integer.

LISTING 3.4   A Demonstration of Putting Too Large a Value in an unsigned Integer

```
 0:   #include <iostream>
 1:   int main()
 2:   {
 3:
 4:       using std::cout;
 5:       using std::endl;
 6:
 7:       unsigned short int smallNumber;
 8:       smallNumber = 65535;
 9:       cout << "small number:" << smallNumber << endl;
10:       smallNumber++;
11:       cout << "small number:" << smallNumber << endl;
12:       smallNumber++;
13:       cout << "small number:" << smallNumber << endl;
14:       return 0;
15:   }
```

OUTPUT
```
small number:65535
small number:0
small number:1
```

ANALYSIS   On line 7, smallNumber is declared to be an unsigned short int, which on my computer is a two-byte variable, able to hold a value between 0 and 65,535. On line 8, the maximum value is assigned to smallNumber, and it is printed on line 9.

On line 10, smallNumber is incremented; that is, 1 is added to it. The symbol for incrementing is ++ (as in the name C++—an incremental increase from C). Thus, the value in smallNumber would be 65,536. However, unsigned short integers can't hold a number larger than 65,535, so the value is wrapped around to 0, which is printed on line 11.

On line 12 smallNumber is incremented again, and then its new value, 1, is printed.

Wrapping Around a **signed** Integer

A signed integer is different from an unsigned integer, in that half of the values you can represent are negative. Instead of picturing a traditional car odometer, you might picture a clock much like the one shown in Figure 3.2, in which the numbers count upward moving clockwise and downward moving counter-clockwise. They cross at the bottom of the clock face (traditional 6 o'clock).

FIGURE 3.2

*If clocks used signed
numbers.*

One number from 0 is either 1 (clockwise) or –1 (counter-clockwise). When you run out of positive numbers, you run right into the largest negative numbers and then count back down to 0. Listing 3.5 shows what happens when you add 1 to the maximum positive number in short integer.

LISTING 3.5   A Demonstration of Adding Too Large a Number to a `signed` Integer

```
0:   #include <iostream>
1:   int main()
2:   {
3:      short int smallNumber;
4:      smallNumber = 32767;
5:      std::cout << "small number:" << smallNumber << std::endl;
6:      smallNumber++;
7:      std::cout << "small number:" << smallNumber << std::endl;
8:      smallNumber++;
9:      std::cout << "small number:" << smallNumber << std::endl;
10:     return 0;
11:  }
```

```
small number:32767
small number:-32768
small number:-32767
```

ANALYSIS On line 4, `smallNumber` is declared this time to be a `signed short` integer (if you don't explicitly say that it is `unsigned`, it is assumed to be `signed`). The program proceeds much as the preceding one, but the output is quite different. To fully understand this output, you must be comfortable with how `signed` numbers are represented as bits in a two-byte integer.

The bottom line, however, is that just like an `unsigned` integer, the `signed` integer wraps around from its highest positive value to its highest negative value.

Characters

Character variables (type `char`) are typically 1 byte, enough to hold 256 values (see Appendix C). A `char` can be interpreted as a small number (0–255) or as a member of the ASCII set. ASCII stands for the American Standard Code for Information Interchange. The ASCII character set and its ISO (International Standards Organization) equivalent are a way to encode all the letters, numerals, and punctuation marks.

> **Note**
>
> Computers do not know about letters, punctuation, or sentences. All they understand are numbers. In fact, all they really know about is whether a sufficient amount of electricity is at a particular junction of wires. If so, it is represented symbolically as a 1; if not, it is represented as a 0. By grouping ones and zeros, the computer is able to generate patterns that can be interpreted as numbers, and these, in turn, can be assigned to letters and punctuation.

In the ASCII code, the lowercase letter "a" is assigned the value 97. All the lower- and uppercase letters, all the numerals, and all the punctuation marks are assigned values between 1 and 128. An additional 128 marks and symbols are reserved for use by the computer maker, although the IBM extended character set has become something of a standard.

> **Note**
>
> ASCII is usually pronounced "Ask-ee."

Characters and Numbers

When you put a character, for example, "a," into a `char` variable, what really is there is a number between 0 and 255. The compiler knows, however, how to translate back and forth between characters (represented by a single quotation mark and then a letter, numeral, or punctuation mark, followed by a closing single quotation mark) and one of the ASCII values.

The value/letter relationship is arbitrary; there is no particular reason that the lowercase "a" is assigned the value 97. As long as everyone (your keyboard, compiler, and screen) agrees, no problem occurs. It is important to realize, however, that a big difference exists between the value 5 and the character "5". The latter is actually valued at 53, much as the letter "a" is valued at 97. This is illustrated in Listing 3.6.

LISTING **3.6**   Printing Characters Based on Numbers

```
0:   #include <iostream>
1:   int main()
2:   {
3:       for (int i = 32; i<128; i++)
4:           std::cout << (char) i;
5:       return 0;
6:   }
```

```
!"#$%&'()*+,-./0123456789:;<=>?@ABCDEFGHIJKLMNOPQRSTUVWXYZ[\]^_`abcdefghijklmno
pqrstuvwxyz{|}~_
```

This simple program prints the character values for the integers 32 through 127.

Special Printing Characters

The C++ compiler recognizes some special characters for formatting. Table 3.2 shows the most common ones. You put these into your code by typing the backslash (called the escape character), followed by the character. Thus, to put a tab character into your code, you would enter a single quotation mark, the slash, the letter t, and then a closing single quotation mark:

```
char tabCharacter = '\t';
```

This example declares a char variable (tabCharacter) and initializes it with the character value \t, which is recognized as a tab. The special printing characters are used when printing either to the screen or to a file or other output device.

An escape character changes the meaning of the character that follows it. For example, normally the character n means the letter n, but when it is preceded by the escape character (\) it means new line.

TABLE 3.2   The Escape Characters

Character	What It Means
\a	Bell (alert)
\b	Backspace
\f	Form feed
\n	New line
\r	Carriage return
\t	Tab
\v	Vertical tab
\'	Single quote
\"	Double quote
\?	Question mark
\\	Backslash
\000	Octal notation
\xhhh	Hexadecimal

3

Constants

Like variables, constants are data storage locations. Unlike variables, and as the name implies, constants don't change. You must initialize a constant when you create it, and you cannot assign a new value later.

Literal Constants

C++ has two types of constants: literal and symbolic.

A literal constant is a value typed directly into your program wherever it is needed. For example:

```
int myAge = 39;
```

myAge is a variable of type int; 39 is a literal constant. You can't assign a value to 39, and its value can't be changed.

Symbolic Constants

A symbolic constant is a constant that is represented by a name, just as a variable is represented. Unlike a variable, however, after a constant is initialized, its value can't be changed.

If your program has one integer variable named `students` and another named `classes`, you could compute how many students you have, given a known number of classes, if you knew each class consisted of 15 students:

```
students = classes * 15;
```

In this example, 15 is a literal constant. Your code would be easier to read, and easier to maintain, if you substituted a symbolic constant for this value:

```
students = classes * studentsPerClass
```

If you later decided to change the number of students in each class, you could do so where you define the constant `studentsPerClass` without having to make a change every place you used that value.

Two ways exist to declare a symbolic constant in C++. The old, traditional, and now obsolete way is with a preprocessor directive, `#define`.

Defining Constants with `#define`

To define a constant the traditional way, you would enter this:

```
#define studentsPerClass 15
```

Note that `studentsPerClass` is of no particular type (`int`, `char`, and so on). `#define` does a simple text substitution. Every time the preprocessor sees the word `studentsPerClass`, it puts in the text 15.

Because the preprocessor runs before the compiler, your compiler never sees your constant; it sees the number 15.

Defining Constants with `const`

Although `#define` works, a new, much better way exists to define constants in C++:

```
const unsigned short int studentsPerClass = 15;
```

This example also declares a symbolic constant named `studentsPerClass`, but this time `studentsPerClass` is typed as an `unsigned short int`. This method has several advantages in making your code easier to maintain and in preventing bugs. The biggest difference is that this constant has a type, and the compiler can enforce that it is used according to its type.

Note   Constants cannot be changed while the program is running. If you need to change `studentsPerClass`, for example, you need to change the code and recompile.

Do	Don't
DO watch for numbers overrunning the size of the integer and wrapping around incorrect values. DO give your variables meaningful names that reflect their use.	DON'T use keywords as variable names.

Enumerated Constants

Enumerated constants enable you to create new types and then to define variables of those types whose values are restricted to a set of possible values. For example, you can declare COLOR to be an enumeration, and you can define five values for COLOR: RED, BLUE, GREEN, WHITE, and BLACK.

The syntax for enumerated constants is to write the keyword enum, followed by the type name, an open brace, each of the legal values separated by a comma, and finally, a closing brace and a semicolon. Here's an example:

```
enum COLOR { RED, BLUE, GREEN, WHITE, BLACK };
```

This statement performs two tasks:

1. It makes COLOR the name of an enumeration; that is, a new type.
2. It makes RED a symbolic constant with the value 0, BLUE a symbolic constant with the value 1, GREEN a symbolic constant with the value 2, and so forth.

Every enumerated constant has an integer value. If you don't specify otherwise, the first constant will have the value 0, and the rest will count up from there. Any one of the constants can be initialized with a particular value, however, and those that are not initialized will count upward from the ones before them. Thus, if you write

```
enum Color { RED=100, BLUE, GREEN=500, WHITE, BLACK=700 };
```

then RED will have the value 100; BLUE, the value 101; GREEN, the value 500; WHITE, the value 501; and BLACK, the value 700.

You can define variables of type COLOR, but they can be assigned only one of the enumerated values (in this case, RED, BLUE, GREEN, WHITE, or BLACK, or else 100, 101, 500, 501, or 700). You can assign any color value to your COLOR variable. In fact, you can assign any integer value, even if it is not a legal color, although a good compiler will issue a warning if you do. It is important to realize that enumerator variables actually are of type unsigned int, and that the enumerated constants equate to integer variables. It is, however, very convenient to be able to name these values when working with colors, days of the week, or similar sets of values. Listing 3.7 presents a program that uses an enumerated type.

LISTING 3.7   A Demonstration of Enumerated Constants

```
0:   #include <iostream>
1:   int main()
2:   {
3:       enum Days { Sunday, Monday, Tuesday,
4:                Wednesday, Thursday, Friday, Saturday };
5:
6:       Days today;
7:       today = Monday;
8:
9:       if (today == Sunday || today == Saturday)
10:          std::cout << "\nGotta' love the weekends!\n";
11:      else
12:          std::cout << "\nBack to work.\n";
13:
14:      return 0;
15:  }
```

OUTPUT   Back to work.

ANALYSIS   On line 3, the enumerated constant DAYS is defined, with seven values. Each of these evaluates to an integer, counting upward from 0; thus, Monday's value is 1.

We create a variable of type Days—that is, the variable will contain a valid value from the list of enumerated constants. We assign the enumerated value Monday to that variable on line 7 and then we test that value on line 9.

The enumerated constant shown in line 7 could be replaced with a series of constant integers, as shown in Listing 3.8.

LISTING 3.8   Same Program Using Constant Integers

```
0:   #include <iostream>
1:   int main()
2:   {
3:       const int Sunday = 0;
4:       const int Monday = 1;
5:       const int Tuesday = 2;
6:       const int Wednesday = 3;
7:       const int Thursday = 4;
8:       const int Friday = 5;
9:       const int Saturday = 6;
```

LISTING 3.8   continued

```
10:
11:     int today;
12:     today = Monday;
13:
14:     if (today == Sunday || today == Saturday)
15:         std::cout << "\nGotta' love the weekends!\n";
16:     else
17:         std::cout << "\nBack to work.\n";
18:
19:     return 0;
20:  }
```

OUTPUT   Back to work.

3

ANALYSIS   The output of this listing is identical to Listing 3.7. Here, each of the constants
(Sunday, Monday, and so on) was explicitly defined, and no enumerated Days
type exists. Enumerated constants have the advantage of being self-documenting—the
intent of the Days enumerated type is immediately clear.

Summary

This chapter discussed numeric and character variables and constants, which are used by
C++ to store data during the execution of your program. Numeric variables are either
integral (char, short, and long int) or they are floating point (float and double).
Numeric variables can also be signed or unsigned. Although all the types can be of various sizes among different computers, the type specifies an exact size on any given computer.

You must declare a variable before it can be used, and then you must store the type of
data that you've declared as correct for that variable. If you put too large a number into
an integral variable, it wraps around and produces an incorrect result.

This chapter also reviewed literal and symbolic constants as well as enumerated constants, and it showed two ways to declare a symbolic constant: using #define and using
the keyword const.

Q&A

Q **If a short `int` can run out of room and wrap around, why not always use long integers?**

A Both short integers and long integers will run out of room and wrap around, but a long integer will do so with a much larger number. For example, an `unsigned short int` will wrap around after 65,535, whereas an `unsigned long int` will not wrap around until 4,294,967,295. However, on most machines, a long integer takes up twice as much memory every time you declare one (four bytes versus two bytes), and a program with 100 such variables will consume an extra 200 bytes of RAM. Frankly, this is less of a problem than it used to be because most personal computers now come with millions (if not billions) of bytes of memory. Optical computers may one day have gigabytes (or even terabytes!) of memory.

Q **What happens if I assign a number with a decimal point to an integer rather than to a float? Consider the following line of code:**

```
int aNumber = 5.4;
```

A A good compiler will issue a warning, but the assignment is completely legal. The number you've assigned will be truncated into an integer. Thus, if you assign 5.4 to an integer variable, that variable will have the value 5. Information will be lost, however, and if you then try to assign the value in that integer variable to a float variable, the float variable will have only 5.

Q **Why not use literal constants; why go to the bother of using symbolic constants?**

A If you use the value in many places throughout your program, a symbolic constant allows all the values to change just by changing the one definition of the constant. Symbolic constants also speak for themselves. It might be hard to understand why a number is being multiplied by 360, but it's much easier to understand what's going on if the number is being multiplied by `degreesInACircle`.

Q **What happens if I assign a negative number to an unsigned variable? Consider the following line of code:**

```
unsigned int aPositiveNumber = -1;
```

A A good compiler will warn, but the assignment is legal. The negative number will be assessed as a bit pattern and assigned to the variable. The value of that variable will then be interpreted as an unsigned number. Thus, −1, whose bit pattern is 11111111 11111111 (0xFF in hex), will be assessed as the unsigned value 65,535. If this information confuses you, refer to Appendix A.

Q Can I work with C++ without understanding bit patterns, binary arithmetic, and hexadecimal?

A Yes, but not as effectively as if you do understand these topics. C++ does not do as good a job as some languages at "protecting" you from what the computer is really doing. This is actually a benefit because it provides you with tremendous power that other languages don't. As with any power tool, however, to get the most out of C++ you must understand how it works. Programmers who try to program in C++ without understanding the fundamentals of the binary system often are confused by their results.

Workshop

The Workshop provides quiz questions to help you solidify your understanding of the material covered and exercises to provide you with experience in using what you've learned. Try to answer the quiz and exercise questions before checking the answers in Appendix D, and make sure that you understand the answers before continuing to the next chapter.

Quiz

1. What is the difference between an integer variable and a floating-point variable?

2. What are the differences between an `unsigned short int` and a `long int`?

3. What are the advantages of using a symbolic constant rather than a literal constant?

4. What are the advantages of using the `const` keyword rather than `#define`?

5. What makes for a good or bad variable name?

6. Given this enum, what is the value of BLUE?

   `enum COLOR { WHITE, BLACK = 100, RED, BLUE, GREEN = 300 };`

7. Which of the following variable names are good, which are bad, and which are invalid?

   a. `Age`

   b. `!ex`

   c. `R79J`

   d. `TotalIncome`

   e. `__Invalid`

Exercises

1. What would be the correct variable type in which to store the following information?

   a. Your age.

   b. The area of your backyard.

   c. The number of stars in the galaxy.

   d. The average rainfall for the month of January.

2. Create good variable names for this information.

3. Declare a constant for pi as 3.14159.

4. Declare a `float` variable and initialize it using your pi constant.

DAY 4

Expressions and Statements

At its heart, a program is a set of commands executed in sequence. The power in a program comes from its capability to execute one or another set of commands, based on whether a particular condition is true or false.

Today you will learn

- What statements are.
- What blocks are.
- What expressions are.
- How to branch your code based on conditions.
- What truth is, and how to act on it.

Statements

In C++ a statement controls the sequence of execution, evaluates an expression, or does nothing (the null statement). All C++ statements end with a semicolon, even the null statement, which is just the semicolon and nothing else. One of the most common statements is the following assignment statement:

```
x = a + b;
```

Unlike in algebra, this statement does not mean that x equals a+b. This is read, "Assign the value of the sum of a and b to x," or "Assign to x, a+b," or "Set x equal to a plus b." Even though this statement is doing two things, it is one statement and thus has one semicolon. The assignment operator assigns whatever is on the right side of the equal sign to whatever is on the left side.

Whitespace

Whitespace (tabs, spaces, and newlines) is generally ignored in statements. The assignment statement previously discussed could be written as

```
x=a+b;
```

or as

```
x                           =a
+             b             ;
```

Although this last variation is perfectly legal, it is also perfectly foolish. Whitespace can be used to make your programs more readable and easier to maintain, or it can be used to create horrific and indecipherable code. In this, as in all things, C++ provides the power; you supply the judgment.

Whitespace characters cannot be seen. If these characters are printed, you see only the white of the paper.

Blocks and Compound Statements

Any place you can put a single statement, you can put a compound statement, also called a block. A block begins with an opening brace ({) and ends with a closing brace (}). Although every statement in the block must end with a semicolon, the block itself does not end with a semicolon, as shown in the following example:

```
{
    temp = a;
    a = b;
    b = temp;
}
```

This block of code acts as one statement and swaps the values in the variables a and b.

> ## Do
>
> **DO** use a closing brace any time you have an opening brace.
>
> **DO** end your statements with a semicolon.
>
> **DO** use whitespace judiciously to make your code clearer.

Expressions

Anything that evaluates to a value is an expression in C++. An expression is said to *return* a value. Thus, the statement 3+2; returns the value 5, so it is an expression. All expressions are statements.

The myriad pieces of code that qualify as expressions might surprise you. Here are three examples:

```
3.2                     // returns the value 3.2

PI                      // float const that returns the value 3.14

SecondsPerMinute        // int const that returns 60
```

Assuming that PI is a constant I created initialized to 3.14 and SecondsPerMinute is a constant equal to 60, all three of these statements are expressions.

The slightly more complicated expression

```
x = a + b;
```

not only adds a and b and assigns the result to x, but returns the value of that assignment (the value of x) as well. Thus, this assignment statement is also an expression. Because it is an expression, it can be on the right side of an assignment operator:

```
y = x = a + b;
```

This line is evaluated in the following order:

Add a to b.

Assign the result of the expression a + b to x.

Assign the result of the assignment expression x = a + b to y.

If a, b, x, and y are all integers, and if a has the value 2 and b has the value 5, both x and y will be assigned the value 7. This is illustrated in Listing 4.1.

LISTING 4.1   Evaluating Complex Expressions

```
 0:   #include <iostream>
 1:   int main()
 2:   {
 3:       using std::cout;
 4:       using std::endl;
 5:
 6:       int a=0, b=0, x=0, y=35;
 7:       cout << "a: " << a << " b: " << b;
 8:       cout << " x: " << x << " y: " << y << endl;
 9:       a = 9;
10:       b = 7;
11:       y = x = a+b;
12:       cout << "a: " << a << " b: " << b;
13:       cout << " x: " << x << " y: " << y << endl;
14:       return 0;
15:   }
```

OUTPUT   a: 0 b: 0 x: 0 y: 35
a: 9 b: 7 x: 16 y: 16

ANALYSIS   On line 6, the four variables are declared and initialized. Their values are printed on lines 7 and 8. On line 9, a is assigned the value 9. One line 10, b is assigned the value 7. On line 11, the values of a and b are summed and the result is assigned to x. This expression (x = a+b) evaluates to a value (the sum of a + b), and that value is, in turn, assigned to y.

Operators

An operator is a symbol that causes the compiler to take an action. Operators act on operands, and in C++ all operands are expressions. In C++ several categories of operators exist. Two of these categories are

- Assignment operators
- Mathematical operators

Assignment Operator

The assignment operator (=) causes the operand on the left side of the assignment operator to have its value changed to the value on the right side of the assignment operator. The expression

x = a + b;

assigns the value that is the result of adding a and b to the operand x.

An operand that legally can be on the left side of an assignment operator is called an l-value. That which can be on the right side is called (you guessed it) an r-value.

Constants are r-values. They cannot be l-values. Thus, you can write

```
x = 35;          // ok
```

but you can't legally write

```
35 = x;          // error, not an l-value!
```

An l-value is an operand that can be on the left side of an expression. An r-value is an operand that can be on the right side of an expression. Note that all l-values are r-values, but not all r-values are l-values. An example of an r-value that is not an l-value is a literal. Thus, you can write x = 5;, but you cannot write 5 = x; (x can be an l-value or an r-value, 5 can only be an r-value).

Mathematical Operators

Five mathematical operators are addition (+), subtraction (–), multiplication (*), division (/), and modulus (%).

Addition and subtraction work as you would expect, although subtraction with `unsigned` integers can lead to surprising results if the result is a negative number. You saw something much like this yesterday, when variable overflow was described. Listing 4.2 shows what happens when you subtract a large unsigned number from a small unsigned number.

LISTING 4.2 A Demonstration of Subtraction and Integer Overflow

```
0:   // Listing 4.2 - demonstrates subtraction and
1:   // integer overflow
2:   #include <iostream>
3:
4:   int main()
5:   {
6:      using std::cout;
7:      using std::endl;
8:
9:      unsigned int difference;
10:     unsigned int bigNumber = 100;
11:     unsigned int smallNumber = 50;
12:     difference = bigNumber - smallNumber;
13:     cout << "Difference is: " << difference;
14:     difference = smallNumber - bigNumber;
15:     cout << "\nNow difference is: " << difference <<endl;
16:     return 0;
17:   }
```

4

OUTPUT
```
Difference is: 50
Now difference is: 4294967246
```

ANALYSIS The subtraction operator is invoked on line 12, and the result is printed on line 13, much as we might expect. The subtraction operator is called again on line 14, but this time a large unsigned number is subtracted from a small unsigned number. The result would be negative, but because it is evaluated (and printed) as an unsigned number, the result is an overflow, as described yesterday. This topic is reviewed in detail in Appendix C, "Operator Precedence."

Integer Division and Modulus

Integer division is the division you learned when you were in second grade. When you divide 21 by 4 (21 / 4), and you are doing integer division the answer is 5 (with a remainder).

The modulus operator tells you the remainder after an integer division. To get the remainder, you take 21 modulus 4 (21 % 4), and the result is 1.

Finding the modulus can be very useful. For example, you might want to print a statement on every 10th action. Any number whose value is 0 when you modulus 10 with that number is an exact multiple of 10. Thus 1 % 10 is 1, 2 % 10 is 2, and so forth, until 10 % 10, whose result is 0. 11 % 10 is back to 1, and this pattern continues until the next multiple of 10, which is 20. 20%10 = 0 again. We'll use this technique when looping is discussed on Day 7, "More Program Flow."

FAQ

When I divide 5/3 I get 1. What is going wrong?

Answer: If you divide one integer by another, you get an integer as a result.

Thus 5/3 will be 1. (The actual answer is 1 with a remainder of 2. To get the remainder, try 5%3, whose value is 2.)

To get a fractional return value, you must use floats.

5.0 / 3.0 will give you a fractional answer: 1.66667

If either the divisor or the dividend is a floating point, the compiler generates a floating point quotient.

Combining the Assignment and Mathematical Operators

It is not uncommon to want to add a value to a variable and then to assign the result back into the variable. If you have a variable myAge and you want to increase the value by two, you can write

```
int myAge = 5;
int temp;
temp = myAge + 2;   // add 5 + 2 and put it in temp
myAge = temp;               // put it back in myAge
```

This method, however, is terribly convoluted and wasteful. In C++, you can put the same variable on both sides of the assignment operator; thus, the preceding becomes

```
myAge = myAge + 2;
```

which is much better. In algebra, this expression would be meaningless, but in C++ it is read as "add two to the value in myAge and assign the result to myAge."

Even simpler to write, but perhaps a bit harder to read is

```
myAge += 2;
```

The self-assigned addition operator (+=) adds the r-value to the l-value and then reassigns the result into the l-value. This operator is pronounced "plus-equals." The statement would be read "myAge plus-equals two." If myAge had the value 4 to start, it would have 6 after this statement.

Self-assigned subtraction (-=), division (/=), multiplication (*=), and modulus (%=) operators exist as well.

Increment and Decrement

The most common value to add (or subtract) and then reassign into a variable is 1. In C++, increasing a value by 1 is called incrementing, and decreasing by 1 is called decrementing. Special operators perform these actions.

The increment operator (++) increases the value of the variable by 1, and the decrement operator (--) decreases it by 1. Thus, if you have a variable, C, and you want to increment it, you would use the following statement:

```
C++;                // Start with C and increment it.
```

This statement is equivalent to the more verbose statement

```
C = C + 1;
```

that you learned is also equivalent to the moderately verbose statement

```
C += 1;
```

 Note

> As you may have guessed, C++ got its name by applying the increment operator to the name of its predecessor language: C. The idea is that C++ is an incremental improvement over C.

Prefix and Postfix

Both the increment operator (++) and the decrement operator(--) come in two varieties: prefix and postfix. The prefix variety is written before the variable name (++myAge); the postfix variety is written after (myAge++).

In a simple statement, it doesn't much matter which you use, but in a complex statement when you are incrementing (or decrementing) a variable and then assigning the result to another variable, it matters very much. The prefix operator is evaluated before the assignment; the postfix is evaluated after.

The semantics of prefix is this: Increment the value and then fetch it. The semantics of postfix is different: Fetch the value and then increment the original.

This can be confusing at first, but if x is an integer whose value is 5 and you write

```
int a = ++x;
```

you have told the compiler to increment x (making it 6) and then fetch that value and assign it to a. Thus, a is now 6 and x is now 6.

If, after doing this, you write

```
int b = x++;
```

you have now told the compiler to fetch the value in x (6) and assign it to b, and then go back and increment x. Thus, b is now 6, but x is now 7. Listing 4.3 shows the use and implications of both types.

LISTING 4.3   A Demonstration of Prefix and Postfix Operators

```
0:  // Listing 4.3 - demonstrates use of
1:  // prefix and postfix increment and
2:  // decrement operators
3:  #include <iostream>
4:  int main()
```

LISTING 4.3 continued

```
 5:  {
 6:      using std::cout;
 7:
 8:      int myAge = 39;       // initialize two integers
 9:      int yourAge = 39;
10:      cout << "I am: " << myAge << " years old.\n";
11:      cout << "You are: " << yourAge << " years old\n";
12:      myAge++;            // postfix increment
13:      ++yourAge;          // prefix increment
14:      cout << "One year passes...\n";
15:      cout << "I am: " << myAge << " years old.\n";
16:      cout << "You are: " << yourAge << " years old\n";
17:      cout << "Another year passes\n";
18:      cout << "I am: " << myAge++ << " years old.\n";
19:      cout << "You are: " << ++yourAge << " years old\n";
20:      cout << "Let's print it again.\n";
21:      cout << "I am: " << myAge << " years old.\n";
22:      cout << "You are: " << yourAge << " years old\n";
23:      return 0;
24:  }
```

OUTPUT

```
I am       39 years old
You are    39 years old
One year passes
I am       40 years old
You are    40 years old
Another year passes
I am       40 years old
You are    41 years old
Let's print it again
I am       41 years old
You are    41 years old
```

ANALYSIS On lines 8 and 9, two integer variables are declared, and each is initialized with the value 39. Their values are printed on lines 10 and 11.

On line 12, myAge is incremented using the postfix increment operator, and on line 13, yourAge is incremented using the prefix increment operator. The results are printed on lines 15 and 16, and they are identical (both 40).

On line 18, myAge is incremented as part of the printing statement, using the postfix increment operator. Because it is postfix, the increment happens after the print, and so the value 40 is printed again. In contrast, on line 19, yourAge is incremented using the prefix increment operator. Thus, it is incremented before being printed, and the value displays as 41.

Finally, on lines 21 and 22, the values are printed again. Because the increment statement has completed, the value in myAge is now 41, as is the value in yourAge.

Precedence

In the complex statement

```
x = 5 + 3 * 8;
```

which is performed first, the addition or the multiplication? If the addition is performed first, the answer is 8 * 8, or 64. If the multiplication is performed first, the answer is 5 + 24, or 29.

Every operator has a precedence value, and the complete list is shown in Appendix C.

Multiplication has higher precedence than addition; thus, the value of the expression is 29.

When two mathematical operators have the same precedence, they are performed in left-to-right order. Thus,

```
x = 5 + 3 + 8 * 9 + 6 * 4;
```

is evaluated multiplication first, left to right. Thus, 8*9 = 72, and 6*4 = 24. Now the expression is essentially

```
x = 5 + 3 + 72 + 24;
```

Now the addition, left to right, is 5 + 3 = 8; 8 + 72 = 80; 80 + 24 = 104.

Be careful with this. Some operators, such as assignment, are evaluated in right-to-left order!

In any case, what if the precedence order doesn't meet your needs? Consider the expression

```
TotalSeconds = NumMinutesToThink + NumMinutesToType * 60
```

In this expression, you do not want to multiply the NumMinutesToType variable by 60 and then add it to NumMinutesToThink. You want to add the two variables to get the total number of minutes, and then you want to multiply that number by 60 to get the total seconds.

In this case, you use parentheses to change the precedence order. Items in parentheses are evaluated at a higher precedence than any of the mathematical operators. Thus,

```
TotalSeconds = (NumMinutesToThink + NumMinutesToType) * 60
```

will accomplish what you want.

Nesting Parentheses

For complex expressions, you might need to nest parentheses one within another. For example, you might need to compute the total seconds and then compute the total number of people who are involved before multiplying seconds times people:

```
TotalPersonSeconds = ( ( (NumMinutesToThink + NumMinutesToType) * 60) *
(PeopleInTheOffice + PeopleOnVacation) )
```

This complicated expression is read from the inside out. First, `NumMinutesToThink` is added to `NumMinutesToType` because these are in the innermost parentheses. Then this sum is multiplied by 60. Next, `PeopleInTheOffice` is added to `PeopleOnVacation`. Finally, the total number of people found is multiplied by the total number of seconds.

This example raises an important related issue. This expression is easy for a computer to understand, but very difficult for a human to read, understand, or modify. Here is the same expression rewritten, using some temporary integer variables:

```
TotalMinutes = NumMinutesToThink + NumMinutesToType;
TotalSeconds = TotalMinutes * 60;
TotalPeople = PeopleInTheOffice + PeopleOnVacation;
TotalPersonSeconds = TotalPeople * TotalSeconds;
```

This example takes longer to write and uses more temporary variables than the preceding example, but it is far easier to understand. Add a comment at the top to explain what this code does and change the 60 to a symbolic constant. You then will have code that is easy to understand and maintain.

4

Do	Don't
DO remember that expressions have a value.	**DON'T** nest too deeply because the expression becomes hard to understand and maintain.
DO use the prefix operator (`++variable`) to increment or decrement the variable before it is used in the expression.	
DO use the postfix operator (`variable++`) to increment or decrement the variable after it is used.	
DO use parentheses to change the order of precedence.	

The Nature of Truth

In previous versions of C++ all truth and falsity was represented by integers, but the ANSI standard introduced the type: bool. A bool can only have one of two values: `false` or `true`.

Every expression can be evaluated for its truth or falsity. Expressions that evaluate mathematically to zero will return false; all others will return true.

> **Note**   Many compilers previously offered a bool type, which was represented internally as a long int and thus had a size of four bytes. Now ANSI-compliant compilers often provide a one byte bool.

Relational Operators

The relational operators are used to determine whether two numbers are equal or if one is greater or less than the other. Every relational statement evaluates either true or false. The relational operators are presented later, in Table 4.1.

> **Note**   All relational operators return a value of type bool: either true or false. In previous versions of C++ these operators returned either 0 for false or a non-zero value (usually 1) for true.

If the integer variable myAge has the value 45, and the integer variable yourAge has the value 50, you can determine whether they are equal by using the relational "equals" operator:

```
myAge == yourAge;   // is the value in myAge the same as in yourAge?
```

This expression evaluates to false, because the variables are not equal. The expression

```
myAge < yourAge;   // is myAge greater than yourAge?
```

evaluates to true.

> **Caution**   Many novice C++ programmers confuse the assignment operator (=) with the equals operator (==). This can create a nasty bug in your program.

The six relational operators are equals (==), less than (<), greater than (>), less than or equal to (<=), greater than or equal to (>=), and not equals (!=). Table 4.1 shows each relational operator and a sample code use.

TABLE 4.1 The Relational Operators

Name	Operator	Sample	Evaluates
Equals	==	100 == 50;	false
		50 == 50;	true
Not Equals	!=	100 != 50;	true
		50 != 50;	false
Greater Than	>	100 > 50;	true
		50 > 50;	false
Greater Than or Equals	>=	100 >= 50;	true
		50 >= 50;	true
Less Than	<	100 < 50;	false
		50 < 50;	false
Less Than or Equals	<=	100 <= 50;	false
		50 <= 50;	true

4

Do	Don't
DO remember that relational operators return the value true or false.	**DON'T** confuse the assignment operator (=) with the equals relational operator (==). This is one of the most common C++ programming mistakes—be on guard for it.

The if Statement

Normally, your program flows along line by line in the order in which it appears in your source code. The if statement enables you to test for a condition (such as whether two variables are equal) and branch to different parts of your code, depending on the result.

The simplest form of an if statement is the following:

```
if (expression)
    statement;
```

The expression in the parentheses can be any expression at all, but it usually contains one of the relational expressions. If the expression has the value false, the statement is skipped. If it evaluates true, the statement is executed. Consider the following example:

```
if (bigNumber > smallNumber)
    bigNumber = smallNumber;
```

This code compares `bigNumber` and `smallNumber`. If `bigNumber` is larger, the second line sets its value to the value of `smallNumber`.

Because a block of statements surrounded by braces is equivalent to a single statement, the branch can be quite large and powerful:

```
if (expression)
{
    statement1;
    statement2;
    statement3;
}
```

Here's a simple example of this usage:

```
if (bigNumber > smallNumber)
{
    bigNumber = smallNumber;
    std::cout << "bigNumber: " << bigNumber << "\n";
    std::cout << "smallNumber: " << smallNumber << "\n";
}
```

This time, if `bigNumber` is larger than `smallNumber`, not only is it set to the value of `smallNumber`, but an informational message is printed. Listing 4.4 shows a more detailed example of branching based on relational operators.

LISTING 4.4   A Demonstration of Branching Based on Relational Operators

```
 0:  // Listing 4.5 - demonstrates if statement
 1:  // used with relational operators
 2:  #include <iostream>
 3:  int main()
 4:  {
 5:     using std::cout;
 6:     using std::cin;
 7:
 8:     int MetsScore, YankeesScore;
 9:     cout << "Enter the score for the Mets: ";
10:     cin >> MetsScore;
11:
12:     cout << "\nEnter the score for the Yankees: ";
13:     cin >> YankeesScore;
14:
```

LISTING 4.4   continued

```
15:    cout << "\n";
16:
17:    if (MetsScore > YankeesScore)
18:        cout << "Let's Go Mets!\n";
19:
20:    if (MetsScore < YankeesScore)
21:    {
22:        cout << "Go Yankees!\n";
23:    }
24:
25:    if (MetsScore == YankeesScore)
26:    {
27:        cout << "A tie? Naah, can't be.\n";
28:        cout << "Give me the real score for the Yanks: ";
29:        cin >> YankeesScore;
30:
31:        if (MetsScore > YankeesScore)
32:            cout << "Knew it! Let's Go Mets!";
33:
34:        if (YankeesScore > MetsScore)
35:            cout << "Knew it! Go Yanks!";
36:
37:        if (YankeesScore == MetsScore)
38:            cout << "Wow, it really was a tie!";
39:    }
40:
41:    cout << "\nThanks for telling me.\n";
42:    return 0;
43: }
```

OUTPUT

```
Enter the score for the Mets: 10

Enter the score for the Yankees: 10

A tie? Naah, can't be.
Give me the real score for the Yanks: 8
Knew it! Let's Go Mets!
Thanks for telling me.
```

ANALYSIS   This program asks for user input of scores for two baseball teams; the scores are stored in integer variables. The variables are compared in the if statement on lines 17, 20, and 25. (In earlier editions of this book, it was the Yanks against the Red Sox. This year is the Subway Series, so I've updated the example!)

If one score is higher than the other, an informational message is printed. If the scores are equal, the block of code that begins on line 25 and ends on line 39 is entered. The second score is requested again, and then the scores are compared again.

Note that if the initial Yankees' score was higher than the Mets score, the `if` statement on line 17 would evaluate as false, and line 18 would not be invoked. The test on line 20 would evaluate as true, and the statement on 22 would be invoked. Then the `if` statement on line 25 would be tested and this would be false (if line 17 was true). Thus, the program would skip the entire block, falling through to line 39.

This example illustrates that getting a true result in one `if` statement does not stop other `if` statements from being tested.

Note that the action for the first two if statements is one line (printing "Let's Go Mets!" or "Go Yankees!"). In the first example (on line 18) I do not put that line in braces; a single line block doesn't need them. The braces are legal, however, and I use them in lines 21–23.

Caution

Many novice C++ programmers inadvertently put a semicolon after their `if` statements:

```
if(SomeValue < 10);
    SomeValue = 10;
```

What was intended here was to test whether `SomeValue` is less than 10, and if so, to set it to 10, making 10 the minimum value for `SomeValue`. Running this code snippet will show that `SomeValue` is always set to 10! Why? The `if` statement terminates with the semicolon (the do-nothing operator).

Remember that indentation has no meaning to the compiler. This snippet could more accurately have been written as

```
if (SomeValue < 10)  // test
;   // do nothing
SomeValue = 10;  // assign
```

Removing the semicolon will make the final line part of the `if` statement and will make this code do what was intended.

Indentation Styles

Listing 4.3 shows one style of indenting `if` statements. Nothing is more likely to create a religious war, however, than to ask a group of programmers what is the best style for brace alignment. Although dozens of variations are possible, the following appear to be the favorite three:

- Putting the initial brace after the condition and aligning the closing brace under the `if` to close the statement block:

```
if (expression){
    statements
}
```

- Aligning the braces under the `if` and indenting the statements:

```
if (expression)
{
    statements
}
```

- Indenting the braces and statements:

```
if (expression)
    {
    statements
    }
```

This book uses the middle alternative because I find it easier to understand where blocks of statements begin and end if the braces line up with each other and with the condition being tested. Again, it doesn't matter much which style you choose, so long as you are consistent with it.

else

Often your program will want to take one branch if your condition is true, another if it is false. In Listing 4.4, you wanted to print one message (`Let's Go Mets!`) if the first test (`MetsScore > YankeesScore`) evaluated true, and another message (`Go Yankees!`) if it evaluated false.

The method shown so far—testing first one condition and then the other—works fine but is a bit cumbersome. The keyword `else` can make for far more readable code:

```
if (expression)
    statement;
else
    statement;
```

Listing 4.5 demonstrates the use of the keyword `else`.

LISTING 4.5 Demonstrating the `else` Keyword

```
0:   // Listing 4.5 - demonstrates if statement
1:   // with else clause
2:   #include <iostream>
3:   int main()
4:   {
5:       using std::cout;
6:       using std::cin;
7:
8:       int firstNumber, secondNumber;
9:       cout << "Please enter a big number: ";
10:      cin >> firstNumber;
11:      cout << "\nPlease enter a smaller number: ";
```

LISTING 4.5 continued

```
12:     cin >> secondNumber;
13:     if (firstNumber > secondNumber)
14:         cout << "\nThanks!\n";
15:     else
16:         cout << "\nOops. The second is bigger!";
17:
18:     return 0;
19: }
```

OUTPUT

```
Please enter a big number: 10

Please enter a smaller number: 12

Oops. The second is bigger!
```

ANALYSIS The if statement on line 13 is evaluated. If the condition is true, the statement on line 14 is run; if it is false, the statement on line 16 is run. If the else clause on line 15 was removed, the statement on line 16 would run whether or not the if statement was true. Remember, the if statement ends after line 14. If the else was not there, line 16 would just be the next line in the program.

Remember that either or both of these statements could be replaced with a block of code in braces.

The if Statement

The syntax for the if statement is as follows:

Form 1

```
if (expression)
statement;
next statement;
```

If the expression is evaluated as true, the statement is executed and the program continues with the next statement. If the expression is not true, the statement is ignored and the program jumps to the next statement.

Remember that the statement can be a single statement ending with a semicolon or a block enclosed in braces.

Form 2

```
if (expression)
    statement1;
else
    statement2;
next statement;
```

> If the expression evaluates true, statement1 is executed; otherwise, statement2 is executed. Afterward, the program continues with the next statement.
>
> **Example 1**
> ```
> Example
> if (SomeValue < 10)
>   cout << "SomeValue is less than 10");
> else
>   cout << "SomeValue is not less than 10!");
> cout << "Done." << endl;
> ```

Advanced `if` Statements

It is worth noting that any statement can be used in an `if` or `else` clause, even another `if` or `else` statement. Thus, you might see complex `if` statements in the following form:

```
if (expression1)
{
    if (expression2)
        statement1;
    else
    {
        if (expression3)
            statement2;
        else
            statement3;
    }
}
else
    statement4;
```

This cumbersome `if` statement says, "If expression1 is true and expression2 is true, execute statement1. If expression1 is true but expression2 is not true, then if expression3 is true execute statement2. If expression1 is true but expression2 and expression3 are false, execute statement3. Finally, if expression1 is not true, execute statement4." As you can see, complex `if` statements can be confusing!

Listing 4.6 gives an example of one such complex `if` statement.

LISTING 4.6   A Complex, Nested `if` Statement

```
0:  // Listing 4.6 - a complex nested
1:  // if statement
2:  #include <iostream>
3:  int main()
4:  {
```

LISTING 4.6   continued

```
 5:      // Ask for two numbers
 6:      // Assign the numbers to bigNumber and littleNumber
 7:      // If bigNumber is bigger than littleNumber,
 8:      // see if they are evenly divisible
 9:      // If they are, see if they are the same number
10:
11:      using namespace std;
12:
13:      int firstNumber, secondNumber;
14:      cout << "Enter two numbers.\nFirst: ";
15:      cin >> firstNumber;
16:      cout << "\nSecond: ";
17:      cin >> secondNumber;
18:        cout << "\n\n";
19:
20:      if (firstNumber >= secondNumber)
21:      {
22:         if ( (firstNumber % secondNumber) == 0) // evenly divisible?
23:         {
24:            if (firstNumber == secondNumber)
25:               cout << "They are the same!\n";
26:            else
27:               cout << "They are evenly divisible!\n";
28:         }
29:         else
30:            cout << "They are not evenly divisible!\n";
31:      }
32:      else
33:         cout << "Hey! The second one is larger!\n";
34:      return 0;
35:   }
```

OUTPUT   Enter two numbers.
              First: 10

              Second: 2
              They are evenly divisible!

ANALYSIS Two numbers are prompted for one at a time, and then compared. The first `if`
              statement, on line 20, checks to ensure that the first number is greater than or
equal to the second. If not, the `else` clause on line 32 is executed.

If the first `if` is true, the block of code beginning on line 21 is executed, and the second
`if` statement is tested on line 22. This checks to see whether the first number modulo the
second number yields no remainder. If so, the numbers are either evenly divisible or

equal. The if statement on line 24 checks for equality and displays the appropriate message either way.

If the if statement on line 22 fails, the else statement on line 29 is executed.

Using Braces in Nested if Statements

Although it is legal to leave out the braces on if statements that are only a single statement, and it is legal to nest if statements, such as

```
if (x > y)              // if x is bigger than y
   if (x < z)           // and if x is smaller than z
      x = y;            // then set x to the value in y
```

when you're writing large nested statements, this can cause enormous confusion. Remember, whitespace and indentation are a convenience for the programmer; they make no difference to the compiler. It is easy to confuse the logic and inadvertently assign an else statement to the wrong if statement. Listing 4.7 illustrates this problem.

LISTING 4.7   A Demonstration of Why Braces Help Clarify Which else Statement Goes with Which if Statement

```
0:  // Listing 4.7 - demonstrates why braces
1:  // are important in nested if statements
2:  #include <iostream>
3:  int main()
4:  {
5:     int x;
6:     std::cout << "Enter a number less than 10 or greater than 100: ";
7:     std::cin >> x;
8:     std::cout << "\n";
9:
10:    if (x >= 10)
11:       if (x > 100)
12:          std::cout << "More than 100, Thanks!\n";
13:    else                        // not the else intended!
14:       std::cout << "Less than 10, Thanks!\n";
15:
16:    return 0;
17: }
```

OUTPUT

```
Enter a number less than 10 or greater than 100: 20

Less than 10, Thanks!
```

ANALYSIS   The programmer intended to ask for a number less than 10 or greater than 100, check for the correct value, and then print a thank-you note.

If the `if` statement on line 10 evaluates true, the following statement (line 11) is executed. In this case, line 11 executes when the number entered is greater than 10. Line 11 contains an `if` statement also. This `if` statement evaluates true if the number entered is greater than 100. If the number is greater than 100, the statement on line 12 is executed.

If the number entered is less than 10, the `if` statement on line 10 evaluates false. Program control goes to the next line following the `if` statement, in this case line 17. If you enter a number less than 10, the output is as follows:

```
Enter a number less than 10 or greater than 100: 9
```

The `else` clause on line 13 was clearly intended to be attached to the `if` statement on line 10, and thus is indented accordingly. Unfortunately, the `else` statement is really attached to the `if` statement on line 11, and thus this program has a subtle bug.

It is a subtle bug because the compiler will not complain. This is a legal C++ program, but it just doesn't do what was intended. Further, most of the times the programmer tests this program, it will appear to work. As long as a number that is greater than 100 is entered, the program will seem to work just fine.

Listing 4.8 fixes the problem by putting in the necessary braces.

LISTING 4.8   A Demonstration of the Proper Use of Braces with an `if` Statement

```
0:   // Listing 4.8 - demonstrates proper use of braces
1:   // in nested if statements
2:   #include <iostream>
3:   int main()
4:   {
5:     int x;
6:     std::cout << "Enter a number less than 10 or greater than 100: ";
7:     std::cin >> x;
8:     std::cout << "\n";
9:
10:    if (x >= 10)
11:    {
12:      if (x > 100)
13:        std::cout << "More than 100, Thanks!\n";
14:    }
15:    else                          // fixed!
16:      std::cout << "Less than 10, Thanks!\n";
17:    return 0;
18:  }
```

OUTPUT   Enter a number less than 10 or greater than 100: 9

Less than 10, Thanks!

ANALYSIS The braces on lines 11 and 14 make everything between them into one statement, and now the `else` on line 15 applies to the `if` on line 10, as intended.

If the user types 9, the `if` statement on line 11 is true; however, the `if` statement on line 13 is false, so nothing would be printed. It would be better if the programmer put another `else` clause after line 14 so that errors would be caught and a message printed.

Note

> The programs shown in this book are written to demonstrate the particular issues being discussed. They are kept intentionally simple; no attempt is made to "bulletproof" the code to protect against user error. Ideally, in professional-quality code, every possible user error is anticipated and handled gracefully.

Logical Operators

Often you want to ask more than one relational question at a time. "Is it true that x is greater than y, and also true that y is greater than z?" A program might need to determine that both of these conditions are true—or that some other condition is true—in order to take an action.

Imagine a sophisticated alarm system that has this logic: "If the door alarm sounds AND it is after six p.m. AND it is NOT a holiday, OR if it is a weekend, then call the police." C++'s three logical operators are used to make this kind of evaluation. These operators are listed in Table 4.2.

TABLE 4.2   The Logical Operators

Operator	Symbol	Example
AND	&&	expression1 && expression2
OR	||	expression1 || expression2
NOT	!	!expression

Logical AND

A logical AND statement evaluates two expressions, and if both expressions are true, the logical AND statement is true as well. If it is true that you are hungry, AND it is true that you have money, THEN it is true that you can buy lunch. Thus,

```
if ( (x == 5) && (y == 5) )
```

would evaluate true if both x and y are equal to 5, and it would evaluate false if either one is not equal to 5. Note that both sides must be true for the entire expression to be true.

Note that the logical AND is two && symbols. A single & symbol is a different operator, which is discussed on Day 21, "What's Next."

Logical OR

A logical OR statement evaluates two expressions. If either one is true, the expression is true. If you have money OR you have a credit card, you can pay the bill. You don't need both money and a credit card; you need only one, although having both would be fine as well. Thus,

```
if ( (x == 5) || (y == 5) )
```

evaluates true if either x or y is equal to 5, or if both are equal to 5.

Note that the logical OR is two || symbols. A single | symbol is a different operator, which is discussed on Day 21.

Logical NOT

A logical NOT statement evaluates true if the expression being tested is false. Again, if the expression being tested is false, the value of the test is true! Thus

```
if ( !(x == 5) )
```

is true only if x is not equal to 5. This is the same as writing

```
if (x != 5)
```

Short Circuit Evaluation

When the compiler is evaluating an AND statement, such as

```
if ( (x == 5) && (y == 5) )
```

the compiler will evaluate the truth of the first statement (x==5), and if this fails (that is, if x is not equal to 5), the compiler will NOT go on to evaluate the truth or falsity of the second statement (y == 5) because AND requires both to be true.

Similarly, if the compiler is evaluating an OR statement, such as

```
if ( (x == 5) || (y == 5) )
```

if the first statement is true (x == 5), the compiler will never evaluate the second statement (y == 5) because the truth of *either* is sufficient in an OR statement.

Relational Precedence

Relational operators and logical operators, because they are C++ expressions, each return a value: true or false. Like all expressions, they have a precedence order (see Appendix C) that determines which relations are evaluated first. This fact is important when determining the value of the statement

```
if ( x > 5 &&  y > 5  || z > 5)
```

It might be that the programmer wanted this expression to evaluate true if both x and y are greater than 5 or if z is greater than 5. On the other hand, the programmer might have wanted this expression to evaluate true only if x is greater than 5 and if it is also true that either y is greater than 5 or z is greater than 5.

If x is 3, and y and z are both 10, the first interpretation will be true (z is greater than 5, so ignore x and y), but the second will be false (it isn't true that x is greater than 5 and thus it doesn't matter what is on the right side of the && symbol because both sides must be true).

Although precedence will determine which relation is evaluated first, parentheses can both change the order and make the statement clearer:

```
if (   (x > 5)  && (y > 5 ||  z > 5) )
```

Using the values from earlier, this statement is false. Because it is not true that x is greater than 5, the left side of the AND statement fails, and thus the entire statement is false. Remember that an AND statement requires that both sides be true—something isn't both "good tasting" AND "good for you" if it isn't good tasting.

 Note

> It is often a good idea to use extra parentheses to clarify what you want to group. Remember, the goal is to write programs that work and that are easy to read and to understand.

More About Truth and Falsehood

In C++, zero evaluates false, and all other values evaluate true. Because an expression always has a value, many C++ programmers take advantage of this feature in their if statements. A statement such as

```
if (x)          // if x is true (nonzero)
    x = 0;
```

4

can be read as "If x has a nonzero value, set it to 0." This is a bit of a cheat; it would be clearer if written

```
if (x != 0)        // if x is nonzero
   x = 0;
```

Both statements are legal, but the latter is clearer. It is good programming practice to reserve the former method for true tests of logic, rather than for testing for nonzero values.

These two statements also are equivalent:

```
if (!x)            // if x is false (zero)

if (x == 0)        // if x is zero
```

The second statement, however, is somewhat easier to understand and is more explicit if you are testing for the mathematical value of x rather than for its logical state.

Do	Don't
DO put parentheses around your logical tests to make them clearer and to make the precedence explicit.	DON'T use if(x) as a synonym for if(x != 0); the latter is clearer.
DO use braces in nested if statements to make the else statements clearer and to avoid bugs.	DON'T use if(!x) as a synonym for if(x == 0); the latter is clearer.

Conditional (Ternary) Operator

The conditional operator (?:) is C++'s only ternary operator; that is, it is the only operator to take three terms.

The conditional operator takes three expressions and returns a value:

```
(expression1) ? (expression2) : (expression3)
```

This line is read as "If expression1 is true, return the value of expression2; otherwise, return the value of expression3." Typically, this value would be assigned to a variable.

Listing 4.9 shows an if statement rewritten using the conditional operator.

LISTING 4.9   A Demonstration of the Conditional Operator

```
0:   // Listing 4.9 - demonstrates the conditional operator
1:   //
2:   #include <iostream>
```

LISTING 4.9 continued

```
 3:  int main()
 4:  {
 5:      using namespace std;
 6:
 7:      int x, y, z;
 8:      cout << "Enter two numbers.\n";
 9:      cout << "First: ";
10:      cin >> x;
11:      cout << "\nSecond: ";
12:      cin >> y;
13:      cout << "\n";
14:
15:      if (x > y)
16:          z = x;
17:      else
18:          z = y;
19:
20:      cout << "z: " << z;
21:      cout << "\n";
22:
23:      z =  (x > y) ? x : y;
24:
25:      cout << "z: " << z;
26:      cout << "\n";
27:      return 0;
28:  }
```

OUTPUT
```
Enter two numbers.
First: 5

Second: 8

z: 8
z: 8
```

ANALYSIS Three integer variables are created: x, y, and z. The first two are given values by the user. The if statement on line 15 tests to see which is larger and assigns the larger value to z. This value is printed on line 20.

The conditional operator on line 23 makes the same test and assigns z the larger value. It is read like this: "If x is greater than y, return the value of x; otherwise, return the value of y." The value returned is assigned to z. That value is printed on line 25. As you can see, the conditional statement is a shorter equivalent to the if...else statement.

4

Summary

This chapter has covered a lot of material. You have learned what C++ statements and expressions are, what C++ operators do, and how C++ if statements work.

You have seen that a block of statements enclosed by a pair of braces can be used anywhere a single statement can be used.

You have learned that every expression evaluates to a value, and that value can be tested in an if statement or by using the conditional operator. You've also seen how to evaluate multiple statements using the logical operator, how to compare values using the relational operators, and how to assign values using the assignment operator.

You have explored operator precedence. And you have seen how parentheses can be used to change the precedence and to make precedence explicit and thus easier to manage.

Q&A

Q Why use unnecessary parentheses when precedence will determine which operators are acted on first?

A Although it is true that the compiler will know the precedence and that a programmer can look up the precedence order, code that is easy to understand is easier to maintain.

Q If the relational operators always return true or false, why is any non-zero value considered true?

A The relational operators return true or false, but every expression returns a value, and those values can also be evaluated in an if statement. Here's an example:

```
if ( (x = a + b) == 35 )
```

This is a perfectly legal C++ statement. It evaluates to a value even if the sum of a and b is not equal to 35. Also note that x is assigned the value that is the sum of a and b in any case.

Q What effect do tabs, spaces, and new lines have on the program?

A Tabs, spaces, and new lines (known as whitespace) have no effect on the program, although judicious use of whitespace can make the program easier to read.

Q Are negative numbers true or false?

A All nonzero numbers, positive and negative, are true.

Workshop

The Workshop provides quiz questions to help you solidify your understanding of the material covered and exercises to provide you with experience in using what you've learned. Try to answer the quiz and exercise questions before checking the answers in Appendix D, and make sure that you understand the answers before continuing to the next chapter.

Quiz

1. What is an expression?

2. Is x = 5 + 7 an expression? What is its value?

3. What is the value of 201 / 4?

4. What is the value of 201 % 4?

5. If `myAge`, `a`, and `b` are all `int` variables, what are their values after
    ```
    myAge = 39;
    a = myAge++;
    b = ++myAge;
    ```

6. What is the value of 8+2*3?

7. What is the difference between `if(x = 3)` and `if(x == 3)`?

8. Do the following values evaluate True or False?

    a. `0`

    b. `1`

    c. `-1`

    d. `x = 0`

    e. `x == 0 // assume that x has the value of 0`

Exercises

1. Write a single `if` statement that examines two integer variables and changes the larger to the smaller, using only one `else` clause.

2. Examine the following program. Imagine entering three numbers, and write what output you expect.
    ```
    1:    #include <iostream>
    2:    using namespace std;
    3:    int main()
    4:    {
    5:        int a, b, c;
    6:        cout << "Please enter three numbers\n";
    ```

```
7:          cout << "a: ";
8:          cin >> a;
9:          cout << "\nb: ";
10:          cin >> b;
11:         cout << "\nc: ";
12:         cin >> c;
13:
14:      if (c = (a-b))
15:            cout << "a: " << a << " minus b: " << b << "
                                _equals c: " << c;
16:      else
17:            cout << "a-b does not equal c: ";
18:    return 0;
19:  }
```

3. Enter the program from Exercise 2; compile, link, and run it. Enter the numbers 20, 10, and 50. Did you get the output you expected? Why not?

4. Examine this program and anticipate the output:

```
1:     #include <iostream>
2:     using namespace std;
3:      int main()
4:       {
5:           int a = 2, b = 2, c;
6:           if (c = (a-b))
7:                cout << "The value of c is: " << c;
8:      return 0;
9:       }
```

5. Enter, compile, link, and run the program from Exercise 4. What was the output? Why?

DAY 5

Functions

Although object-oriented programming has shifted attention from functions and toward objects, functions nonetheless remain a central component of any program. Global functions exist outside of objects, and member functions (also called member methods) exist within the object and do its work.

Today you will learn

- What a function is and what its parts are.
- How to declare and define functions.
- How to pass parameters into functions.
- How to return a value from a function.

We'll start with global functions; tomorrow you'll see how functions work from within objects as well.

What Is a Function?

A function is, in effect, a subprogram that can act on data and return a value. Every C++ program has at least one function, main(). When your program starts, main() is called automatically. main() might call other functions, some of which might call still others.

Since these functions are not part of an object, they are called "global"—that is, they may be accessed from anywhere in your program. For today, when we talk about functions, we mean global functions unless otherwise noted.

Each function has its own name, and when that name is encountered, the execution of the program branches to the body of that function. This is called *calling* the function. When the function returns, execution resumes on the next line of the calling function. This flow is illustrated in Figure 5.1.

FIGURE 5.1

When a program calls a function, execution switches to the function and then resumes at the line after the function call.

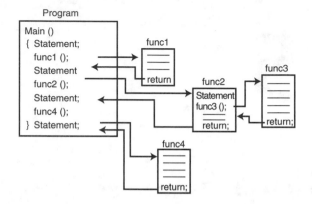

Well-designed functions perform a specific and easily understood task. Complicated tasks should be broken down into multiple functions, and then each can be called in turn.

Functions come in two varieties: user-defined and built-in. Built-in functions are part of your compiler package—they are supplied by the manufacturer for your use. User-defined functions are the functions you write yourself.

Return Values, Parameters, and Arguments

Functions can *return* a value. When you call a function, it can do work and then send back a value as a result of that work. This is called its *return value*, and the type of that return value must be declared. Thus if you write

```
int myFunction();
```

you are declaring that `myFunction` will return an integer value.

You can also send values *into* the function. These values then act as variables that you can manipulate from within the function.

The description of the values you send is called a parameter list.

```
int myFunction(int someValue, float someFloat);
```

This declaration indicates that `myFunction` will not only return an integer, it will take an integer value and a `float` as parameters.

A parameter describes the *type* of the value that will be passed into the function when the function is called. The actual values you pass into the function are called the *arguments*.

```
int theValueReturned = myFunction(5,6.7);
```

Here we see that an integer variable `theValueReturned` is initialized with the value returned by `myFunction`, and that the values 5 and 6.7 are passed in as arguments. The type of the arguments must match the declared parameter types.

Declaring and Defining Functions

Using functions in your program requires that you first declare the function and that you then define the function. The declaration tells the compiler the name, return type, and parameters of the function. The definition tells the compiler how the function works. No function can be called from any other function if it hasn't first been declared. A declaration of a function is called a *prototype*.

Declaring the Function

Three ways exist to declare a function:

- Write your prototype into a file, and then use the `#include` directive to include it in your program.
- Write the prototype into the file in which your function is used.
- Define the function before it is called by any other function. When you do this, the definition acts as its own declaration.

Although you can define the function before using it and thus avoid the necessity of creating a function prototype, this is not good programming practice for three reasons.

First, it is a bad idea to require that functions appear in a file in a particular order. Doing so makes it hard to maintain the program when requirements change.

Second, it is possible that function A() needs to be able to call function B(), but function B() also needs to be able to call function A() under some circumstances. It is not possible to define function A() before you define function B() and also to define function B() before you define function A(), so at least one of them must be declared in any case.

5

Third, function prototypes are a good and powerful debugging technique. If your prototype declares that your function takes a particular set of parameters or that it returns a
particular type of value, and then your function does not match the prototype, the compiler can flag your error instead of waiting for it to show itself when you run the program. This is like double entry bookkeeping. The prototype and the definition check each
other, reducing the likelihood that a simple typo will lead to a bug in your program.

Function Prototypes

Many of the built-in functions you use will have their function prototypes already written
for you. These appear in the files you include in your program by using `#include`. For
functions you write yourself, you must include the prototype.

The function prototype is a statement, which means it ends with a semicolon. It consists
of the function's return type and signature. A function signature is its name and parameter list.

The parameter list is a list of all the parameters and their types, separated by commas.
Figure 5.2 illustrates the parts of the function prototype.

FIGURE 5.2

*Parts of a function
prototype.*

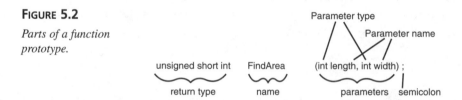

The function prototype and the function definition must agree exactly about the return
type and signature. If they do not agree, you will get a compile-time error. Note, however, that the function prototype does not need to contain the names of the parameters, just
their types. A prototype that looks like this is perfectly legal:

```
long Area(int, int);
```

This prototype declares a function named `Area()` that returns a `long` and that has two
parameters, both integers. Although this is legal, it is not a good idea. Adding parameter
names makes your prototype clearer. The same function with named parameters might be

```
long Area(int length, int width);
```

It is now obvious what this function does and what the parameters are.

Note that all functions have a return type. If none is explicitly stated, the return type
defaults to `int`. Your programs will be easier to understand, however, if you explicitly
declare the return type of every function, including `main()`.

Defining the Function

The definition of a function consists of the function header and its body. The header is like the function prototype except that the parameters must be named, and no terminating semicolon is used.

The body of the function is a set of statements enclosed in braces. Figure 5.3 shows the header and body of a function.

FIGURE 5.3

The header and body of a function.

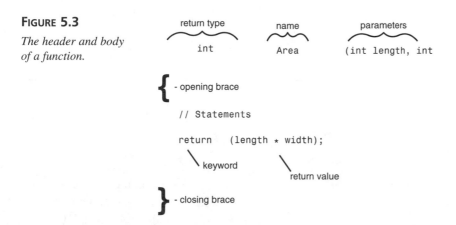

Listing 5.1 demonstrates a program that includes a function prototype for the Area() function.

LISTING 5.1   A Function Declaration and the Definition and Use of That Function

```
0:   // Listing 5.1 - demonstrates the use of function prototypes
1:
2:   #include <iostream>
3:   int Area(int length, int width); //function prototype
4:
5:   int main()
6:   {
7:       using std::cout;
8:       using std::cin;
9:
10:      int lengthOfYard;
11:      int widthOfYard;
12:      int areaOfYard;
13:
14:      cout << "\nHow wide is your yard? ";
15:      cin >> widthOfYard;
16:      cout << "\nHow long is your yard? ";
17:      cin >> lengthOfYard;
```

LISTING 5.1   continued

```
18:
19:     areaOfYard= Area(lengthOfYard,widthOfYard);
20:
21:     cout << "\nYour yard is ";
22:     cout << areaOfYard;
23:     cout << " square feet\n\n";
24:     return 0;
25: }
26:
27: int Area(int l, int w)
28: {
29:     return l * w;
30: }
```

OUTPUT

```
How wide is your yard? 100

How long is your yard? 200

Your yard is 20000 square feet
```

ANALYSIS The prototype for the `Area()` function is on line 3. Compare the prototype with the definition of the function on line 27. Note that the name, the return type, and the parameter types are the same. If they were different, a compiler error would have been generated. In fact, the only required difference is that the function prototype ends with a semicolon and has no body.

Also note that the parameter names in the prototype are length and width, but the parameter names in the definition are `l` and `w`. As discussed, the names in the prototype are not used; they are there as information to the programmer. It is good programming practice to match the prototype parameter names to the implementation parameter names, but this is not required.

The arguments are passed in to the function in the order in which the parameters are declared and defined, but no matching of the names occurs. Had you passed in `widthOfYard`, followed by `lengthOfYard`, the `FindArea()` function would have used the value in `widthOfYard` for length and `lengthOfYard` for width. The body of the function is always enclosed in braces, even when it consists of only one statement, as in this case.

Execution of Functions

When you call a function, execution begins with the first statement after the opening brace (`{`). Branching can be accomplished by using the `if` statement. (The `if` and other related statements will be discussed on Day 7, "More Program Flow"). Functions can also call other functions and can even call themselves (see the section "Recursion," later in this chapter).

Local Variables

Not only can you pass in variables to the function, but you also can declare variables within the body of the function. Variables you declare within the body of the function are called "local" because they exist only locally within the function itself. When the function returns, the local variables are no longer available; they are marked for destruction by the compiler.

Local variables are defined the same as any other variables. The parameters passed in to the function are also considered local variables and can be used exactly as if they had been defined within the body of the function. Listing 5.2 is an example of using parameters and locally defined variables within a function.

LISTING 5.2   The Use of Local Variables and Parameters

```
0:   #include <iostream>
1:
2:   float Convert(float);
3:   int main()
4:   {
5:      using namespace std;
6:
7:      float TempFer;
8:      float TempCel;
9:
10:     cout << "Please enter the temperature in Fahrenheit: ";
11:     cin >> TempFer;
12:     TempCel = Convert(TempFer);
13:     cout << "\nHere's the temperature in Celsius: ";
14:     cout << TempCel << endl;
15:     return 0;
16:  }
17:
18:  float Convert(float TempFer)
19:  {
20:     float TempCel;
21:     TempCel = ((TempFer - 32) * 5) / 9;
22:     return TempCel;
23:  }
```

5

OUTPUT

```
Please enter the temperature in Fahrenheit: 212

Here's the temperature in Celsius: 100

Please enter the temperature in Fahrenheit: 32

Here's the temperature in Celsius: 0

Please enter the temperature in Fahrenheit: 85

Here's the temperature in Celsius: 29.4444
```

ANALYSIS On lines 7 and 8, two `float` variables are declared, one to hold the temperature in Fahrenheit and one to hold the temperature in degrees Celsius. The user is prompted to enter a Fahrenheit temperature on line 10, and that value is passed to the function `Convert()`.

Execution jumps to the first line of the function `Convert()` on line 20, where a local variable, also named `TempCel`, is declared. Note that this local variable is not the same as the variable `TempCel` on line 8. This variable exists only within the function `Convert()`. The value passed as a parameter, `TempFer`, is also just a local copy of the variable passed in by `main()`.

This function could have named the parameter `FerTemp` and the local variable `CelTemp`, and the program would work equally well. You can enter these names again and recompile the program to see this work.

The local function variable `TempCel` is assigned the value that results from subtracting 32 from the parameter `TempFer`, multiplying by 5, and then dividing by 9. This value is then returned as the return value of the function, and on line 12 it is assigned to the variable `TempCel` in the `main()` function. The value is printed on line 14.

The program is run three times. The first time, the value `212` is passed in to ensure that the boiling point of water in degrees Fahrenheit (`212`) generates the correct answer in degrees Celsius (`100`). The second test is the freezing point of water. The third test is a random number chosen to generate a fractional result.

Scope

A variable has scope, which determines how long it is available to your program and where it can be accessed. Variables declared within a block are scoped to that block; they can be accessed only within that block and "go out of existence" when that block ends. Global variables have global scope and are available anywhere within your program.

Global Variables

Variables defined outside of any function have global scope and thus are available from any function in the program, including main().

Local variables with the same name as global variables do not change the global variables. A local variable with the same name as a global variable *hides* the global variable, however. If a function has a variable with the same name as a global variable, the name refers to the local variable—not the global—when used within the function. Listing 5.3 illustrates these points.

LISTING 5.3   Demonstrating Global and Local Variables

```
0:   #include <iostream>
1:   void myFunction();          // prototype
2:
3:   int x = 5, y = 7;           // global variables
4:   int main()
5:   {
6:      using std::cout;
7:
8:      cout << "x from main: " << x << "\n";
9:      cout << "y from main: " << y << "\n\n";
10:     myFunction();
11:     cout << "Back from myFunction!\n\n";
12:     cout << "x from main: " << x << "\n";
13:     cout << "y from main: " << y << "\n";
14:     return 0;
15:  }
16:
17:  void myFunction()
18:  {
19:     using std::cout;
20:
21:     int y = 10;
22:
23:     cout << "x from myFunction: " << x << "\n";
24:     cout << "y from myFunction: " << y << "\n\n"0
25:  }
```

OUTPUT
```
x from main: 5
y from main: 7

x from myFunction: 5
y from myFunction: 10

Back from myFunction!
```

```
x from main: 5
y from main: 7
```

ANALYSIS This simple program illustrates a few key, and potentially confusing, points about local and global variables. On line 3, two global variables, x and y, are declared. The global variable x is initialized with the value 5, and the global variable y is initialized with the value 7.

On lines 8 and 9 in the function main(), these values are printed to the screen. Note that the function main() defines neither variable; because they are global, they are already available to main().

When myFunction() is called on line 10, program execution passes to line 17, and on line 21 a local variable, y, is defined and initialized with the value 10. On line 23, myFunction() prints the value of the variable x, and the global variable x is used, just as it was in main(). On line 24, however, when the variable name y is used, the local variable y is used, hiding the global variable with the same name.

The function call ends, and control returns to main(), which again prints the values in the global variables. Note that the global variable y was totally unaffected by the value assigned to myFunction()'s local y variable.

Global Variables: A Word of Caution

In C++, global variables are legal, but they are almost never used. C++ grew out of C, and in C global variables are a dangerous but necessary tool. They are necessary because there are times when the programmer needs to make data available to many functions, and he does not want to pass that data as a parameter from function to function.

Globals are dangerous because they are shared data, and one function can change a global variable in a way that is invisible to another function. This can and does create bugs that are very difficult to find.

On Day 15, "Special Classes and Functions," you'll see a powerful alternative to global variables called static member variables.

More on Local Variables

You can define variables anywhere within the function, not just at its top. The scope of the variable is the block in which it is defined. Thus, if you define a variable inside a set of braces within the function, that variable is available only within that block. Listing 5.4 illustrates this idea.

LISTING 5.4 Variables Scoped Within a Block

```
0:  // Listing 5.4 - demonstrates variables
1:  // scoped within a block
2:
3:  #include <iostream>
4:
5:  void myFunc();
6:
7:  int main()
8:  {
9:      int x = 5;
10:     std::cout << "\nIn main x is: " << x;
11:
12:     myFunc();
13:
14:     std::cout << "\nBack in main, x is: " << x;
15:     return 0;
16: }
17:
18: void myFunc()
19: {
20:     int x = 8;
21:     std::cout << "\nIn myFunc, local x: " << x << std::endl;
22:
23:     {
24:         std::cout << "\nIn block in myFunc, x is: " << x;
25:
26:         int x = 9;
27:
28:         std::cout << "\nVery local x: " << x;
29:     }
30:
31:     std::cout << "\nOut of block, in myFunc, x: " << x << std::endl;
32: }
```

OUTPUT

```
In main x is: 5
In myFunc, local x: 8

In block in myFunc, x is: 8
Very local x: 9
Out of block, in myFunc, x: 8
Back in main, x is: 5
```

ANALYSIS This program begins with the initialization of a local variable, x, on line 9, in main(). The printout on line 10 verifies that x was initialized with the value 5.

MyFunc() is called, and a local variable, also named x, is initialized with the value 8 on line 20. Its value is printed on line 21.

5

A block is started on line 23, and the variable x from the function is printed again on line 24. A new variable also named x, but local to the block, is created on line 26 and initialized with the value 9.

The value of the newest variable x is printed on line 28. The local block ends on line 29, and the variable created on line 26 goes "out of scope" and is no longer visible.

When x is printed on line 31, it is the x that was declared on line 20. This x was unaffected by the x that was defined on line 26; its value is still 8.

On line 32, MyFunc() goes out of scope, and its local variable x becomes unavailable. Execution returns to line 14, and the value of the local variable x, which was created on line 9, is printed. It was unaffected by either of the variables defined in MyFunc().

Needless to say, this program would be far less confusing if these three variables were given unique names!

Function Statements

Virtually no limit exists to the number or types of statements that can be placed in the body of a function. Although you can't define another function from within a function, you can *call* a function, and of course, main() does just that in nearly every C++ program. Functions can even call themselves, which is discussed soon in the section on recursion.

Although no limit exists to the size of a function in C++, well-designed functions tend to be small. Many programmers advise keeping your functions short enough to fit on a single screen so that you can see the entire function at one time. This is a rule of thumb, often broken by very good programmers, but it is true that a smaller function is easier to understand and maintain.

Each function should carry out a single, easily understood task. If your functions start getting large, look for places where you can divide them into component tasks.

More About Function Arguments

Function arguments do not all have to be of the same type. It is perfectly reasonable to write a function that takes an integer, two longs, and a character as its arguments.

Any valid C++ expression can be a function argument, including constants, mathematical and logical expressions, and other functions that return a value.

Using Functions as Parameters to Functions

Although it is legal for one function to take as a parameter a second function that returns a value, it can make for code that is hard to read and hard to debug.

As an example, suppose you have the functions myDouble(), triple(), square(), and cube(), each of which returns a value. You could write

```
Answer = (myDouble(triple(square(cube(myValue)))));
```

This statement takes a variable, myValue, and passes it as an argument to the function cube(), whose return value is passed as an argument to the function square(), whose return value is in turn passed to triple(), and that return value is passed to myDouble(). The return value of this doubled, tripled, squared, and cubed number is now assigned to Answer.

It is difficult to be certain what this code does (was the value tripled before or after it was squared?), and if the answer is wrong, it will be hard to figure out which function failed.

An alternative is to assign each step to its own intermediate variable:

```
unsigned long myValue = 2;
unsigned long cubed   =  cube(myValue);      // cubed = 8
unsigned long squared = square(cubed);       // squared = 64
unsigned long tripled = triple(squared);     // tripled = 192
unsigned long Answer =  myDouble(tripled);    // Answer = 384
```

Now each intermediate result can be examined, and the order of execution is explicit.

Parameters Are Local Variables

The arguments passed in to the function are local to the function. Changes made to the arguments do not affect the values in the calling function. This is known as passing *by value*, which means a local copy of each argument is made in the function. These local copies are treated the same as any other local variables. Listing 5.5 illustrates this point.

LISTING 5.5   A Demonstration of Passing by Value

```
0:  // Listing 5.5 - demonstrates passing by value
1:
2:  #include <iostream>
3:
4:  void swap(int x, int y);
5:
6:  int main()
7:  {
```

5

LISTING 5.5   continued

```
 8:     int x = 5, y = 10;
 9:
10:     std::cout << "Main. Before swap, x: " << x << " y: " << y << "\n";
11:     swap(x,y);
12:     std::cout << "Main. After swap, x: " << x << " y: " << y << "\n";
13:     return 0;
14: }
15:
16: void swap (int x, int y)
17: {
18:     int temp;
19:
20:     std::cout << "Swap. Before swap, x: " << x << " y: " << y << "\n";
21:
22:     temp = x;
23:     x = y;
24:     y = temp;
25:
26:     std::cout << "Swap. After swap, x: " << x << " y: " << y << "\n";
27: }
```

OUTPUT
```
Main. Before swap, x: 5 y: 10
Swap. Before swap, x: 5 y: 10
Swap. After swap, x: 10 y: 5
Main. After swap, x: 5 y: 10
```

ANALYSIS   This program initializes two variables in main() and then passes them to the swap() function, which appears to swap them. When they are examined again in main(), however, they are unchanged!

The variables are initialized on line 8, and their values are displayed on line 10. swap() is called, and the variables are passed in.

Execution of the program switches to the swap() function, where on line 20 the values are printed again. They are in the same order as they were in main(), as expected. On lines 22 to 24 the values are swapped, and this action is confirmed by the printout on line 26. Indeed, while in the swap() function, the values are swapped.

Execution then returns to line 12, back in main(), where the values are no longer swapped.

As you've figured out, the values passed in to the swap() function are passed by value, meaning that copies of the values are made that are local to swap(). These local variables are swapped in lines 22 to 24, but the variables back in main() are unaffected.

On Day 8, "Pointers," and Day 10, "Advanced Functions," you'll see alternatives to passing by value that will allow the values in main() to be changed.

More About Return Values

Functions return a value or return void. Void is a signal to the compiler that no value will be returned.

To return a value from a function, write the keyword `return` followed by the value you want to return. The value might itself be an expression that returns a value. For example:

```
return 5;
return (x > 5);
return (MyFunction());
```

These are all legal return statements, assuming that the function `MyFunction()` itself returns a value. The value in the second statement, `return (x > 5)`, will be false if x is not greater than 5, or it will be true. What is returned is the value of the expression, false or true, not the value of x.

When the `return` keyword is encountered, the expression following `return` is returned as the value of the function. Program execution returns immediately to the calling function, and any statements following the return are not executed.

It is legal to have more than one return statement in a single function. Listing 5.6 illustrates this idea.

LISTING 5.6   A Demonstration of Multiple Return Statements

```
 0:   // Listing 5.6 - demonstrates multiple return
 1:   // statements
 2:
 3:   #include <iostream>
 4:
 5:   int Doubler(int AmountToDouble);
 6:
 7:   int main()
 8:   {
 9:      using std::cout;
10:
11:      int result = 0;
12:      int input;
13:
14:      cout << "Enter a number between 0 and 10,000 to double: ";
15:      std::cin >> input;
16:
17:      cout << "\nBefore doubler is called... ";
18:      cout << "\ninput: " << input << " doubled: " << result << "\n";
19:
20:      result = Doubler(input);
21:
```

5

LISTING 5.6 continued

```
22:     cout << "\nBack from Doubler...\n";
23:     cout << "\ninput: " << input << "   doubled: " << result << "\n";
24:
25:     return 0;
26: }
27:
28: int Doubler(int original)
29: {
30:     if (original <= 10000)
31:         return original * 2;
32:     else
33:         return -1;
34:     std::cout << "You can't get here!\n";
35: }
```

OUTPUT

```
Enter a number between 0 and 10,000 to double: 9000

Before doubler is called...
input: 9000 doubled: 0

Back from doubler...

input: 9000   doubled: 18000

Enter a number between 0 and 10,000 to double: 11000

Before doubler is called...
input: 11000 doubled: 0

Back from doubler...
input: 11000   doubled: -1
```

ANALYSIS A number is requested on lines 14 and 15 and printed on line 17, along with the local variable result. The function Doubler() is called on line 20, and the input value is passed as a parameter. The result will be assigned to the local variable result, and the values will be reprinted on line 23.

On line 30, in the function Doubler(), the parameter is tested to see whether it is greater than 10,000. If it is not, the function returns twice the original number. If it is greater than 10,000, the function returns -1 as an error value.

The statement on line 34 is never reached because whether or not the value is greater than 10,000, the function returns on either line 31 or line 33—before it gets to line 34. A good compiler will warn that this statement cannot be executed, and a good programmer will take it out!

> **FAQ**
>
> **What is the difference between `int main()` and `void main();` which one should I use? I have used both and they both worked fine, so why do we need to use `int main(){ return 0;}`?**
>
> **Answer**: Both will work on most compilers, but only `int main()` is ANSI compliant, and thus only `int main()` is guaranteed to continue working.
>
> Here's the difference: `int main()` returns a value to the operating system. When your program completes, that value can be captured by, for example, batch programs.
>
> We won't be using the return value (it is rare to bother), but the ANSI standard requires it.

Default Parameters

For every parameter you declare in a function prototype and definition, the calling function must pass in a value. The value passed in must be of the declared type. Thus, if you have a function declared as

```
long myFunction(int);
```

the function must in fact take an integer variable. If the function definition differs, or if you fail to pass in an integer, you will get a compiler error.

The one exception to this rule is if the function prototype declares a default value for the parameter. A default value is a value to use if none is supplied. The preceding declaration could be rewritten as

```
long myFunction (int x = 50);
```

This prototype says, "myFunction() returns a long and takes an integer parameter. If an argument is not supplied, use the default value of 50." Because parameter names are not required in function prototypes, this declaration could have been written as

```
long myFunction (int = 50);
```

The function definition is not changed by declaring a default parameter. The function definition header for this function would be

```
long myFunction (int x)
```

If the calling function did not include a parameter, the compiler would fill x with the default value of 50. The name of the default parameter in the prototype need not be the same as the name in the function header; the default value is assigned by position, not name.

5

Any or all of the function's parameters can be assigned default values. The one restriction is this: If any of the parameters does not have a default value, no previous parameter may have a default value.

If the function prototype looks like

```
long myFunction (int Param1, int Param2, int Param3);
```

you can assign a default value to Param2 only if you have assigned a default value to Param3. You can assign a default value to Param1 only if you've assigned default values to both Param2 and Param3. Listing 5.7 demonstrates the use of default values.

LISTING 5.7   A Demonstration of Default Parameter Values

```
0:  // Listing 5.7 - demonstrates use
1:  // of default parameter values
2:
3:  #include <iostream>
4:
5:  int VolumeCube(int length, int width = 25, int height = 1);
6:
7:  int main()
8:  {
9:     int length = 100;
10:    int width = 50;
11:    int height = 2;
12:    int volume;
13:
14:    volume = VolumeCube(length, width, height);
15:    std::cout << "First volume equals: " << volume << "\n";
16:
17:    volume = VolumeCube(length, width);
18:    std::cout << "Second time volume equals: " << volume << "\n";
19:
20:    volume = VolumeCube(length);
21:    std::cout << "Third time volume equals: " << volume << "\n";
22:    return 0;
23: }
24:
25: VolumeCube(int length, int width, int height)
26: {
27:
28:    return (length * width * height);
29: }
```

OUTPUT
```
First volume equals: 10000
Second time volume equals: 5000
Third time volume equals: 2500
```

ANALYSIS On line 5, the VolumeCube() prototype specifies that the VolumeCube() function takes three integer parameters. The last two have default values.

This function computes the volume of the cube whose dimensions are passed in. If no width is passed in, a width of 25 is used and a height of 1 is used. If the width but not the height is passed in, a height of 1 is used. It is not possible to pass in the height without passing in a width.

On lines 9 to 11, the dimensions length, height, and width are initialized, and they are passed to the VolumeCube() function on line 14. The values are computed, and the result is printed on line 15.

Execution returns to line 17, where VolumeCube() is called again, but with no value for height. The default value is used, and again the dimensions are computed and printed.

Execution returns to line 20, and this time neither the width nor the height is passed in. Execution branches for a third time to line 25. The default values are used. The volume is computed and then printed.

Do	Don't
DO remember that function parameters act as local variables within the function.	**DON'T** try to create a default value for a first parameter if no default value exists for the second.
	DON'T forget that arguments passed by value cannot affect the variables in the calling function.
	DON'T forget that changes to a global variable in one function change that variable for all functions.

5

Overloading Functions

C++ enables you to create more than one function with the same name. This is called *function overloading*. The functions must differ in their parameter list with a different type of parameter, a different number of parameters, or both. Here's an example:

```
int myFunction (int, int);
int myFunction (long, long);
int myFunction (long);
```

myFunction() is overloaded with three parameter lists. The first and second versions differ in the types of the parameters, and the third differs in the number of parameters.

The return types can be the same or different on overloaded functions.

Note Two functions with the same name and parameter list, but different return types, generate a compiler error. To change the return type, you must also change the signature (name and/or parameter list).

Function overloading is also called *function polymorphism*. Poly means many, and morph means form: a polymorphic function is many-formed.

Function polymorphism refers to the capability to "overload" a function with more than one meaning. By changing the number or type of the parameters, you can give two or more functions the same function name, and the right one will be called by matching the parameters used. This enables you to create a function that can average integers, doubles, and other values without having to create individual names for each function, such as AverageInts(), AverageDoubles(), and so on.

Suppose you write a function that doubles whatever input you give it. You would like to be able to pass in an int, a long, a float, or a double. Without function overloading, you would have to create four function names:

```
int DoubleInt(int);
long DoubleLong(long);
float DoubleFloat(float);
double DoubleDouble(double);
```

With function overloading, you make this declaration:

```
int Double(int);
long Double(long);
float Double(float);
double Double(double);
```

This is easier to read and easier to use. You don't have to worry about which one to call; you just pass in a variable, and the right function is called automatically. Listing 5.8 illustrates the use of function overloading.

LISTING 5.8   A Demonstration of Function Polymorphism

```
0:  // Listing 5.8 - demonstrates
1:  // function polymorphism
2:
3:  #include <iostream>
4:
5:  int Double(int);
6:  long Double(long);
7:  float Double(float);
8:  double Double(double);
```

LISTING 5.8   continued

```
 9:
10:   using namespace std;
11:
12:   int main()
13:   {
14:       int      myInt = 6500;
15:       long     myLong = 65000;
16:       float    myFloat = 6.5F;
17:       double   myDouble = 6.5e20;
18:
19:       int      doubledInt;
20:       long     doubledLong;
21:       float    doubledFloat;
22:       double   doubledDouble;
23:
24:       cout << "myInt: " << myInt << "\n";
25:       cout << "myLong: " << myLong << "\n";
26:       cout << "myFloat: " << myFloat << "\n";
27:       cout << "myDouble: " << myDouble << "\n";
28:
29:       doubledInt = Double(myInt);
30:       doubledLong = Double(myLong);
31:       doubledFloat = Double(myFloat);
32:       doubledDouble = Double(myDouble);
33:
34:       cout << "doubledInt: " << doubledInt << "\n";
35:       cout << "doubledLong: " << doubledLong << "\n";
36:       cout << "doubledFloat: " << doubledFloat << "\n";
37:       cout << "doubledDouble: " << doubledDouble << "\n";
38:
39:       return 0;
40:   }
41:
42:   int Double(int original)
43:   {
44:       cout << "In Double(int)\n";
45:       return 2 * original;
46:   }
47:
48:   long Double(long original)
49:   {
50:       cout << "In Double(long)\n";
51:       return 2 * original;
52:   }
53:
54:   float Double(float original)
55:   {
56:       cout << "In Double(float)\n";
```

5

LISTING 5.8   continued

```
57:       return 2 * original;
58:    }
59:
60:    double Double(double original)
61:    {
62:       cout << "In Double(double)\n";
63:       return 2 * original;
64:    }
```

OUTPUT
```
myInt: 6500
myLong: 65000
myFloat: 6.5
myDouble: 6.5e+20
In Double(int)
In Double(long)
In Double(float)
In Double(double)
DoubledInt: 13000
DoubledLong: 130000
DoubledFloat: 13
DoubledDouble: 1.3e+21
```

ANALYSIS   The MyDouble() function is overloaded with int, long, float, and double. The prototypes are on lines 5–8, and the definitions are on lines 42–64.

Note that in this example, I added the statement using namespace std; on line 10, outside of any particular function. This makes the statement global to this file, and thus the namespace is used in all the functions declared within this file.

In the body of the main program, eight local variables are declared. On lines 14–17, four of the values are initialized, and on lines 29–32, the other four are assigned the results of passing the first four to the MyDouble() function. Note that when MyDouble() is called, the calling function does not distinguish which one to call; it just passes in an argument, and the correct one is invoked.

The compiler examines the arguments and chooses which of the four MyDouble() functions to call. The output reveals that each of the four was called in turn, as you would expect.

Special Topics About Functions

Because functions are so central to programming, a few special topics arise which might be of interest when you confront unusual problems. Used wisely, inline functions can help you squeak out that last bit of performance. Function recursion is one of those wonderful, esoteric bits of programming, which, every once in a while, can cut through a thorny problem otherwise not easily solved.

Inline Functions

When you define a function, normally the compiler creates just one set of instructions in memory. When you call the function, execution of the program jumps to those instructions, and when the function returns, execution jumps back to the next line in the calling function. If you call the function 10 times, your program jumps to the same set of instructions each time. This means only one copy of the function exists, not 10.

A small performance overhead occurs in jumping in and out of functions. It turns out that some functions are very small, just a line or two of code, and an efficiency might be gained if the program can avoid making these jumps just to execute one or two instructions. When programmers speak of efficiency, they usually mean speed; the program runs faster if the function call can be avoided.

If a function is declared with the keyword inline, the compiler does not create a real function; it copies the code from the inline function directly into the calling function. No jump is made; it is just as if you had written the statements of the function right into the calling function.

Note that inline functions can bring a heavy cost. If the function is called 10 times, the inline code is copied into the calling functions each of those 10 times. The tiny improvement in speed you might achieve is more than swamped by the increase in size of the executable program, which might in fact actually slow the program!

The reality is that today's optimizing compilers can almost certainly do a better job of making this decision than you can; and so it is generally a good idea not to declare a function inline unless it is only one or at most two statements in length. When in doubt, though, leave it out.

Listing 5.9 demonstrates an inline function.

LISTING 5.9   Demonstrates an Inline Function

```
0:   // Listing 5.9 - demonstrates inline functions
1:
2:   #include <iostream>
3:
4:   inline int Double(int);
5:
6:   int main()
7:   {
8:      int target;
```

LISTING 5.9   continued

```
 9:        using std::cout;
10:        using std::cin;
11:        using std::endl;
12:
13:        cout << "Enter a number to work with: ";
14:        cin >> target;
15:        cout << "\n";
16:
17:        target = Double(target);
18:        cout << "Target: " << target << endl;
19:
20:        target = Double(target);
21:        cout << "Target: " << target << endl;
22:
23:
24:        target = Double(target);
25:        cout << "Target: " << target << endl;
26:        return 0;
27:    }
28:
29:    int Double(int target)
30:    {
31:        return 2*target;
32:    }
```

OUTPUT

```
Enter a number to work with: 20

Target: 40
Target: 80
Target: 160
```

ANALYSIS   On line 4, `MyDouble()` is declared to be an inline function taking an `int` parameter and returning an `int`. The declaration is just like any other prototype except that the keyword `inline` is prepended just before the return value.

This compiles into code that is the same as if you had written the following:

```
target = 2 * target;
```

everywhere you entered

```
target = Double(target);
```

By the time your program executes, the instructions are already in place, compiled into the `.obj` file. This saves a jump in the execution of the code at the cost of a larger program.

Inline is a hint to the compiler that you would like the function to be inlined. The compiler is free to ignore the hint and make a real function call.

Recursion

A function can call itself. This is called *recursion*, and recursion can be direct or indirect. It is direct when a function calls itself; it is indirect recursion when a function calls another function that then calls the first function.

Some problems are most easily solved by recursion, usually those in which you act on data and then act in the same way on the result. Both types of recursion, direct and indirect, come in two varieties: those that eventually end and produce an answer, and those that never end and produce a runtime failure. Programmers think that the latter is quite funny (when it happens to someone else).

It is important to note that when a function calls itself, a new copy of that function is run. The local variables in the second version are independent of the local variables in the first, and they cannot affect one another directly, any more than the local variables in `main()` can affect the local variables in any function it calls, as was illustrated in Listing 5.4.

To illustrate solving a problem using recursion, consider the Fibonacci series:

1,1,2,3,5,8,13,21,34...

Each number, after the second, is the sum of the two numbers before it. A Fibonacci problem might be to determine what the 12th number in the series is.

To solve this problem, we must examine the series carefully. The first two numbers are 1. Each subsequent number is the sum of the previous two numbers. Thus, the seventh number is the sum of the sixth and fifth numbers. More generally, the nth number is the sum of n–2 and n–1, as long as n > 2.

Recursive functions need a stop condition. Something must happen to cause the program to stop recursing, or it will never end. In the Fibonacci series, n < 3 is a stop condition (that is, when n is less than 3 we can stop working on the problem).

An algorithm is a set of steps you follow to solve a problem. One algorithm for the Fibonacci series is the following:

1. Ask the user for a position in the series.
2. Call the `fib()` function with that position, passing in the value the user entered.

3. The fib() function examines the argument (*n*). If n < 3 it returns 1; otherwise, fib() calls itself (recursively) passing in n-2. It then calls itself again passing in n-1, and returns the sum of the first call and the second.

If you call fib(1), it returns 1. If you call fib(2), it returns 1. If you call fib(3), it returns the sum of calling fib(2) and fib(1). Because fib(2) returns 1 and fib(1) returns 1, fib(3) will return 2 (the sum of 1 + 1).

If you call fib(4), it returns the sum of calling fib(3) and fib(2). We've established that fib(3) returns 2 (by calling fib(2) and fib(1)) and that fib(2) returns 1, so fib(4) will sum these numbers and return 3, which is the fourth number in the series.

Taking this one more step, if you call fib(5), it will return the sum of fib(4) and fib(3). We've established that fib(4) returns 3 and fib(3) returns 2, so the sum returned will be 5.

This method is not the most efficient way to solve this problem (in fib(20) the fib() function is called 13,529 times!), but it does work. Be careful—if you feed in too large a number, you'll run out of memory. Every time fib() is called, memory is set aside. When it returns, memory is freed. With recursion, memory continues to be set aside before it is freed, and this system can eat memory very quickly. Listing 5.10 implements the fib() function.

> **Caution**
>
> When you run Listing 5.10, use a small number (less than 15). Because this uses recursion, it can consume a lot of memory.

LISTING 5.10   Demonstrates Recursion Using the Fibonacci Series

```
0:  // Fibonacci series using recursion
1:  #include <iostream>
2:
3:  int fib (int n);
4:
5:  int main()
6:  {
7:
8:      int n, answer;
9:      std::cout << "Enter number to find: ";
10:     std::cin >> n;
11:
12:     std::cout << "\n\n";
13:
14:     answer = fib(n);
15:
```

LISTING 5.10   continued

```
16:      std::cout << answer << " is the " << n;
17:          std::cout << "th Fibonacci number\n";
18:      return 0;
19:  }
20:
21:  int fib (int n)
22:  {
23:      std::cout << "Processing fib(" << n << ")... ";
24:
25:      if (n < 3 )
26:      {
27:          std::cout << "Return 1!\n";
28:          return (1);
29:      }
30:      else
31:      {
32:          std::cout << "Call fib(" << n-2 << ") ";
33:              std::cout << "and fib(" << n-1 << ").\n";
34:          return( fib(n-2) + fib(n-1));
35:      }
36:  }
```

```
Enter number to find: 6
```

OUTPUT
```
Processing fib(6)... Call fib(4) and fib(5).
Processing fib(4)... Call fib(2) and fib(3).
Processing fib(2)... Return 1!
Processing fib(3)... Call fib(1) and fib(2).
Processing fib(1)... Return 1!
Processing fib(2)... Return 1!
Processing fib(5)... Call fib(3) and fib(4).
Processing fib(3)... Call fib(1) and fib(2).
Processing fib(1)... Return 1!
Processing fib(2)... Return 1!
Processing fib(4)... Call fib(2) and fib(3).
Processing fib(2)... Return 1!
Processing fib(3)... Call fib(1) and fib(2).
Processing fib(1)... Return 1!
Processing fib(2)... Return 1!
8 is the 6th Fibonacci number
```

5

Note

Some compilers have difficulty with the use of operators in a cout statement. If you receive a warning on line 32, place parentheses around the subtraction operation so that lines 32 and 33 become:

```
32:          std::cout << "Call fib(" << (n-2) << ") ";
33:              std::cout << "and fib(" << (n-1) << ").\n";
```

ANALYSIS The program asks for a number to find on line 9 and assigns that number to n. It then calls fib() with n. Execution branches to the fib() function, where, on line 23, it prints its argument.

The argument n is tested to see whether it is less than 3 on line 25; if so, fib() returns the value 1. Otherwise, it returns the sum of the values returned by calling fib() on n-2 and n-1.

It cannot return these values until the call (to fib()) is resolved. Thus, you can picture the program diving into fib repeatedly until it hits a call to fib which returns a value. The only calls that return a value are the calls to fib(2) and fib(1). These values are then passed up to the waiting callers, which, in turn, add the return value to their own, and then they return. Figures 5.4 and 5.5 illustrate this recursion into fib().

FIGURE 5.4

Using recursion.

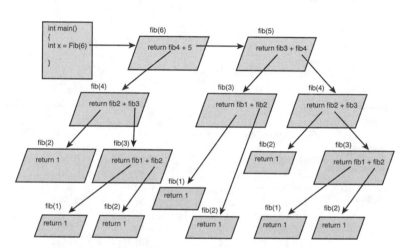

FIGURE 5.5

Returning from recursion.

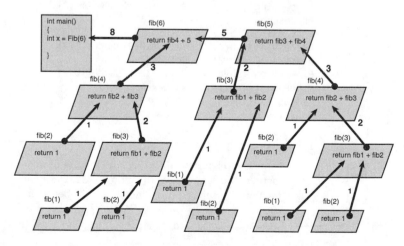

In the example, n is 6 so `fib(6)` is called from `main()`. Execution jumps to the `fib()` function, and n is tested for a value less than 3 on line 25. The test fails, so `fib(6)` returns the sum of the values returned by `fib(4)` and `fib(5)`.

```
34:          return( fib(n-2) + fib(n-1));
```

That means that a call is made to `fib(4)` [since n == 6, `fib(n-2)` is the same as `fib(4)`] and another call is made to `fib(5)` [`fib(n-1)`], and then the function you are in [`fib(6)`] *waits* until these calls return a value. When these return a value, then this function can return the result of summing those two values.

Because `fib(5)` passes in an argument that is not less than 3, `fib()` will be called again, this time with 4 and 3. `fib(4)` will in turn call `fib(3)` and `fib(2)`.

The output traces these calls and the return values. Compile, link, and run this program, entering first 1, then 2, then 3, building up to 6, and watch the output carefully.

This would be a great time to start experimenting with your debugger. Put a break point on line 21 and then trace *into* each call to `fib`, keeping track of the value of *n* as you work your way into each recursive call to `fib`.

Recursion is not used often in C++ programming, but it can be a powerful and elegant tool for certain needs.

> **Note**
>
> Recursion is a tricky part of advanced programming. It is presented here because it can be useful to understand the fundamentals of how it works, but don't worry too much if you don't fully understand all the details.

5

How Functions Work—A Peek Under the Hood

When you call a function, the code branches to the called function, parameters are passed in, and the body of the function is executed. When the function completes, a value is returned (unless the function returns void), and control returns to the calling function.

How is this task accomplished? How does the code know where to branch? Where are the variables kept when they are passed in? What happens to variables that are declared in the body of the function? How is the return value passed back out? How does the code know where to resume?

Most introductory books don't try to answer these questions, but without understanding this information, you'll find that programming remains a fuzzy mystery. The explanation requires a brief tangent into a discussion of computer memory.

Levels of Abstraction

One of the principal hurdles for new programmers is grappling with the many layers of intellectual abstraction. Computers, of course, are only electronic machines. They don't know about windows and menus, they don't know about programs or instructions, and they don't even know about ones and zeros. All that is really going on is that voltage is being measured at various places on an integrated circuit. Even this is an abstraction: electricity itself is just an intellectual concept representing the behavior of subatomic particles, which arguably are themselves intellectual abstractions(!).

Few programmers bother with any level of detail below the idea of values in RAM. After all, you don't need to understand particle physics to drive a car, make toast, or hit a baseball, and you don't need to understand the electronics of a computer to program one.

You do need to understand how memory is organized, however. Without a reasonably strong mental picture of where your variables are when they are created and how values are passed among functions, it will all remain an unmanageable mystery.

Partitioning RAM

When you begin your program, your operating system (such as DOS, Unix, or Microsoft Windows) sets up various areas of memory based on the requirements of your compiler. As a C++ programmer, you'll often be concerned with the global name space, the free store, the registers, the code space, and the stack.

Global variables are in global name space. We'll talk more about global name space and the free store in coming days, but for now we'll focus on the registers, code space, and stack.

Registers are a special area of memory built right into the Central Processing Unit (or CPU). They take care of internal housekeeping. A lot of what goes on in the registers is beyond the scope of this book, but what we are concerned with is the set of registers responsible for pointing, at any given moment, to the next line of code. We'll call these registers, together, the instruction pointer. It is the job of the instruction pointer to keep track of which line of code is to be executed next.

The code itself is in code space, which is that part of memory set aside to hold the binary form of the instructions you created in your program. Each line of source code is translated into a series of instructions, and each of these instructions is at a particular address in memory. The instruction pointer has the address of the next instruction to execute. Figure 5.6 illustrates this idea.

FIGURE 5.6

The instruction pointer.

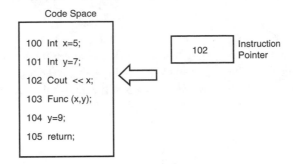

Code Space

```
100  Int  x=5;
101  Int  y=7;
102  Cout  << x;
103  Func (x,y);
104  y=9;
105  return;
```

```
102
```
Instruction Pointer

The stack is a special area of memory allocated for your program to hold the data required by each of the functions in your program. It is called a stack because it is a last-in, first-out queue, much like a stack of dishes at a cafeteria, as shown in Figure 5.7.

FIGURE 5.7

A stack.

Last-in, first-out means that whatever is added to the stack last will be the first thing taken off. Most queues are like a line at a theater: The first one on line is the first one off. A stack is more like a stack of coins: If you stack 10 pennies on a tabletop and then take some back, the last three you put on will be the first three you take off.

When data is *pushed* onto the stack, the stack grows; as data is *popped* off the stack, the stack shrinks. It isn't possible to pop a dish off the stack without first popping off all the dishes placed on after that dish.

A stack of dishes is the common analogy. It is fine as far as it goes, but it is wrong in a fundamental way. A more accurate mental picture is of a series of cubbyholes aligned top to bottom. The top of the stack is whatever cubby the stack pointer (which is another register) happens to be pointing to.

Each of the cubbies has a sequential address, and one of those addresses is kept in the stack pointer register. Everything below that magic address, known as the top of the stack, is considered to be on the stack. Everything above the top of the stack is considered to be off the stack and invalid. Figure 5.8 illustrates this idea.

FIGURE 5.8

The stack pointer.

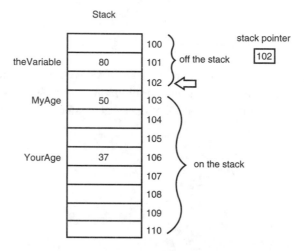

When data is put on the stack, it is placed into a cubby above the stack pointer, and then the stack pointer is moved to the new data. When data is popped off the stack, all that really happens is that the address of the stack pointer is changed by moving it down the stack. Figure 5.9 makes this rule clear.

The data *above* the stack pointer (off the stack) may or may not be changed at any time. We refer to these values as "garbage" to remind us that we can't rely on their value.

The Stack and Functions

The following is an approximation of what happens when your program branches to a function. (The details will differ depending on the operating system and compiler.)

1. The address in the instruction pointer is incremented to the next instruction past the function call. That address is then placed on the stack, and it will be the return address when the function returns.

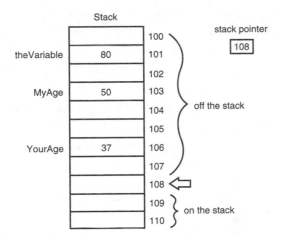

FIGURE 5.9

Moving the stack pointer.

2. Room is made on the stack for the return type you've declared. On a system with two-byte integers, if the return type is declared to be `int`, another two bytes are added to the stack, but no value is placed in these bytes (that means that whatever "garbage" was in those two bytes remains until the local variable is initialized).

3. The address of the called function, which is kept in a special area of memory set aside for that purpose, is loaded into the instruction pointer, so the next instruction executed will be in the called function.

4. The current top of the stack is now noted and is held in a special pointer called the stack frame. Everything added to the stack from now until the function returns will be considered "local" to the function.

5. All the arguments to the function are placed on the stack.

6. The instruction now in the instruction pointer is executed, thus executing the first instruction in the function.

7. Local variables are pushed onto the stack as they are defined.

When the function is ready to return, the return value is placed in the area of the stack reserved at step 2. The stack is then popped all the way up to the stack frame pointer, which effectively throws away all the local variables and the arguments to the function.

The return value is popped off the stack and assigned as the value of the function call itself, and the address stashed away in step 1 is retrieved and put into the instruction pointer. The program thus resumes immediately after the function call, with the value of the function retrieved.

5

Some of the details of this process change from compiler to compiler, or between computers, but the essential ideas are consistent across environments. In general, when you call a function, the return address and the parameters are put on the stack. During the life of the function, local variables are added to the stack. When the function returns, these are all removed by popping the stack.

In coming days we'll look at other places in memory that are used to hold data that must persist beyond the life of the function.

Summary

This chapter introduced functions. A function is, in effect, a subprogram into which you can pass parameters and from which you can return a value. Every C++ program starts in the main() function, and main(), in turn, can call other functions.

A function is declared with a function prototype, which describes the return value, the function name, and its parameter types. A function can optionally be declared inline. A function prototype can also declare default variables for one or more of the parameters.

The function definition must match the function prototype in return type, name, and parameter list. Function names can be overloaded by changing the number or type of parameters; the compiler finds the right function based on the argument list.

Local function variables, and the arguments passed in to the function, are local to the block in which they are declared. Parameters passed by value are copies and cannot affect the value of variables in the calling function.

Q&A

Q Why not make all variables global?

A At one time, this was exactly how programming was done. As programs became more complex, however, it became very difficult to find bugs in programs because data could be corrupted by any of the functions—global data can be changed anywhere in the program. Years of experience have convinced programmers that data should be kept as local as possible, and access to changing that data should be narrowly defined.

Q When should the keyword inline be used in a function prototype?

A If the function is very small, no more than a line or two, and won't be called from many places in your program, it is a candidate for inlining.

Q Why aren't changes to the value of function arguments reflected in the calling function?

A Arguments passed to a function are passed by value. That means that the argument in the function is actually a copy of the original value. This concept is explained in depth in the section "How Functions Work—A Peek Under the Hood."

Q If arguments are passed by value, what do I do if I need to reflect the changes back in the calling function?

A On Day 8, pointers will be discussed and on Day 9 you'll learn about references. Use of pointers or references will solve this problem, as well as provide a way around the limitation of returning only a single value from a function.

Q What happens if I have the following two functions?

```
int Area (int width, int length = 1); int Area (int size);
```

Will these overload? A different number of parameters exist, but the first one has a default value.

A The declarations will compile, but if you invoke Area with one parameter, you will receive a compile-time error: ambiguity between Area(int, int) and Area(int).

Workshop

The Workshop provides quiz questions to help you solidify your understanding of the material covered and exercises to provide you with experience in using what you've learned. Try to answer the quiz and exercise questions before checking the answers in Appendix D, and make sure that you understand the answers before continuing to the next chapter.

Quiz

1. What are the differences between the function prototype and the function definition?

2. Do the names of parameters have to agree in the prototype, definition, and call to the function?

3. If a function doesn't return a value, how do you declare the function?

4. If you don't declare a return value, what type of return value is assumed?

5. What is a local variable?

6. What is scope?

7. What is recursion?

8. When should you use global variables?

5

9. What is function overloading?

10. What is polymorphism?

Exercises

1. Write the prototype for a function named `Perimeter()`, which returns an `unsigned long int` and takes two parameters, both `unsigned short ints`.

2. Write the definition of the function `Perimeter()` as described in Exercise 1. The two parameters represent the length and width of a rectangle. Have the function return the perimeter (twice the length plus twice the width).

3. **BUG BUSTERS:** What is wrong with the function in the following code?

```
#include <iostream>
void myFunc(unsigned short int x);
int main()
{
    unsigned short int x, y;
    y = myFunc(int);
    std::cout << "x: " << x << " y: " << y << "\n";
return 0;
}

void myFunc(unsigned short int x)
{
    return (4*x);
}
```

4. **BUG BUSTERS:** What is wrong with the function in the following code?

```
#include <iostream>
int myFunc(unsigned short int x);
int main()
{
    unsigned short int x, y;
    x = 7;
    y = myFunc(x);
    std::cout << "x: " << x << " y: " << y << "\n";
return 0;
}

int myFunc(unsigned short int x);
{
    return (4*x);
}
```

5. Write a function that takes two `unsigned short` integer arguments and returns the result of dividing the first by the second. Do not do the division if the second number is zero, but do return -1.

6. Write a program that asks the user for two numbers and calls the function you wrote in Exercise 5. Print the answer, or print an error message if you get -1.

7. Write a program that asks for a number and a power. Write a recursive function that takes the number to the power. Thus, if the number is 2 and the power is 4, the function will return 16.

5

DAY 6

Object-Oriented Programming

Classes extend the built-in capabilities of C++ to assist you in representing and solving complex, real-world problems.

Today you will learn

- What classes and objects are.
- How to define a new class and create objects of that class.
- What member functions and member data are.
- What constructors are and how to use them.

Is C++ Object-Oriented?

C++ was created as a bridge between object-oriented programming and C, the world's most popular programming language for commercial software development. The goal was to provide object-oriented design to a fast, commercial software development platform.

C was developed as a middle ground between high-level business application languages such as COBOL and the pedal-to-the-metal, high-performance, but difficult-to-use Assembler language. C was to enforce "structured" programming, in which problems were "decomposed" into smaller units of repeatable activities called *procedures*.

The programs we're writing early in the twenty-first century are much more complex than those written at the end of the twentieth. Programs created in procedural languages tend to be difficult to manage, hard to maintain, and impossible to extend. Graphical user interfaces, the Internet, digital and wireless telephony, and a host of new technologies have dramatically increased the complexity of our projects at the same time that consumer expectations for the quality of the user interface are rising.

In the face of this increasing complexity, developers took a long, hard look at the state of the industry. What they found was disheartening, at best. Software was late, broken, defective, bug ridden, unreliable, and expensive. Projects routinely ran over budget and were delivered late to market. The cost of maintaining these projects was prohibitive, and a tremendous amount of money was being wasted.

Object-oriented software development offers a path out of the abyss. Object-oriented programming languages build a strong link between the data structures and the methods that manipulate that data. More importantly, in object-oriented programming, you no longer think about data structures and manipulating functions; you think instead about objects. Things.

The world is populated by things: cars, dogs, trees, clouds, flowers. Things. Each *thing* has characteristics (fast, friendly, brown, puffy, pretty). Most things have behavior (move, bark, grow, rain, wilt). We don't think about a dog's data and how we might manipulate it—we think about a dog as a thing in the world, what it is like, and what it does.

Creating New Types

You've already learned about a number of variable types, including unsigned integers and characters. The type of a variable tells you quite a bit about it. For example, if you declare Height and Width to be unsigned short integers, you know that each one can hold a number between 0 and 65,535, assuming an unsigned short integer is two bytes. That is the meaning of saying they are unsigned integers; trying to hold anything else in these variables causes an error. You can't store your name in an unsigned short integer, and you shouldn't try.

Just by declaring these variables to be unsigned short integers, you know that it is possible to add Height to Width and to assign that number to another number.

The type of these variables tells you

- Their size in memory
- What information they can hold
- What actions can be performed on them

In traditional languages such as C, types were built in to the language. In C++, the programmer can extend the language by creating any type needed, and each of these new types can have all the functionality and power of the built-in types.

Why Create a New Type?

Programs are usually written to solve real-world problems, such as keeping track of employee records or simulating the workings of a heating system. Although it is possible to solve complex problems by using programs written with only integers and characters, it is far easier to grapple with large, complex problems if you can create representations of the objects that you are talking about. In other words, simulating the workings of a heating system is easier if you can create variables that represent rooms, heat sensors, thermostats, and boilers. The closer these variables correspond to reality, the easier it is to write the program.

Classes and Members

You make a new type by declaring a class. A class is just a collection of variables—often of different types—combined with a set of related functions.

One way to think about a car is as a collection of wheels, doors, seats, windows, and so forth. Another way is to think about what a car can do: It can move, speed up, slow down, stop, park, and so on. A class enables you to encapsulate, or bundle, these various parts and various functions into one collection, which is called an object.

Encapsulating everything you know about a car into one class has a number of advantages for a programmer. Everything is in one place, which makes it easy to refer to, copy, and manipulate the data. Likewise, clients of your class—that is, the parts of the program that use your class—can use your object without worrying about what is in it or how it works.

A class can consist of any combination of the variable types and also other class types. The variables in the class are referred to as the member variables or data members. A Car class might have member variables representing the seats, radio type, tires, and so forth.

Member variables, also known as data members, are the variables in your class. Member variables are part of your class, just as the wheels and engine are part of your car.

6

The functions in the class typically manipulate the member variables. They are referred to as member functions or methods of the class. Methods of the Car class might include Start() and Brake(). A Cat class might have data members that represent age and weight; its methods might include Sleep(), Meow(), and ChaseMice().

Member functions, also known as methods, are the functions in your class. Member functions are as much a part of your class as the member variables. They determine what your class can do.

Declaring a Class

To declare a class, use the class keyword followed by an opening brace, and then list the data members and methods of that class. End the declaration with a closing brace and a semicolon. Here's the declaration of a class called Cat:

```
class Cat
{
   unsigned int  itsAge;
   unsigned int  itsWeight;
   void Meow();
};
```

Declaring this class doesn't allocate memory for a Cat. It just tells the compiler what a Cat is, what data it contains (itsAge and itsWeight), and what it can do (Meow()). It also tells the compiler how big a Cat is—that is, how much room the compiler must set aside for each Cat that you create. In this example, if an integer is four bytes, a Cat is eight bytes big: itsAge is four bytes, and itsWeight is another four bytes. Meow() takes up no room because no storage space is set aside for member functions (methods).

A Word on Naming Conventions

As a programmer, you must name all your member variables, member functions, and classes. As you learned on Day 3, "Variables and Constants," these should be easily understood and meaningful names. Cat, Rectangle, and Employee are good class names. Meow(), ChaseMice(), and StopEngine() are good function names because they tell you what the functions do. Many programmers name the member variables with the prefix "its," as in itsAge, itsWeight, and itsSpeed. This helps to distinguish member variables from nonmember variables.

Other programmers use different prefixes. Some prefer myAge, myWeight, and mySpeed. Still others simply use the letter m (for member), possibly with an underscore (_) such as mAge or m_age, mWeight or m_weight, or mSpeed or m_speed.

C++ is case sensitive, and all class names should follow the same pattern so that you never have to check how to spell your class name; was it Rectangle, rectangle, or RECTANGLE?

Some programmers like to prefix every class name with a particular letter—for example, cCat or cPerson—whereas others put the name in all uppercase or all lowercase. The convention that I use is to name all classes with initial capitalization, as in Cat and Person.

Similarly, many programmers begin all functions with capital letters and all variables with lowercase. Words are usually separated with an underscore—as in Chase_Mice—or by capitalizing each word—for example, ChaseMice or DrawCircle.

The important idea is that you should pick one style and stay with it through each program. Over time, your style will evolve to include not only naming conventions, but also indentation, alignment of braces, and commenting style.

Note   It's common for development companies to have house standards for many style issues. This ensures that all developers can easily read one another's code.

Defining an Object

You define an object of your new type the same as you define an integer variable:

```
unsigned int GrossWeight;      // define an unsigned integer
Cat Frisky;                    // define a Cat
```

This code defines a variable called GrossWeight, whose type is an unsigned integer. It also defines Frisky, which is an object whose class (or type) is Cat.

Classes Versus Objects

You never pet the definition of a cat; you pet individual cats. You draw a distinction between the idea of a cat and the particular cat that right now is shedding all over your living room. In the same way, C++ differentiates between the class Cat, which is the idea of a cat, and each individual Cat object. Thus, Frisky is an object of type Cat in the same way that GrossWeight is a variable of type unsigned int.

An object is an individual instance of a class.

6

Accessing Class Members

Once you define an actual `Cat` object—for example, `Frisky`—you use the dot operator
(`.`) to access the members of that object. Therefore, to assign 50 to `Frisky`'s `Weight`
member variable, you would write

```
Frisky.itsWeight = 50;
```

In the same way, to call the `Meow()` function, you would write

```
Frisky.Meow();
```

When you use a class method, you call the method. In this example, you are calling
`Meow()` on `Frisky`.

Assign to Objects, Not to Classes

In C++ you don't assign values to types; you assign values to variables. For example,
you would never write

```
int = 5;                 // wrong
```

The compiler would flag this as an error because you can't assign 5 to an integer. Rather,
you must define an integer variable and assign 5 to that variable. For example,

```
int  x;            // define x to be an int
x = 5;             // set x's value to 5
```

This is a shorthand way of saying, "Assign 5 to the variable x, which is of type int." In
the same way, you wouldn't write

```
Cat.itsAge=5;            // wrong
```

The compiler would flag this as an error because you can't assign 5 to the age part of a
`Cat`. Rather, you must define a `Cat` object and assign 5 to that object. For example,

```
Cat Frisky;            // just like  int x;
Frisky.itsAge = 5;     // just like  x = 5;
```

If You Don't Declare It, Your Class Won't Have It

Try this experiment: Walk up to a three-year-old and show her a cat. Then say, "This is
Frisky. Frisky knows a trick. Frisky, bark." The child will giggle and say, "No, silly, cats
can't bark."

If you wrote

```
Cat  Frisky;            // make a Cat named Frisky
Frisky.Bark()           // tell Frisky to bark
```

the compiler would say, "No, silly, Cats can't bark." (Your compiler's wording may vary.) The compiler knows that Frisky can't bark because the Cat class doesn't have a Bark() method. The compiler wouldn't even let Frisky meow if you didn't define a Meow() function.

Do	**DON'T**
DO use the keyword class to declare a class. **DO** use the dot operator (.) to access class members and functions.	**DON'T** confuse a declaration with a definition. A declaration says what a class is. A definition sets aside memory for an object. **DON'T** confuse a class with an object. **DON'T** assign values to a class. Assign values to the data members of an object.

Private Versus Public

Other keywords are used in the declaration of a class. Two of the most important are public and private.

All members of a class—data and methods—are private by default. Private members can be accessed only within methods of the class itself. Public members can be accessed through any object of the class. This distinction is both important and confusing. To make it a bit clearer, consider an example from earlier in this chapter:

```
class Cat
{
  unsigned int  itsAge;
  unsigned int  itsWeight;
  void Meow();
};
```

In this declaration, itsAge, itsWeight, and Meow() are all private because all members of a class are private by default. This means that unless you specify otherwise, they are private.

However, if you write the following in main (for example):

```
Cat  Boots;
Boots.itsAge=5;        // error! can't access private data!
```

the compiler flags this as an error. In effect, you've said to the compiler, "I'll access itsAge, itsWeight, and Meow() only from within member functions of the Cat class." Yet here you've accessed the itsAge member variable of the Boots object from outside a Cat method. Just because Boots is an object of class Cat, that doesn't mean that you can access the parts of Boots that are private.

6

This is a source of endless confusion to new C++ programmers. I can almost hear you yelling, "Hey! I just said Boots is a cat. Why can't Boots access his own age?" The answer is that Boots can, but you can't. Boots, in his own methods, can access all his parts—public and private. Even though you've created a Cat, that doesn't mean that you can see or change the parts of it that are private.

The way to use Cat so that you can access the data members is

```
class Cat
{
public:
   unsigned int  itsAge;
   unsigned int  itsWeight;
   void Meow();
};
```

Now itsAge, itsWeight, and Meow() are all public. Boots.itsAge=5 compiles without problems.

Listing 6.1 shows the declaration of a Cat class with public member variables.

LISTING 6.1   Accessing the Public Members of a Simple Class

```
0:  // Demonstrates declaration of a class and
1:  // definition of an object of the class,
2:
3:  #include <iostream>
4:
5:  class Cat                  // declare the Cat class
6:  {
7:  public:                    // members which follow are public
8:     int itsAge;      // member variable
9:     int itsWeight;       // member variable
10: };          // note the semicolon
11:
12:
13: int main()
14: {
15:    Cat Frisky;
16:    Frisky.itsAge = 5;    // assign to the member variable
17:    std::cout << "Frisky is a cat who is " ;
18:    std::cout << Frisky.itsAge << " years old.\n";
19:    return 0;
20: }
```

OUTPUT

Frisky is a cat who is 5 years old.

ANALYSIS Line 5 contains the keyword class. This tells the compiler that what follows is a declaration. The name of the new class comes after the keyword class. In this case, it is Cat.

The body of the declaration begins with the opening brace in line 6 and ends with a closing brace and a semicolon in line 10. Line 7 contains the keyword public, which indicates that everything that follows is public until the keyword private or the end of the class declaration.

Lines 8 and 9 contain the declarations of the class members itsAge and itsWeight.

Line 13 begins the main() function of the program. Frisky is defined in line 15 as an instance of a Cat—that is, as a Cat object. In line 16, Frisky's age is set to 5. In lines 17 and 18, the itsAge member variable is used to print out a message about Frisky.

Note

Try commenting out line 7 and try to recompile. You will receive an error on line 16 because itsAge will no longer have public access. The default for classes is private access.

Make Member Data Private

As a general rule of design, you should keep the member data of a class private. Therefore, you must create public functions known as accessor methods to set and get the private member variables. These accessor methods are the member functions that other parts of your program call to get and set your private member variables.

A public accessor method is a class member function used either to read the value of a private class member variable or to set its value.

Why bother with this extra level of indirect access? After all, it is simpler and easier to use the data instead of working through accessor functions.

Accessor functions enable you to separate the details of how the data is stored from how it is used. This enables you to change how the data is stored without having to rewrite functions that use the data.

If a function that needs to know a Cat's age accesses itsAge directly, that function would need to be rewritten if you, as the author of the Cat class, decided to change how that data is stored. By having the function call GetAge(), your Cat class can easily return the right value no matter how you arrive at the age. The calling function doesn't need to know whether you are storing it as an unsigned integer or a long, or whether you are computing it as needed.

6

This technique makes your program easier to maintain. It gives your code a longer life because design changes don't make your program obsolete.

Listing 6.2 shows the Cat class modified to include private member data and public accessor methods. Note that this is not an executable listing.

LISTING 6.2   A Class with Accessor Methods

```
0:  // Cat class declaration
1:  // Data members are private, public accessor methods
2:  // mediate setting and getting the values of the private data
3:
4:  class Cat
5:  {
6:  public:
7:      // public accessors
8:      unsigned int GetAge();
9:      void SetAge(unsigned int Age);
10:
11:     unsigned int GetWeight();
12:     void SetWeight(unsigned int Weight);
13:
14:     // public member functions
15:     void Meow();
16:
17:     // private member data
18: private:
19:     unsigned int  itsAge;
20:     unsigned int  itsWeight;
21:
22: };
```

ANALYSIS   This class has five public methods. Lines 8 and 9 contain the accessor methods for itsAge. Lines 11 and 12 contain the accessor methods for itsWeight. These accessor functions set the member variables and return their values.

The public member function Meow() is declared in line 15. Meow() is not an accessor function. It doesn't get or set a member variable; it performs another service for the class, printing the word Meow.

The member variables themselves are declared in lines 19 and 20.

To set Frisky's age, you would pass the value to the SetAge() method, as in

```
Cat  Frisky;
Frisky.SetAge(5);    // set Frisky's age using the public accessor
```

Privacy Versus Security

Declaring methods or data private enables the compiler to find programming mistakes before they become bugs. Any programmer worth his consulting fees can find a way around privacy if he wants to. Stroustrup, the inventor of C++, said, "The C++ access control mechanisms provide protection against accident—not against fraud." (ARM, 1990.)

The `class` Keyword

Syntax for the `class` keyword is as follows:

```
class class_name
{
// access control keywords here
// class variables and methods declared here
};
```

You use the `class` keyword to declare new types. A class is a collection of class member data, which are variables of various types, including other classes. The class also contains class functions—or methods—which are functions used to manipulate the data in the class and to perform other services for the class.

You define objects of the new type in much the same way in which you define any variable. State the type (`class`) and then the variable name (the object). You access the class members and functions by using the dot (.) operator.

You use access control keywords to declare sections of the class as public or private. The default for access control is private. Each keyword changes the access control from that point on to the end of the class or until the next access control keyword. Class declarations end with a closing brace and a semicolon.

Example 1

```
class Cat
{
        public:
        unsigned int Age;
        unsigned int Weight;
        void Meow();
};

Cat  Frisky;
Frisky.Age = 8;
Frisky.Weight = 18;
Frisky.Meow();
```

Example 2

```
class Car
{
public:                                 // the next five are public
```

6

```
        void Start();
        void Accelerate();
        void Brake();
        void SetYear(int year);
        int GetYear();

    private:                        // the rest is private

        int Year;
        Char Model [255];
    };                              // end of class declaration

    Car OldFaithful;                // make an instance of car
    int bought;                     // a local variable of type int
    OldFaithful.SetYear(84) ;       // assign 84 to the year
    bought = OldFaithful.GetYear(); // set bought to 84
    OldFaithful.Start();            // call the start method
```

Do	**Don't**
DO declare member variables private.	**DON'T** try to use private member variables from outside the class.
DO use public accessor methods.	
DO access private member variables from within class member functions.	

Implementing Class Methods

As you've seen, an accessor function provides a public interface to the private member data of the class. Each accessor function, along with any other class methods that you declare, must have an implementation. The implementation is called the function definition.

A member function definition begins with the name of the class, followed by two colons, the name of the function, and its parameters. Listing 6.3 shows the complete declaration of a simple Cat class and the implementation of its accessor function and one general class member function.

LISTING **6.3**   Implementing the Methods of a Simple Class

```
0:  // Demonstrates declaration of a class and
1:  // definition of class methods,
2:
3:  #include <iostream>       // for cout
```

LISTING 6.3   continued

```
 4:
 5:   class Cat                    // begin declaration of the class
 6:   {
 7:   public:                   // begin public section
 8:       int GetAge();            // accessor function
 9:       void SetAge (int age);  // accessor function
10:       void Meow();             // general function
11:   private:                  // begin private section
12:       int itsAge;              // member variable
13:   };
14:
15:   // GetAge, Public accessor function
16:   // returns value of itsAge member
17:   int Cat::GetAge()
18:   {
19:       return itsAge;
20:   }
21:
22:   // definition of SetAge, public
23:   // accessor function
24:   // sets itsAge member
25:   void Cat::SetAge(int age)
26:   {
27:       // set member variable itsAge to
28:       // value passed in by parameter age
29:       itsAge = age;
30:   }
31:
32:   // definition of Meow method
33:   // returns: void
34:   // parameters: None
35:   // action: Prints "meow" to screen
36:   void Cat::Meow()
37:   {
38:       std::cout << "Meow.\n";
39:   }
40:
41:   // create a cat, set its age, have it
42:   // meow, tell us its age, then meow again.
43:   int main()
44:   {
45:       Cat Frisky;
46:       Frisky.SetAge(5);
47:       Frisky.Meow();
48:       std::cout << "Frisky is a cat who is " ;
49:       std::cout << Frisky.GetAge() << " years old.\n";
50:       Frisky.Meow();
51:       return 0;
52:   }
```

6

```
Meow.
Frisky is a cat who is 5 years old.
Meow.
```

ANALYSIS   Lines 5–13 contain the definition of the Cat class. Line 7 contains the keyword
public, which tells the compiler that what follows is a set of public members.
Line 8 has the declaration of the public accessor method GetAge(). GetAge() provides
access to the private member variable itsAge, which is declared in line 12. Line 9 has
the public accessor function SetAge(). SetAge() takes an integer as an argument and
sets itsAge to the value of that argument.

Line 10 has the declaration of the class method Meow(). Meow() is not an accessor function. Here it is a general method that prints the word Meow to the screen.

Line 11 begins the private section, which includes only the declaration in line 12 of the
private member variable itsAge. The class declaration ends with a closing brace and
semicolon in line 13.

Lines 17–20 contain the definition of the member function GetAge(). This method takes
no parameters; it returns an integer. Note that class methods include the class name followed by two colons and the function name (line 17). This syntax tells the compiler that
the GetAge() function you are defining here is the one that you declared in the Cat class.
With the exception of this header line, the GetAge() function is created the same as any
other function.

The GetAge() function takes only one line; it returns the value in itsAge. Note that the
main() function cannot access itsAge because itsAge is private to the Cat class. The
main() function has access to the public method GetAge(). Because GetAge() is a member function of the Cat class, it has full access to the itsAge variable. This access
enables GetAge() to return the value of itsAge to main().

Line 25 contains the definition of the SetAge() member function. It takes an integer
parameter and sets the value of itsAge to the value of that parameter in line 29. Because
it is a member of the Cat class, SetAge() has direct access to the member variable
itsAge.

Line 36 begins the definition, or implementation, of the Meow() method of the Cat class.
It is a one-line function that prints the word Meow to the screen, followed by a new line.
Remember that the \n character prints a new line to the screen.

Line 43 begins the body of the program with the familiar main() function. In this case, it
takes no arguments. In line 45, main() declares a Cat named Frisky. In line 46, the
value 5 is assigned to the itsAge member variable by way of the SetAge() accessor
method. Note that the method is called by using the object name (Frisky) followed by

the member operator (.) and the method name (SetAge()). In this same way, you can call any of the other methods in a class.

Line 47 calls the Meow() member function, and line 48 prints a message using the GetAge() accessor. Line 50 calls Meow() again.

Constructors and Destructors

Two ways exist to define an integer variable. You can define the variable and then assign a value to it later in the program. For example:

```
int Weight;            // define a variable
...                    // other code here
Weight = 7;            // assign it a value
```

Or you can define the integer and immediately initialize it. For example:

```
int Weight = 7;        // define and initialize to 7
```

Initialization combines the definition of the variable with its initial assignment. Nothing stops you from changing that value later. Initialization ensures that your variable is never without a meaningful value.

How do you initialize the member data of a class? Classes have a special member function called a constructor. The constructor can take parameters as needed, but it cannot have a return value—not even void. The constructor is a class method with the same name as the class itself.

Whenever you declare a constructor, you'll also want to declare a destructor. Just as constructors create and initialize objects of your class, destructors clean up after your object and free any memory you might have allocated. A destructor always has the name of the class, preceded by a tilde (~). Destructors take no arguments and have no return value. Therefore, the Cat declaration includes

```
~Cat();
```

Default Constructors and Destructors

If you don't declare a constructor or a destructor, the compiler makes one for you.

There are many types of constructors; some take arguments, others do not. The one that takes no arguments is called the default constructor. There is only one destructor. It too, takes no arguments.

6

It turns out that if you don't create a constructor or a destructor, the compiler will provide one for you. The constructor that is provided by the compiler is the default constructor—the constructor with no arguments. You can, however, create your own default constructor.

The default constructor and destructor created by the compiler not only have no arguments, they do nothing!

Using the Default Constructor

What good is a constructor that does nothing? In part, it is a matter of form. All objects must be constructed and destructed, and these do-nothing functions are called at the right time. However, to declare an object without passing in parameters, such as

```
Cat Rags;          // Rags gets no parameters
```

you must have a constructor in the form

```
Cat();
```

When you define an object of a class, the constructor is called. If the Cat constructor took two parameters, you might define a Cat object by writing

```
Cat Frisky (5,7);
```

If the constructor took one parameter, you would write

```
Cat Frisky (3);
```

In the event that the constructor takes no parameters at all (that is, that it is a *default* constructor), you leave off the parentheses and write

```
Cat Frisky;
```

This is an exception to the rule that states all functions require parentheses, even if they take no parameters. This is why you are able to write

```
Cat Frisky;
```

This is interpreted as a call to the default constructor. It provides no parameters, and it leaves off the parentheses.

Note that you don't have to use the compiler-provided default constructor. You are always free to write your own default constructor—that is, a constructor with no parameters. You are free to give your default constructor a function body in which you might initialize the object.

As a matter of form, if you declare a constructor, be sure to declare a destructor, even if your destructor does nothing. Although it is true that the default destructor would work correctly, it doesn't hurt to declare your own. It makes your code clearer.

Listing 6.4 rewrites the Cat class to use a constructor to initialize the Cat object, setting its age to whatever initial age you provide, and it demonstrates where the destructor is called.

LISTING 6.4   Using Constructors and Destructors

```
0:  // Demonstrates declaration of  constructors and
1:  // destructor for the Cat class
2:  // Programmer created default constructor
3:
4:  #include <iostream>       // for cout
5:
6:  class Cat                     // begin declaration of the class
7:  {
8:  public:                  // begin public section
9:     Cat(int initialAge);   // constructor
10:    ~Cat();                // destructor
11:    int GetAge();          // accessor function
12:    void SetAge(int age);    // accessor function
13:    void Meow();
14: private:                 // begin private section
15:    int itsAge;            // member variable
16: };
17:
18: // constructor of Cat,
19: Cat::Cat(int initialAge)
20: {
21:    itsAge = initialAge;
22: }
23:
24: Cat::~Cat()                  // destructor, takes no action
25: {
26: }
27:
28: // GetAge, Public accessor function
29: // returns value of itsAge member
30: int Cat::GetAge()
31: {
32:    return itsAge;
33: }
34:
35: // Definition of SetAge, public
36: // accessor function
37:
38: void Cat::SetAge(int age)
```

6

LISTING 6.4   continued

```
39:  {
40:      // set member variable itsAge to
41:      // value passed in by parameter age
42:      itsAge = age;
43:  }
44:
45:  // definition of Meow method
46:  // returns: void
47:  // parameters: None
48:  // action: Prints "meow" to screen
49:  void Cat::Meow()
50:  {
51:      std::cout << "Meow.\n";
52:  }
53:
54:  // create a cat, set its age, have it
55:  // meow, tell us its age, then meow again.
56:  int main()
57:  {
58:      Cat Frisky(5);
59:      Frisky.Meow();
60:      std::cout << "Frisky is a cat who is " ;
61:      std::cout << Frisky.GetAge() << " years old.\n";
62:      Frisky.Meow();
63:      Frisky.SetAge(7);
64:      std::cout << "Now Frisky is " ;
65:      std::cout << Frisky.GetAge() << " years old.\n";
66:      return 0;
67:  }
```

OUTPUT

```
Meow.
Frisky is a cat who is 5 years old.
Meow.
Now Frisky is 7 years old.
```

ANALYSIS   Listing 6.4 is similar to Listing 6.3, except that line 9 adds a constructor that takes an integer. Line 10 declares the destructor, which takes no parameters. Destructors never take parameters, and neither constructors nor destructors return a value—not even void.

Lines 19–22 show the implementation of the constructor. It is similar to the implementation of the SetAge() accessor function. There is no return value.

Lines 24–26 show the implementation of the destructor ~Cat(). This function does nothing, but you must include the definition of the function if you declare it in the class declaration.

Line 58 contains the definition of a Cat object, Frisky. The value 5 is passed in to Frisky's constructor. No need exists to call SetAge() because Frisky was created with the value 5 in its member variable itsAge, as shown in line 61. In line 63, Frisky's itsAge variable is reassigned to 7. Line 65 prints the new value.

Do	Don't
DO use constructors to initialize your objects.	**DON'T** give constructors or destructors a return value.
	DON'T give destructors parameters.

const Member Functions

If you declare a class method const, you are promising that the method won't change the value of any of the members of the class. To declare a class method constant, put the keyword const after the parentheses but before the semicolon. The declaration of the constant member function SomeFunction() takes no arguments and returns void. It looks like this:

```
void SomeFunction() const;
```

Accessor functions are often declared as constant functions by using the const modifier. The Cat class has two accessor functions:

```
void SetAge(int anAge);
int GetAge();
```

SetAge() cannot be const because it changes the member variable itsAge. GetAge(), on the other hand, can and should be const because it doesn't change the class at all. GetAge() simply returns the current value of the member variable itsAge. Therefore, the declaration of these functions should be written like this:

```
void SetAge(int anAge);
int GetAge() const;
```

If you declare a function to be const, and the implementation of that function changes the object by changing the value of any of its members, the compiler flags it as an error. For example, if you wrote GetAge() in such a way that it kept count of the number of times that the Cat was asked its age, it would generate a compiler error. This is because you would be changing the Cat object by calling this method.

6

> **Note**   Use const whenever possible. Declare member functions to be const when-
> ever they should not change the object. This enables the compiler to help
> you find errors; it's faster and less expensive than doing it yourself.

It is good programming practice to declare as many methods to be const as possible. Each time you do, you enable the compiler to catch your errors instead of letting your errors become bugs that will show up when your program is running.

Interface Versus Implementation

As you've learned, clients are the parts of the program that create and use objects of your class. You can think of the public interface to your class—the class declaration—as a contract with these clients. The contract tells how your class will behave.

In the Cat class declaration, for example, you create a contract that every Cat's age can be initialized in its constructor, assigned to by its SetAge() accessor function, and read by its GetAge() accessor. You also promise that every Cat will know how to Meow(). Note that you say nothing in the public interface about the member variable itsAge; that is an implementation detail that is not part of your contract. You will provide an age (GetAge()) and you will set an age (SetAge()), but the mechanism (itsAge) is invisible.

If you make GetAge() a const function—as you should—the contract also promises that GetAge() won't change the Cat on which it is called.

C++ is strongly typed, which means that the compiler enforces these contracts by giving you a compiler error when you violate them. Listing 6.5 demonstrates a program that doesn't compile because of violations of these contracts.

> **Caution**   Listing 6.5 does not compile!

LISTING 6.5   A Demonstration of Violations of the Interface

```
0:  // Demonstrates compiler errors
1:  // This program does not compile!
2:
3:  #include <iostream>          // for cout
4:
5:  class Cat
```

LISTING 6.5 continued

```
6:  {
7:  public:
8:     Cat(int initialAge);
9:     ~Cat();
10:    int GetAge() const;          // const accessor function
11:    void SetAge (int age);
12:    void Meow();
13: private:
14:    int itsAge;
15: };
16:
17: // constructor of Cat,
18: Cat::Cat(int initialAge)
19: {
20:    itsAge = initialAge;
21:    std::cout << "Cat Constructor\n";
22: }
23:
24: Cat::~Cat()                     // destructor, takes no action
25: {
26:    std::cout << "Cat Destructor\n";
27: }
28: // GetAge, const function
29: // but we violate const!
30: int Cat::GetAge() const
31: {
32:    return (itsAge++);           // violates const!
33: }
34:
35: // definition of SetAge, public
36: // accessor function
37:
38: void Cat::SetAge(int age)
39: {
40:    // set member variable its age to
41:    // value passed in by parameter age
42:    itsAge = age;
43: }
44:
45: // definition of Meow method
46: // returns: void
47: // parameters: None
48: // action: Prints "meow" to screen
49: void Cat::Meow()
50: {
51:    std::cout << "Meow.\n";
52: }
53:
54: // demonstrate various violations of the
```

6

LISTING 6.5 continued

```
55:   // interface, and resulting compiler errors
56:   int main()
57:   {
58:       Cat Frisky;                  // doesn't match declaration
59:       Frisky.Meow();
60:       Frisky.Bark();               // No, silly, cat's can't bark.
61:       Frisky.itsAge = 7;           // itsAge is private
62:       return 0;
63:   }
```

ANALYSIS As it is written, this program doesn't compile. Therefore, there is no output.

This program was fun to write because so many errors are in it.

Line 10 declares GetAge() to be a const accessor function—as it should be. In the body of GetAge(), however, in line 32, the member variable itsAge is incremented. Because this method is declared to be const, it must not change the value of itsAge. Therefore, it is flagged as an error when the program is compiled.

In line 12, Meow() is not declared const. Although this is not an error, it is bad programming practice. A better design takes into account that this method doesn't change the member variables of Cat. Therefore, Meow() should be const.

Line 58 shows the definition of a Cat object, Frisky. Cat now has a constructor, which takes an integer as a parameter. This means that you must pass in a parameter. Because no parameter exists in line 58, it is flagged as an error.

Note If you provide *any* constructor, the compiler will not provide one at all. Thus, if you create a constructor that takes a parameter, you will then have no default constructor unless you write your own.

Line 60 shows a call to a class method, Bark(). Bark() was never declared. Therefore, it is illegal.

Line 61 shows itsAge being assigned the value 7. Because itsAge is a private data member, it is flagged as an error when the program is compiled.

Why Use the Compiler to Catch Errors?

Although it would be wonderful to write 100 percent bug-free code, few programmers have been able to do so. However, many programmers have developed a system to help minimize bugs by catching and fixing them early in the process.

Although compiler errors are infuriating and are the bane of a programmer's existence, they are far better than the alternative. A weakly typed language enables you to violate your contracts without a peep from the compiler, but your program will crash at run-time—when, for example, your boss is watching.

Compile-time errors—that is, errors found while you are compiling—are far better than runtime errors—that is, errors found while you are executing the program. This is because compile-time errors can be found much more reliably. It is possible to run a program many times without going down every possible code path. Thus, a runtime error can hide for quite a while. Compile-time errors are found every time you compile. Thus, they are easier to identify and fix. It is the goal of quality programming to ensure that the code has no runtime bugs. One tried-and-true technique to accomplish this is to use the compiler to catch your mistakes early in the development process.

Where to Put Class Declarations and Method Definitions

Each function that you declare for your class must have a definition. The definition is also called the function implementation. Like other functions, the definition of a class method has a function header and a function body.

The definition must be in a file that the compiler can find. Most C++ compilers want that file to end with .c or .cpp. This book uses .cpp, but check your compiler to see what it prefers.

Note

Many compilers assume that files ending with .c are C programs, and that C++ program files end with .cpp. You can use any extension, but .cpp will minimize confusion.

6

You are free to put the declaration in this file as well, but that is not good programming practice. The convention that most programmers adopt is to put the declaration into what is called a header file, usually with the same name but ending in .h, .hp, or .hpp. This book names the header files with .hpp, but check your compiler to see what it prefers.

For example, you put the declaration of the Cat class into a file named CAT.hpp, and you put the definition of the class methods into a file called CAT.cpp. You then attach the header file to the .cpp file by putting the following code at the top of CAT.cpp:

```
#include "Cat.hpp"
```

This tells the compiler to read CAT.hpp into the file, the same as if you had typed in its contents at this point. Note: Some compilers insist that the capitalization agree between your #include statement and your file system.

Why bother separating the contents of your .hpp file and your .cpp file if you're just going to read the .hpp file back into the .cpp file? Most of the time, clients of your class don't care about the implementation specifics. Reading the header file tells them everything they need to know; they can ignore the implementation files. In addition, you might very well end up including the .hpp file into more than one .cpp file.

> **Note**
>
> The declaration of a class tells the compiler what the class is, what data it holds, and what functions it has. The declaration of the class is called its interface because it tells the user how to interact with the class. The interface is usually stored in an .hpp file, which is referred to as a header file.
>
> The function definition tells the compiler how the function works. The function definition is called the implementation of the class method, and it is kept in a .cpp file. The implementation details of the class are of concern only to the author of the class. Clients of the class—that is, the parts of the program that use the class—don't need to know, and don't care, how the functions are implemented.

Inline Implementation

Just as you can ask the compiler to make a regular function inline, you can make class methods inline. The keyword inline appears before the return type. The inline implementation of the GetWeight() function, for example, looks like this:

```
inline int Cat::GetWeight()
{
return itsWeight;          // return the Weight data member
}
```

You can also put the definition of a function into the declaration of the class, which automatically makes that function inline. For example,

```
class Cat
{
```

```
public:
int GetWeight() { return itsWeight; }    // inline
void SetWeight(int aWeight);
};
```

Note the syntax of the GetWeight() definition. The body of the inline function begins immediately after the declaration of the class method; no semicolon is used after the parentheses. Like any function, the definition begins with an opening brace and ends with a closing brace. As usual, whitespace doesn't matter; you could have written the declaration as

```
class Cat
{
public:
int GetWeight() const
{
return itsWeight;
}                              // inline
void SetWeight(int aWeight);
};
```

Listings 6.6 and 6.7 re-create the Cat class, but they put the declaration in CAT.hpp and the implementation of the functions in CAT.cpp. Listing 6.7 also changes the accessor functions and the Meow() function to inline.

LISTING 6.6   Cat Class Declaration in CAT.hpp

```
0:   #include <iostream>
1:   class Cat
2:   {
3:   public:
4:       Cat (int initialAge);
5:       ~Cat();
6:       int GetAge() const { return itsAge;}       // inline!
7:       void SetAge (int age) { itsAge = age;}      // inline!
8:       void Meow() const  { std::cout << "Meow.\n";}   // inline!
9:   private:
10:      int itsAge;
11:  };
```

6

LISTING 6.7   Cat Implementation in CAT.cpp

```
0:   // Demonstrates inline functions
1:   // and inclusion of header files
2:
3:   // be sure to include the header files!
4:   #include "cat.hpp"
```

LISTING 6.7   continued

```
 5:
 6:
 7:  Cat::Cat(int initialAge)    //constructor
 8:  {
 9:      itsAge = initialAge;
10:  }
11:
12:  Cat::~Cat()                 //destructor, takes no action
13:  {
14:  }
15:
16:  // Create a cat, set its age, have it
17:  // meow, tell us its age, then meow again.
18:  int main()
19:  {
20:      Cat Frisky(5);
21:      Frisky.Meow();
22:      std::cout << "Frisky is a cat who is " ;
23:      std::cout << Frisky.GetAge() << " years old.\n";
24:      Frisky.Meow();
25:      Frisky.SetAge(7);
26:      std::cout << "Now Frisky is " ;
27:      std::cout << Frisky.GetAge() << " years old.\n";
28:      return 0;
29:  }
```

OUTPUT
```
Meow.
Frisky is a cat who is 5 years old.
Meow.
Now Frisky is 7 years old.
```

ANALYSIS The code presented in Listing 6.6 and Listing 6.7 is similar to the code in Listing 6.4, except that three of the methods are written inline in the declaration file and the declaration has been separated into CAT.hpp (Listing 6.6).

GetAge() is declared in line 6, and its inline implementation is provided. Lines 7 and 8 provide more inline functions, but the functionality of these functions is unchanged from the previous "outline" implementations.

Line 4 of Listing 6.7 shows #include "cat.hpp", which brings in the listings from CAT.hpp. By including cat.hpp, you have told the precompiler to read cat.hpp into the file as if it had been typed there, starting on line 5.

This technique enables you to put your declarations into a different file from your implementation, yet have that declaration available when the compiler needs it. This is a very common technique in C++ programming. Typically, class declarations are in an .hpp file that is then #included into the associated .cpp file.

Lines 18–29 repeat the main function from Listing 6.4. This shows that making these functions inline doesn't change their performance.

Classes with Other Classes as Member Data

It is not uncommon to build up a complex class by declaring simpler classes and including them in the declaration of the more complicated class. For example, you might declare a wheel class, a motor class, a transmission class, and so forth, and then combine them into a car class. This declares a has-a relationship. A car has a motor, it has wheels, and it has a transmission.

Consider a second example. A rectangle is composed of lines. A line is defined by two points. A point is defined by an x coordinate and a y coordinate. Listing 6.8 shows a complete declaration of a Rectangle class, as might appear in RECTANGLE.hpp. Because a rectangle is defined as four lines connecting four points, and each point refers to a coordinate on a graph, we first declare a Point class to hold the x,y coordinates of each point. Listing 6.9 provides the implementation for both classes.

LISTING 6.8   Declaring a Complete Class

```
0:  // Begin Rect.hpp
1:
2:  #include <iostream>
3:  class Point      // holds x,y coordinates
4:  {
5:  // no constructor, use default
6:  public:
7:      void SetX(int x) { itsX = x; }
8:      void SetY(int y) { itsY = y; }
9:      int GetX()const { return itsX;}
10:     int GetY()const { return itsY;}
11: private:
12:     int itsX;
13:     int itsY;
14: };    // end of Point class declaration
15:
16:
17: class  Rectangle
18: {
19: public:
20:     Rectangle (int top, int left, int bottom, int right);
21:     ~Rectangle () {}
22:
23:     int GetTop() const { return itsTop; }
24:     int GetLeft() const { return itsLeft; }
25:     int GetBottom() const { return itsBottom; }
```

6

LISTING 6.8 continued

```
26:     int GetRight() const { return itsRight; }
27:
28:     Point  GetUpperLeft() const { return itsUpperLeft; }
29:     Point  GetLowerLeft() const { return itsLowerLeft; }
30:     Point  GetUpperRight() const { return itsUpperRight; }
31:     Point  GetLowerRight() const { return itsLowerRight; }
32:
33:     void SetUpperLeft(Point Location)   {itsUpperLeft = Location;}
34:     void SetLowerLeft(Point Location)   {itsLowerLeft = Location;}
35:     void SetUpperRight(Point Location)  {itsUpperRight = Location;}
36:     void SetLowerRight(Point Location)  {itsLowerRight = Location;}
37:
38:     void SetTop(int top) { itsTop = top; }
39:     void SetLeft (int left) { itsLeft = left; }
40:     void SetBottom (int bottom) { itsBottom = bottom; }
41:     void SetRight (int right) { itsRight = right; }
42:
43:     int GetArea() const;
44:
45: private:
46:     Point  itsUpperLeft;
47:     Point  itsUpperRight;
48:     Point  itsLowerLeft;
49:     Point  itsLowerRight;
50:     int    itsTop;
51:     int    itsLeft;
52:     int    itsBottom;
53:     int    itsRight;
54: };
55: // end Rect.hpp
```

LISTING 6.9 RECT.cpp

```
0:  // Begin rect.cpp
1:
2:  #include "rect.hpp"
3:  Rectangle::Rectangle(int top, int left, int bottom, int right)
4:  {
5:      itsTop = top;
6:      itsLeft = left;
7:      itsBottom = bottom;
8:      itsRight = right;
9:
10:     itsUpperLeft.SetX(left);
11:     itsUpperLeft.SetY(top);
12:
13:     itsUpperRight.SetX(right);
14:     itsUpperRight.SetY(top);
```

LISTING 6.9   continued

```
15:
16:      itsLowerLeft.SetX(left);
17:      itsLowerLeft.SetY(bottom);
18:
19:      itsLowerRight.SetX(right);
20:      itsLowerRight.SetY(bottom);
21:  }
22:
23:
24:  // compute area of the rectangle by finding cornerssides,
25:  // establish width and height and then multiply
26:  int Rectangle::GetArea() const
27:  {
28:      int Width = itsRight-itsLeft;
29:      int Height = itsTop - itsBottom;
30:      return (Width * Height);
31:  }
32:
33:  int main()
34:  {
35:      //initialize a local Rectangle variable
36:      Rectangle MyRectangle (100, 20, 50, 80 );
37:
38:      int Area = MyRectangle.GetArea();
39:
40:      std::cout << "Area: " << Area << "\n";
41:      std::cout << "Upper Left X Coordinate: ";
42:      std::cout << MyRectangle.GetUpperLeft().GetX();
43:      return 0;
44:  }
```

OUTPUT
```
Area: 3000
Upper Left X Coordinate: 20
```

ANALYSIS   Lines 3–14 in Listing 6.8 declare the class Point, which is used to hold a specific x,y coordinate on a graph. As written, this program doesn't use Points much. However, other drawing methods require Points.

Note

> Some compilers report an error if you declare a class named Rectangle. If you have this problem, simply rename the class to myRectangle.

Within the declaration of the class Point, you declare two member variables (itsX and itsY) on lines 12 and 13. These variables hold the values of the coordinates. As the x coordinate increases, you move to the right on the graph. As the y coordinate increases, you move upward on the graph. Other graphs use different systems. Some windowing programs, for example, increase the y coordinate as you move down in the window.

The `Point` class uses inline accessor functions to get and set the X and Y points declared on lines 7–10. Points use the default constructor and destructor. Therefore, you must set their coordinates explicitly.

Line 17 begins the declaration of a `Rectangle` class. A `Rectangle` consists of four points that represent the corners of the `Rectangle`.

The constructor for the `Rectangle` (line 20) takes four integers, known as `top`, `left`, `bottom`, and `right`. The four parameters to the constructor are copied into four member variables (Listing 6.9), and then the four `Point`s are established.

In addition to the usual accessor functions, `Rectangle` has a function `GetArea()` declared in line 43. Instead of storing the area as a variable, the `GetArea()` function computes the area on lines 28 and 29 of Listing 6.9. To do this, it computes the width and the height of the rectangle, and then it multiplies these two values.

Getting the x coordinate of the upper-left corner of the rectangle requires that you access the `UpperLeft` point and ask that point for its X value. Because `GetUpperLeft()` is a method of `Rectangle`, it can directly access the private data of `Rectangle`, including `itsUpperLeft`. Because `itsUpperLeft` is a `Point` and `Point`'s `itsX` value is private, `GetUpperLeft()` cannot directly access this data. Rather, it must use the public accessor function `GetX()` to obtain that value.

Line 33 of Listing 6.9 is the beginning of the body of the actual program. Until line 36, no memory has been allocated, and nothing has really happened. The only thing you've done is tell the compiler how to make a point and how to make a rectangle, in case one is ever needed.

In line 36, you define a `Rectangle` by passing in values for `Top`, `Left`, `Bottom`, and `Right`.

In line 38, you make a local variable, `Area`, of type int. This variable holds the area of the `Rectangle` that you've created. You initialize `Area` with the value returned by `Rectangle`'s `GetArea()` function.

A client of `Rectangle` could create a `Rectangle` object and get its area without ever looking at the implementation of `GetArea()`.

`RECT.hpp` is shown in Listing 6.8. Just by looking at the header file, which contains the declaration of the `Rectangle` class, the programmer knows that `GetArea()` returns an int. How `GetArea()` does its magic is not of concern to the user of class `Rectangle`. In fact, the author of `Rectangle` could change `GetArea()` without affecting the programs that use the `Rectangle` class.

FAQ

What is the difference between declaring and defining?

Answer: A declaration introduces a name of something but does not allocate memory. A definition allocates memory.

With a few exceptions, all declarations are also definitions. The most important exceptions are the declaration of a global function (a prototype) and the declaration of a class (usually in a header file).

Structures

A very close cousin to the `class` keyword is the keyword `struct`, which is used to declare a structure. In C++, a structure is the same as a class, except that its members are public by default. You can declare a structure exactly as you declare a class, and you can give it the same data members and functions. In fact, if you follow the good programming practice of always explicitly declaring the private and public sections of your class, no difference will exist whatsoever.

Try re-entering Listing 6.8 with these changes:

- In line 3, change class `Point` to struct `Point`.
- In line 17, change class `Rectangle` to struct `Rectangle`.

Now run the program again and compare the output. No change should have occurred.

Why Two Keywords Do the Same Thing

You're probably wondering why two keywords do the same thing. This is an accident of history. When C++ was developed, it was built as an extension of the C language. C has structures, although C structures don't have class methods. Bjarne Stroustrup, the creator of C++, built upon structs, but he changed the name to class to represent the new, expanded functionality.

6

Do

DO put your class declaration in an .hpp file and your member functions in a .cpp file.

DO use const whenever you can.

DO understand classes before you move on.

Summary

Today you learned how to create new data types called classes. You learned how to define variables of these new types, which are called objects.

A class has data members, which are variables of various types, including other classes. A class also includes member functions—also known as methods. You use these member functions to manipulate the member data and to perform other services.

Class members, both data and functions, can be public or private. Public members are accessible to any part of your program. Private members are accessible only to the member functions of the class.

It is good programming practice to isolate the interface, or declaration, of the class in a header file. You usually do this in a file with an .hpp extension. The implementation of the class methods is written in a file with a .cpp extension.

Class constructors initialize objects. Class destructors destroy objects and are often used to free memory allocated by methods of the class.

Q&A

Q How big is a class object?

A A class object's size in memory is determined by the sum of the sizes of its member variables. Class methods don't take up room as part of the memory set aside for the object.

Some compilers align variables in memory in such a way that two-byte variables actually consume somewhat more than two bytes. Check your compiler manual to be sure, but at this point you do not need to be concerned with these details.

Q If I declare a class Cat with a private member itsAge and then define two Cat objects, Frisky and Boots, can Boots access Frisky's itsAge member variable?

A Yes. Private data is available to the member functions of a class, and different instances of the class can access each other's data. In other words, if Frisky and Boots are both instances of Cat, Frisky's member functions can access Frisky's data and also Boots's data.

Q Why shouldn't I make all the member data public?

A Making member data private enables the client of the class to use the data without worrying about how it is stored or computed. For example, if the Cat class has a method GetAge(), clients of the Cat class can ask for the cat's age without knowing or caring if the cat stores its age in a member variable or computes its age on-the-fly.

Q If using a const function to change the class causes a compiler error, why shouldn't I just leave out the word const and be sure to avoid errors?

A If your member function logically shouldn't change the class, using the keyword const is a good way to enlist the compiler in helping you find silly mistakes. For example, GetAge() might have no reason to change the Cat class, but your implementation has this line:

```
if (itsAge = 100) cout << "Hey! You're 100 years old\n";
```

Declaring GetAge() to be const causes this code to be flagged as an error. You meant to check whether itsAge is equal to 100, but instead you inadvertently assigned 100 to itsAge. Because this assignment changes the class—and you said this method would not change the class—the compiler is able to find the error.

This kind of mistake can be hard to find just by scanning the code. The eye often sees only what it expects to see. More importantly, the program might appear to run correctly, but itsAge has now been set to a bogus number. This will cause problems sooner or later.

Q Is there ever a reason to use a structure in a C++ program?

A Many C++ programmers reserve the struct keyword for classes that have no functions. This is a throwback to the old C structures, which could not have functions. Frankly, I find it confusing and poor programming practice. Today's methodless structure might need methods tomorrow. Then you'll be forced either to change the type to class or to break your rule and end up with a structure with methods.

6

Workshop

The Workshop provides quiz questions to help you solidify your understanding of the material covered and exercises to provide you with experience in using what you've learned. Try to answer the quiz and exercise questions before checking the answers in Appendix D, and make sure you understand the answers before continuing to the next chapter.

Quiz

1. What is the dot operator, and what is it used for?

2. Which sets aside memory—declaration or definition?

3. Is the declaration of a class its interface or its implementation?

4. What is the difference between public and private data members?

5. Can member functions be private?

6. Can member data be public?

7. If you declare two Cat objects, can they have different values in their itsAge member data?

8. Do class declarations end with a semicolon? Do class method definitions?

9. What would the header be for a Cat function, Meow(), that takes no parameters and returns void?

10. What function is called to initialize a class?

Exercises

1. Write the code that declares a class called Employee with these data members: age, yearsOfService, and Salary.

2. Rewrite the Employee class to make the data members private, and provide public accessor methods to get and set each of the data members.

3. Write a program with the Employee class that makes two employees; sets their age, YearsOfService, and Salary; and prints their values.

4. Continuing from Exercise 3, provide a method of Employee that reports how many thousands of dollars the employee earns, rounded to the nearest 1,000.

5. Change the Employee class so that you can initialize age, YearsOfService, and Salary when you create the employee.

6. **BUG BUSTERS:** What is wrong with the following declaration?
```
class Square
{
public:
    int Side;
}
```

7. **BUG BUSTERS:** Why isn't the following class declaration very useful?
```
class Cat
{
    int GetAge()const;
private:
    int itsAge;
};
```

8. **BUG BUSTERS:** What three bugs in this code will the compiler find?

```cpp
class  TV
{
public:
    void SetStation(int Station);
    int GetStation() const;
private:
    int itsStation;
};

main()
{
    TV myTV;
    myTV.itsStation = 9;
    TV.SetStation(10);
    TV myOtherTv(2);
}
```

6

DAY 7

More Program Flow

Programs accomplish most of their work by branching and looping. On Day 4, "Expressions and Statements," you learned how to branch your program using the if statement.

Today you will learn

- What loops are and how they are used.
- How to build various loops.
- An alternative to deeply nested if/else statements.

Looping

Many programming problems are solved by repeatedly acting on the same data. Two ways to do this are recursion (discussed on Day 5, "Functions") and iteration. Iteration means doing the same thing again and again. The principal method of iteration is the loop.

The Roots of Looping goto

In the primitive days of early computer science, programs were nasty, brutish, and short. Loops consisted of a label, some statements, and a jump.

In C++, a label is just a name followed by a colon (:). The label is placed to the left of a legal C++ statement, and a jump is accomplished by writing goto followed by the label name. Listing 7.1 illustrates this.

LISTING 7.1   Looping with the Keyword goto

```
0:   // Listing 7.1
1:   // Looping with goto
2:
3:   #include <iostream>
4:
5:   int main()
6:   {
7:        int counter = 0;       // initialize counter
8:   loop:    counter ++;             // top of the loop
9:        std::cout << "counter: " << counter << "\n";
10:       if (counter < 5)              // test the value
11:         goto loop;                  // jump to the top
12:
13:       std::cout << "Complete. Counter: " << counter << ".\n";
14:       return 0;
15:  }
```

OUTPUT
```
counter: 1
counter: 2
counter: 3
counter: 4
counter: 5
Complete. Counter: 5.
```

ANALYSIS   On line 7, counter is initialized to 0. The label loop is on line 8, marking the top of the loop. counter is incremented and its new value is printed. The value of counter is tested on line 10. If it is less than 5, the if statement is true and the goto statement is executed. This causes program execution to jump back to line 8. The program continues looping until counter is equal to 5, at which time it "falls through" the loop and the final output is printed.

Why goto Is Shunned

As a rule, programmers avoid goto, and with good reason. goto statements can cause a jump to any location in your source code, backward or forward. The indiscriminate use of goto statements has caused tangled, miserable, impossible-to-read programs known as "spaghetti code."

> **The** goto **Statement**
>
> To use the goto statement, you write goto followed by a label name. This causes an unconditioned jump to the label.
>
> **Example**
>
> ```
>         if (value > 10)
>             goto end;
>         if (value < 10)
>             goto end;
>         cout << "value is 10!";
>         end:
>             cout << "done";
> ```
>
> To avoid the use of goto, more sophisticated, tightly controlled looping commands have been introduced: for, while, and do...while.

while Loops

A while loop causes your program to repeat a sequence of statements as long as the starting condition remains true. In the example of goto in Listing 7.1, the counter was incremented until it was equal to 5. Listing 7.2 shows the same program rewritten to take advantage of a while loop.

LISTING 7.2   while Loops

```
0:  // Listing 7.2
1:  // Looping with while
2:
3:  #include <iostream>
4:
5:  int main()
6:  {
7:      int counter = 0;              // initialize the condition
8:
9:      while(counter < 5)      // test condition still true
10:     {
11:         counter++;              // body of the loop
12:         std::cout << "counter: " << counter << "\n";
13:     }
14:
15:     std::cout << "Complete. Counter: " << counter << ".\n";
16:     return 0;
17: }
```

7

OUTPUT
```
counter: 1
counter: 2
counter: 3
counter: 4
counter: 5
Complete. Counter: 5.
```

ANALYSIS This simple program demonstrates the fundamentals of the while loop. A condition is tested, and if it is true, the body of the while loop is executed. In this case, the condition tested on line 9 is whether counter is less than 5. If the condition is true, the body of the loop is executed; on line 11 the counter is incremented, and on line 12 the value is printed. When the conditional statement on line 9 fails (when counter is no longer less than 5), the entire body of the while loop (lines 10–13) is skipped. Program execution falls through to line 14.

The while Statement

The syntax for the while statement is as follows:

```
while ( condition )
statement;
```

condition is any C++ expression, and statement is any valid C++ statement or block of statements. When condition evaluates true (1), statement is executed, and then condition is tested again. This continues until condition tests false, at which time the while loop terminates and execution continues on the first line below statement.

Example

```
// count to 10
int x = 0;
while (x < 10)
cout << "X: " << x++;
```

More Complicated while Statements

The condition tested by a while loop can be as complex as any legal C++ expression. This can include expressions produced using the logical && (AND), || (OR), and ! (NOT) operators. Listing 7.3 is a somewhat more complicated while statement.

LISTING 7.3   Complex while Loops

```
0:  // Listing 7.3
1:  // Complex while statements
2:
3:  #include <iostream>
4:  using namespace std;
```

LISTING 7.3 continued

```
 5:
 6:  int main()
 7:  {
 8:      unsigned short small;
 9:      unsigned long  large;
10:      const unsigned short MAXSMALL=65535;
11:
12:      cout << "Enter a small number: ";
13:      cin >> small;
14:      cout << "Enter a large number: ";
15:      cin >> large;
16:
17:      cout << "small: " << small << "...";
18:
19:      // for each iteration, test three conditions
20:      while (small < large && large > 0 && small < MAXSMALL)
21:      {
22:         if (small % 5000 == 0)  // write a dot every 5k lines
23:             cout << ".";
24:
25:         small++;
26:
27:         large-=2;
28:      }
29:
30:      cout << "\nSmall: " << small << " Large: " << large << endl;
31:      return 0;
32:  }
```

OUTPUT

```
Enter a small number: 2
Enter a large number: 100000
small: 2........
Small: 33335 Large: 33334
```

ANALYSIS This program is a game. Enter two numbers, one small and one large. The smaller number will count up by ones, and the larger number will count down by twos. The goal of the game is to guess when they'll meet.

On lines 12–15, the numbers are entered. Line 20 sets up a while loop, which will continue only as long as three conditions are met:

1. Small is not bigger than large.

2. Large isn't negative or zero.

3. Small doesn't overrun the size of a small integer (MAXSMALL).

7

On line 23, the value in `small` is calculated modulo 5,000. This does not change the value in `small`; however, it only returns the value 0 when `small` is an exact multiple of 5,000. Each time it is, a dot (.) is printed to the screen to show progress. On line 26, `small` is incremented, and on line 28, `large` is decremented by 2.

When any of the three conditions in the `while` loop fails, the loop ends and execution of the program continues after the `while` loop's closing brace on line 29.

Note

> The modulus operator (%) and compound conditions are covered on Day 3, "Variables and Constants."

continue and break

At times you'll want to return to the top of a `while` loop before the entire set of statements in the `while` loop is executed. The `continue` statement jumps back to the top of the loop.

At other times, you may want to exit the loop before the exit conditions are met. The `break` statement immediately exits the `while` loop, and program execution resumes after the closing brace.

Listing 7.4 demonstrates the use of these statements. This time the game has become more complicated. The user is invited to enter a small number and a large number, a skip number, and a target number. The small number will be incremented by one, and the large number will be decremented by 2. The decrement will be skipped each time the small number is a multiple of the skip. The game ends if `small` becomes larger than `large`. If the large number reaches the target exactly, a statement is printed and the game stops.

The user's goal is to put in a target number for the large number that will stop the game.

LISTING 7.4   break and continue

```
0:  // Listing 7.4
1:  // Demonstrates break and continue
2:
3:  #include <iostream>
4:
5:  int main()
6:  {
7:      using namespace std;
8:      unsigned short small;
9:      unsigned long  large;
```

LISTING 7.4   continued

```
10:     unsigned long  skip;
11:     unsigned long target;
12:     const unsigned short MAXSMALL=65535;
13:
14:     cout << "Enter a small number: ";
15:     cin >> small;
16:     cout << "Enter a large number: ";
17:     cin >> large;
18:     cout << "Enter a skip number: ";
19:     cin >> skip;
20:     cout << "Enter a target number: ";
21:     cin >> target;
22:
23:     cout << "\n";
24:
25:     // set up 3 stop conditions for the loop
26:     while (small < large && large > 0 && small < MAXSMALL)
27:
28:     {
29:
30:        small++;
31:
32:        if (small % skip == 0)  // skip the decrement?
33:        {
34:           cout << "skipping on " << small << endl;
35:           continue;
36:        }
37:
38:        if (large == target)     // exact match for the target?
39:        {
40:           cout << "Target reached!";
41:           break;
42:        }
43:
44:        large-=2;
45:     }                     // end of while loop
46:
47:     cout << "\nSmall: " << small << " Large: " << large << endl;
48:     return 0;
49: }
```

OUTPUT

```
Enter a small number: 2
Enter a large number: 20
Enter a skip number: 4
Enter a target number: 6

skipping on 4
skipping on 8

Small: 10 Large: 8
```

7

ANALYSIS In this play, the user lost; small became larger than large before the target number of 6 was reached.

On line 26, the while conditions are tested. If small continues to be smaller than large, large is larger than 0, and small hasn't overrun the maximum value for a small int, the body of the while loop is entered.

On line 32, the small value is taken modulo the skip value. If small is a multiple of skip, the continue statement is reached and program execution jumps to the top of the loop at line 26. This effectively skips over the test for the target and the decrement of large.

On line 38, target is tested against the value for large. If they are the same, the user has won. A message is printed and the break statement is reached. This causes an immediate break out of the while loop, and program execution resumes on line 46.

Note

> Both continue and break should be used with caution. They are the next most dangerous commands after goto, for much the same reason. Programs that suddenly change direction are harder to understand, and liberal use of continue and break can render even a small while loop unreadable.

The continue Statement

continue; causes a while or for loop to begin again at the top of the loop.

See Listing 7.4 for an example of using continue.

The break Statement

break; causes the immediate end of a while or for loop. Execution jumps to the closing brace.

Example

```
while (condition)
{
    if (condition2)
        break;
    // statements;
}
```

while (true) Loops

The condition tested in a while loop can be any valid C++ expression. As long as that condition remains true, the while loop will continue. You can create a loop that will never end by using the value true for the condition to be tested. Listing 7.5 demonstrates counting to 10 using this construct.

LISTING 7.5 while Loops

```
0:  // Listing 7.5
1:  // Demonstrates a while true loop
2:
3:  #include <iostream>
4:
5:  int main()
6:  {
7:     int counter = 0;
8:
9:     while (true)
10:    {
11:       counter ++;
12:       if (counter > 10)
13:          break;
14:    }
15:    std::cout << "Counter: " << counter << "\n";
16:    return 0;
17: }
```

OUTPUT

Counter: 11

ANALYSIS On line 9, a while loop is set up with a condition that can never be false. The loop increments the counter variable on line 11, and then on line 12 it tests to see whether counter has gone past 10. If it hasn't, the while loop iterates. If counter is greater than 10, the break on line 13 ends the while loop, and program execution falls through to line 15, where the results are printed.

This program works, but it isn't pretty. This is a good example of using the wrong tool for the job. The same thing can be accomplished by putting the test of counter's value where it belongs—in the while condition.

Caution Eternal loops such as while (true) can cause your computer to hang if the exit condition is never reached. Use these with caution and test them thoroughly.

7

C++ gives you many ways to accomplish the same task. The real trick is picking the right tool for the particular job.

Do	Don't
DO use while loops to iterate while a condition is true. **DO** exercise caution when using continue and break statements. **DO** make sure your loop will eventually end.	**DON'T** use the goto statement.

do...while Loops

It is possible that the body of a while loop will never execute. The while statement checks its condition before executing any of its statements, and if the condition evaluates false, the entire body of the while loop is skipped. Listing 7.6 illustrates this.

LISTING 7.6   Skipping the Body of the while Loop

```
0:   // Listing 7.6
1:   // Demonstrates skipping the body of
2:   // the while loop when the condition is false.
3:
4:   #include <iostream>
5:
6:   int main()
7:   {
8:
9:       int counter;
10:      std::cout << "How many hellos?: ";
11:      std::cin >> counter;
12:      while (counter > 0)
13:      {
14:          std::cout << "Hello!\n";
15:          counter--;
16:      }
17:      std::cout << "Counter is OutPut: " << counter;
18:      return 0;
19:  }
```

OUTPUT

```
How many hellos?: 2
Hello!
Hello!
Counter is OutPut: 0

How many hellos?: 0
Counter is OutPut: 0
```

ANALYSIS The user is prompted for a starting value on line 10. This starting value is stored in the integer variable `counter`. The value of `counter` is tested on line 12 and decremented in the body of the `while` loop. The first time through, `counter` was set to 2, and so the body of the `while` loop ran twice. The second time through, however, the user typed in 0. The value of `counter` was tested on line 12 and the condition was false; `counter` was not greater than 0. The entire body of the `while` loop was skipped, and `Hello` was never printed.

What if you want to ensure that `Hello` is always printed at least once? The `while` loop can't accomplish this because the `if` condition is tested before any printing is done. You can force the issue with an `if` statement just before entering the `while` loop

```
if (counter < 1)  // force a minimum value
counter = 1;
```

but that is what programmers call a "kludge" (pronounced klooj to rhyme with stooge), an ugly and inelegant solution.

do...while

The `do...while` loop executes the body of the loop before its condition is tested and ensures that the body always executes at least one time. Listing 7.7 rewrites Listing 7.6, this time using a `do...while` loop.

LISTING 7.7 Demonstrates do...while Loop

```
0:  // Listing 7.7
1:  // Demonstrates do while
2:
3:  #include <iostream>
4:
5:  int main()
6:  {
7:      using namespace std;
8:      int counter;
9:      cout << "How many hellos? ";
10:     cin >> counter;
11:     do
```

7

LISTING 7.7   continued

```
12:    {
13:        cout << "Hello\n";
14:        counter--;
15:    }  while (counter >0 );
16:    cout << "Counter is: " << counter << endl;
17:    return 0;
18:  }
```

OUTPUT

```
How many hellos? 2
Hello
Hello
Counter is: 0
```

ANALYSIS   The user is prompted for a starting value on line 9, which is stored in the integer variable counter. In the do...while loop, the body of the loop is entered before the condition is tested, and therefore, the body of the loop is guaranteed to run at least once. On line 13 the message is printed, on line 14 the counter is decremented, and on line 15 the condition is tested. If the condition evaluates true, execution jumps to the top of the loop on line 13; otherwise, it falls through to line 16.

The continue and break statements work in the do...while loop exactly as they do in the while loop. The only difference between a while loop and a do...while loop is when the condition is tested.

The do...while Statement

The syntax for the do...while statement is as follows:

```
do
statement
while (condition);
```

statement is executed, and then condition is evaluated. If condition is true, the loop is repeated; otherwise, the loop ends. The statements and conditions are otherwise identical to the while loop.

Example 1

```
// count to 10
int x = 0;
do
cout << "X: " << x++;
while (x < 10)
```

Example 2

```
// print lowercase alphabet.
char ch = 'a';
do
{
cout << ch << ' ';
ch++;
} while ( ch <= 'z' );
```

Do

DO use do...while when you want to ensure the loop is executed at least once.

DO use while loops when you want to skip the loop if the condition is false.

DO test all loops to make sure they do what you expect.

for Loops

When programming while loops, you'll often find yourself setting up a starting condition, testing to see if the condition is true, and incrementing or otherwise changing a variable each time through the loop. Listing 7.8 demonstrates this.

LISTING 7.8 while Reexamined

```
0:  // Listing 7.8
1:  // Looping with while
2:
3:  #include <iostream>
4:
5:  int main()
6:  {
7:
8:      int counter = 0;
9:
10:     while(counter < 5)
11:     {
12:         counter++;
13:         std::cout << "Looping!   ";
14:     }
15:
16:     std::cout << "\nCounter: " << counter << ".\n";
17:     return 0;
18: }
```

7

OUTPUT
Looping! Looping! Looping! Looping! Looping!
Counter: 5.

ANALYSIS
The condition is set on line 8: counter is initialized to 0. On line 10, counter is
tested to see whether it is less than 5. counter is incremented on line 12. On line
16, a simple message is printed, but you can imagine that more important work could be
done for each increment of the counter.

A for loop combines three steps into one statement. The three steps are initialization,
test, and increment. A for statement consists of the keyword for followed by a pair of
parentheses. Within the parentheses are three statements separated by semicolons.

The first statement is the initialization. Any legal C++ statement can be put here, but typically this is used to create and initialize a counting variable. Statement 2 is the test, and
any legal C++ expression can be used here. This serves the same role as the condition in
the while loop. Statement 3 is the action. Typically a value is incremented or decremented, though any legal C++ statement can be put here. Note that statements 1 and 3 can be
any legal C++ statement, but statement 2 must be an expression—a C++ statement that
returns a value. Listing 7.9 demonstrates a for loop.

LISTING 7.9   Demonstrating the for Loop

```
0:   // Listing 7.9
1:   // Looping with for
2:
3:   #include <iostream>
4:
5:   int main()
6:   {
7:
8:       int counter;
9:       for (counter = 0; counter < 5; counter++)
10:          std::cout << "Looping! ";
11:
12:      std::cout << "\nCounter: " << counter << ".\n";
13:      return 0;
14:  }
```

OUTPUT
Looping! Looping! Looping! Looping! Looping!
Counter: 5.

ANALYSIS
The for statement on line 9 combines the initialization of counter, the test that
counter is less than 5, and the increment of counter all into one line. The body
of the for statement is on line 10. Of course, a block could be used here as well.

> **The** `for` **Statement**
>
> The syntax for the `for` statement is as follows:
>
> ```
> for (initialization; test; action )
>     statement;
> ```
>
> The `initialization` statement is used to initialize the state of a counter, or to otherwise prepare for the loop. `test` is any C++ expression and is evaluated each time through the loop. If `test` is true, the body of the `for` loop is executed and then the action in the header is executed (typically the counter is incremented).
>
> **Example 1**
>
> ```
> // print Hello ten times
> for (int i = 0; i<10; i++)
>     cout << "Hello! ";
> ```
>
> **Example 2**
>
> ```
> for (int i = 0; i < 10; i++)
> {
>     cout << "Hello!" << endl;
>     cout << "the value of i is: " << i << endl;
> }
> ```

Advanced `for` Loops

`for` statements are powerful and flexible. The three independent statements (`initialization`, `test`, and `action`) lend themselves to a number of variations.

A `for` loop works in the following sequence:

1. Performs the operations in the initialization
2. Evaluates the condition
3. If the condition is true, executes the body of the `for` loop, and then executes the action statement

After each time through, the loop repeats steps 2 and 3.

Multiple Initialization and Increments

It is not uncommon to initialize more than one variable, to test a compound logical expression, and to execute more than one statement. The initialization and the action may be replaced by multiple C++ statements, each separated by a comma. Listing 7.10 demonstrates the initialization and increment of two variables.

7

LISTING 7.10   Demonstrating Multiple Statements in for Loops

```
0:    //listing 7.10
1:    // demonstrates multiple statements in
2:    // for loops
3:
4:    #include <iostream>
5:
6:    int main()
7:    {
8:
9:        for (int i=0, j=0; i<3; i++, j++)
10:           std::cout << "i: " << i << " j: " << j << std::endl;
11:        return 0;
12:    }
```

OUTPUT
```
i: 0   j: 0
i: 1   j: 1
i: 2   j: 2
```

ANALYSIS On line 9, two variables, i and j, are each initialized with the value 0. The test (i<3) is evaluated, and because it is true, the body of the for statement is executed, and the values are printed. Finally, the third clause in the for statement is executed, and i and j are incremented.

After line 10 completes, the condition is evaluated again, and if it remains true, the actions are repeated (i and j are again incremented), and the body of loop is executed again. This continues until the test fails, in which case the action statement is not executed, and control falls out of the loop.

Null Statements in for Loops

Any or all the statements in a for loop can be null. To accomplish this, use the semicolon (;) to mark where the statement would have been. To create a for loop that acts exactly like a while loop, leave out the first and third statements. Listing 7.11 illustrates this idea.

LISTING 7.11   Null Statements in for Loops

```
0:    // Listing 7.11
1:    // For loops with null statements
2:
3:    #include <iostream>
4:
5:    int main()
6:    {
7:
```

LISTING 7.11   continued

```
 8:     int counter = 0;
 9:
10:     for( ; counter < 5; )
11:     {
12:        counter++;
13:        std::cout << "Looping!  ";
14:     }
15:
16:     std::cout << "\nCounter: " << counter << ".\n";
17:     return 0;
18:  }
```

OUTPUT
```
Looping!  Looping!  Looping!  Looping!  Looping!
Counter: 5.
```

ANALYSIS   You may recognize this as exactly like the `while` loop illustrated in Listing 7.8. On line 8, the `counter` variable is initialized. The `for` statement on line 10 does not initialize any values, but it does include a test for `counter < 5`. No increment statement exists, so this loop behaves exactly as if it had been written:

```
while (counter < 5)
```

Once again, C++ gives you several ways to accomplish the same thing. No experienced C++ programmer would use a `for` loop in this way, but it does illustrate the flexibility of the `for` statement. In fact, it is possible, using `break` and `continue`, to create a `for` loop with none of the three statements. Listing 7.12 illustrates how.

LISTING 7.12   Illustrating Empty for Loop Statement

```
 0:  //Listing 7.12 illustrating
 1:  //empty for loop statement
 2:
 3:  #include <iostream>
 4:
 5:  int main()
 6:  {
 7:
 8:     int counter=0;       // initialization
 9:     int max;
10:     std::cout << "How many hellos?";
11:     std::cin >> max;
12:     for (;;)             // a for loop that doesn't end
13:     {
14:        if (counter < max)       // test
15:        {
16:           std::cout << "Hello!\n";
```

7

LISTING 7.12   continued

```
17:           counter++;        // increment
18:        }
19:        else
20:           break;
21:     }
22:     return 0;
23:  }
```

OUTPUT

```
How many hellos?3
Hello!
Hello!
Hello!
```

ANALYSIS   The for loop has now been pushed to its absolute limit. Initialization, test, and action have all been taken out of the for statement. The initialization is done on line 8, before the for loop begins. The test is done in a separate if statement on line 14, and if the test succeeds, the action, an increment to counter, is performed on line 17. If the test fails, breaking out of the loop occurs on line 20.

Although this particular program is somewhat absurd, sometimes a for(;;) loop or a while (true) loop is just what you'll want. You'll see an example of a more reasonable use of such loops when switch statements are discussed later today.

Empty for Loops

Because so much can be done in the header of a for statement, at times you won't need the body to do anything at all. In that case, be sure to put a null statement (;) as the body of the loop. The semicolon can be on the same line as the header, but this is easy to overlook. Listing 7.13 illustrates how to use a null body in a for loop.

LISTING 7.13   Illustrates the Null Statement in a for Loop

```
0:  //Listing 7.13
1:  //Demonstrates null statement
2:  // as body of for loop
3:
4:  #include <iostream>
5:  int main()
6:  {
7:
8:     for (int i = 0; i<5; std::cout << "i: " << i++ << std::endl)
9:        ;
10:    return 0;
11: }
```

OUTPUT
```
i: 0
i: 1
i: 2
i: 3
i: 4
```

ANALYSIS The `for` loop on line 8 includes three statements: The `initialization` statement establishes the counter `i` and initializes it to 0. The `condition` statement tests for `i<5`, and the `action` statement prints the value in `i` and increments it.

Nothing is left to do in the body of the `for` loop, so the null statement (`;`) is used. Note that this is not a well-designed `for` loop: the action statement is doing far too much. This would be better rewritten as

```
8:          for (int i = 0; i<5; i++)
9:              cout << "i: " << i << endl;
```

Although both do the same thing, this example is easier to understand.

Nested Loops

Loops may be nested with one loop sitting in the body of another. The inner loop will be executed in full for every execution of the outer loop. Listing 7.14 illustrates writing marks into a matrix using nested `for` loops.

LISTING 7.14   Illustrates Nested `for` Loops

```
0:  //Listing 7.14
1:  //Illustrates nested for loops
2:
3:  #include <iostream>
4:
5:  int main()
6:  {
7:      using namespace std;
8:      int rows, columns;
9:      char theChar;
10:     cout << "How many rows? ";
11:     cin >> rows;
12:     cout << "How many columns? ";
13:     cin >> columns;
14:     cout << "What character? ";
15:     cin >> theChar;
16:     for (int i = 0; i<rows; i++)
17:     {
18:         for (int j = 0; j<columns; j++)
19:             cout << theChar;
20:         cout << "\n";
```

7

LISTING 7.14   continued

```
21:    }
22:    return 0;
23: }
```

OUTPUT

```
How many rows? 4
How many columns? 12
What character? x
xxxxxxxxxxxx
xxxxxxxxxxxx
xxxxxxxxxxxx
xxxxxxxxxxxx
```

ANALYSIS The user is prompted for the number of rows and columns and for a character to print. The first for loop, on line 16, initializes a counter (i) to 0, and then the body of the outer for loop is run.

On line 18, the first line of the body of the outer for loop, another for loop, is established. A second counter (j) is also initialized to 0, and the body of the inner for loop is executed. On line 19, the chosen character is printed, and control returns to the header of the inner for loop. Note that the inner for loop is only one statement (the printing of the character). The condition is tested (j < columns) and if it evaluates true, j is incremented and the next character is printed. This continues until j equals the number of columns.

Once the inner for loop fails its test, in this case after 12 Xs are printed, execution falls through to line 20, and a new line is printed. The outer for loop now returns to its header, where its condition (i < rows) is tested. If this evaluates true, i is incremented and the body of the loop is executed.

In the second iteration of the outer for loop, the inner for loop is started over. Thus, j is reinitialized to 0 and the entire inner loop is run again.

The important idea here is that by using a nested loop, the inner loop is executed for each iteration of the outer loop. Thus, the character is printed columns times for each row.

Note

As an aside, many C++ programmers use the letters i and j as counting variables. This tradition goes all the way back to FORTRAN, in which the letters i, j, k, l, m, and n were the only counting variables.

Other programmers prefer to use more descriptive counter variable names, such as Ctr1 and Ctr2. Using i and j in for loop headers should not cause much confusion, however.

Scoping in `for` Loops

In the past, variables declared in the `for` loop were scoped to the outer block. The ANSI standard changes this to scope these variables only to the block of the `for` loop itself; however, not every compiler supports this change. You can test your compiler with the following code:

```
#include <iostream>
int main()
{
    // i scoped to the for loop?
    for (int i = 0; i<5; i++)
    {
        std::cout << "i: " << i << std::endl;
    }

    i = 7;  // should not be in scope!
    return 0;
}
```

If this compiles without complaint, your compiler does not yet support this aspect of the ANSI standard.

If your compiler complains that `i` is not yet defined (in the line `i=7`), then your compiler does support the new standard. You can write code that will compile on either compiler by changing this to

```
#include <iostream>
int main()
{
    int i; //declare outside the for loop
    for (i = 0; i<5; i++)
    {
        std::cout << "i: " << i << std::endl;
    }

    i = 7;  // now this is in scope for all compilers
    return 0;
}
```

Summing Up Loops

On Day 5, "Functions," you learned how to solve the Fibonacci series problem using recursion. To review briefly, a Fibonacci series starts with 1, 1, 2, 3, and all subsequent numbers are the sum of the previous two:

1,1,2,3,5,8,13,21,34...

7

The nth Fibonacci number is the sum of the n-1 and the n-2 Fibonacci numbers. The problem solved on Day 5 was finding the value of the nth Fibonacci number. This was done with recursion. Listing 7.15 offers a solution using iteration.

LISTING 7.15   Solving the nth Fibonacci Number Using Iteration

```cpp
0:  // Listing 7.15
1:  // Demonstrates solving the nth
2:  // Fibonacci number using iteration
3:
4:  #include <iostream>
5:
6:  int fib(int position);
7:  int main()
8:  {
9:     using namespace std;
10:    int answer, position;
11:    cout << "Which position? ";
12:    cin >> position;
13:    cout << "\n";
14:
15:    answer = fib(position);
16:    cout << answer << " is the ";
17:    cout << position << "th Fibonacci number.\n";
18:    return 0;
19: }
20:
21: int fib(int n)
22: {
23:    int minusTwo=1, minusOne=1, answer=2;
24:
25:    if (n < 3)
26:       return 1;
27:
28:    for (n -= 3; n; n--)
29:    {
30:       minusTwo = minusOne;
31:       minusOne = answer;
32:       answer = minusOne + minusTwo;
33:    }
34:
35:    return answer;
36: }
```

OUTPUT

```
Which position? 4
3 is the 4th Fibonacci number.
Which position? 5
5 is the 5th Fibonacci number.
Which position? 20
6765 is the 20th Fibonacci number.
Which position? 100
3314859971 is the 100th Fibonacci number.
```

ANALYSIS Listing 7.15 solves the Fibonacci series using iteration rather than recursion. This approach is faster and uses less memory than the recursive solution.

On line 11, the user is asked for the position to check. The function `fib()` is called, which evaluates the position. If the position is less than 3, the function returns the value 1. Starting with position 3, the function iterates using the following algorithm:

1. Establish the starting position: Fill variable answer with 2, minusTwo with 1, and minusOne with 1. Decrement the position by 3 because the first two numbers are handled by the starting position.

2. For every number, count up the Fibonacci series. This is done by

    a. Putting the value currently in minusOne into minusTwo.

    b. Putting the value currently in answer into minusOne.

    c. Adding minusOne and minusTwo and putting the sum in answer.

    d. Decrementing n.

3. When n reaches 0, return the answer.

This is exactly how you would solve this problem with pencil and paper. If you were asked for the fifth Fibonacci number, you would write

1, 1, 2,

and think, "two more to do." You would then add 2+1 and write 3, and think, "one more to find." Finally, you would write 3+2 and the answer would be 5. In effect, you are shifting your attention right one number each time through and decrementing the number remaining to be found.

Note the condition tested on line 28 (n). This is a C++ idiom, and is equivalent to n != 0. This for loop relies on the fact that when n reaches 0 it will evaluate false, because 0 is false in C++. The for loop header could have been written

```
for (n-=3; n!=0; n--)
```

which might have been clearer. However, this idiom is so common in C++ that there is little sense in fighting it.

7

Compile, link, and run this program, along with the recursive solution offered on Day 5. Try finding position 25 and compare the time it takes each program. Recursion is elegant, but because the function call brings a performance overhead, and because it is called so many times, its performance is noticeably slower than iteration. Microcomputers tend to be optimized for the arithmetic operations, so the iterative solution should be blazingly fast.

Be careful how large a number you enter. `fib` grows quickly, and long integers will overflow after a while.

switch Statements

On Day 4, you saw how to write `if` and `if/else` statements. These can become quite confusing when nested too deeply, and C++ offers an alternative. Unlike `if`, which evaluates one value, `switch` statements enable you to branch on any of several values. The general form of the `switch` statement is

```
switch (expression)
{
case valueOne: statement;
               break;
case valueTwo: statement;
               break;
....
case valueN:   statement;
               break;
default:       statement;
}
```

`expression` is any legal C++ expression, and the statements are any legal C++ statements or block of statements which evaluate (or can be unambiguously converted to) an integer value. Note, however, that the evaluation is for equality only; relational operators may not be used here, nor can Boolean operations.

If one of the `case` values matches the expression, execution jumps to those statements and continues to the end of the `switch` block unless a `break` statement is encountered. If nothing matches, execution branches to the optional default statement. If no default and no matching value exist, execution falls through the `switch` statement and the statement ends.

Note

It is almost always a good idea to have a default case in `switch` statements. If you have no other need for the default, use it to test for the supposedly impossible case, and print out an error message; this can be a tremendous aid in debugging.

It is important to note that if no break statement is at the end of a case statement, execution will fall through to the next case statement. This is sometimes necessary, but usually is an error. If you decide to let execution fall through, be sure to put a comment indicating that you didn't just forget the break.

Listing 7.16 illustrates use of the switch statement.

LISTING 7.16   Demonstrating the switch Statement

```
0:  //Listing 7.16
1:  // Demonstrates switch statement
2:
3:  #include <iostream>
4:
5:  int main()
6:  {
7:      using namespace std;
8:      unsigned short int number;
9:      cout << "Enter a number between 1 and 5: ";
10:     cin >> number;
11:     switch (number)
12:     {
13:     case 0:     cout << "Too small, sorry!";
14:             break;
15:     case 5:     cout << "Good job!\n";  // fall through
16:     case 4:     cout << "Nice Pick!\n"; // fall through
17:     case 3:     cout << "Excellent!\n"; // fall through
18:     case 2:     cout << "Masterful!\n"; // fall through
19:     case 1:     cout << "Incredible!\n";
20:             break;
21:     default:  cout << "Too large!\n";
22:             break;
23:     }
24:     cout << "\n\n";
25:     return 0;
26:  }
```

OUTPUT
```
Enter a number between 1 and 5: 3
Excellent!
Masterful!
Incredible!

Enter a number between 1 and 5: 8
Too large!
```

ANALYSIS   The user is prompted for a number. That number is given to the switch statement. If the number is 0, the case statement on line 13 matches, the message Too small, sorry! is printed, and the break statement ends the switch. If the value is 5, execution switches to line 15 where a message is printed, and then falls through to line 16, another message is printed, and so forth until hitting the break on line 20.

The net effect of these statements is that for a number between 1 and 5, that many messages are printed. If the value of number is not 0 to 5, it is assumed to be too large, and the default statement is invoked on line 21.

The switch Statement

The syntax for the switch statement is as follows:

```
switch (expression)
{
case valueOne: statement;
case valueTwo: statement;
....
case valueN: statement;
default: statement;
}
```

The switch statement allows for branching on multiple values of expression. The expression is evaluated, and if it matches any of the case values, execution jumps to that line. Execution continues until either the end of the switch statement or a break statement is encountered.

If expression does not match any of the case statements, and if there is a default statement, execution switches to the default statement, otherwise the switch statement ends.

Example 1

```
switch (choice)
{
case 0:
        cout << "Zero!" << endl;
        break;
case 1:
        cout << "One!" << endl;
        break;
case 2:
        cout << "Two!" << endl;
default:
        cout << "Default!" << endl;
}
```

Example 2

```
switch (choice)
{
case 0:
case 1:
```

```
case 2:
        cout << "Less than 3!";
        break;
case 3:
        cout << "Equals 3!";
        break;
default:
        cout << "greater than 3!";
}
```

Using a `switch` Statement with a Menu

Listing 7.17 returns to the for(;;) loop discussed earlier. These loops are also called forever loops, as they will loop forever if a break is not encountered. The forever loop is used to put up a menu, solicit a choice from the user, act on the choice, and then return to the menu. This will continue until the user chooses to exit.

 Note

Some programmers like to write

```
#define EVER ;;
for (EVER)
{
    // statements...
}
```

A forever loop is a loop that does not have an exit condition. In order to exit the loop, a break statement must be used. forever loops are also known as eternal loops.

LISTING 7.17   Demonstrating a forever Loop

```
0:   //Listing 7.17
1:   //Using a forever loop to manage
2:   //user interaction
3:   #include <iostream>
4:
5:   // prototypes
6:   int menu();
7:   void DoTaskOne();
8:   void DoTaskMany(int);
9:
10:  using namespace std;
11:
12:  int main()
```

7

LISTING 7.17 continued

```
13:  {
14:      bool exit = false;
15:      for (;;)
16:      {
17:          int choice = menu();
18:          switch(choice)
19:          {
20:          case (1):
21:              DoTaskOne();
22:              break;
23:          case (2):
24:              DoTaskMany(2);
25:              break;
26:          case (3):
27:              DoTaskMany(3);
28:              break;
29:          case (4):
30:              continue;  // redundant!
31:              break;
32:          case (5):
33:              exit=true;
34:              break;
35:          default:
36:              cout << "Please select again!\n";
37:              break;
38:          }            // end switch
39:
40:          if (exit)
41:              break;
42:      }                        // end forever
43:      return 0;
44:  }                            // end main()
45:
46:  int menu()
47:  {
48:      int choice;
49:
50:      cout << " **** Menu ****\n\n";
51:      cout << "(1) Choice one.\n";
52:      cout << "(2) Choice two.\n";
53:      cout << "(3) Choice three.\n";
54:      cout << "(4) Redisplay menu.\n";
55:      cout << "(5) Quit.\n\n";
56:      cout << ": ";
57:      cin >> choice;
58:      return choice;
59:  }
60:
61:  void DoTaskOne()
```

LISTING 7.17   continued

```
62:  {
63:     cout << "Task One!\n";
64:  }
65:
66:  void DoTaskMany(int which)
67:  {
68:     if (which == 2)
69:        cout << "Task Two!\n";
70:     else
71:        cout << "Task Three!\n";
72:  }
```

OUTPUT

```
**** Menu ****

(1) Choice one.
(2) Choice two.
(3) Choice three.
(4) Redisplay menu.
(5) Quit.

: 1
Task One!
 **** Menu ****
(1) Choice one.
(2) Choice two.
(3) Choice three.
(4) Redisplay menu.
(5) Quit.

: 3
Task Three!
 **** Menu ****
(1) Choice one.
(2) Choice two.
(3) Choice three.
(4) Redisplay menu.
(5) Quit.

: 5
```

ANALYSIS   This program brings together a number of concepts from today and previous days. It also shows a common use of the switch statement.

The forever loop begins on line 15. The menu() function is called, which prints the menu to the screen and returns the user's selection. The switch statement, which begins on line 18 and ends on line 38, switches on the user's choice.

7

If the user enters 1, execution jumps to the `case 1:` statement on line 20. Line 21 switches execution to the `DoTaskOne()` function, which prints a message and returns. On its return, execution resumes on line 22, where the break ends the `switch` statement, and execution falls through to line 39. On line 40, the variable `exit` is evaluated. If it evaluates true, the break on line 41 will be executed and the `for(;;)` loop will end; but if it evaluates false, execution resumes at the top of the loop on line 15.

Note that the `continue` statement on line 30 is redundant. If it were left out and the `break` statement were encountered, the switch would end, `exit` would evaluate false, the loop would reiterate, and the menu would be reprinted. The `continue` does, however, bypass the test of `exit`.

Do	Don't
DO use `switch` statements to avoid deeply nested `if` statements.	**DON'T** forget break at the end of each case unless you wish to fall through.
DO carefully document all intentional fall-through cases.	
DO put a default case in `switch` statements, if only to detect seemingly impossible situations.	

Summary

Different ways exist to cause a C++ program to loop. `while` loops check a condition, and if it is true, execute the statements in the body of the loop. `do...while` loops execute the body of the loop and then test the condition. `for` loops initialize a value, then test an expression. If an expression is true, the final statement in the `for` header is executed, as is the body of the loop. Each subsequent time through the loop, the expression is tested again.

The `goto` statement is generally avoided because it causes an unconditional jump to a seemingly arbitrary location in the code and thus makes source code difficult to understand and maintain. `continue` causes `while`, `do...while`, and `for` loops to start over, and `break` causes `while`, `do...while`, `for`, and `switch` statements to end.

Q&A

Q How do you choose between `if/else` and `switch`?

A If more than just one or two `else` clauses are used, and all are testing the same value, consider using a `switch` statement.

Q How do you choose between `while` and `do...while`?

A If the body of the loop should always execute at least once, consider a `do...while` loop; otherwise, try to use the `while` loop.

Q How do you choose between `while` and `for`?

A If you are initializing a counting variable, testing that variable, and incrementing it each time through the loop, consider the `for` loop. If your variable is already initialized and is not incremented on each loop, a `while` loop may be the better choice.

Q How do you choose between recursion and iteration?

A Some problems cry out for recursion, but most problems will yield to iteration as well. Put recursion in your back pocket; it may come in handy someday.

Q Is it better to use `while (true)` or `for (;;)`?

A No significant difference exists.

Workshop

The Workshop provides quiz questions to help you solidify your understanding of the material covered as well as exercises to provide you with experience in using what you've learned. Try to answer the quiz and exercise questions before checking the answers in Appendix D, and make sure you understand the answers before continuing to the next chapter.

Quiz

1. How do you initialize more than one variable in a `for` loop?
2. Why is `goto` avoided?
3. Is it possible to write a `for` loop with a body that is never executed?
4. Is it possible to nest `while` loops within `for` loops?
5. Is it possible to create a loop that never ends? Give an example.
6. What happens if you create a loop that never ends?

Exercises

1. What is the value of x when the `for` loop completes?

   ```
   for (int x = 0; x < 100; x++)
   ```

2. Write a nested `for` loop that prints a 10×10 pattern of 0s.
3. Write a `for` statement to count from 100 to 200 by twos.

7

4. Write a `while` loop to count from 100 to 200 by twos.

5. Write a `do...while` loop to count from 100 to 200 by twos.

6. **BUG BUSTERS:** What is wrong with this code?

```
int counter = 0;
while (counter < 10)
{
    cout << "counter: " << counter;
}
```

7. **BUG BUSTERS:** What is wrong with this code?

```
for (int counter = 0; counter < 10; counter++);
    cout << counter << "\n ";
```

8. **BUG BUSTERS:** What is wrong with this code?

```
int counter = 100;
while (counter < 10)
{
    cout << "counter now: " << counter;
    counter--;
}
```

9. **BUG BUSTERS:** What is wrong with this code?

```
cout << "Enter a number between 0 and 5: ";
cin >> theNumber;
switch (theNumber)
{
    case 0:
          doZero();
    case 1:              // fall through
    case 2:              // fall through
    case 3:              // fall through
    case 4:              // fall through
    case 5:
          doOneToFive();
          break;
    default:
          doDefault();
          break;
}
```

WEEK 1

In Review

1

2

3

4

5

6

7

LISTING R1.1   Week 1 in Review Listing

```
0:    #include <iostream>
1:    using namespace std;
2:    enum CHOICE { DrawRect = 1, GetArea, GetPerim,
3:        ChangeDimensions, Quit};
4:
5:    // Rectangle class declaration
6:    class Rectangle
7:    {
8:    public:
9:        // constructors
10:        Rectangle(int width, int height);
11:        ~Rectangle();
12:
13:        // accessors
14:        int GetHeight() const { return itsHeight; }
15:        int GetWidth() const { return itsWidth; }
16:        int GetArea() const { return itsHeight * itsWidth; }
17:        int GetPerim() const { return 2*itsHeight + 2*itsWidth; }
18:        void SetSize(int newWidth, int newHeight);
19:
20:        // Misc. methods
21:
22:
23:     private:
24:        int itsWidth;
25:        int itsHeight;
26:    };
27:
28:    // Class method implementations
29:    void Rectangle::SetSize(int newWidth, int newHeight)
30:    {
31:        itsWidth = newWidth;
32:        itsHeight = newHeight;
33:    }
34:
35:
36:    Rectangle::Rectangle(int width, int height)
37:    {
38:        itsWidth = width;
39:        itsHeight = height;
40:    }
41:
42:    Rectangle::~Rectangle() {}
43:
44:    int DoMenu();
45:    void DoDrawRect(Rectangle);
46:    void DoGetArea(Rectangle);
47:    void DoGetPerim(Rectangle);
48:
```

```
49:   int main ()
50:   {
51:       // initialize a rectangle to 30,5
52:       Rectangle theRect(30,5);
53:
54:       int choice = DrawRect;
55:       int fQuit = false;
56:
57:       while (!fQuit)
58:       {
59:         choice = DoMenu();
60:         if (choice < DrawRect || choice >  Quit)
61:         {
62:           cout << "\nInvalid Choice, please try again.\n\n";
63:           continue;
64:         }
65:         switch (choice)
66:         {
67:         case  DrawRect:
68:           DoDrawRect(theRect);
69:           break;
70:         case GetArea:
71:           DoGetArea(theRect);
72:           break;
73:         case GetPerim:
74:           DoGetPerim(theRect);
75:           break;
76:         case ChangeDimensions:
77:           int newLength, newWidth;
78:           cout << "\nNew width: ";
79:           cin >> newWidth;
80:           cout << "New height: ";
81:           cin >> newLength;
82:           theRect.SetSize(newWidth, newLength);
83:           DoDrawRect(theRect);
84:           break;
85:         case Quit:
86:           fQuit = true;
87:           cout << "\nExiting...\n\n";
88:           break;
89:         default:
90:           cout << "Error in choice!\n";
91:           fQuit = true;
92:           break;
93:         }    // end switch
94:       }      // end while
95:     return 0;
96:   }          // end main
97:
```

LISTING R1.1   continued

```
 98:   int DoMenu()
 99:   {
100:      int choice;
101:       cout << "\n\n    *** Menu *** \n";
102:       cout << "(1) Draw Rectangle\n";
103:       cout << "(2) Area\n";
104:       cout << "(3) Perimeter\n";
105:       cout << "(4) Resize\n";
106:       cout << "(5) Quit\n";
107:
108:     cin >> choice;
109:     return choice;
110:   }
111:
112:    void DoDrawRect(Rectangle theRect)
113:    {
114:      int height = theRect.GetHeight();
115:      int width = theRect.GetWidth();
116:
117:      for (int i = 0; i<height; i++)
118:      {
119:        for (int j = 0; j< width; j++)
120:          cout << "*";
121:        cout << "\n";
122:      }
123:    }
124:
125:
126:    void DoGetArea(Rectangle theRect)
127:    {
128:      cout << "Area: " <<  theRect.GetArea() << endl;
129:    }
130:
131:    void DoGetPerim(Rectangle theRect)
132:    {
133:      cout << "Perimeter: " <<  theRect.GetPerim() << endl;
134:    }
```

```
*** Menu ***
(1) Draw Rectangle
(2) Area
(3) Perimeter
(4) Resize
(5) Quit
1
```

LISTING R1.1 continued

```
******************************
******************************
******************************
******************************
******************************

     *** Menu ***
(1) Draw Rectangle
(2) Area
(3) Perimeter
(4) Resize
(5) Quit
2
Area: 150

     *** Menu ***
(1) Draw Rectangle
(2) Area
(3) Perimeter
(4) Resize
(5) Quit
3
Perimeter: 70

     *** Menu ***
(1) Draw Rectangle
(2) Area
(3) Perimeter
(4) Resize
(5) Quit
4

New Width: 10
New height: 8
**********
**********
**********
**********
**********
**********
**********
**********

     *** Menu ***
(1) Draw Rectangle
(2) Area
(3) Perimeter
(4) Resize
(5) Quit
```

LISTING R1.1   continued

```
2
Area: 80

      *** Menu ***
(1) Draw Rectangle
(2) Area
(3) Perimeter
(4) Resize
(5) Quit
3
Perimeter: 36

      *** Menu ***
(1) Draw Rectangle
(2) Area
(3) Perimeter
(4) Resize
(5) Quit
5

Exiting...
```

This program utilizes most of the skills you learned this week. You should not only be able to enter, compile, link, and run this program, but also understand what it does and how it works, based on the work you've done this week.

The first six lines set up the new types and definitions that will be used throughout the program.

Lines 6–26 declare the Rectangle class. There are public accessor methods for obtaining and setting the width and height of the rectangle, as well as for computing the area and perimeter. Lines 29–40 contain the class function definitions that were not declared inline.

The function prototypes, for the non-class member functions, are on lines 44–47, and the program begins on line 49. The essence of this program is to generate a rectangle, and then to print out a menu offering five options: Draw the rectangle, determine its area, determine its perimeter, resize the rectangle, or quit.

A flag is set on line 55, and when that flag is not set to true the menu loop continues. The flag is only set to true if the user picks Quit from the menu.

Each of the other choices, with the exception of ChangeDimensions, calls out to a function. This makes the switch statement cleaner. ChangeDimensions cannot call out to a function because it must change the dimensions of the rectangle. If the rectangle were passed (by value) to a function such as DoChangeDimensions(), the dimensions would be changed on the local copy of the rectangle in DoChangeDimensions() and not on the rectangle in main(). On Day 8, "Pointers," and Day 10, "Advanced Functions," you'll learn how to overcome this restriction, but for now the change is made in the main() function.

Note how the use of an enumeration makes the switch statement much cleaner and easier to understand. Had the switch depended on the numeric choices (1–5) of the user, you would have to constantly refer to the description of the menu to see which pick was which.

On line 60, the user's choice is checked to make sure it is in range. If not, an error message is printed and the menu is reprinted. Note that the switch statement includes an "impossible" default condition. This is an aid in debugging. If the program is working, that statement can never be reached.

Week in Review

Congratulations! You've completed the first week! Now you can create and understand sophisticated C++ programs. Of course, there's much more to do, and next week starts with one of the most difficult concepts in C++: pointers. Don't give up now, you're about to delve deeply into the meaning and use of object-oriented programming, virtual functions, and many of the advanced features of this powerful language.

Take a break, bask in the glory of your accomplishment, and then turn the page to start Week 2.

WEEK 2

At a Glance

You have finished the first week of learning how to program in C++. By now you should feel comfortable entering programs, using your compiler, and thinking about objects, classes, and program flow.

Where You Are Going

Week 2 begins with pointers. Pointers are traditionally a difficult subject for new C++ programmers, but you will find them explained fully and clearly, and they should not be a stumbling block. Day 9, "References," teaches references, which are a close cousin to pointers. On Day 10, "Advanced Functions," you will see how to overload functions.

Day 11, "Object-Oriented Analysis and Design," is a departure: Rather than focusing on the syntax of the language, you take a day out to learn about object-oriented analysis and design. Day 12, "Inheritance," introduces inheritance, a fundamental concept in object-oriented programming. On Day 13, "Arrays and Linked Lists," you will learn how to work with arrays and collections. Day 14, "Polymorphism," extends the lessons of Day 12 to discuss polymorphism.

8

9

10

11

12

13

14

DAY 8

Pointers

One of the most powerful tools available to a C++ programmer is the capability to manipulate computer memory directly by using pointers.

Today you will learn

- What pointers are.
- How to declare and use pointers.
- What the free store is and how to manipulate memory.

Pointers present two special challenges when you're learning C++: They can be somewhat confusing, and it isn't immediately obvious why they are needed. This chapter explains how pointers work, step by step. You will fully understand the need for pointers, however, only as the book progresses.

What Is a Pointer?

A pointer is a variable that holds a memory address. That's it. If you understand this simple sentence, then you know all there is to know about pointers. A pointer is a variable that holds a memory address.

A Bit About Memory

To understand pointers, you must know a little about computer memory. Computer memory is divided into sequentially numbered memory locations. Each variable is located at a unique location in memory, known as its address. Figure 8.1 shows a schematic representation of the storage of an unsigned long integer variable named theAge.

FIGURE 8.1

A schematic representation of theAge.

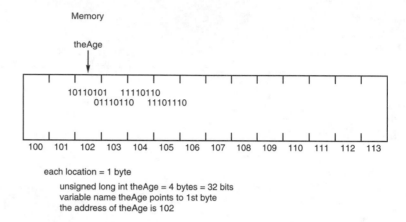

Memory

theAge

10110101 11110110
   01110110 11101110

100 101 102 103 104 105 106 107 108 109 110 111 112 113

each location = 1 byte
unsigned long int theAge = 4 bytes = 32 bits
variable name theAge points to 1st byte
the address of theAge is 102

Using the Address Of Operator (&)

Different computers number this memory using different complex schemes. Usually, programmers don't need to know the particular address of any given variable because the compiler handles the details. If you want this information, though, you can use the address of operator (&), which returns the address of an object in memory, and which is illustrated in Listing 8.1.

LISTING 8.1   Demonstrating the Address Of Operator

```
0:   // Listing 8.1 Demonstrates address of operator
1:   // and addresses of local variables
2:
3:   #include <iostream>
4:
5:   int main()
6:   {
7:      using namespace std;
8:      unsigned short shortVar=5;
9:      unsigned long  longVar=65535;
10:     long sVar = -65535;
11:
12:     cout << "shortVar:\t" << shortVar;
13:     cout << "\tAddress of shortVar:\t";
```

LISTING 8.1   continued

```
14:     cout << &shortVar << "\n";
15:
16:     cout << "longVar:\t" << longVar;
17:     cout << "\tAddress of longVar:\t" ;
18:     cout << &longVar << "\n";
19:
20:     cout << "sVar:\t\t" << sVar;
21:     cout << "\tAddress of sVar:\t" ;
22:     cout << &sVar << "\n";
23:
24:     return 0;
25: }
```

OUTPUT
```
shortVar:    5      Address of shortVar:    0012FF7C
longVar:     65535  Address of longVar:     0012FF78
sVar:        -65535 Address of sVar:        0012FF74
```

(Your printout may look different.)

ANALYSIS Three variables are declared and initialized: an unsigned short on line 8, an unsigned long on line 9, and a long on line 10. Their values and addresses are printed on lines 12–16 by using the address-of operator (&).

The value of shortVar is 5, as expected, and its address is 0012FF7C when run on my Pentium (32-bit) computer. This address is computer-specific and may change slightly each time the program is run. Your results will be different.

You tell the compiler how much memory to allow for your variables by declaring the variable type; the compiler automatically assigns an address for it. A long integer is typically 4 bytes, for example, meaning that the variable has an address to four bytes of memory.

Note that your compiler, like mine, might insist on assigning new variables on 4-byte boundaries (thus, longVar was assigned an address 4 bytes after shortVar even though shortVar only needed 2 bytes!)

Storing the Address in a Pointer

Every variable has an address. Even without knowing the specific address of a given variable, you can store that address in a pointer.

Suppose, for example, that howOld is an integer. To declare a pointer called pAge to hold its address, you would write

```
int *pAge = 0;
```

This declares pAge to be a pointer to int. That is, pAge is declared to hold the address of an integer.

Note that pAge is a variable. When you declare an integer variable (type int), the compiler sets aside enough memory to hold an integer. When you declare a pointer variable such as pAge, the compiler sets aside enough memory to hold an address (on most computers, 4 bytes). pAge is just a different type of variable.

Null and Wild Pointers

In this example, pAge is initialized to zero. A pointer whose value is zero is called a *null* pointer. All pointers, when they are created, should be initialized to something. If you don't know what you want to assign to the pointer, assign 0. A pointer that is not initialized is called a *wild* pointer. Wild pointers are very dangerous.

 Note | Practice safe computing: Initialize your pointers!

You must specifically assign the address of howOld to pAge. The following is an example that shows how to do that:

```
unsigned short int howOld = 50;       // make a variable
unsigned short int * pAge = 0;        // make a pointer
pAge = &howOld;                       // put howOld's address in pAge
```

The first line creates a variable—howOld, whose type is unsigned short int—and initializes it with the value 50. The second line declares pAge to be a pointer to type unsigned short int and initializes it to zero. You know that pAge is a pointer because of the asterisk (*) after the variable type and before the variable name.

The third and final line assigns the address of howOld to the pointer pAge. You can tell that the address of howOld is being assigned because of the address-of operator (&). If the address-of operator had not been used, the value of howOld would have been assigned. That might, or might not, have been a valid address.

At this point, pAge has as its value the address of howOld. howOld, in turn, has the value 50. You could have accomplished this with one fewer step, as in

```
unsigned short int howOld = 50;       // make a variable
unsigned short int * pAge = &howOld;  // make pointer to howOld
```

pAge is a pointer that now contains the address of the howOld variable. Using pAge, you can actually determine the value of howOld, which in this case is 50. Accessing howOld by using the pointer pAge is called *indirection* because you are indirectly accessing howOld by means of pAge. Later today you will see how to use indirection to access a variable's value.

Indirection means accessing the value at the address held by a pointer. The pointer provides an indirect way to get the value held at that address.

> **Note**
>
> With a normal variable, the type tells the compiler how much memory is needed to hold the value. With a pointer, the type does not do this: all pointers are 4 bytes. The type tells the compiler how much memory is needed for the object at the address which the pointer holds!
>
> In the declaration
>
> ```
> unsigned short int * pAge = 0;      // make a pointer
> ```
>
> pAge is declared to be a pointer to an unsigned short integer. This tells the compiler that the pointer (which needs 4 bytes to hold an address) will hold the address of an object of type unsigned short int, which itself requires two bytes.

Pointer Names

Pointers can have any name that is legal for other variables. Many programmers follow the convention of naming all pointers with an initial p, as in pAge or pNumber.

The Indirection Operator

The indirection operator (*) is also called the *dereference* operator. When a pointer is dereferenced, the value at the address stored by the pointer is retrieved.

Normal variables provide direct access to their own values. If you create a new variable of type unsigned short int called yourAge, and you want to assign the value in howOld to that new variable, you would write

```
unsigned short int yourAge;
yourAge = howOld;
```

A pointer provides *indirect* access to the value of the variable whose address it stores. To assign the value in howOld to the new variable yourAge by way of the pointer pAge, you would write

```
unsigned short int yourAge;
yourAge = *pAge;
```

The indirection operator (*) in front of the variable pAge means "the value stored at." This assignment says, "Take the value stored at the address in pAge and assign it to yourAge."

Note

> The asterisk (*) is used in two distinct ways with pointers: as part of the pointer declaration and also as the dereference operator.
>
> When you declare a pointer, the * is part of the declaration and it follows the type of the object pointed to. For example:
>
> ```
> // make a pointer to an unsigned short
> unsigned short * pAge = 0;
> ```
>
> When the pointer is dereferenced, the dereference (or indirection) operator indicates that the value at the memory location stored in the pointer is to be accessed, rather than the address itself.
>
> ```
> // assign 5 to the value at pAge
> *pAge = 5;
> ```
>
> Also note that this same character (*) is used as the multiplication operator. The compiler knows which operator to call based on context.

Pointers, Addresses, and Variables

It is important to distinguish between a pointer, the address that the pointer holds, and the value at the address held by the pointer. This is the source of much of the confusion about pointers.

Consider the following code fragment:

```
int theVariable = 5;
int * pPointer = &theVariable ;
```

theVariable is declared to be an integer variable initialized with the value 5. pPointer is declared to be a pointer to an integer; it is initialized with the address of theVariable. pPointer is the pointer. The address that pPointer holds is the address of theVariable. The value at the address that pPointer holds is 5. Figure 8.2 shows a schematic representation of theVariable and pPointer.

In this figure the value 5 is stored at address location 101. This is shown in the binary number

```
0000 0000 0000 0101
```

This is two bytes (16 bits) whose decimal value is 5.

FIGURE 8.2

A schematic represen-
tation of memory.

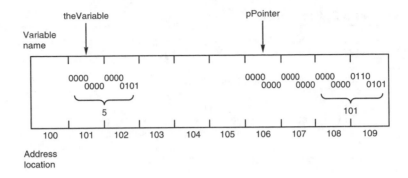

The pointer variable is at location 106. Its value is

```
000 0000 0000 0000 0000 0000 0110 0101
```

This is the binary representation of the value one hundred and one, which is the address of `theVariable`, whose value is 5.

The memory layout here is schematic, but it illustrates the idea of how pointers store an address.

Manipulating Data by Using Pointers

After a pointer is assigned the address of a variable, you can use that pointer to access the data in that variable. Listing 8.2 demonstrates how the address of a local variable is assigned to a pointer and how the pointer manipulates the values in that variable.

LISTING 8.2   Manipulating Data by Using Pointers

```cpp
0:    // Listing 8.2 Using pointers
1:
2:    #include <iostream>
3:
4:    typedef unsigned short int USHORT;
5:
6:    int main()
7:    {
8:
9:        using std::cout;
10:
11:       USHORT myAge;          // a variable
12:       USHORT * pAge = 0;     // a pointer
13:
14:       myAge = 5;
15:
16:       cout << "myAge: " << myAge << "\n";
```

LISTING 8.2   continued

```
17:      pAge = &myAge;      // assign address of myAge to pAge
18:      cout << "*pAge: " << *pAge << "\n\n";
19:
20:      cout << "Setting *pAge = 7...\n";
21:      *pAge = 7;          // sets myAge to 7
22:
23:      cout << "*pAge: " << *pAge << "\n";
24:      cout << "myAge: " << myAge << "\n\n";
25:
26:      cout << "Setting myAge = 9…\n";
27:      myAge = 9;
28:
29:      cout << "myAge: " << myAge << "\n";
30:      cout << "*pAge: " << *pAge << "\n";
31:
32:      return 0;
33:  }
```

OUTPUT

```
myAge: 5
*pAge: 5

Setting *pAge = 7...
*pAge: 7
myAge: 7

Setting myAge = 9...
myAge: 9
*pAge: 9
```

ANALYSIS   This program declares two variables: an unsigned short, myAge, and a pointer to an unsigned short, pAge. myAge is assigned the value 5 on line 14; this is verified by the printout on line 16.

On line 17, pAge is assigned the address of myAge. On line 18, pAge is dereferenced and printed, showing that the value at the address that pAge stores is the 5 stored in myAge. On line 21, the value 7 is assigned to the variable at the address stored in pAge. This sets myAge to 7, and the printouts on lines 23 and 24 confirm this.

On line 27, the value 9 is assigned to the variable myAge. This value is obtained directly on line 29 and indirectly (by dereferencing pAge) on line 30.

Examining the Address

Pointers enable you to manipulate addresses without ever knowing their real value. After today, you'll take it on faith that when you assign the address of a variable to a pointer, it really has the address of that variable as its value. But just this once, why not check to make sure? Listing 8.3 illustrates this idea.

LISTING 8.3   Finding Out What Is Stored in Pointers

```
0:    // Listing 8.3 What is stored in a pointer.
1:
2:    #include <iostream>
3:
4:
5:    int main()
6:    {
7:       using std::cout;
8:
9:       unsigned short int myAge = 5, yourAge = 10;
10:
11:        // a pointer
12:       unsigned short int * pAge = &myAge;
13:
14:       cout << "myAge:\t" << myAge
15:          <<  "\t\tyourAge:\t" << yourAge << "\n";
16:
17:       cout << "&myAge:\t" << &myAge
18:          << "\t&yourAge:\t" << &yourAge <<"\n";
19:
20:       cout << "pAge:\t" << pAge << "\n";
21:       cout << "*pAge:\t" << *pAge << "\n";
22:
23:
24:       cout << "\nReassigning: pAge = &yourAge...\n\n";
25:       pAge = &yourAge;        // reassign the pointer
26:
27:       cout << "myAge:\t" << myAge <<
28:          "\t\tyourAge:\t" << yourAge << "\n";
29:
30:       cout << "&myAge:\t" << &myAge
31:          << "\t&yourAge:\t" << &yourAge <<"\n";
32:
33:       cout << "pAge:\t" << pAge << "\n";
34:       cout << "*pAge:\t" << *pAge << "\n";
35:
36:       cout << "\n&pAge:\t" << &pAge << "\n";
37:
38:       return 0;
39:    }
```

OUTPUT

```
myAge:    5              yourAge:        10
&myAge: 0012FF7C         &yourAge:       0012FF78
pAge:     0012FF7C
*pAge:    5

Reassigning: pAge = &yourAge...
```

```
myAge:    5                    yourAge:         10
&myAge:   0012FF7C             &yourAge:        0012FF78
pAge:     0012FF78
*pAge:    10

&pAge:    0012FF74
```

(Your output may look different.)

ANALYSIS On line 9, myAge and yourAge are declared to be variables of type unsigned short integer. On line 12, pAge is declared to be a pointer to an unsigned short integer, and it is initialized with the address of the variable myAge.

Lines 14–18 print the values and the addresses of myAge and yourAge. Line 20 prints the *contents* of pAge, which is the address of myAge. Line 21 prints the result of dereferencing pAge, which prints the value at pAge—the value in myAge, or 5.

This is the essence of pointers. Line 20 shows that pAge stores the address of myAge, and line 21 shows how to get the value stored in myAge by dereferencing the pointer pAge. Make sure that you understand this fully before you go on. Study the code and look at the output.

On line 25, pAge is reassigned to point to the address of yourAge. The values and addresses are printed again. The output shows that pAge now has the address of the variable yourAge and that dereferencing obtains the value in yourAge.

Line 36 prints the address of pAge itself. Like any variable, it has an address, and that address can be stored in a pointer. (Assigning the address of a pointer to another pointer will be discussed shortly.)

Do

DO use the indirection operator (*) to access the data stored at the address in a pointer.

DO initialize all pointers either to a valid address or to null (0).

DO remember the difference between the address in a pointer and the value at that address.

Using Pointers

To declare a pointer, write the type of the variable or object whose address will be stored in the pointer, followed by the pointer operator (*) and the name of the pointer. For example:

```
unsigned short int * pPointer = 0;
```

8

> To assign or initialize a pointer, prepend the name of the variable whose address is being assigned with the address-of operator (&). For example,
>
> ```
> unsigned short int theVariable = 5;
> unsigned short int * pPointer = & theVariable;
> ```
>
> To dereference a pointer, prepend the pointer name with the dereference operator (*). For example:
>
> ```
> unsigned short int theValue = *pPointer
> ```

Why Would You Use Pointers?

So far you've seen step-by-step details of assigning a variable's address to a pointer. In practice, though, you would never do this. After all, why bother with a pointer when you already have a variable with access to that value? The only reason for this kind of pointer manipulation of an automatic variable is to demonstrate how pointers work. Now that you are comfortable with the syntax of pointers, you can put them to good use. Pointers are used, most often, for three tasks:

- Managing data on the free store
- Accessing class member data and functions
- Passing variables by reference to functions

This rest of this chapter focuses on managing data on the free store and accessing class member data and functions. Tomorrow you will learn about passing variables by reference.

The Stack and the Free Store (Heap)

In the section "How Functions Work—A Peek Under the Hood" on Day 5, five areas of memory are mentioned:

- Global name space
- The free store
- Registers
- Code space
- The stack

Local variables are on the stack, along with function parameters. Code is in code space, of course, and global variables are in global name space. The registers are used for internal housekeeping functions, such as keeping track of the top of the stack and the instruction pointer. Just about all remaining memory is given over to the free store, which is sometimes referred to as the heap.

The problem with local variables is that they don't persist; when the function returns, the local variables are thrown away. Global variables solve that problem at the cost of unrestricted access throughout the program, which leads to the creation of code that is difficult to understand and maintain. Putting data in the free store solves both of these problems.

You can think of the free store as a massive section of memory in which thousands of sequentially numbered cubbyholes lie waiting for your data. You can't label these cubbyholes, though, as you can with the stack. You must ask for the address of the cubbyhole that you reserve and then stash that address away in a pointer.

One way to think about this is with an analogy: A friend gives you the 800 number for Acme Mail Order. You go home and program your telephone with that number, and then you throw away the piece of paper with the number on it. If you push the button, a telephone rings somewhere, and Acme Mail Order answers. You don't remember the number, and you don't know where the other telephone is located, but the button gives you access to Acme Mail Order. Acme Mail Order is your data on the free store. You don't know where it is, but you know how to get to it. You access it by using its address—in this case, the telephone number. You don't have to know that number; you just have to put it into a pointer (the button). The pointer gives you access to your data without bothering you with the details.

The stack is cleaned automatically when a function returns. All the local variables go out of scope, and they are removed from the stack. The free store is not cleaned until your program ends, and it is your responsibility to free any memory that you've reserved when you are done with it.

The advantage to the free store is that the memory you reserve remains available until you explicitly free it. If you reserve memory on the free store while in a function, the memory is still available when the function returns.

The advantage of accessing memory in this way, rather than using global variables, is that only functions with access to the pointer have access to the data. This provides a tightly controlled interface to that data, and it eliminates the problem of one function changing that data in unexpected and unanticipated ways.

For this to work, you must be able to create a pointer to an area on the free store and to pass that pointer among functions. The following sections describe how to do this.

new

You allocate memory on the free store in C++ by using the new keyword. new is followed by the type of the object that you want to allocate, so that the compiler knows how much memory is required. Therefore, new unsigned short int allocates two bytes in the free store, and new long allocates four.

The return value from new is a memory address. It must be assigned to a pointer. To create an unsigned short on the free store, you might write

```
unsigned short int * pPointer;
pPointer = new unsigned short int;
```

You can, of course, initialize the pointer at its creation with

```
unsigned short int * pPointer = new unsigned short int;
```

In either case, pPointer now points to an unsigned short int on the free store. You can use this like any other pointer to a variable and assign a value into that area of memory by writing

```
*pPointer = 72;
```

This means "Put 72 at the value in pPointer," or "Assign the value 72 to the area on the free store to which pPointer points."

> **Note**
> If new cannot create memory on the free store (memory is, after all, a limited resource) it throws an exception (see Day 20, "Exceptions and Error Handling").

delete

When you are finished with your area of memory, you must call delete on the pointer. delete returns the memory to the free store. Remember that the pointer itself—as opposed to the memory to which it points—is a local variable. When the function in which it is declared returns, that pointer goes out of scope and is lost. The memory allocated with new is not freed automatically, however. That memory becomes unavailable—a situation called a *memory leak*. It's called a memory leak because that memory can't be recovered until the program ends. It is as though the memory has leaked out of your computer.

To restore the memory to the free store, you use the keyword delete. For example:

```
delete pPointer;
```

When you delete the pointer, what you are really doing is freeing up the memory whose address is stored in the pointer. You are saying, "Return to the free store the memory that this pointer points to." The pointer is still a pointer, and it can be reassigned. Listing 8.4 demonstrates allocating a variable on the heap, using that variable, and deleting it.

> **Caution**
>
> When you call `delete` on a pointer, the memory it points to is freed. Calling `delete` on that pointer again will crash your program! When you delete a pointer, set it to zero (null). Calling `delete` on a null pointer is guaranteed to be safe. For example:
>
> ```
> Animal *pDog = new Animal;
> delete pDog; //frees the memory
>    pDog = 0; //sets pointer to null
>    //...
> delete pDog; //harmless
> ```

LISTING 8.4   Allocating, Using, and Deleting Pointers

```
 0:  // Listing 8.4
 1:  // Allocating and deleting a pointer
 2:
 3:  #include <iostream>
 4:  int main()
 5:  {
 6:     using std::cout;
 7:     int localVariable = 5;
 8:     int * pLocal= &localVariable;
 9:     int * pHeap = new int;
10:     *pHeap = 7;
11:     cout << "localVariable: " << localVariable << "\n";
12:     cout << "*pLocal: " << *pLocal << "\n";
13:     cout << "*pHeap: " << *pHeap << "\n";
14:     delete pHeap;
15:     pHeap = new int;
16:     *pHeap = 9;
17:     cout << "*pHeap: " << *pHeap << "\n";
18:     delete pHeap;
19:     return 0;
20:  }
```

OUTPUT
```
localVariable: 5
*pLocal: 5
*pHeap: 7
*pHeap: 9
```

8

ANALYSIS Line 7 declares and initializes a local variable. Line 8 declares and initializes a pointer with the address of the local variable. Line 9 declares another pointer but initializes it with the result obtained from calling `new int`. This allocates space on the free store for an int.

Line 10 assigns the value 7 to the newly allocated memory. Line 11 prints the value of the local variable, and line 12 prints the value pointed to by pLocal. As expected, these are the same. Line 13 prints the value pointed to by pHeap. It shows that the value assigned on line 10 is, in fact, accessible.

On line 14, the memory allocated on line 9 is returned to the free store by a call to `delete`. This frees the memory and disassociates the pointer from that memory. pHeap is now free to point to other memory. It is reassigned on lines 15 and 16, and line 17 prints the result. Line 18 restores that memory to the free store.

Although line 18 is redundant (the end of the program would have returned that memory) it is a good idea to free this memory explicitly. If the program changes or is extended, having already taken care of this step will be beneficial.

Memory Leaks

Another way you might inadvertently create a memory leak is by reassigning your pointer before deleting the memory to which it points. Consider this code fragment:

```
0:    unsigned short int * pPointer = new unsigned short int;
1:    *pPointer = 72;
2:    pPointer = new unsigned short int;
3:    *pPointer = 84;
```

Line 0 creates pPointer and assigns it the address of an area on the free store. Line 1 stores the value 72 in that area of memory. Line 2 reassigns pPointer to another area of memory. Line 3 places the value 84 in that area. The original area—in which the value 72 is now held—is unavailable because the pointer to that area of memory has been reassigned. No way exists to access that original area of memory, nor is there any way to free it before the program ends.

The code should have been written like this:

```
0: unsigned short int * pPointer = new unsigned short int;
1: *pPointer = 72;
2: delete pPointer;
3: pPointer = new unsigned short int;
4: *pPointer = 84;
```

Now the memory originally pointed to by pPointer is deleted, and thus freed, on line 2.

Note

> For every time in your program that you call new, there should be a call to
> delete. It is important to keep track of which pointer owns an area of mem-
> ory and to ensure that the memory is returned to the free store when you
> are done with it.

Creating Objects on the Free Store

Just as you can create a pointer to an integer, you can create a pointer to any object. If
you have declared an object of type Cat, you can declare a pointer to that class and
instantiate a Cat object on the free store, just as you can make one on the stack. The syntax is the same as for integers:

```
Cat *pCat = new Cat;
```

This calls the default constructor—the constructor that takes no parameters. The constructor is called whenever an object is created (on the stack or on the free store).

Deleting Objects

When you call delete on a pointer to an object on the free store, that object's destructor
is called before the memory is released. This gives your class a chance to clean up, just
as it does for objects destroyed on the stack. Listing 8.5 illustrates creating and deleting
objects on the free store.

LISTING 8.5   Creating and Deleting Objects on the Free Store

```
0:  // Listing 8.5
1:  // Creating objects on the free store
2:  // using new and delete
3:
4:  #include <iostream>
5:
6:  class SimpleCat
7:  {
8:  public:
9:     SimpleCat();
10:    ~SimpleCat();
11: private:
12:    int itsAge;
13: };
14:
15: SimpleCat::SimpleCat()
16: {
17:    std::cout << "Constructor called.\n";
```

LISTING 8.5   continued

```
18:      itsAge = 1;
19:  }
20:
21:  SimpleCat::~SimpleCat()
22:  {
23:      std::cout << "Destructor called.\n";
24:  }
25:
26:  int main()
27:  {
28:      std::cout << "SimpleCat Frisky...\n";
29:      SimpleCat Frisky;
30:      std::cout << "SimpleCat *pRags = new SimpleCat...\n";
31:      SimpleCat * pRags = new SimpleCat;
32:      std::cout << "delete pRags...\n";
33:      delete pRags;
34:      std::cout << "Exiting, watch Frisky go...\n";
35:      return 0;
36:  }
```

OUTPUT

```
SimpleCat Frisky...
Constructor called.
SimpleCat *pRags = new SimpleCat..
Constructor called.
delete pRags...
Destructor called.
Exiting, watch Frisky go...
Destructor called.
```

ANALYSIS Lines 6–13 declare the stripped-down class SimpleCat. Line 9 declares SimpleCat's constructor, and lines 15–19 contain its definition. Line 10 declares SimpleCat's destructor, and lines 21–24 contain its definition.

On line 29, Frisky is created on the stack, which causes the constructor to be called. On line 31, the SimpleCat pointed to by pRags is created on the heap; the constructor is called again. On line 33, delete is called on pRags, and the destructor is called. When the function ends, Frisky goes out of scope, and the destructor is called.

Accessing Data Members

You accessed data members and functions by using the dot (.) operator for Cat objects created locally. To access the Cat object on the free store, you must dereference the pointer and call the dot operator on the object pointed to by the pointer. Therefore, to access the GetAge member function, you would write

```
(*pRags).GetAge();
```

Parentheses are used to ensure that pRags is dereferenced before GetAge() is accessed.

Because this is cumbersome, C++ provides a shorthand operator for indirect access: the points-to operator (->), which is created by typing the dash (-) immediately followed by the greater-than symbol (>). C++ treats this as a single symbol. Listing 8.6 demonstrates accessing member variables and functions of objects created on the free store.

LISTING 8.6   Accessing Member Data of Objects on the Free Store

```
0:   // Listing 8.6
1:   // Accessing data members of objects on the heap
2:   // using the -> operator
3:
4:   #include <iostream>
5:
6:   class SimpleCat
7:   {
8:   public:
9:       SimpleCat() {itsAge = 2; }
10:      ~SimpleCat() {}
11:      int GetAge() const { return itsAge; }
12:      void SetAge(int age) { itsAge = age; }
13:  private:
14:      int itsAge;
15:  };
16:
17:  int main()
18:  {
19:      SimpleCat * Frisky = new SimpleCat;
20:      std::cout << "Frisky is " << Frisky->GetAge() << " years old\n";
21:      Frisky->SetAge(5);
22:      std::cout << "Frisky is " << Frisky->GetAge() << " years old\n";
23:      delete Frisky;
24:      return 0;
25:  }
```

OUTPUT
Frisky is 2 years old
Frisky is 5 years old

ANALYSIS On line 19, a SimpleCat object is instantiated on the free store. The default constructor sets its age to 2, and the GetAge() method is called on line 20. Because this is a pointer, the indirection operator (->) is used to access the member data and functions. On line 21, the SetAge() method is called, and GetAge() is accessed again on line 22.

Member Data on the Free Store

One or more of the data members of a class can be a pointer to an object on the free store. The memory can be allocated in the class constructor or in one of its methods, and it can be deleted in its destructor, as Listing 8.7 illustrates.

LISTING 8.7 Pointers as Member Data

```cpp
0:   // Listing 8.7
1:   // Pointers as data members
2:   // accessed with -> operator
3:
4:   #include <iostream>
5:
6:   class SimpleCat
7:   {
8:   public:
9:      SimpleCat();
10:     ~SimpleCat();
11:     int GetAge() const { return *itsAge; }
12:     void SetAge(int age) { *itsAge = age; }
13:
14:     int GetWeight() const { return *itsWeight; }
15:     void setWeight (int weight) { *itsWeight = weight; }
16:
17:  private:
18:     int * itsAge;
19:     int * itsWeight;
20:  };
21:
22:  SimpleCat::SimpleCat()
23:  {
24:     itsAge = new int(2);
25:     itsWeight = new int(5);
26:  }
27:
28:  SimpleCat::~SimpleCat()
29:  {
30:     delete itsAge;
31:     delete itsWeight;
32:  }
33:
34:  int main()
35:  {
36:     SimpleCat *Frisky = new SimpleCat;
37:     std::cout << "Frisky is " << Frisky->GetAge() << " years old\n";
38:     Frisky->SetAge(5);
39:     std::cout << "Frisky is " << Frisky->GetAge() << " years old\n";
40:     delete Frisky;
41:     return 0;
42:  }
```

OUTPUT
```
Frisky is 2 years old
Frisky is 5 years old
```

ANALYSIS The class `SimpleCat` is declared to have two member variables—both of which are pointers to integers—on lines 18 and 19. The constructor (lines 22–26) initializes the pointers to memory on the free store and to the default values.

Notice that we can call a pseudo-constructor on the new integer, passing in the value for the integer. This creates an integer on the heap and initializes its value (on line 24 to the value 2 and on line 25 to the value 5).

The destructor (lines 28–32) cleans up the allocated memory. Because this is the destructor, there is no point in assigning these pointers to null because they will no longer be accessible. This is one of the safe places to break the rule that deleted pointers should be assigned to null, although following the rule doesn't hurt.

The calling function (in this case, `main()`) is unaware that `itsAge` and `itsWeight` are pointers to memory on the free store. `main()` continues to call `GetAge()` and `SetAge()`, and the details of the memory management are hidden in the implementation of the class—as they should be.

When `Frisky` is deleted on line 40, its destructor is called. The destructor deletes each of its member pointers. If these, in turn, point to objects of other user-defined classes, their destructors are called as well.

Now this would be pretty silly in a real program unless a good reason existed for the `Cat` object to hold its members by reference. In this case, there is no good reason, but in other cases, this would make a lot of sense.

This brings up the obvious question: What are you trying to accomplish? Understand, too, that you must start with design. If what you've designed is an object that refers to another object, but the second object may come into existence before the first object and continue after the first object is gone, then the first object must contain the second by reference.

For example, the first object might be a window and the second object might be a document. The window needs access to the document, but it doesn't control the lifetime of the document. Thus, the window needs to hold the document by reference.

We implement this in C++ by using pointers or references. References are covered on Day 9.

**If I declare an object on the stack that has member variables on the
heap, what is on the stack and what is on the heap? For example**

```cpp
#include <iostream.h>

class SimpleCat
{
public:
     SimpleCat();
     ~SimpleCat();
     int GetAge() const { return *itsAge; }
     // other methods

private:
     int * itsAge;
     int * itsWeight;
};

SimpleCat::SimpleCat()
{
     itsAge = new int(2);
     itsWeight = new int(5);
}

SimpleCat::~SimpleCat()
{
     delete itsAge;
     delete itsWeight;
}

int main()
{
     SimpleCat Frisky;
     cout << "Frisky is " <<
                 Frisky.GetAge() <<
                       " years old\n";
     Frisky.SetAge(5);
     cout << "Frisky is " <<
             Frisky.GetAge() << " years old\n";
     return 0;
}
```

Answer: What is on the stack is the local object `Frisky`. That object has two pointers,
each of which is taking up four bytes of stack space and holding the address of an integer allocated on the heap. Thus, in the example, eight bytes are on the stack and eight
bytes are on the heap.

8

The this Pointer

Every class member function has a hidden parameter: the this pointer. this points to the individual object. Therefore, in each call to GetAge() or SetAge(), the this pointer for the object is included as a hidden parameter.

It is possible to use the this pointer explicitly, as Listing 8.8 illustrates.

LISTING 8.8   Using the this Pointer

```
0:   // Listing 8.8
1:   // Using the this pointer
2:
3:
4:   #include <iostream.h>
5:
6:   class Rectangle
7:   {
8:   public:
9:       Rectangle();
10:      ~Rectangle();
11:      void SetLength(int length)
12:          { this->itsLength = length; }
13:      int GetLength() const
14:          { return this->itsLength; }
15:
16:      void SetWidth(int width)
17:          { itsWidth = width; }
18:      int GetWidth() const
19:          { return itsWidth; }
20:
21:  private:
22:      int itsLength;
23:      int itsWidth;
24:  };
25:
26:  Rectangle::Rectangle()
27:  {
28:      itsWidth = 5;
29:      itsLength = 10;
30:  }
31:  Rectangle::~Rectangle()
32:  {}
33:
34:  int main()
35:  {
36:      Rectangle theRect;
37:      cout << "theRect is " << theRect.GetLength()
38:          << " feet long.\n";
39:      cout << "theRect is " << theRect.GetWidth()
```

LISTING 8.8   continued

```
40:          << " feet wide.\n";
41:       theRect.SetLength(20);
42:       theRect.SetWidth(10);
43:       cout << "theRect is " << theRect.GetLength()
44:          << " feet long.\n";
45:       cout << "theRect is " << theRect.GetWidth()
46:          << " feet wide.\n";
47:       return 0;
48:    }
```

OUTPUT
```
theRect is 10 feet long.
theRect is 5 feet wide.
theRect is 20 feet long.
theRect is 10 feet wide.
```

ANALYSIS The SetLength() and GetLength() accessor functions explicitly use the this pointer to access the member variables of the Rectangle object. The SetWidth and GetWidth accessors do not. No difference exists in their behavior, although the syntax is easier to understand.

If that were all there was to the this pointer, there would be little point in bothering you with it. The this pointer, however, is a pointer; it stores the memory address of an object. As such, it can be a powerful tool.

You'll see a practical use for the this pointer on Day 10, "Advanced Functions," when operator overloading is discussed. For now, your goal is to know about the this pointer and to understand what it is: a pointer to the object itself.

You don't have to worry about creating or deleting the this pointer. The compiler takes care of that.

Stray, Wild, or Dangling Pointers

One source of bugs that are nasty and difficult to find is stray pointers. A stray pointer (also called a wild or dangling pointer) is created when you call delete on a pointer—thereby freeing the memory that it points to—and then you don't set it to null. If you then try to use that pointer again without reassigning it, the result is unpredictable and, if you are lucky, your program will crash.

It is as though the Acme Mail Order company moved away, but you still pressed the programmed button on your phone. It is possible that nothing terrible happens—a telephone rings in a deserted warehouse. On the other hand, perhaps the telephone number has been reassigned to a munitions factory, and your call detonates an explosive and blows up your whole city!

In short, be careful not to use a pointer after you have called `delete` on it. The pointer still points to the old area of memory, but the compiler is free to put other data there; using the pointer can cause your program to crash. Worse, your program might proceed merrily on its way and crash several minutes later. This is called a time bomb, and it is no fun. To be safe, after you delete a pointer, set it to null (0). This disarms the pointer.

> **Note**   Stray pointers are often called wild pointers or dangling pointers.

Listing 8.9 illustrates creating a stray pointer.

> **Caution**   This program intentionally creates a stray pointer. Do NOT run this program—it will crash, if you are lucky.

LISTING 8.9   Creating a Stray Pointer

```
0:  // Listing 8.9
1:  // Demonstrates a stray pointer
2:
3:  typedef unsigned short int USHORT;
4:  #include <iostream>
5:
6:  int main()
7:  {
8:      USHORT * pInt = new USHORT;
9:      *pInt = 10;
10:     std::cout << "*pInt: " << *pInt << std::endl;
11:     delete pInt;
12:
13:     long * pLong = new long;
14:     *pLong = 90000;
15:     std::cout << "*pLong: " << *pLong << std::endl;
16:
17:     *pInt = 20;       // uh oh, this was deleted!
18:
19:     std::cout << "*pInt: " << *pInt  << std::endl;
20:     std::cout << "*pLong: " << *pLong  << std::endl;
21:     delete pLong;
22:     return 0;
23: }
```

8

OUTPUT

```
*pInt:    10
*pLong:   90000
*pInt:    20
*pLong:   65556
```

(Do not try to re-create this output; yours will differ if you are lucky; or your computer will crash if you are not.)

ANALYSIS Line 8 declares pInt to be a pointer to USHORT, and pInt is pointed to newly allocated memory. Line 9 puts the value 10 in that memory, and line 10 prints its value. After the value is printed, delete is called on the pointer. pInt is now a stray, or dangling, pointer.

Line 13 declares a new pointer, pLong, which is pointed at the memory allocated by new. Line 14 assigns the value 90000 to pLong, and line 15 prints its value.

Line 17 assigns the value 20 to the memory that pInt points to, but pInt no longer points anywhere that is valid. The memory that pInt points to was freed by the call to delete, so assigning a value to that memory is certain disaster.

Line 19 prints the value at pInt. Sure enough, it is 20. Line 20 prints 20, the value at pLong; it has suddenly been changed to 65556. Two questions arise:

1. How could pLong's value change, given that pLong wasn't touched?
2. Where did the 20 go when pInt was used on line 17?

As you might guess, these are related questions. When a value was placed at pInt on line 17, the compiler happily placed the value 20 at the memory location that pInt previously pointed to. However, because that memory was freed on line 11, the compiler was free to reassign it. When pLong was created on line 13, it was given pInt's old memory location. (On some computers this may not happen, depending on where in memory these values are stored.) When the value 20 was assigned to the location that pInt previously pointed to, it wrote over the value pointed to by pLong. This is called "stomping on a pointer." It is often the unfortunate outcome of using a stray pointer.

This is a particularly nasty bug because the value that changed wasn't associated with the stray pointer. The change to the value at pLong was a side effect of the misuse of pInt. In a large program, this would be very difficult to track down.

Just for fun, here are the details of how 65,556 got into that memory address:

1. pInt was pointed at a particular memory location, and the value 10 was assigned.
2. delete was called on pInt, which told the compiler that it could put something else at that location. Then pLong was assigned the same memory location.

3. The value 90000 was assigned to *pLong. The particular computer used in this example stored the four-byte value of 90,000 (00 01 5F 90) in byte-swapped order. Therefore, it was stored as 5F 90 00 01.

4. pInt was assigned the value 20—or 00 14 in hexadecimal notation. Because pInt still pointed to the same address, the first two bytes of pLong were overwritten, leaving 00 14 00 01.

5. The value at pLong was printed, reversing the bytes back to their correct order of 00 01 00 14, which was translated into the DOS value of 65556.

What is the difference between a null pointer and a stray pointer?

Answer: When you delete a pointer, you tell the compiler to free the memory, but the pointer itself continues to exist. It is now a stray pointer.

When you then write myPtr = 0; you change it from being a stray pointer to being a null pointer.

Normally, if you delete a pointer and then delete it again, your program is undefined. That is, anything might happen—if you are lucky, the program will crash. If you delete a null pointer, nothing happens; it is safe.

Using a stray *or* a null pointer (for example, writing myPtr = 5;) is illegal, and it might crash. If the pointer is null it *will* crash, another benefit of null over stray. We prefer predictable crashes because they are easier to debug.

---

const Pointers

You can use the keyword const for pointers before the type, after the type, or in both places. For example, all the following are legal declarations:

```
const int * pOne;
int * const pTwo;
const int * const pThree;
```

pOne is a pointer to a constant integer. The value that is pointed to can't be changed.

pTwo is a constant pointer to an integer. The integer can be changed, but pTwo can't point to anything else.

pThree is a constant pointer to a constant integer. The value that is pointed to can't be changed, and pThree can't be changed to point to anything else.

8

The trick to keeping this straight is to look to the right of the keyword const to find out what is being declared constant. If the type is to the right of the keyword, it is the value that is constant. If the variable is to the right of the keyword const, it is the pointer variable itself that is constant.

```
const int * p1;   // the int pointed to is constant
int * const p2;   // p2 is constant, it can't point to anything else
```

const Pointers and const Member Functions

On Day 6, "Object-Oriented Programming," you learned that you can apply the keyword const to a member function. When a function is declared const, the compiler flags as an error any attempt to change data in the object from within that function.

If you declare a pointer to a const object, the only methods that you can call with that pointer are const methods. Listing 8.10 illustrates this.

LISTING 8.10   Using Pointers to const Objects

```
0:   // Listing 8.10
1:   // Using pointers with const methods
2:
3:   #include <iostream>
4:   using namespace std;
5:
6:   class Rectangle
7:   {
8:   public:
9:       Rectangle();
10:      ~Rectangle();
11:      void SetLength(int length) { itsLength = length; }
12:      int GetLength() const { return itsLength; }
13:      void SetWidth(int width) { itsWidth = width; }
14:      int GetWidth() const { return itsWidth; }
15:
16:   private:
17:      int itsLength;
18:      int itsWidth;
19:   };
20:
21:   Rectangle::Rectangle()
22:   {
23:      itsWidth = 5;
24:      itsLength = 10;
25:   }
26:
27:   Rectangle::~Rectangle()
28:   {}
```

LISTING 8.10   continued

```
29:
30:   int main()
31:   {
32:      Rectangle* pRect =  new Rectangle;
33:      const Rectangle * pConstRect = new Rectangle;
34:      Rectangle * const pConstPtr = new Rectangle;
35:
36:      cout << "pRect width: " << pRect->GetWidth()
37:         << " feet\n";
38:      cout << "pConstRect width: " << pConstRect->GetWidth()
39:         << " feet\n";
40:      cout << "pConstPtr width: " << pConstPtr->GetWidth()
41:         << " feet\n";
42:
43:      pRect->SetWidth(10);
44:      // pConstRect->SetWidth(10);
45:      pConstPtr->SetWidth(10);
46:
47:      cout << "pRect width: " << pRect->GetWidth()
48:         << " feet\n";
49:      cout << "pConstRect width: " << pConstRect->GetWidth()
50:         << " feet\n";
51:      cout << "pConstPtr width: " << pConstPtr->GetWidth()
52:         << " feet\n";
53:      return 0;
54:   }
```

OUTPUT
```
pRect width: 5 feet
pConstRect width: 5 feet
pConstPtr width: 5 feet
pRect width: 10 feet
pConstRect width: 5 feet
pConstPtr width: 10 feet
```

ANALYSIS   Lines 6–19 declare Rectangle. Line 14 declares the GetWidth() member method const. Line 32 declares a pointer to Rectangle. Line 33 declares pConstRect, which is a pointer to a constant Rectangle. Line 34 declares pConstPtr, which is a constant pointer to Rectangle.

Lines 36–41 print their values.

On line 43, pRect is used to set the width of the rectangle to 10. On line 44, pConstRect would be used, but it was declared to point to a constant Rectangle. Therefore, it cannot legally call a non-const member function; it is commented out. On line 45, pConstPtr calls SetWidth(). pConstPtr is declared to be a constant pointer to a rectangle. In other words, the pointer is constant and cannot point to anything else, but the rectangle is not constant.

const this Pointers

When you declare an object to be const, you are in effect declaring that the this pointer is a pointer to a const object. A const this pointer can be used only with const member functions.

Constant objects and constant pointers will be discussed again tomorrow, when references to constant objects are discussed.

Do	Don't
DO protect objects passed by reference with const if they should not be changed.	**DON'T** delete pointers more than once.
DO pass by reference when the object can be changed.	
DO pass by value when small objects should not be changed.	

Pointer Arithmetic—An Advanced Topic

Pointers can be subtracted, one from another. One powerful technique is to point two pointers at different elements in an array and to take their difference to see how many elements separate the two members. This can be very useful when parsing arrays of characters as illustrated in Listing 8.11.

LISTING 8.11   Illustrates How to Parse Out Words from a Character String

```
0:  #include <iostream>
1:  #include <ctype.h>
2:  #include <string.h>
3:
4:  bool GetWord(char* theString,
5:          char* word, int& wordOffset);
6:
7:  // driver program
8:  int main()
9:  {
10:     const int bufferSize = 255;
11:     char buffer[bufferSize+1];   // hold the entire string
12:     char word[bufferSize+1];   // hold the word
13:     int wordOffset = 0;          // start at the beginning
14:
15:     std::cout << "Enter a string: ";
```

LISTING 8.11   continued

```
16:        std::cin.getline(buffer,bufferSize);
17:
18:        while (GetWord(buffer,word,wordOffset))
19:        {
20:            std::cout << "Got this word: " << word << std::endl;
21:        }
22:
23:        return 0;
24:
25:    }
26:
27:
28:    // function to parse words from a string.
29:    bool GetWord(char* theString, char* word, int& wordOffset)
30:    {
31:
32:        if (!theString[wordOffset])  // end of string?
33:            return false;
34:
35:        char *p1, *p2;
36:        p1 = p2 = theString+wordOffset;  // point to the next word
37:
38:        // eat leading spaces
39:        for (int i = 0; i<(int)strlen(p1) && !isalnum(p1[0]); i++)
40:            p1++;
41:
42:        // see if you have a word
43:        if (!isalnum(p1[0]))
44:            return false;
45:
46:        // p1 now points to start of next word
47:        // point p2 there as well
48:        p2 = p1;
49:
50:        // march p2 to end of word
51:        while (isalnum(p2[0]))
52:            p2++;
53:
54:        // p2 is now at end of word
55:        // p1 is at beginning of word
56:        // length of word is the difference
57:        int len = int (p2 - p1);
58:
59:        // copy the word into the buffer
60:        strncpy (word,p1,len);
61:
62:        // null terminate it
63:        word[len]='\0';
64:
```

LISTING 8.11   continued

```
65:      // now find the beginning of the next word
66:      for (int j = int(p2-theString); j<(int)strlen(theString)
67:         && !isalnum(p2[0]); j++)
68:      {
69:          p2++;
70:      }
71:
72:      wordOffset = int(p2-theString);
73:
74:      return true;
75:  }
```

OUTPUT

```
Enter a string: this code first appeared in C++ Report
Got this word: this
Got this word: code
Got this word: first
Got this word: appeared
Got this word: in
Got this word: C
Got this word: Report
```

ANALYSIS On line 15, the user is prompted to enter a string. This is fed to GetWord on line 18, along with a buffer to hold the first word and an integer variable WordOffset, which is initialized on line 13 to zero. As words are returned from GetWord they are printed until GetWord() returns false.

Each call to GetWord causes a jump to line 29. On line 32, we check to see if the value of string[wordOffset]) is zero. This will be true if we are past the end of the string, at which time GetWord() will return false.

Notice that we take advantage of the fact that C++ considers the value 0 to be false. We could rewrite this line to

```
32:        if (theString[wordOffset] == 0)  // end of string?
```

On line 35, two character pointers, p1 and p2, are declared, and on line 36, they are set to point into string offset by wordOffset. Initially, wordOffset is zero, so they point to the beginning of the string.

Lines 39 and 40 tick through the string, pushing p1 to the first alphanumeric character. Lines 43 and 44 ensure that we have found an alphanumeric character; if not, we return false.

p1 now points to the start of the next word, and line 48 sets p2 to point to the same position.

Lines 51 and 52 then cause p2 to march through the word, stopping at the first non-alphanumeric character. p2 is now pointing to the end of the word that p1 points to the beginning of. By subtracting p1 from p2 on line 55 and casting the result to an integer, we are able to establish the length of the word. We then copy that word into the buffer *word*, passing in as the starting point p1 and as the length the difference we've established.

On line 63, we append a null to mark the end of the word. p2 is then incremented to point to the beginning of the next word, and the offset of that word is pushed into the integer reference wordOffset. Finally, we return true to indicate that a word has been found.

This is a classic example of code that is best understood by putting it into a debugger and stepping through its execution.

Summary

Pointers provide a powerful way to access data by indirection. Every variable has an address, which can be obtained using the address-of operator (&). The address can be stored in a pointer.

Pointers are declared by writing the type of object that they point to, followed by the indirection operator (*) and the name of the pointer. Pointers should be initialized to point to an object or to null (0).

You access the value at the address stored in a pointer by using the indirection operator (*). You can declare const pointers, which can't be reassigned to point to other objects, and pointers to const objects, which can't be used to change the objects to which they point.

To create new objects on the free store, you use the new keyword and assign the address that is returned to a pointer. You free that memory by calling the delete keyword on the pointer. delete frees the memory, but it doesn't destroy the pointer. Therefore, you must reassign the pointer after its memory has been freed.

Q&A

Q Why are pointers so important?

A Today you saw how pointers are used to hold the address of objects on the free store and how they are used to pass arguments by reference. In addition, on Day 14, "Polymorphism," you'll see how pointers are used in class polymorphism.

8

Q Why should I bother to declare anything on the free store?

A Objects on the free store persist after the return of a function. Additionally, the capability to store objects on the free store enables you to decide at runtime how many objects you need, instead of having to declare this in advance. This is explored in greater depth tomorrow.

Q Why should I declare an object `const` if it limits what I can do with it?

A As a programmer, you want to enlist the compiler in helping you find bugs. One serious bug that is difficult to find is a function that changes an object in ways that aren't obvious to the calling function. Declaring an object `const` prevents such changes.

Workshop

The Workshop provides quiz questions to help you solidify your understanding of the material covered and exercises to provide you with experience in using what you've learned. Try to answer the quiz and exercise questions before checking the answers in Appendix D, and make sure you understand the answers before continuing to the next chapter.

Quiz

1. What operator is used to determine the address of a variable?

2. What operator is used to find the value stored at an address held in a pointer?

3. What is a pointer?

4. What is the difference between the address stored in a pointer and the value at that address?

5. What is the difference between the indirection operator and the address of operator?

6. What is the difference between `const int * ptrOne` and `int * const ptrTwo`?

Exercises

1. What do these declarations do?

   a. `int * pOne;`

   b. `int vTwo;`

   c. `int * pThree = &vTwo;`

2. If you have an `unsigned short` variable named `yourAge`, how would you declare a pointer to manipulate `yourAge`?

3. Assign the value 50 to the variable yourAge by using the pointer that you declared in Exercise 2.

4. Write a small program that declares an integer and a pointer to integer. Assign the address of the integer to the pointer. Use the pointer to set a value in the integer variable.

5. **BUG BUSTERS:** What is wrong with this code?

```
#include <iostream>
using namespace std;
int main()
{
    int *pInt;
    *pInt = 9;
    cout << "The value at pInt: " << *pInt;
return 0;
}
```

6. **BUG BUSTERS:** What is wrong with this code?

```
int main()
{
    int SomeVariable = 5;
    cout << "SomeVariable: " << SomeVariable << "\n";
    int *pVar = & SomeVariable;
    pVar = 9;
    cout << "SomeVariable: " << *pVar << "\n";
return 0;
}
```

DAY 9

References

Yesterday you learned how to use pointers to manipulate objects on the free store and how to refer to those objects indirectly. References, the topic of today's chapter, give you almost all the power of pointers but with a much easier syntax.

Today you will learn

- What references are.
- How references differ from pointers.
- How to create references and use them.
- What the limitations of references are.
- How to pass values and objects into and out of functions by reference.

What Is a Reference?

A reference is an alias; when you create a reference, you initialize it with the name of another object, the target. From that moment on, the reference acts as an alternative name for the target, and anything you do to the reference is really done to the target.

You create a reference by writing the type of the target object, followed by the reference operator (&), followed by the name of the reference.

References can use any legal variable name, but many programmers prefer to prefix all reference names with "r". Thus, if you have an integer variable named someInt, you can make a reference to that variable by writing the following:

```
int &rSomeRef = someInt;
```

This is read as "rSomeRef is a reference to an integer. The reference is initialized to refer to someInt." Listing 9.1 shows how references are created and used.

Note

Note that the reference operator (&) is the same symbol as the one used for the address of operator. These are not the same operators, however, although clearly they are related.

The space before the reference operator is required, the space between the reference operator and the name of the reference variable is optional. Thus

```
int &rSomeRef = someInt;   // ok
int & rSomeRef = someInt; // ok
```

LISTING 9.1   Creating and Using References

```cpp
0:   //Listing 9.1
1:   // Demonstrating the use of References
2:
3:   #include <iostream>
4:
5:   int main()
6:   {
7:       using namespace std;
8:       int  intOne;
9:       int &rSomeRef = intOne;
10:
11:      intOne = 5;
12:      cout << "intOne: " << intOne << endl;
13:      cout << "rSomeRef: " << rSomeRef << endl;
14:
15:      rSomeRef = 7;
16:      cout << "intOne: " << intOne << endl;
17:      cout << "rSomeRef: " << rSomeRef << endl;
18:
19:      return 0;
20:   }
```

```
intOne: 5
rSomeRef: 5
intOne: 7
rSomeRef: 7
```

ANALYSIS On line 8, a local int variable, intOne, is declared. On line 9, a reference to an int, rSomeRef, is declared and initialized to refer to intOne. If you declare a reference but don't initialize it, you will get a compile-time error. References must be initialized.

On line 11, intOne is assigned the value 5. On lines 12 and 13, the values in intOne and rSomeRef are printed, and are, of course, the same.

On line 15, 7 is assigned to rSomeRef. Because this is a reference, it is an alias for intOne, and thus the 7 is really assigned to intOne, as is shown by the printouts on lines 16 and 17.

Using the Address Of Operator & on References

If you ask a reference for its address, it returns the address of its target. That is the nature of references. They are aliases for the target. Listing 9.2 demonstrates this.

LISTING 9.2 Taking the Address of a Reference

```
0:   //Listing 9.2
1:   // Demonstrating the use of References
2:
3:   #include <iostream>
4:
5:   int main()
6:   {
7:      using namespace std;
8:      int  intOne;
9:      int &rSomeRef = intOne;
10:
11:     intOne = 5;
12:     cout << "intOne: " << intOne << endl;
13:     cout << "rSomeRef: " << rSomeRef << endl;
14:
15:     cout << "&intOne: "  << &intOne << endl;
16:     cout << "&rSomeRef: " << &rSomeRef << endl;
17:
18:     return 0;
19:   }
```

```
intOne: 5
rSomeRef: 5
&intOne:  0x3500
&rSomeRef: 0x3500
```

> **Note**   Your output may differ on the last two lines.

ANALYSIS   Once again, rSomeRef is initialized as a reference to intOne. This time the addresses of the two variables are printed, and they are identical. C++ gives you no way to access the address of the reference itself because it is not meaningful as it would be if you were using a pointer or other variable. References are initialized when created, and they always act as a synonym for their target, even when the address of operator is applied.

For example, if you have a class called President, you might declare an instance of that class as follows:

```
President George_Washington;
```

You might then declare a reference to President and initialize it with this object:

```
President &FatherOfOurCountry = George_Washington;
```

Only one President exists; both identifiers refer to the same object of the same class. Any action you take on FatherOfOurCountry will be taken on George_Washington as well.

Be careful to distinguish between the & symbol on line 9 of Listing 9.2, which declares a reference to int named rSomeRef, and the & symbols on lines 15 and 16, which return the addresses of the integer variable intOne and the reference rSomeRef.

Normally, when you use a reference, you do not use the address of operator. You simply use the reference as you would use the target variable. This is shown on line 13.

References Cannot Be Reassigned

Even experienced C++ programmers who know the rule that references cannot be reassigned and are always aliases for their target can be confused by what happens when you try to reassign a reference. What appears to be a reassignment turns out to be the assignment of a new value to the target. Listing 9.3 illustrates this fact.

LISTING 9.3   Assigning to a Reference

```
0:   //Listing 9.3
1:   //Reassigning a reference
2:
3:   #include <iostream>
4:
5:   int main()
6:   {
7:      using namespace std;
8:      int  intOne;
9:      int &rSomeRef = intOne;
10:
11:     intOne = 5;
12:     cout << "intOne:\t" << intOne << endl;
13:     cout << "rSomeRef:\t" << rSomeRef << endl;
14:     cout << "&intOne:\t"  << &intOne << endl;
15:     cout << "&rSomeRef:\t" << &rSomeRef << endl;
16:
17:     int intTwo = 8;
18:     rSomeRef = intTwo;   // not what you think!
19:     cout << "\nintOne:\t" << intOne << endl;
20:     cout << "intTwo:\t" << intTwo << endl;
21:     cout << "rSomeRef:\t" << rSomeRef << endl;
22:     cout << "&intOne:\t"  << &intOne << endl;
23:     cout << "&intTwo:\t"  << &intTwo << endl;
24:     cout << "&rSomeRef:\t" << &rSomeRef << endl;
25:     return 0;
26:  }
```

OUTPUT

```
intOne:                 5
rSomeRef:       5
&intOne:                0x213e
&rSomeRef:      0x213e

intOne:                 8
intTwo:                 8
rSomeRef:       8
&intOne:                0x213e
&intTwo:                0x2130
&rSomeRef:      0x213e
```

ANALYSIS   Once again, on lines 8 and 9, an integer variable and a reference to an integer are declared. The integer is assigned the value 5 on line 11, and the values and their addresses are printed on lines 12–15.

On line 17, a new variable, intTwo, is created and initialized with the value 8. On line 18, the programmer tries to reassign rSomeRef to now be an alias to the variable intTwo, but that is not what happens. What actually happens is that rSomeRef continues to act as an alias for intOne, so this assignment is equivalent to the following:

```
intOne = intTwo;
```

Sure enough, when the values of intOne and rSomeRef are printed (lines 19–21), they are the same as intTwo. In fact, when the addresses are printed on lines 22–24, you see that rSomeRef continues to refer to intOne and not intTwo.

Do	Don't
DO use references to create an alias to an object. **DO** initialize all references.	**DON'T** try to reassign a reference. **DON'T** confuse the address of operator with the reference operator.

What Can Be Referenced?

Any object can be referenced, including user-defined objects. Note that you create a reference to an object, but not to a class. You do not write this:

```
int & rIntRef = int;     // wrong
```

You must initialize rIntRef to a particular integer, such as this:

```
int howBig = 200;
int & rIntRef = howBig;
```

In the same way, you don't initialize a reference to a CAT:

```
CAT & rCatRef = CAT;     // wrong
```

You must initialize rCatRef to a particular CAT object:

```
CAT frisky;
CAT & rCatRef = frisky;
```

References to objects are used just like the object itself. Member data and methods are accessed using the normal class member access operator (.), and just as with the built-in types, the reference acts as an alias to the object. Listing 9.4 illustrates this.

LISTING 9.4   References to Objects

```
0:   // Listing 9.4
1:   // References to class objects
2:
3:   #include <iostream>
4:
5:   class SimpleCat
6:   {
7:   public:
8:      SimpleCat (int age, int weight);
9:      ~SimpleCat() {}
10:     int GetAge() { return itsAge; }
11:     int GetWeight() { return itsWeight; }
12:  private:
13:     int itsAge;
14:     int itsWeight;
15:  };
16:
17:  SimpleCat::SimpleCat(int age, int weight)
18:  {
19:     itsAge = age;
20:     itsWeight = weight;
21:  }
22:
23:  int main()
24:  {
25:     SimpleCat Frisky(5,8);
26:     SimpleCat & rCat = Frisky;
27:
28:     std::cout << "Frisky is: ";
29:     std::cout << Frisky.GetAge() << " years old. \n";
30:     std::cout << "And Frisky weighs: ";
31:     std::cout << rCat.GetWeight() << " pounds. \n";
32:     return 0;
33:  }
```

OUTPUT
```
Frisky is: 5 years old.
And Frisky weighs 8 pounds.
```

ANALYSIS On line 25, Frisky is declared to be a SimpleCat object. On line 26, a
SimpleCat reference, rCat, is declared and initialized to refer to Frisky. On lines
29 and 31, the SimpleCat accessor methods are accessed by using first the SimpleCat
object and then the SimpleCat reference. Note that the access is identical. Again, the reference is an alias for the actual object.

Null Pointers and Null References

When pointers are not initialized or when they are deleted, they ought to be assigned to null (0). This is not true for references. In fact, a reference *cannot* be null, and a program with a reference to a null object is considered an invalid program. When a program is invalid, just about anything can happen. It can appear to work, or it can erase all the files on your disk.

Most compilers will support a null object without much complaint, crashing only if you try to use the object in some way. Taking advantage of this, however, is still not a good idea. When you move your program to another machine or compiler, mysterious bugs may develop if you have null objects.

Passing Function Arguments by Reference

On Day 5, "Functions," you learned that functions have two limitations: Arguments are passed by value, and the return statement can return only one value.

Passing values to a function by reference can overcome both of these limitations. In C++, passing by reference is accomplished in two ways: using pointers and using references. Note the difference: you pass *by* reference using a pointer, or you pass *by* reference using a reference.

The syntax of using a pointer is different from that of using a reference, but the net effect is the same. Rather than a copy being created within the scope of the function, the actual original object is (effectively) passed into the function.

On Day 5 you learned that functions are passed their parameters on the stack. When a function is passed a value by reference (using either pointers or references), the address of the object is put on the stack, not the entire object.

In fact, on some computers the address is actually held in a register and nothing is put on the stack. In either case, the compiler now knows how to get to the original object, and changes are made there and not in a copy.

Passing an object by reference enables the function to change the object being referred to.

Recall that Listing 5.5 in Day 5 demonstrated that a call to the swap() function did not affect the values in the calling function. Listing 5.5 is reproduced here as Listing 9.5, for your convenience.

LISTING 9.5 Demonstrating Passing by Value

```
0:   //Listing 9.5 Demonstrates passing by value
1:
2:   #include <iostream>
3:
4:   using namespace std;
5:   void swap(int x, int y);
6:
7:   int main()
8:   {
9:      int x = 5, y = 10;
10:
11:     cout << "Main. Before swap, x: " << x << " y: " << y << "\n";
12:     swap(x,y);
13:     cout << "Main. After swap, x: " << x << " y: " << y << "\n";
14:     return 0;
15:  }
16:
17:  void swap (int x, int y)
18:  {
19:     int temp;
20:
21:     cout << "Swap. Before swap, x: " << x << " y: " << y << "\n";
22:
23:     temp = x;
24:     x = y;
25:     y = temp;
26:
27:     cout << "Swap. After swap, x: " << x << " y: " << y << "\n";
28:
29:  }
```

OUTPUT
```
Main. Before swap, x: 5 y: 10
Swap. Before swap, x: 5 y: 10
Swap. After swap, x: 10 y: 5
Main. After swap, x: 5 y: 10
```

ANALYSIS This program initializes two variables in `main()` and then passes them to the `swap()` function, which appears to swap them. When they are examined again in `main()`, they are unchanged!

The problem here is that x and y are being passed to `swap()` by value. That is, local copies were made in the function. What you want is to pass x and y by reference.

Two ways to solve this problem are possible in C++: You can make the parameters of `swap()` pointers to the original values, or you can pass in references to the original values.

Making `swap()` Work with Pointers

When you pass in a pointer, you pass in the address of the object, and thus the function can manipulate the value at that address. To make `swap()` change the actual values using pointers, the function, `swap()`, should be declared to accept two int pointers. Then, by dereferencing the pointers, the values of x and y will, in fact, be swapped. Listing 9.6 demonstrates this idea.

LISTING 9.6   Passing by Reference Using Pointers

```
0:   //Listing 9.6 Demonstrates passing by reference
1:
2:   #include <iostream>
3:
4:   using namespace std;
5:   void swap(int *x, int *y);
6:
7:   int main()
8:   {
9:      int x = 5, y = 10;
10:
11:     cout << "Main. Before swap, x: " << x << " y: " << y << "\n";
12:     swap(&x,&y);
13:     cout << "Main. After swap, x: " << x << " y: " << y << "\n";
14:     return 0;
15:   }
16:
17:  void swap (int *px, int *py)
18:  {
19:     int temp;
20:
21:     cout << "Swap. Before swap, *px: " << *px <<
22:        " *py: " << *py << "\n";
23:
24:     temp = *px;
25:     *px = *py;
```

LISTING 9.6   continued

```
26:    *py = temp;
27:
28:    cout << "Swap. After swap, *px: " << *px <<
29:        " *py: " << *py << "\n";
30:
31: }
```

OUTPUT

```
Main. Before swap, x: 5 y: 10
Swap. Before swap, *px: 5 *py: 10
Swap. After swap, *px: 10 *py: 5
Main. After swap, x: 10 y: 5
```

ANALYSIS   Success! On line 5, the prototype of swap() is changed to indicate that its two parameters will be pointers to int rather than int variables. When swap() is called on line 12, the addresses of x and y are passed as the arguments.

On line 19, a local variable, temp, is declared in the swap() function. temp need not be a pointer; it will just hold the value of *px (that is, the value of x in the calling function) for the life of the function. After the function returns, temp will no longer be needed.

On line 24, temp is assigned the value at px. On line 25, the value at px is assigned to the value at py. On line 26, the value stashed in temp (that is, the original value at px) is put into py.

The net effect of this is that the values in the calling function, whose address was passed to swap(), are, in fact, swapped.

Implementing swap() with References

The preceding program works, but the syntax of the swap() function is cumbersome in two ways. First, the repeated need to dereference the pointers within the swap() function makes it error-prone and hard to read. Second, the need to pass the address of the variables in the calling function makes the inner workings of swap() overly apparent to its users.

It is a goal of C++ to prevent the user of a function from worrying about how it works. Passing by pointers puts the burden on the calling function rather than where it belongs—on the called function. Listing 9.7 rewrites the swap() function, using references.

LISTING 9.7   swap() Rewritten with References

```
0:    //Listing 9.7 Demonstrates passing by reference
1:    // using references!
2:
3:    #include <iostream>
4:
5:    using namespace std;
6:    void swap(int &x, int &y);
7:
8:    int main()
9:    {
10:       int x = 5, y = 10;
11:
12:       cout << "Main. Before swap, x: " << x << " y: "
13:          << y << "\n";
14:
15:       swap(x,y);
16:
17:       cout << "Main. After swap, x: " << x << " y: "
18:          << y << "\n";
19:
20:       return 0;
21:    }
22:
23:    void swap (int &rx, int &ry)
24:    {
25:       int temp;
26:
27:       cout << "Swap. Before swap, rx: " << rx << " ry: "
28:          << ry << "\n";
29:
30:       temp = rx;
31:       rx = ry;
32:       ry = temp;
33:
34:
35:       cout << "Swap. After swap, rx: " << rx << " ry: "
36:          << ry << "\n";
37:
38:    }
```

OUTPUT
```
Main. Before swap, x:5 y: 10
Swap. Before swap, rx:5 ry:10
Swap. After swap, rx:10 ry:5
Main. After swap, x:10, y:5
```

ANALYSIS   Just as in the example with pointers, two variables are declared on line 10, and
their values are printed on line 12. On line 15, the function swap() is called, but
note that x and y, not their addresses, are passed. The calling function simply passes the
variables.

When `swap()` is called, program execution jumps to line 23, where the variables are identified as references. Their values are printed on line 27, but note that no special operators are required. These are aliases for the original values and can be used as such.

On lines 30–32, the values are swapped, and then they're printed on line 35. Program execution jumps back to the calling function, and on line 17, the values are printed in `main()`. Because the parameters to `swap()` are declared to be references, the values from `main()` are passed by reference, and thus are changed in `main()` as well.

References provide the convenience and ease of use of normal variables, with the power and pass-by-reference capability of pointers!

Understanding Function Headers and Prototypes

Listing 9.6 shows `swap()` using pointers, and Listing 9.7 shows it using references. Using the function that takes references is easier, and the code is easier to read, but how does the calling function know if the values are passed by reference or by value? As a client (or user) of `swap()`, the programmer must ensure that `swap()` will, in fact, change the parameters.

This is another use for the function prototype. By examining the parameters declared in the prototype, which is typically in a header file along with all the other prototypes, the programmer knows that the values passed into `swap()` are passed by reference, and thus will be swapped properly.

If `swap()` had been a member function of a class, the class declaration, also available in a header file, would have supplied this information.

In C++, clients of classes and functions rely on the header file to tell all that is needed; it acts as the interface to the class or function. The actual implementation is hidden from the client. This enables the programmer to focus on the problem at hand and to use the class or function without concern for how it works.

When Colonel John Roebling designed the Brooklyn Bridge, he worried in detail about how the concrete was poured and how the wire for the bridge was manufactured. He was intimately involved in the mechanical and chemical processes required to create his materials. Today, however, engineers make more efficient use of their time by using well-understood building materials, without regard to how their manufacturer produced them.

It is the goal of C++ to enable programmers to rely on well-understood classes and functions without regard to their internal workings. These "component parts" can be assembled to produce a program, much the same way wires, pipes, clamps, and other parts are assembled to produce buildings and bridges.

In much the same way that an engineer examines the spec sheet for a pipe to determine its load-bearing capacity, volume, fitting size, and so forth, a C++ programmer reads the interface of a function or class to determine what services it provides, what parameters it takes, and what values it returns.

Returning Multiple Values

As discussed, functions can only return one value. What if you need to get two values back from a function? One way to solve this problem is to pass two objects into the function, by reference. The function can then fill the objects with the correct values. Because passing by reference allows a function to change the original objects, this effectively enables the function to return two pieces of information. This approach bypasses the return value of the function, which can then be reserved for reporting errors.

Once again, this can be done with references or pointers. Listing 9.8 demonstrates a function that returns three values: two as pointer parameters and one as the return value of the function.

LISTING 9.8   Returning Values with Pointers

```
 0:  //Listing 9.8
 1:  // Returning multiple values from a function
 2:
 3:  #include <iostream>
 4:
 5:  using namespace std;
 6:  short Factor(int n, int* pSquared, int* pCubed);
 7:
 8:  int main()
 9:  {
10:      int number, squared, cubed;
11:      short error;
12:
13:      cout << "Enter a number (0 - 20): ";
14:      cin >> number;
15:
16:      error = Factor(number, &squared, &cubed);
17:
18:      if (!error)
19:      {
20:          cout << "number: " << number << "\n";
21:          cout << "square: " << squared << "\n";
22:          cout << "cubed: "  << cubed   << "\n";
```

LISTING 9.8   continued

```
23:      }
24:      else
25:         cout << "Error encountered!!\n";
26:      return 0;
27:   }
28:
29:   short Factor(int n, int *pSquared, int *pCubed)
30:   {
31:      short Value = 0;
32:      if (n > 20)
33:         Value = 1;
34:      else
35:      {
36:         *pSquared = n*n;
37:         *pCubed = n*n*n;
38:         Value = 0;
39:      }
40:      return Value;
41:   }
```

OUTPUT
```
Enter a number (0-20): 3
number: 3
square: 9
cubed: 27
```

ANALYSIS   On line 10, number, squared, and cubed are defined as short integers. number is assigned a value based on user input. This number and the addresses of squared and cubed are passed to the function Factor().

Factor() examines the first parameter, which is passed by value. If it is greater than 20 (the maximum value this function can handle), it sets return Value to a simple error value. Note that the return value from Function() is reserved for either this error value or the value 0, indicating all went well, and note that the function returns this value on line 40.

The actual values needed, the square and cube of number, are returned not by using the return mechanism, but rather by changing the pointers that were passed into the function.

On lines 36 and 37, the pointers are assigned their return values. On line 38, return Value is assigned a success value. On line 40, return Value is returned.

One improvement to this program might be to declare the following:

```
enum ERROR_VALUE { SUCCESS, FAILURE};
```

Then, rather than returning 0 or 1, the program could return SUCCESS or FAILURE.

Returning Values by Reference

Although Listing 9.8 works, it can be made easier to read and maintain by using references rather than pointers. Listing 9.9 shows the same program rewritten to use references and to incorporate the ERROR enumeration.

LISTING 9.9   Listing 9.8 Rewritten Using References

```
0:   //Listing 9.9
1:   // Returning multiple values from a function
2:   // using references
3:
4:   #include <iostream>
5:
6:   using namespace std;
7:   typedef unsigned short USHORT;
8:   enum ERR_CODE { SUCCESS, ERROR };
9:
10:  ERR_CODE Factor(USHORT, USHORT&, USHORT&);
11:
12:  int main()
13:  {
14:     USHORT number, squared, cubed;
15:     ERR_CODE result;
16:
17:     cout << "Enter a number (0 - 20): ";
18:     cin >> number;
19:
20:     result = Factor(number, squared, cubed);
21:
22:     if (result == SUCCESS)
23:     {
24:        cout << "number: " << number << "\n";
25:        cout << "square: " << squared << "\n";
26:        cout << "cubed: "  << cubed   << "\n";
27:     }
28:     else
29:        cout << "Error encountered!!\n";
30:     return 0;
31:  }
32:
33:  ERR_CODE Factor(USHORT n, USHORT &rSquared, USHORT &rCubed)
34:  {
35:     if (n > 20)
36:        return ERROR;   // simple error code
37:     else
38:     {
39:        rSquared = n*n;
40:        rCubed = n*n*n;
```

LISTING 9.9   continued

```
41:        return SUCCESS;
42:     }
43:  }
```

OUTPUT
```
Enter a number (0 - 20): 3
number: 3
square: 9
cubed: 27
```

ANALYSIS   Listing 9.9 is identical to 9.8, with two exceptions. The ERR_CODE enumeration makes the error reporting a bit more explicit on lines 36 and 41, as well as the error handling on line 22.

The larger change, however, is that Factor() is now declared to take references to squared and cubed rather than to pointers. This makes the manipulation of these parameters far simpler and easier to understand.

Passing by Reference for Efficiency

Each time you pass an object into a function by value, a copy of the object is made. Each time you return an object from a function by value, another copy is made.

On Day 5, you learned that these objects are copied onto the stack. Doing so takes time and memory. For small objects, such as the built-in integer values, this is a trivial cost.

However, with larger, user-created objects, the cost is greater. The size of a user-created object on the stack is the sum of each of its member variables. These, in turn, can each be user-created objects, and passing such a massive structure by copying it onto the stack can be very expensive in performance and memory consumption.

Another cost occurs as well. With the classes you create, each of these temporary copies is created when the compiler calls a special constructor: the copy constructor. Tomorrow you will learn how copy constructors work and how you can make your own, but for now it is enough to know that the copy constructor is called each time a temporary copy of the object is put on the stack.

When the temporary object is destroyed, which happens when the function returns, the object's destructor is called. If an object is returned by the function by value, a copy of that object must be made and destroyed as well.

With large objects, these constructor and destructor calls can be expensive in speed and use of memory. To illustrate this idea, Listing 9.9 creates a stripped-down, user-created object: SimpleCat. A real object would be larger and more expensive, but this is sufficient to show how often the copy constructor and destructor are called.

Listing 9.10 creates the SimpleCat object and then calls two functions. The first function receives the Cat by value and then returns it by value. The second one receives a pointer to the object, rather than the object itself, and returns a pointer to the object.

LISTING 9.10   Passing Objects by Reference Using Pointers

```
0:   //Listing 9.10
1:   // Passing pointers to objects
2:
3:   #include <iostream>
4:
5:   using namespace std;
6:   class SimpleCat
7:   {
8:   public:
9:       SimpleCat ();                        // constructor
10:      SimpleCat(SimpleCat&);      // copy constructor
11:      ~SimpleCat();                        // destructor
12:  };
13:
14:  SimpleCat::SimpleCat()
15:  {
16:      cout << "Simple Cat Constructor...\n";
17:  }
18:
19:  SimpleCat::SimpleCat(SimpleCat&)
20:  {
21:      cout << "Simple Cat Copy Constructor...\n";
22:  }
23:
24:  SimpleCat::~SimpleCat()
25:  {
26:      cout << "Simple Cat Destructor...\n";
27:  }
28:
29:  SimpleCat FunctionOne (SimpleCat theCat);
30:  SimpleCat* FunctionTwo (SimpleCat *theCat);
31:
32:  int main()
33:  {
34:      cout << "Making a cat...\n";
35:      SimpleCat Frisky;
36:      cout << "Calling FunctionOne...\n";
37:      FunctionOne(Frisky);
```

LISTING 9.10   continued

```
38:      cout << "Calling FunctionTwo...\n";
39:      FunctionTwo(&Frisky);
40:      return 0;
41:   }
42:
43:   // FunctionOne, passes by value
44:   SimpleCat FunctionOne(SimpleCat theCat)
45:   {
46:      cout << "Function One. Returning...\n";
47:      return theCat;
48:   }
49:
50:   // functionTwo, passes by reference
51:   SimpleCat* FunctionTwo (SimpleCat  *theCat)
52:   {
53:      cout << "Function Two. Returning...\n";
54:      return theCat;
55:   }
```

OUTPUT
```
Making a cat...
Simple Cat Constructor...
Calling FunctionOne...
Simple Cat Copy Constructor...
Function One. Returning...
Simple Cat Copy Constructor...
Simple Cat Destructor...
Simple Cat Destructor...
Calling FunctionTwo...
Function Two. Returning...
Simple Cat Destructor...
```

ANALYSIS   A very simplified SimpleCat class is declared on lines 6–12. The constructor, copy constructor, and destructor all print an informative message so that you can tell when they've been called.

On line 34, main() prints out a message, and that is seen on output line 1. On line 35, a SimpleCat object is instantiated. This causes the constructor to be called, and the output from the constructor is seen on output line 2.

On line 36, main() reports that it is calling FunctionOne, which creates output line 3. Because FunctionOne() is called passing the SimpleCat object by value, a copy of the SimpleCat object is made on the stack as an object local to the called function. This causes the copy constructor to be called, which creates output line 4.

Program execution jumps to line 46 in the called function, which prints an informative message, output line 5. The function then returns, and returns the SimpleCat object by value. This creates yet another copy of the object, calling the copy constructor and producing line 6.

The return value from FunctionOne() is not assigned to any object, and so the temporary created for the return is thrown away, calling the destructor, which produces output line 7. Because FunctionOne() has ended, its local copy goes out of scope and is destroyed, calling the destructor and producing line 8.

Program execution returns to main(), and FunctionTwo() is called, but the parameter is passed by reference. No copy is produced, so there's no output. FunctionTwo() prints the message that appears as output line 10 and then returns the SimpleCat object, again by reference, and so again produces no calls to the constructor or destructor.

Finally, the program ends and Frisky goes out of scope, causing one final call to the destructor and printing output line 11.

The net effect of this is that the call to FunctionOne(), because it passed the cat by value, produced two calls to the copy constructor and two to the destructor, while the call to FunctionTwo() produced none.

Passing a const Pointer

Although passing a pointer to FunctionTwo() is more efficient, it is dangerous. FunctionTwo() is not meant to be allowed to change the SimpleCat object it is passed, yet it is given the address of the SimpleCat. This seriously exposes the object to change and defeats the protection offered in passing by value.

Passing by value is like giving a museum a photograph of your masterpiece instead of the real thing. If vandals mark it up, there is no harm done to the original. Passing by reference is like sending your home address to the museum and inviting guests to come over and look at the real thing.

The solution is to pass a pointer to a constant SimpleCat. Doing so prevents calling any non-const method on SimpleCat, and thus protects the object from change.

Passing a const reference allows your guests to see the original painting, but not to alter it in any way. Listing 9.11 demonstrates this idea.

LISTING 9.11   Passing Pointer to a Constant Object

```
0:  //Listing 9.11
1:  // Passing pointers to objects
2:
```

LISTING 9.11   continued

```
 3:  #include <iostream>
 4:
 5:  using namespace std;
 6:  class SimpleCat
 7:  {
 8:  public:
 9:      SimpleCat();
10:      SimpleCat(SimpleCat&);
11:      ~SimpleCat();
12:
13:      int GetAge() const { return itsAge; }
14:      void SetAge(int age) { itsAge = age; }
15:
16:  private:
17:      int itsAge;
18:  };
19:
20:  SimpleCat::SimpleCat()
21:  {
22:      cout << "Simple Cat Constructor...\n";
23:      itsAge = 1;
24:  }
25:
26:  SimpleCat::SimpleCat(SimpleCat&)
27:  {
28:      cout << "Simple Cat Copy Constructor...\n";
29:  }
30:
31:  SimpleCat::~SimpleCat()
32:  {
33:      cout << "Simple Cat Destructor...\n";
34:  }
35:
36:  const SimpleCat * const FunctionTwo
37:      (const SimpleCat * const theCat);
38:
39:  int main()
40:  {
41:      cout << "Making a cat...\n";
42:      SimpleCat Frisky;
43:      cout << "Frisky is " ;
44:      cout << Frisky.GetAge();
45:      cout << " years old\n";
46:      int age = 5;
47:      Frisky.SetAge(age);
48:      cout << "Frisky is " ;
49:      cout << Frisky.GetAge();
50:      cout << " years old\n";
51:      cout << "Calling FunctionTwo...\n";
```

9

LISTING 9.11   continued

```
52:        FunctionTwo(&Frisky);
53:        cout << "Frisky is " ;
54:        cout << Frisky.GetAge();
55:        cout << " years old\n";
56:        return 0;
57:   }
58:
59:   // functionTwo, passes a const pointer
60:   const SimpleCat * const FunctionTwo
61:       (const SimpleCat * const theCat)
62:   {
63:       cout << "Function Two. Returning...\n";
64:       cout << "Frisky is now " << theCat->GetAge();
65:       cout << " years old \n";
66:       // theCat->SetAge(8);    const!
67:       return theCat;
68:   }
```

OUTPUT

```
Making a cat...
Simple Cat constructor...
Frisky is 1 years old
Frisky is 5 years old
Calling FunctionTwo...
FunctionTwo. Returning...
Frisky is now 5 years old
Frisky is 5 years old
Simple Cat Destructor...
```

ANALYSIS   SimpleCat has added two accessor functions, GetAge() on line 13, which is a const function, and SetAge() on line 14, which is not a const function. It has also added the member variable itsAge on line 17.

The constructor, copy constructor, and destructor are still defined to print their messages. The copy constructor is never called, however, because the object is passed by reference and so no copies are made. On line 42, an object is created, and its default age is printed, starting on line 43.

On line 47, itsAge is set using the accessor SetAge, and the result is printed on line 48. FunctionOne is not used in this program, but FunctionTwo() is called. FunctionTwo() has changed slightly; the parameter and return value are now declared, on line 36, to take a constant pointer to a constant object and to return a constant pointer to a constant object.

Because the parameter and return value are still passed by reference, no copies are made and the copy constructor is not called. The object being pointed to in FunctionTwo(), however, is now constant, and thus cannot call the non-const method, SetAge(). If the call to SetAge() on line 66 was not commented out, the program would not compile.

Note that the object created in main() is not constant, and Frisky can call SetAge(). The address of this non-constant object is passed to FunctionTwo(), but because FunctionTwo()'s declaration declares the pointer to be a constant pointer to a constant object, the object is treated as if it were constant!

References as an Alternative

Listing 9.11 solves the problem of making extra copies, and thus saves the calls to the copy constructor and destructor. It uses constant pointers to constant objects, and thereby solves the problem of the function changing the object. It is still somewhat cumbersome, however, because the objects passed to the function are pointers.

Because you know the object will never be null, it would be easier to work within the function if a reference were passed in, rather than a pointer. Listing 9.12 illustrates this.

LISTING 9.12 Passing References to Objects

```
0:   //Listing 9.12
1:   // Passing references to objects
2:
3:   #include <iostream>
4:
5:   using namespace std;
6:   class SimpleCat
7:   {
8:   public:
9:      SimpleCat();
10:     SimpleCat(SimpleCat&);
11:     ~SimpleCat();
12:
13:     int GetAge() const { return itsAge; }
14:     void SetAge(int age) { itsAge = age; }
15:
16:  private:
17:     int itsAge;
18:  };
19:
20:  SimpleCat::SimpleCat()
21:  {
22:     cout << "Simple Cat Constructor...\n";
23:     itsAge = 1;
24:  }
```

LISTING 9.12   continued

```
25:
26:   SimpleCat::SimpleCat(SimpleCat&)
27:   {
28:      cout << "Simple Cat Copy Constructor...\n";
29:   }
30:
31:   SimpleCat::~SimpleCat()
32:   {
33:      cout << "Simple Cat Destructor...\n";
34:   }
35:
36:   const    SimpleCat & FunctionTwo (const SimpleCat & theCat);
37:
38:   int main()
39:   {
40:      cout << "Making a cat...\n";
41:      SimpleCat Frisky;
42:      cout << "Frisky is " << Frisky.GetAge() << " years old\n";
43:      int age = 5;
44:      Frisky.SetAge(age);
45:      cout << "Frisky is " << Frisky.GetAge() << " years old\n";
46:      cout << "Calling FunctionTwo...\n";
47:      FunctionTwo(Frisky);
48:      cout << "Frisky is " << Frisky.GetAge() << " years old\n";
49:      return 0;
50:   }
51:
52:   // functionTwo, passes a ref to a const object
53:   const SimpleCat & FunctionTwo (const SimpleCat & theCat)
54:   {
55:      cout << "Function Two. Returning...\n";
56:      cout << "Frisky is now " << theCat.GetAge();
57:      cout << " years old \n";
58:      // theCat.SetAge(8);    const!
59:      return theCat;
60:   }
```

OUTPUT
```
Making a cat...
Simple Cat constructor...
Frisky is 1 years old
Frisky is 5 years old
Calling FunctionTwo...
FunctionTwo. Returning...
Frisky is now 5 years old
Frisky is 5 years old
Simple Cat Destructor...
```

ANALYSIS The output is identical to that produced by Listing 9.11. The only significant change is that FunctionTwo() now takes and returns a reference to a constant object. Once again, working with references is somewhat simpler than working with pointers, and the same savings and efficiency are achieved, as well as the safety provided by using const.

9

---

const References

C++ programmers do not usually differentiate between "constant reference to a SimpleCat object" and "reference to a constant SimpleCat object." References themselves can never be reassigned to refer to another object, and so they are always constant. If the keyword const is applied to a reference, it is to make the object referred to constant.

When to Use References and When to Use Pointers

C++ programmers strongly prefer references to pointers. References are cleaner and easier to use, and they do a better job of hiding information, as we saw in the previous example.

References cannot be reassigned, however. If you need to point first to one object and then to another, you must use a pointer. References cannot be null, so if any chance exists that the object in question may be null, you must not use a reference. You must use a pointer.

An example of the latter concern is the operator new. If new cannot allocate memory on the free store, it returns a null pointer. Because a reference can't be null, you must not initialize a reference to this memory until you've checked that it is not null. The following example shows how to handle this:

```
int *pInt = new int;
if (pInt != NULL)
int &rInt = *pInt;
```

In this example a pointer to int, pInt, is declared and initialized with the memory returned by the operator new. The address in pInt is tested, and if it is not null, pInt is dereferenced. The result of dereferencing an int variable is an int object, and rInt is initialized to refer to that object. Thus, rInt becomes an alias to the int returned by the operator new.

Do	**Don't**
DO pass parameters by reference whenever possible.	**DON'T** use pointers if references will work.
DO return by reference whenever possible.	
DO use const to protect references and pointers whenever possible.	

Mixing References and Pointers

It is perfectly legal to declare both pointers and references in the same function parameter list, along with objects passed by value. Here's an example:

```
CAT * SomeFunction (Person &theOwner, House *theHouse, int age);
```

This declaration says that SomeFunction takes three parameters. The first is a reference to a Person object, the second is a pointer to a House object, and the third is an integer. It returns a pointer to a CAT object.

The question of where to put the reference (&) or indirection (*) operator when declaring these variables is a great controversy. You may legally write any of the following:

```
1:  CAT&  rFrisky;

2:  CAT & rFrisky;

3:  CAT  &rFrisky;
```

Note

Whitespace is completely ignored, so anywhere you see a space here you may put as many spaces, tabs, and new lines as you like.

Setting aside freedom of expression issues, which is best? Here are the arguments for all three:

The argument for case 1 is that rFrisky is a variable whose name is rFrisky and whose type can be thought of as "reference to CAT object." Thus, this argument goes, the & should be with the type.

The counterargument is that the type is CAT. The & is part of the "declarator," which includes the variable name and the ampersand. More important, having the & near the CAT can lead to the following bug:

```
CAT&  rFrisky, rBoots;
```

Casual examination of this line would lead you to think that both rFrisky and rBoots are references to CAT objects, but you'd be wrong. This really says that rFrisky is a reference to a CAT, and rBoots (despite its name) is not a reference but a plain old CAT variable. This should be rewritten as follows:

```
CAT    &rFrisky, rBoots;
```

The answer to this objection is that declarations of references and variables should never be combined like this. Here's the right answer:

```
CAT& rFrisky;
CAT  boots;
```

Finally, many programmers opt out of the argument and go with the middle position, that of putting the & in the middle of the two, as illustrated in case 2.

Of course, everything said so far about the reference operator (&) applies equally well to the indirection operator (*). The important thing is to recognize that reasonable people differ in their perceptions of the one true way. Choose a style that works for you, and be consistent within any one program; clarity is, and remains, the goal.

Many programmers like the following conventions for declaring references and pointers:

1. Put the ampersand and asterisk in the middle, with a space on either side.

2. Never declare references, pointers, and variables all on the same line.

Don't Return a Reference to an Object That Isn't in Scope!

Once C++ programmers learn to pass by reference, they have a tendency to go hog-wild. It is possible, however, to overdo it. Remember that a reference is always an alias to some other object. If you pass a reference into or out of a function, be sure to ask yourself, "What is the object I'm aliasing, and will it still exist every time it's used?"

Listing 9.13 illustrates the danger of returning a reference to an object that no longer exists.

LISTING 9.13   Returning a Reference to a Non-existent Object

```
0:  // Listing 9.13
1:  // Returning a reference to an object
2:  // which no longer exists
3:
```

LISTING 9.13   continued

```
 4:  #include <iostream>
 5:
 6:
 7:  class SimpleCat
 8:  {
 9:  public:
10:     SimpleCat (int age, int weight);
11:     ~SimpleCat() {}
12:     int GetAge() { return itsAge; }
13:     int GetWeight() { return itsWeight; }
14:  private:
15:     int itsAge;
16:     int itsWeight;
17:  };
18:
19:  SimpleCat::SimpleCat(int age, int weight)
20:  {
21:     itsAge = age;
22:     itsWeight = weight;
23:  }
24:
25:  SimpleCat &TheFunction();
26:
27:  int main()
28:  {
29:     SimpleCat &rCat = TheFunction();
30:     int age = rCat.GetAge();
31:     std::cout << "rCat is " << age << " years old!\n";
32:     return 0;
33:  }
34:
35:  SimpleCat &TheFunction()
36:  {
37:     SimpleCat Frisky(5,9);
38:     return Frisky;
39:  }
```

OUTPUT   Compile error: Attempting to return a reference to a local object!

Caution   This program won't compile on the Borland compiler. It will compile on Microsoft compilers; however, it should be noted that it is a bad coding practice.

ANALYSIS On lines 7–17, SimpleCat is declared. On line 29, a reference to a SimpleCat is initialized with the results of calling TheFunction(), which is declared on line 25 to return a reference to a SimpleCat.

The body of TheFunction() declares a local object of type SimpleCat and initializes its age and weight. It then returns that local object by reference. Some compilers are smart enough to catch this error and won't let you run the program. Others will let you run the program, with unpredictable results.

When TheFunction() returns, the local object, Frisky, will be destroyed (painlessly, I assure you). The reference returned by this function will be an alias to a non-existent object, and this is a bad thing.

Returning a Reference to an Object on the Heap

You might be tempted to solve the problem in Listing 9.13 by having TheFunction() create Frisky on the heap. That way, when you return from TheFunction(), Frisky will still exist.

The problem with this approach is: What do you do with the memory allocated for Frisky when you are done with it? Listing 9.14 illustrates this problem.

LISTING 9.14   Memory Leaks

```
0:  // Listing 9.14
1:  // Resolving memory leaks
2:
3:  #include <iostream>
4:
5:  class SimpleCat
6:  {
7:  public:
8:     SimpleCat (int age, int weight);
9:     ~SimpleCat() {}
10:    int GetAge() { return itsAge; }
11:    int GetWeight() { return itsWeight; }
12:
13: private:
14:    int itsAge;
15:    int itsWeight;
16: };
17:
18: SimpleCat::SimpleCat(int age, int weight)
19: {
```

LISTING 9.14   continued

```
20:        itsAge = age;
21:        itsWeight = weight;
22:    }
23:
24:    SimpleCat & TheFunction();
25:
26:    int main()
27:    {
28:        SimpleCat & rCat = TheFunction();
29:        int age = rCat.GetAge();
30:        std::cout << "rCat is " << age << " years old!\n";
31:        std::cout << "&rCat: " << &rCat << std::endl;
32:        // How do you get rid of that memory?
33:        SimpleCat * pCat = &rCat;
34:        delete pCat;
35:        // Uh oh, rCat now refers to ??
36:        return 0;
37:    }
38:
39:    SimpleCat &TheFunction()
40:    {
41:        SimpleCat * pFrisky = new SimpleCat(5,9);
42:        std::cout << "pFrisky: " << pFrisky << std::endl;
43:        return *pFrisky;
44:    }
```

OUTPUT
```
pFrisky: 0x00431C60
rCat is 5 years old!
&rCat: 0x00431C60
```

Caution This compiles, links, and appears to work. But it is a time bomb waiting to go off.

`TheFunction()` has been changed so that it no longer returns a reference to a local variable. Memory is allocated on the free store and assigned to a pointer on line 41. The address that pointer holds is printed, and then the pointer is dereferenced and the `SimpleCat` object is returned by reference.

On line 28, the return of `TheFunction()` is assigned to a reference to `SimpleCat`, and that object is used to obtain the cat's age, which is printed on line 30.

To prove that the reference declared in main() is referring to the object put on the free store in TheFunction(), the address of operator is applied to rCat. Sure enough, it displays the address of the object it refers to, and this matches the address of the object on the free store.

So far, so good. But how will that memory be freed? You can't call delete on the reference. One clever solution is to create another pointer and initialize it with the address obtained from rCat. This does delete the memory, and it plugs the memory leak. One small problem, though: What is rCat referring to after line 34? As stated earlier, a reference must always alias an actual object; if it references a null object (as this does now), the program is invalid.

Note

> It cannot be overemphasized that a program with a reference to a null object may compile, but it is invalid and its performance is unpredictable.

Three solutions exist to this problem. The first is to declare a SimpleCat object on line 28 and to return that cat from TheFunction by value. The second is to go ahead and declare the SimpleCat on the free store in TheFunction(), but have TheFunction() return a pointer to that memory. Then the calling function can delete the pointer when it is done.

The third workable solution, and the right one, is to declare the object in the calling function and then to pass it to TheFunction() by reference.

Pointer, Pointer, Who Has the Pointer?

When your program allocates memory on the free store, a pointer is returned. It is imperative that you keep a pointer to that memory because once the pointer is lost, the memory cannot be deleted and becomes a memory leak.

As you pass this block of memory between functions, someone will "own" the pointer. Typically, the value in the block will be passed using references, and the function that created the memory is the one that deletes it. But this is a general rule, not an ironclad one.

It is dangerous for one function to create memory and another to free it, however. Ambiguity about who owns the pointer can lead to one of two problems: forgetting to delete a pointer or deleting it twice. Either one can cause serious problems in your program. It is safer to build your functions so that they delete the memory they create.

If you are writing a function that needs to create memory and then pass it back to the calling function, consider changing your interface. Have the calling function allocate the memory and then pass it into your function by reference. This moves all memory management out of your program and back to the function that is prepared to delete it.

Do	Don't
DO pass parameters by value when you must.	**DON'T** pass by reference if the item referred to may go out of scope.
DO return by value when you must.	**DON'T** use references to null objects.

Summary

Today you learned what references are and how they compare to pointers. You saw that references must be initialized to refer to an existing object and cannot be reassigned to refer to anything else. Any action taken on a reference is in fact taken on the reference's target object. Proof of this is that taking the address of a reference returns the address of the target.

You saw that passing objects by reference can be more efficient than passing by value. Passing by reference also allows the called function to change the value in the arguments back in the calling function.

You saw that arguments to functions and values returned from functions can be passed by reference, and that this can be implemented with pointers or with references.

You saw how to use pointers to constant objects and constant references to pass values between functions safely while achieving the efficiency of passing by reference.

Q&A

Q Why have references if pointers can do everything references can?

A References are easier to use and to understand. The indirection is hidden, and no need exists to repeatedly dereference the variable.

Q Why have pointers if references are easier?

A References cannot be null, and they cannot be reassigned. Pointers offer greater flexibility but are slightly more difficult to use.

Q Why would you ever return by value from a function?

A If the object being returned is local, you must return by value or you will be returning a reference to a non-existent object.

Q Given the danger in returning by reference, why not always return by value?

A Far greater efficiency is achieved in returning by reference. Memory is saved and the program runs faster.

Workshop

The Workshop contains quiz questions to help solidify your understanding of the material covered and exercises to provide you with experience in using what you've learned. Try to answer the quiz and exercise questions before checking the answers in Appendix D, and make sure you understand the answers before going to the next chapter.

Quiz

1. What is the difference between a reference and a pointer?

2. When must you use a pointer rather than a reference?

3. What does new return if there is insufficient memory to make your new object?

4. What is a constant reference?

5. What is the difference between passing by reference and passing a reference?

Exercises

1. Write a program that declares an int, a reference to an int, and a pointer to an int. Use the pointer and the reference to manipulate the value in the int.

2. Write a program that declares a constant pointer to a constant integer. Initialize the pointer to an integer variable, varOne. Assign 6 to varOne. Use the pointer to assign 7 to varOne. Create a second integer variable, varTwo. Reassign the pointer to varTwo. Do not compile this exercise yet.

3. Now compile the program in Exercise 2. What produces errors? What produces warnings?

4. Write a program that produces a stray pointer.

5. Fix the program from Exercise 4.

6. Write a program that produces a memory leak.

7. Fix the program from Exercise 6.

8. **BUG BUSTERS:** What is wrong with this program?

```
1:     #include <iostream>
2:     using namespace std;
3:     class CAT
4:     {
5:        public:
```

```
6:            CAT(int age) { itsAge = age; }
7:            ~CAT(){}
8:            int GetAge() const { return itsAge;}
9:        private:
10:           int itsAge;
11:     };
12:
13:     CAT & MakeCat(int age);
14:     int main()
15:     {
16:        int age = 7;
17:        CAT Boots = MakeCat(age);
18:        cout << "Boots is " << Boots.GetAge() << " years old\n";
19:      return 0;
20:     }
21:
22:     CAT & MakeCat(int age)
23:     {
24:        CAT * pCat = new CAT(age);
25:        return *pCat;
26:     }
```

9. Fix the program from Exercise 8.

DAY 10

Advanced Functions

On Day 5, "Functions," you learned the fundamentals of working with functions. Now that you know how pointers and references work, you can do more with functions.

Today you will learn

- How to overload member functions.
- How to overload operators.
- How to write functions to support classes with dynamically allocated variables.

Overloaded Member Functions

On Day 5, you learned how to implement function polymorphism, or function overloading, by writing two or more functions with the same name but with different parameters. Class member functions can be overloaded as well, in much the same way.

The `Rectangle` class, demonstrated in Listing 10.1, has two `DrawShape()` functions. One, which takes no parameters, draws the rectangle based on the class's current values. The other takes two values, width and length, and draws the rectangle based on those values, ignoring the current class values.

LISTING 10.1   Overloading Member Functions

```
0:   //Listing 10.1 Overloading class member functions
1:
2:   #include <iostream>
3:
4:   // Rectangle class declaration
5:   class Rectangle
6:   {
7:   public:
8:       // constructors
9:       Rectangle(int width, int height);
10:      ~Rectangle(){}
11:
12:      // overloaded class function DrawShape
13:      void DrawShape() const;
14:      void DrawShape(int aWidth, int aHeight) const;
15:
16:  private:
17:      int itsWidth;
18:      int itsHeight;
19:  };
20:
21:  //Constructor implementation
22:  Rectangle::Rectangle(int width, int height)
23:  {
24:      itsWidth = width;
25:      itsHeight = height;
26:  }
27:
28:
29:  // Overloaded DrawShape - takes no values
30:  // Draws based on current class member values
31:  void Rectangle::DrawShape() const
32:  {
33:      DrawShape( itsWidth, itsHeight);
34:  }
35:
36:
37:  // overloaded DrawShape - takes two values
38:  // draws shape based on the parameters
39:  void Rectangle::DrawShape(int width, int height) const
40:  {
41:      for (int i = 0; i<height; i++)
```

LISTING 10.1 continued

```
42:     {
43:         for (int j = 0; j< width; j++)
44:         {
45:             std::cout << "*";
46:         }
47:     std::cout << "\n";
48:     }
49: }
50:
51: // Driver program to demonstrate overloaded functions
52: int main()
53: {
54:     // initialize a rectangle to 30,5
55:     Rectangle theRect(30,5);
56:     std::cout << "DrawShape(): \n";
57:     theRect.DrawShape();
58:     std::cout << "\nDrawShape(40,2): \n";
59:     theRect.DrawShape(40,2);
60:     return 0;
61: }
```

OUTPUT

```
DrawShape():
******************************
******************************
******************************
******************************
******************************

DrawShape(40,2):
********************************************************************
********************************************************************
```

ANALYSIS Listing 10.1 represents a stripped-down version of the Week in Review project from Week 1. The test for illegal values has been taken out to save room, as have some of the accessor functions. The main program has been stripped down to a simple driver program, rather than a menu.

The important code, however, is on lines 13 and 14, where DrawShape() is overloaded. The implementation for these overloaded class methods is on lines 29–49. Note that the version of DrawShape() that takes no parameters simply calls the version that takes two parameters, passing in the current member variables. Try very hard to avoid duplicating code in two functions. Otherwise, keeping them in sync when changes are made to one or the other will be difficult and error prone.

The driver program on lines 51–61 creates a rectangle object and then calls DrawShape(), first passing in no parameters and then passing in two unsigned short integers.

The compiler decides which method to call based on the number and type of parameters entered. One can imagine a third overloaded function named DrawShape() that takes one dimension and an enumeration for whether it is the width or height, at the user's choice.

Using Default Values

Just as global functions can have one or more default values, so can each member function of a class. The same rules apply for declaring the default values, as illustrated in Listing 10.2.

LISTING 10.2   Using Default Values

```
0:   //Listing 10.2 Default values in member functions
1:
2:   #include <iostream>
3:
4:   using namespace std;
5:
6:   // Rectangle class declaration
7:   class Rectangle
8:   {
9:   public:
10:      // constructors
11:      Rectangle(int width, int height);
12:      ~Rectangle(){}
13:      void DrawShape(int aWidth, int aHeight,
14:         bool UseCurrentVals = false) const;
15:
16:   private:
17:      int itsWidth;
18:      int itsHeight;
19:   };
20:
21:   //Constructor implementation
22:   Rectangle::Rectangle(int width, int height):
23:   itsWidth(width),         // initializations
24:   itsHeight(height)
25:   {}                       // empty body
26:
27:
28:   // default values used for third parameter
29:   void Rectangle::DrawShape(
30:   int width,
31:   int height,
32:   bool UseCurrentValue
33:   ) const
34:   {
35:      int printWidth;
```

LISTING 10.2   continued

```
36:        int printHeight;
37:
38:        if (UseCurrentValue == true)
39:        {
40:           printWidth = itsWidth;        // use current class values
41:           printHeight = itsHeight;
42:        }
43:        else
44:        {
45:           printWidth = width;           // use parameter values
46:           printHeight = height;
47:        }
48:
49:
50:        for (int i = 0; i<printHeight; i++)
51:        {
52:           for (int j = 0; j< printWidth; j++)
53:           {
54:              cout << "*";
55:           }
56:           cout << "\n";
57:        }
58:   }
59:
60:   // Driver program to demonstrate overloaded functions
61:   int main()
62:   {
63:      // initialize a rectangle to 30,5
64:      Rectangle theRect(30,5);
65:      cout << "DrawShape(0,0,true)...\n";
66:      theRect.DrawShape(0,0,true);
67:      cout <<"DrawShape(40,2)...\n";
68:      theRect.DrawShape(40,2);
69:      return 0;
70:   }
```

OUTPUT

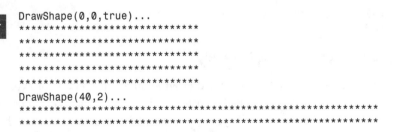

```
DrawShape(0,0,true)...
*****************************
*****************************
*****************************
*****************************
*****************************
DrawShape(40,2)...
**********************************************************
**********************************************************
```

ANALYSIS Listing 10.2 replaces the overloaded DrawShape() function with a single function with default parameters. The function is declared on line 13 to take three parameters. The first two, aWidth and aHeight, are USHORTs, and the third, UseCurrentVals, is a bool that defaults to false.

The implementation for this somewhat awkward function begins on line 28. The third parameter, UseCurrentValue, is evaluated. If it is true, the member variables itsWidth and itsHeight are used to set the local variables printWidth and printHeight, respectively.

If UseCurrentValue is false, either because it has defaulted false or was set by the user, the first two parameters are used for setting printWidth and printHeight.

Note that if UseCurrentValue is true, the values of the other two parameters are completely ignored.

Choosing Between Default Values and Overloaded Functions

Listings 10.1 and 10.2 accomplish the same thing, but the overloaded functions in Listing 10.1 are easier to understand and more natural to use. Also, if a third variation is needed—perhaps the user wants to supply either the width or the height, but not both—it is easy to extend the overloaded functions. The default value, however, will quickly become unusably complex as new variations are added.

How do you decide whether to use function overloading or default values? Here's a rule of thumb:

Use function overloading when

- No reasonable default value exists.
- You need different algorithms.
- You need to support variant types in your parameter list.

The Default Constructor

As discussed on Day 6, "Object-Oriented Programming," if you do not explicitly declare a constructor for your class, a default constructor is created that takes no parameters and does nothing. You are free to make your own default constructor, however, that takes no arguments but that "sets up" your object as required.

The constructor provided for you is called the "default" constructor, but by convention so is any constructor that takes no parameters. This can be a bit confusing, but it is usually clear from the context which one is meant.

Take note that if you make any constructors at all, the default constructor is not provided by the compiler. So if you want a constructor that takes no parameters and you've created any other constructors, you must add the default constructor yourself!

Overloading Constructors

The point of a constructor is to establish the object; for example, the point of a Rectangle constructor is to make a valid rectangle object. Before the constructor runs, no rectangle exists, only an area of memory. After the constructor finishes, there is a complete, ready-to-use rectangle object.

Constructors, like all member functions, can be overloaded. The capability to overload constructors is very powerful and very flexible.

For example, you might have a rectangle object that has two constructors: The first takes a length and a width and makes a rectangle of that size. The second takes no values and makes a default-sized rectangle. Listing 10.3 implements this idea.

LISTING 10.3   Overloading the Constructor

```
0:   // Listing 10.3
1:   // Overloading constructors
2:
3:   #include <iostream>
4:   using namespace std;
5:
6:   class Rectangle
7:   {
8:   public:
9:      Rectangle();
10:     Rectangle(int width, int length);
11:     ~Rectangle() {}
12:     int GetWidth() const { return itsWidth; }
13:     int GetLength() const { return itsLength; }
14:  private:
15:     int itsWidth;
16:     int itsLength;
17:  };
18:
19:  Rectangle::Rectangle()
20:  {
21:     itsWidth = 5;
```

LISTING 10.3   continued

```
22:        itsLength = 10;
23:    }
24:
25:    Rectangle::Rectangle (int width, int length)
26:    {
27:        itsWidth = width;
28:        itsLength = length;
29:    }
30:
31:    int main()
32:    {
33:        Rectangle Rect1;
34:        cout << "Rect1 width: " << Rect1.GetWidth() << endl;
35:        cout << "Rect1 length: " << Rect1.GetLength() << endl;
36:
37:        int aWidth, aLength;
38:        cout << "Enter a width: ";
39:        cin >> aWidth;
40:        cout << "\nEnter a length: ";
41:        cin >> aLength;
42:
43:        Rectangle Rect2(aWidth, aLength);
44:        cout << "\nRect2 width: " << Rect2.GetWidth() << endl;
45:        cout << "Rect2 length: " << Rect2.GetLength() << endl;
46:        return 0;
47:    }
```

OUTPUT
```
Rect1 width: 5
Rect1 length: 10
Enter a width: 20

Enter a length: 50

Rect2 width: 20
Rect2 length: 50
```

ANALYSIS The Rectangle class is declared on lines 6–17. Two constructors are declared: the "default constructor" on line 9 and a second constructor on line 10, which takes two integer variables.

On line 33, a rectangle is created using the default constructor, and its values are printed on lines 34 and 35. On lines 38–41, the user is prompted for a width and length, and the constructor taking two parameters is called on line 43. Finally, the width and height for this rectangle are printed on lines 44 and 45.

Just as it does any overloaded function, the compiler chooses the right constructor, based on the number and type of the parameters.

Initializing Objects

Up to now, you've been setting the member variables of objects in the body of the constructor. Constructors, however, are invoked in two stages: the initialization stage and the body.

Most variables can be set in either stage, either by initializing in the initialization stage or by assigning in the body of the constructor. It is cleaner, and often more efficient, to initialize member variables at the initialization stage. The following example shows how to initialize member variables:

```
CAT():           // constructor name and parameters
itsAge(5),       // initialization list
itsWeight(8)
{ }                      // body of constructor
```

After the closing parentheses on the constructor's parameter list, write a colon. Then write the name of the member variable and a pair of parentheses. Inside the parentheses, write the expression to be used to initialize that member variable. If more than one initialization exists, separate each one with a comma. Listing 10.4 shows the definition of the constructors from Listing 10.3 with initialization of the member variables rather than assignment.

LISTING 10.4   A Code Snippet Showing Initialization of Member Variables

```
0: Listing 10.4 - Initializing Member Variables
1:   Rectangle::Rectangle():
2:       itsWidth(5),
3:       itsLength(10)
4:   {
5:   }
6:
7:   Rectangle::Rectangle (int width, int length):
8:       itsWidth(width),
9:       itsLength(length)
10:  {
11:  }
```

No output.

Some variables must be initialized and cannot be assigned to, such as references and constants. It is common to have other assignments or action statements in the body of the constructor; however, it is best to use initialization as much as possible.

The Copy Constructor

In addition to providing a default constructor and destructor, the compiler provides a default copy constructor. The copy constructor is called every time a copy of an object is made.

When you pass an object by value, either into a function or as a function's return value, a temporary copy of that object is made. If the object is a user-defined object, the class's copy constructor is called, as you saw yesterday in Listing 9.6.

All copy constructors take one parameter, a reference to an object of the same class. It is a good idea to make it a constant reference because the constructor will not have to alter the object passed in. For example:

```
CAT(const CAT & theCat);
```

Here the CAT constructor takes a constant reference to an existing CAT object. The goal of the copy constructor is to make a copy of theCat.

The default copy constructor simply copies each member variable from the object passed as a parameter to the member variables of the new object. This is called a member-wise (or shallow) copy, and although this is fine for most member variables, it breaks pretty quickly for member variables that are pointers to objects on the free store.

A shallow or member-wise copy copies the exact values of one object's member variables into another object. Pointers in both objects end up pointing to the same memory. A deep copy copies the values allocated on the heap to newly allocated memory.

If the CAT class includes a member variable, itsAge, that points to an integer on the free store, the default copy constructor will copy the passed-in CAT's itsAge member variable to the new CAT's itsAge member variable. The two objects will now point to the same memory, as illustrated in Figure 10.1.

FIGURE 10.1

Using the default copy constructor.

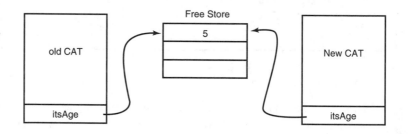

This will lead to a disaster when either CAT goes out of scope. As mentioned on Day 8, "Pointers," the job of the destructor is to clean up this memory. If the original CAT's destructor frees this memory and the new CAT is still pointing to the memory, a stray pointer has been created, and the program is in mortal danger. Figure 10.2 illustrates this problem.

FIGURE 10.2

Creating a stray pointer.

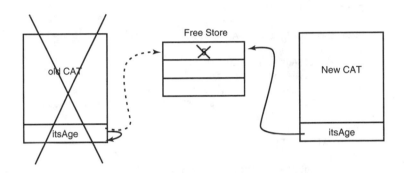

The solution to this is to create your own copy constructor and to allocate the memory as required. After the memory is allocated, the old values can be copied into the new memory. This is called a deep copy. Listing 10.5 illustrates how to do this.

LISTING 10.5   Copy Constructors

```
0:  // Listing 10.5
1:  // Copy constructors
2:
3:  #include <iostream>
4:  using namespace std;
5:
6:  class CAT
7:  {
8:  public:
9:     CAT();                  // default constructor
10:    CAT (const CAT &);   // copy constructor
11:    ~CAT();                 // destructor
12:    int GetAge()    const   { return *itsAge; }
13:    int GetWeight()   const   { return *itsWeight; }
14:    void SetAge(int age)    { *itsAge = age; }
15:
16:  private:
17:     int *itsAge;
18:     int *itsWeight;
19:  };
20:
21:  CAT::CAT()
```

10

LISTING 10.5   continued

```
22:    {
23:        itsAge = new int;
24:        itsWeight = new int;
25:        *itsAge = 5;
26:        *itsWeight = 9;
27:    }
28:
29:    CAT::CAT(const CAT & rhs)
30:    {
31:        itsAge = new int;
32:        itsWeight = new int;
33:        *itsAge = rhs.GetAge();   // public access
34:        *itsWeight = *(rhs.itsWeight); // private access
35:    }
36:
37:    CAT::~CAT()
38:    {
39:        delete itsAge;
40:        itsAge = 0;
41:        delete itsWeight;
42:        itsWeight = 0;
43:    }
44:
45:    int main()
46:    {
47:        CAT frisky;
48:        cout << "frisky's age: " << frisky.GetAge() << endl;
49:        cout << "Setting frisky to 6...\n";
50:        frisky.SetAge(6);
51:        cout << "Creating boots from frisky\n";
52:        CAT boots(frisky);
53:        cout << "frisky's age: " <<     frisky.GetAge() << endl;
54:        cout << "boots' age: " << boots.GetAge() << endl;
55:        cout << "setting frisky to 7...\n";
56:        frisky.SetAge(7);
57:        cout << "frisky's age: " <<     frisky.GetAge() << endl;
58:        cout << "boot's age: " << boots.GetAge() << endl;
59:        return 0;
60:    }
```

OUTPUT

```
frisky's age: 5
Setting frisky to 6...
Creating boots from frisky
frisky's age: 6
boots' age:  6
setting frisky to 7...
frisky's age: 7
boots' age: 6
```

ANALYSIS On lines 6–19, the CAT class is declared. Note that on line 9 a default constructor is declared, and on line 10 a copy constructor is declared.

On lines 17 and 18, two member variables are declared, each as a pointer to an integer. Typically there would be little reason for a class to store int member variables as pointers, but this was done to illustrate how to manage member variables on the free store.

The default constructor on lines 21–27 allocates room on the free store for two int variables and then assigns values to them.

The copy constructor begins on line 29. Note that the parameter is rhs. It is common to refer to the parameter to a copy constructor as rhs, which stands for right-hand side. When you look at the assignments in lines 33 and 34, you'll see that the object passed in as a parameter is on the right-hand side of the equal sign. Here's how it works:

On lines 31 and 32, memory is allocated on the free store. Then, on lines 33 and 34, the value at the new memory location is assigned the values from the existing CAT.

The parameter rhs is a CAT that is passed into the copy constructor as a constant reference. As a CAT object, rhs has all the member variables of any other CAT.

Any CAT object can access private member variables of any other CAT object; however, it is good programming practice to use public accessor methods when possible. The member function rhs.GetAge() returns the value stored in the memory pointed to by rhs's member variable itsAge.

Figure 10.3 diagrams what is happening here. The values pointed to by the existing CAT's member variables are copied to the memory allocated for the new CAT.

FIGURE 10.3

Deep copy illustrated.

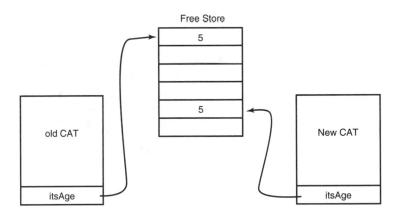

On line 47, a CAT called frisky is created. frisky's age is printed, and then his age is set to 6 on line 50. On line 52, a new CAT, boots, is created, using the copy constructor and passing in frisky. Had frisky been passed as a parameter to a function by value (not by reference), this same call to the copy constructor would have been made by the compiler.

On lines 53 and 54, the ages of both CATs are printed. Sure enough, boots has frisky's age, 6, not the default age of 5. On line 56, frisky's age is set to 7, and then the ages are printed again. This time frisky's age is 7, but boots's age is still 6, demonstrating that they are stored in separate areas of memory.

When the CATs fall out of scope, their destructors are automatically invoked. The implementation of the CAT destructor is shown on lines 37–43. delete is called on both pointers, itsAge and itsWeight, returning the allocated memory to the free store. Also, for safety, the pointers are reassigned to NULL.

Operator Overloading

C++ has a number of built-in types, including int, real, char, and so forth. Each of these has a number of built-in operators, such as addition (+) and multiplication (*). C++ enables you to add these operators to your own classes as well.

To explore operator overloading fully, Listing 10.6 creates a new class, Counter. A Counter object will be used in counting (surprise!) in loops and other applications where a number must be incremented, decremented, or otherwise tracked.

LISTING 10.6   The Counter Class

```
0:   // Listing 10.6
1:   // The Counter class
2:
3:   #include <iostream>
4:   using namespace std;
5:
6:   class Counter
7:   {
8:   public:
9:       Counter();
10:      ~Counter(){}
11:      int GetItsVal()const { return itsVal; }
12:      void SetItsVal(int x) {itsVal = x; }
13:
14:  private:
15:      int itsVal;
16:
17:  };
```

LISTING 10.6   continued

```
18:
19:  Counter::Counter():
20:  itsVal(0)
21:  {}
22:
23:  int main()
24:  {
25:      Counter i;
26:      cout << "The value of i is " << i.GetItsVal() << endl;
27:      return 0;
28:  }
```

OUTPUT

```
The value of i is 0
```

ANALYSIS   As it stands, this is a pretty useless class. It is defined on lines 6–17. Its only member variable is an int. The default constructor, which is declared on line 9 and whose implementation is on line 19, initializes the one member variable, itsVal, to zero.

Unlike an honest, red-blooded int, the Counter object cannot be incremented, decremented, added, assigned, or otherwise manipulated. In exchange for this, it makes printing its value far more difficult!

Writing an Increment Function

Operator overloading restores much of the functionality that has been stripped out of this class. Two ways exist, for example, to add the capability to increment a Counter object. The first is to write an increment method, as shown in Listing 10.7.

LISTING 10.7   Adding an Increment Operator

```
0:   // Listing 10.7
1:   // The Counter class
2:
3:   #include <iostream>
4:   using namespace std;
5:
6:   class Counter
7:   {
8:   public:
9:       Counter();
10:      ~Counter(){}
11:      int GetItsVal()const { return itsVal; }
12:      void SetItsVal(int x) {itsVal = x; }
```

LISTING 10.7   continued

```
13:      void Increment() { ++itsVal; }
14:
15:  private:
16:     int itsVal;
17:
18:  };
19:
20:  Counter::Counter():
21:  itsVal(0)
22:  {}
23:
24:  int main()
25:  {
26:     Counter i;
27:     cout << "The value of i is " << i.GetItsVal() << endl;
28:     i.Increment();
29:     cout << "The value of i is " << i.GetItsVal() << endl;
30:     return 0;
31:  }
```

OUTPUT
```
The value of i is 0
The value of i is 1
```

ANALYSIS   Listing 10.7 adds an Increment function, defined on line 13. Although this
            works, it is cumbersome to use. The program cries out for the capability to add
a ++ operator, and of course, this can be done.

Overloading the Prefix Operator

Prefix operators can be overloaded by declaring functions with the form:

```
returnType Operator op()
```

Here, op is the operator to overload. Thus, the ++ operator can be overloaded with the
following syntax:

```
void operator++ ()
```

Listing 10.8 demonstrates this alternative.

LISTING 10.8   Overloading operator++

```
0:  // Listing 10.8
1:  // The Counter class
2:  // prefix increment operator
3:
4:  #include <iostream>
```

LISTING 10.8   continued

```
 5:  using namespace std;
 6:
 7:  class Counter
 8:  {
 9:  public:
10:      Counter();
11:      ~Counter(){}
12:      int GetItsVal()const { return itsVal; }
13:      void SetItsVal(int x) {itsVal = x; }
14:      void Increment() { ++itsVal; }
15:      void operator++ () { ++itsVal; }
16:
17:  private:
18:      int itsVal;
19:
20:  };
21:
22:  Counter::Counter():
23:  itsVal(0)
24:  {}
25:
26:  int main()
27:  {
28:      Counter i;
29:      cout << "The value of i is " << i.GetItsVal() << endl;
30:      i.Increment();
31:      cout << "The value of i is " << i.GetItsVal() << endl;
32:      ++i;
33:      cout << "The value of i is " << i.GetItsVal() << endl;
34:      return 0;
35:  }
```

OUTPUT

```
The value of i is 0
The value of i is 1
The value of i is 2
```

ANALYSIS   On line 15, operator++ is overloaded, and it's used on line 32. This is much closer to the syntax of a built-in type such as int. At this point, you might consider putting in the extra capabilities for which Counter was created in the first place, such as detecting when the Counter overruns its maximum size.

A significant defect exists in the way the increment operator was written, however. If you want to put the Counter on the right side of an assignment, it will fail. For example:

Counter a = ++i;

This code intends to create a new `Counter`, a, and then assign to it the value in i after i is incremented. The built-in copy constructor will handle the assignment, but the current increment operator does not return a `Counter` object. It returns void. You can't assign a void object to a `Counter` object. (You can't make something from nothing!)

Returning Types in Overloaded Operator Functions

Clearly, what you want is to return a `Counter` object so that it can be assigned to another `Counter` object. Which object should be returned? One approach would be to create a temporary object and return that. Listing 10.9 illustrates this approach.

LISTING 10.9   Returning a Temporary Object

```
0:   // Listing 10.9
1:   // operator++ returns a temporary object
2:
3:   #include <iostream>
4:
5:   using namespace std;
6:
7:   class Counter
8:   {
9:   public:
10:      Counter();
11:      ~Counter(){}
12:      int GetItsVal()const { return itsVal; }
13:      void SetItsVal(int x) {itsVal = x; }
14:      void Increment() { ++itsVal; }
15:      Counter operator++ ();
16:
17:   private:
18:      int itsVal;
19:
20:   };
21:
22:   Counter::Counter():
23:   itsVal(0)
24:   {}
25:
26:   Counter Counter::operator++()
27:   {
28:      ++itsVal;
29:      Counter temp;
30:      temp.SetItsVal(itsVal);
31:      return temp;
32:   }
33:
34:   int main()
```

LISTING 10.9   continued

```
35:  {
36:     Counter i;
37:     cout << "The value of i is " << i.GetItsVal() << endl;
38:     i.Increment();
39:     cout << "The value of i is " << i.GetItsVal() << endl;
40:     ++i;
41:     cout << "The value of i is " << i.GetItsVal() << endl;
42:     Counter a = ++i;
43:     cout << "The value of a: " << a.GetItsVal();
44:     cout << " and i: " << i.GetItsVal() << endl;
45:     return 0;
46:  }
```

OUTPUT

```
The value of i is 0
The value of i is 1
The value of i is 2
The value of a: 3 and i: 3
```

10

ANALYSIS In this version, operator++ has been declared on line 15 to return a Counter object. On line 29, a temporary variable, temp, is created, and its value is set to match that in the current object. That temporary variable is returned and immediately assigned to a on line 42.

Returning Nameless Temporaries

There is really no need to name the temporary object created on line 29. If Counter had a constructor that took a value, you could simply return the result of that constructor as the return value of the increment operator. Listing 10.10 illustrates this idea.

LISTING 10.10   Returning a Nameless Temporary Object

```
0:  // Listing 10.10
1:  // operator++ returns a nameless temporary object
2:
3:  #include <iostream>
4:
5:  using namespace std;
6:
7:  class Counter
8:  {
9:  public:
10:     Counter();
11:     Counter(int val);
12:     ~Counter(){}
13:     int GetItsVal()const { return itsVal; }
14:     void SetItsVal(int x) {itsVal = x; }
```

LISTING 10.10   continued

```
15:        void Increment() { ++itsVal; }
16:        Counter operator++ ();
17:
18:    private:
19:        int itsVal;
20:
21:    };
22:
23:    Counter::Counter():
24:    itsVal(0)
25:    {}
26:
27:    Counter::Counter(int val):
28:    itsVal(val)
29:    {}
30:
31:    Counter Counter::operator++()
32:    {
33:        ++itsVal;
34:        return Counter (itsVal);
35:    }
36:
37:    int main()
38:    {
39:        Counter i;
40:        cout << "The value of i is " << i.GetItsVal() << endl;
41:        i.Increment();
42:        cout << "The value of i is " << i.GetItsVal() << endl;
43:        ++i;
44:        cout << "The value of i is " << i.GetItsVal() << endl;
45:        Counter a = ++i;
46:        cout << "The value of a: " << a.GetItsVal();
47:        cout << " and i: " << i.GetItsVal() << endl;
48:        return 0;
49:    }
```

OUTPUT
```
The value of i is 0
The value of i is 1
The value of i is 2
The value of a: 3 and i: 3
```

ANALYSIS On line 11, a new constructor is declared that takes an int. The implementation is on lines 27–29. It initializes itsVal with the passed-in value.

The implementation of operator++ is now simplified. On line 33, itsVal is incremented. Then on line 34, a temporary Counter object is created, initialized to the value in itsVal, and then returned as the result of the operator++.

This is more elegant, but raises the question, "Why create a temporary object at all?" Remember that each temporary object must be constructed and later destroyed—each of these is potentially an expensive operation. Also, the object i already exists and already has the right value, so why not return it? We'll solve this problem by using the this pointer.

Using the this Pointer

The this pointer is passed to all member functions, including overloaded operators such as operator++(). The this pointer points to i, and if it is dereferenced it will return the object i, which already has the right value in its member variable itsVal. Listing 10.11 illustrates returning the dereferenced this pointer and avoiding the creation of an unneeded temporary object.

10

LISTING 10.11   Returning the this Pointer

```
0:   // Listing 10.11
1:   // Returning the dereferenced this pointer
2:
3:   #include <iostream>
4:
5:   using namespace std;
6:
7:   class Counter
8:   {
9:   public:
10:      Counter();
11:      ~Counter(){}
12:      int GetItsVal()const { return itsVal; }
13:      void SetItsVal(int x) {itsVal = x; }
14:      void Increment() { ++itsVal; }
15:      const Counter& operator++ ();
16:
17:   private:
18:      int itsVal;
19:
20:   };
21:
22:   Counter::Counter():
23:   itsVal(0)
24:   {};
25:
26:   const Counter& Counter::operator++()
27:   {
28:      ++itsVal;
29:      return *this;
30:   }
31:
```

LISTING 10.11   continued

```
32:  int main()
33:  {
34:      Counter i;
35:      cout << "The value of i is " << i.GetItsVal() << endl;
36:      i.Increment();
37:      cout << "The value of i is " << i.GetItsVal() << endl;
38:      ++i;
39:      cout << "The value of i is " << i.GetItsVal() << endl;
40:      Counter a = ++i;
41:      cout << "The value of a: " << a.GetItsVal();
42:      cout << " and i: " << i.GetItsVal() << endl;
43:      return 0;
44:  }
```

OUTPUT
```
The value of i is 0
The value of i is 1
The value of i is 2
The value of a: 3 and i: 3
```

ANALYSIS The implementation of `operator++`, on lines 26–30, has been changed to dereference the `this` pointer and to return the current object. This provides a `Counter` object to be assigned to a. As discussed, if the `Counter` object allocated memory, it would be important to override the copy constructor. In this case, the default copy constructor works fine.

Note that the value returned is a `Counter` reference, thereby avoiding the creation of an extra temporary object. It is a const reference because the value should not be changed by the function using the returned `Counter`.

Why Constant?

The returned `Counter` object must be constant. If it were not, it would be possible to perform operations on that returned object that might change its values. For example, if the returned value were not constant, then you might write

```
40:      Counter a = ++++i;
```

This would translate to calling the increment operator (++) on the result of calling the increment operator, which we'd like to block.

Try this: Change the return value to non-constant in both the declaration and the implementation (lines 15 and 26), and change line 40 as shown (++++i). Put a break point in your debugger on line 40 and step in. You will find that you step into the increment operator twice. The increment is being applied to the (now non-constant) return value.

It is to prevent this that we declare the return value to be constant. If you change lines 15 and 26 back to constant, and leave line 40 as shown (++++i) the compiler will complain that you can't call the increment operator on a constant object.

Overloading the Postfix Operator

So far, you've overloaded the prefix operator. What if you want to overload the postfix increment operator? Here the compiler has a problem: How is it to differentiate between prefix and postfix? By convention, an integer variable is supplied as a parameter to the operator declaration. The parameter's value is ignored; it is just a signal that this is the postfix operator.

Difference Between Prefix and Postfix

Before we can write the postfix operator, we must understand how it is different from the prefix operator. We reviewed this in detail on Day 4, "Expressions and Statements" (see Listing 4.3).

To review, prefix says "increment, and then fetch," but postfix says "fetch, and then increment."

Thus, although the prefix operator can simply increment the value and then return the object itself, the postfix must return the value that existed before it was incremented. To do this, we must create a temporary object that will hold the original value, then increment the value of the original object, and then return the temporary.

Let's go over that again. Consider the following line of code:

```
a = x++;
```

If x was 5, after this statement a is 5, but x is 6. Thus, we returned the value in x and assigned it to a, and then we increased the value of x. If x is an object, its postfix increment operator must stash away the original value (5) in a temporary object, increment x's value to 6, and then return that temporary object to assign its original value to a.

Note that because we are returning the temporary, we must return it by value and not by reference, because the temporary will go out of scope as soon as the function returns.

Listing 10.12 demonstrates the use of both the prefix and the postfix operators.

LISTING 10.12   Prefix and Postfix Operators

```
0:  // Listing 10.12
1:  // Returning the dereferenced this pointer
2:
3:  #include <iostream>
```

LISTING **10.12**   continued

```
4:
5:   using namespace std;
6:
7:   class Counter
8:   {
9:   public:
10:     Counter();
11:     ~Counter(){}
12:     int GetItsVal()const { return itsVal; }
13:     void SetItsVal(int x) {itsVal = x; }
14:     const Counter& operator++ ();        // prefix
15:     const Counter operator++ (int); // postfix
16:
17:   private:
18:     int itsVal;
19:   };
20:
21:   Counter::Counter():
22:   itsVal(0)
23:   {}
24:
25:   const Counter& Counter::operator++()
26:   {
27:       ++itsVal;
28:       return *this;
29:   }
30:
31:   const Counter Counter::operator++(int theFlag)
32:   {
33:       Counter temp(*this);
34:       ++itsVal;
35:       return temp;
36:   }
37:
38:   int main()
39:   {
40:       Counter i;
41:       cout << "The value of i is " << i.GetItsVal() << endl;
42:       i++;
43:       cout << "The value of i is " << i.GetItsVal() << endl;
44:       ++i;
45:       cout << "The value of i is " << i.GetItsVal() << endl;
46:       Counter a = ++i;
47:       cout << "The value of a: " << a.GetItsVal();
48:       cout << " and i: " << i.GetItsVal() << endl;
49:       a = i++;
50:       cout << "The value of a: " << a.GetItsVal();
51:       cout << " and i: " << i.GetItsVal() << endl;
52:       return 0;
53:   }
```

```
The value of i is 0
The value of i is 1
The value of i is 2
The value of a: 3 and i: 3
The value of a: 3 and i: 4
```

The postfix operator is declared on line 15 and implemented on lines 31–36. The prefix operator is declared on line 14.

The parameter passed into the postfix operator on line 32 (theFlag) serves to signal that it is the postfix operator, but this value is never used.

The Addition Operator

The increment operator is a unary operator. It operates on only one object. The addition operator (+) is a binary operator, in which two objects are involved. How do you implement overloading the + operator for Count?

The goal is to be able to declare two Counter variables and then add them, as in the following example:

```
Counter varOne, varTwo, varThree;
VarThree = VarOne + VarTwo;
```

Once again, you could start by writing a function, Add(), which would take a Counter as its argument, add the values, and then return a Counter with the result. Listing 10.13 illustrates this approach.

LISTING 10.13   The Add() Function

```
0:   // Listing 10.13
1:   // Add function
2:
3:   #include <iostream.h>
4:
5:   using namespace std;
6:
7:   class Counter
8:   {
9:   public:
10:      Counter();
11:      Counter(int initialValue);
12:      ~Counter(){}
13:      int GetItsVal()const { return itsVal; }
14:      void SetItsVal(int x) {itsVal = x; }
15:      Counter Add(const Counter &);
16:
17:   private:
18:      int itsVal;
```

LISTING 10.13   continued

```
19:
20:  };
21:
22:  Counter::Counter(int initialValue):
23:  itsVal(initialValue)
24:  {}
25:
26:  Counter::Counter():
27:  itsVal(0)
28:  {}
29:
30:  Counter Counter::Add(const Counter & rhs)
31:  {
32:      return Counter(itsVal+ rhs.GetItsVal());
33:  }
34:
35:  int main()
36:  {
37:      Counter varOne(2), varTwo(4), varThree;
38:      varThree = varOne.Add(varTwo);
39:      cout << "varOne: " << varOne.GetItsVal()<< endl;
40:      cout << "varTwo: " << varTwo.GetItsVal() << endl;
41:      cout << "varThree: " << varThree.GetItsVal() << endl;
42:
43:    return 0;
44:  }
```

OUTPUT
```
varOne: 2
varTwo: 4
varThree: 6
```

ANALYSIS The Add() function is declared on line 15. It takes a constant Counter reference, which is the number to add to the current object. It returns a Counter object, which is the result to be assigned to the left side of the assignment statement, as shown on line 38. That is, VarOne is the object, varTwo is the parameter to the Add() function, and the result is assigned to VarThree.

In order to create varThree without having to initialize a value for it, a default constructor is required. The default constructor initializes itsVal to 0, as shown on lines 26–28. Because varOne and varTwo need to be initialized to a nonzero value, another constructor was created, as shown on lines 22–24. Another solution to this problem is to provide the default value 0 to the constructor declared on line 11.

Overloading operator+

The Add() function itself is shown on lines 30–33 of Listing 10.13. It works, but its use is unnatural. Overloading the + operator would make for a more natural use of the Counter class. Listing 10.14 illustrates this.

LISTING 10.14   operator+

```
0:  // Listing 10.14
1:  //Overload operator plus (+)
2:
3:  #include <iostream>
4:
5:  using namespace std;
6:
7:  class Counter
8:  {
9:  public:
10:     Counter();
11:     Counter(int initialValue);
12:     ~Counter(){}
13:     int GetItsVal()const { return itsVal; }
14:     void SetItsVal(int x) {itsVal = x; }
15:     Counter operator+ (const Counter &);
16:  private:
17:     int itsVal;
18:  };
19:
20:  Counter::Counter(int initialValue):
21:  itsVal(initialValue)
22:  {}
23:
24:  Counter::Counter():
25:  itsVal(0)
26:  {}
27:
28:  Counter Counter::operator+ (const Counter & rhs)
29:  {
30:      return Counter(itsVal + rhs.GetItsVal());
31:  }
32:
33:  int main()
34:  {
35:      Counter varOne(2), varTwo(4), varThree;
36:      varThree = varOne + varTwo;
37:      cout << "varOne: " << varOne.GetItsVal()<< endl;
38:      cout << "varTwo: " << varTwo.GetItsVal() << endl;
39:      cout << "varThree: " << varThree.GetItsVal() << endl;
40:
41:      return 0;
42:  }
```

10

varOne: 2
varTwo: 4
varThree: 6

 operator+ is declared on line 15 and defined on lines 28–31.

Compare these with the declaration and definition of the Add() function in the previous listing; they are nearly identical. The syntax of their use, however, is quite different. It is more natural to say this:

```
varThree = varOne + varTwo;
```

than to say:

```
varThree = varOne.Add(varTwo);
```

Not a big change, but enough to make the program easier to use and understand.

On line 36 the operator is used

```
36:        varThree = varOne + varTwo;
```

This is translated by the compiler into

```
VarThree = varOne.Operator+(varTwo);
```

You could, of course, have written it this way yourself, and the compiler would have been equally happy.

The operator+ method is called on the left-hand operand, passing in the right-hand operand.

Issues in Operator Overloading

Overloaded operators can be member functions, as described in this chapter, or nonmember functions. The latter will be described on Day 15, "Special Classes and Functions," when we discuss friend functions.

The only operators that must be class members are the assignment (=), subscript ([ ]), function call (( )), and indirection (->) operators.

Operator [ ] will be discussed on Day 13, when arrays are covered. Overloading operator -> will be discussed on Day 15, when smart pointers are discussed.

Limitations on Operator Overloading

Operators forfor built-in types (such as int) cannot be overloaded. The precedence order cannot be changed, and the arity of the operator, that is, whether it is unary or binary, cannot be changed. You cannot make up new operators, so you cannot declare ** to be the "power of" operator.

Arity refers to how many terms are used in the operator. Some C++ operators are unary and use only one term (myValue++). Some operators are binary and use two terms (a+b). Only one operator is ternary and uses three terms. The ? operator is often called the ternary operator because it is the only ternary operator in C++ (a > b ? x : y).

What to Overload

Operator overloading is one of the aspects of C++ most overused and abused by new programmers. It is tempting to create new and interesting uses for some of the more obscure operators, but these invariably lead to code that is confusing and difficult to read.

Of course, making the + operator subtract and the * operator add can be fun, but no professional programmer would do that. The greater danger lies in the well-intentioned but idiosyncratic use of an operator—using + to mean concatenate a series of letters or / to mean split a string. There is good reason to consider these uses, but there is even better reason to proceed with caution. Remember, the goal of overloading operators is to increase usability and understanding.

Do	Don't
DO use operator overloading when it will clarify the program.	DON'T create counterintuitive operators.
DO return an object of the class from overloaded operators.	

The Assignment Operator

The fourth and final function that is supplied by the compiler, if you don't specify one, is the assignment operator (operator=()). This operator is called whenever you assign to an object. For example:

```
CAT catOne(5,7);
CAT catTwo(3,4);
// ... other code here
catTwo = catOne;
```

Here, catOne is created and initialized with itsAge equal to 5 and itsWeight equal to 7. catTwo is then created and assigned the values 3 and 4.

After a while, catTwo is assigned the values in catOne. Two issues are raised here: What happens if itsAge is a pointer, and what happens to the original values in catTwo?

Handling member variables that store their values on the free store was discussed earlier during the examination of the copy constructor. The same issues arise here, as you saw illustrated in Figures 10.1 and 10.2.

C++ programmers differentiate between a shallow, or memberwise, copy on the one hand and a deep copy on the other. A shallow copy just copies the members, and both objects end up pointing to the same area on the free store. A deep copy allocates the necessary memory. This is illustrated in Figure 10.3.

An added wrinkle occurs with the assignment operator, however. The object catTwo already exists and has memory already allocated. That memory must be deleted if there is to be no memory leak. But what happens if you assign catTwo to itself?

```
catTwo = catTwo;
```

No one is likely to do this on purpose, but it is possible for this to happen by accident when references and dereferenced pointers hide the fact that the assignment is to itself.

If you did not handle this problem carefully, catTwo would delete its memory allocation. Then, when it was ready to copy in the memory from the right-hand side of the assignment, it would have a very big problem: The value would be gone!

To protect against this, your assignment operator must check to see if the right-hand side of the assignment operator is the object itself. It does this by examining the this pointer. Listing 10.15 shows a class with an assignment operator.

LISTING 10.15   An Assignment Operator

```
0:   // Listing 10.15
1:   // Copy constructors
2:
3:   #include <iostream>
4:
5:   using namespace std;
6:
7:   class CAT
8:   {
9:   public:
10:      CAT();              // default constructor
11:      // copy constructor and destructor elided!
12:      int GetAge() const { return *itsAge; }
13:      int GetWeight() const { return *itsWeight; }
14:      void SetAge(int age) { *itsAge = age; }
15:      CAT & operator=(const CAT &);
16:
17:   private:
18:      int *itsAge;
19:      int *itsWeight;
20:   };
21:
22:   CAT::CAT()
23:   {
```

LISTING 10.15 continued

```
24:     itsAge = new int;
25:     itsWeight = new int;
26:     *itsAge = 5;
27:     *itsWeight = 9;
28:  }
29:
30:
31:  CAT & CAT::operator=(const CAT & rhs)
32:  {
33:     if (this == &rhs)
34:     return *this;
35:     *itsAge = rhs.GetAge();
36:     *itsWeight = rhs.GetWeight();
37:     return *this;
38:  }
39:
40:
41:  int main()
42:  {
43:     CAT frisky;
44:     cout << "frisky's age: " << frisky.GetAge() << endl;
45:     cout << "Setting frisky to 6...\n";
46:     frisky.SetAge(6);
47:     CAT whiskers;
48:     cout << "whiskers' age: " << whiskers.GetAge() << endl;
49:     cout << "copying frisky to whiskers...\n";
50:     whiskers = frisky;
51:     cout << "whiskers' age: " << whiskers.GetAge() << endl;
52:     return 0;
53:  }
```

OUTPUT
```
frisky's age: 5
Setting frisky to 6...
whiskers' age: 5
copying frisky to whiskers...
whiskers' age: 6
```

ANALYSIS Listing 10.15 brings back the CAT class and leaves out the copy constructor and destructor to save room. On line 15, the assignment operator is declared, and on lines 31–38, it is defined.

On line 33, the current object (the CAT being assigned to) is tested to see whether it is the same as the CAT being assigned. This is done by checking whether the address of rhs is the same as the address stored in the this pointer.

Of course, the equality operator (==) can be overloaded as well, enabling you to determine for yourself what it means for your objects to be equal.

Handling Data Type Conversion

What happens when you try to assign a variable of a built-in type, such as int or unsigned short, to an object of a user-defined class? Listing 10.16 brings back the Counter class and attempts to assign a variable of type int to a Counter object.

 Caution   Listing 10.16 will not compile!

LISTING 10.16   Attempting to Assign a Counter to an int

```
0:   // Listing 10.16
1:   // This code won't compile!
2:
3:   #include <iostream>
4:
5:   #using namespace std;
6:
7:   class Counter
8:   {
9:   public:
10:      Counter();
11:      ~Counter(){}
12:      int GetItsVal()const { return itsVal; }
13:      void SetItsVal(int x) {itsVal = x; }
14:   private:
15:      int itsVal;
16:
17:   };
18:
19:   Counter::Counter():
20:   itsVal(0)
21:   {}
22:
23:   int main()
24:   {
25:      int theShort = 5;
26:      Counter theCtr = theShort;
27:      cout << "theCtr: " << theCtr.GetItsVal() << endl;
28:      return 0;
29:   }
```

OUTPUT   Compiler error! Unable to convert int to Counter

ANALYSIS The Counter class declared on lines 7–17 has only a default constructor. It declares no particular method for turning an int into a Counter object, and so line 26 causes a compile error. The compiler cannot figure out, unless you tell it that, given an int, it should assign that value to the member variable itsVal.

Listing 10.17 corrects this by creating a conversion operator: a constructor that takes an int and produces a Counter object.

LISTING 10.17 Converting int to Counter

```
0:  // Listing 10.17
1:  // Constructor as conversion operator
2:
3:  #include <iostream>
4:
5:  using namespace std;
6:
7:  class Counter
8:  {
9:  public:
10:     Counter();
11:     Counter(int val);
12:     ~Counter(){}
13:     int GetItsVal()const { return itsVal; }
14:     void SetItsVal(int x) {itsVal = x; }
15:  private:
16:     int itsVal;
17:
18:  };
19:
20:  Counter::Counter():
21:  itsVal(0)
22:  {}
23:
24:  Counter::Counter(int val):
25:  itsVal(val)
26:  {}
27:
28:
29:  int main()
30:  {
31:     int theShort = 5;
32:     Counter theCtr = theShort;
33:     cout << "theCtr: " << theCtr.GetItsVal() << endl;
34:     return 0;
35:  }
```

OUTPUT   theCtr: 5

ANALYSIS The important change is on line 11, where the constructor is overloaded to take an int, and on lines 24–26, where the constructor is implemented. The effect of this constructor is to create a Counter out of an int.

Given this, the compiler is able to call the constructor that takes an int as its argument. Here's how:

Step 1: Create a counter called theCtr.

This is like saying int x = 5; which creates an integer variable x and then initializes it with the value 5. In this case, we're creating a Counter object theCtr and initializing it with the short integer variable theShort.

Step 2: Assign to theCtr *the value of* theShort.

But theShort is a short, not a counter! First we have to convert it into a Counter. The compiler will try to make certain conversions for you automatically, but you have to teach it how. You teach the compiler how to make the conversion by creating a constructor for Counter that takes a short as its only parameter:

```
class Counter
{
Counter (short int x);
// ..
};
```

This constructor creates Counter objects from shorts. It does this by creating a temporary and unnamed counter. For illustration purposes, suppose that the temporary Counter object we create from the short is called wasShort.

Step 3: Assign wasShort *to* theCtr, *which is equivalent to*

```
"theCtr = wasShort";
```

In this step, wasShort (the temporary created when you ran the constructor) is substituted for what was on the right-hand side of the assignment operator. That is, now that the compiler has made a temporary for you, it initializes theCtr with that temporary.

To understand this, you must understand that *all* operator overloading works the same way—you declare an overloaded operator using the keyword operator. With binary operators (such as = or +) the right-hand side variable becomes the parameter. This is done by the constructor. Thus

```
a = b;
```

becomes

```
a.operator=(b);
```

What happens, however, if you try to reverse the assignment with the following?

```
1:  Counter theCtr(5);
2:  int theShort = theCtr;
3:  cout << "theShort : " << theShort  << endl;
```

Again, this will generate a compile error. Although the compiler now knows how to create a `Counter` out of an `int`, it does not know how to reverse the process.

Conversion Operators

To solve this and similar problems, C++ provides conversion operators that can be added to your class. This enables your class to specify how to do implicit conversions to built-in types. Listing 10.18 illustrates this. One note, however: Conversion operators do not specify a return value, even though they do, in effect, return a converted value.

LISTING 10.18   Converting from `Counter` to unsigned `short()`

```
0:  // Listing 10.18 - Conversion Operators
1:
2:  #include <iostream>
3:
4:  class Counter
5:  {
6:  public:
7:     Counter();
8:     Counter(int val);
9:     ~Counter(){}
10:    int GetItsVal()const { return itsVal; }
11:    void SetItsVal(int x) {itsVal = x; }
12:    operator unsigned short();
13: private:
14:    int itsVal;
15:
16: };
17:
18: Counter::Counter():
19: itsVal(0)
20: {}
21:
22: Counter::Counter(int val):
23: itsVal(val)
24: {}
25:
26: Counter::operator unsigned short ()
27: {
28:    return ( int (itsVal) );
29: }
30:
```

10

LISTING 10.18   continued

```
31:  int main()
32:  {
33:     Counter ctr(5);
34:     int theShort = ctr;
35:     std::cout << "theShort: " << theShort << std::endl;
36:     return 0;
37:  }
```

OUTPUT   theShort: 5

ANALYSIS   On line 12, the conversion operator is declared. Note that it has no return value. The implementation of this function is on lines 26–29. Line 28 returns the value of itsVal, converted to an int.

Now the compiler knows how to turn ints into Counter objects and vice versa, and they can be assigned to one another freely.

Summary

Today you learned how to overload member functions of your classes. You also learned how to supply default values to functions and how to decide when to use default values and when to overload.

Overloading class constructors enables you to create flexible classes that can be created from other objects. Initialization of objects happens at the initialization stage of construction and is more efficient than assigning values in the body of the constructor.

The copy constructor and the assignment operator are supplied by the compiler if you don't create your own, but they do a memberwise copy of the class. In classes in which member data includes pointers to the free store, these methods must be overridden so that you allocate memory for the target object.

Almost all C++ operators can be overloaded, although you want to be cautious not to create operators whose use is counterintuitive. You cannot change the arity of operators, nor can you invent new operators.

The this pointer refers to the current object and is an invisible parameter to all member functions. The dereferenced this pointer is often returned by overloaded operators.

Conversion operators enable you to create classes that can be used in expressions that expect a different type of object. They are exceptions to the rule that all functions return an explicit value; like constructors and destructors, they have no return type.

Q&A

Q Why would you ever use default values when you can overload a function?

A It is easier to maintain one function than two, and it is often easier to understand a function with default parameters than to study the bodies of two functions. Furthermore, updating one of the functions and neglecting to update the second is a common source of bugs.

Q Given the problems with overloaded functions, why not always use default values instead?

A Overloaded functions supply capabilities not available with default variables, such as varying the list of parameters by type rather than just by number.

Q When writing a class constructor, how do you decide what to put in the initialization and what to put in the body of the constructor?

A A simple rule of thumb is to do as much as possible in the initialization phase—that is, initialize all member variables there. Some things, like computations and print statements, must be in the body of the constructor.

Q Can an overloaded function have a default parameter?

A Yes. No reason exists not to combine these powerful features. One or more of the overloaded functions can have its own default values, following the normal rules for default variables in any function.

Q Why are some member functions defined within the class declaration and others are not?

A Defining the implementation of a member function within the declaration makes it inline. Generally, this is done only if the function is extremely simple. Note that you can also make a member function inline by using the keyword `inline`, even if the function is declared outside the class declaration.

Workshop

The Workshop provides quiz questions to help solidify your understanding of the material covered and exercises to provide you with experience in using what you've learned. Try to answer the quiz and exercise questions before checking the answers in Appendix D, and make sure you understand the answers before going to the next chapter.

Quiz

1. When you overload member functions, in what ways must they differ?
2. What is the difference between a declaration and a definition?

3. When is the copy constructor called?

4. When is the destructor called?

5. How does the copy constructor differ from the assignment operator (=)?

6. What is the `this` pointer?

7. How do you differentiate between overloading the prefix and postfix increment operators?

8. Can you overload the `operator+` for `short` integers?

9. Is it legal in C++ to overload the `operator++` so that it decrements a value in your class?

10. What return value must conversion operators have in their declarations?

Exercises

1. Write a `SimpleCircle` class declaration (only) with one member variable: `itsRadius`. Include a default constructor, a destructor, and accessor methods for radius.

2. Using the class you created in Exercise 1, write the implementation of the default constructor, initializing `itsRadius` with the value 5.

3. Using the same class, add a second constructor that takes a value as its parameter and assigns that value to `itsRadius`.

4. Create a prefix and postfix increment operator for your `SimpleCircle` class that increments `itsRadius`.

5. Change `SimpleCircle` to store `itsRadius` on the free store, and fix the existing methods.

6. Provide a copy constructor for `SimpleCircle`.

7. Provide an assignment operator for `SimpleCircle`.

8. Write a program that creates two `SimpleCircle` objects. Use the default constructor on one and instantiate the other with the value 9. Call the increment operator on each and then print their values. Finally, assign the second to the first and print its values.

9. **BUG BUSTERS:** What is wrong with this implementation of the assignment operator?

```
SQUARE SQUARE ::operator=(const SQUARE & rhs)
{
     itsSide = new int;
     *itsSide = rhs.GetSide();
     return *this;
}
```

10. **BUG BUSTERS:** What is wrong with this implementation of the addition operator?

```
VeryShort  VeryShort::operator+ (const VeryShort& rhs)
{
   itsVal += rhs.GetItsVal();
   return *this;
}
```

10

Object-Oriented Analysis and Design

It is easy to become focused on the syntax of C++ and to lose sight of how and why you use these techniques to build programs.

Today you will learn

- How to use object-oriented analysis to understand the problem you are trying to solve.
- How to use object-oriented design to create a robust, extensible, and reliable solution.
- How to use the Unified Modeling Language (UML) to document your analysis and design.

Building Models

If we are to manage complexity, we must create a model of the universe. The goal of the model is to create a meaningful abstraction of the real world. Such an abstraction should be simpler than the real world but should also accurately reflect the real world so that we can use the model to predict the behavior of things in the real world.

A child's globe is a classic model. The model isn't the thing itself; we would never confuse a child's globe with the Earth, but one maps the other well enough that we can learn about the Earth by studying the globe.

There are, of course, significant simplifications. My daughter's globe never has rain, floods, globe-quakes, and so forth, but I can use her globe to predict how long it will take me to fly from my home to Indianapolis should I ever need to come in and explain myself to the Sams senior management when they ask me why my manuscript was late ("you see, I was doing great, but then I got lost in a metaphor and it took me hours to get out").

A model that is not simpler than the thing being modeled is not much use. The comedian Steve Wright quips: "I have a map on which one inch equals one inch. I live at E5."

Object-oriented software design is about building good models. It consists of two significant pieces: a modeling language and a process.

Software Design: The Modeling Language

The *modeling language* is the least important aspect of object-oriented analysis and design; unfortunately, it tends to get the most attention. A modeling language is nothing more than a convention for how we'll draw our model on paper. We can easily decide that we'll draw our classes as triangles and that we'll draw the inheritance relationship as a dotted line. If so, we might model a geranium as shown in Figure 11.1.

FIGURE 11.1

Generalization/special-ization.

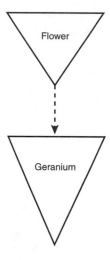

In the figure, you see that a Geranium is a special kind of Flower. If you and I agree to draw our inheritance (generalization/specialization) diagrams like this, we'll understand each other perfectly. Over time, we'll probably want to model lots of complex relationships, and so we'll develop our own complicated set of diagramming conventions and rules.

Of course, we'll need to explain our conventions to everyone else with whom we work, and each new employee or collaborator will have to learn our conventions. We may interact with other companies that have their own conventions, and we'll need to allow time to negotiate a common convention and to compensate for the inevitable misunderstandings.

It would be more convenient if everyone in the industry agreed on a common modeling language. (For that matter, it would be convenient if everyone in the world agreed on a single spoken language, but one thing at a time.) The *lingua franca* of software development is UML—The Unified Modeling Language. The job of the UML is to answer questions such as, "How do we draw an inheritance relationship?" The geranium drawing shown in Figure 11.1 would be drawn in UML as shown in Figure 11.2.

FIGURE 11.2

UML drawing of specialization.

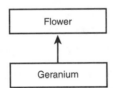

11

In UML, classes are drawn as rectangles, and inheritance is drawn as a line with an arrowhead. Interestingly, the arrowhead points from the more specialized class to the more general class. The direction of the arrow is counter-intuitive for most folks, but it doesn't matter much; when we all agree, the system works just fine.

The details of the UML are rather straightforward. The diagrams are not hard to use or to understand, and I'll explain them as we go along. Although it is possible to write a whole book on the UML, the truth is that 90 percent of the time, you use only a small subset of the UML notation, and that subset is easily learned.

Software Design: The Process

The *process* of object-oriented analysis and design is much more complex and important than the modeling language. So of course, it is what you hear much less about. That is because the debate about modeling languages is pretty much settled; as an industry, we've decided to use the UML. The debate about process rages on.

A *methodologist* is someone who develops or studies one or more methods. Typically, methodologists develop and publish their own methods. A *method* is a modeling language and a process. Three of the leading methodologists and their methods are Grady Booch, who developed the Booch method, Ivar Jacobson, who developed object-oriented software engineering, and James Rumbaugh, who developed Object Modeling Technology (OMT). Together, these three men have created what is now called the *Rational Unified Process* (formerly known as Objectory), a method and a commercial product from Rational Software, Inc. All three men are employed at Rational Software, where they are affectionately known as the *Three Amigos*.

This chapter loosely follows their process. I won't follow it rigidly because I don't believe in slavish adherence to academic theory—I'm much more interested in shipping product than in adhering to a method. Other methods have something to offer, and I tend to be eclectic, picking up bits and pieces as I go along and stitching them together into a workable framework.

The process of software design is *iterative*. That means that as we develop software, we go through the entire process repeatedly as we strive for enhanced understanding of the requirements. The design directs the implementation, but the details uncovered during implementation feed back into the design. Most important, we do not try to develop any sizable project in a single, orderly, straight line; rather, we iterate over pieces of the project, constantly improving our design and refining our implementation.

Iterative development can be distinguished from waterfall development. In waterfall development, the output from one stage becomes the input to the next, and there is no going back (see Figure 11.3). In a waterfall development process, the requirements are detailed, and the clients sign off ("Yes, this is what I want"); the requirements are then passed on to the designer, set in stone. The designer creates the design (and a wonder to behold it is) and passes it off to the programmer who implements the design. The programmer in turn hands the code to a QA person who tests the code and then releases it to the customer. Great in theory, disaster in practice.

FIGURE 11.3

The waterfall method.

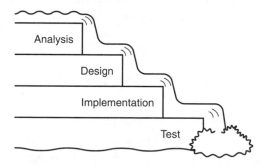

In iterative design, we start with a concept; an idea of what we might want to build. As we examine the details, the vision may grow and evolve.

When we have a good start on the requirements, we begin the design, knowing full well that the questions that arise during design may cause modifications back in the requirements. As we work on design, we begin prototyping and then implementing the product. The issues that arise in development feed back into design and may even influence our understanding of the requirements. Most important, we design and implement only pieces of the full product, iterating over the design and implementation phases repeatedly.

Although the steps of the process are repeated iteratively, it is nearly impossible to describe them in such a cyclical manner. Therefore, I will describe them in sequence: initial concept, analysis, design, implementation, testing, rollout. Don't misunderstand me—in reality, we run through each of these steps many times during the course of the development of a single product. The iterative design process is just hard to present and understand if we cycle through each step, so I'll describe them one after the other.

The following are the steps of the iterative design process:

1. Conceptualization
2. Analysis
3. Design
4. Implementation
5. Testing
6. Rollout

Conceptualization is the "vision thing." It is the single sentence that describes the great idea.

Analysis is the process of understanding the requirements.

Design is the process of creating the model of your classes, from which you will generate your code.

Implementation is writing it in code (for example, in C++).

Testing is making sure that you did it right.

Rollout is getting it to your customers.

Piece of cake. All the rest is details.

> **Controversies**
>
> Endless controversies exist about what happens in each stage of the iterative design process, and even about what you name those stages. Here's a secret: *It doesn't matter.* The essential steps are the same in just about every object-oriented process: Find out what you need to build, design a solution, and implement that design.
>
> Although the newsgroups and object-technology mailing lists thrive on splitting hairs, the essentials of object-oriented analysis and design are fairly straightforward. In this chapter, I'll lay out a practical approach to the process as the bedrock on which you can build the architecture of your application.
>
> The goal of all this work is to produce code that meets the stated requirements and that is reliable, extensible, and maintainable. Most important, the goal is to produce high-quality code on time and on budget.

Extreme Programming

There is a new approach to analysis and design called *Extreme Programming*, which is discussed in the book *Extreme Programming Explained: Embrace Change* by Kent Beck (Addison-Wesley, 1999 ISBN 0201616416).

In this book Beck makes a number of radical and wonderful suggestions, including the idea of coding nothing until you can test whether it works, and programming in pairs (two programmers at one computer). The most important point he makes, from our perspective, however, is this: Requirements are going to change. Get something working and keep it working; design for what you know, and do not over-design; after all tomorrow may never come.

This is a terrible simplification of what Beck says, and for all I know he might think it is a distortion, but in any case, I believe in the essence of it: Get your program working, build for the requirements as you understand them, and try not to code yourself into a corner.

It is difficult to create a robust maintainable program if you don't invest time in understanding the requirements (analysis) and planning your approach (design), but beware of trying to control more than you possibly can.

The Vision

All great software starts with a vision. One individual has an insight into a product he or she thinks would be good to build. Rarely do committees create compelling visions. The very first phase of object-oriented analysis and design is to capture this vision in a single sentence (or at most, a short paragraph). The vision becomes the guiding principle of development, and the team that comes together to implement the vision ought to refer back to it—and update it if necessary—as it goes forward.

Even if the vision statement comes out of a committee in the marketing department, one person should be designated as the "visionary." It is his or her job to be the keeper of the sacred light. As you progress, the requirements will evolve. Scheduling and time-to-market demands may (and should) modify what you try to accomplish in the first iteration of the program, but the visionary must keep an eye on the essential idea, to ensure that whatever is produced reflects the core vision with high fidelity. It is this ruthless dedication—this passionate commitment—that sees the project through to completion. If you lose sight of the vision, your product is doomed.

Requirements Analysis

The conceptualization phase, in which the vision is articulated, is very brief. It may be no longer than a flash of insight followed by the time it takes to write down what the visionary has in mind. Often, as the object-oriented expert, you join the project after the vision is already articulated.

11

Some companies confuse the vision statement with the requirements. A strong vision is necessary, but it is not sufficient. To move on to analysis, you must understand how the product will be used and how it must perform. The goal of the analysis phase is to articulate and capture these requirements. The outcome of the analysis phase is the production of a requirements document. The first section in the requirements document is the use-case analysis.

Use Cases

The driving force in analysis, design, and implementation is the use cases. A *use case* is nothing more than a high-level description of how the product will be used. Use cases drive not only the analysis, they drive the design, they help you find the classes, and they are especially important in testing the product.

Creating a robust and comprehensive set of use cases may be the single most important task in analysis. It is here that you depend most heavily on your domain experts; the domain experts have the most information about the business requirements you are trying to capture.

Use cases pay little attention to user interface, and they pay no attention to the internals of the system you are building. Any system or person who interacts with the system is called an *actor*.

To summarize, the following are some definitions:

- Use case—A description of how the software will be used.
- Domain experts—People with expertise in the *domain* (area) of business for which you are creating the product.
- Actor—Any person or system that interacts with the system you are developing.

A use case is a description of the interaction between an actor and the system itself. For purposes of use-case analysis, the system is treated as a "black box." An actor "sends a message" to the system, and something happens: Information is returned; the state of the system is changed; the space ship changes direction; whatever.

Identify the Actors

It is important to note that not all actors are people. Systems that interact with the system you are building are also actors. Thus, if we were building an automated teller machine (ATM), the customer and the bank clerk can both be actors—as can other systems with which our new system interacts, such as a mortgage-tracking or student-loan system. The essential characteristics of actors are as follows:

- They are external to the system
- They interact with the system

Getting started is often the hardest part of use-case analysis. Often, the best way to get going is with a "brainstorming" session. Simply write down the list of people and systems that will interact with your new system. Remember that when we discuss *people*, we really mean *roles*—the bank clerk, the manager, the customer, and so forth. One person can have more than one role.

For the ATM example just mentioned, we can expect such a list to include the following roles:

- The customer
- The bank personnel
- A back-office system
- The person who fills the ATM with money and supplies

No need exists to go beyond the obvious list at first. Generating even three or four actors may be enough to get you started on generating use cases. Each of these actors interacts with the system in different ways. We'll want to capture these interactions in our use cases.

Determine the First Use Cases

Let's start with the customer role. We might brainstorm the following use cases for a *customer*:

- Customer checks his or her balances.
- Customer deposits money to his or her account.
- Customer withdraws money from his or her account.
- Customer transfers money between accounts.
- Customer opens an account.
- Customer closes an account.

Should we distinguish between "Customer deposits money in his or her checking account" and "Customer deposits money in his or her savings account," or should we combine these actions (as we did in the preceding list) into "Customer deposits money to his or her account?" The answer to this question lies in whether this distinction is meaningful in the domain (the domain is the real-world environment we're modeling—in this case, banking).

To determine whether these actions are one use case or two, you must ask whether the *mechanisms* are different (does the customer do something significantly different with these deposits) and whether the *outcomes* are different (does the system reply in a different way). The answer to both questions for the deposit issue is "no": The customer deposits money to either account in essentially the same way, and the outcome is pretty much the same; the ATM responds by incrementing the balance in the appropriate account.

Given that the actor and the system behave and respond more or less identically, regardless of whether the deposit is made to the checking or the savings account, these two use cases are actually a single use case. Later, when we flesh out use-case scenarios, we can try the two variations to see whether they make any difference at all.

As you think about each actor, you may discover additional use cases by asking these questions:

- Why is the actor using this system?

  The customer is using the system to get cash, to make a deposit, or to check an account balance.

- What outcome does the actor want from each request?

  Add cash to an account or get cash to make a purchase.

11

- What happened to cause the actor to use this system now?

  He or she may recently have been paid or may be on the way to make a purchase.

- What must the actor do to use the system?

  Put an ATM card into the slot in the machine.

  Aha! We need a use case for the customer logging in to the system.

- What information must the actor provide to the system?

  Enter a Personal ID number.

  Aha! We need use cases for obtaining and editing the Personal ID number.

- What information does the actor hope to get from the system?

  Balances, and so on.

You can often can find additional use cases by focusing on the attributes of the objects in the domain. The customer has a name, a PIN, and an account number; do we have use cases to manage these objects? An account has an account number, a balance, and a transaction history; have we captured these elements in the use cases?

After we've explored the customer use cases in detail, the next step in fleshing out the list of use cases is to develop the use cases for each of the other actors. The following list shows a reasonable first set of use cases for the ATM example:

- Customer checks his or her balances.
- Customer deposits money to his or her account.
- Customer withdraws money from his or her account.
- Customer transfers money between accounts.
- Customer opens an account.
- Customer closes an account.
- Customer logs in to his or her account.
- Customer checks recent transactions.
- Bank clerk logs in to special management account.
- Bank clerk makes an adjustment to a customer's account.
- A back office system updates a user's account based on external activity.
- Changes in a user's account are reflected in a back office system.
- The ATM signals it is out of cash to dispense.
- The bank technician fills the ATM with cash and supplies.

Create the Domain Model

After you have a first cut at your use cases, you can begin to flesh out your requirements document with a detailed domain model. The *domain model* is a document that captures all you know about the domain (the field of business you are working in). As part of your domain model, you create domain objects that describe all the objects mentioned in your use cases. So far, the ATM example includes these objects: customer, bank personnel, back office systems, checking account, savings account, and so forth.

For each of these domain objects, we want to capture such essential data as the name of the object (for example, customer, account, and so on), whether the object is an actor, the object's principal attributes and behavior, and so forth. Many modeling tools support capturing this information in "class" descriptions. Figure 11.4 shows how this information is captured with Rational Rose.

FIGURE 11.4

Rational Rose.

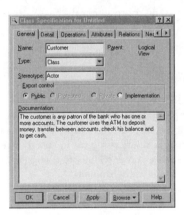

It is important to realize that what we are describing here are *not* design objects, but rather objects in the domain. This is documentation of how the world works, not documentation of how our system will work.

We can diagram the relationship among the objects in the domain of the ATM example using the UML—with the same diagramming conventions we'll use later to describe the relationships among classes in the domain. This is one of the great strengths of the UML: We can use the same tools at every stage of the project.

For example, we can capture that checking accounts and savings accounts are both specializations of the more general concept of bank account by using the UML conventions for classes and generalization relationships, as shown in Figure 11.5.

FIGURE 11.5

Specialization.

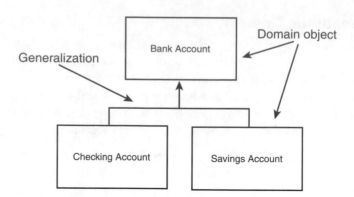

In the diagram in Figure 11.5, the boxes represent the various domain objects, and the line with an arrow head indicates generalization. The UML specifies that this line is drawn from the *specialized* class to the more general "base" class. Thus, both Checking Account and Savings Account point up to Bank Account, indicating that each is a specialized form of Bank Account.

 Note

> Again, it is important to note that what we are showing at this time are relationships among objects in the domain. Later, you may decide to have a CheckingAccount object in your design as well as a BankAccount object, and you may implement this relationship using inheritance; but these are design-time decisions. At analysis time, all we are doing is documenting our understanding of these objects in the domain.

The UML is a rich modeling language, and you can capture any number of relationships. The principal relationships captured in analysis, however, are generalization (or specialization), containment, and association.

Generalization

Generalization is often equated with "inheritance," but a sharp and meaningful distinction exists between the two. Generalization describes the relationship; inheritance is the programming implementation of generalization—it is *how we* manifest generalization in code. The obverse side of the generalization coin is specialization. A cat is a specialized form of animal; animal is a generalized form of cat and dog.

Specialization implies that the derived object *is a* subtype of the base object. Thus, a checking account *is a* bank account. The relationship is symmetrical: Bank account *generalizes* the common behavior and attributes of checking and savings accounts.

During domain analysis, we seek to capture these relationships *as they exist in the real world.*

Containment

Often, one object is composed of many sub-objects. For example, a car is composed of a steering wheel, tires, doors, radio, and so forth. A checking account is composed of a balance, a transaction history, a customer ID, and so on. We say that the checking account *has* these items; containment models the *has a* relationship. The UML illustrates the containment relationship by drawing a line with a diamond from the containing object to the contained object, as shown in Figure 11.6.

FIGURE 11.6

Containment.

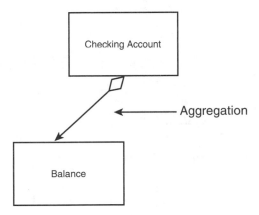

The diagram in Figure 11.6 suggests that the Checking Account *has a* Balance. You can combine these diagrams to show a fairly complex set of relationships (see Figure 11.7).

The diagram in Figure 11.7 states that a Checking Account and a Savings Account are both Bank Accounts, and that all Bank Accounts have both a Balance and a Transaction History.

Association

The third relationship commonly captured in the domain analysis is a simple association. An association suggests that two objects interact in some way. This definition will become much more precise in the design stage, but for analysis, we are suggesting only that Object A and Object B interact, but that neither contains the other and neither is a specialization of the other. We show this association in the UML with a simple straight line between the objects, as shown in Figure 11.8.

FIGURE 11.7

Object relationships.

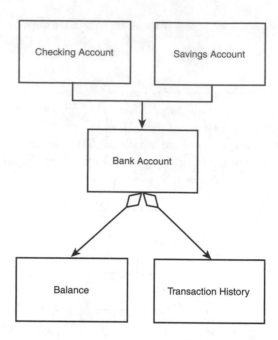

The diagram in Figure 11.8 indicates that Object A associates in some way with Object B.

FIGURE 11.8

Association.

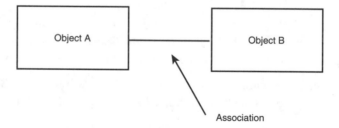

Establish Scenarios

Now that we have a preliminary set of use cases and the tools with which to diagram the relationship among the objects in the domain, we are ready to formalize the use cases and give them more depth.

Each use case can be broken into a series of scenarios. A *scenario* is a description of a specific set of circumstances that distinguish among the various contingent elements of the use case. For example, the use case "Customer withdraws money from his or her account" might have the following scenarios:

- Customer requests a $300 withdrawal from checking, takes the cash from the cash slot, and the system prints a receipt.

- Customer requests a $300 withdrawal from checking, but his or her balance is $200. Customer is informed that not enough cash is in the checking account to accomplish the withdrawal.

- Customer requests a $300 withdrawal from checking, but he or she has already withdrawn $100 today and the limit is $300 per day. Customer is informed of the problem, and he or she chooses to withdraw only $200.

- Customer requests a $300 withdrawal from checking, but the receipt roll is out of paper. Customer is informed of the problem, and he or she chooses to proceed without a receipt.

And so forth. Each scenario explores a variation on the original use case. Often, these variations are exception conditions (not enough money in account, not enough money in machine, and so on). Sometimes, the variations explore nuances of decisions in the use case itself (for example, did the customer want to transfer money before making the withdrawal).

Not every possible scenario must be explored. We are looking for those scenarios that tease out requirements of the system or details of the interaction with the actor.

Establish Guidelines

As part of your methodology, you will want to create guidelines for documenting each scenario. You capture these guidelines in your requirements document. Typically, you'll want to ensure that each scenario includes the following:

- Preconditions—What must be true for the scenario to begin.
- Triggers—What causes the scenario to begin.
- What actions the actors take.
- What results or changes are caused by the system.
- What feedback the actors receive.
- Whether repeating activities occur, and what causes them to conclude.
- A description of the logical flow of the scenario.
- What causes the scenario to end.
- Postconditions—What must be true when the scenario is complete.

In addition, you will want to name each use case and each scenario. Thus, you might have the following situation:

Use Case:	Customer withdraws cash.
Scenario:	Successful cash withdrawal from checking.
Preconditions:	Customer is already logged on to system.
Trigger:	Customer requests "withdrawal."
Description:	Customer chooses to withdraw cash from a checking account. Sufficient cash is in the account, sufficient cash and receipt paper are in the ATM, and the network is up and running. The ATM asks the customer to indicate the amount of the withdrawal, and the customer asks for $300, a legal amount to withdraw at this time. The machine dispenses $300 and prints a receipt, and the customer takes the money and the receipt.
Postconditions:	Customer account is debited $300, and customer has $300 cash.

This use case can be shown with the incredibly simple diagram given in Figure 11.9.

FIGURE 11.9

Use-case diagram.

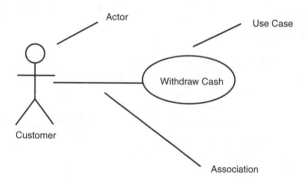

Little information is captured here except a high-level abstraction of an interaction between an actor (the customer) and the system. This diagram becomes slightly more useful when you show the interaction among use cases. I say only *slightly* more useful because only two interactions are possible: <<uses>> and <<extends>>. The <<uses>> stereotype indicates that one use case is a superset of another. For example, it isn't possible to *withdraw cash* without first *logging on*. We can show this relationship with the diagram shown in Figure 11.10.

FIGURE 11.10

The <<uses>> stereo-type.

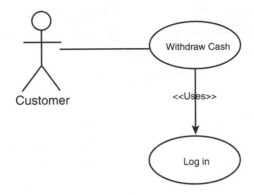

Figure 11.10 indicates that the Withdraw Cash use case "uses" the Log In use case, and thus fully implements Log In as part of Withdraw Cash.

The <<extends>> use case was intended to indicate conditional relationships and something akin to inheritance, but so much confusion exists in the object-modeling community about the distinction between <<uses>> and <<extends>> that many developers have simply set aside <<extends>>, feeling that its meaning is not sufficiently well-understood. Personally, I use <<uses>> when I would otherwise copy and paste the entire use case in place, and I use <<extends>> when I only *use* the use case under certain definable conditions.

Interaction Diagrams

Although the diagram of the use case itself may be of limited value, you can associate diagrams with the use case that can dramatically improve the documentation and under-standing of the interactions. For example, we know that the Withdraw Cash scenario represents the interactions among the following domain objects: customer, checking account, and the user interface. We can document this interaction with an interaction diagram, as shown in Figure 11.11.

The interaction diagram in Figure 11.11 captures details of the scenario that may not be evident by reading the text. The objects that are interacting are *domain* objects, and the entire ATM/UI is treated as a single object, with only the specific bank account called out in any detail.

This rather simple ATM example shows only a fanciful set of interactions, but nailing down the specifics of these interactions can be a powerful tool in understanding both the problem domain and the requirements of your new system.

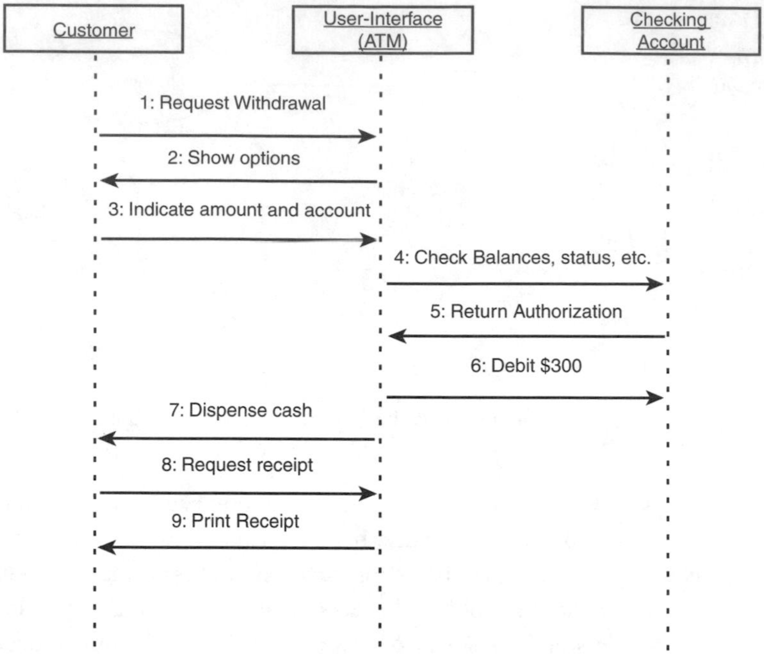

FIGURE **11.11**

UML interaction diagram.

Create Packages

Because you generate many use cases for any problem of significant complexity, the UML enables you to group your use cases in packages.

A *package* is like a directory or a folder—it is a collection of modeling objects (classes, actors, and so forth). To manage the complexity of use cases, you can create packages aggregated by whatever characteristics make sense for your problem. Thus, you can aggregate your use cases by account type (everything affecting checking or savings), by credit or debit, by customer type, or by whatever characteristics make sense to you. More important, a single use case can appear in different packages, allowing you great flexibility of design.

Application Analysis

In addition to creating use cases, the requirements document will capture your customer's assumptions, constraints, and requirements about hardware and operating systems. Application requirements are your *particular* customer's prerequisites—those things that you would normally determine during design and implementation but that your client has decided for you.

The application requirements are often driven by the need to interface with existing (legacy) systems. In this case, understanding what the existing systems do and how they work is an essential component of your analysis.

Ideally, you'll analyze the problem, design the solution, and then decide which platform and operating system best fits your design. That scenario is as ideal as it is rare. More often, the client has a standing investment in a particular operating system or hardware platform. The client's business plan depends on your software running on the existing system, and you must capture these requirements early and design accordingly.

Systems Analysis

Some software is written to stand alone, interacting only with the end user. Often, however, you will be called on to interface to an existing system. *Systems analysis* is the process of collecting all the details of the systems with which you will interact. Will your new system be a server, providing services to the existing system, or will it be a client? Will you be able to negotiate an interface between the systems, or must you adapt to an existing standard? Will the other system be stable, or must you continually hit a moving target?

These and related questions must be answered in the analysis phase, before you begin to design your new system. In addition, you will want to try to capture the constraints and limitations implicit in interacting with the other systems. Will they slow down the responsiveness of your system? Will they put high demands on your new system, consuming resources and computing time?

Planning Documents

After you understand what your system must do and how it must behave, it is time to take a first stab at creating a time and budget document. Often, the timeline is dictated, top-down, by the client: "You have 18 months to get this done." Ideally, you'll examine the requirements and estimate the time it will take to design and implement the solution. That is the ideal; the practical reality is that most systems come with an imposed time limit and cost limit, and the real trick is to figure out how much of the required functionality you can build in the allotted time—and at the allotted cost.

Here are a couple guidelines to keep in mind when you are creating a project budget and timeline:

- If you are given a range, the outer number is probably optimistic.
- Liberty's Law states that everything takes longer than you expect—even if you take into account Liberty's Law.

11

Given these realities, it is imperative that you prioritize your work. *You will not finish*—it is that simple. It is important that when you run out of time, what you have works and is adequate for a first release. If you are building a bridge and run out of time, if you didn't get a chance to put in the bicycle path, that is too bad; but you can still open the bridge and start collecting tolls. If you run out of time and you're only halfway across the river, that is not as good.

An essential thing to know about planning documents is that they are wrong. This early in the process, it is virtually impossible to offer a reliable estimate of the duration of the project. After you have the requirements, you can get a good handle on how long the design will take, a fair estimate of how long the implementation will take, and a reasonable guesstimate of the testing time. Then you must allow yourself at least 20 to 25 percent "wiggle room," which you can tighten as you move forward and learn more.

Note

The inclusion of "wiggle room" in your planning document is not an excuse to avoid planning documents. It is merely a warning not to rely on them too much early on. As the project goes forward, you'll strengthen your understanding of how the system works, and your estimates will become increasingly precise.

Visualizations

The final piece of the requirements document is the visualization. The visualization is a fancy name for the diagrams, pictures, screen shots, prototypes, and any other visual representations created to help you think through and design the graphical user interface of your product.

For many large projects, you may develop a full prototype to help you (and your customers) understand how the system will behave. On some teams, the prototype becomes the living requirements document; the "real" system is designed to implement the functionality demonstrated in the prototype.

Artifacts

At the end of each phase of analysis and design, you will create a series of documents or "artifacts." Table 11.1 shows some of the artifacts of the analysis phase. These documents are used by the customer to make sure that you understand what the customer needs, by end users to give feedback and guidance to the project, and by the project team to design and implement the code. Many of these documents also provide material crucial both to your documentation team and to Quality Assurance to tell them how the system *ought* to behave.

TABLE 11.1   Artifacts Created During the Analysis Stage of Project Development

Artifact	Description
Use case report	A document detailing the use cases, scenarios, stereotypes, preconditions, postconditions, and visualizations
Domain analysis	Document and diagrams describing the relationships among the domain objects
Analysis collaboration diagrams	Collaboration diagrams describing interactions among objects in the problem domain
Analysis activity diagrams	Activity diagrams describing interactions among objects in the problem domain
Systems analysis	Report and diagrams describing low-level and hardware systems on which the project will be built
Application analysis document	Report and diagrams describing the customer's requirements specific to this particular project
Operational constraints report	Report describing performance characteristics and constraints imposed by this client
Cost and planning document	Report with Gantt and Pert charts indicating projected scheduling, milestones, and costs

Design

Analysis focuses on understanding the problem domain, whereas design focuses on creating the solution. *Design* is the process of transforming our understanding of the requirements into a model that can be implemented in software. The result of this process is the production of a design document.

The design document is divided into two sections: Class Design and Architectural Mechanisms. The Class Design section, in turn, is divided into static design (which details the various classes and their relationships and characteristics) and dynamic design (which details how the classes interact).

The Architectural Mechanisms section of the design document provides details about how you will implement object persistence, concurrency, a distributed object system, and so forth. The rest of this chapter focuses on the class design aspect of the design document; other chapters in the rest of this book explain how to implement various architecture mechanisms.

What Are the Classes?

As a C++ programmer, you are used to creating classes. Formal design methodology requires you to separate the C++ class from the design class, although they will be intimately related. The C++ class you write in code is the implementation of the class you designed. These are isomorphic: Each class in your design will correspond to a class in your code, but don't confuse one for the other. It is certainly possible to implement your design classes in another language, and the *syntax* of the class definitions might be changed.

That said, most of the time we talk about these classes without distinguishing them because the differences are highly abstract. When you say that in your model your Cat class will have a Meow() method, understand that this means that you will put a Meow() method into your C++ class as well.

You capture the model's classes in UML diagrams, and you capture the C++ classes in code which can be compiled. The distinction is meaningful, yet subtle.

In any case, the biggest stumbling block for many novices is finding the initial set of classes and understanding what makes a well-designed class. One simplistic technique suggests writing out the use-case scenarios and then creating a class for every noun. Consider the following use-case scenario:

> **Customer** chooses to withdraw **cash** from **checking**. Sufficient cash is in the **account**, sufficient cash and **receipts** are in the **ATM**, and the **network** is up and running. The ATM asks the customer to indicate an **amount** for the **withdrawal**, and the customer asks for $300, a legal amount to withdraw at this time. The **machine** dispenses $300 and prints a receipt, and the customer takes the **money** and the receipt.

You might pull out of this scenario the following classes:

- Customer
- Cash
- Checking
- Account
- Receipts
- ATM
- Network
- Amount
- Withdrawal
- Machine
- Money

You might then aggregate the synonyms to create this list, and then create classes for each of these nouns:

- Customer
- Cash (money, amount, withdrawal)
- Checking
- Account
- Receipts
- ATM (machine)
- Network

This is not a bad way to start, as far as it goes. You might then go on to diagram the obvious relationships among some of these classes as shown in Figure 11.12.

FIGURE 11.12

Preliminary classes.

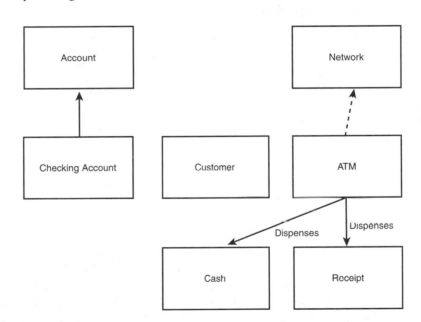

Transformations

What you began to do in the preceding section was not so much extract the nouns from the scenario as to begin transforming objects from the domain analysis into objects in the design. That is a fine first step. Often, many of the objects in the domain will have *surrogates* in the design. An object is called a surrogate to distinguish between the actual physical receipt dispensed by an ATM and the object in your design that is merely an intellectual abstraction implemented in code.

You will likely find that *most* of the domain objects have an isomorphic representation in the design—that is, a one-to-one correspondence exists between the domain object and the design object. Other times, however, a single domain object is represented in the design by an entire series of design objects. And at times, a series of domain objects may be represented by a single design object.

In Figure 11.12, note that we have already captured the fact that CheckingAccount is a specialization of Account. We didn't set out to find the generalization relationship, but this one was self-evident, so we captured it. Similarly, we knew, from the domain analysis, that the ATM dispenses both Cash and Receipts, so we captured that information immediately in the design.

The relationship between Customer and CheckingAccount is less obvious. We know that such a relationship exists, but the details are not obvious, so we hold off.

Other Transformations

After you have transformed the domain objects, you can begin to look for other useful design-time objects. A good starting place is with interfaces. Each interface between your new system and any existing (legacy) systems should be encapsulated in an interface class. If you will interact with a database of any type, this is also a good candidate for an interface class.

These interface classes offer encapsulation of the interface protocol and thus shield your code from changes in the other system. Interface classes allow you to change your own design, or to accommodate changes in the design of other systems, without breaking the rest of the code. As long as the two systems continue to support the agreed-on interface, they can move independently of one another.

Data Manipulation

Similarly, you will create classes for data manipulation. If you have to transform data from one format into another format (for example, from Fahrenheit to Celsius or from English to Metric), you may want to encapsulate these manipulations behind a data manipulation class. You can use this technique when messaging data into required formats for other systems or for transmission over the Internet—in short, any time you must manipulate data into a specified format, you will encapsulate the protocol behind a data manipulation class.

Views

Every "view" or "report" your system generates (or, if you generate many reports, every set of reports) is a candidate for a class. The rules behind the report—both how the information is gathered and how it is to be displayed—can be productively encapsulated inside a view class.

Devices

If your system interacts with or manipulates devices (such as printers, modems, scanners, and so forth), the specifics of the device protocol ought to be encapsulated in a class. Again, by creating classes for the interface to the device, you can plug in new devices with new protocols and not break any of the rest of your code; just create a new interface class that supports the same interface (or a derived interface), and off you go.

Static Model

When you have established your preliminary set of classes, it is time to begin modeling their relationships and interactions. For purposes of clarity, this chapter first explains the static model and then explains the dynamic model. In the actual design process, you will move freely between the static and dynamic models, filling in details of both—and, in fact, adding new classes and sketching them in as you go.

The static model focuses on three areas of concern: responsibilities, attributes, and relationships. The most important of these—and the one you focus on first—is the set of responsibilities for each class. The most important guiding principal is this: *Each class should be responsible for one thing.*

That is not to say that each class has only one method. Far from it; many classes will have dozens of methods. But all these methods must be coherent and cohesive; that is, they must all relate to one another and contribute to the class's capability to accomplish a single area of responsibility.

In a well-designed system, each object is an instance of a well-defined and well-understood class that is responsible for one area of concern. Classes typically delegate extraneous responsibilities to other, related classes. By creating classes that have only a single area of concern, you promote the creation of highly maintainable code.

To get a handle on the responsibilities of your classes, you may find it beneficial to begin your design work with the use of CRC cards.

CRC Cards

CRC stands for Class, Responsibility, and Collaboration. A CRC card is nothing more than a 4×6 index card. This simple, low-tech device enables you to work with other people in understanding the primary responsibilities of your initial set of classes. You assemble a stack of blank 4×6 index cards and meet around a conference table for a series of CRC card sessions.

How to Conduct a CRC Session

Each CRC session should be attended, ideally, by a group of three to six people; any more becomes unwieldy. You should have a *facilitator*, whose job it is to keep the session on track and to help the participants capture what they learn. At least one senior software architect should be present, ideally someone with significant experience in object-oriented analysis and design. In addition, you will want to include at least one or two "domain experts" who understand the system requirements and who can provide expert advice in how things ought to work.

The most essential ingredient in a CRC session is the conspicuous absence of managers. This is a creative, free-wheeling session that must be unencumbered by the need to impress one's boss. The goal here is to explore, to take risks, to tease out the responsibilities of the classes, and to understand how they might interact with one another.

You begin the CRC session by assembling your group around a conference table, with a small stack of 4×6 index cards. At the top of each CRC card you will write the name of a single class. Draw a line down the center of the card and write *Responsibilities* on the left and *Collaborations* on the right.

Begin by filling out cards for the most important classes you've identified. For each card, write a one-sentence or two-sentence definition on the back. You may also capture what other class this class specializes if that is obvious at the time you're working with the CRC card. Just write *Superclass:* below the class name and fill in the name of the class this class derives from.

Focus on Responsibilities

The point of the CRC session is to identify the *responsibilities* of each class. Pay little attention to the attributes, capturing only the most essential and obvious attributes as you go. The important work is to identify the responsibilities. If, in fulfilling a responsibility, the class must delegate work to another class, you capture that information under *collaborations*.

As you progress, keep an eye on your list of responsibilities. If you run out of room on your 4×6 card, it may make sense to wonder whether you're asking this class to do too much. Remember, each class should be responsible for one general area of work, and the various responsibilities listed should be cohesive and coherent—that is, they should work together to accomplish the overall responsibility of the class.

At this point, you do *not* want to focus on relationships, nor do you want to worry about the class interface or which methods will be public and which will be private. The focus is only on understanding what each class *does*.

Anthropomorphic and Use-Case Driven

The key feature of CRC cards is to make them anthropomorphic—that is, you attribute humanlike qualities to each class. Here's how it works: After you have a preliminary set of classes, return to your CRC scenarios. Divide the cards around the table arbitrarily, and walk through the scenario together. For example, let's return to the following scenario:

> Customer chooses to withdraw cash from checking. Sufficient cash is in the account, sufficient cash and receipts are in the ATM, and the network is up and running. The ATM asks the customer to indicate an amount for the withdrawal, and the customer asks for $300, a legal amount to withdraw at this time. The machine dispenses $300 and prints a receipt, and the customer takes the money and the receipt.

Assume we have five participants in our CRC session: Amy, the facilitator and object-oriented designer; Barry, the lead programmer; Charlie, the client; Dorris, the domain expert; and Ed, a programmer.

Amy holds up a CRC card representing `CheckingAccount` and says "I tell the customer how much money is available. He asks me to give him $300. I send a message to the dispenser telling him to give out $300 cash." Barry holds up his card and says "I'm the dispenser; I spit out $300 and send Amy a message telling her to decrement her balance by $300. Who do I tell that the machine now has $300 less? Do I keep track of that?" Charlie says, "I think we need an object to keep track of cash in the machine." Ed says, "No, the dispenser should know how much cash it has; that's part of being a dispenser." Amy disagrees: "No, someone has to coordinate the dispensing of cash. The dispenser needs to know whether cash is available and whether the customer has enough in the account, and it has to count out the money and know when to close the drawer. It should delegate responsibility for keeping track of cash on hand—some kind of internal account. Whoever knows about cash on hand can also notify the back office when it is time to be refilled. Otherwise, that's asking the dispenser to do too much."

The discussion continues. By holding up cards and interacting with one another, the requirements and opportunities to delegate are teased out; each class comes alive, and its responsibilities are clarified. When the group becomes bogged down in design questions, the facilitator can make a decision and help the group move on.

Limitations of CRC Cards

Although CRC cards can be a powerful tool for getting started with design, they have inherent limitations. The first problem is that they don't scale well. In a very complex project, you can be overwhelmed with CRC cards; just keeping track of them all can be difficult.

CRC cards also don't capture the interrelationship among classes. Although it is true that collaborations are noted, the nature of the collaboration is not modeled well. Looking at the CRC cards, you can't tell whether classes aggregate one another, who creates whom, and so forth. CRC cards also don't capture attributes, so it is difficult to go from CRC cards to code. Most important, CRC cards are static; although you can act out the interactions among the classes, the CRC cards themselves do not capture this information.

In short, CRC cards are a good start, but you need to move the classes into the UML if you are to build a robust and complete model of your design. Although the transition *into* the UML is not terribly difficult, it is a one-way street. Once you move your classes into UML diagrams, there is no turning back; you set aside the CRC cards and don't come back to them. It is simply too difficult to keep the two models synchronized with one another.

Transforming CRC Cards to UML

Each CRC card can be translated directly into a class modeled with the UML. Responsibilities are translated into class methods, and whatever attributes you have captured are added as well. The class definition from the back of the card is put into the class documentation. Figure 11.13 shows the relationship between the CheckingAccount CRC card and the UML class created from that card.

Class: CheckingAccount

SuperClass: Account

Responsibilities:

>>> Track current balance

>>> Accept deposits and transfers in

>>> Write checks

>>> Transfer cash out

>>> Keep current day's ATM withdrawal balance

Collaborations:

>>> Other accounts

>>> Back-office systems

>>> Cash dispenser

Class Relationships

After the classes are in the UML, you can begin to turn your attention to the relationships among the various classes. The principal relationships you'll model are the following:

- Generalization
- Association
- Aggregation
- Composition

11

FIGURE 11.13

CRC card.

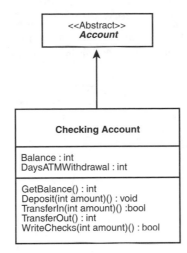

The generalization relationship is implemented in C++ through public inheritance. From a design perspective, however, we focus less on the mechanism and more on the semantics: what it is that this relationship implies.

We examined the generalization relationship in the analysis phase, but now we turn our attention not just to the objects in the domain, but also to the objects in our design. Our efforts now are to "factor out" common functionality in related classes into base classes that can encapsulate the shared responsibilities.

When you "factor out" common functionality, you move that functionality out of the specialized classes and up into the more general class. Thus, if I notice that both my checking and my savings account need methods for transferring money in and out, I'll move the TransferFunds() method up into the account base class. The more you factor out of the derived classes, the more polymorphic your design will be.

One of the capabilities available in C++, which is not available in Java, is *multiple inheritance* (although Java has a similar, if limited, capability with its multiple *interfaces*). Multiple inheritance allows a class to inherit from more than one base class, bringing in the members and methods of two or more classes.

Experience has shown that you should use multiple inheritance judiciously because it can complicate both your design and the implementation. Many problems initially solved with multiple inheritance are today solved using aggregation. That said, multiple inheritance is a powerful tool, and your design may require that a single class specializes the behavior of two or more other classes.

Multiple Inheritance Versus Containment

Is an object the sum of its parts? Does it make sense to model a `Car` object as a specialization of `SteeringWheel`, `Door`, and `Tire`, as shown in Figure 11.14?

FIGURE 11.14

False inheritance.

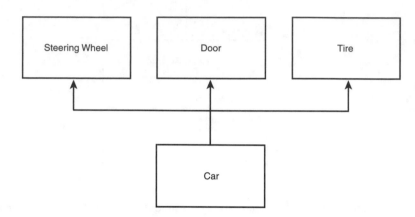

It is important to come back to the fundamentals: Public inheritance should always model generalization. The common expression for this is that inheritance should model *is-a* relationships. If you want to model the has-a relationship (for example, a car *has-a* steering wheel), you do so with aggregation, as shown in Figure 11.15.

FIGURE 11.15

Aggregation.

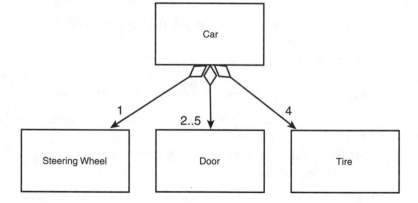

The diagram in Figure 11.15 indicates that a car has a steering wheel, four wheels, and 2–5 doors. This is a more accurate model of the relationship among a car and its parts. Notice that the diamond in the diagram is not filled in; this is so because we are modeling this relationship as an aggregation, not as a composition. Composition implies control for the lifetime of the object. Although the car *has* tires and a door, the tires and door can exist before they are part of the car and can continue to exist after they are no longer part of the car.

Figure 11.16 models composition. This model says that the body is not only an aggregation of a head, two arms, and two legs, but that these objects (head, arms, legs) are created when the body is created and disappear when the body disappears. That is, they have no independent existence; the body is composed of these things and their lifetimes are intertwined.

FIGURE 11.16

Composition.

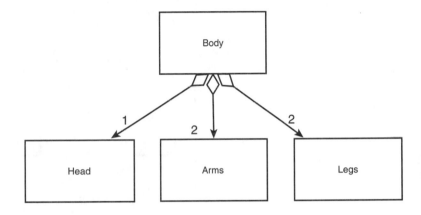

Discriminators and Powertypes

How might you design the classes required to reflect the various model lines of a typical car manufacturer? Suppose that you've been hired to design a system for Acme Motors, which currently manufactures five cars: the Pluto (a slow, compact car with a small engine), the Venus (a four-door sedan with a middle-sized engine), the Mars (a sport coupe with the company's biggest engine, engineered for maximum performance), the Jupiter (a minivan with the same engine as the sports coupe but designed to shift at a lower RPM and to use its power to move its greater weight), and the Earth (a station wagon with a small engine but high RPM).

You might start by creating subtypes of car that reflect the various models, and then create instances of each model as it rolls off the assembly line, as shown in Figure 11.17.

How are these models differentiated? As we saw, they are differentiated by the engine size, body type, and performance characteristics. These various discriminating characteristics can be mixed and matched to create various models. We can model this in the UML with the *discriminator* stereotype, as shown in Figure 11.18.

FIGURE **11.17**

Modeling subtypes.

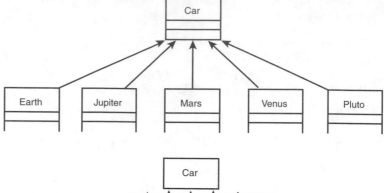

FIGURE **11.18**

Modeling the discrimi-nator.

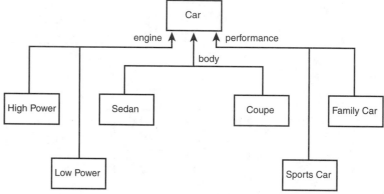

The diagram in Figure 11.18 indicates that classes can be derived from Car based on mixing and matching three discriminating attributes. The size of the engine dictates how powerful the car is, and the performance characteristics indicate how sporty the car is. Thus, you can have a powerful and sporty station wagon, a low-power family sedan, and so forth.

Each attribute can be implemented with a simple enumerator. Thus, the body type might be implemented with the following statement in code:

```
enum BodyType = { sedan, coupe, minivan, stationwagon };
```

It may turn out, however, that a simple value is insufficient to model a particular discriminator. For example, the performance characteristic may be rather complex. In this case, the discriminator can be modeled as a class, and the discrimination can be encapsulated in an instance of that type.

Thus, the car might model the performance characteristics in a *performance* type, which contains information about where the engine shifts and how fast it can turn. The UML stereotype for a class that encapsulates a discriminator, and that can be used to create *instances* of a class (Car) that are logically of different types (for example, SportsCar versus LuxuryCar) is <<powertype>>. In this case, the Performance class is a powertype for car. When you instantiate `Car`, you also instantiate a `Performance` object, and you associate a given `Performance` object with a given `Car`, as shown in Figure 11.19.

FIGURE 11.19

A discriminator as a powertype.

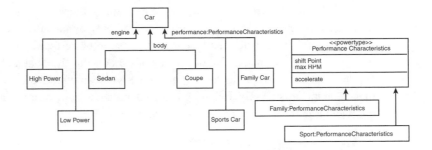

Powertypes enable you to create a variety of *logical* types without using inheritance. You can thus manage a large and complex set of types without the combinatorial explosion you might encounter with inheritance.

Typically, you *implement* the powertype in C++ with pointers. In this case, the `Car` class holds a pointer to an instance of `PerformanceCharacteristics` class (see Figure 11.20). I'll leave it as an exercise to the ambitious reader to convert the body and engine discriminators into powertypes.

FIGURE 11.20

The relationship between a Car object and its powertype.

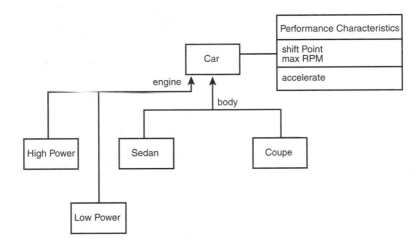

```
Class Car : public Vehicle
{
public:
    Car();
    ~Car();
    // other public methods elided
```

```
private:
    PerformanceCharacteristics * pPerformance;
};
```

As a final note, powertypes enable you to create new *types* (not just instances) at run-time. Because each logical type is differentiated only by the attributes of the associated powertype, these attributes can be parameters to the powertype's constructor. This means that you can, at runtime, create new *types* of cars on-the-fly. That is, by passing different engine sizes and shift points to the powertype, you can effectively create new performance characteristics. By assigning those characteristics to various cars, you can effectively enlarge the set of types of cars *at runtime*.

Dynamic Model

In addition to modeling the relationships among the classes, it is critical to model how they interact. For example, the CheckingAccount, ATM, and Receipt classes may interact with the Customer in fulfilling the "Withdraw Cash" use case. We return to the kinds of sequence diagrams first used in analysis, but now flesh out the details based on the methods we've developed in the classes, as shown in Figure 11.21.

FIGURE 11.21

Sequence diagram.

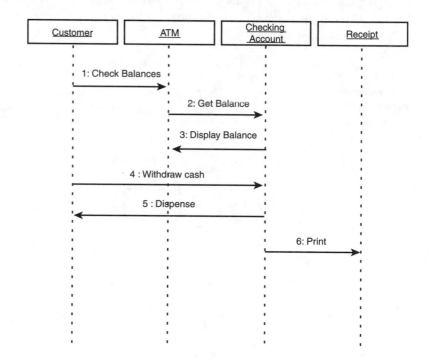

This simple interaction diagram shows the interaction among a number of design classes over time. It suggests that the ATM class will delegate to the CheckingAccount class all responsibility for managing the balance, while the CheckingAccount will call on the ATM to manage display to the user.

Interaction diagrams comes in two flavors. The one in Figure 11.21 is called a *sequence diagram.* Another view on the same information is provided by the *collaboration diagram.* The sequence diagram emphasizes the sequence of events over time; the collaboration diagram emphasizes the interactions among the classes. You can generate a collaboration diagram directly from a sequence diagram; tools such as Rational Rose automate this task at the click of a button (see Figure 11.22).

FIGURE 11.22

Collaboration diagram.

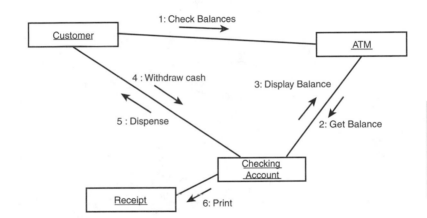

State Transition Diagrams

As we come to understand the interactions among the objects, we have to understand the various possible *states* of each individual object. We can model the transitions among the various states in a state diagram (or state transition diagram). Figure 11.23 shows the various states of the CustomerAccount class as the customer logs in to the system.

Every state diagram begins with a single start state and ends with zero or more end states. The individual states are named, and the transitions may be labeled. The guard indicates a condition that must be satisfied for an object to move from one state to another.

Super States

The customer can change his mind at any time and decide not to log in. He can do this after he swipes his card to identify his account or after he enters his password. In either case, the system must accept his request to cancel and return to the "not logged in state" (see Figure 11.24).

FIGURE 11.23

*Customer account
state.*

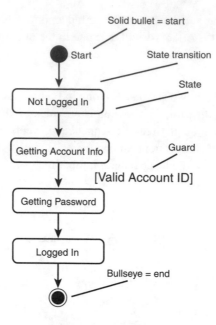

FIGURE 11.24

User may cancel.

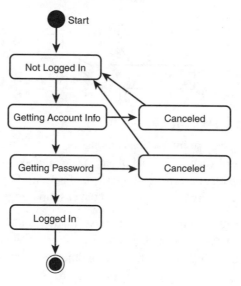

As you can see, in a more complicated diagram, the `Canceled` state will quickly become a distraction. This is particularly annoying because canceling is an exceptional condition that should not be given prominence in the diagram. We can simplify this diagram by using a *super state*, as shown in Figure 11.25.

FIGURE 11.25

Super state.

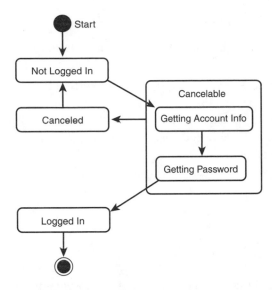

The diagram in Figure 11.24 provides the same information in Figure 11.23 but is much cleaner and easier to read. From the time you start logging in until the system finalizes your login, you can cancel the process. If you do cancel, you return to the state "not logged in."

Summary

This chapter provided an introduction to the issues involved in object-oriented analysis and design. The essence of this approach is to analyze how your system will be used (use cases) and how it must perform, and then to design the classes and model their relationships and interactions.

In the old days, we sketched out a quick idea of what we wanted to accomplish and began writing code. The problem is that complex projects are never finished; and if they are, they are unreliable and brittle. By investing up front in understanding the requirements and modeling the design, we ensure a finished product that is correct (that is, it meets the design) and that is robust, reliable, and extensible.

Much of the rest of this book focuses on the details of implementation. Issues relating to testing and rollout are beyond the scope of this book, except to mention that you want to plan your unit testing as you implement, and that you will use your requirements document as the foundation of your test plan prior to rollout.

11

Q&A

Q **In what way is object-oriented analysis and design fundamentally different from other approaches?**

A Prior to the development of these object-oriented techniques, analysts and programmers tended to think of programs as groups of functions that acted on data. Object-oriented programming focuses on the integrated data and functionality as discrete units that have both knowledge (data) and capabilities (functions). Procedural programs, on the other hand, focus on functions and how they act on data. It has been said that Pascal and C programs are collections of procedures, and C++ programs are collections of classes.

Q **Is object-oriented programming finally the silver bullet that will solve all programming problems?**

A No, it was never intended to be. For large, complex problems, however, object-oriented analysis, design, and programming can provide the programmer with tools to manage enormous complexity in ways that were previously impossible.

Q **Is C++ the perfect object-oriented language?**

A C++ has a number of advantages and disadvantages when compared with alternative object-oriented programming languages, but it has one killer advantage above and beyond all others: It is the single most popular object-oriented programming language on the face of the Earth. Frankly, most programmers don't decide to program in C++ after an exhaustive analysis of the alternative object-oriented programming languages; they go where the action is, and these days the action is with C++. There are good reasons for that; C++ has a lot to offer, but this book exists—and I'd wager you are reading it—because C++ is the development language of choice at so many corporations.

Workshop

The Workshop provides quiz questions to help you solidify your understanding of the material covered and exercises to provide you with experience in using what you've learned. Try to answer the quiz and exercise questions before checking the answers in Appendix D, and make sure you understand the answers before continuing to the next chapter.

Quiz

1. What is the difference between object-oriented programming and procedural programming?

2. What are the phases of object-oriented analysis and design?

3. What is encapsulation?

Exercises

1. Suppose you had to simulate the intersection of Massachusetts Avenue and Vassar Street—two typical two-lane roads, with traffic lights and crosswalks. The purpose of the simulation is to determine whether the timing of the traffic signal allows for a smooth flow of traffic.

   What kinds of objects should be modeled in the simulation? What would the classes be for the simulation?

2. Suppose the intersection from Exercise 1 were in a suburb of Boston, which has arguably the least friendly streets in the United States. At any time three kinds of Boston drivers exist:

   Locals, who continue to drive through intersections after the light turns red; tourists, who drive slowly and cautiously (in a rental car, typically); and taxis, who have a wide variation of driving patterns, depending on the kinds of passengers in the cabs.

   Also, Boston has two kinds of pedestrians: locals, who cross the street whenever they feel like it and seldom use the crosswalk buttons; and tourists, who always use the crosswalk buttons and only cross when the Walk/Don't Walk light permits.

   Finally, Boston has bicyclists who never pay attention to stop lights.

   How do these considerations change the model?

3. You are asked to design a group scheduler. The software enables you to arrange meetings among individuals or groups and to reserve a limited number of conference rooms. Identify the principal subsystems.

4. Design and show the interfaces to the classes in the room reservation portion of the program discussed in Exercise 3.

11

DAY 12

Inheritance

Yesterday you learned about a number of object-oriented relationships, including Specialization/Generalization. C++ implements this relationship through Inheritance.

Today you will learn

- What inheritance is.
- How to derive one class from another.
- What protected access is and how to use it.
- What virtual functions are.

What Is Inheritance?

What is a dog? When you look at your pet, what do you see? I see four legs in service to a mouth. A biologist sees a network of interacting organs, a physicist sees atoms and forces at work, and a taxonomist sees a representative of the species *canine domesticus*.

It is that last assessment that interests us at the moment. A dog is a kind of canine, a canine is a kind of mammal, and so forth. Taxonomists divide the world of living things into Kingdom, Phylum, Class, Order, Family, Genus, and Species.

This specialization/generalization hierarchy establishes an *is-a* relationship. A Homo sapien is a kind of primate. We see this relationship everywhere: A station wagon is a kind of car, which is a kind of vehicle. A sundae is a kind of dessert, which is a kind of food.

When we say something is a kind of something else, we imply that it is a specialization of that thing. That is, a car is a special kind of vehicle.

Inheritance and Derivation

The concept dog inherits—that is, it automatically gets—all the features of a mammal. Because it is a mammal, we know that it moves and that it breathes air. All mammals, by definition, move and breathe air. The concept of a dog adds the idea of barking, wagging its tail, eating my revisions to this chapter just when I was finally done, barking when I'm trying to sleep... Sorry. Where was I? Oh yes:

We can divide dogs into working dogs, sporting dogs, and terriers, and we can divide sporting dogs into retrievers, spaniels, and so forth. Finally, each of these can be specialized further; for example, retrievers can be subdivided into Labradors and Goldens.

A Golden is a kind of retriever, which is a sporting dog, which is a dog, and thus a kind of mammal, which is a kind of animal, and therefore, a kind of living thing. This hierarchy is represented in Figure 12.1.

C++ attempts to represent these relationships by enabling you to define classes that derive from one another. Derivation is a way of expressing the *is-a* relationship. You derive a new class, Dog, from the class Mammal. You don't have to state explicitly that dogs move because they inherit that from Mammal.

A class that adds new functionality to an existing class is said to derive from that original class. The original class is said to be the new class's base class.

If the Dog class derives from the Mammal class, then Mammal is a base class of Dog. Derived classes are supersets of their base classes. Just as dog adds certain features to the idea of mammal, the Dog class will add certain methods or data to the Mammal class.

Typically, a base class will have more than one derived class. Because dogs, cats, and horses are all types of mammals, their classes would all derive from the Mammal class.

The Animal Kingdom

To facilitate the discussion of derivation and inheritance, this chapter will focus on the relationships among a number of classes representing animals. You can imagine that you have been asked to design a children's game—a simulation of a farm.

FIGURE 12.1

Hierarchy of animals.

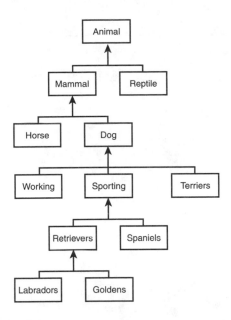

In time you will develop a whole set of farm animals, including horses, cows, dogs, cats, sheep, and so forth. You will create methods for these classes so that they can act in the ways the child might expect, but for now you'll stub-out each method with a simple print statement.

Stubbing-out a function means you'll write only enough to show that the function was called, leaving the details for later when you have more time. Please feel free to extend the minimal code provided in this chapter to enable the animals to act more realistically.

The Syntax of Derivation

When you declare a class, you can indicate what class it derives from by writing a colon after the class name, the type of derivation (public or otherwise), and the class from which it derives. The following is an example:

```
class Dog : public Mammal
```

The type of derivation will be discussed later in this chapter. For now, always use public. The class from which you derive must have been declared earlier, or you will get a compiler error. Listing 12.1 illustrates how to declare a Dog class that is derived from a Mammal class.

LISTING 12.1   Simple Inheritance

```
0:   //Listing 12.1 Simple inheritance
1:
2:   #include <iostream>
```

12

LISTING 12.1   continued

```
3:   using namespace std;
4:
5:   enum BREED { GOLDEN, CAIRN, DANDIE, SHETLAND, DOBERMAN, LAB };
6:
7:   class Mammal
8:   {
9:   public:
10:      // constructors
11:      Mammal();
12:      ~Mammal();
13:
14:      //accessors
15:      int GetAge()          const;
16:      void SetAge(int);
17:      int GetWeight() const;
18:      void SetWeight();
19:
20:      //Other methods
21:      void Speak() const;
22:      void Sleep() const;
23:
24:
25:   protected:
26:      int itsAge;
27:      int itsWeight;
28:   };
29:
30:   class Dog : public Mammal
31:   {
32:   public:
33:
34:      // Constructors
35:      Dog();
36:      ~Dog();
37:
38:      // Accessors
39:      BREED GetBreed() const;
40:      void  SetBreed(BREED);
41:
42:      // Other methods
43:      WagTail();
44:      BegForFood();
45:
46:   protected:
47:      BREED itsBreed;
48:   };
```

This program has no output because it is only a set of class declarations without their
implementations. Nonetheless, there is much to see here.

ANALYSIS On lines 7–28, the `Mammal` class is declared. Note that in this example, `Mammal` does not derive from any other class. In the real world, mammals do derive—that is, mammals are kinds of animals. In a C++ program, you can represent only a fraction of the information you have about any given object. Reality is far too complex to capture all of it, so every C++ hierarchy is an arbitrary representation of the data available. The trick of good design is to represent the areas that you care about in a way that maps back to reality in a reasonably faithful manner.

The hierarchy has to begin somewhere; this program begins with `Mammal`. Because of this decision, some member variables that might properly belong in a higher base class are now represented here. Certainly all animals have an age and weight, for example, so if `Mammal` is derived from `Animal`, we might expect to inherit those attributes. As it is, the attributes appear in the `Mammal` class.

To keep the program reasonably simple and manageable, only six methods have been put in the `Mammal` class—four accessor methods, `Speak()`, and `Sleep()`.

The `Dog` class inherits from `Mammal`, as indicated on line 30. Every `Dog` object will have three member variables: `itsAge`, `itsWeight`, and `itsBreed`. Note that the class declaration for `Dog` does not include the member variables `itsAge` and `itsWeight`. Dog objects inherit these variables from the `Mammal` class, along with all `Mammal`'s methods except the copy operator and the constructors and destructor.

Private Versus Protected

You may have noticed that a new access keyword, `protected`, has been introduced on lines 25 and 46 of Listing 12.1. Previously, class data had been declared private. However, private members are not available to derived classes. You could make `itsAge` and `itsWeight` public, but that is not desirable. You don't want other classes accessing these data members directly.

 Note

> There is an argument to be made that you ought to make all member data private and never protected. Stroustrup (the creator of C++) makes this argument in *The Design and Evolution of C++* ISBN 0-201-543330-3 Addison Wesley, 1994. Protected methods, however, are not generally regarded as problematic, and can be very useful.

What you want is a designation that says, "Make these visible to this class and to classes that derive from this class." That designation is protected. Protected data members and functions are fully visible to derived classes, but are otherwise private.

12

In total, three access specifiers exist: public, protected, and private. If a function has an object of your class, it can access all the public member data and functions. The member functions, in turn, can access all private data members and functions of their own class and all protected data members and functions of any class from which they derive.

Thus, the function `Dog::WagTail()` can access the private data `itsBreed` and can access the protected data in the `Mammal` class.

Even if other classes are layered between `Mammal` and `Dog` (for example, `DomesticAnimals`), the `Dog` class will still be able to access the protected members of `Mammal`, assuming that these other classes all use public inheritance. Private inheritance is discussed on Day 16, "Advanced Inheritance."

Listing 12.2 demonstrates how to create objects of type `Dog` and access the data and functions of that type.

LISTING 12.2   Using a Derived Object

```
0:  //Listing 12.2 Using a derived object
1:
2:  #include <iostream>
3:  using std::cout;
4:
5:  enum BREED { GOLDEN, CAIRN, DANDIE, SHETLAND, DOBERMAN, LAB };
6:
7:  class Mammal
8:  {
9:  public:
10:     // constructors
11:     Mammal():itsAge(2), itsWeight(5){}
12:     ~Mammal(){}
13:
14:     //accessors
15:     int GetAge() const   { return itsAge; }
16:     void SetAge(int age) { itsAge = age; }
17:     int GetWeight() const { return itsWeight; }
18:     void SetWeight(int weight) { itsWeight = weight; }
19:
20:     //Other methods
21:     void Speak()const { cout << "Mammal sound!\n"; }
22:     void Sleep()const { cout << "shhh. I'm sleeping.\n"; }
23:
24:
25:  protected:
26:     int itsAge;
27:     int itsWeight;
28:  };
29:
```

LISTING 12.2   continued

```
30:    class Dog : public Mammal
31:    {
32:    public:
33:
34:        // Constructors
35:        Dog():itsBreed(GOLDEN){}
36:        ~Dog(){}
37:
38:        // Accessors
39:        BREED GetBreed() const { return itsBreed; }
40:        void SetBreed(BREED breed) { itsBreed = breed; }
41:
42:        // Other methods
43:        void WagTail() const { cout << "Tail wagging...\n"; }
44:        void BegForFood() const { cout << "Begging for food...\n"; }
45:
46:    private:
47:        BREED itsBreed;
48:    };
49:
50:    int main()
51:    {
52:        Dog fido;
53:        fido.Speak();
54:        fido.WagTail();
55:        cout << "Fido is " << fido.GetAge() << " years old\n";
56:        return 0;
57:    }
```

OUTPUT
```
Mammal sound!
Tail wagging...
Fido is 2 years old
```

ANALYSIS   On lines 7–28, the Mammal class is declared (all its functions are inline to save space here). On lines 30–48, the Dog class is declared as a derived class of Mammal. Thus, by these declarations, all Dogs have an age, a weight, and a breed.

On line 52, a Dog is declared: Fido. Fido inherits all the attributes of a Mammal, as well as all the attributes of a Dog. Thus, Fido knows how to WagTail(), but he also knows how to Speak() and Sleep().

Constructors and Destructors

Dog objects are Mammal objects. This is the essence of the is-a relationship. When Fido is created, his base constructor is called first, creating a Mammal. Then the Dog constructor is called, completing the construction of the Dog object. Because we gave Fido no parameters, the default constructor was called in each case. Fido doesn't exist until he is completely constructed, which means that both his Mammal part and his Dog part must be constructed. Thus, both constructors must be called.

When Fido is destroyed, first the Dog destructor will be called and then the destructor for the Mammal part of Fido. Each destructor is given an opportunity to clean up after its own part of Fido. Remember to clean up after your Dog! Listing 12.3 demonstrates this.

LISTING 12.3   Constructors and Destructors Called

```
0:   //Listing 12.3 Constructors and destructors called.
1:
2:   #include <iostream>
3:   enum BREED { GOLDEN, CAIRN, DANDIE, SHETLAND, DOBERMAN, LAB };
4:
5:   class Mammal
6:   {
7:   public:
8:       // constructors
9:       Mammal();
10:      ~Mammal();
11:
12:      //accessors
13:      int GetAge() const { return itsAge; }
14:      void SetAge(int age) { itsAge = age; }
15:      int GetWeight() const { return itsWeight; }
16:      void SetWeight(int weight) { itsWeight = weight; }
17:
18:      //Other methods
19:      void Speak() const { std::cout << "Mammal sound!\n"; }
20:      void Sleep() const { std::cout << "shhh. I'm sleeping.\n"; }
21:
22:
23:   protected:
24:      int itsAge;
25:      int itsWeight;
26:   };
27:
28:   class Dog : public Mammal
29:   {
30:   public:
31:
32:      // Constructors
33:      Dog();
34:      ~Dog();
35:
36:      // Accessors
37:      BREED GetBreed() const { return itsBreed; }
```

LISTING 12.3   continued

```
38:        void SetBreed(BREED breed) { itsBreed = breed; }
39:
40:        // Other methods
41:        void WagTail() const { std::cout << "Tail wagging...\n"; }
42:        void BegForFood() const { std::cout << "Begging for food...\n"; }
43:
44:   private:
45:        BREED itsBreed;
46:   };
47:
48:   Mammal::Mammal():
49:   itsAge(1),
50:   itsWeight(5)
51:   {
52:        std::cout << "Mammal constructor...\n";
53:   }
54:
55:   Mammal::~Mammal()
56:   {
57:        std::cout << "Mammal destructor...\n";
58:   }
59:
60:   Dog::Dog():
61:   itsBreed(GOLDEN)
62:   {
63:        std::cout << "Dog constructor...\n";
64:   }
65:
66:   Dog::~Dog()
67:   {
68:        std::cout << "Dog destructor...\n";
69:   }
70:   int main()
71:   {
72:        Dog fido;
73:        fido.Speak();
74:        fido.WagTail();
75:        std::cout << "Fido is " << fido.GetAge() << " years old\n";
76:        return 0;
77:   }
```

OUTPUT

```
Mammal constructor...
Dog constructor...
Mammal sound!
Tail wagging...
Fido is 1 years old
Dog destructor...
Mammal destructor...
```

12

ANALYSIS Listing 12.3 is like Listing 12.2, except that the constructors and destructors now print to the screen when called. Mammal's constructor is called, then Dog's. At that point the Dog fully exists, and its methods can be called. When Fido goes out of scope, Dog's destructor is called, followed by a call to Mammal's destructor.

Passing Arguments to Base Constructors

It is possible that you'll want to overload the constructor of Mammal to take a specific age, and that you'll want to overload the Dog constructor to take a breed. How do you get the age and weight parameters passed up to the right constructor in Mammal? What if Dogs want to initialize weight but Mammals don't?

Base class initialization can be performed during class initialization by writing the base class name, followed by the parameters expected by the base class. Listing 12.4 demonstrates this.

LISTING 12.4   Overloading Constructors in Derived Classes

```
0:   //Listing 12.4 Overloading constructors in derived classes
1:
2:   #include <iostream>
3:   using namespace std;
4:
5:   enum BREED { GOLDEN, CAIRN, DANDIE, SHETLAND, DOBERMAN, LAB };
6:
7:   class Mammal
8:   {
9:   public:
10:      // constructors
11:      Mammal();
12:      Mammal(int age);
13:      ~Mammal();
14:
15:      //accessors
16:      int GetAge() const { return itsAge; }
17:      void SetAge(int age) { itsAge = age; }
18:      int GetWeight() const { return itsWeight; }
19:      void SetWeight(int weight) { itsWeight = weight; }
20:
21:      //Other methods
22:      void Speak() const { cout << "Mammal sound!\n"; }
23:      void Sleep() const { cout << "shhh. I'm sleeping.\n"; }
24:
25:
26:   protected:
27:      int itsAge;
28:      int itsWeight;
29:   };
```

LISTING 12.4   continued

```
30:
31:    class Dog : public Mammal
32:    {
33:    public:
34:
35:        // Constructors
36:        Dog();
37:        Dog(int age);
38:        Dog(int age, int weight);
39:        Dog(int age, BREED breed);
40:        Dog(int age, int weight, BREED breed);
41:        ~Dog();
42:
43:        // Accessors
44:        BREED GetBreed() const { return itsBreed; }
45:        void SetBreed(BREED breed) { itsBreed = breed; }
46:
47:        // Other methods
48:        void WagTail() const { cout << "Tail wagging...\n"; }
49:        void BegForFood() const { cout << "Begging for food...\n"; }
50:
51:    private:
52:        BREED itsBreed;
53:    };
54:
55:    Mammal::Mammal():
56:    itsAge(1),
57:    itsWeight(5)
58:    {
59:        cout << "Mammal constructor...\n";
60:    }
61:
62:    Mammal::Mammal(int age):
63:    itsAge(age),
64:    itsWeight(5)
65:    {
66:        cout << "Mammal(int) constructor...\n";
67:    }
68:
69:    Mammal::~Mammal()
70:    {
71:        cout << "Mammal destructor...\n";
72:    }
73:
74:    Dog::Dog():
75:    Mammal(),
76:    itsBreed(GOLDEN)
77:    {
78:        cout << "Dog constructor...\n";
```

12

LISTING 12.4   continued

```
79:    }
80:
81:    Dog::Dog(int age):
82:    Mammal(age),
83:    itsBreed(GOLDEN)
84:    {
85:        cout << "Dog(int) constructor...\n";
86:    }
87:
88:    Dog::Dog(int age, int weight):
89:    Mammal(age),
90:    itsBreed(GOLDEN)
91:    {
92:        itsWeight = weight;
93:        cout << "Dog(int, int) constructor...\n";
94:    }
95:
96:    Dog::Dog(int age, int weight, BREED breed):
97:    Mammal(age),
98:    itsBreed(breed)
99:    {
100:        itsWeight = weight;
101:        cout << "Dog(int, int, BREED) constructor...\n";
102:    }
103:
104:    Dog::Dog(int age, BREED breed):
105:    Mammal(age),
106:    itsBreed(breed)
107:    {
108:        cout << "Dog(int, BREED) constructor...\n";
109:    }
110:
111:    Dog::~Dog()
112:    {
113:        cout << "Dog destructor...\n";
114:    }
115:    int main()
116:    {
117:        Dog fido;
118:        Dog rover(5);
119:        Dog buster(6,8);
120:        Dog yorkie (3,GOLDEN);
121:        Dog dobbie (4,20,DOBERMAN);
122:        fido.Speak();
123:        rover.WagTail();
124:        cout << "Yorkie is " << yorkie.GetAge() << " years old\n";
125:        cout << "Dobbie weighs ";
126:        cout << dobbie.GetWeight() << " pounds\n";
127:        return 0;
128:    }
```

Note | The output has been numbered here so that each line can be referred to in the analysis.

OUTPUT

```
 1: Mammal constructor...
 2: Dog constructor...
 3: Mammal(int) constructor...
 4: Dog(int) constructor...
 5: Mammal(int) constructor...
 6: Dog(int, int) constructor...
 7: Mammal(int) constructor...
 8: Dog(int, BREED) constructor....
 9: Mammal(int) constructor...
10: Dog(int, int, BREED) constructor...
11: Mammal sound!
12: Tail wagging...
13: Yorkie is 3 years old.
14: Dobbie weighs 20 pounds.
15: Dog destructor. . .
16: Mammal destructor...
17: Dog destructor...
18: Mammal destructor...
19: Dog destructor...
20: Mammal destructor...
21: Dog destructor...
22: Mammal destructor...
23: Dog destructor...
24: Mammal destructor...
```

12

ANALYSIS In Listing 12.4, Mammal's constructor has been overloaded on line 11 to take an integer, the Mammal's age. The implementation on lines 62–67 initializes itsAge with the value passed into the constructor and initializes itsWeight with the value 5.

Dog has overloaded five constructors on lines 36–40. The first is the default constructor. The second takes the age, which is the same parameter that the Mammal constructor takes. The third constructor takes both the age and the weight, the fourth takes the age and the breed, and the fifth takes the age, the weight, and the breed.

Note that on line 75, Dog's default constructor calls Mammal's default constructor. Although it is not strictly necessary to do this, it serves as documentation that you intended to call the base constructor, which takes no parameters. The base constructor would be called in any case, but actually doing so makes your intentions explicit.

The implementation for the Dog constructor, which takes an integer, is on lines 81–86. In its initialization phase (lines 82 and 83), Dog initializes its base class, passing in the parameter, and then it initializes its breed.

Another `Dog` constructor is on lines 88–94. This one takes two parameters. Once again it initializes its base class by calling the appropriate constructor, but this time it also assigns weight to its base class's variable `itsWeight`. Note that you cannot assign to the base class variable in the initialization phase. Because `Mammal` does not have a constructor that takes this parameter, you must do this within the body of the `Dog`'s constructor.

Walk through the remaining constructors to make sure you are comfortable with how they work. Note what is initialized and what must wait for the body of the constructor.

The output has been numbered so that each line can be referred to in this analysis. The first two lines of output represent the instantiation of `Fido`, using the default constructor.

In the output, lines 3 and 4 represent the creation of `rover`. Lines 5 and 6 represent `buster`. Note that the `Mammal` constructor that was called is the constructor that takes one integer, but the `Dog` constructor is the constructor that takes two integers.

After all the objects are created, they are used and then go out of scope. As each object is destroyed, first the `Dog` destructor and then the `Mammal` destructor is called, five of each in total.

Overriding Functions

A `Dog` object has access to all the member functions in class `Mammal`, as well as to any member functions, such as `WagTail()`, that the declaration of the `Dog` class might add. It can also override a base class function. Overriding a function means changing the implementation of a base class function in a derived class. When you make an object of the derived class, the correct function is called.

When a derived class creates a function with the same return type and signature as a member function in the base class, but with a new implementation, it is said to be overriding that function.

When you override a function, its signature must agree with signature of the function in the base class. The signature is the function prototype other than the return type; that is, the name, the parameter list, and the keyword const, if used. The return types may differ.

Listing 12.5 illustrates what happens if the `Dog` class overrides the `Speak()` method in `Mammal`. To save room, the accessor functions have been left out of these classes.

LISTING 12.5   Overriding a Base Class Method in a Derived Class

```
0:    //Listing 12.5 Overriding a base class method in a derived class
1:
2:    #include <iostream>
3:    using std::cout;
4:
5:    enum BREED { GOLDEN, CAIRN, DANDIE, SHETLAND, DOBERMAN, LAB };
6:
7:    class Mammal
8:    {
9:    public:
10:       // constructors
11:       Mammal() { cout << "Mammal constructor...\n"; }
12:       ~Mammal() { cout << "Mammal destructor...\n"; }
13:
14:       //Other methods
15:       void Speak()const { cout << "Mammal sound!\n"; }
16:       void Sleep()const { cout << "shhh. I'm sleeping.\n"; }
17:
18:
19:    protected:
20:       int itsAge;
21:       int itsWeight;
22:    };
23:
24:    class Dog : public Mammal
25:    {
26:    public:
27:
28:       // Constructors
29:       Dog(){ cout << "Dog constructor...\n"; }
30:       ~Dog(){ cout << "Dog destructor...\n"; }
31:
32:       // Other methods
33:       void WagTail() const  { cout << "Tail wagging...\n"; }
34:       void BegForFood() const  { cout << "Begging for food...\n"; }
35:       void Speak() const { cout << "Woof!\n"; }
36:
37:    private:
38:       BREED itsBreed;
39:    };
40:
41:    int main()
42:    {
43:       Mammal bigAnimal;
44:       Dog fido;
45:       bigAnimal.Speak();
46:       fido.Speak();
47:       return 0;
48:    }
```

12

OUTPUT

```
Mammal constructor...
Mammal constructor...
Dog constructor...
Mammal sound!
Woof!
Dog destructor...
Mammal destructor...
Mammal destructor...
```

ANALYSIS   On line 35, the Dog class overrides the Speak() method, causing Dog objects to say Woof! when the Speak() method is called. On line 43, a Mammal object, bigAnimal, is created, causing the first line of output when the Mammal constructor is called. On line 44, a Dog object, fido, is created, causing the next two lines of output, where the Mammal constructor and then the Dog constructor are called.

On line 45, the Mammal object calls its Speak() method; then on line 46 the Dog object calls its Speak() method. The output reflects that the correct methods were called. Finally, the two objects go out of scope and the destructors are called.

Overloading Versus Overriding

These terms are similar, and they do similar things. When you overload a method, you create more than one method with the same name, but with a different signature. When you override a method, you create a method in a derived class with the same name as a method in the base class and the same signature.

Hiding the Base Class Method

In the previous listing, the Dog class's Speak() method hides the base class's method. This is just what is wanted, but it can have unexpected results. If Mammal has a method, Move(), which is overloaded, and Dog overrides that method, the Dog method will hide all the Mammal methods with that name.

If Mammal overloads Move() as three methods—one that takes no parameters, one that takes an integer, and one that takes an integer and a direction—and Dog overrides just the Move() method that takes no parameters, it will not be easy to access the other two methods using a Dog object. Listing 12.6 illustrates this problem.

LISTING **12.6**   Hiding Methods

```
0:  //Listing 12.6 Hiding methods
1:
2:  #include <iostream>
```

LISTING 12.6   continued

```
3:
4:
5:   class Mammal
6:   {
7:   public:
8:       void Move() const { std::cout << "Mammal move one step\n"; }
9:       void Move(int distance) const
10:      {
11:          std::cout << "Mammal move ";
12:          std::cout << distance <<" steps.\n";
13:      }
14:  protected:
15:      int itsAge;
16:      int itsWeight;
17:  };
18:
19:  class Dog : public Mammal
20:  {
21:  public:
22:      // You may receive a warning that you are hiding a function!
23:      void Move() const { std::cout << "Dog move 5 steps.\n"; }
24:  };
25:
26:  int main()
27:  {
28:      Mammal bigAnimal;
29:      Dog fido;
30:      bigAnimal.Move();
31:      bigAnimal.Move(2);
32:      fido.Move();
33:      // fido.Move(10);
34:      return 0;
35:  }
```

OUTPUT

```
Mammal move one step
Mammal move 2 steps.
Dog move 5 steps.
```

ANALYSIS   All the extra methods and data have been removed from these classes. On lines 8 and 9, the Mammal class declares the overloaded Move() methods. On line 23, Dog overrides the version of Move() with no parameters. These are invoked on lines 30–32, and the output reflects this as executed.

Line 33, however, is commented out because it causes a compile-time error. Although the Dog class could have called the Move(int) method if it had not overridden the version of Move() without parameters, now that it has done so, it must override both if it wishes to use both. Otherwise, it will *hide* the method that it doesn't override. This is reminiscent of the rule that if you supply any constructor, the compiler will no longer supply a default constructor.

The rule is this: Once you override any overloaded method, all the other overrides of that method are hidden. If you want them not to be hidden, you must override them all.

It is a common mistake to hide a base class method when you intend to override it, by forgetting to include the keyword const. const is part of the signature, and leaving it off changes the signature and thus hides the method rather than overriding it.

Overriding Versus Hiding

In the next section, virtual methods are described. Overriding a virtual method supports polymorphism—hiding it undermines polymorphism. You'll see more on this very soon.

Calling the Base Method

If you have overridden the base method, it is still possible to call it by fully qualifying the name of the method. You do this by writing the base name, followed by two colons and then the method name. For example: `Mammal::Move()`.

It would have been possible to rewrite line 33 in Listing 12.6 so that it would compile, by writing

```
33:      fido.Mammal::Move(10);
```

This calls the `Mammal` method explicitly. Listing 12.7 fully illustrates this idea.

LISTING 12.7   Calling Base Method from Overridden Method

```
0:  //Listing 12.7 Calling base method from overridden method.
1:
2:  #include <iostream>
3:  using namespace std;
4:
5:  class Mammal
6:  {
7:  public:
8:      void Move() const { cout << "Mammal move one step\n"; }
9:      void Move(int distance) const
10:     {
11:        cout << "Mammal move " << distance;
12:        cout << " steps.\n";
13:     }
```

LISTING 12.7   continued

```
14:
15:   protected:
16:       int itsAge;
17:       int itsWeight;
18:   };
19:
20:   class Dog : public Mammal
21:   {
22:   public:
23:       void Move()const;
24:
25:   };
26:
27:   void Dog::Move() const
28:   {
29:       cout << "In dog move...\n";
30:       Mammal::Move(3);
31:   }
32:
33:   int main()
34:   {
35:       Mammal bigAnimal;
36:       Dog fido;
37:       bigAnimal.Move(2);
38:       fido.Mammal::Move(6);
39:       return 0;
40:   }
```

OUTPUT

```
Mammal move 2 steps.
Mammal move 6 steps.
```

ANALYSIS   On line 35, a `Mammal`, `bigAnimal`, is created, and on line 36, a `Dog`, `fido`, is created. The method call on line 37 invokes the `Move()` method of `Mammal`, which takes an `int`.

The programmer wanted to invoke `Move(int)` on the `Dog` object, but had a problem. `Dog` overrides the `Move()` method, but does not overload it and does not provide a version that takes an `int`. This is solved by the explicit call to the base class `Move(int)` method on line 38.

12

Do	Don't
DO extend the functionality of tested classes by deriving. **DO** change the behavior of certain functions in the derived class by overriding the base class methods.	**DON'T** hide a base class function by changing the function signature.

Virtual Methods

This chapter has emphasized the fact that a `Dog` object is a `Mammal` object. So far that has meant only that the `Dog` object has inherited the attributes (data) and capabilities (methods) of its base class. In C++ the is-a relationship runs deeper than that, however.

C++ extends its polymorphism to allow pointers to base classes to be assigned to derived class objects. Thus, you can write

```
Mammal* pMammal = new Dog;
```

This creates a new `Dog` object on the heap and returns a pointer to that object, which it assigns to a pointer to Mammal. This is fine because a dog is a mammal.

 Note

This is the essence of polymorphism. For example, you could create many types of windows, including dialog boxes, scrollable windows, and list boxes, and give them each a virtual `draw()` method. By creating a pointer to a window and assigning dialog boxes and other derived types to that pointer, you can call `draw()` without regard to the actual runtime type of the object pointed to. The correct `draw()` function will be called.

You can then use this pointer to invoke any method on `Mammal`. What you would like is for those methods that are overridden in `Dog()` to call the correct function. Virtual functions enable you to do that. Listing 12.8 illustrates how this works, and what happens with nonvirtual methods.

LISTING 12.8   Using Virtual Methods

```
0:  //Listing 12.8 Using virtual methods
1:
2:  #include <iostream>
3:  using std::cout;
4:
```

LISTING 12.8 continued

```
5:  class Mammal
6:  {
7:  public:
8:      Mammal():itsAge(1) { cout << "Mammal constructor...\n"; }
9:      virtual ~Mammal() { cout << "Mammal destructor...\n"; }
10:     void Move() const { cout << "Mammal move one step\n"; }
11:     virtual void Speak() const { cout << "Mammal speak!\n"; }
12: protected:
13:     int itsAge;
14:
15: };
16:
17: class Dog : public Mammal
18: {
19: public:
20:     Dog() { cout << "Dog Constructor...\n"; }
21:     virtual ~Dog() { cout << "Dog destructor...\n"; }
22:     void WagTail() { cout << "Wagging Tail...\n"; }
23:     void Speak()const { cout << "Woof!\n"; }
24:     void Move()const { cout << "Dog moves 5 steps...\n"; }
25: };
26:
27: int main()
28: {
29:
30:     Mammal *pDog = new Dog;
31:     pDog->Move();
32:     pDog->Speak();
33:
34:     return 0;
35: }
```

OUTPUT

```
Mammal constructor...
Dog Constructor...
Mammal move one step
Woof!
```

ANALYSIS On line 11, Mammal is provided a virtual method—Speak(). The designer of this class thereby signals that she expects this class eventually to be another class's base type. The derived class will probably want to override this function.

On line 30, a pointer to Mammal is created (pDog), but it is assigned the address of a new Dog object. Because a dog is a mammal, this is a legal assignment. The pointer is then used to call the Move() function. Because the compiler knows pDog only to be a Mammal, it looks to the Mammal object to find the Move() method.

12

On line 32, the pointer then calls the Speak() method. Because Speak() is virtual, the Speak() method overridden in Dog is invoked.

This is almost magical. As far as the calling function knew, it had a Mammal pointer, but here a method on Dog was called. In fact, if you had an array of pointers to Mammal, each of which pointed to a subclass of Mammal, you could call each in turn, and the correct function would be called. Listing 12.9 illustrates this idea.

LISTING 12.9 Multiple Virtual Functions Called in Turn

```
0:  //Listing 12.9 Multiple virtual functions called in turn
1:
2:  #include <iostream>
3:  using namespace std;
4:
5:  class Mammal
6:  {
7:  public:
8:      Mammal():itsAge(1) {  }
9:      virtual ~Mammal() { }
10:     virtual void Speak() const { cout << "Mammal speak!\n"; }
11: protected:
12:     int itsAge;
13: };
14:
15: class Dog : public Mammal
16: {
17: public:
18:     void Speak()const { cout << "Woof!\n"; }
19: };
20:
21:
22: class Cat : public Mammal
23: {
24: public:
25:     void Speak()const { cout << "Meow!\n"; }
26: };
27:
28:
29: class Horse : public Mammal
30: {
31: public:
32:     void Speak()const { cout << "Winnie!\n"; }
33: };
34:
35: class Pig : public Mammal
36: {
37: public:
38:     void Speak()const { cout << "Oink!\n"; }
```

LISTING 12.9   continued

```
39:   };
40:
41:   int main()
42:   {
43:      Mammal* theArray[5];
44:      Mammal* ptr;
45:      int choice, i;
46:      for ( i = 0; i<5; i++)
47:      {
48:         cout << "(1)dog (2)cat (3)horse (4)pig: ";
49:         cin >> choice;
50:         switch (choice)
51:         {
52:         case 1: ptr = new Dog;
53:               break;
54:         case 2: ptr = new Cat;
55:               break;
56:         case 3: ptr = new Horse;
57:               break;
58:         case 4: ptr = new Pig;
59:               break;
60:         default: ptr = new Mammal;
61:               break;
62:         }
63:         theArray[i] = ptr;
64:      }
65:      for (i=0;i<5;i++)
66:         theArray[i]->Speak();
67:      return 0;
68:   }
```

12

OUTPUT
```
(1)dog (2)cat (3)horse (4)pig: 1
(1)dog (2)cat (3)horse (4)pig: 2
(1)dog (2)cat (3)horse (4)pig: 3
(1)dog (2)cat (3)horse (4)pig: 4
(1)dog (2)cat (3)horse (4)pig: 5
Woof!
Meow!
Whinny!
Oink!
Mammal speak!
```

ANALYSIS   This stripped-down program, which provides only the barest functionality to each class, illustrates virtual functions in their purest form. Four classes are declared: Dog, Cat, Horse, and Pig are all derived from Mammal.

On line 10, Mammal's Speak() function is declared to be virtual. On lines 18, 25, 32, and 38, the four derived classes override the implementation of Speak().

The user is prompted to pick which objects to create, and the pointers are added to the array on lines 47–65.

Note

At compile time, it is impossible to know which objects will be created, and thus which Speak() methods will be invoked. The pointer ptr is bound to its object at runtime. This is called dynamic binding, or runtime binding, as opposed to static binding, or compile-time binding.

FAQ

If I mark a member method as virtual in the base class, do I need to also mark it as virtual in derived classes?

Answer: No, once a method is virtual, if you override it in derived classes, it remains virtual. It is a good idea (though not required) to continue to mark it virtual—this makes the code easier to understand.

How Virtual Functions Work

When a derived object, such as a Dog object, is created, first the constructor for the base class is called, and then the constructor for the derived class is called. Figure 12.2 shows what the Dog object looks like after it is created. Note that the Mammal part of the object is contiguous in memory with the Dog part.

FIGURE 12.2

The Dog object after it is created.

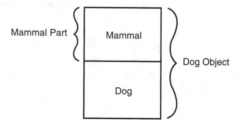

When a virtual function is created in an object, the object must keep track of that function. Many compilers build a virtual function table, called a v-table. One of these is kept for each type, and each object of that type keeps a virtual table pointer (called a vptr or v-pointer), which points to that table.

Although implementations vary, all compilers must accomplish the same thing, so you won't be too wrong with this description.

Each object's vptr points to the v-table which, in turn, has a pointer to each of the virtual functions. (Note: pointers to functions will be discussed in depth on Day 15, "Special Classes and Functions.") When the `Mammal` part of the `Dog` is created, the vptr is initialized to point to the correct part of the v-table, as shown in Figure 12.3.

FIGURE 12.3

The v-table of a
`Mammal`.

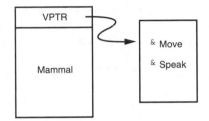

When the `Dog` constructor is called, and the `Dog` part of this object is added, the vptr is adjusted to point to the virtual function overrides (if any) in the `Dog` object (see Figure 12.4).

FIGURE 12.4

The v-table of a `Dog`.

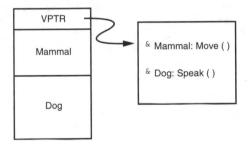

When a pointer to a `Mammal` is used, the vptr continues to point to the correct function, depending on the "real" type of the object. Thus, when `Speak()` is invoked, the correct function is invoked.

You Can't Get There from Here

If the `Dog` object had a method, `WagTail()`, which is not in the `Mammal`, you could not use the pointer to `Mammal` to access that method (unless you cast it to be a pointer to `Dog`). Because `WagTail()` is not a virtual function, and because it is not in a `Mammal` object, you can't get there without either a `Dog` object or a `Dog` pointer.

Although you can transform the `Mammal` pointer into a `Dog` pointer, usually much better and safer ways exist to call the `WagTail()` method. C++ frowns on explicit casts because they are error-prone. This subject will be addressed in depth when multiple inheritance is

12

covered on Day 15, and again when templates are covered on Day 20, "Exceptions and Error Handling."

Slicing

Note that the virtual function magic operates only on pointers and references. Passing an object by value will not enable the virtual functions to be invoked. Listing 12.10 illustrates this problem.

LISTING **12.10**   Data Slicing When Passing by Value

```
0:   //Listing 12.10 Data slistd:std::cing with passing by value
1:
2:   #include <iostream>
3:
4:   class Mammal
5:   {
6:   public:
7:       Mammal():itsAge(1) {  }
8:       virtual ~Mammal() { }
9:       virtual void Speak() const { std::cout << "Mammal speak!\n"; }
10:  protected:
11:      int itsAge;
12:  };
13:
14:  class Dog : public Mammal
15:  {
16:  public:
17:      void Speak()const { std::cout << "Woof!\n"; }
18:  };
19:
20:  class Cat : public Mammal
21:  {
22:  public:
23:      void Speak()const { std::cout << "Meow!\n"; }
24:  };
25:
26:  void ValueFunction (Mammal);
27:  void PtrFunction   (Mammal*);
28:  void RefFunction (Mammal&);
29:  int main()
30:  {
31:     Mammal* ptr=0;
32:     int choice;
33:     while (1)
34:     {
35:        bool fQuit = false;
36:        std::cout << "(1)dog (2)cat (0)Quit: ";
37:        std::cin >> choice;
```

LISTING 12.10 continued

```
38:        switch (choice)
39:        {
40:        case 0: fQuit = true;
41:            break;
42:        case 1: ptr = new Dog;
43:            break;
44:        case 2: ptr = new Cat;
45:            break;
46:        default: ptr = new Mammal;
47:            break;
48:        }
49:        if (fQuit)
50:            break;
51:        PtrFunction(ptr);
52:        RefFunction(*ptr);
53:        ValueFunction(*ptr);
54:    }
55:    return 0;
56: }
57:
58: void ValueFunction (Mammal MammalValue)
59: {
60:    MammalValue.Speak();
61: }
62:
63: void PtrFunction (Mammal * pMammal)
64: {
65:    pMammal->Speak();
66: }
67:
68: void RefFunction (Mammal & rMammal)
69: {
70:    rMammal.Speak();
71: }
```

12

OUTPUT

```
(1)dog (2)cat (0)Quit: 1
Woof
Woof
Mammal Speak!
(1)dog (2)cat (0)Quit: 2
Meow!
Meow!
Mammal Speak!
(1)dog (2)cat (0)Quit: 0
```

ANALYSIS On lines 4–24, stripped-down versions of the Mammal, Dog, and Cat classes are
declared. Three functions are declared—PtrFunction(), RefFunction(), and
ValueFunction(). They take a pointer to a Mammal, a Mammal reference, and a Mammal
object, respectively. All three functions then do the same thing—they call the Speak()
method.

The user is prompted to choose a Dog or a Cat, and based on the choice he makes, a
pointer to the correct type is created on lines 42–45.

In the first line of the output, the user chooses Dog. The Dog object is created on the free
store on line 42. The Dog is then passed as a pointer, as a reference, and by value to the
three functions.

The pointer and references all invoke the virtual functions, and the Dog->Speak() member function is invoked. This is shown on the first two lines of output after the user's
choice.

The dereferenced pointer, however, is passed by value. The function expects a Mammal
object, and so the compiler slices down the Dog object to just the Mammal part. At that
point, the Mammal Speak() method is called, as reflected in the third line of output after
the user's choice.

This experiment is then repeated for the Cat object, with similar results.

Virtual Destructors

It is legal and common to pass a pointer to a derived object when a pointer to a base
object is expected. What happens when that pointer to a derived subject is deleted? If the
destructor is virtual, as it should be, the right thing happens—the derived class's destructor is called. Because the derived class's destructor will automatically invoke the base
class's destructor, the entire object will be properly destroyed.

The rule of thumb is this: If any of the functions in your class are virtual, the destructor
should be as well.

Virtual Copy Constructors

Constructors cannot be virtual, and so, technically, no such thing exists as a virtual copy
constructor. Nonetheless, at times your program desperately needs to be able to pass in a
pointer to a base object and have a copy of the correct derived object that is created. A
common solution to this problem is to create a Clone() method in the base class and to
make that be virtual. The Clone() method creates a new object copy of the current class
and returns that object.

Because each derived class overrides the `Clone()` method, a copy of the derived class is created. Listing 12.11 illustrates how this is used.

LISTING 12.11   Virtual Copy Constructor

```
0:   //Listing 12.11 Virtual copy constructor
1:
2:   #include <iostream>
3:   using namespace std;
4:
5:   class Mammal
6:   {
7:   public:
8:       Mammal():itsAge(1) { cout << "Mammal constructor...\n"; }
9:       virtual ~Mammal() { cout << "Mammal destructor...\n"; }
10:      Mammal (const Mammal & rhs);
11:      virtual void Speak() const { cout << "Mammal speak!\n"; }
12:      virtual Mammal* Clone() { return new Mammal(*this); }
13:      int GetAge()const { return itsAge; }
14:  protected:
15:      int itsAge;
16:  };
17:
18:  Mammal::Mammal (const Mammal & rhs):itsAge(rhs.GetAge())
19:  {
20:      cout << "Mammal Copy Constructor...\n";
21:  }
22:
23:  class Dog : public Mammal
24:  {
25:  public:
26:      Dog() { cout << "Dog constructor...\n"; }
27:      virtual ~Dog() { cout << "Dog destructor...\n"; }
28:      Dog (const Dog & rhs);
29:      void Speak()const { cout << "Woof!\n"; }
30:      virtual Mammal* Clone() { return new Dog(*this); }
31:  };
32:
33:  Dog::Dog(const Dog & rhs):
34:  Mammal(rhs)
35:  {
36:      cout << "Dog copy constructor...\n";
37:  }
38:
39:  class Cat : public Mammal
40:  {
41:  public:
42:      Cat() { cout << "Cat constructor...\n"; }
43:      ~Cat() { cout << "Cat destructor...\n"; }
44:      Cat (const Cat &);
```

LISTING **12.11**   continued

```
45:        void Speak()const { cout << "Meow!\n"; }
46:        virtual Mammal* Clone() { return new Cat(*this); }
47:    };
48:
49:    Cat::Cat(const Cat & rhs):
50:    Mammal(rhs)
51:    {
52:        cout << "Cat copy constructor...\n";
53:    }
54:
55:    enum ANIMALS { MAMMAL, DOG, CAT};
56:    const int NumAnimalTypes = 3;
57:    int main()
58:    {
59:        Mammal *theArray[NumAnimalTypes];
60:        Mammal* ptr;
61:        int choice, i;
62:        for ( i = 0; i<NumAnimalTypes; i++)
63:        {
64:            cout << "(1)dog (2)cat (3)Mammal: ";
65:            cin >> choice;
66:            switch (choice)
67:            {
68:            case DOG:   ptr = new Dog;
69:                    break;
70:            case CAT:   ptr = new Cat;
71:                    break;
72:            default:    ptr = new Mammal;
73:                    break;
74:            }
75:            theArray[i] = ptr;
76:        }
77:        Mammal *OtherArray[NumAnimalTypes];
78:        for (i=0;i<NumAnimalTypes;i++)
79:        {
80:            theArray[i]->Speak();
81:            OtherArray[i] = theArray[i]->Clone();
82:        }
83:        for (i=0;i<NumAnimalTypes;i++)
84:            OtherArray[i]->Speak();
85:        return 0;
86:    }
```

OUTPUT

```
1:  (1)dog (2)cat (3)Mammal: 1
2:  Mammal constructor...
3:  Dog constructor...
4:  (1)dog (2)cat (3)Mammal: 2
5:  Mammal constructor...
```

```
 6: Cat constructor...
 7: (1)dog (2)cat (3)Mammal: 3
 8: Mammal constructor...
 9: Woof!
10: Mammal Copy Constructor...
11: Dog copy constructor...
12: Meow!
13: Mammal Copy Constructor...
14: Cat copy constructor...
15: Mammal speak!
16: Mammal Copy Constructor...
17: Woof!
18: Meow!
19: Mammal speak!
```

ANALYSIS Listing 12.11 is very similar to the previous two listings, except that a new virtual method has been added to the Mammal class: Clone(). This method returns a pointer to a new Mammal object by calling the copy constructor, passing in itself (*this) as a const reference.

Dog and Cat both override the Clone() method, initializing their data and passing in copies of themselves to their own copy constructors. Because Clone() is virtual, this will effectively create a virtual copy constructor, as shown on line 81.

The user is prompted to choose dogs, cats, or mammals, and these are created on lines 62–74. A pointer to each choice is stored in an array on line 75.

As the program iterates over the array, each object has its Speak() and its Clone() methods called, in turn, on lines 80 and 81. The result of the Clone() call is a pointer to a copy of the object, which is then stored in a second array on line 81.

On line 1 of the output, the user is prompted and responds with 1, choosing to create a dog. The Mammal and Dog constructors are invoked. This is repeated for Cat and for Mammal on lines 4–8 of the constructor.

Line 9 of the output represents the call to Speak() on the first object, the Dog. The virtual Speak() method is called, and the correct version of Speak() is invoked. The Clone() function is then called, and because this is also virtual, Dog's Clone() method is invoked, causing the Mammal constructor and the Dog copy constructor to be called.

The same is repeated for Cat on lines 12–14, and then for Mammal on lines 15 and 16. Finally, the new array is iterated, and each of the new objects has Speak() invoked.

The Cost of Virtual Methods

Because objects with virtual methods must maintain a v-table, some overhead occurs in having virtual methods. If you have a very small class from which you do not expect to derive other classes, there may be no reason to have any virtual methods at all.

Once you declare any methods virtual, you've paid most of the price of the v-table (although each entry does add a small memory overhead). At that point, you'll want the destructor to be virtual, and the assumption will be that all other methods probably will be virtual as well. Take a long, hard look at any nonvirtual methods, and be certain you understand why they are not virtual.

Do	Don't
DO use virtual methods when you expect to derive from a class. **DO** use a virtual destructor if any methods are virtual.	**DON'T** mark the constructor as virtual.

Summary

Today you learned how derived classes inherit from base classes. This chapter discussed public inheritance and virtual functions. Classes inherit all the public and protected data and functions from their base classes.

Protected access is public to derived classes and private to all other objects. Even derived classes cannot access private data or functions in their base classes.

Constructors can be initialized before the body of the constructor. At that time, the base constructors are invoked and parameters can be passed to the base class.

Functions in the base class can be overridden in the derived class. If the base class functions are virtual, and if the object is accessed by pointer or reference, the derived class's functions will be invoked, based on the runtime type of the object pointed to.

Methods in the base class can be invoked by explicitly naming the function with the prefix of the base class name and two colons. For example, if Dog inherits from Mammal, Mammal's walk() method can be called with Mammal::walk().

In classes with virtual methods, the destructor should almost always be made virtual. A virtual destructor ensures that the derived part of the object will be freed when delete is called on the pointer. Constructors cannot be virtual. Virtual copy constructors can be effectively created by making a virtual member function that calls the copy constructor.

Q&A

Q **Are inherited members and functions passed along to subsequent generations? If `Dog` derives from `Mammal`, and `Mammal` derives from `Animal`, does `Dog` inherit `Animal`'s functions and data?**

A Yes. As derivation continues, derived classes inherit the sum of all the functions and data in all their base classes.

Q **If, in the example above, `Mammal` overrides a function in `Animal`, which does `Dog` get, the original or the overridden function?**

A If `Dog` inherits from `Mammal`, it gets the function in the state `Mammal` has it: the overridden function.

Q **Can a derived class make a public base function private?**

A Yes, the derived class can override the method and make it private. It then remains private for all subsequent derivation.

Q **Why not make all class functions virtual?**

A Overhead occurs with the first virtual function in the creation of a v-table. After that, the overhead is trivial. Many C++ programmers feel that if one function is virtual, all others should be. Other programmers disagree, feeling that there should always be a reason for what you do.

Q **If a function (`SomeFunc()`) is virtual in a base class and is also overloaded, so as to take either an integer or two integers, and the derived class overrides the form taking one integer, what is called when a pointer to a derived object calls the two-integer form?**

A The overriding of the one-int form hides the entire base class function, and thus you will get a compile error complaining that that function requires only one int.

Workshop

The Workshop provides quiz questions to help you solidify your understanding of the material that was covered and exercises to provide you with experience in using what you've learned. Try to answer the quiz and exercise questions before checking the answers in Appendix D, and make sure you understand the answers before continuing to the next chapter.

Quiz

1. What is a v-table?

2. What is a virtual destructor?

3. How do you show the declaration of a virtual constructor?

4. How can you create a virtual copy constructor?

5. How do you invoke a base member function from a derived class in which you've overridden that function?

6. How do you invoke a base member function from a derived class in which you have not overridden that function?

7. If a base class declares a function to be virtual, and a derived class does not use the term `virtual` when overriding that class, is it still virtual when inherited by a third-generation class?

8. What is the `protected` keyword used for?

Exercises

1. Show the declaration of a virtual function that takes an integer parameter and returns void.

2. Show the declaration of a class `Square`, which derives from `Rectangle`, which in turn derives from `Shape`.

3. If, in Exercise 2, `Shape` takes no parameters, `Rectangle` takes two (length and width), but `Square` takes only one (length), show the constructor initialization for `Square`.

4. Write a virtual copy constructor for the class `Square` (in Exercise 3).

5. **BUG BUSTERS:** What is wrong with this code snippet?
```
void SomeFunction (Shape);
Shape * pRect = new Rectangle;
SomeFunction(*pRect);
```

6. **BUG BUSTERS:** What is wrong with this code snippet?
```
class Shape()
{
public:
    Shape();
    virtual ~Shape();
    virtual Shape(const Shape&);
};
```

WEEK 2

DAY 13

Arrays and Linked Lists

In previous chapters, you declared a single int, char, or other object. You often want to declare a collection of objects, such as 20 ints or a litter of CATs.

Today you will learn

- What arrays are and how to declare them.
- What strings are and how to use character arrays to make them.
- The relationship between arrays and pointers.
- How to use pointer arithmetic with arrays.

What Is an Array?

An array is a collection of data storage locations, each of which holds the same type of data. Each storage location is called an element of the array.

You declare an array by writing the type, followed by the array name and the subscript. The subscript is the number of elements in the array, surrounded by square brackets. For example

```
long LongArray[25];
```

declares an array of 25 long integers, named LongArray. When the compiler sees this declaration, it sets aside enough memory to hold all 25 elements. Because each long integer requires four bytes, this declaration sets aside 100 contiguous bytes of memory, as illustrated in Figure 13.1.

FIGURE 13.1

Declaring an array.

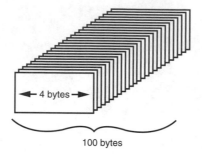

← 4 bytes →

100 bytes

Array Elements

You access each of the array elements by referring to an offset from the array name. Array elements are counted from zero. Therefore, the first array element is arrayName[0]. In the LongArray example, LongArray[0] is the first array element, LongArray[1] the second, and so forth.

This can be somewhat confusing. The array SomeArray[3] has three elements. They are: SomeArray[0], SomeArray[1], and SomeArray[2]. More generally, SomeArray[n] has n elements that are numbered SomeArray[0] through SomeArray[n-1].

Therefore, LongArray[25] is numbered from LongArray[0] through LongArray[24]. Listing 13.1 shows how to declare an array of five integers and fill each with a value.

LISTING 13.1   Using an Integer Array

```
0:  //Listing 13.1 - Arrays
1:  #include <iostream>
2:
3:  int main()
4:  {
5:      int myArray[5];
6:      int i;
7:      for ( i=0; i<5; i++)  // 0-4
8:      {
9:          std::cout << "Value for myArray[" << i << "]: ";
10:         std::cin >> myArray[i];
11:     }
```

LISTING 13.1 continued

```
12:    for (i = 0; i<5; i++)
13:        std::cout << i << ": " << myArray[i] << "\n";
14:    return 0;
15:  }
```

OUTPUT

```
Value for myArray[0]:  3
Value for myArray[1]:  6
Value for myArray[2]:  9
Value for myArray[3]:  12
Value for myArray[4]:  15
0: 3
1: 6
2: 9
3: 12
4: 15
```

ANALYSIS Line 5 declares an array called myArray, which holds five integer variables. Line 7 establishes a loop that counts from 0 through 4, which is the proper set of offsets for a five-element array. The user is prompted for a value, and that value is saved at the correct offset into the array.

The first value is saved at myArray[0], the second at myArray[1], and so forth. The second for loop prints each value to the screen.

Note

> Arrays count from 0, not from 1. This is the cause of many bugs in programs written by C++ novices. Whenever you use an array, remember that an array with 10 elements counts from ArrayName[0] to ArrayName[9]. ArrayName[10] is not used.

Writing Past the End of an Array

13

When you write a value to an element in an array, the compiler computes where to store the value based on the size of each element and the subscript. Suppose that you ask to write over the value at LongArray[5], which is the sixth element. The compiler multiplies the offset (5) by the size of each element—in this case, 4. It then moves that many bytes (20) from the beginning of the array and writes the new value at that location.

If you ask to write at LongArray[50], the compiler ignores the fact that no such element exists. It computes how far past the first element it should look (200 bytes) and then writes over whatever is at that location. This can be virtually any data, and writing your new value there might have unpredictable results. If you're lucky, your program will crash immediately. If you're unlucky, you'll get strange results much later in your program, and you'll have a difficult time figuring out what went wrong.

The compiler is like a blind man pacing off the distance from a house. He starts out at the first house, MainStreet[0]. When you ask him to go to the sixth house on Main Street, he says to himself, "I must go five more houses. Each house is four big paces. I must go an additional 20 steps." If you ask him to go to MainStreet[100] and Main Street is only 25 houses long, he will pace off 400 steps. Long before he gets there, he will, no doubt, step in front of a truck. So be careful where you send him.

Listing 13.2 shows what happens when you write past the end of an array.

Caution   Do not run this program; it may crash your system!

LISTING **13.2**   Writing Past the End of an Array

```
0:   //Listing 13.2
1:   // Demonstrates what happens when you write past the end
2:   // of an array
3:
4:   #include <iostream>
5:   using namespace std;
6:
7:   int main()
8:   {
9:       // sentinels
10:      long sentinelOne[3];
11:      long TargetArray[25]; // array to fill
12:      long sentinelTwo[3];
13:      int i;
14:      for (i=0; i<3; i++)
15:          sentinelOne[i] = sentinelTwo[i] = 0;
16:
17:      for (i=0; i<25; i++)
18:          TargetArray[i] = 0;
19:
20:      cout << "Test 1: \n";  // test current values (should be 0)
21:      cout << "TargetArray[0]: " << TargetArray[0] << "\n";
22:      cout << "TargetArray[24]: " << TargetArray[24] << "\n\n";
23:
24:      for (i = 0; i<3; i++)
25:      {
26:          cout << "sentinelOne[" << i << "]: ";
27:          cout << sentinelOne[i] << "\n";
28:          cout << "sentinelTwo[" << i << "]: ";
```

LISTING 13.2   continued

```
29:         cout << sentinelTwo[i]<< "\n";
30:     }
31:
32:     cout << "\nAssigning...";
33:     for (i = 0; i<=25; i++)
34:        TargetArray[i] = 20;
35:
36:     cout << "\nTest 2: \n";
37:     cout << "TargetArray[0]: " << TargetArray[0] << "\n";
38:     cout << "TargetArray[24]: " << TargetArray[24] << "\n";
39:     cout << "TargetArray[25]: " << TargetArray[25] << "\n\n";
40:     for (i = 0; i<3; i++)
41:     {
42:        cout << "sentinelOne[" << i << "]: ";
43:        cout << sentinelOne[i]<< "\n";
44:        cout << "sentinelTwo[" << i << "]: ";
45:        cout << sentinelTwo[i]<< "\n";
46:     }
47:
48:     return 0;
49: }
```

OUTPUT

```
Test 1:
TargetArray[0]: 0
TargetArray[24]: 0

SentinelOne[0]: 0
SentinelTwo[0]: 0
SentinelOne[1]: 0
SentinelTwo[1]: 0
SentinelOne[2]: 0
SentinelTwo[2]: 0

Assigning...
Test 2:
TargetArray[0]: 20
TargetArray[24]: 20
TargetArray[25]: 20

SentinelOne[0]: 20
SentinelTwo[0]: 0
SentinelOne[1]: 0
SentinelTwo[1]: 0
SentinelOne[2]: 0
SentinelTwo[2]: 0
```

13

ANALYSIS Lines 10 and 12 declare two arrays of three integers that act as sentinels around TargetArray. These sentinel arrays are initialized with the value 0. If memory is written to beyond the end of TargetArray, the sentinels are likely to be changed. Some compilers count down in memory; others count up. For this reason, the sentinels are placed on both sides of TargetArray.

Lines 20–30 confirm the sentinel values in Test 1. In line 34, TargetArray's members are all initialized to the value 20, but the counter counts to TargetArray offset 25, which doesn't exist in TargetArray.

Lines 37–39 print TargetArray's values in Test 2. Note that TargetArray[25] is perfectly happy to print the value 20. However, when SentinelOne and SentinelTwo are printed, SentinelOne[0] reveals that its value has changed. This is because the memory that is 25 elements after TargetArray[0] is the same memory that is at SentinelOne[0]. When the nonexistent TargetArray[25] was accessed, what was actually accessed was SentinelOne[0].

This nasty bug can be very hard to find, because SentinelOne [0]'s value was changed in a part of the code that was not writing to SentinelOne at all.

This code uses "magic numbers" such as 3 for the size of the sentinel arrays and 25 for the size of TargetArray. It is safer to use constants so that you can change all these values in one place.

Note that because all compilers use memory differently, your results may vary.

Fence Post Errors

It is so common to write to one past the end of an array that this bug has its own name. It is called a fence post error. This refers to the problem in counting how many fence posts you need for a 10-foot fence if you need one post for every foot. Most people answer 10, but of course you need 11. Figure 13.2 makes this clear.

FIGURE 13.2

Fence post errors.

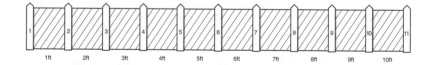

This type of "off by one" counting can be the bane of any programmer's life. Over time, however, you'll get used to the idea that a 25-element array counts only to element 24, and that everything counts from 0.

Note

> Some programmers refer to `ArrayName[0]` as the zeroth element. Getting into this habit is a mistake. If `ArrayName[0]` is the zeroth element, what is `ArrayName[1]`? The oneth? If so, when you see `ArrayName[24]`, will you real-ize that it is not the 24th element, but rather the 25th? It is far less confus-ing to say that `ArrayName[0]` is at offset zero and is the first element.

Initializing Arrays

You can initialize a simple array of built-in types, such as integers and characters, when you first declare the array. After the array name, you put an equal sign (=) and a list of comma-separated values enclosed in braces. For example

```
int IntegerArray[5] = { 10, 20, 30, 40, 50 };
```

declares `IntegerArray` to be an array of five integers. It assigns `IntegerArray[0]` the value `10`, `IntegerArray[1]` the value `20`, and so forth.

If you omit the size of the array, an array just big enough to hold the initialization is cre-ated. Therefore, if you write

```
int IntegerArray[] = { 10, 20, 30, 40, 50 };
```

you will create the same array as you did in the previous example.

If you need to know the size of the array, you can ask the compiler to compute it for you. For example

```
const USHORT IntegerArrayLength = sizeof(IntegerArray)/sizeof(IntegerArray[0]);
```

sets the constant USHORT variable `IntegerArrayLength` to the result obtained from divid-ing the size of the entire array by the size of each individual entry in the array. That quo-tient is the number of members in the array.

You cannot initialize more elements than you've declared for the array. Therefore,

```
int IntegerArray[5] = { 10, 20, 30, 40, 50, 60};
```

generates a compiler error because you've declared a five-member array and initialized six values. It is legal, however, to write

```
int IntegerArray[5] = {10, 20};
```

13

Do	Don't
DO let the compiler set the size of initial-ized arrays. **DO** give arrays meaningful names, as you would with any variable. **DO** remember that the first member of the array is at offset 0.	**DON'T** write past the end of the array.

Declaring Arrays

Arrays can have any legal variable name, but they cannot have the same name as another variable or array within their scope. Therefore, you cannot have an array named myCats[5] and a variable named myCats at the same time.

You can dimension the array size with a const or with an enumeration. Listing 13.3 illustrates this.

LISTING 13.3   Using Consts and Enums in Arrays

```
0:   // Listing 13.3
1:   // Dimensioning arrays with consts and enumerations
2:
3:   #include <iostream>
4:   int main()
5:   {
6:       enum WeekDays { Sun, Mon, Tue,
7:               Wed, Thu, Fri, Sat, DaysInWeek };
8:       int ArrayWeek[DaysInWeek] = { 10, 20, 30, 40, 50, 60, 70 };
9:
10:      std::cout << "The value at Tuesday is: " << ArrayWeek[Tue];
11:      return 0;
12:  }
```

OUTPUT

```
The value at Tuesday is: 30
```

ANALYSIS   Line 6 creates an enumeration called WeekDays. It has eight members. Sunday is equal to 0, and DaysInWeek is equal to 7.

Line 10 uses the enumerated constant Tue as an offset into the array. Because Tue evaluates to 2, the third element of the array, ArrayWeek[2], is returned and printed in line 10.

Arrays of Objects

Any object, whether built-in or user defined, can be stored in an array. When you declare the array, you tell the compiler the type of object to store and the number of objects for which to allocate room. The compiler knows how much room is needed for each object based on the class declaration. The class must have a default constructor that takes no arguments so that the objects can be created when the array is defined.

Accessing member data in an array of objects is a two-step process. You identify the member of the array by using the index operator ([ ]), and then you add the member operator (.) to access the particular member variable. Listing 13.4 demonstrates how you would create an array of five CATs.

13

LISTING 13.4   Creating an Array of Objects

```
0:  // Listing 13.4 - An array of objects
1:
2:  #include <iostream>
3:  using namespace std;
4:
5:  class CAT
6:  {
7:  public:
8:      CAT() { itsAge = 1; itsWeight=5; }
9:      ~CAT() {}
10:     int GetAge() const { return itsAge; }
11:     int GetWeight() const { return itsWeight; }
```

LISTING 13.4   continued

```
12:        void SetAge(int age) { itsAge = age; }
13:
14:    private:
15:        int itsAge;
16:        int itsWeight;
17:    };
18:
19:    int main()
20:    {
21:        CAT Litter[5];
22:        int i;
23:      for (i = 0; i < 5; i++)
24:          Litter[i].SetAge(2*i +1);
25:
26:        for (i = 0; i < 5; i++)
27:        {
28:          cout << "Cat #" << i+1<< ": ";
29:          cout << Litter[i].GetAge() << endl;
30:        }
31:        return 0;
32:    }
```

OUTPUT
```
cat #1: 1
cat #2: 3
cat #3: 5
cat #4: 7
cat #5: 9
```

ANALYSIS   Lines 5–17 declare the CAT class. The CAT class must have a default constructor so that CAT objects can be created in an array. Remember that if you create any other constructor, the compiler-supplied default constructor is not created; you must create your own.

The first for loop (lines 23 and 24) sets the age of each of the five CATs in the array. The second for loop (lines 26–30) accesses each member of the array and calls GetAge().

Each individual CAT's GetAge() method is called by accessing the member in the array, Litter[i], followed by the dot operator (.), and the member function.

Multidimensional Arrays

It is possible to have arrays of more than one dimension. Each dimension is represented as a subscript in the array. Therefore, a two-dimensional array has two subscripts; a three-dimensional array has three subscripts; and so on. Arrays can have any number of dimensions, although it is likely that most of the arrays you create will be of one or two dimensions.

A good example of a two-dimensional array is a chess board. One dimension represents the eight rows; the other dimension represents the eight columns. Figure 13.3 illustrates this idea.

FIGURE 13.3

A chess board and a two-dimensional array.

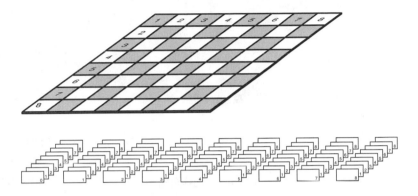

Suppose that you have a class named SQUARE. The declaration of an array named Board that represents it would be

```
SQUARE Board[8][8];
```

You could also represent the same data with a one-dimensional, 64-square array. For example:

```
SQUARE Board[64];
```

This doesn't correspond as closely to the real-world object as the two-dimension. When the game begins, the king is located in the fourth position in the first row, that position corresponds to

```
Board[0][3];
```

assuming that the first subscript corresponds to row and the second to column.

Initializing Multidimensional Arrays

You can initialize multidimensional arrays. You assign the list of values to array elements in order, with the last array subscript changing while each of the former holds steady. Therefore, if you have an array

```
int theArray[5][3];
```

the first three elements go into theArray[0]; the next three into theArray[1]; and so forth.

13

You initialize this array by writing

```
int theArray[5][3] = { 1,2,3,4,5,6,7,8,9,10,11,12,13,14,15 };
```

For the sake of clarity, you could group the initializations with braces. For example:

```
int theArray[5][3] = {  {1,2,3},
{4,5,6},
{7,8,9},
{10,11,12},
{13,14,15} };
```

The compiler ignores the inner braces, but they do make it easier to understand how the numbers are distributed.

Each value must be separated by a comma, without regard to the braces. The entire initialization set must be within braces, and it must end with a semicolon.

Listing 13.5 creates a two-dimensional array. The first dimension is the set of numbers from 0 to 4. The second dimension consists of the double of each value in the first dimension.

LISTING 13.5   Creating a Multidimensional Array

```
0:   // Listing 13.5 - Creating a Multidimensional Array
1:
2:   #include <iostream>
3:   using namespace std;
4:
5:   int main()
6:   {
7:       int SomeArray[5][2] = { {0,0}, {1,2}, {2,4}, {3,6}, {4,8}};
8:       for (int i = 0; i<5; i++)
9:          for (int j=0; j<2; j++)
10:         {
11:             cout << "SomeArray[" << i << "][" << j << "]: ";
12:             cout << SomeArray[i][j]<< endl;
13:         }
14:
15:      return 0;
16:  }
```

OUTPUT

```
SomeArray[0][0]: 0
SomeArray[0][1]: 0
SomeArray[1][0]: 1
SomeArray[1][1]: 2
SomeArray[2][0]: 2
SomeArray[2][1]: 4
SomeArray[3][0]: 3
```

```
SomeArray[3][1]: 6
SomeArray[4][0]: 4
SomeArray[4][1]: 8
```

 Line 7 declares SomeArray to be a two-dimensional array. The first dimension consists of five integers; the second dimension consists of two integers. This creates a 5×2 grid, as Figure 13.4 shows.

FIGURE 13.4

A 5×2 array.

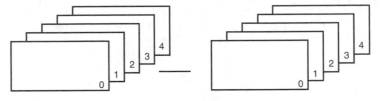

Some Array [5] [2]

The values are initialized in pairs, although they could be computed as well. Lines 8 and 9 create a nested for loop. The outer for loop ticks through each member of the first dimension. For every member in that dimension, the inner for loop ticks through each member of the second dimension. This is consistent with the printout. SomeArray[0][0] is followed by SomeArray[0][1]. The first dimension is incremented only after the second dimension is incremented by 1. Then the second dimension starts over.

A Word About Memory

When you declare an array, you tell the compiler exactly how many objects you expect to store in it. The compiler sets aside memory for all the objects, even if you never use it. This isn't a problem with arrays for which you have a good idea of how many objects you'll need. For example, a chess board has 64 squares, and cats have between 1 and 10 kittens. When you have no idea of how many objects you'll need, however, you must use more advanced data structures.

This book looks at arrays of pointers, arrays built on the free store, and various other collections. We'll look at a few advanced data structures, but you can learn more in my book *C++ Unleashed* from Sams Publishing. Two of the great things about programming are that there are always more things to learn and that there are always more books from which to learn.

Arrays of Pointers

The arrays discussed so far store all their members on the stack. Usually stack memory is severely limited, whereas free store memory is much larger. It is possible to declare

13

each object on the free store and then to store only a pointer to the object in the array. This dramatically reduces the amount of stack memory used. Listing 13.6 rewrites the array from Listing 13.4, but it stores all the objects on the free store. As an indication of the greater memory that this enables, the array is expanded from 5 to 500, and the name is changed from Litter to Family.

LISTING 13.6   Storing an Array on the Free Store

```
0:   // Listing 13.6 - An array of pointers to objects
1:
2:   #include <iostream>
3:   using namespace std;
4:
5:   class CAT
6:   {
7:   public:
8:       CAT() { itsAge = 1; itsWeight=5; }
9:       ~CAT() {}                                 // destructor
10:      int GetAge() const { return itsAge; }
11:      int GetWeight() const { return itsWeight; }
12:      void SetAge(int age) { itsAge = age; }
13:
14:  private:
15:      int itsAge;
16:      int itsWeight;
17:  };
18:
19:  int main()
20:  {
21:      CAT * Family[500];
22:      int i;
23:      CAT * pCat;
24:      for (i = 0; i < 500; i++)
25:      {
26:         pCat = new CAT;
27:         pCat->SetAge(2*i +1);
28:         Family[i] = pCat;
29:      }
30:
31:      for (i = 0; i < 500; i++)
32:      {
33:         cout << "Cat #" << i+1 << ": ";
34:         cout << Family[i]->GetAge() << endl;
35:      }
36:      return 0;
37:  }
```

OUTPUT
```
Cat #1: 1
Cat #2: 3
Cat #3: 5
...
Cat #499: 997
Cat #500: 999
```

ANALYSIS The CAT object declared in lines 5–17 is identical to the CAT object declared in Listing 13.4. This time, however, the array declared in line 21 is named Family, and it is declared to hold 500 pointers to CAT objects.

In the initial loop (lines 24–29), 500 new CAT objects are created on the free store, and each one has its age set to twice the index plus one. Therefore, the first CAT is set to 1, the second CAT to 3, the third CAT to 5, and so on. Finally, the pointer is added to the array.

Because the array has been declared to hold pointers, the pointer—rather than the dereferenced value in the pointer—is added to the array.

The second loop (lines 31–35) prints each of the values. The pointer is accessed by using the index, Family[i]. That address is then used to access the GetAge() method.

In this example, the array Family and all its pointers are stored on the stack, but the 500 CATs that are created are stored on the free store.

Declaring Arrays on the Free Store

It is possible to put the entire array on the free store, also known as the heap. You do this by calling new and using the subscript operator. The result is a pointer to an area on the free store that holds the array. For example

```
CAT *Family = new CAT[500];
```

declares Family to be a pointer to the first in an array of 500 CATs. In other words, Family points to—or has the address of—Family[0].

The advantage of using Family in this way is that you can use pointer arithmetic to access each member of Family. For example, you can write

```
CAT *Family = new CAT[500];
CAT *pCat = Family;        //pCat points to Family[0]
pCat->SetAge(10);          // set Family[0] to 10
pCat++;                    // advance to Family[1]
pCat->SetAge(20);          // set Family[1] to 20
```

This declares a new array of 500 CATs and a pointer to point to the start of the array. Using that pointer, the first CAT's SetAge() function is called with a value of 10. The

13

pointer is then incremented to point to the next CAT, and the second Cat's SetAge() method is then called.

A Pointer to an Array Versus an Array of Pointers

Examine the following three declarations:

```
1:  Cat    FamilyOne[500];
2:  CAT * FamilyTwo[500];
3:  CAT * FamilyThree = new CAT[500];
```

FamilyOne is an array of 500 CATs. FamilyTwo is an array of 500 pointers to CATs. FamilyThree is a pointer to an array of 500 CATs.

The differences among these three code lines dramatically affect how these arrays operate. What is perhaps even more surprising is that FamilyThree is a variant of FamilyOne, but it is very different from FamilyTwo.

This raises the thorny issue of how pointers relate to arrays. In the third case, FamilyThree is a pointer to an array. That is, the address in FamilyThree is the address of the first item in that array. This is exactly the case for FamilyOne.

Pointers and Array Names

In C++ an array name is a constant pointer to the first element of the array. Therefore, in the declaration

```
CAT Family[50];
```

Family is a pointer to &Family[0], which is the address of the first element of the array Family.

It is legal to use array names as constant pointers, and vice versa. Therefore, Family + 4 is a legitimate way of accessing the data at Family[4].

The compiler does all the arithmetic when you add to, increment, and decrement pointers. The address accessed when you write Family + 4 isn't four bytes past the address of Family—it is four objects. If each object is four bytes long, Family + 4 is 16 bytes past the start of the array. If each object is a CAT that has four long member variables of four bytes each and two short member variables of two bytes each, each CAT is 20 bytes, and Family + 4 is 80 bytes past the start of the array.

Listing 13.7 illustrates declaring and using an array on the free store.

LISTING 13.7   Creating an Array by Using new

```
0:    // Listing 13.7 - An array on the free store
1:
2:    #include <iostream>
3:
4:    class CAT
5:    {
6:    public:
7:        CAT() { itsAge = 1; itsWeight=5; }
8:        ~CAT();
9:        int GetAge() const { return itsAge; }
10:       int GetWeight() const { return itsWeight; }
11:       void SetAge(int age) { itsAge = age; }
12:
13:   private:
14:       int itsAge;
15:       int itsWeight;
16:   };
17:
18:   CAT :: ~CAT()
19:   {
20:       // std::cout << "Destructor called!\n";
21:   }
22:
23:   int main()
24:   {
25:       CAT * Family = new CAT[500];
26:       int i;
27:
28:       for (i = 0; i < 500; i++)
29:       {
30:           Family[i].SetAge(2*i +1);
31:       }
32:
33:       for (i = 0; i < 500; i++)
34:       {
35:           std::cout << "Cat #" << i+1 << ": ";
36:           std::cout << Family[i].GetAge() << std::endl;
37:       }
38:
39:       delete [] Family;
40:
41:       return 0;
42:   }
```

OUTPUT

```
Cat #1: 1
Cat #2: 3
Cat #3: 5

...
Cat #499: 997
Cat #500: 999
```

13

Line 25 declares the array Family, which holds 500 CAT objects. The entire array is created on the free store with the call to new CAT[500].

Deleting Arrays on the Free Store

What happens to the memory allocated for these Cat objects when the array is destroyed? Is there a chance of a memory leak? Deleting Family automatically returns all the memory set aside for the array if you use the delete [] operator, remembering to include the square brackets. The compiler is smart enough to destroy each object in the array and to return its memory to the free store.

To see this, change the size of the array from 500 to 10 in lines 25, 28, and 36. Then uncomment the cout statement in line 20. When line 39 is reached and the array is destroyed, each CAT object destructor is called.

When you create an item on the heap by using new, you always delete that item and free its memory with delete. Similarly, when you create an array by using new <class>[size], you delete that array and free all its memory with delete[]. The brackets signal the compiler that this array is being deleted.

If you leave the brackets off, only the first object in the array will be deleted. You can prove this to yourself by removing the bracket on line 39. If you edited line 20 so that the destructor prints, you should now see only one CAT object destroyed. Congratulations! You just created a memory leak.

Do	Don't
DO remember that an array of n items is numbered from zero through n–1.	**DON'T** write or read past the end of an array.
DO use array indexing with pointers that point to arrays.	**DON'T** confuse an array of pointers with a pointer to an array.

char Arrays

A C-style string is an array of characters terminated by a null. The only C-style strings you've seen until now have been unnamed C-style string constants used in cout statements, such as

```
cout << "hello world.\n";
```

You can declare and initialize a C-style string the same as you would any other array. For example:

```
char Greeting[] =
{ 'H', 'e', 'l', 'l', 'o', ' ', 'W','o','r','l','d', '\0' };
```

The last character, `'\0'`, is the null character, which many C++ functions recognize as the terminator for a C-style string. Although this character-by-character approach works, it is difficult to type and admits too many opportunities for error. C++ enables you to use a shorthand form of the previous line of code. It is

```
char Greeting[] = "Hello World";
```

You should note two things about this syntax:

- Instead of single-quoted characters separated by commas and surrounded by braces, you have a double-quoted C-style string, no commas, and no braces.

- You don't need to add the null character because the compiler adds it for you.

The C-style string Hello World is 12 bytes. Hello is 5 bytes, the space 1, World 5, and the null character 1.

You can also create uninitialized character arrays. As with all arrays, it is important to ensure that you don't put more into the buffer than there is room for.

Listing 13.8 demonstrates the use of an uninitialized buffer.

LISTING 13.8 Filling an Array

```
0:  //Listing 13.8 char array buffers
1:
2:  #include <iostream>
3:
4:  int main()
5:  {
6:      char buffer[80];
7:      std::cout << "Enter the string: ";
8:      std::cin >> buffer;
9:      std::cout << "Here is's the buffer:  " << buffer << std::endl;
10:     return 0;
11: }
```

13

OUTPUT
```
Enter the string: Hello World
Here's the buffer:  Hello
```

ANALYSIS On line 6, a buffer is declared to hold 80 characters. This is large enough to hold a 79-character C-style string and a terminating null character.

On line 7, the user is prompted to enter a C-style string, which is entered into buffer on line 8. It is the syntax of cin to write a terminating null to buffer after it writes the string.

Two problems occur with the program in Listing 13.8. First, if the user enters more than 79 characters, cin writes past the end of the buffer. Second, if the user enters a space, cin thinks that it is the end of the string, and it stops writing to the buffer.

To solve these problems, you must call a special method on cin: get(). cin.get() takes three parameters:

- The buffer to fill
- The maximum number of characters to get
- The delimiter that terminates input

The default delimiter is newline. Listing 13.9 illustrates its use.

LISTING 13.9   Filling an Array

```
//Listing 13.9 using cin.get()
1:
2:  #include <iostream>
3:  using namespace std;
4:
5:  int main()
6:  {
7:      char buffer[80];
8:      cout << "Enter the string: ";
9:      cin.get(buffer, 79);        // get up to 79 or newline
10:     cout << "Here's the buffer:  " << buffer << endl;
11:     return 0;
12: }
```

OUTPUT
```
Enter the string: Hello World
Here's the buffer:  Hello World
```

ANALYSIS   Line 9 calls the method get() of cin. The buffer declared in line 7 is passed in as the first argument. The second argument is the maximum number of characters to get. In this case, it must be 79 to allow for the terminating null. No need exists to provide a terminating character because the default value of newline is sufficient.

strcpy() and strncpy()

C++ inherits from C a library of functions for dealing with C-style strings. Among the many functions provided are two for copying one string into another: strcpy() and strncpy(). strcpy() copies the entire contents of one string into a designated buffer. Listing 13.10 demonstrates the use of strcpy().

LISTING 13.10 Using `strcpy()`

```
0:  //Listing 13.10 Using strcpy()
1:
2:  #include <iostream>
3:  #include <string.h>
4:  using namespace std;
5:
6:  int main()
7:  {
8:      char String1[] = "No man is an island";
9:      char String2[80];
10:
11:     strcpy(String2,String1);
12:
13:     cout << "String1: " << String1 << endl;
14:     cout << "String2: " << String2 << endl;
15:     return 0;
16: }
```

OUTPUT

```
String1: No man is an island
String2: No man is an island
```

ANALYSIS The header file `string.h` is included in line 3. This file contains the prototype of the `strcpy()` function. `strcpy()` takes two character arrays—a destination followed by a source. If the source were larger than the destination, `strcpy()` would overwrite past the end of the buffer.

To protect against this, the standard library also includes `strncpy()`. This variation takes a maximum number of characters to copy. `strncpy()` copies up to the first null character or the maximum number of characters specified into the destination buffer.

Listing 13.11 illustrates the use of `strncpy()`.

LISTING 13.11 Using `strncpy()`

```
0:  //Listing 13.11 Using strncpy()
1:
2:  #include <iostream>
3:  #include <string.h>
4:
5:  int main()
6:  {
7:      const int MaxLength = 80;
8:      char String1[] = "No man is an island";
9:      char String2[MaxLength+1];
10:
11:
```

13

LISTING 13.11   continued

```
12:        strncpy(String2,String1,MaxLength);
13:
14:        std::cout << "String1: " << String1 << std::endl;
15:        std::cout << "String2: " << String2 << std::endl;
16:        return 0;
17:   }
```

OUTPUT
```
String1: No man is an island
String2: No man is an island
```

ANALYSIS In line 12, the call to strcpy() has been changed to a call to strncpy(), which takes a third parameter: the maximum number of characters to copy. The buffer String2 is declared to take MaxLength+1 characters. The extra character is for the null, which both strcpy() and strncpy() automatically add to the end of the string.

String Classes

C++ inherited the null-terminated C-style string and the library of functions that includes strcpy() from C, but these functions aren't integrated into an object-oriented framework. The Standard Library includes a String class that provides an encapsulated set of data and functions for manipulating that data, as well as accessor functions so that the data itself is hidden from the clients of the String class.

We will now create a custom String class as an exercise in understanding the issues involved. At a minimum, our String class should overcome the basic limitations of character arrays. Like all arrays, character arrays are static. You define how large they are. They always take up that much room in memory, even if you don't need it all. Writing past the end of the array is disastrous.

 Note | This custom String class is quite limited and is by no means complete, robust, or ready for commercial use. That is fine, however, as the Standard Library does provide a complete and robust String class.

A good String class allocates only as much memory as it needs and always enough to hold whatever it is given. If it can't allocate enough memory, it should fail gracefully.

Listing 13.12 provides a first approximation of a String class.

LISTING **13.12**   Using a String class

```
0:   //Listing 13.12 Using a String class
1:
2:   #include <iostream>
3:   #include <string.h>
4:   using namespace std;
5:
6:   // Rudimentary string class
7:   class String
8:   {
9:   public:
10:      // constructors
11:      String();
12:      String(const char *const);
13:      String(const String &);
14:      ~String();
15:
16:      // overloaded operators
17:      char & operator[](unsigned short offset);
18:      char operator[](unsigned short offset) const;
19:      String operator+(const String&);
20:      void operator+=(const String&);
21:      String & operator= (const String &);
22:
23:      // General accessors
24:      unsigned short GetLen()const { return itsLen; }
25:      const char * GetString() const { return itsString; }
26:
27:   private:
28:      String (unsigned short);          // private constructor
29:      char * itsString;
30:      unsigned short itsLen;
31:   };
32:
33:   // default constructor creates string of 0 bytes
34:   String::String()
35:   {
36:      itsString = new char[1];
37:      itsString[0] = '\0';
38:      itsLen=0;
39:   }
40:
41:   // private (helper) constructor, used only by
42:   // class methods for creating a new string of
43:   // required size. Null filled.
44:   String::String(unsigned short len)
45:   {
46:      itsString = new char[len+1];
47:      for (unsigned short i = 0; i<=len; i++)
48:          itsString[i] = '\0';
```

LISTING **13.12** continued

```
49:        itsLen=len;
50:    }
51:
52:    // Converts a character array to a String
53:    String::String(const char * const cString)
54:    {
55:        itsLen = strlen(cString);
56:        itsString = new char[itsLen+1];
57:        for (unsigned short i = 0; i<itsLen; i++)
58:            itsString[i] = cString[i];
59:        itsString[itsLen]='\0';
60:    }
61:
62:    // copy constructor
63:    String::String (const String & rhs)
64:    {
65:        itsLen=rhs.GetLen();
66:        itsString = new char[itsLen+1];
67:        for (unsigned short i = 0; i<itsLen;i++)
68:            itsString[i] = rhs[i];
69:        itsString[itsLen] = '\0';
70:    }
71:
72:    // destructor, frees allocated memory
73:    String::~String ()
74:    {
75:        delete [] itsString;
76:        itsLen = 0;
77:    }
78:
79:    // operator equals, frees existing memory
80:    // then copies string and size
81:    String& String::operator=(const String & rhs)
82:    {
83:        if (this == &rhs)
84:            return *this;
85:        delete [] itsString;
86:        itsLen=rhs.GetLen();
87:        itsString = new char[itsLen+1];
88:        for (unsigned short i = 0; i<itsLen;i++)
89:            itsString[i] = rhs[i];
90:        itsString[itsLen] = '\0';
91:        return *this;
92:    }
93:
94:    //nonconstant offset operator, returns
95:    // reference to character so it can be
96:    // changed!
97:    char & String::operator[](unsigned short offset)
```

LISTING 13.12   continued

```
98:  {
99:     if (offset > itsLen)
100:          return itsString[itsLen-1];
101:     else
102:          return itsString[offset];
103:  }
104:
105:  // constant offset operator for use
106:  // on const objects (see copy constructor!)
107:  char String::operator[](unsigned short offset) const
108:  {
109:     if (offset > itsLen)
110:          return itsString[itsLen-1];
111:     else
112:          return itsString[offset];
113:  }
114:
115:  // creates a new string by adding current
116:  // string to rhs
117:  String String::operator+(const String& rhs)
118:  {
119:     unsigned short  totalLen = itsLen + rhs.GetLen();
120:     String temp(totalLen);
121:     unsigned short i;
122:     for ( i= 0; i<itsLen; i++)
123:          temp[i] = itsString[i];
124:     for (unsigned short j = 0; j<rhs.GetLen(); j++, i++)
125:          temp[i] = rhs[j];
126:     temp[totalLen]='\0';
127:     return temp;
128:  }
129:
130:  // changes current string, returns nothing
131:  void String::operator+=(const String& rhs)
132:  {
133:     unsigned short rhsLen = rhs.GetLen();
134:     unsigned short totalLen = itsLen + rhsLen;
135:     String  temp(totalLen);
136:     unsigned short i;
137:     for (i = 0; i<itsLen; i++)
138:          temp[i] = itsString[i];
139:     for (unsigned short j = 0; j<rhs.GetLen(); j++, i++)
140:          temp[i] = rhs[i-itsLen];
141:     temp[totalLen]='\0';
142:     *this = temp;
143:  }
144:
145:  int main()
146:  {
```

13

LISTING **13.12**   continued

```
147:      String s1("initial test");
148:      cout << "S1:\t" << s1.GetString() << endl;
149:
150:      char * temp = "Hello World";
151:      s1 = temp;
152:      cout << "S1:\t" << s1.GetString() << endl;
153:
154:      char tempTwo[20];
155:      strcpy(tempTwo,"; nice to be here!");
156:      s1 += tempTwo;
157:      cout << "tempTwo:\t" << tempTwo << endl;
158:      cout << "S1:\t" << s1.GetString() << endl;
159:
160:      cout << "S1[4]:\t" << s1[4] << endl;
161:      s1[4]='x';
162:      cout << "S1:\t" << s1.GetString() << endl;
163:
164:      cout << "S1[999]:\t" << s1[999] << endl;
165:
166:      String s2(" Another string");
167:      String s3;
168:      s3 = s1+s2;
169:      cout << "S3:\t" << s3.GetString() << endl;
170:
171:      String s4;
172:      s4 = "Why does this work?";
173:      cout << "S4:\t" << s4.GetString() << endl;
174:      return 0;
175:  }
```

OUTPUT
```
S1:      initial test
S1:      Hello World
tempTwo:          ; nice to be here!
S1:      Hello World; nice to be here!
S1[4]:   o
S1:      Hellx World; nice to be here!
S1[999]:          !
S3:      Hellx World; nice to be here! Another string
S4:      Why does this work?
```

ANALYSIS   Lines 7–31 are the declaration of a simple String class. Lines 11–13 contain three constructors: the default constructor, the copy constructor, and a constructor that takes an existing null-terminated (C-style) string.

This String class overloads the offset operator ([ ]), operator plus (+), and operator plus-equals (+=). The offset operator is overloaded twice: once as a constant function returning a char and again as a nonconstant function returning a reference to a char.

The nonconstant version is used in statements such as

```
SomeString[4]='x';
```

as seen in line 161. This enables direct access to each of the characters in the string. A reference to the character is returned so that the calling function can manipulate it.

The constant version is used when a constant `String` object is being accessed, such as in the implementation of the copy constructor (line 63). Note that `rhs[i]` is accessed, yet `rhs` is declared as a const `String` &. It isn't legal to access this object by using a nonconstant member function. Therefore, the offset operator must be overloaded with a constant accessor.

If the object being returned were large, you might want to declare the return value to be a constant reference. However, because a char is only one byte, there would be no point in doing that.

The default constructor is implemented in lines 33–39. It creates a string whose length is 0. It is the convention of this `String` class to report its length not counting the terminating null. This default string contains only a terminating null.

The copy constructor is implemented in lines 63–70. It sets the new string's length to that of the existing string—plus 1 for the terminating null. It copies each character from the existing string to the new string, and it null-terminates the new string.

Lines 53–60 implement the constructor that takes an existing C-style string. This constructor is similar to the copy constructor. The length of the existing string is established by a call to the standard `String` library function `strlen()`.

On line 28, another constructor, `String(unsigned short)`, is declared to be a private member function. It is the intent of the designer of this class that no client class ever create a `String` of arbitrary length. This constructor exists only to help in the internal creation of Strings as required, for example, by `operator+=`, on line 130. This will be discussed in depth when `operator+=` is described later.

The `String(unsigned short)` constructor fills every member of its array with NULL. Therefore, the `for` loop checks for `i<=len` rather than `i<len`.

The destructor, implemented in lines 73–77, deletes the character string maintained by the class. Be sure to include the brackets in the call to the delete operator so that every member of the array is deleted, instead of only the first.

The assignment operator first checks whether the right-hand side of the assignment is the same as the left-hand side. If it isn't, the current string is deleted, and the new string is created and copied into place. A reference is returned to facilitate assignments such as

```
String1 = String2 = String3;
```

13

The offset operator is overloaded twice. Rudimentary bounds checking is performed both times. If the user attempts to access a character at a location beyond the end of the array, the last character—that is, `len-1`—is returned.

Lines 117–127 implement operator plus (+) as a concatenation operator. It is convenient to be able to write

```
String3 = String1 + String2;
```

and have `String3` be the concatenation of the other two strings. To accomplish this, the operator plus function computes the combined length of the two strings and creates a temporary string `temp`. This invokes the private constructor, which takes an integer, and creates a string filled with nulls. The nulls are then replaced by the contents of the two strings. The left-hand side string (`*this`) is copied first, followed by the right-hand side string (`rhs`).

The first `for` loop counts through the string on the left-hand side and adds each character to the new string. The second `for` loop counts through the right-hand side. Note that `i` continues to count the place for the new string, even as `j` counts into the rhs string.

Operator plus returns the temp string by value, which is assigned to the string on the left-hand side of the assignment (`string1`). Operator += operates on the existing string—that is, the left-hand side of the statement `string1 += string2`. It works the same as operator plus, except that the temp value is assigned to the current string (`*this = temp`) in line 142.

The `main()` function (lines 145–175) acts as a test driver program for this class. Line 147 creates a `String` object by using the constructor that takes a null-terminated C-style string. Line 148 prints its contents by using the accessor function `GetString()`. Line 150 creates another C-style string. Line 151 tests the assignment operator, and line 152 prints the results.

Line 154 creates a third C-style string, `tempTwo`. Line 155 invokes `strcpy` to fill the buffer with the characters `; nice to be here!` Line 156 invokes operator += and concatenates `tempTwo` onto the existing string s1. Line 158 prints the results.

In line 160, the fifth character in s1 is accessed and printed. It is assigned a new value in line 161. This invokes the nonconstant offset operator (`[ ]`). Line 162 prints the result, which shows that the actual value has, in fact, been changed.

Line 164 attempts to access a character beyond the end of the array. The last character of the array is returned, as designed.

Lines 166 and 167 create two more `String` objects, and line 168 calls the addition operator. Line 169 prints the results.

Line 171 creates a new `String` object, s4. Line 172 invokes the assignment operator. Line 173 prints the results. You might be thinking, "The assignment operator is defined to take a constant `String` reference in line 21, but here the program passes in a C-style string. Why is this legal?"

The answer is that the compiler expects a `String`, but it is given a character array. Therefore, it checks whether it can create a `String` from what it is given. In line 12, you declared a constructor that creates `String`s from character arrays. The compiler creates a temporary `String` from the character array and passes it to the assignment operator. This is known as implicit casting, or promotion. If you had not declared—and provided the implementation for—the constructor that takes a character array, this assignment would have generated a compiler error.

Linked Lists and Other Structures

Arrays are much like Tupperware. They are great containers, but they are of a fixed size. If you pick a container that is too large, you waste space in your storage area. If you pick one that is too small, its contents spill all over and you have a big mess.

One way to solve this problem is with a linked list. A linked list is a data structure that consists of small containers that are designed to link together as needed. The idea is to write a class that holds one object of your data—such as one `CAT` or one `Rectangle`—and that can point at the next container. You create one container for each object that you need to store, and you chain them together as needed.

The containers are called nodes. The first node in the list is called the head, and the last node in the list is called the tail.

Lists come in three fundamental forms. From simplest to most complex, they are

- Singly linked
- Doubly linked
- Trees

In a singly linked list, each node points forward to the next one, but not backward. To find a particular node, start at the top and go from node to node, as in a treasure hunt ("The next node is under the sofa"). A doubly linked list enables you to move backward and forward in the chain. A tree is a complex structure built from nodes, each of which can point in two or three directions. Figure 13.5 shows these three fundamental structures.

13

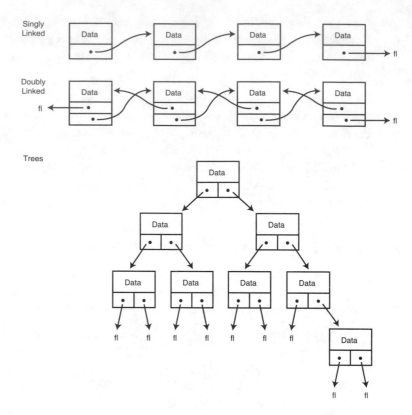

Figure 13.5

Linked lists.

A Linked List Case Study

In this section, we will examine a linked list in detail as a case study both of how you create complex structures and, more importantly, how you use inheritance, polymorphism, and encapsulation to manage large projects.

Delegation of Responsibility

A fundamental premise of object-oriented programming is that each object does *one* thing very well and delegates to other objects anything that is not its core mission.

An automobile is a perfect example of this idea in hardware: The engine's job is to produce the power. Distribution of that power is not the engine's job; that is up to the transmission. Turning is not the job of the engine nor the transmission; that is delegated to the wheels.

A well-designed machine has lots of small, well-understood parts, each doing its own job and working together to accomplish a greater good. A well-designed program is much the same: Each class sticks to its own knitting, but together they create one heck of an afghan.

The Component Parts

The linked list will consist of nodes. The node class itself will be abstract; we'll use three subtypes to accomplish the work. There will be a head node whose job is to manage the head of the list, a tail node (guess what its job is!), and zero or more internal nodes. The internal nodes will keep track of the actual data to be held in the list.

Note that the data and the list are quite distinct. You can, in theory, save any type of data you like in a list. It isn't the data that is linked together; it is the node that *holds* the data.

The driver program doesn't know about the nodes; it works with the list. The list, however, does little work; it simply delegates to the nodes.

Listing 13.13 shows the code; we'll examine it in excruciating detail:

LISTING 13.13 Linked List

```
0:  // ************************************************
1:  //     FILE:        Listing 13.13
2:  //
3:  //     PURPOSE:     Demonstrate ilinked list
4:  //     NOTES:
5:  //
6:  //  COPYRIGHT:   Copyright (C) 2000 Liberty Associates, Inc.
7:  //                    All Rights Reserved
8:  //
9:  // Demonstrates an object-oriented approach to
10: // linked lists. The list delegates to the node.
11: // The node is an abstract data type. Three types of
12: // nodes are used, head nodes, tail nodes and internal
13: // nodes. Only the internal nodes hold data.
14: //
15: // The Data class is created to serve as an object to
16: // hold in the linked list.
17: //
18: // ************************************************
19:
20:
21: #include <iostream>
22: using namespace std;
23:
24: enum { kIsSmaller, kIsLarger, kIsSame};
```

13

LISTING 13.13   continued

```
25:
26:  // Data class to put into the linked list
27:  // Any class in this linked list must support two methods:
28:  // Show (displays the value) and
29:  // Compare (returns relative position)
30:  class Data
31:  {
32:  public:
33:     Data(int val):myValue(val){}
34:     ~Data(){}
35:     int Compare(const Data &);
36:     void Show() { cout << myValue << endl; }
37:  private:
38:     int myValue;
39:  };
40:
41:  // Compare is used to decide where in the list
42:  // a particular object belongs.
43:  int Data::Compare(const Data & theOtherData)
44:  {
45:     if (myValue < theOtherData.myValue)
46:        return kIsSmaller;
47:     if (myValue > theOtherData.myValue)
48:        return kIsLarger;
49:     else
50:        return kIsSame;
51:  }
52:
53:  // forward declarations
54:  class Node;
55:  class HeadNode;
56:  class TailNode;
57:  class InternalNode;
58:
59:  // ADT representing the node object in the list
60:  // Every derived class must override Insert and Show
61:  class Node
62:  {
63:  public:
64:     Node(){}
65:     virtual ~Node(){}
66:     virtual Node * Insert(Data * theData)=0;
67:     virtual void Show() = 0;
68:  private:
69:  };
70:
71:  // This is the node which holds the actual object
72:  // In this case the object is of type Data
73:  // We'll see how to make this more general when
```

LISTING 13.13   continued

```
74:    // we cover templates
75:    class InternalNode: public Node
76:    {
77:    public:
78:       InternalNode(Data * theData, Node * next);
79:       ~InternalNode(){ delete myNext; delete myData; }
80:       virtual Node * Insert(Data * theData);
81:       // delegate!
82:       virtual void Show() { myData->Show(); myNext->Show(); }
83:
84:    private:
85:       Data * myData;   // the data itself
86:       Node * myNext;    // points to next node in the linked list
87:    };
88:
89:    // All the constructor does is to initialize
90:    InternalNode::InternalNode(Data * theData, Node * next):
91:    myData(theData),myNext(next)
92:    {
93:    }
94:
95:    // the meat of the list
96:    // When you put a new object into the list
97:    // it is passed ot the node which figures out
98:    // where it goes and inserts it into the list
99:    Node * InternalNode::Insert(Data * theData)
100:   {
101:
102:       // is the new guy bigger or smaller than me?
103:       int result = myData->Compare(*theData);
104:
105:
106:       switch(result)
107:       {
108:       // by convention if it is the same as me it comes first
109:       case kIsSame:         // fall through
110:       case kIsLarger:     // new data comes before me
111:          {
112:             InternalNode * dataNode = new InternalNode(theData, this);
113:             return dataNode;
114:          }
115:
116:       // it is bigger than I am so pass it on to the next
117:       // node and let HIM handle it.
118:       case kIsSmaller:
119:          myNext = myNext->Insert(theData);
120:          return this;
121:       }
122:       return this;   // appease MSC
```

13

LISTING 13.13   continued

```
123:    }
124:
125:
126:    // Tail node is just a sentinel
127:
128:    class TailNode : public Node
129:    {
130:    public:
131:        TailNode(){}
132:        ~TailNode(){}
133:        virtual Node * Insert(Data * theData);
134:        virtual void Show() { }
135:
136:    private:
137:
138:    };
139:
140:    // If data comes to me, it must be inserted before me
141:    // as I am the tail and NOTHING comes after me
142:    Node * TailNode::Insert(Data * theData)
143:    {
144:        InternalNode * dataNode = new InternalNode(theData, this);
145:        return dataNode;
146:    }
147:
148:    // Head node has no data, it just points
149:    // to the very beginning of the list
150:    class HeadNode : public Node
151:    {
152:    public:
153:        HeadNode();
154:        ~HeadNode() { delete myNext; }
155:        virtual Node * Insert(Data * theData);
156:        virtual void Show() { myNext->Show(); }
157:    private:
158:        Node * myNext;
159:    };
160:
161:    // As soon as the head is created
162:    // it creates the tail
163:    HeadNode::HeadNode()
164:    {
165:        myNext = new TailNode;
166:    }
167:
168:    // Nothing comes before the head so just
169:    // pass the data on to the next node
170:    Node * HeadNode::Insert(Data * theData)
171:    {
```

LISTING 13.13   continued

```
172:      myNext = myNext->Insert(theData);
173:      return this;
174:  }
175:
176:  // I get all the credit and do none of the work
177:  class LinkedList
178:  {
179:  public:
180:      LinkedList();
181:      ~LinkedList() { delete myHead; }
182:      void Insert(Data * theData);
183:      void ShowAll() { myHead->Show(); }
184:  private:
185:      HeadNode * myHead;
186:  };
187:
188:  // At birth, I create the head node
189:  // It creates the tail node
190:  // So an empty list points to the head which
191:  // points to the tail and has nothing between
192:  LinkedList::LinkedList()
193:  {
194:      myHead = new HeadNode;
195:  }
196:
197:  // Delegate, delegate, delegate
198:  void LinkedList::Insert(Data * pData)
199:  {
200:      myHead->Insert(pData);
201:  }
202:
203:  // test driver program
204:  int main()
205:  {
206:      Data * pData;
207:      int val;
208:      LinkedList ll;
209:
210:      // ask the user to produce some values
211:      // put them in the list
212:      for (;;)
213:      {
214:         cout << "What value? (0 to stop): ";
215:         cin >> val;
216:         if (!val)
217:            break;
218:         pData = new Data(val);
219:         ll.Insert(pData);
220:      }
```

13

LISTING 13.13   continued

```
221:
222:    // now walk the list and show the data
223:    ll.ShowAll();
224:    return 0;  // ll falls out of scope and is destroyed!
225: }
```

OUTPUT

```
What value? (0 to stop): 5
What value? (0 to stop): 8
What value? (0 to stop): 3
What value? (0 to stop): 9
What value? (0 to stop): 2
What value? (0 to stop): 10
What value? (0 to stop): 0
2
3
5
8
9
10
```

ANALYSIS   The first thing to note is the enumerated constant, which provides three constant values: kIsSmaller, kIsLarger, and kIsSame. Every object that may be held in this linked list must support a Compare() method. These constants will be the result value returned by the Compare() method.

For illustration purposes, the class Data is created on lines 30–39, and the Compare() method is implemented on lines 41–51. A Data object holds a value and can compare itself with other Data objects. It also supports a Show() method to display the value of the Data object.

The easiest way to understand the workings of the linked list is to step through an example of using one. On line 203 a driver program is declared; on line 206 a pointer to a Data object is declared; and on line 208 a local linked list is defined.

When the linked list is created, the constructor on line 192 is called. The only work done in the constructor is to allocate a HeadNode object and to assign that object's address to the pointer held in the linked list on line 185.

This allocation of a HeadNode invokes the HeadNode constructor shown on lines 163–166. This in turn allocates a TailNode and assigns its address to the head node's myNext pointer. The creation of the TailNode calls the TailNode constructor shown on line 131, which is inline and which does nothing.

Thus, by the simple act of allocating a linked list on the stack, the list is created, a head and a tail node are created, and their relationship is established, as illustrated in Figure 13.6.

FIGURE 13.6

The linked list after it is created.

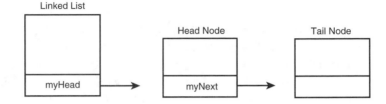

Line 212 begins an infinite loop. The user will be prompted for values to add to the linked list. He can add as many values as he likes, entering 0 when he is finished. The code on line 216 evaluates the value entered; if it is 0, it breaks out of the loop.

If the value is not 0, a new Data object is created on line 218, and that is inserted into the list on line 219. For illustration purposes, assume the user enters the value 15. This invokes the Insert method on line 198.

The linked list immediately delegates responsibility for inserting the object to its head node. This invokes the method Insert on line 170. The head node immediately passes the responsibility to whatever node its myNext is pointing to. In this (first) case, it is pointing to the tail node (remember, when the head node was born, it created a link to a tail node). This, therefore, invokes the method Insert on line 142.

TailNode::Insert knows that the object it has been handed must be inserted immediately before itself—that is, the new object will be in the list right before the tail node. Therefore, on line 144 it creates a new InternalNode object, passing in the data and a pointer to itself. This invokes the constructor for the InternalNode object, shown on line 90.

The InternalNode constructor does nothing more than initialize its Data pointer with the address of the Data object it was passed and its myNext pointer with the node's address it was passed. In this case, the node it will point to is the tail node (remember, the tail node passed in its own this pointer).

Now that the InternalNode has been created, the address of that internal node is assigned to the pointer dataNode on line 144, and that address is in turn returned from the TailNode::Insert() method. This returns us to HeadNode::Insert(), where the address of the InternalNode is assigned to the HeadNode's myNext pointer (on line 172). Finally, the HeadNode's address is returned to the linked list where, on line 200, it is thrown away (nothing is done with it because the linked list already knows the address of the head node).

13

Why bother returning the address if it is not used? Insert is declared in the base class, Node. The return value is needed by the other implementations. If you change the return value of HeadNode::Insert(), you will get a compiler error; it is simpler just to return the HeadNode and let the linked list throw its address on the floor.

So what happened? The data was inserted into the list. The list passed it to the head. The head, blindly, passed the data to whatever the head happened to be pointing to. In this (first) case, the head was pointing to the tail. The tail immediately created a new internal node, initializing the new node to point to the tail. The tail then returned the address of the new node to the head, which reassigned its myNext pointer to point to the new node. Hey! Presto! The data is in the list in the right place, as illustrated in Figure 13.7.

FIGURE 13.7

The linked list after the first node is inserted.

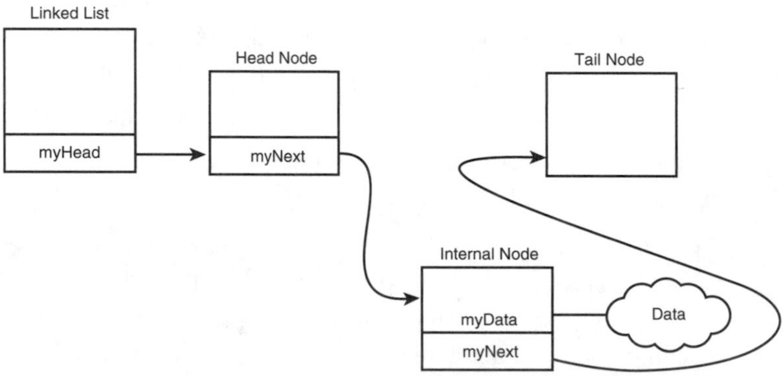

After inserting the first node, program control resumes at line 214. Once again, the value is evaluated. For illustration purposes, assume that the value 3 is entered. This causes a new Data object to be created on line 218 and to be inserted into the list on line 219.

Once again, on line 200, the list passes the data to its HeadNode. The HeadNode::Insert() method, in turn, passes the new value to whatever its myNext happens to be pointing to. As you know, it is now pointing to the node that contains the Data object whose value is 15. This invokes the InternalNode::Insert() method on line 99.

On line 103, the InternalNode uses its myData pointer to tell its Data object (the one whose value is 15) to call its Compare() method, passing in the new Data object (whose value is 3). This invokes the Compare() method shown on line 43.

The two values are compared, and, because myValue will be 15 and theOtherData.myValue will be 3, the returned value will be kIsLarger. This will cause program flow to jump to line 112.

A new `InternalNode` is created for the new `Data` object. The new node will point to the current `InternalNode` object, and the new `InternalNode`'s address is returned from the `InternalNode::Insert()` method to the `HeadNode`. Thus, the new node, whose object's value is smaller than the current node's object's value, is inserted into the list, and the list now looks like Figure 13.8.

FIGURE 13.8

The linked list after the second node is inserted.

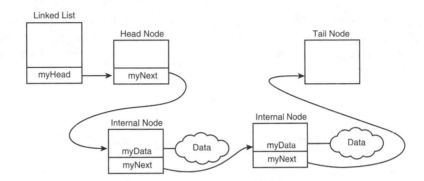

In the third invocation of the loop, the customer adds the value 8. This is larger than 3 but smaller than 15, and so it should be inserted between the two existing nodes. Progress will be like the previous example, except that when the node whose object's value is 3 does the compare, rather than returning `kIsLarger`, it will return `kIsSmaller` (meaning that the object whose value is 3 is smaller than the new object, whose value is 8).

This will cause the `InternalNode::Insert()` method to branch to line 119. Rather than creating a new node and inserting it, the `InternalNode` will just pass the new data on to the `Insert` method of whatever its `myNext` pointer happens to be pointing to. In this case, it will invoke `InsertNode` on the `InternalNode` whose `Data` object's value is 15.

The comparison will be done again, and a new `InternalNode` will be created. This new `InternalNode` will point to the `InternalNode` whose `Data` object's value is 15, and its address will be passed back to the `InternalNode` whose `Data` object's value is 3, as shown on line 119.

The net effect is that the new node will be inserted into the list at the right location.

If at all possible, you'll want to step through the insertion of a number of nodes in your debugger. You should be able to watch these methods invoke one another and the pointers be properly adjusted.

13

What Have You Learned, Dorothy?

"If I ever go looking for my heart's desire again, I won't look any further than my own backyard." Although it is true there is no place like home, it is also true that this is nothing like procedural programming. In procedural programming, a controlling method would examine data and invoke functions.

In this object-oriented approach, each individual object is given a narrow and well-defined set of responsibilities. The linked list is responsible for maintaining the head node. The head node immediately passes the new data on to whatever it points to, without regard to what that might be.

The tail node creates a new node and inserts it whenever it is handed data. It knows only one thing: If this came to me, it gets inserted right before me.

Internal nodes are marginally more complicated; they ask their existing object to compare itself with the new object. Depending on the result, they then insert or they just pass it along.

Note that the `InternalNode` has *no idea* how to do the comparison; that is properly left to the object itself. All the `InternalNode` knows is to ask the objects to compare themselves and to expect one of three possible answers. Given one answer, it inserts; otherwise it just passes it along, not knowing or caring where it will end up.

So who's in charge? In a well-designed object-oriented program, *no one* is in charge. Each object does its own little job, and the net effect is a well-running machine.

Array Classes

Writing your own array class has many advantages over using the built-in arrays. For starters, you can prevent array overruns. You might also consider making your array class dynamically sized: At creation it might have only one member, growing as needed during the course of the program.

You might want to sort or otherwise order the members of the array. You might consider a number of powerful array variants. Among the most popular are

- **Ordered collection:** Each member is in sorted order.
- **Set:** No member appears more than once.
- **Dictionary:** This uses matched pairs in which one value acts as a key to retrieve the other value.

- **Sparse array:** Indices are permitted for a large set, but only those values actually added to the array consume memory. Thus, you can ask for `SparseArray[5]` or `SparseArray[200]`, but it is possible that memory is allocated only for a small number of entries.
- **Bag:** An unordered collection that is added to and retrieved in random order.

By overloading the index operator (`[ ]`), you can turn a linked list into an ordered collection. By excluding duplicates, you can turn a collection into a set. If each object in the list has a pair of matched values, you can use a linked list to build a dictionary or a sparse array.

Summary

Today you learned how to create arrays in C++. An array is a fixed-size collection of objects that are all the same type.

Arrays don't do bounds checking. Therefore it is legal—even if disastrous—to read or write past the end of an array. Arrays count from 0. A common mistake is to write to offset n of an array of n members.

Arrays can be one dimensional or multidimensional. In either case, the members of the array can be initialized, as long as the array contains either built-in types, such as `int`, or objects of a class that has a default constructor.

Arrays and their contents can be on the free store or on the stack. If you delete an array on the free store, remember to use the brackets in the call to delete.

Array names are constant pointers to the first elements of the array. Pointers and arrays use pointer arithmetic to find the next element of an array.

You can create linked lists to manage collections whose size you won't know at compile time. From linked lists, you can create any number of more complex data structures.

Strings are arrays of characters, or chars. C++ provides special features for managing `char` arrays, including the capability to initialize them with quoted strings.

13

Q&A

Q **What happens if I write to element 25 in a 24-member array?**

A You will write to other memory, with potentially disastrous effects on your program.

Q What is in an uninitialized array element?

A Whatever happens to be in memory at a given time. The results of using this member without assigning a value are unpredictable.

Q Can I combine arrays?

A Yes. With simple arrays you can use pointers to combine them into a new, larger array. With strings, you can use some of the built-in functions, such as `strcat`, to combine strings.

Q Why should I create a linked list if an array will work?

A An array must have a fixed size, whereas a linked list can be sized dynamically at runtime.

Q Why would I ever use built-in arrays if I can make a better array class?

A Built-in arrays are quick and easy to use.

Q Must a string class use a `char *` to hold the contents of the string?

A No. It can use any memory storage the designer thinks is best.

Workshop

The Workshop provides quiz questions to help you solidify your understanding of the material covered and exercises to provide you with experience in using what you've learned. Try to answer the quiz and exercise questions before checking the answers in Appendix D, and make sure you understand the answers before continuing to the next chapter.

Quiz

1. What are the first and last elements in `SomeArray[25]`?

2. How do you declare a multidimensional array?

3. Initialize the members of the array in Question 2.

4. How many elements are in the array `SomeArray[10][5][20]`?

5. What is the maximum number of elements that you can add to a linked list?

6. Can you use subscript notation on a linked list?

7. What is the last character in the string "Brad is a nice guy"?

Exercises

1. Declare a two-dimensional array that represents a tic-tac-toe game board.

2. Write the code that initializes all the elements in the array you created in Exercise 1 to the value `0`.

3. Write the declaration for a Node class that holds integers.

4. **BUG BUSTERS:** What is wrong with this code fragment?

```
unsigned short SomeArray[5][4];
for (int i = 0; i<4; i++)
    for (int j = 0; j<5; j++)
        SomeArray[i][j] = i+j;
```

5. **BUG BUSTERS:** What is wrong with this code fragment?

```
unsigned short SomeArray[5][4];
for (int i = 0; i<=5; i++)
    for (int j = 0; j<=4; j++)
        SomeArray[i][j] = 0;
```

13

DAY 14

Polymorphism

On Day 12, you learned how to write virtual functions in derived classes. This is the fundamental building block of polymorphism: the capability to bind specific, derived class objects to base class pointers at runtime.

Today you will learn

- What multiple inheritance is and how to use it.
- What virtual inheritance is.
- What abstract data types are.
- What pure virtual functions are.

Problems with Single Inheritance

Suppose you've been working with your animal classes for a while, and you've divided the class hierarchy into Birds and Mammals. The Bird class includes the member function Fly(). The Mammal class has been divided into a number of types of Mammals, including Horse. The Horse class includes the member functions Whinny() and Gallop().

Suddenly, you realize you need a Pegasus object: a cross between a Horse and a Bird. A Pegasus can Fly(), it can Whinny(), and it can Gallop(). With single inheritance, you're in quite a jam.

You can make Pegasus a Bird, but then it won't be able to Whinny() or Gallop(). You can make it a Horse, but then it won't be able to Fly().

Your first solution is to copy the Fly() method into the Pegasus class and derive Pegasus from Horse. This works fine, at the cost of having the Fly() method in two places (Bird and Pegasus). If you change one, you must remember to change the other. Of course, a developer who comes along months or years later to maintain your code must also know to fix both places.

Soon, however, you have a new problem. You want to create a list of Horse objects and a list of Bird objects. You'd like to be able to add your Pegasus objects to either list, but if a Pegasus is a Horse, you can't add it to a list of Birds.

You have a couple of potential solutions. You can rename the Horse method Gallop() to Move(), and then override Move() in your Pegasus object to do the work of Fly(). You would then override Move() in your other horses to do the work of Gallop(). Perhaps Pegasus could be clever enough to gallop short distances and fly longer distances.

```
Pegasus::Move(long distance)
{
if (distance > veryFar)
fly(distance);
else
gallop(distance);
}
```

This is a bit limiting. Perhaps one day Pegasus will want to fly a short distance or gallop a long distance. Your next solution might be to move Fly() up into Horse, as illustrated in Listing 14.1. The problem is that most horses can't fly, so you have to make this method do nothing unless it is a Pegasus.

LISTING 14.1   If Horses Could Fly...

```
0:  // Listing 14.1. If horses could fly...
1:  // Percolating Fly() up into Horse
2:
3:  #include <iostream>
4:  using namespace std;
5:
6:  class Horse
7:  {
8:  public:
9:      void Gallop(){ cout << "Galloping...\n"; }
```

LISTING 14.1   continued

```
10:      virtual void Fly() { cout << "Horses can't fly.\n" ; }
11:  private:
12:      int itsAge;
13:  };
14:
15:  class Pegasus : public Horse
16:  {
17:  public:
18:      virtual void Fly() {cout<<"I can fly! I can fly! I can fly!\n";}
19:  };
20:
21:  const int NumberHorses = 5;
22:  int main()
23:  {
24:      Horse* Ranch[NumberHorses];
25:      Horse* pHorse;
26:      int choice,i;
27:      for (i=0; i<NumberHorses; i++)
28:      {
29:         cout << "(1)Horse (2)Pegasus: ";
30:         cin >> choice;
31:         if (choice == 2)
32:            pHorse = new Pegasus;
33:         else
34:            pHorse = new Horse;
35:         Ranch[i] = pHorse;
36:      }
37:      cout << "\n";
38:      for (i=0; i<NumberHorses; i++)
39:      {
40:         Ranch[i]->Fly();
41:         delete Ranch[i];
42:      }
43:      return 0;
44:  }
```

OUTPUT
```
(1)Horse (2)Pegasus: 1
(1)Horse (2)Pegasus: 2
(1)Horse (2)Pegasus: 1
(1)Horse (2)Pegasus: 2
(1)Horse (2)Pegasus: 1

Horses can't fly.
I can fly! I can fly! I can fly!
Horses can't fly.
I can fly! I can fly! I can fly!
Horses can't fly.
```

14

ANALYSIS   This program certainly works, although at the expense of the Horse class having a Fly() method. On line 10, the method Fly() is provided to Horse. In a real-world class, you might have it issue an error, or fail quietly. On line 18, the Pegasus class overrides the Fly() method to "do the right thing," represented here by printing a happy message.

The array of Horse pointers on line 24 is used to demonstrate that the correct Fly() method is called, based on the runtime binding of the Horse or Pegasus object.

> **Note**   These examples have been stripped down to their bare essentials to illustrate the points under consideration. Constructors, virtual destructors, and so on have been removed to keep the code simple.

Percolating Upward

Putting the required function higher in the class hierarchy is a common solution to this problem and results in many functions "percolating up" into the base class. The base class is then in grave danger of becoming a global namespace for all the functions that might be used by any of the derived classes. This can seriously undermine the class typing of C++, and can create a large and cumbersome base class.

In general, you want to percolate shared functionality up the hierarchy, without migrating the interface of each class. This means that if two classes that share a common base class (for example, Horse and Bird both share Animal) and have a function in common (both birds and horses eat, for example), you'll want to move that functionality up into the base class and create a virtual function.

What you'll want to avoid, however, is percolating an interface (such as Fly up where it doesn't belong) just so you can call that function only on some derived classes.

Casting Down

An alternative to this approach, still within single inheritance, is to keep the Fly() method within Pegasus and only call it if the pointer is actually pointing to a Pegasus object. To make this work, you'll need to be able to ask your pointer what type it is really pointing to. This is known as Run Time Type Identification (RTTI). Using RTTI has only recently become an official part of C++.

If your compiler does not support RTTI, you can mimic it by putting a method that returns an enumerated type in each of the classes. You can then test that type at runtime and call Fly() if it returns Pegasus.

Note

Beware of using RTTI in your programs. Use of it may be an indication of poor design. Consider using virtual functions, templates, or multiple inheritance instead.

To call `Fly()`, however, you must cast the pointer, telling it that the object it is pointing to is a `Pegasus` object, not a `Horse`. This is called casting down because you are casting the `Horse` object down to a more derived type.

C++ now officially, though perhaps reluctantly, supports casting down using the new `dynamic_cast` operator. Here's how it works.

If you have a pointer to a base class such as `Horse`, and you assign to it a pointer to a derived class, such as `Pegasus`, you can use the `Horse` pointer polymorphically. If you then need to get at the `Pegasus` object, you create a `Pegasus` pointer and use the `dynamic_cast` operator to make the conversion.

At runtime, the base pointer will be examined. If the conversion is proper, your new `Pegasus` pointer will be fine. If the conversion is improper, if you didn't really have a `Pegasus` object after all, then your new pointer will be null. Listing 14.2 illustrates this point.

LISTING 14.2   Casting Down

```
0:  // Listing 14.2 Using dynamic_cast.
1:  // Using rtti
2:
3:  #include <iostream>
4:  using namespace std;
5:
6:  enum TYPE { HORSE, PEGASUS };
7:
8:  class Horse
9:  {
10: public:
11:     virtual void Gallop(){ cout << "Galloping...\n"; }
12:
13: private:
14:     int itsAge;
15: };
16:
17: class Pegasus : public Horse
18: {
19: public:
20:
```

14

LISTING 14.2   continued

```
21:     virtual void Fly() {cout<<"I can fly! I can fly! I can fly!\n";}
22:   };
23:
24:   const int NumberHorses = 5;
25:   int main()
26:   {
27:       Horse* Ranch[NumberHorses];
28:       Horse* pHorse;
29:       int choice,i;
30:       for (i=0; i<NumberHorses; i++)
31:       {
32:           cout << "(1)Horse (2)Pegasus: ";
33:           cin >> choice;
34:           if (choice == 2)
35:               pHorse = new Pegasus;
36:           else
37:               pHorse = new Horse;
38:           Ranch[i] = pHorse;
39:       }
40:       cout << "\n";
41:       for (i=0; i<NumberHorses; i++)
42:       {
43:           Pegasus *pPeg = dynamic_cast< Pegasus *> (Ranch[i]);
44:           if (pPeg)
45:               pPeg->Fly();
46:           else
47:               cout << "Just a horse\n";
48:
49:           delete Ranch[i];
50:       }
51:       return 0;
52:   }
```

OUTPUT

```
(1)Horse (2)Pegasus: 1
(1)Horse (2)Pegasus: 2
(1)Horse (2)Pegasus: 1
(1)Horse (2)Pegasus: 2
(1)Horse (2)Pegasus: 1

Just a horse
I can fly! I can fly! I can fly!
Just a horse
I can fly! I can fly! I can fly!
Just a horse
```

FAQ

When compiling I got a warning from Microsoft Visual C++: warning C4541: 'dynamic_cast' used on polymorphic type 'class Horse' with /GR-; unpredictable behavior may result. What should I do?

Answer: This is one of this compiler's most confusing error messages. To fix it do the following:

1. In your project, choose Project/Settings.

2. Go to the C++ Tab.

3. Change the drop-down to C++ Language.

4. Click Enable Runtime Type Information (RTTI).

5. Rebuild your entire project.

ANALYSIS This solution also works. Fly() is kept out of Horse, and it is not called on Horse objects. When it is called on Pegasus objects, however, they must be explicitly cast; Horse objects don't have the method Fly(), so the pointer must be told it is pointing to a Pegasus object before being used.

The need for you to cast the Pegasus object is a warning that something may be wrong with your design. This program effectively undermines the virtual function polymorphism because it depends on casting the object to its real runtime type.

Adding to Two Lists

The other problem with these solutions is that you've declared Pegasus to be a type of Horse, so you cannot add a Pegasus object to a list of Birds. You've paid the price of either moving Fly() up into Horse or casting down the pointer, and yet you still don't have the full functionality you need.

One final, single inheritance solution presents itself. You can push Fly(), Whinny(), and Gallop() all up into a common base class of both Bird and Horse: Animal. Now, instead of having a list of Birds and a list of Horses, you can have one unified list of Animals. This works, but percolates more functionality up into the base classes.

Alternatively, you can leave the methods where they are but cast down Horses and Birds and Pegasus objects, but that is even worse!

14

Do	Don't
DO move functionality up the inheritance hierarchy.	**DON'T** move interface up the inheritance hierarchy.
DO avoid switching on the runtime type of the object—use virtual methods, templates, and multiple inheritance.	**DON'T** cast pointers to base objects down to derived objects.

Multiple Inheritance

It is possible to derive a new class from more than one base class. This is called multiple inheritance. To derive from more than the base class, you separate each base class by commas in the class designation. Listing 14.3 illustrates how to declare `Pegasus` so that it derives from both `Horses` and `Birds`. The program then adds `Pegasus` objects to both types of lists.

LISTING 14.3   Multiple Inheritance

```
0:  // Listing 14.3. Multiple inheritance.
1:  // Multiple Inheritance
2:
3:  #include <iostream>
4:  using std::cout;
5:  using std::cin;
6:
7:  class Horse
8:  {
9:  public:
10:     Horse() { cout << "Horse constructor... "; }
11:     virtual ~Horse() { cout << "Horse destructor... "; }
12:     virtual void Whinny() const { cout << "Whinny!... "; }
13:  private:
14:     int itsAge;
15:  };
16:
17:  class Bird
18:  {
19:  public:
20:     Bird() { cout << "Bird constructor... "; }
21:     virtual ~Bird() { cout << "Bird destructor... "; }
22:     virtual void Chirp() const { cout << "Chirp... "; }
23:     virtual void Fly() const
24:     {
25:         cout << "I can fly! I can fly! I can fly! ";
26:     }
27:  private:
```

LISTING 14.3   continued

```
28:      int itsWeight;
29:    };
30:
31:    class Pegasus : public Horse, public Bird
32:    {
33:    public:
34:      void Chirp() const { Whinny(); }
35:      Pegasus() { cout << "Pegasus constructor... "; }
36:      ~Pegasus() { cout << "Pegasus destructor...  "; }
37:    };
38:
39:    const int MagicNumber = 2;
40:    int main()
41:    {
42:      Horse* Ranch[MagicNumber];
43:      Bird* Aviary[MagicNumber];
44:      Horse * pHorse;
45:      Bird * pBird;
46:      int choice,i;
47:      for (i=0; i<MagicNumber; i++)
48:      {
49:        cout << "\n(1)Horse (2)Pegasus: ";
50:        cin >> choice;
51:        if (choice == 2)
52:          pHorse = new Pegasus;
53:        else
54:          pHorse = new Horse;
55:        Ranch[i] = pHorse;
56:      }
57:      for (i=0; i<MagicNumber; i++)
58:      {
59:        cout << "\n(1)Bird (2)Pegasus: ";
60:        cin >> choice;
61:        if (choice == 2)
62:          pBird = new Pegasus;
63:        else
64:          pBird = new Bird;
65:        Aviary[i] = pBird;
66:      }
67:
68:      cout << "\n";
69:      for (i=0; i<MagicNumber; i++)
70:      {
71:        cout << "\nRanch[" << i << "]: " ;
72:        Ranch[i]->Whinny();
73:        delete Ranch[i];
74:      }
75:
76:      for (i=0; i<MagicNumber; i++)
```

14

LISTING **14.3**   continued

```
77:      {
78:         cout << "\nAviary[" << i << "]: " ;
79:         Aviary[i]->Chirp();
80:         Aviary[i]->Fly();
81:         delete Aviary[i];
82:      }
83:      return 0;
84:  }
```

OUTPUT

```
(1)Horse (2)Pegasus: 1
Horse constructor...
(1)Horse (2)Pegasus: 2
Horse constructor... Bird constructor... Pegasus constructor...
(1)Bird (2)Pegasus: 1
Bird constructor...
(1)Bird (2)Pegasus: 2
Horse constructor... Bird constructor... Pegasus constructor...

Ranch[0]: Whinny!... Horse destructor...
Ranch[1]: Whinny!... Pegasus destructor...  Bird destructor...
Horse destructor...
Aviary[0]: Chirp... I can fly! I can fly! I can fly! Bird destructor...
Aviary[1]: Whinny!... I can fly! I can fly! I can fly!
Pegasus destructor... Bird destructor... Horse destructor...
```

ANALYSIS   On lines 7–15, a Horse class is declared. The constructor and destructor print out a message, and the Whinny() method prints the word Whinny!

On lines 17–29, a Bird class is declared. In addition to its constructor and destructor, this class has two methods: Chirp() and Fly(), both of which print identifying messages. In a real program these might, for example, activate the speaker or generate animated images.

Finally, on lines 31–37, the class Pegasus is declared. It derives both from Horse and from Bird. The Pegasus class overrides the Chirp() method to call the Whinny() method, which it inherits from Horse.

Two lists are created: a Ranch with pointers to Horse on line 42, and an Aviary with pointers to Bird on line 43. On lines 47–56, Horse and Pegasus objects are added to the Ranch. On lines 57–66, Bird and Pegasus objects are added to the Aviary.

Invocations of the virtual methods on both the Bird pointers and the Horse pointers do the right things for Pegasus objects. For example, on line 79 the members of the Aviary array are used to call Chirp() on the objects to which they point. The Bird class declares this to be a virtual method, so the right function is called for each object.

Note that each time a `Pegasus` object is created, the output reflects that both the `Bird` part and the `Horse` part of the `Pegasus` object are also created. When a `Pegasus` object is destroyed, the `Bird` and `Horse` parts are destroyed as well, thanks to the destructors being made virtual.

Declaring Multiple Inheritance

Declare an object to inherit from more than one class by listing the base classes following the colon after the class name. Separate the base classes by commas.

Example 1

```
class Pegasus : public Horse, public Bird
```

Example 2

```
class Schnoodle : public Schnauzer, public Poodle
```

The Parts of a Multiply Inherited Object

When the `Pegasus` object is created in memory, both the base classes form part of the `Pegasus` object, as illustrated in Figure 14.1.

FIGURE 14.1

Multiply inherited objects.

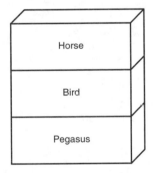

Several issues arise with objects with multiple base classes. For example, what happens if two base classes that happen to have the same name have virtual functions or data? How are multiple base class constructors initialized? What happens if multiple base classes both derive from the same class? The next sections will answer these questions and explore how multiple inheritance can be put to work.

Constructors in Multiply Inherited Objects

If `Pegasus` derives from both `Horse` and `Bird`, and each of the base classes has constructors that take parameters, the Pegasus class initializes these constructors in turn. Listing 14.4 illustrates how this is done.

14

LISTING 14.4   Calling Multiple Constructors

```
0:   // Listing 14.4
1:   // Calling multiple constructors
2:
3:   #include <iostream>
4:   using namespace std;
5:
6:   typedef int HANDS;
7:   enum COLOR { Red, Green, Blue, Yellow, White, Black, Brown } ;
8:
9:   class Horse
10:  {
11:  public:
12:      Horse(COLOR color, HANDS height);
13:      virtual ~Horse() { cout << "Horse destructor...\n"; }
14:      virtual void Whinny()const { cout << "Whinny!... "; }
15:      virtual HANDS GetHeight() const { return itsHeight; }
16:      virtual COLOR GetColor() const { return itsColor; }
17:  private:
18:      HANDS itsHeight;
19:      COLOR itsColor;
20:  };
21:
22:  Horse::Horse(COLOR color, HANDS height):
23:  itsColor(color),itsHeight(height)
24:  {
25:      cout << "Horse constructor...\n";
26:  }
27:
28:  class Bird
29:  {
30:  public:
31:      Bird(COLOR color, bool migrates);
32:      virtual ~Bird() {cout << "Bird destructor...\n";  }
33:      virtual void Chirp()const { cout << "Chirp... ";  }
34:      virtual void Fly()const
35:      {
36:         cout << "I can fly! I can fly! I can fly! ";
37:      }
38:      virtual COLOR GetColor()const { return itsColor; }
39:      virtual bool GetMigration() const { return itsMigration; }
40:
41:  private:
42:      COLOR itsColor;
43:      bool itsMigration;
44:  };
45:
46:  Bird::Bird(COLOR color, bool migrates):
47:  itsColor(color), itsMigration(migrates)
48:  {
```

LISTING 14.4   continued

```
49:      cout << "Bird constructor...\n";
50:  }
51:
52:  class Pegasus : public Horse, public Bird
53:  {
54:  public:
55:      void Chirp()const { Whinny(); }
56:      Pegasus(COLOR, HANDS, bool,long);
57:      ~Pegasus() {cout << "Pegasus destructor...\n";}
58:      virtual long GetNumberBelievers() const
59:      {
60:          return  itsNumberBelievers;
61:      }
62:
63:  private:
64:      long itsNumberBelievers;
65:  };
66:
67:  Pegasus::Pegasus(
68:      COLOR aColor,
69:      HANDS height,
70:      bool migrates,
71:      long NumBelieve):
72:      Horse(aColor, height),
73:      Bird(aColor, migrates),
74:      itsNumberBelievers(NumBelieve)
75:  {
76:  cout << "Pegasus constructor...\n";
77:  }
78:
79:  int main()
80:  {
81:      Pegasus *pPeg = new Pegasus(Red, 5, true, 10);
82:      pPeg->Fly();
83:      pPeg->Whinny();
84:      cout << "\nYour Pegasus is " << pPeg->GetHeight();
85:      cout << " hands tall and ";
86:      if (pPeg->GetMigration())
87:          cout << "it does migrate.";
88:      else
89:          cout << "it does not migrate.";
90:      cout << "\nA total of " << pPeg->GetNumberBelievers();
91:      cout << " people believe it exists.\n";
92:      delete pPeg;
93:      return 0;
94:  }
```

14

OUTPUT
```
Horse constructor...
Bird constructor...
Pegasus constructor...
I can fly! I can fly! I can fly! Whinny!...
Your Pegasus is 5 hands tall and it does migrate.
A total of 10 people believe it exists.

Pegasus destructor...
Bird destructor...
Horse destructor...
```

ANALYSIS
On lines 9–20, the Horse class is declared. The constructor takes two parameters: One is an enumeration declared on line 7 and the other is a typedef declared on line 6. The implementation of the constructor on lines 22–26 simply initializes the member variables and prints a message.

On lines 28–44, the Bird class is declared, and the implementation of its constructor is on lines 46–50. Again, the Bird class takes two parameters. Interestingly, the Horse constructor takes color (so that you can detect horses of different colors), and the Bird constructor takes the color of the feathers (so those of one feather can stick together). This leads to a problem when you want to ask the Pegasus for its color, which you'll see in the next example.

The Pegasus class itself is declared on lines 52–65, and its constructor is on lines 67–77. The initialization of the Pegasus object includes three statements. First, the Horse constructor is initialized with color and height. Then the Bird constructor is initialized with color and the Boolean. Finally, the Pegasus member variable itsNumberBelievers is initialized. After all that is accomplished, the body of the Pegasus constructor is called.

In the main() function, a Pegasus pointer is created and used to access the member functions of the base objects.

Ambiguity Resolution

In Listing 14.4, both the Horse class and the Bird class have a method GetColor(). You may need to ask the Pegasus object to return its color, but you have a problem—the Pegasus class inherits from both Bird and Horse. They both have a color, and their methods for getting that color have the same names and signature. This creates an ambiguity for the compiler, which you must resolve.

If you simply write

```
COLOR currentColor = pPeg->GetColor();
```

you will get a compiler error:

```
Member is ambiguous: 'Horse::GetColor' and 'Bird::GetColor'
```

You can resolve the ambiguity with an explicit call to the function you want to invoke:

```
COLOR currentColor = pPeg->Horse::GetColor();
```

Any time you need to resolve which class a member function or member data inherits from, you can fully qualify the call by prepending the class name to the base class data or function.

Note that if Pegasus were to override this function, the problem would be moved, as it should be, into the Pegasus member function:

```
virtual COLOR GetColor()const { return Horse::GetColor(); }
```

This hides the problem from clients of the Pegasus class and encapsulates within Pegasus the knowledge of which base class it wishes to inherit its color from. A client is still free to force the issue by writing

```
COLOR currentColor = pPeg->Bird::GetColor();
```

Inheriting from Shared Base Class

What happens if both Bird and Horse inherit from a common base class, such as Animal? Figure 14.2 illustrates what this looks like.

FIGURE 14.2

Common base classes.

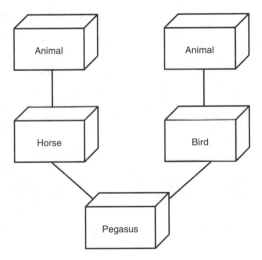

As you can see in Figure 14.2, two base class objects exist. When a function or data member is called in the shared base class, another ambiguity exists. For example, if Animal declares itsAge as a member variable and GetAge() as a member function, and you call pPeg->GetAge(), did you mean to call the GetAge() function you inherit from

14

Animal by way of Horse, or by way of Bird? You must resolve this ambiguity as well, as
illustrated in Listing 14.5.

LISTING **14.5**   Common Base Classes

```
0:   // Listing 14.5
1:   // Common base classes
2:
3:   #include <iostream>
4:   using namespace std;
5:
6:   typedef int HANDS;
7:   enum COLOR { Red, Green, Blue, Yellow, White, Black, Brown } ;
8:
9:   class Animal        // common base to both horse and bird
10:  {
11:  public:
12:     Animal(int);
13:     virtual ~Animal() { cout << "Animal destructor...\n"; }
14:     virtual int GetAge() const { return itsAge; }
15:     virtual void SetAge(int age) { itsAge = age; }
16:  private:
17:     int itsAge;
18:  };
19:
20:  Animal::Animal(int age):
21:  itsAge(age)
22:  {
23:     cout << "Animal constructor...\n";
24:  }
25:
26:  class Horse : public Animal
27:  {
28:  public:
29:     Horse(COLOR color, HANDS height, int age);
30:     virtual ~Horse() { cout << "Horse destructor...\n"; }
31:     virtual void Whinny()const { cout << "Whinny!... "; }
32:     virtual HANDS GetHeight() const { return itsHeight; }
33:     virtual COLOR GetColor() const { return itsColor; }
34:  protected:
35:     HANDS itsHeight;
36:     COLOR itsColor;
37:  };
38:
39:  Horse::Horse(COLOR color, HANDS height, int age):
40:  Animal(age),
41:  itsColor(color),itsHeight(height)
42:  {
43:     cout << "Horse constructor...\n";
44:  }
```

LISTING 14.5   continued

```
45:
46:  class Bird : public Animal
47:  {
48:  public:
49:      Bird(COLOR color, bool migrates, int age);
50:      virtual ~Bird() {cout << "Bird destructor...\n";  }
51:      virtual void Chirp()const { cout << "Chirp... ";  }
52:      virtual void Fly()const
53:              { cout << "I can fly! I can fly! I can fly! "; }
54:      virtual COLOR GetColor()const { return itsColor; }
55:      virtual bool GetMigration() const { return itsMigration; }
56:  protected:
57:      COLOR itsColor;
58:      bool itsMigration;
59:  };
60:
61:  Bird::Bird(COLOR color, bool migrates, int age):
62:  Animal(age),
63:  itsColor(color), itsMigration(migrates)
64:  {
65:      cout << "Bird constructor...\n";
66:  }
67:
68:  class Pegasus : public Horse, public Bird
69:  {
70:  public:
71:      void Chirp()const { Whinny(); }
72:      Pegasus(COLOR, HANDS, bool, long, int);
73:      virtual ~Pegasus() {cout << "Pegasus destructor...\n";}
74:      virtual long GetNumberBelievers() const
75:      { return  itsNumberBelievers; }
76:      virtual COLOR GetColor()const { return Horse::itsColor; }
77:      virtual int GetAge() const { return Horse::GetAge(); }
78:  private:
79:      long itsNumberBelievers;
80:  };
81:
82:  Pegasus::Pegasus(
83:      COLOR aColor,
84:      HANDS height,
85:      bool migrates,
86:      long NumBelieve,
87:      int age):
88:      Horse(aColor, height,age),
89:      Bird(aColor, migrates,age),
90:      itsNumberBelievers(NumBelieve)
91:  {
92:      cout << "Pegasus constructor...\n";
93:  }
```

14

LISTING 14.5   continued

```
94:
95:   int main()
96:   {
97:       Pegasus *pPeg = new Pegasus(Red, 5, true, 10, 2);
98:       int age = pPeg->GetAge();
99:       cout << "This pegasus is " << age << " years old.\n";
100:      delete pPeg;
101:      return 0;
102:  }
```

OUTPUT

```
Animal constructor...
Horse constructor...
Animal constructor...
Bird constructor...
Pegasus constructor...
This pegasus is 2 years old.
Pegasus destructor...
Bird destructor...
Animal destructor...
Horse destructor...
Animal destructor...
```

ANALYSIS   Several interesting features are in this listing. The Animal class is declared on lines 9–18. Animal adds one member variable, itsAge, and two accessors: GetAge() and SetAge().

On line 26, the Horse class is declared to derive from Animal. The Horse constructor now has a third parameter, age, which it passes to its base class, Animal. Note that the Horse class does not override GetAge(), it simply inherits it.

On line 46, the Bird class is declared to derive from Animal. Its constructor also takes an age and uses it to initialize its base class, Animal. It also inherits GetAge() without over-riding it.

Pegasus inherits from both Bird and Animal, and so has two Animal classes in its inheritance chain. If you were to call GetAge() on a Pegasus object, you would have to disambiguate, or fully qualify, the method you want if Pegasus did not override the method.

This is solved on line 77 when the Pegasus object overrides GetAge() to do nothing more than to chain up—that is, to call the same method in a base class.

Chaining up is done for two reasons: either to disambiguate which base class to call, as in this case, or to do some work and then let the function in the base class do some more work. At times, you may want to do work and then chain up, or chain up and then do the work when the base class function returns.

The Pegasus constructor takes five parameters: the creature's color, its height (in HANDS), whether it migrates, how many believe in it, and its age. The constructor initializes the Horse part of the Pegasus with the color, height, and age on line 89. It initializes the Bird part with color, whether it migrates, and age on line 88. Finally, it initializes itsNumberBelievers on line 90.

The call to the Horse constructor on line 88 invokes the implementation shown on line 39. The Horse constructor uses the age parameter to initialize the Animal part of the Horse part of the Pegasus. It then goes on to initialize the two member variables of Horse—itsColor and itsHeight.

The call to the Bird constructor on line 89 invokes the implementation shown on line 61. Here too, the age parameter is used to initialize the Animal part of the Bird.

Note that the color parameter to the Pegasus is used to initialize member variables in each of Bird and Horse. Note also that the age is used to initialize itsAge in the Horse's base Animal and in the Bird's base Animal.

Virtual Inheritance

In Listing 14.5, the Pegasus class went to some lengths to disambiguate which of its Animal base classes it meant to invoke. Most of the time, the decision as to which one to use is arbitrary—after all, the Horse and the Bird have the same base class.

It is possible to tell C++ that you do not want two copies of the shared base class, as shown in Figure 14.2, but rather to have a single shared base class, as shown in Figure 14.3.

You accomplish this by making Animal a virtual base class of both Horse and Bird. The Animal class does not change at all. The Horse and Bird classes change only in their use of the term virtual in their declarations. Pegasus, however, changes substantially.

Normally, a class's constructor initializes only its own variables and its base class. Virtually inherited base classes are an exception, however. They are initialized by their most derived class. Thus, Animal is initialized not by Horse and Bird, but by Pegasus. Horse and Bird have to initialize Animal in their constructors, but these initializations will be ignored when a Pegasus object is created.

Listing 14.6 rewrites Listing 14.5 to take advantage of virtual derivation.

14

FIGURE 14.3

A diamond inheritance.

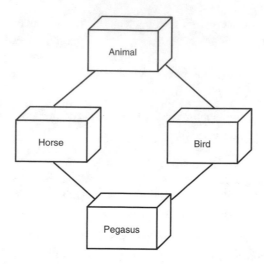

LISTING 14.6   Illustration of the Use of Virtual Inheritance

```
0:   // Listing 14.6
1:   // Virtual inheritance
2:   #include <iostream>
3:   using namespace std;
4:
5:   typedef int HANDS;
6:   enum COLOR { Red, Green, Blue, Yellow, White, Black, Brown } ;
7:
8:   class Animal        // common base to both horse and bird
9:   {
10:  public:
11:      Animal(int);
12:      virtual ~Animal() { cout << "Animal destructor...\n"; }
13:      virtual int GetAge() const { return itsAge; }
14:      virtual void SetAge(int age) { itsAge = age; }
15:  private:
16:      int itsAge;
17:  };
18:
19:  Animal::Animal(int age):
20:  itsAge(age)
21:  {
22:      cout << "Animal constructor...\n";
23:  }
24:
25:  class Horse : virtual public Animal
26:  {
27:  public:
```

LISTING 14.6   continued

```
28:      Horse(COLOR color, HANDS height, int age);
29:      virtual ~Horse() { cout << "Horse destructor...\n"; }
30:      virtual void Whinny()const { cout << "Whinny!... "; }
31:      virtual HANDS GetHeight() const { return itsHeight; }
32:      virtual COLOR GetColor() const { return itsColor; }
33:   protected:
34:      HANDS itsHeight;
35:      COLOR itsColor;
36:   };
37:
38:   Horse::Horse(COLOR color, HANDS height, int age):
39:   Animal(age),
40:   itsColor(color),itsHeight(height)
41:   {
42:      cout << "Horse constructor...\n";
43:   }
44:
45:   class Bird : virtual public Animal
46:   {
47:   public:
48:      Bird(COLOR color, bool migrates, int age);
49:      virtual ~Bird() {cout << "Bird destructor...\n";   }
50:      virtual void Chirp()const { cout << "Chirp... ";   }
51:      virtual void Fly()const
52:              { cout << "I can fly! I can fly! I can fly! "; }
53:      virtual COLOR GetColor()const { return itsColor; }
54:      virtual bool GetMigration() const { return itsMigration; }
55:   protected:
56:      COLOR itsColor;
57:      bool itsMigration;
58:   };
59:
60:   Bird::Bird(COLOR color, bool migrates, int age):
61:   Animal(age),
62:   itsColor(color), itsMigration(migrates)
63:   {
64:      cout << "Bird constructor...\n";
65:   }
66:
67:   class Pegasus : public Horse, public Bird
68:   {
69:   public:
70:      void Chirp()const { Whinny(); }
71:      Pegasus(COLOR, HANDS, bool, long, int);
72:      virtual ~Pegasus() {cout << "Pegasus destructor...\n";}
73:      virtual long GetNumberBelievers() const
74:              { return  itsNumberBelievers; }
```

14

LISTING 14.6   continued

```
75:       virtual COLOR GetColor()const { return Horse::itsColor; }
76:    private:
77:       long itsNumberBelievers;
78:    };
79:
80:    Pegasus::Pegasus(
81:       COLOR aColor,
82:       HANDS height,
83:       bool migrates,
84:       long NumBelieve,
85:       int age):
86:       Horse(aColor, height,age),
87:       Bird(aColor, migrates,age),
88:       Animal(age*2),
89:       itsNumberBelievers(NumBelieve)
90:    {
91:       cout << "Pegasus constructor...\n";
92:    }
93:
94:    int main()
95:    {
96:       Pegasus *pPeg = new Pegasus(Red, 5, true, 10, 2);
97:       int age = pPeg->GetAge();
98:       cout << "This pegasus is " << age << " years old.\n";
99:       delete pPeg;
100:      return 0;
101:   }
```

OUTPUT
```
Animal constructor...
Horse constructor...
Bird constructor...
Pegasus constructor...
This pegasus is 4 years old.
Pegasus destructor...
Bird destructor...
Horse destructor...
Animal destructor...
```

ANALYSIS   On line 25, Horse declares that it inherits virtually from Animal, and on line 45, Bird makes the same declaration. Note that the constructors for both Bird and Animal still initialize the Animal object.

Pegasus inherits from both Bird and Animal, and as the most derived object of Animal, it also initializes Animal. It is Pegasus's initialization which is called, however, and the calls to Animal's constructor in Bird and Horse are ignored. You can see this because the value 2 is passed in, and Horse and Bird pass it along to Animal, but Pegasus doubles it. The result, 4, is reflected in the printout on line 98 and as shown in the output.

Pegasus no longer has to disambiguate the call to GetAge(), and so is free to simply inherit this function from Animal. Note that Pegasus must still disambiguate the call to GetColor() because this function is in both of its base classes and not in Animal.

Declaring Classes for Virtual Inheritance

To ensure that derived classes have only one instance of common base classes, declare the intermediate classes to inherit virtually from the base class.

Example 1

```
class Horse : virtual public Animal
class Bird : virtual public Animal
class Pegasus : public Horse, public Bird
```

Example 2

```
class Schnauzer : virtual public Dog
class Poodle : virtual public Dog
class Schnoodle : public Schnauzer, public Poodle
```

Problems with Multiple Inheritance

Although multiple inheritance offers several advantages over single inheritance, many C++ programmers are reluctant to use it. The problems they cite are that many compilers don't support it yet, that it makes debugging harder, and that nearly everything that can be done with multiple inheritance can be done without it.

These are valid concerns, and you will want to be on your guard against installing needless complexity into your programs. Some debuggers have a hard time with multiple inheritance, and some designs are needlessly made complex by using multiple inheritance when it is not needed.

Do	Don't
DO use multiple inheritance when a new class needs functions and features from more than one base class.	DON'T use multiple inheritance when single inheritance will do.
DO use virtual inheritance when the most derived classes must have only one instance of the shared base class.	
DO initialize the shared base class from the most derived class when using virtual base classes.	

14

Mixins and Capabilities Classes

One way to strike a middle ground between multiple inheritance and single inheritance is to use what are called mixins. Thus, you might have your Horse class derive from Animal and from Displayable. Displayable would just add a few methods for displaying any object onscreen.

A mixin, or capability class, is a class that adds functionality without adding much or any data.

Capability classes are mixed into a derived class the same as any other class might be, by declaring the derived class to inherit publicly from them. The only difference between a capability class and any other class is that the capability class has little or no data. This is an arbitrary distinction, of course, and is just a shorthand way of noting that at times all you want to do is mix in some additional capabilities without complicating the derived class.

This will, for some debuggers, make it easier to work with mixins than with more complex multiply inherited objects. In addition, less likelihood exists of ambiguity in accessing the data in the other principal base class.

For example, if Horse derives from Animal and from Displayable, Displayable would have no data. Animal would be just as it always was, so all the data in Horse would derive from Animal, but the functions in Horse would derive from both.

The term mixin comes from an ice cream store in Sommerville, Massachusetts, where candies and cakes were mixed into the basic ice cream flavors. This seemed like a good metaphor to some of the object-oriented programmers who used to take a summer break there, especially while working with the object-oriented programming language SCOOPS.

Abstract Data Types

Often, you will create a hierarchy of classes together. For example, you might create a Shape class, and derive from that Rectangle and Circle. From Rectangle, you might derive Square as a special case of Rectangle.

Each of the derived classes will override the Draw() method, the GetArea() method, and so forth. Listing 14.7 illustrates a bare-bones implementation of the Shape class and its derived Circle and Rectangle classes.

LISTING 14.7 Shape Classes

```
0:  //Listing 14.7. Shape classes.
1:
2:  #include <iostream>
3:  using std::cout;
4:  using std::cin;
5:  using std::endl;
6:
7:  class Shape
8:  {
9:  public:
10:     Shape(){}
11:     virtual ~Shape(){}
12:     virtual long GetArea() { return -1; } // error
13:     virtual long GetPerim() { return -1; }
14:     virtual void Draw() {}
15:  private:
16:  };
17:
18:  class Circle : public Shape
19:  {
20:  public:
21:     Circle(int radius):itsRadius(radius){}
22:     ~Circle(){}
23:     long GetArea() { return 3 * itsRadius * itsRadius; }
24:     long GetPerim() { return 6 * itsRadius; }
25:     void Draw();
26:  private:
27:     int itsRadius;
28:     int itsCircumference;
29:  };
30:
31:  void Circle::Draw()
32:  {
33:     cout << "Circle drawing routine here!\n";
34:  }
35:
36:
37:  class Rectangle : public Shape
38:  {
39:  public:
40:     Rectangle(int len, int width):
41:     itsLength(len), itsWidth(width){}
42:     virtual ~Rectangle(){}
43:     virtual long GetArea() { return itsLength * itsWidth; }
44:     virtual long GetPerim() {return 2*itsLength + 2*itsWidth; }
45:     virtual int GetLength() { return itsLength; }
46:     virtual int GetWidth() { return itsWidth; }
47:     virtual void Draw();
```

14

LISTING 14.7   continued

```
48:   private:
49:      int itsWidth;
50:      int itsLength;
51:   };
52:
53:   void Rectangle::Draw()
54:   {
55:      for (int i = 0; i<itsLength; i++)
56:      {
57:         for (int j = 0; j<itsWidth; j++)
58:            cout << "x ";
59:
60:         cout << "\n";
61:      }
62:   }
63:
64:   class Square : public Rectangle
65:   {
66:   public:
67:      Square(int len);
68:      Square(int len, int width);
69:      ~Square(){}
70:      long GetPerim() {return 4 * GetLength();}
71:   };
72:
73:   Square::Square(int len):
74:   Rectangle(len,len)
75:   {}
76:
77:   Square::Square(int len, int width):
78:   Rectangle(len,width)
79:   {
80:      if (GetLength() != GetWidth())
81:      cout << "Error, not a square... a Rectangle??\n";
82:   }
83:
84:   int main()
85:   {
86:      int choice;
87:      bool fQuit = false;
88:      Shape * sp;
89:
90:      while ( !fQuit )
91:      {
92:         cout << "(1)Circle (2)Rectangle (3)Square (0)Quit: ";
93:         cin >> choice;
94:
95:         switch (choice)
96:         {
```

LISTING 14.7   continued

```
97:          case 0:    fQuit = true;
98:               break;
99:          case 1: sp = new Circle(5);
100:              break;
101:         case 2: sp = new Rectangle(4,6);
102:              break;
103:         case 3: sp = new Square(5);
104:              break;
105:         default: cout<<"Please enter a number between 0 and 3"<<endl;
106:              continue;
107:              break;
108:         }
109:         if( !fQuit )
110:             sp->Draw();
111:         delete sp;
112:         sp = 0;
113:         cout << "\n";
114:      }
115:    return 0;
116: }
```

OUTPUT

```
(1)Circle (2)Rectangle (3)Square (0)Quit: 2
x x x x x x
x x x x x x
x x x x x x
x x x x x x

(1)Circle (2)Rectangle (3)Square (0)Quit:3
x x x x x
x x x x x
x x x x x
x x x x x
x x x x x

(1)Circle (2)Rectangle (3)Square (0)Quit:0
```

ANALYSIS   On lines 7–16, the Shape class is declared. The GetArea() and GetPerim() methods return an error value, and Draw() takes no action. After all, what does it mean to draw a Shape? Only types of shapes (circles, rectangles, and so on) can be drawn; Shapes as an abstraction cannot be drawn.

Circle derives from Shape and overrides the three virtual methods. Note that no reason exists to add the word "virtual," because that is part of their inheritance. But there is no harm in doing so either, as shown in the Rectangle class on lines 43, 44, and 47. It is a good idea to include the term virtual as a reminder, a form of documentation.

14

Square derives from Rectangle, and it, too, overrides the GetPerim() method, inheriting the rest of the methods defined in Rectangle.

It is troubling, though, that a client might try to instantiate a Shape object, and it might be desirable to make that impossible. The Shape class exists only to provide an interface for the classes derived from it; as such, it is an abstract data type, or ADT.

An abstract data type represents a concept (such as shape) rather than an object (such as circle). In C++, an ADT is always the base class to other classes, and it is not valid to make an instance of an ADT.

Pure Virtual Functions

C++ supports the creation of abstract data types with pure virtual functions. A virtual function is made pure by initializing it with zero, as in

```
virtual void Draw() = 0;
```

Any class with one or more pure virtual functions is an ADT, and it is illegal to instantiate an object of a class that is an ADT. Trying to do so will cause a compile-time error. Putting a pure virtual function in your class signals two things to clients of your class:

- Don't make an object of this class, derive from it.
- Make sure you override the pure virtual function.

Any class that derives from an ADT inherits the pure virtual function as pure, and so must override every pure virtual function if it wants to instantiate objects. Thus, if Rectangle inherits from Shape, and Shape has three pure virtual functions, Rectangle must override all three or it, too, will be an ADT. Listing 14.8 rewrites the Shape class to be an abstract data type. To save space, the rest of Listing 14.7 is not reproduced here. Replace the declaration of Shape in Listing 14.7, lines 7–16, with the declaration of Shape in Listing 14.8 and run the program again.

LISTING 14.8   Abstract Data Types

```
0:  //Listing 14.8 Abstract Data Types
1:
2:  class Shape
3:  {
4:  public:
5:        Shape(){}
6:        ~Shape(){}
7:        virtual long GetArea() = 0;
8:        virtual long GetPerim()= 0;
9:        virtual void Draw() = 0;
10: private:
11: };
```

OUTPUT

```
(1)Circle (2)Rectangle (3)Square (0)Quit: 2
x x x x x x
x x x x x x
x x x x x x
x x x x x x

(1)Circle (2)Rectangle (3)Square (0)Quit: 3
x x x x x
x x x x x
x x x x x
x x x x x
x x x x x

(1)Circle (2)Rectangle (3)Square (0)Quit: 0
```

ANALYSIS   As you can see, the workings of the program are totally unaffected. The only difference is that it would now be impossible to make an object of class Shape.

Abstract Data Types

Declare a class to be an abstract data type by including one or more pure virtual functions in the class declaration. Declare a pure virtual function by writing = 0 after the function declaration.

Example

```
class Shape
{
virtual void Draw() = 0;    // pure virtual
};
```

Implementing Pure Virtual Functions

Typically, the pure virtual functions in an abstract base class are never implemented. Because no objects of that type are ever created, no reason exists to provide implementations, and the ADT works purely as the definition of an interface to objects which derive from it.

It is possible, however, to provide an implementation to a pure virtual function. The function can then be called by objects derived from the ADT, perhaps to provide common functionality to all the overridden functions. Listing 14.9 reproduces Listing 14.7, this time with Shape as an ADT and with an implementation for the pure virtual function Draw(). The Circle class overrides Draw(), as it must, but it then chains up to the base class function for additional functionality.

14

In this example, the additional functionality is simply an additional message printed, but one can imagine that the base class provides a shared drawing mechanism, perhaps setting up a window that all derived classes will use.

LISTING 14.9   Implementing Pure Virtual Functions

```
0:   //Listing 14.9 Implementing pure virtual functions
1:
2:   #include <iostream>
3:   using namespace std;
4:
5:   class Shape
6:   {
7:   public:
8:       Shape(){}
9:       virtual ~Shape(){}
10:      virtual long GetArea() = 0; // error
11:      virtual long GetPerim()= 0;
12:      virtual void Draw() = 0;
13:   private:
14:   };
15:
16:   void Shape::Draw()
17:   {
18:       cout << "Abstract drawing mechanism!\n";
19:   }
20:
21:   class Circle : public Shape
22:   {
23:   public:
24:      Circle(int radius):itsRadius(radius){}
25:      virtual ~Circle(){}
26:      long GetArea() { return 3 * itsRadius * itsRadius; }
27:      long GetPerim() { return 9 * itsRadius; }
28:      void Draw();
29:   private:
30:      int itsRadius;
31:      int itsCircumference;
32:   };
33:
34:   void Circle::Draw()
35:   {
36:      cout << "Circle drawing routine here!\n";
37:      Shape::Draw();
38:   }
39:
40:
41:   class Rectangle : public Shape
42:   {
43:   public:
```

LISTING 14.9   continued

```
44:     Rectangle(int len, int width):
45:     itsLength(len), itsWidth(width){}
46:     virtual ~Rectangle(){}
47:     long GetArea() { return itsLength * itsWidth; }
48:     long GetPerim() {return 2*itsLength + 2*itsWidth; }
49:     virtual int GetLength() { return itsLength; }
50:     virtual int GetWidth() { return itsWidth; }
51:     void Draw();
52:  private:
53:     int itsWidth;
54:     int itsLength;
55:  };
56:
57:  void Rectangle::Draw()
58:  {
59:     for (int i = 0; i<itsLength; i++)
60:     {
61:        for (int j = 0; j<itsWidth; j++)
62:           cout << "x ";
63:
64:     cout << "\n";
65:     }
66:     Shape::Draw();
67:  }
68:
69:
70:  class Square : public Rectangle
71:  {
72:  public:
73:     Square(int len);
74:     Square(int len, int width);
75:     virtual ~Square(){}
76:     long GetPerim() {return 4 * GetLength();}
77:  };
78:
79:  Square::Square(int len):
80:  Rectangle(len,len)
81:  {}
82:
83:  Square::Square(int len, int width):
84:  Rectangle(len,width)
85:
86:  {
87:     if (GetLength() != GetWidth())
88:     cout << "Error, not a square... a Rectangle??\n";
89:  }
90:
91:  int main()
92:  {
```

14

LISTING 14.9   continued

```
 93:     int choice;
 94:     bool fQuit = false;
 95:     Shape * sp;
 96:
 97:     while (1)
 98:     {
 99:        cout << "(1)Circle (2)Rectangle (3)Square (0)Quit: ";
100:        cin >> choice;
101:
102:        switch (choice)
103:        {
104:         case 1: sp = new Circle(5);
105:               break;
106:         case 2: sp = new Rectangle(4,6);
107:               break;
108:         case 3: sp = new Square (5);
109:               break;
110:         default: fQuit = true;
111:               break;
112:        }
113:        if (fQuit)
114:           break;
115:
116:        sp->Draw();
117:        delete sp;
118:        cout << "\n";
119:     }
120:    return 0;
121: }
```

OUTPUT

```
(1)Circle (2)Rectangle (3)Square (0)Quit: 2
x x x x x x
x x x x x x
x x x x x x
x x x x x x
Abstract drawing mechanism!

(1)Circle (2)Rectangle (3)Square (0)Quit: 3
x x x x x
x x x x x
x x x x x
x x x x x
x x x x x
Abstract drawing mechanism!

(1)Circle (2)Rectangle (3)Square (0)Quit: 0
```

ANALYSIS   On lines 5–14, the abstract data type Shape is declared, with all three of its accessor methods declared to be pure virtual. Note that this is not necessary. If any one were declared pure virtual, the class would have been an ADT.

The GetArea() and GetPerim() methods are not implemented, but Draw() is. Circle and Rectangle both override Draw(), and both chain up to the base method, taking advantage of shared functionality in the base class.

Complex Hierarchies of Abstraction

At times, you will derive ADTs from other ADTs. It may be that you will want to make some of the derived pure virtual functions non-pure, and leave others pure.

If you create the Animal class, you may make Eat(), Sleep(), Move(), and Reproduce() all be pure virtual functions. Perhaps from Animal you derive Mammal and Fish.

On examination, you decide that every Mammal will reproduce in the same way, and so you make Mammal::Reproduce() be non-pure, but you leave Eat(), Sleep(), and Move() as pure virtual functions.

From Mammal you derive Dog, and Dog must override and implement the three remaining pure virtual functions so that you can make objects of type Dog.

What you've said, as class designer, is that no Animals or Mammals can be instantiated, but that all Mammals may inherit the provided Reproduce() method without overriding it.

Listing 14.10 illustrates this technique with a bare-bones implementation of these classes.

LISTING 14.10   Deriving ADTs from Other ADTs

```
0:  // Listing 14.10
1:  // Deriving ADTs from other ADTs
2:  #include <iostream>
3:  using namespace std;
4:
5:  enum COLOR { Red, Green, Blue, Yellow, White, Black, Brown } ;
6:
7:  class Animal          // common base to both Mammal and Fish
8:  {
9:  public:
10:     Animal(int);
11:     virtual ~Animal() { cout << "Animal destructor...\n"; }
12:     virtual int GetAge() const { return itsAge; }
13:     virtual void SetAge(int age) { itsAge = age; }
14:     virtual void Sleep() const = 0;
15:     virtual void Eat() const = 0;
```

14

LISTING **14.10**   continued

```
16:        virtual void Reproduce() const = 0;
17:        virtual void Move() const = 0;
18:        virtual void Speak() const = 0;
19:    private:
20:        int itsAge;
21:    };
22:
23:    Animal::Animal(int age):
24:    itsAge(age)
25:    {
26:        cout << "Animal constructor...\n";
27:    }
28:
29:    class Mammal : public Animal
30:    {
31:    public:
32:        Mammal(int age):Animal(age)
33:            { cout << "Mammal constructor...\n";}
34:        virtual ~Mammal() { cout << "Mammal destructor...\n";}
35:        virtual void Reproduce() const
36:            { cout << "Mammal reproduction depicted...\n"; }
37:    };
38:
39:    class Fish : public Animal
40:    {
41:    public:
42:        Fish(int age):Animal(age)
43:            { cout << "Fish constructor...\n";}
44:        virtual ~Fish() {cout << "Fish destructor...\n";  }
45:        virtual void Sleep() const { cout << "fish snoring...\n"; }
46:        virtual void Eat() const { cout << "fish feeding...\n"; }
47:        virtual void Reproduce() const
48:            { cout << "fish laying eggs...\n"; }
49:        virtual void Move() const
50:            { cout << "fish swimming...\n";    }
51:        virtual void Speak() const { }
52:    };
53:
54:    class Horse : public Mammal
55:    {
56:    public:
57:        Horse(int age, COLOR color ):
58:        Mammal(age), itsColor(color)
59:            { cout << "Horse constructor...\n"; }
60:        virtual ~Horse() { cout << "Horse destructor...\n"; }
61:        virtual void Speak()const { cout << "Whinny!... \n"; }
62:        virtual COLOR GetItsColor() const { return itsColor; }
63:        virtual void Sleep() const
64:            { cout << "Horse snoring...\n"; }
```

LISTING **14.10** continued

```
65:       virtual void Eat() const { cout << "Horse feeding...\n"; }
66:       virtual void Move() const { cout << "Horse running...\n";}
67:
68:   protected:
69:       COLOR itsColor;
70:   };
71:
72:   class Dog : public Mammal
73:   {
74:   public:
75:       Dog(int age, COLOR color ):
76:       Mammal(age), itsColor(color)
77:           { cout << "Dog constructor...\n"; }
78:       virtual ~Dog() { cout << "Dog destructor...\n"; }
79:       virtual void Speak()const { cout << "Whoof!... \n"; }
80:       virtual void Sleep() const { cout << "Dog snoring...\n"; }
81:       virtual void Eat() const { cout << "Dog eating...\n"; }
82:       virtual void Move() const  { cout << "Dog running...\n"; }
83:       virtual void Reproduce() const
84:           { cout << "Dogs reproducing...\n"; }
85:
86:   protected:
87:       COLOR itsColor;
88:   };
89:
90:   int main()
91:   {
92:       Animal *pAnimal=0;
93:       int choice;
94:       bool fQuit = false;
95:
96:       while (1)
97:       {
98:           cout << "(1)Dog (2)Horse (3)Fish (0)Quit: ";
99:           cin >> choice;
100:
101:          switch (choice)
102:          {
103:           case 1: pAnimal = new Dog(5,Brown);
104:               break;
105:           case 2: pAnimal = new Horse(4,Black);
106:               break;
107:           case 3: pAnimal = new Fish (5);
108:               break;
109:           default: fQuit = true;
110:               break;
111:          }
112:          if (fQuit)
113:              break;
```

14

LISTING 14.10 continued

```
114:
115:        pAnimal->Speak();
116:        pAnimal->Eat();
117:        pAnimal->Reproduce();
118:        pAnimal->Move();
119:        pAnimal->Sleep();
120:        delete pAnimal;
121:        cout << "\n";
122:    }
123:    return 0;
124: }
```

OUTPUT

```
(1)Dog (2)Horse (3)Bird (0)Quit: 1
Animal constructor...
Mammal constructor...
Dog constructor...
Whoof!...
Dog eating...
Dog reproducing....
Dog running...
Dog snoring...
Dog destructor...
Mammal destructor...
Animal destructor...

(1)Dog (2)Horse (3)Bird (0)Quit: 0
```

ANALYSIS On lines 7–21, the abstract data type Animal is declared. Animal has non-pure virtual accessors for itsAge, which are shared by all Animal objects. It has five pure virtual functions, Sleep(), Eat(), Reproduce(), Move(), and Speak().

Mammal is derived from Animal, is declared on lines 29–37, and adds no data. It overrides Reproduce(), however, providing a common form of reproduction for all mammals. Fish must override Reproduce() because Fish derives directly from Animal and cannot take advantage of Mammalian reproduction (and a good thing, too!).

Mammal classes no longer have to override the Reproduce() function, but they are free to do so if they choose, as Dog does on line 83. Fish, Horse, and Dog all override the remaining pure virtual functions, so that objects of their type can be instantiated.

In the body of the program, an Animal pointer is used to point to the various derived objects in turn. The virtual methods are invoked, and based on the runtime binding of the pointer, the correct method is called in the derived class.

It would be a compile-time error to try to instantiate an Animal or a Mammal, as both are abstract data types.

Which Types Are Abstract?

In one program, the class `Animal` is abstract; in another, it is not. What determines whether to make a class abstract?

The answer to this question is decided not by any real-world intrinsic factor, but by what makes sense in your program. If you are writing a program that depicts a farm or a zoo, you may want `Animal` to be an abstract data type, but `Dog` to be a class from which you can instantiate objects.

On the other hand, if you are making an animated kennel, you may want to keep `Dog` as an abstract data type and only instantiate types of dogs: retrievers, terriers, and so forth. The level of abstraction is a function of how finely you need to distinguish your types.

Do	Don't
DO use abstract data types to provide common functionality for a number of related classes. DO override all pure virtual functions. DO make pure virtual any function that must be overridden.	DON'T try to instantiate an object of an abstract data type.

Summary

Today you learned how to overcome some of the limitations in single inheritance. You learned about the danger of percolating interfaces up the inheritance hierarchy and the risks in casting down the inheritance hierarchy. You also learned how to use multiple inheritance, what problems multiple inheritance can create, and how to solve them using virtual inheritance.

You also learned what abstract data types are and how to create abstract classes using pure virtual functions. You learned how to implement pure virtual functions and when and why you might do so.

Q&A

Q What does percolating functionality upward mean?

A This refers to the idea of moving shared functionality upward into a common base class. If more than one class shares a function, it is desirable to find a common base class in which that function can be stored.

14

Q Is percolating upward always a good thing?

A Yes, if you are percolating shared functionality upward. No, if all you are moving is interface. That is, if all the derived classes can't use the method, it is a mistake to move it up into a common base class. If you do, you'll have to switch on the runtime type of the object before deciding if you can invoke the function.

Q Why is switching on the runtime type of an object bad?

A With large programs, the switch statements become big and hard to maintain. The point of virtual functions is to let the virtual table, rather than the programmer, determine the runtime type of the object.

Q Why is casting bad?

A Casting isn't bad if it is done in a way that is type-safe. If a function is called that knows that the object must be of a particular type, casting to that type is fine. Casting can be used to undermine the strong type checking in C++, and that is what you want to avoid. If you are switching on the runtime type of the object and then casting a pointer, that may be a warning sign that something is wrong with your design.

Q Why not make all functions virtual?

A Virtual functions are supported by a virtual function table, which incurs runtime overhead, both in the size of the program and in the performance of the program. If you have very small classes that you don't expect to subclass, you may not want to make any of the functions virtual.

Q When should the destructor be made virtual?

A Any time you think the class will be subclassed, and a pointer to the base class will be used to access an object of the subclass. As a general rule of thumb, if you've made any functions in your class virtual, be sure to make the destructor virtual as well.

Q Why bother making an Abstract Data Type—why not just make it non-abstract and avoid creating any objects of that type?

A The purpose of many of the conventions in C++ is to enlist the compiler in finding bugs, so as to avoid runtime bugs in code that you give your customers. Making a class abstract—that is, giving it pure virtual functions—causes the compiler to flag any objects created of that abstract type as errors.

Workshop

The Workshop provides quiz questions to help you solidify your understanding of the material covered and exercises to provide you with experience in using what you've learned. Try to answer the quiz and exercise questions before checking the answers in Appendix D, and make sure you understand the answers before continuing to the next chapter.

Quiz

1. What is a down cast?

2. What is the v-ptr?

3. If a round-rectangle has straight edges and rounded corners, and your `RoundRect` class inherits both from `Rectangle` and from `Circle`, and they in turn both inherit from `Shape`, how many `Shapes` are created when you create a `RoundRect`?

4. If `Horse` and `Bird` inherit from `Animal` using public virtual inheritance, do their constructors initialize the `Animal` constructor? If `Pegasus` inherits from both `Horse` and `Bird`, how does it initialize `Animal`'s constructor?

5. Declare a class vehicle and make it an abstract data type.

6. If a base class is an ADT, and it has three pure virtual functions, how many of these must be overridden in its derived classes?

Exercises

1. Show the declaration for a class `JetPlane`, which inherits from `Rocket` and `Airplane`.

2. Show the declaration for `Seven47`, which inherits from the `JetPlane` class described in Exercise 1.

3. Write a program that derives `Car` and `Bus` from the class `Vehicle`. Make `Vehicle` be an ADT with two pure virtual functions. Make `Car` and `Bus` not be ADTs.

4. Modify the program in Exercise 3 so that `Car` is an ADT, and derive `SportsCar` and `Coupe` from `Car`. In the `Car` class, provide an implementation for one of the pure virtual functions in `Vehicle` and make it non-pure.

14

WEEK 2

In Review

The Week in Review program for Week 2 brings together many of the skills you've acquired over the past fortnight and produces a powerful program.

This demonstration of linked lists utilizes virtual functions, pure virtual functions, function overriding, polymorphism, public inheritance, function overloading, forever loops, pointers, references, and more. Note that this is a different linked list from the one shown earlier; in C++ there are many ways to accomplish the same thing.

The goal of this program is to create a linked list. The nodes on the list are designed to hold parts, as might be used in a factory. While this is not the final form of this program, it does make a good demonstration of a fairly advanced data structure. The code list is 311 lines. Try to analyze the code on your own before reading the analysis that follows the output.

LISTING R2.1   Week 2 in Review Listing

```
 0:   // **************************************************
 1:   //
 2:   // Title:        Week 2 in Review
 3:   //
 4:   // File:         Week2
 5:   //
 6:   // Description:  Provide a linked list demonstration program
 7:   //
 8:   // Classes:      PART - holds part numbers and potentially other
 9:   //                      information about parts
10:   //
11:   //               PartNode - acts as a node in a PartsList
12:   //
13:   //               PartsList - provides the mechanisms for
14:   //                           a linked list of parts
15:   //
16:   //
17:   // **************************************************
18:
19:   #include <iostream>
20:   using namespace std;
21:
22:
23:
24:   // *************** Part ***********
25:
26:   // Abstract base class of parts
27:   class Part
28:   {
29:   public:
30:       Part():itsPartNumber(1) {}
31:       Part(int PartNumber):itsPartNumber(PartNumber){}
32:       virtual ~Part(){};
33:       int GetPartNumber() const { return itsPartNumber; }
34:       virtual void Display() const =0;  // must be overridden
35:   private:
36:       int itsPartNumber;
37:   };
38:
39:   // implementation of pure virtual function so that
40:   // derived classes can chain up
41:   void Part::Display() const
42:   {
43:       cout << "\nPart Number: " << itsPartNumber << endl;
44:   }
45:
46:   // *************** Car Part ***********
47:
48:   class CarPart : public Part
```

```
49:    {
50:    public:
51:       CarPart():itsModelYear(94){}
52:       CarPart(int year, int partNumber);
53:       virtual void Display() const
54:       {
55:          Part::Display(); cout << "Model Year: ";
56:          cout << itsModelYear << endl;
57:       }
58:    private:
59:       int itsModelYear;
60:    };
61:
62:    CarPart::CarPart(int year, int partNumber):
63:       itsModelYear(year),
64:       Part(partNumber)
65:    {}
66:
67:
68:    // *************** AirPlane Part ************
69:
70:    class AirPlanePart : public Part
71:    {
72:    public:
73:       AirPlanePart():itsEngineNumber(1){};
74:       AirPlanePart(int EngineNumber, int PartNumber);
75:       virtual void Display() const
76:       {
77:          Part::Display(); cout << "Engine No.: ";
78:          cout << itsEngineNumber << endl;
79:       }
80:    private:
81:       int itsEngineNumber;
82:    };
83:
84:    AirPlanePart::AirPlanePart(int EngineNumber, int PartNumber):
85:       itsEngineNumber(EngineNumber),
86:       Part(PartNumber)
87:    {}
88:
89:    // *************** Part Node ************
90:    class PartNode
91:    {
92:    public:
93:       PartNode (Part*);
94:       ~PartNode();
95:       void SetNext(PartNode * node) { itsNext = node; }
96:       PartNode * GetNext() const;
97:       Part * GetPart() const;
```

LISTING R2.1   continued

```
98:    private:
99:       Part *itsPart;
100:      PartNode * itsNext;
101:    };
102:
103:    // PartNode Implementations...
104:
105:    PartNode::PartNode(Part* pPart):
106:    itsPart(pPart),
107:    itsNext(0)
108:    {}
109:
110:    PartNode::~PartNode()
111:    {
112:       delete itsPart;
113:       itsPart = 0;
114:       delete itsNext;
115:       itsNext = 0;
116:    }
117:
118:    // Returns NULL if no next PartNode
119:    PartNode * PartNode::GetNext() const
120:    {
121:          return itsNext;
122:    }
123:
124:    Part * PartNode::GetPart() const
125:    {
126:       if (itsPart)
127:          return itsPart;
128:       else
129:          return NULL; //error
130:    }
131:
132:    // *************** Part List ************
133:    class PartsList
134:    {
135:    public:
136:       PartsList();
137:       ~PartsList();
138:       // needs copy constructor and operator equals!
139:       Part*      Find(int & position, int PartNumber)  const;
140:       int        GetCount() const { return itsCount; }
141:       Part*      GetFirst() const;
142:       void       Insert(Part *);
143:       void       Iterate() const;
144:       Part*      operator[](int) const;
```

LISTING R2.1 continued

```
145:    private:
146:        PartNode * pHead;
147:        int itsCount;
148:    };
149:
150:    // Implementations for Lists...
151:
152:    PartsList::PartsList():
153:        pHead(0),
154:        itsCount(0)
155:        {}
156:
157:    PartsList::~PartsList()
158:    {
159:        delete pHead;
160:    }
161:
162:    Part*   PartsList::GetFirst() const
163:    {
164:        if (pHead)
165:            return pHead->GetPart();
166:        else
167:            return NULL;   // error catch here
168:    }
169:
170:    Part *   PartsList::operator[](int offSet) const
171:    {
172:        PartNode* pNode = pHead;
173:
174:        if (!pHead)
175:            return NULL; // error catch here
176:
177:        if (offSet > itsCount)
178:            return NULL; // error
179:
180:        for (int i=0;i<offSet; i++)
181:            pNode = pNode->GetNext();
182:
183:      return    pNode->GetPart();
184:    }
185:
186:    Part*   PartsList::Find(int & position, int PartNumber)  const
187:    {
188:        PartNode * pNode = 0;
189:        for (pNode = pHead, position = 0;
190:                pNode!=NULL;
191:                pNode = pNode->GetNext(), position++)
192:        {
193:            if (pNode->GetPart()->GetPartNumber() == PartNumber)
```

```
194:                  break;
195:              }
196:          if (pNode == NULL)
197:              return NULL;
198:          else
199:              return pNode->GetPart();
200:      }
201:
202:      void PartsList::Iterate() const
203:      {
204:          if (!pHead)
205:              return;
206:          PartNode* pNode = pHead;
207:          do
208:              pNode->GetPart()->Display();
209:          while (pNode = pNode->GetNext());
210:      }
211:
212:      void PartsList::Insert(Part* pPart)
213:      {
214:          PartNode * pNode = new PartNode(pPart);
215:          PartNode * pCurrent = pHead;
216:          PartNode * pNext = 0;
217:
218:          int New =  pPart->GetPartNumber();
219:          int Next = 0;
220:          itsCount++;
221:
222:          if (!pHead)
223:          {
224:              pHead = pNode;
225:              return;
226:          }
227:
228:          // if this one is smaller than head
229:          // this one is the new head
230:          if (pHead->GetPart()->GetPartNumber() > New)
231:          {
232:              pNode->SetNext(pHead);
233:              pHead = pNode;
234:              return;
235:          }
236:
237:          for (;;)
238:          {
239:              // if there is no next, append this new one
240:              if (!pCurrent->GetNext())
241:              {
242:                  pCurrent->SetNext(pNode);
```

LISTING R2.1 continued

```
243:              return;
244:          }
245:
246:          // if this goes after this one and before the next
247:          // then insert it here, otherwise get the next
248:          pNext = pCurrent->GetNext();
249:          Next = pNext->GetPart()->GetPartNumber();
250:          if (Next > New)
251:          {
252:              pCurrent->SetNext(pNode);
253:              pNode->SetNext(pNext);
254:              return;
255:          }
256:          pCurrent = pNext;
257:      }
258:  }
259:
260:  int main()
261:  {
262:      // PartsList&pl = PartsList::GetGlobalPartsList();
263:      PartsList pl;
264:
265:      Part * pPart = 0;
266:      int PartNumber;
267:      int value;
268:      int choice;
269:
270:      while (1)
271:      {
272:          cout << "(0)Quit (1)Car (2)Plane: ";
273:          cin >> choice;
274:
275:          if (!choice)
276:              break;
277:
278:          cout << "New PartNumber?: ";
279:          cin >>  PartNumber;
280:
281:          if (choice == 1)
282:          {
283:              cout << "Model Year?: ";
284:              cin >> value;
285:              pPart = new CarPart(value,PartNumber);
286:          }
287:          else
288:          {
289:              cout << "Engine Number?: ";
290:              cin >> value;
```

```
291:                    pPart = new AirPlanePart(value,PartNumber);
292:             }
293:
294:            pl.Insert(pPart);
295:          }
296:        pl.Iterate();
297:      return 0;
298:    }
```

```
(0)Quit (1)Car (2)Plane: 1
New PartNumber?: 2837
Model Year? 90
(0)Quit (1)Car (2)Plane: 2
New PartNumber?: 378
Engine Number?: 4938
(0)Quit (1)Car (2)Plane: 1
New PartNumber?: 4499
Model Year? 94
(0)Quit (1)Car (2)Plane: 1
New PartNumber?: 3000
Model Year? 93
(0)Quit (1)Car (2)Plane: 0

Part Number: 378
Engine No.: 4938

Part Number: 2837
Model Year: 90

Part Number: 3000
Model Year: 93

Part Number: 4499
Model Year: 94
```

The Week 2 in Review listing provides a linked list implementation for Part objects. A linked list is a dynamic data structure; that is, it is like an array but it is sized to fit as objects are added and deleted.

This particular linked list is designed to hold objects of class Part, where Part is an abstract data type serving as a base class to any objects with a part number. In this example, Part has been subclassed into CarPart and AirPlanePart.

Class Part is declared on lines 27–37, and consists of a part number and some accessors. Presumably this class could be fleshed out to hold other important information about the parts, such as what components they are used in, how many are in stock, and so forth. Part is an abstract data type, enforced by the pure virtual function Display().

Note that Display() does have an implementation, on lines 41–44. It is the designer's intention that derived classes will be forced to create their own Display() method, but may chain up to this method as well.

Two simple derived classes, CarPart and AirPlanePart, are provided on lines 48–60 and 70–88, respectively. Each provides an overridden Display() method, which does in fact chain up to the base class Display() method.

The class PartNode serves as the interface between the Part class and the PartList class. It contains a pointer to a part and a pointer to the next node in the list. Its only methods are to get and set the next node in the list and to return the Part to which it points.

The intelligence of the list is, appropriately, in the class PartsList, whose declaration is on lines 133–148. PartsList keeps a pointer to the first element in the list (pHead) and uses that to access all other methods by walking the list. Walking the list means asking each node in the list for the next node, until you reach a node whose next pointer is NULL.

This is only a partial implementation; a fully developed list would provide either greater access to its first and last nodes, or would provide an iterator object, which allows clients to easily walk the list.

PartsList nonetheless provides a number of interesting methods, which are listed in alphabetical order. This is often a good idea, as it makes finding the functions easier.

Find() takes a PartNumber and an int. If the part corresponding to PartNumber is found, it returns a pointer to the Part and fills the int with the position of that part in the list. If PartNumber is not found, it returns NULL, and the position is meaningless.

GetCount() returns the number of elements in the list. PartsList keeps this number as a member variable, itsCount, though it could, of course, compute this number by walking the list.

GetFirst() returns a pointer to the first Part in the list, or returns NULL if the list is empty.

GetGlobalPartsList() returns a reference to the static member variable GlobalPartsList. This is a static instance of this class; every program with a PartsList also has one GlobalPartsList, though, of course, it is free to make other PartsLists as well. A full implementation of this idea would modify the constructor of Part to ensure that every part is created on the GlobalPartsList.

Insert takes a pointer to a Part, creates a PartNode for it, and adds the Part to the list, ordered by PartNumber.

Iterate takes a pointer to a member function of Part, which takes no parameters, returns void, and is const. It calls that function for every Part object in the list. In the sample program this is called on Display(), which is a virtual function, so the appropriate Display() method will be called based on the runtime type of the Part object called.

Operator[] allows direct access to the Part at the offset provided. Rudimentary bounds checking is provided; if the list is NULL or if the offset requested is greater than the size of the list, NULL is returned as an error condition.

Note that in a real program these comments on the functions would be written into the class declaration.

The driver program is on lines 260–298. The PartList object is created on line 263.

On line 278, the user is repeatedly prompted to choose whether to enter a car part or an airplane part. Depending on the choice the right value is requested, and the appropriate part is created. Once created, the part is inserted into the list on line 294.

The implementation for the Insert() method of PartsList is on lines 212–258. When the first part number is entered, 2837, a CarPart with that part number and the model year 90 is created and passed in to LinkedList::Insert().

On line 214, a new PartNode is created with that part, and the variable New is initialized with the part number. The PartsList's itsCount member variable is incremented on line 220.

On line 222, the test that pHead is NULL will evaluate TRUE. Since this is the first node, it is true that the PartsList's pHead pointer has zero. Thus, on line 224, pHead is set to point to the new node and this function returns.

The user is prompted to enter a second part, and this time an AirPlane part with part number 37 and engine number 4938 is entered. Once again PartsList::Insert() is called, and once again pNode is initialized with the new node. The static member variable itsCount is incremented to 2, and pHead is tested. Since pHead was assigned last time, it is no longer null and the test fails.

On line 230, the part number held by pHead, 2837, is compared against the current part number, 378. Since the new one is smaller than the one held by pHead, the new one must become the new head pointer, and the test on line 230 is true.

On line 232, the new node is set to point to the node currently pointed to by pHead. Note that this does not point the new node to pHead, but rather to the node that pHead was pointing to! On line 233, pHead is set to point to the new node.

The third time through the loop, the user enters the part number 4499 for a Car with model year 94. The counter is incremented and the number this time is not less than the number pointed to by pHead, so the for loop that begins on line 237 is entered.

The value pointed to by pHead is 378. The value pointed to by the second node is 2837. The current value is 4499. The pointer pCurrent points to the same node as pHead and so has a next value; pCurrent points to the second node, and so the test on line 240 fails.

The pointer pCurrent is set to point to the next node and the loop repeats. This time the test on line 240 succeeds. There is no next item, so the current node is told to point to the new node on line 242, and the insert is finished.

The fourth time through, the part number 3000 is entered. This proceeds just like the previous iteration, but this time when the current node is pointing to 2837 and the next node has 4499, the test on line 250 returns TRUE and the new node is inserted into position.

When the user finally presses 0, the test on line 275 evaluates true and the while(1) loop breaks. Execution falls to line 296 where Iterate() is called, branching to line 202 where on line 208 the PNode is used to access the Part and the Display() method is called on that Part object.

Week 3

At a Glance

You have finished the second week of learning C++. By now you should feel comfortable with some of the more advanced aspects of object-oriented programming, including encapsulation and polymorphism.

Where You Are Going

The last week begins with a discussion of static functions and friends. Day 16 discusses advanced inheritance. On Day 17, "Streams," you will learn about streams in depth, and on Day 18, "Namespaces," you will how to work with this exciting addition to the C++ Standard. On Day 19, "Templates," templates are introduced, and on Day 20, "Exceptions and Error Handling," exceptions are explained. Day 21, "What's Next," the last day of this book, covers some miscellaneous subjects not covered elsewhere, and then there is a discussion of the next steps to take in becoming a C++ guru.

15

16

17

18

19

20

21

Special Classes and Functions

C++ offers several ways to limit the scope and impact of variables and pointers. So far, you've seen how to create global variables, local function variables, pointers to variables, and class member variables.

Today you will learn

- What static member variables and static member functions are.
- How to use static member variables and static member functions.
- How to create and manipulate pointers to functions and pointers to member functions.
- How to work with arrays of pointers to functions.

Static Member Data

Until now, you have probably thought of the data in each object as unique to that object and not shared among objects in a class. If you have five Cat objects, for example, each has its own age, weight, and other data. The age of one does not affect the age of another.

At times, however, you'll want to keep track of a pool of data. For example, you might want to know how many objects for a specific class have been created in your program, and how many are still in existence. Static member variables are shared among all instances of a class. They are a compromise between global data, which is available to all parts of your program, and member data, which is usually available only to each object.

You can think of a static member as belonging to the class rather than to the object. Normal member data is one per object, but static members are one per class. Listing 15.1 declares a Cat object with a static data member, HowManyCats. This variable keeps track of how many Cat objects have been created. This is done by incrementing the static variable, HowManyCats, with each construction and decrementing it with each destruction.

LISTING 15.1   Static Member Data

```
0:   //Listing 15.1 static data members
1:
2:   #include <iostream>
3:   using namespace std;
4:
5:   class Cat
6:   {
7:   public:
8:       Cat(int age):itsAge(age){HowManyCats++; }
9:       virtual ~Cat() { HowManyCats--; }
10:      virtual int GetAge() { return itsAge; }
11:      virtual void SetAge(int age) { itsAge = age; }
12:      static int HowManyCats;
13:
14:  private:
15:      int itsAge;
16:
17:  };
18:
19:  int Cat::HowManyCats = 0;
20:
21:  int main()
22:  {
23:      const int MaxCats = 5; int i;
24:      Cat *CatHouse[MaxCats];
25:      for (i = 0; i<MaxCats; i++)
26:         CatHouse[i] = new Cat(i);
27:
28:      for (i = 0; i<MaxCats; i++)
29:      {
30:         cout << "There are ";
31:         cout << Cat::HowManyCats;
32:         cout << " cats left!\n";
33:         cout << "Deleting the one which is ";
```

LISTING 15.1 continued

```
34:        cout << CatHouse[i]->GetAge();
35:        cout << " years old\n";
36:        delete CatHouse[i];
37:        CatHouse[i] = 0;
38:     }
39:     return 0;
40: }
```

OUTPUT

```
There are 5 cats left!
Deleting the one which is 0 years old
There are 4 cats left!
Deleting the one which is 1 years old
There are 3 cats left!
Deleting the one which is 2 years old
There are 2 cats left!
Deleting the one which is 3 years old
There are 1 cats left!
Deleting the one which is 4 years old
```

ANALYSIS On lines 5–17, the simplified class Cat is declared. On line 12, HowManyCats is declared to be a static member variable of type int.

The declaration of HowManyCats does not define an integer; no storage space is set aside. Unlike the non-static member variables, no storage space is set aside by instantiating a Cat object because the HowManyCats member variable is not in the object. Thus, on line 19, the variable is defined and initialized.

It is a common mistake to forget to define the static member variables of classes. Don't let this happen to you! Of course, if it does, the linker will catch it with a pithy error message such as the following:

```
undefined symbol Cat::HowManyCats
```

You don't need to do this for itsAge because it is a non-static member variable and is defined each time you make a Cat object, which you do here on line 26.

The constructor for Cat increments the static member variable on line 8. The destructor decrements it on line 9. Thus, at any moment, HowManyCats has an accurate measure of how many Cat objects were created but not yet destroyed.

The driver program on lines 21–40 instantiates five Cats and puts them in an array. This calls five Cat constructors, and thus HowManyCats is incremented five times from its initial value of 0.

The program then loops through each of the five positions in the array and prints out the value of HowManyCats before deleting the current Cat pointer. The printout reflects that the starting value is 5 (after all, 5 are constructed), and that each time the loop is run, one fewer Cat remains.

Note that HowManyCats is public and is accessed directly by main(). No reason exists to expose this member variable in this way. It is preferable to make it private along with the other member variables and provide a public accessor method, as long as you will always access the data through an instance of Cat. On the other hand, if you'd like to access this data directly, without necessarily having a Cat object available, you have two options: keep it public, as shown in Listing 15.2, or provide a static member function, as discussed later in this chapter.

LISTING 15.2   Accessing Static Members Without an Object

```
0:  //Listing 15.2 static data members
1:
2:  #include <iostream>
3:  using namespace std;
4:
5:  class Cat
6:  {
7:  public:
8:      Cat(int age):itsAge(age){HowManyCats++; }
9:      virtual ~Cat() { HowManyCats--; }
10:     virtual int GetAge() { return itsAge; }
11:     virtual void SetAge(int age) { itsAge = age; }
12:     static int HowManyCats;
13:
14: private:
15:     int itsAge;
16:
17: };
18:
19: int Cat::HowManyCats = 0;
20:
21: void TelepathicFunction();
22:
23: int main()
24: {
25:     const int MaxCats = 5; int i;
26:     Cat *CatHouse[MaxCats];
27:     for (i = 0; i<MaxCats; i++)
28:     {
29:         CatHouse[i] = new Cat(i);
30:         TelepathicFunction();
31:     }
32:
```

LISTING 15.2   continued

```
33:        for ( i = 0; i<MaxCats; i++)
34:        {
35:           delete CatHouse[i];
36:           TelepathicFunction();
37:        }
38:        return 0;
39:   }
40:
41:   void TelepathicFunction()
42:   {
43:        cout << "There are ";
44:        cout << Cat::HowManyCats << " cats alive!\n";
45:   }
```

OUTPUT

```
There are 1 cats alive!
There are 2 cats alive!
There are 3 cats alive!
There are 4 cats alive!
There are 5 cats alive!
There are 4 cats alive!
There are 3 cats alive!
There are 2 cats alive!
There are 1 cats alive!
There are 0 cats alive!
```

ANALYSIS   Listing 15.2 is much like Listing 15.1 except for the addition of a new function, TelepathicFunction(). This function does not create a Cat object, nor does it take a Cat object as a parameter, yet it can access the HowManyCats member variable. Again, it is worth reemphasizing that this member variable is not in any particular object; it is in the class as a whole, and, if public, can be accessed by any function in the program.

The alternative to making this member variable public is to make it private. If you do, you can access it through a member function, but then you must have an object of that class available. Listing 15.3 shows this approach. The alternative, static member functions, is discussed immediately after the analysis of Listing 15.3.

LISTING 15.3   Accessing Static Members Using Non-static Member Functions

```
0:   //Listing 15.3 private static data members
1:
2:   #include <iostream>
3:   using std::cout;
4:
5:   class Cat
```

LISTING 15.3   continued

```
6:  {
7:  public:
8:      Cat(int age):itsAge(age){HowManyCats++; }
9:      virtual ~Cat() { HowManyCats--; }
10:     virtual int GetAge() { return itsAge; }
11:     virtual void SetAge(int age) { itsAge = age; }
12:     virtual int GetHowMany() { return HowManyCats; }
13:
14:
15: private:
16:     int itsAge;
17:     static int HowManyCats;
18: };
19:
20: int Cat::HowManyCats = 0;
21:
22: int main()
23: {
24:     const int MaxCats = 5; int i;
25:     Cat *CatHouse[MaxCats];
26:     for (i = 0; i<MaxCats; i++)
27:         CatHouse[i] = new Cat(i);
28:
29:     for (i = 0; i<MaxCats; i++)
30:     {
31:         cout << "There are ";
32:         cout << CatHouse[i]->GetHowMany();
33:         cout << " cats left!\n";
34:         cout << "Deleting the one which is ";
35:         cout << CatHouse[i]->GetAge()+2;
36:         cout << " years old\n";
37:         delete CatHouse[i];
38:         CatHouse[i] = 0;
39:     }
40:     return 0;
41: }
```

OUTPUT
```
There are 5 cats left!
Deleting the one which is 2 years old
There are 4 cats left!
Deleting the one which is 3 years old
There are 3 cats left!
Deleting the one which is 4 years old
There are 2 cats left!
Deleting the one which is 5 years old
There are 1 cats left!
Deleting the one which is 6 years old
```

ANALYSIS On line 17, the static member variable HowManyCats is declared to have private access. Now you cannot access this variable from nonmember functions, such as TelepathicFunction from the previous listing.

Even though HowManyCats is static, it is still within the scope of the class. Any class function, such as GetHowMany(), can access it, just as member functions can access any member data. However, for a function to call GetHowMany(), it must have an object on which to call the function.

Do	Don't
DO use static member variables to share data among all instances of a class. **DO** make static member variables protected or private if you want to restrict access to them.	**DON'T** use static member variables to store data for one object. Static member data is shared among all objects of its class.

Static Member Functions

Static member functions are like static member variables: They exist not in an object but in the scope of the class. Thus, they can be called without having an object of that class, as illustrated in Listing 15.4.

LISTING 15.4   Static Member Functions

```
0:   //Listing 15.4 static data members
1:
2:   #include <iostream>
3:
4:   class Cat
5:   {
6:   public:
7:       Cat(int age):itsAge(age){HowManyCats++; }
8:       virtual ~Cat() { HowManyCats--; }
9:       virtual int GetAge() { return itsAge; }
10:      virtual void SetAge(int age) { itsAge = age; }
11:      static int GetHowMany() { return HowManyCats; }
12:  private:
13:      int itsAge;
14:       static int HowManyCats;
15:  };
16:
17:  int Cat::HowManyCats = 0;
18:
19:  void TelepathicFunction();
```

LISTING 15.4   continued

```
20:
21:   int main()
22:   {
23:       const int MaxCats = 5;
24:       Cat *CatHouse[MaxCats]; int i;
25:       for (i = 0; i<MaxCats; i++)
26:       {
27:           CatHouse[i] = new Cat(i);
28:           TelepathicFunction();
29:       }
30:
31:       for ( i = 0; i<MaxCats; i++)
32:       {
33:           delete CatHouse[i];
34:           TelepathicFunction();
35:       }
36:       return 0;
37:   }
38:
39:   void TelepathicFunction()
40:   {
41:       std::cout<<"There are "<< Cat::GetHowMany()<<" cats alive!\n";
42:   }
```

OUTPUT

```
There are 1 cats alive!
There are 2 cats alive!
There are 3 cats alive!
There are 4 cats alive!
There are 5 cats alive!
There are 4 cats alive!
There are 3 cats alive!
There are 2 cats alive!
There are 1 cats alive!
There are 0 cats alive!
```

ANALYSIS The static member variable HowManyCats is declared to have private access on line 14 of the Cat declaration. The public accessor function, GetHowMany(), is declared to be both public and static on line 11.

Because GetHowMany() is public, it can be accessed by any function, and because it is static, no need exists to have an object of type Cat on which to call it. Thus, on line 41, the function TelepathicFunction() is able to access the public static accessor, even though it has no access to a Cat object. Of course, you could have called GetHowMany() on the Cat objects available in main(), the same as with any other accessor functions.

Note

Static member functions do not have a this pointer. Therefore, they cannot be declared const. Also, because member data variables are accessed in member functions using the this pointer, static member functions cannot access any non-static member variables!

Static Member Functions

You can access static member functions by calling them on an object of the class the same as you do any other member function, or you can call them without an object by fully qualifying the class and object name.

Example

```
class Cat
{
public:
static int GetHowMany() { return HowManyCats; }
private:
static int HowManyCats;
};
int Cat::HowManyCats = 0;
int main()
{
int howMany;
Cat theCat;                       // define a cat
howMany = theCat.GetHowMany();    // access through an object
howMany = Cat::GetHowMany();      // access without an object
}
```

Pointers to Functions

Just as an array name is a constant pointer to the first element of the array, a function name is a constant pointer to the function. It is possible to declare a pointer variable that points to a function and to invoke the function by using that pointer. This can be very useful; it enables you to create programs that decide which functions to invoke based on user input.

The only tricky part about function pointers is understanding the type of the object being pointed to. A pointer to int points to an integer variable, and a pointer to a function must point to a function of the appropriate return type and signature.

In the declaration

```
long (* funcPtr) (int);
```

funcPtr is declared to be a pointer (note the * in front of the name) that points to a function that takes an integer parameter and returns a long. The parentheses around * funcPtr are necessary because the parentheses around int bind more tightly; that is, they have higher precedence than the indirection operator (*). Without the first parentheses, this would declare a function that takes an integer and returns a pointer to a long. (Remember that spaces are meaningless here.)

Examine these two declarations:

```
long * Function (int);
```

```
long (* funcPtr) (int);
```

The first, Function (), is a function taking an integer and returning a pointer to a variable of type long. The second, funcPtr, is a pointer to a function taking an integer and returning a variable of type long.

The declaration of a function pointer will always include the return type and the parentheses indicating the type of the parameters, if any. Listing 15.5 illustrates the declaration and use of function pointers.

LISTING 15.5   Pointers to Functions

```
0:  // Listing 15.5 Using function pointers
1:
2:  #include <iostream>
3:  using namespace std;
4:
5:  void Square (int&,int&);
6:  void Cube (int&, int&);
7:  void Swap (int&, int &);
8:  void GetVals(int&, int&);
9:  void PrintVals(int, int);
10:
11:  int main()
12:  {
13:      void (* pFunc) (int &, int &);
14:      bool fQuit = false;
15:
16:      int valOne=1, valTwo=2;
17:      int choice;
18:      while (fQuit == false)
19:      {
20:          cout << "(0)Quit (1)Change Values (2)Square (3)Cube (4)Swap: ";
```

LISTING 15.5   continued

```
21:         cin >> choice;
22:         switch (choice)
23:         {
24:         case 1: pFunc = GetVals; break;
25:         case 2: pFunc = Square; break;
26:         case 3: pFunc = Cube; break;
27:         case 4: pFunc = Swap; break;
28:         default : fQuit = true; break;
29:         }
30:
31:         if (fQuit)
32:             break;
33:
34:         PrintVals(valOne, valTwo);
35:         pFunc(valOne, valTwo);
36:         PrintVals(valOne, valTwo);
37:     }
38:     return 0;
39: }
40:
41: void PrintVals(int x, int y)
42: {
43:     cout << "x: " << x << " y: " << y << endl;
44: }
45:
46: void Square (int & rX, int & rY)
47: {
48:     rX *= rX;
49:     rY *= rY;
50: }
51:
52: void Cube (int & rX, int & rY)
53: {
54:     int tmp;
55:
56:     tmp = rX;
57:     rX *= rX;
58:     rX = rX * tmp;
59:
60:     tmp = rY;
61:     rY *= rY;
62:     rY = rY * tmp;
63: }
64:
65: void Swap(int & rX, int & rY)
66: {
67:     int temp;
68:     temp = rX;
69:     rX = rY;
```

LISTING 15.5   continued

```
70:        rY = temp;
71:    }
72:
73:    void GetVals (int & rValOne, int & rValTwo)
74:    {
75:        cout << "New value for ValOne: ";
76:        cin >> rValOne;
77:        cout << "New value for ValTwo: ";
78:        cin >> rValTwo;
79:    }
```

OUTPUT

```
(0)Quit (1)Change Values (2)Square (3)Cube (4)Swap: 1
x: 1 y: 2
New value for ValOne: 2
New value for ValTwo: 3
x: 2 y: 3
(0)Quit (1)Change Values (2)Square (3)Cube (4)Swap: 3
x: 2 y: 3
x: 8 y: 27
(0)Quit (1)Change Values (2)Square (3)Cube (4)Swap: 2
x: 8 y: 27
x: 64 y: 729
(0)Quit (1)Change Values (2)Square (3)Cube (4)Swap: 4
x: 64 y: 729
x: 729 y: 64
(0)Quit (1)Change Values (2)Square (3)Cube (4)Swap: 0
```

ANALYSIS   On lines 5–8, four functions are declared, each with the same return type and signature, returning void and taking two references to integers.

On line 13, pFunc is declared to be a pointer to a function that returns void and takes two integer reference parameters. Any of the previous functions can be pointed to by pFunc. The user is repeatedly offered the choice of which functions to invoke, and pFunc is assigned accordingly. On lines 34–36, the current value of the two integers is printed, the currently assigned function is invoked, and then the values are printed again.

Pointer to Function

A pointer to function is invoked the same as the functions it points to, except that the function pointer name is used instead of the function name.

Assign a pointer to function to a specific function by assigning to the function name without the parentheses. The function name is a constant pointer to the function itself. Use the pointer to function the same as you would the function name. The pointer to function must agree in return value and signature with the function to which you assign it.

Example

```
long (*pFuncOne) (int, int);
long SomeFunction (int, int);
pFuncOne = SomeFunction;
pFuncOne(5,7);
```

15

Why Use Function Pointers?

You certainly could write the program in Listing 15.5 without function pointers, but the use of these pointers makes the intent and use of the program explicit: Pick a function from a list, and then invoke it.

Listing 15.6 uses the function prototypes and definitions from Listing 15.5, but the body of the program does not use a function pointer. Examine the differences between these two listings.

LISTING 15.6   Rewriting Listing 15.5 Without the Pointer to Function

```
0:  // Listing 15.6 Without function pointers
1:
2:  #include <iostream>
3:  using namespace std;
4:
5:  void Square (int&,int&);
6:  void Cube (int&, int&);
7:  void Swap (int&, int &);
8:  void GetVals(int&, int&);
9:  void PrintVals(int, int);
10:
11:  int main()
12:  {
13:     bool fQuit = false;
14:     int valOne=1, valTwo=2;
15:     int choice;
16:     while (fQuit == false)
17:     {
18:        cout << "(0)Quit (1)Change Values (2)Square (3)Cube (4)Swap: ";
19:        cin >> choice;
20:        switch (choice)
21:        {
22:        case 1:
23:           PrintVals(valOne, valTwo);
24:           GetVals(valOne, valTwo);
25:           PrintVals(valOne, valTwo);
26:           break;
```

LISTING 15.6   continued

```
27:
28:          case 2:
29:              PrintVals(valOne, valTwo);
30:              Square(valOne,valTwo);
31:              PrintVals(valOne, valTwo);
32:              break;
33:
34:          case 3:
35:              PrintVals(valOne, valTwo);
36:              Cube(valOne, valTwo);
37:              PrintVals(valOne, valTwo);
38:              break;
39:
40:          case 4:
41:              PrintVals(valOne, valTwo);
42:              Swap(valOne, valTwo);
43:              PrintVals(valOne, valTwo);
44:              break;
45:
46:          default :
47:              fQuit = true;
48:              break;
49:          }
50:
51:          if (fQuit)
52:              break;
53:      }
54:      return 0;
55: }
56:
57: void PrintVals(int x, int y)
58: {
59:      cout << "x: " << x << " y: " << y << endl;
60: }
61:
62: void Square (int & rX, int & rY)
63: {
64:      rX *= rX;
65:      rY *= rY;
66: }
67:
68: void Cube (int & rX, int & rY)
69: {
70:      int tmp;
71:
72:      tmp = rX;
73:      rX *= rX;
74:      rX = rX * tmp;
75:
```

15

LISTING 15.6 continued

```
76:       tmp = rY;
77:       rY *= rY;
78:       rY = rY * tmp;
79:    }
80:
81:    void Swap(int & rX, int & rY)
82:    {
83:       int temp;
84:       temp = rX;
85:       rX = rY;
86:       rY = temp;
87:    }
88:
89:    void GetVals (int & rValOne, int & rValTwo)
90:    {
91:       cout << "New value for ValOne: ";
92:       cin >> rValOne;
93:       cout << "New value for ValTwo: ";
94:       cin >> rValTwo;
95:    }
```

OUTPUT

```
(0)Quit (1)Change Values (2)Square (3)Cube (4)Swap: 1
x: 1 y: 2
New value for ValOne: 2
New value for ValTwo: 3
(0)Quit (1)Change Values (2)Square (3)Cube (4)Swap: 3
x: 2 y: 3
x: 8 y: 27
(0)Quit (1)Change Values (2)Square (3)Cube (4)Swap: 2
x: 8 y: 27
x: 64 y: 729
(0)Quit (1)Change Values (2)Square (3)Cube (4)Swap: 4
x: 64 y: 729
x: 729 y: 64
(0)Quit (1)Change Values (2)Square (3)Cube (4)Swap: 0
```

ANALYSIS It was tempting to put PrintVals() at the top of the while loop and again at the bottom, rather than in each case statement. This would have called PrintVals() even for the exit case, however, and that was not part of the specification.

Setting aside the increased size of the code and the repeated calls to do the same thing, the overall clarity is somewhat diminished. This is an artificial case, however, created to show how pointers to functions work. In real-world conditions, the advantages are even clearer: Pointers to functions can eliminate duplicate code, clarify your program, and enable you to make tables of functions to call based on runtime conditions.

Shorthand Invocation

The pointer to function does not need to be dereferenced, although you are free to do so. Therefore, if pFunc is a pointer to a function taking an integer and returning a variable of type long, and you assign pFunc to a matching function, you can invoke that function with either

        pFunc(x);

or

        (*pFunc)(x);

The two forms are identical. The former is just a shorthand version of the latter.

Arrays of Pointers to Functions

Just as you can declare an array of pointers to integers, you can declare an array of pointers to functions returning a specific value type and with a specific signature. Listing 15.7 again rewrites Listing 15.5, this time using an array to invoke all the choices at once.

LISTING 15.7   Demonstrates Use of an Array of Pointers to Functions

```
0:  // Listing 15.7
1:  //demonstrates use of an array of pointers to functions
2:
3:  #include <iostream>
4:  using namespace std;
5:
6:  void Square (int&,int&);
7:  void Cube (int&, int&);
8:  void Swap (int&, int &);
9:  void GetVals(int&, int&);
10:  void PrintVals(int, int);
11:
12:  int main()
13:  {
14:     int valOne=1, valTwo=2;
15:     int choice, i;
16:     const MaxArray = 5;
17:     void (*pFuncArray[MaxArray])(int&, int&);
18:
19:     for (i=0;i<MaxArray;i++)
20:     {
21:        cout << "(1)Change Values (2)Square (3)Cube (4)Swap: ";
22:        cin >> choice;
23:        switch (choice)
24:        {
25:        case 1:    pFuncArray[i] = GetVals; break;
```

LISTING 15.7 continued

```
26:        case 2:   pFuncArray[i] = Square; break;
27:        case 3:   pFuncArray[i] = Cube; break;
28:        case 4:   pFuncArray[i] = Swap; break;
29:        default:pFuncArray[i] = 0;
30:        }
31:    }
32:
33:    for (i=0;i<MaxArray; i++)
34:    {
35:        if ( pFuncArray[i] == 0 )
36:            continue;
37:        pFuncArray[i](valOne,valTwo);
38:        PrintVals(valOne,valTwo);
39:    }
40:    return 0;
41: }
42:
43: void PrintVals(int x, int y)
44: {
45:    cout << "x: " << x << " y: " << y << endl;
46: }
47:
48: void Square (int & rX, int & rY)
49: {
50:    rX *= rX;
51:    rY *= rY;
52: }
53:
54: void Cube (int & rX, int & rY)
55: {
56:    int tmp;
57:
58:    tmp = rX;
59:    rX *= rX;
60:    rX = rX * tmp;
61:
62:    tmp = rY;
63:    rY *= rY;
64:    rY = rY * tmp;
65: }
66:
67: void Swap(int & rX, int & rY)
68: {
69:    int temp;
70:    temp = rX;
71:    rX = rY;
72:    rY = temp;
73: }
74:
```

LISTING 15.7   continued

```
75:   void GetVals (int & rValOne, int & rValTwo)
76:   {
77:      cout << "New value for ValOne: ";
78:      cin >> rValOne;
79:      cout << "New value for ValTwo: ";
80:      cin >> rValTwo;
81:   }
```

OUTPUT

```
(1)Change Values (2)Square (3)Cube (4)Swap: 1
(1)Change Values (2)Square (3)Cube (4)Swap: 2
(1)Change Values (2)Square (3)Cube (4)Swap: 3
(1)Change Values (2)Square (3)Cube (4)Swap: 4
(1)Change Values (2)Square (3)Cube (4)Swap: 2
New Value for ValOne: 2
New Value for ValTwo: 3
x: 2 y: 3
x: 4 y: 9
x: 64 y: 729
x: 729 y: 64
x: 531441 y:4096
```

ANALYSIS   On line 17, the array `pFuncArray` is declared to be an array of five pointers to functions that return void and that take two integer references.

On lines 19–31, the user is asked to pick the functions to invoke, and each member of the array is assigned the address of the appropriate function. On lines 33–39, each function is invoked in turn. The result is printed after each invocation.

Passing Pointers to Functions to Other Functions

The pointers to functions (and arrays of pointers to functions, for that matter) can be passed to other functions, which may take action and then call the right function using the pointer.

You might improve Listing 15.5, for example, by passing the chosen function pointer to another function (outside of `main()`), which prints the values, invokes the function, and then prints the values again. Listing 15.8 illustrates this variation.

LISTING 15.8   Passing Pointers to Functions as Function Arguments

```
0:   // Listing 15.8 Without function pointers
1:
2:   #include <iostream>
3:   using namespace std;
4:
5:   void Square (int&,int&);
```

LISTING 15.8   continued

```
6:  void Cube (int&, int&);
7:  void Swap (int&, int &);
8:  void GetVals(int&, int&);
9:  void PrintVals(void (*)(int&, int&),int&, int&);
10:
11:  int main()
12:  {
13:     int valOne=1, valTwo=2;
14:     int choice;
15:     bool fQuit = false;
16:
17:     void (*pFunc)(int&, int&);
18:
19:     while (fQuit == false)
20:     {
21:        cout << "(0)Quit (1)Change Values (2)Square (3)Cube (4)Swap: ";
22:        cin >> choice;
23:        switch (choice)
24:        {
25:        case 1:   pFunc = GetVals; break;
26:        case 2:   pFunc = Square; break;
27:        case 3:   pFunc = Cube; break;
28:        case 4:   pFunc = Swap; break;
29:        default:fQuit = true; break;
30:        }
31:        if (fQuit == true)
32:           break;
33:        PrintVals ( pFunc, valOne, valTwo);
34:     }
35:
36:     return 0;
37:  }
38:
39:  void PrintVals( void (*pFunc)(int&, int&),int& x, int& y)
40:  {
41:     cout << "x: " << x << " y: " << y << endl;
42:     pFunc(x,y);
43:     cout << "x: " << x << " y: " << y << endl;
44:  }
45:
46:  void Square (int & rX, int & rY)
47:  {
48:     rX *= rX;
49:     rY *= rY;
50:  }
51:
52:  void Cube (int & rX, int & rY)
53:  {
54:     int tmp;
```

LISTING 15.8   continued

```
55:
56:        tmp = rX;
57:        rX *= rX;
58:        rX = rX * tmp;
59:
60:        tmp = rY;
61:        rY *= rY;
62:        rY = rY * tmp;
63:    }
64:
65:    void Swap(int & rX, int & rY)
66:    {
67:        int temp;
68:        temp = rX;
69:        rX = rY;
70:        rY = temp;
71:    }
72:
73:    void GetVals (int & rValOne, int & rValTwo)
74:    {
75:        cout << "New value for ValOne: ";
76:        cin >> rValOne;
77:        cout << "New value for ValTwo: ";
78:        cin >> rValTwo;
79:    }
```

OUTPUT

```
(0)Quit (1)Change Values (2)Square (3)Cube (4)Swap: 1
x: 1 y: 2
New value for ValOne: 2
New value for ValTwo: 3
x: 2 y: 3
(0)Quit (1)Change Values (2)Square (3)Cube (4)Swap: 3
x: 2 y: 3
x: 8 y: 27
(0)Quit (1)Change Values (2)Square (3)Cube (4)Swap: 2
x: 8 y: 27
x: 64 y: 729
(0)Quit (1)Change Values (2)Square (3)Cube (4)Swap: 4
x: 64 y: 729
x: 729 y:64
(0)Quit (1)Change Values (2)Square (3)Cube (4)Swap: 0
```

ANALYSIS   On line 17, pFunc is declared to be a pointer to a function returning void and taking two parameters, both integer references. On line 9, PrintVals is declared to be a function taking three parameters. The first is a pointer to a function that returns void but takes two integer reference parameters, and the second and third arguments to PrintVals are integer references. The user is again prompted for which functions to call, and then on line 33 PrintVals is called.

Go find a C++ programmer and ask him what this declaration means:

```
void PrintVals(void (*)(int&, int&),int&, int&);
```

This is the kind of declaration that you use infrequently and probably look up in the book each time you need it, but it will save your program on those rare occasions when it is exactly the required construct.

Using `typedef` with Pointers to Functions

The construct `void (*)(int&, int&)` is cumbersome, at best. You can use `typedef` to simplify this, by declaring a type (in this case we've called it VPF) as a pointer to a function returning void and taking two integer references. Listing 15.9 rewrites Listing 15.8 using this `typedef` statement.

LISTING 15.9   Using `typedef` to Make Pointers to Functions More Readable

```
0:   // Listing 15.9.
1:   // Using typedef to make pointers to functions more readable
2:
3:   #include <iostream>
4:   using namespace std;
5:
6:   void Square (int&,int&);
7:   void Cube (int&, int&);
8:   void Swap (int&, int &);
9:   void GetVals(int&, int&);
10:  typedef  void (*VPF) (int&, int&) ;
11:  void PrintVals(VPF,int&, int&);
12:
13:  int main()
14:  {
15:     int valOne=1, valTwo=2;
16:     int choice;
17:     bool fQuit = false;
18:
19:     VPF pFunc;
20:
21:     while (fQuit == false)
22:     {
23:        cout << "(0)Quit (1)Change Values (2)Square (3)Cube (4)Swap: ";
24:        cin >> choice;
25:        switch (choice)
26:        {
27:        case 1:   pFunc = GetVals; break;
28:        case 2:   pFunc = Square; break;
29:        case 3:   pFunc = Cube; break;
30:        case 4:   pFunc = Swap; break;
31:        default:fQuit = true; break;
```

LISTING 15.9   continued

```
32:          }
33:          if (fQuit == true)
34:             break;
35:          PrintVals ( pFunc, valOne, valTwo);
36:       }
37:       return 0;
38:  }
39:
40:  void PrintVals( VPF pFunc,int& x, int& y)
41:  {
42:       cout << "x: " << x << " y: " << y << endl;
43:       pFunc(x,y);
44:       cout << "x: " << x << " y: " << y << endl;
45:  }
46:
47:  void Square (int & rX, int & rY)
48:  {
49:       rX *= rX;
50:       rY *= rY;
51:  }
52:
53:  void Cube (int & rX, int & rY)
54:  {
55:       int tmp;
56:
57:       tmp = rX;
58:       rX *= rX;
59:       rX = rX * tmp;
60:
61:       tmp = rY;
62:       rY *= rY;
63:       rY = rY * tmp;
64:  }
65:
66:  void Swap(int & rX, int & rY)
67:  {
68:       int temp;
69:       temp = rX;
70:       rX = rY;
71:       rY = temp;
72:  }
73:
74:  void GetVals (int & rValOne, int & rValTwo)
75:  {
76:       cout << "New value for ValOne: ";
77:       cin >> rValOne;
78:       cout << "New value for ValTwo: ";
79:       cin >> rValTwo;
80:  }
```

OUTPUT

```
(0)Quit (1)Change Values (2)Square (3)Cube (4)Swap: 1
x: 1 y: 2
New value for ValOne: 2
New value for ValTwo: 3
x: 2 y: 3
(0)Quit (1)Change Values (2)Square (3)Cube (4)Swap: 3
x: 2 y: 3
x: 8 y: 27
(0)Quit (1)Change Values (2)Square (3)Cube (4)Swap: 2
x: 8 y: 27
x: 64 y: 729
(0)Quit (1)Change Values (2)Square (3)Cube (4)Swap: 4
x: 64 y: 729
x: 729 y: 64
(0)Quit (1)Change Values (2)Square (3)Cube (4)Swap: 0
```

ANALYSIS

On line 10, `typedef` is used to declare `VPF` to be of the type "pointer to function that returns void and takes two parameters, both integer references."

On line 11, the function `PrintVals()` is declared to take three parameters: a `VPF` and two integer references. On line 19, `pFunc` is now declared to be of type `VPF`.

After the type `VPF` is defined, all subsequent uses to declare `pFunc` and `PrintVals()` are much cleaner. As you can see, the output is identical.

Pointers to Member Functions

Up until this point, all the function pointers you've created have been for general, non-class functions. It is also possible to create pointers to functions that are members of classes.

To create a pointer to member function, use the same syntax as with a pointer to function, but include the class name and the scoping operator (::). Thus, if `pFunc` points to a member function of the class `Shape`, which takes two integers and returns `void`, the declaration for `pFunc` is the following:

```
void (Shape::*pFunc) (int, int);
```

Pointers to member functions are used in the same way as pointers to functions, except that they require an object of the correct class on which to invoke them. Listing 15.10 illustrates the use of pointers to member functions.

LISTING 15.10   Pointers to Member Functions

```
0:   //Listing 15.10 Pointers to member functions using virtual methods
1:
2:   #include <iostream>
3:   using namespace std;
4:
5:   class Mammal
6:   {
7:   public:
8:       Mammal():itsAge(1) {  }
9:       virtual ~Mammal() { }
10:      virtual void Speak() const = 0;
11:      virtual void Move() const = 0;
12:  protected:
13:      int itsAge;
14:  };
15:
16:  class Dog : public Mammal
17:  {
18:  public:
19:      void Speak()const { cout << "Woof!\n"; }
20:      void Move() const { cout << "Walking to heel...\n"; }
21:  };
22:
23:
24:  class Cat : public Mammal
25:  {
26:  public:
27:      void Speak()const { cout << "Meow!\n"; }
28:      void Move() const { cout << "slinking...\n"; }
29:  };
30:
31:
32:  class Horse : public Mammal
33:  {
34:  public:
35:      void Speak()const { cout << "Winnie!\n"; }
36:      void Move() const { cout << "Galloping...\n"; }
37:  };
38:
39:
40:  int main()
41:  {
42:      void (Mammal::*pFunc)() const =0;
43:      Mammal* ptr =0;
44:      int Animal;
45:      int Method;
46:      bool fQuit = false;
47:
48:      while (fQuit == false)
```

LISTING 15.10   continued

```
49:    {
50:        cout << "(0)Quit (1)dog (2)cat (3)horse: ";
51:        cin >> Animal;
52:        switch (Animal)
53:        {
54:        case 1:   ptr = new Dog; break;
55:        case 2:   ptr = new Cat; break;
56:        case 3:   ptr = new Horse; break;
57:        default: fQuit = true; break;
58:        }
59:        if (fQuit)
60:            break;
61:
62:        cout << "(1)Speak   (2)Move: ";
63:        cin >> Method;
64:        switch (Method)
65:        {
66:        case 1: pFunc = Mammal::Speak; break;
67:        default: pFunc = Mammal::Move; break;
68:        }
69:
70:        (ptr->*pFunc)();
71:        delete ptr;
72:    }
73:    return 0;
74: }
```

OUTPUT

```
(0)Quit (1)dog (2)cat (3)horse: 1
(1)Speak (2)Move: 1
Woof!
(0)Quit (1)dog (2)cat (3)horse: 2
(1)Speak (2)Move: 1
Meow!
(0)Quit (1)dog (2)cat (3)horse: 3
(1)Speak (2)Move: 2
Galloping
(0)Quit (1)dog (2)cat (3)horse: 0
```

ANALYSIS   On lines 5–14, the abstract data type Mammal is declared with two pure virtual methods: Speak() and Move(). Mammal is subclassed into Dog, Cat, and Horse, each of which overrides Speak() and Move().

The driver program in main() asks the user to choose which type of animal to create, and then a new subclass of Animal is created on the free store and assigned to ptr on lines 54–56.

The user is then prompted for which method to invoke, and that method is assigned to the pointer pFunc. On line 70, the method chosen is invoked by the object created, by using the pointer ptr to access the object and pFunc to access the function.

Finally, on line 71, delete is called on the pointer ptr to return the memory set aside for the object to the free store. Note that no reason exists to call delete on pFunc because this is a pointer to code, not to an object on the free store. In fact, attempting to do so will generate a compile-time error.

Arrays of Pointers to Member Functions

As with pointers to functions, pointers to member functions can be stored in an array. The array can be initialized with the addresses of various member functions, and these can be invoked by offsets into the array. Listing 15.11 illustrates this technique.

LISTING 15.11   Array of Pointers to Member Functions

```
0:   //Listing 15.11 Array of pointers to member functions
1:
2:   #include <iostream>
3:   using std::cout;
4:
5:   class Dog
6:   {
7:   public:
8:       void Speak()const { cout << "Woof!\n"; }
9:       void Move() const { cout << "Walking to heel...\n"; }
10:      void Eat() const { cout << "Gobbling food...\n"; }
11:      void Growl() const { cout << "Grrrrr\n"; }
12:      void Whimper() const { cout << "Whining noises...\n"; }
13:      void RollOver() const { cout << "Rolling over...\n"; }
14:      void PlayDead() const { cout << "The end of Little Caesar?\n"; }
15:   };
16:
17:   typedef void (Dog::*PDF)()const ;
18:   int main()
19:   {
20:       const int MaxFuncs = 7;
21:       PDF DogFunctions[MaxFuncs] =
22:          {Dog::Speak,
23:           Dog::Move,
24:           Dog::Eat,
25:           Dog::Growl,
26:           Dog::Whimper,
27:           Dog::RollOver,
28:           Dog::PlayDead };
29:
30:       Dog* pDog =0;
```

15

LISTING 15.11 continued

```
31:     int Method;
32:     bool fQuit = false;
33:
34:     while (!fQuit)
35:     {
36:         cout << "(0)Quit (1)Speak (2)Move (3)Eat (4)Growl";
37:         cout << " (5)Whimper (6)Roll Over (7)Play Dead: ";
38:         std::cin >> Method;
39:         if (Method == 0)
40:         {
41:             fQuit = true;
42:         }
43:         else
44:         {
45:             pDog = new Dog;
46:             (pDog->*DogFunctions[Method-1])();
47:             delete pDog;
48:         }
49:     }
50:     return 0;
51: }
```

OUTPUT

```
(0)Quit (1)Speak (2)Move (3)Eat (4)Growl (5)Whimper (6)Roll Over (7)Play
Dead: 1
Woof!
 (0)Quit (1)Speak (2)Move (3)Eat (4)Growl (5)Whimper (6)Roll Over
(7)Play Dead: 4
Grrr
 (0)Quit (1)Speak (2)Move (3)Eat (4)Growl (5)Whimper (6)Roll Over
(7)Play Dead: 7
The end of Little Caesar?
 (0)Quit (1)Speak (2)Move (3)Eat (4)Growl (5)Whimper (6)Roll Over
(7)Play Dead: 0
```

ANALYSIS
On lines 5–15, the class Dog is created, with seven member functions all sharing the same return type and signature. On line 17, a typedef declares PDF to be a pointer to a member function of Dog that takes no parameters and returns no values, and that is const: the signature of the seven member functions of Dog.

On lines 21–28, the array DogFunctions is declared to hold seven such member functions, and it is initialized with the addresses of these functions.

On lines 36 and 37, the user is prompted to pick a method. Unless Quit is picked, a new Dog is created on the heap, and then the correct method is invoked on the array on line 46. Here's another good line to show to the hotshot C++ programmers in your company; ask them what this does:

```
(pDog->*DogFunctions[Method-1])();
```

Once again, this is a bit esoteric, but when you need a table built from member functions, it can make your program much easier to read and understand.

Do	Don't
DO invoke pointers to member functions on a specific object of a class.	DON'T use pointer to member functions when simpler solutions are possible.
DO use typedef to make pointer to member function declarations easier to read.	

Summary

Today you learned how to create static member variables in your class. Each class, rather than each object, has one instance of the static member variable. It is possible to access this member variable without an object of the class type by fully qualifying the name, assuming you've declared the static member to have public access.

Static member variables can be used as counters across instances of the class. Because they are not part of the object, the declaration of static member variables does not allocate memory, and static member variables must be defined and initialized outside the declaration of the class.

Static member functions are part of the class in the same way that static member variables are. They can be accessed without a particular object of the class and can be used to access static member data. Static member functions cannot be used to access non-static member data because they do not have a this pointer.

Because static member functions do not have a this pointer, they also cannot be made const. const in a member function indicates that the this pointer is const.

You also learned how to declare and use pointers to functions and pointers to member functions. You saw how to create arrays of these pointers and how to pass them to functions.

Pointers to functions and pointers to member functions can be used to create tables of functions that can be selected from at runtime. This can give your program flexibility that is not easily achieved without these pointers.

Q&A

Q **Why use static data when you can use global data?**

A Static data is scoped to the class. In this manner, static data is available only through an object of the class, through an explicit call using the class name if they are public, or by using a static member function. Static data is typed to the class type, however, and the restricted access and strong typing makes static data safer than global data.

Q **Why use static member functions when you can use global functions?**

A Static member functions are scoped to the class and can be called only by using an object of the class or an explicit full specification (such as
`ClassName::FunctionName()`).

Q **Is it common to use many pointers to functions and pointers to member functions?**

A No, these have their special uses, but are not common constructs. Many complex and powerful programs have neither.

Workshop

The Workshop contains quiz questions to help solidify your understanding of the material covered and exercises to provide you with experience in using what you've learned. Try to answer the quiz and exercise questions before checking the answers in Appendix D, and make sure you understand the answers before going to the next chapter.

Quiz

1. Can static member variables be private?

2. Show the declaration for a static member variable.

3. Show the declaration for a static function.

4. Show the declaration for a pointer to function returning `long` and taking an integer parameter.

5. Modify the pointer in Question 4 so it's a pointer to member function of class `Car`.

6. Show the declaration for an array of 10 pointers as defined in Question 5.

Exercises

1. Write a short program declaring a class with one member variable and one static member variable. Have the constructor initialize the member variable and increment the static member variable. Have the destructor decrement the member variable.

2. Using the program from Exercise 1, write a short driver program that makes three objects and then displays their member variables and the static member variable. Then destroy each object and show the effect on the static member variable.

3. Modify the program from Exercise 2 to use a static member function to access the static member variable. Make the static member variable private.

4. Write a pointer to member function to access the non-static member data in the program in Exercise 3, and use that pointer to print the value of that data.

5. Add two more member variables to the class from the previous exercises. Add accessor functions that get the value of these data and give all the member functions the same return values and signatures. Use the pointer to member function to access these functions.

DAY 16

Advanced Inheritance

So far, you have worked with single and multiple inheritance to create *is-a* relationships.

Today you will learn

- What containment is and how to model it.
- What delegation is and how to model it.
- How to implement one class in terms of another.
- How to use private inheritance.

Containment

As you have seen in previous examples, it is possible for the member data of a class to include objects of another class. C++ programmers say that the outer class contains the inner class. Thus, an Employee class might contain string objects (for the name of the employee), as well as integers (for the employee's salary and so forth).

Listing 16.1 describes an incomplete, but still useful, String class, not unlike the String class created on Day 13. This listing does not produce any output. Instead, Listing 16.1 will be used with later listings.

LISTING 16.1   The String Class

```
0:    // Listing 16.1 The String Class
1:
2:    #include <iostream>
3:    #include <string.h>
4:    using namespace std;
5:
6:    class String
7:    {
8:    public:
9:        // constructors
10:        String();
11:        String(const char *const);
12:        String(const String &);
13:        ~String();
14:
15:        // overloaded operators
16:        char & operator[](int offset);
17:        char operator[](int offset) const;
18:        String operator+(const String&);
19:        void operator+=(const String&);
20:        String & operator= (const String &);
21:
22:        // General accessors
23:        int GetLen()const { return itsLen; }
24:        const char * GetString() const { return itsString; }
25:        static int ConstructorCount;
26:
27:    private:
28:        String (int);          // private constructor
29:        char * itsString;
30:        unsigned short itsLen;
31:
32:    };
33:
34:    // default constructor creates string of 0 bytes
35:    String::String()
36:    {
37:        itsString = new char[1];
38:        itsString[0] = '\0';
39:        itsLen=0;
40:        // cout << "\tDefault string constructor\n";
41:        // ConstructorCount++;
42:    }
43:
44:    // private (helper) constructor, used only by
45:    // class methods for creating a new string of
46:    // required size.  Null filled.
47:    String::String(int len)
48:    {
```

LISTING **16.1** continued

```
49:        itsString = new char[len+1];
50:        for (int i = 0; i<=len; i++)
51:            itsString[i] = '\0';
52:        itsLen=len;
53:        // cout << "\tString(int) constructor\n";
54:        // ConstructorCount++;
55:    }
56:
57:    // Converts a character array to a String
58:    String::String(const char * const cString)
59:    {
60:        itsLen = strlen(cString);
61:        itsString = new char[itsLen+1];
62:        for (int i = 0; i<itsLen; i++)
63:            itsString[i] = cString[i];
64:        itsString[itsLen]='\0';
65:        // cout << "\tString(char*) constructor\n";
66:        // ConstructorCount++;
67:    }
68:
69:    // copy constructor
70:    String::String (const String & rhs)
71:    {
72:        itsLen=rhs.GetLen();
73:        itsString = new char[itsLen+1];
74:        for (int i = 0; i<itsLen;i++)
75:            itsString[i] = rhs[i];
76:        itsString[itsLen] = '\0';
77:        // cout << "\tString(String&) constructor\n";
78:        // ConstructorCount++;
79:    }
80:
81:    // destructor, frees allocated memory
82:    String::~String ()
83:    {
84:        delete [] itsString;
85:        itsLen = 0;
86:        // cout << "\tString destructor\n";
87:    }
88:
89:    // operator equals, frees existing memory
90:    // then copies string and size
91:    String& String::operator=(const String & rhs)
92:    {
93:        if (this == &rhs)
94:            return *this;
95:        delete [] itsString;
96:        itsLen=rhs.GetLen();
97:        itsString = new char[itsLen+1];
```

LISTING 16.1   continued

```
 98:     for (int i = 0;  i<itsLen;i++)
 99:         itsString[i] = rhs[i];
100:     itsString[itsLen] = '\0';
101:     return *this;
102:     // cout << "\tString operator=\n";
103:   }
104:
105:  //non constant offset operator, returns
106:  // reference to character so it can be
107:  // changed!
108:  char & String::operator[](int offset)
109:  {
110:     if (offset > itsLen)
111:         return itsString[itsLen-1];
112:     else
113:         return itsString[offset];
114:  }
115:
116:  // constant offset operator for use
117:  // on const objects (see copy constructor!)
118:  char String::operator[](int offset) const
119:  {
120:     if (offset > itsLen)
121:         return itsString[itsLen-1];
122:     else
123:         return itsString[offset];
124:  }
125:
126:  // creates a new string by adding current
127:  // string to rhs
128:  String String::operator+(const String& rhs)
129:  {
130:     int  totalLen = itsLen + rhs.GetLen();
131:     String temp(totalLen);
132:     int i, j;
133:     for (i = 0; i<itsLen; i++)
134:         temp[i] = itsString[i];
135:     for (j = 0; j<rhs.GetLen(); j++, i++)
136:         temp[i] = rhs[j];
137:     temp[totalLen]='\0';
138:     return temp;
139:  }
140:
141:  // changes current string, returns nothing
142:  void String::operator+=(const String& rhs)
143:  {
144:     unsigned short rhsLen = rhs.GetLen();
145:     unsigned short totalLen = itsLen + rhsLen;
```

LISTING 16.1   continued

```
146:      String  temp(totalLen);
147:      int i, j;
148:      for (i = 0; i<itsLen; i++)
149:          temp[i] = itsString[i];
150:      for (j = 0; j<rhs.GetLen(); j++, i++)
151:          temp[i] = rhs[i-itsLen];
152:      temp[totalLen]='\0';
153:      *this = temp;
154:  }
155:
156:   // int String::ConstructorCount = 0;
```

> **Note**
>
> Put the code from Listing 16.1 into a file called String.hpp. Then any time you need the String class you can include Listing 16.1 by using #include "String.hpp", such as in this listing.

OUTPUT   None.

ANALYSIS   Listing 16.1 provides a String class much like the one used in Listing 13.12 of Day 13, "Arrays and Linked Lists." The significant difference here is that the constructors and a few other functions in Listing 13.12 have print statements to show their use, which are currently commented out in Listing 16.1. These functions will be used in later examples.

On line 25, the static member variable ConstructorCount is declared, and on line 156 it is initialized. This variable is incremented in each string constructor. All this is currently commented out; it will be used in a later listing.

Listing 16.2 describes an Employee class that contains three string objects.

LISTING 16.2   The Employee Class and Driver Program

```
0:   // Listing 16.2 The Employee Class and Driver Program
1:   #include "String.hpp"
2:
3:   class Employee
4:   {
5:   public:
6:       Employee();
7:       Employee(char *, char *, char *, long);
8:       ~Employee();
```

LISTING 16.2   continued

```
9:         Employee(const Employee&);
10:        Employee & operator= (const Employee &);
11:
12:        const String & GetFirstName() const
13:           { return itsFirstName; }
14:        const String & GetLastName() const { return itsLastName; }
15:        const String & GetAddress() const { return itsAddress; }
16:        long GetSalary() const { return itsSalary; }
17:
18:        void SetFirstName(const String & fName)
19:           { itsFirstName = fName; }
20:        void SetLastName(const String & lName)
21:           { itsLastName = lName; }
22:        void SetAddress(const String & address)
23:           { itsAddress = address; }
24:        void SetSalary(long salary) { itsSalary = salary; }
25:    private:
26:        String    itsFirstName;
27:        String    itsLastName;
28:        String    itsAddress;
29:        long      itsSalary;
30:    };
31:
32:    Employee::Employee():
33:        itsFirstName(""),
34:        itsLastName(""),
35:        itsAddress(""),
36:        itsSalary(0)
37:    {}
38:
39:    Employee::Employee(char * firstName, char * lastName,
40:        char * address, long salary):
41:        itsFirstName(firstName),
42:        itsLastName(lastName),
43:        itsAddress(address),
44:        itsSalary(salary)
45:    {}
46:
47:    Employee::Employee(const Employee & rhs):
48:        itsFirstName(rhs.GetFirstName()),
49:        itsLastName(rhs.GetLastName()),
50:        itsAddress(rhs.GetAddress()),
51:        itsSalary(rhs.GetSalary())
52:    {}
53:
54:    Employee::~Employee() {}
55:
56:    Employee & Employee::operator= (const Employee & rhs)
57:    {
```

LISTING 16.2   continued

```
58:      if (this == &rhs)
59:         return *this;
60:
61:      itsFirstName = rhs.GetFirstName();
62:      itsLastName = rhs.GetLastName();
63:      itsAddress = rhs.GetAddress();
64:      itsSalary = rhs.GetSalary();
65:
66:      return *this;
67:   }
68:
69:   int main()
70:   {
71:      Employee Edie("Jane","Doe","1461 Shore Parkway", 20000);
72:      Edie.SetSalary(50000);
73:      String LastName("Levine");
74:      Edie.SetLastName(LastName);
75:      Edie.SetFirstName("Edythe");
76:
77:      cout << "Name: ";
78:      cout << Edie.GetFirstName().GetString();
79:      cout << " " << Edie.GetLastName().GetString();
80:      cout << ".\nAddress: ";
81:      cout << Edie.GetAddress().GetString();
82:      cout << ".\nSalary: " ;
83:      cout << Edie.GetSalary();
84:      return 0;
85:   }
```

For convenience I've included the implementation with the declaration of the class. In a real-world program, you would save the class declaration in String.hpp and the implementation in String.cpp. You would then add String.cpp into your program (using add files or a make file) and have String.cpp #include String.hpp.

Of course, in a real program you'd use the C++ Standard Library String class, and not this string class in the first place.

```
Name: Edythe Levine.
Address: 1461 Shore Parkway.
Salary: 50000
```

Listing 16.2 shows the Employee class, which contains three string objects: itsFirstName, itsLastName, and itsAddress.

On line 71, an Employee object is created, and four values are passed in to initialize the Employee object. On line 72, the Employee access function SetSalary() is called, with the constant value 50000. Note that in a real program, this would be either a dynamic value (set at runtime) or a constant.

On line 73, a string is created and initialized using a C++ string constant. This string object is then used as an argument to SetLastName() on line 74.

On line 75, the Employee function SetFirstName() is called with yet another string constant. However, if you are paying close attention, you will notice that Employee does not have a function SetFirstName() that takes a character string as its argument; SetFirstName() requires a constant string reference.

The compiler resolves this because it knows how to make a string from a constant character string. It knows this because you told it how to do so on line 11 of Listing 16.1.

FAQ

Why do you tack on GetString() to lines 78, 79, and 81?

```
78:     cout << Edie.GetFirstName().GetString();
```

Answer: The Edie Object's GetFirstName() method returns a String. Unfortunately, our String object does not yet support the cout << operator. To satisfy cout, we need to return a C-Style string. GetString() is a method on our String object that returns a C-Style string. We'll fix this problem soon.

Accessing Members of the Contained Class

Employee objects do not have special access to the member variables of String. If the Employee object Edie tried to access the member variable itsLen of its own itsFirstName member variable, it would get a compile-time error. This is not much of a burden, however. The accessor functions provide an interface for the String class, and the Employee class need not worry about the implementation details, any more than it worries about how the integer variable, itsSalary, stores its information.

Filtering Access to Contained Members

Note that the String class provides the operator+. The designer of the Employee class has blocked access to the operator+ being called on Employee objects by declaring that all the string accessors, such as GetFirstName(), return a constant reference. Because operator+ is not (and can't be) a const function (it changes the object it is called on), attempting to write the following will cause a compile-time error:

```
String buffer = Edie.GetFirstName() + Edie.GetLastName();
```

`GetFirstName()` returns a constant `String`, and you can't call `operator+` on a constant object.

To fix this, overload `GetFirstName()` to be non-const:

```
const String & GetFirstName() const { return itsFirstName; }
String & GetFirstName()  { return itsFirstName; }
```

Note that the return value is no longer `const` and that the member function itself is no longer `const`. Changing the return value is not sufficient to overload the function name; you must change the constancy of the function itself.

Cost of Containment

It is important to note that the user of an `Employee` class pays the price of each of those string objects each time one is constructed or a copy of the `Employee` is made.

Uncommenting the `cout` statements in Listing 16.1 reveals how often these are called. Listing 16.3 rewrites the driver program to add print statements indicating where in the program objects are being created:

 Note

To compile this listing, uncomment lines 40, 53, 65, 77, 86, and 102 in Listing 16.1.

LISTING 16.3   Contained Class Constructors

```
0:  //Listing 16.3 Contained Class Constructors
1:  #include "String.hpp"
2:
3:  class Employee
4:  {
5:  public:
6:      Employee();
7:      Employee(char *, char *, char *, long);
8:      ~Employee();
9:      Employee(const Employee&);
10:     Employee & operator= (const Employee &);
11:
12:     const String & GetFirstName() const
13:         { return itsFirstName; }
14:     const String & GetLastName() const { return itsLastName; }
15:     const String & GetAddress() const { return itsAddress; }
16:     long GetSalary() const { return itsSalary; }
17:
18:     void SetFirstName(const String & fName)
19:         { itsFirstName = fName; }
```

16

LISTING 16.3   continued

```
20:     void SetLastName(const String & lName)
21:        { itsLastName = lName; }
22:     void SetAddress(const String & address)
23:        { itsAddress = address; }
24:     void SetSalary(long salary) { itsSalary = salary; }
25:  private:
26:     String    itsFirstName;
27:     String    itsLastName;
28:     String    itsAddress;
29:     long      itsSalary;
30:  };
31:
32:  Employee::Employee():
33:     itsFirstName(""),
34:     itsLastName(""),
35:     itsAddress(""),
36:     itsSalary(0)
37:  {}
38:
39:  Employee::Employee(char * firstName, char * lastName,
40:     char * address, long salary):
41:     itsFirstName(firstName),
42:     itsLastName(lastName),
43:     itsAddress(address),
44:     itsSalary(salary)
45:  {}
46:
47:  Employee::Employee(const Employee & rhs):
48:     itsFirstName(rhs.GetFirstName()),
49:     itsLastName(rhs.GetLastName()),
50:     itsAddress(rhs.GetAddress()),
51:     itsSalary(rhs.GetSalary())
52:  {}
53:
54:  Employee::~Employee() {}
55:
56:  Employee & Employee::operator= (const Employee & rhs)
57:  {
58:     if (this == &rhs)
59:        return *this;
60:
61:     itsFirstName = rhs.GetFirstName();
62:     itsLastName = rhs.GetLastName();
63:     itsAddress = rhs.GetAddress();
64:     itsSalary = rhs.GetSalary();
65:
66:     return *this;
67:  }
68:
```

LISTING 16.3 continued

```
69:  int main()
70:  {
71:      cout << "Creating Edie...\n";
72:      Employee Edie("Jane","Doe","1461 Shore Parkway", 20000);
73:      Edie.SetSalary(20000);
74:      cout << "Calling SetFirstName with char *...\n";
75:      Edie.SetFirstName("Edythe");
76:      cout << "Creating temporary string LastName...\n";
77:      String LastName("Levine");
78:      Edie.SetLastName(LastName);
79:
80:      cout << "Name: ";
81:      cout << Edie.GetFirstName().GetString();
82:      cout << " " << Edie.GetLastName().GetString();
83:      cout << "\nAddress: ";
84:      cout << Edie.GetAddress().GetString();
85:      cout << "\nSalary: " ;
86:      cout << Edie.GetSalary();
87:      cout << endl;
88:      return 0;
89:  }
```

16

OUTPUT

```
1:   Creating Edie...
2:           String(char*) constructor
3:           String(char*) constructor
4:           String(char*) constructor
5:   Calling SetFirstName with char *...
6:           String(char*) constructor
7:           String destructor
8:   Creating temporary string LastName...
9:           String(char*) constructor
10:  Name: Edythe Levine
11:  Address: 1461 Shore Parkway
12:  Salary: 20000
13:          String destructor
14:          String destructor
15:          String destructor
16:          String destructor
```

ANALYSIS Listing 16.3 uses the same class declarations as Listings 16.1 and 16.2. However, the cout statements have been uncommented. The output from Listing 16.3 has been numbered to make analysis easier.

On line 71 of Listing 16.3, the statement Creating Edie... is printed, as reflected on line 1 of the output. On line 72, an Employee object, Edie, is created with four parameters. The output reflects the constructor for String being called three times, as expected.

Line 74 prints an information statement, and then on line 75 is the statement
`Edie.SetFirstName("Edythe")`. This statement causes a temporary string to be created
from the character string `"Edythe"`, as reflected on lines 5 and 6 of the output. Note that
the temporary is destroyed immediately after it is used in the assignment statement.

On line 77, a `String` object is created in the body of the program. Here the programmer
is doing explicitly what the compiler did implicitly on the previous statement. This time
you see the constructor on line 8 of the output, but no destructor. This object will not be
destroyed until it goes out of scope at the end of the function.

On lines 81–87, the strings in the employee object are destroyed as the `Employee` object
falls out of scope, and the string `LastName`, created on line 77, is destroyed as well when
it falls out of scope.

Copying by Value

Listing 16.3 illustrates how the creation of one `Employee` object caused five string
constructor calls. Listing 16.4 again rewrites the driver program. This time the print
statements are not used, but the string static member variable `ConstructorCount` is
uncommented and used.

Examination of Listing 16.1 shows that `ConstructorCount` is incremented each time a
string constructor is called. The driver program in 16.4 calls the print functions, passing
in the `Employee` object, first by reference and then by value. `ConstructorCount` keeps
track of how many string objects are created when the employee is passed as a parameter.

 Note   To compile this listing, leave in the lines that you uncommented in Listing
16.1 to run Listing 16.3, and in addition, uncomment lines 25, 41, 54, 66, 78,
and 155 from Listing 16.1.

LISTING 16.4   Passing by Value

```
0:   // Listing 16.4 Passing by Value
1:   #include "String.hpp"
2:
3:   class Employee
4:   {
5:   public:
6:       Employee();
7:       Employee(char *, char *, char *, long);
8:       ~Employee();
9:       Employee(const Employee&);
```

LISTING 16.4 continued

```
10:     Employee & operator= (const Employee &);
11:
12:     const String & GetFirstName() const
13:         { return itsFirstName; }
14:     const String & GetLastName() const { return itsLastName; }
15:     const String & GetAddress() const { return itsAddress; }
16:     long GetSalary() const { return itsSalary; }
17:
18:     void SetFirstName(const String & fName)
19:         { itsFirstName = fName; }
20:     void SetLastName(const String & lName)
21:         { itsLastName = lName; }
22:     void SetAddress(const String & address)
23:         { itsAddress = address; }
24:     void SetSalary(long salary) { itsSalary = salary; }
25: private:
26:     String    itsFirstName;
27:     String    itsLastName;
28:     String    itsAddress;
9:     long      itsSalary;
30: };
31:
32: Employee::Employee():
33:     itsFirstName(""),
34:     itsLastName(""),
35:     itsAddress(""),
36:     itsSalary(0)
37: {}
38:
39: Employee::Employee(char * firstName, char * lastName,
40:     char * address, long salary):
41:     itsFirstName(firstName),
42:     itsLastName(lastName),
43:     itsAddress(address),
44:     itsSalary(salary)
45: {}
46:
47: Employee::Employee(const Employee & rhs):
48:     itsFirstName(rhs.GetFirstName()),
49:     itsLastName(rhs.GetLastName()),
50:     itsAddress(rhs.GetAddress()),
51:     itsSalary(rhs.GetSalary())
52: {}
53:
54: Employee::~Employee() {}
55:
56: Employee & Employee::operator= (const Employee & rhs)
57: {
58:     if (this == &rhs)
```

16

LISTING 16.4 continued

```
59:        return *this;
60:
61:     itsFirstName = rhs.GetFirstName();
62:     itsLastName = rhs.GetLastName();
63:     itsAddress = rhs.GetAddress();
64:     itsSalary = rhs.GetSalary();
65:
66:     return *this;
67:  }
68:
69:  void PrintFunc(Employee);
70:  void rPrintFunc(const Employee&);
71:
72:  int main()
73:  {
74:     Employee Edie("Jane","Doe","1461 Shore Parkway", 20000);
75:     Edie.SetSalary(20000);
76:     Edie.SetFirstName("Edythe");
77:     String LastName("Levine");
78:     Edie.SetLastName(LastName);
79:
80:     cout << "Constructor count: " ;
81:     cout << String::ConstructorCount << endl;
82:     rPrintFunc(Edie);
83:     cout << "Constructor count: ";
84:     cout << String::ConstructorCount << endl;
85:     PrintFunc(Edie);
86:     cout << "Constructor count: ";
87:     cout << String::ConstructorCount << endl;
88:     return 0;
89:  }
90:  void PrintFunc (Employee Edie)
91:  {
92:     cout << "Name: ";
93:     cout << Edie.GetFirstName().GetString();
94:     cout << " " << Edie.GetLastName().GetString();
95:     cout << ".\nAddress: ";
96:     cout << Edie.GetAddress().GetString();
97:     cout << ".\nSalary: " ;
98:     cout << Edie.GetSalary();
99:     cout << endl;
100: }
101:
102: void rPrintFunc (const Employee& Edie)
103: {
104:     cout << "Name: ";
105:     cout << Edie.GetFirstName().GetString();
106:     cout << " " << Edie.GetLastName().GetString();
107:     cout << "\nAddress: ";
```

LISTING 16.4   continued

```
108:      cout << Edie.GetAddress().GetString();
109:      cout << "\nSalary: " ;
110:      cout << Edie.GetSalary();
111:      cout << endl;
112:  }
```

16

OUTPUT
```
String(char*) constructor
        String(char*) constructor
        String(char*) constructor
        String(char*) constructor
        String destructor
        String(char*) constructor
Constructor count: 5
Name: Edythe Levine
Address: 1461 Shore Parkway
Salary: 20000
Constructor count: 5
        String(String&) constructor
        String(String&) constructor
        String(String&) constructor
Name: Edythe Levine.
Address: 1461 Shore Parkway.
Salary: 20000
        String destructor
        String destructor
        String destructor
Constructor count: 8
String destructor
        String destructor
        String destructor
        String destructor
```

ANALYSIS   The output shows that five string objects were created as part of creating one Employee object. When the Employee object is passed to rPrintFunc() by reference, no additional Employee objects are created, and so no additional String objects are created. (They, too, are passed by reference.)

When, on line 85, the Employee object is passed to PrintFunc() by value, a copy of the Employee is created, and three more string objects are created (by calls to the copy constructor).

Implementation in Terms of Inheritance/ Containment Versus Delegation

At times, one class wants to draw on some of the attributes of another class. For example, suppose you need to create a PartsCatalog class. The specification you've been given defines a PartsCatalog as a collection of parts; each part has a unique part number. The PartsCatalog does not allow duplicate entries and does allow access by part number.

The listing for the Week in Review for Week 2 provides a PartsList class. This PartsList is well tested and understood, and you'd like to build on that technology when making your PartsCatalog, rather than inventing it from scratch.

You could create a new PartsCatalog class and have it contain a PartsList. The PartsCatalog could delegate management of the linked list to its contained PartsList object.

An alternative would be to make the PartsCatalog derive from PartsList and thereby inherit the properties of a PartsList. Remembering, however, that public inheritance provides an *is-a* relationship, you should question whether a PartsCatalog really is a type of PartsList.

One way to answer the question of whether PartsCatalog is a PartsList is to assume that PartsList is the base and PartsCatalog is the derived class, and then to ask these other questions:

1. Is anything in the base class that should not be in the derived? For example, does the PartsList base class have functions that are inappropriate for the PartsCatalog class? If so, you probably don't want public inheritance.

2. Might the class you are creating have more than one of the base? For example, might a PartsCatalog need two PartsLists in each object? If it might, you almost certainly want to use containment.

3. Do you need to inherit from the base class so that you can take advantage of virtual functions or access protected members? If so, you must use inheritance, public or private.

Based on the answers to these questions, you must choose between public inheritance (the *is-a* relationship) and either private inheritance (explained later today) or containment.

- **Contained**—An object declared as a member of another class contained by that class.

- **Delegation**—Using the attributes of a contained class to accomplish functions not otherwise available to the containing class.
- **Implemented in terms of**—Building one class on the capabilities of another without using public inheritance.

Delegation

Why not derive `PartsCatalog` from `PartsList`? The `PartsCatalog` isn't a `PartsList` because `PartsLists` are ordered collections, and each member of the collection can repeat. The `PartsCatalog` has unique entries that are not ordered. The fifth member of the `PartsCatalog` is not part number 5.

Certainly, it would have been possible to inherit publicly from `PartsList` and then override `Insert()` and the offset operators (`[]`) to do the right thing, but then you would have changed the essence of the `PartsList` class. Instead, you'll build a `PartsCatalog` that has no offset operator, does not allow duplicates, and defines the `operator+` to combine two sets.

The first way to accomplish this is with containment. The `PartsCatalog` will delegate list management to a contained `PartsList`. Listing 16.5 illustrates this approach.

LISTING 16.5   Delegating to a Contained `PartsList`

```
0:  // Listing 16.5 Delegating to a Contained PartsList
1:
2:  #include <iostream>
3:  using namespace std;
4:
5:  // *************** Part ************
6:
7:  // Abstract base class of parts
8:  class Part
9:  {
10:  public:
11:      Part():itsPartNumber(1) {}
12:      Part(int PartNumber):
13:      itsPartNumber(PartNumber){}
14:      virtual ~Part(){}
15:      int GetPartNumber() const
16:          { return itsPartNumber; }
17:      virtual void Display() const =0;
18:  private:
19:      int itsPartNumber;
20:  };
21:
22:  // implementation of pure virtual function so that
```

LISTING **16.5**   continued

```
23:   // derived classes can chain up
24:   void Part::Display() const
25:   {
26:       cout << "\nPart Number: " << itsPartNumber << endl;
27:   }
28:
29:   // *************** Car Part ************
30:
31:   class CarPart : public Part
32:   {
33:   public:
34:       CarPart():itsModelYear(94){}
35:       CarPart(int year, int partNumber);
36:       virtual void Display() const
37:       {
38:       Part::Display();
39:       cout << "Model Year: ";
40:       cout << itsModelYear << endl;
41:       }
42:   private:
43:       int itsModelYear;
44:   };
45:
46:   CarPart::CarPart(int year, int partNumber):
47:       itsModelYear(year),
48:       Part(partNumber)
49:   {}
50:
51:
52:   // *************** AirPlane Part ************
53:
54:   class AirPlanePart : public Part
55:   {
56:   public:
57:       AirPlanePart():itsEngineNumber(1){};
58:       AirPlanePart
59:       (int EngineNumber, int PartNumber);
60:       virtual void Display() const
61:       {
62:       Part::Display();
63:       cout << "Engine No.: ";
64:       cout << itsEngineNumber << endl;
65:       }
66:   private:
67:       int itsEngineNumber;
68:   };
69:
70:   AirPlanePart::AirPlanePart
```

LISTING 16.5 continued

16

```
71:  (int EngineNumber, int PartNumber):
72:      itsEngineNumber(EngineNumber),
73:      Part(PartNumber)
74:  {}
75:
76:  // *************** Part Node ************
77:  class PartNode
78:  {
79:  public:
80:      PartNode (Part*);
81:      ~PartNode();
82:      void SetNext(PartNode * node)
83:          { itsNext = node; }
84:      PartNode * GetNext() const;
85:      Part * GetPart() const;
86:  private:
87:      Part *itsPart;
88:      PartNode * itsNext;
89:  };
90:  // PartNode Implementations...
91:
92:  PartNode::PartNode(Part* pPart):
93:      itsPart(pPart),
94:      itsNext(0)
95:  {}
96:
97:  PartNode::~PartNode()
98:  {
99:      delete itsPart;
100:     itsPart = 0;
101:     delete itsNext;
102:     itsNext = 0;
103: }
104:
105: // Returns NULL if no next PartNode
106: PartNode * PartNode::GetNext() const
107: {
108:     return itsNext;
109: }
110:
111: Part * PartNode::GetPart() const
112: {
113:     if (itsPart)
114:         return itsPart;
115:     else
116:         return NULL; //error
117: }
118:
119:
```

LISTING 16.5   continued

```
120:
121:   // **************** Part List ************
122:   class PartsList
123:   {
124:   public:
125:      PartsList();
126:      ~PartsList();
127:      // needs copy constructor and operator equals!
128:      void      Iterate(void (Part::*f)()const) const;
129:      Part*     Find(int & position, int PartNumber)  const;
130:      Part*     GetFirst() const;
131:      void      Insert(Part *);
132:      Part*     operator[](int) const;
133:      int       GetCount() const { return itsCount; }
134:      static    PartsList& GetGlobalPartsList()
135:      {
136:      return  GlobalPartsList;
137:      }
138:   private:
139:      PartNode * pHead;
140:      int itsCount;
141:      static PartsList GlobalPartsList;
142:   };
143:
144:   PartsList PartsList::GlobalPartsList;
145:
146:
147:   PartsList::PartsList():
148:      pHead(0),
149:      itsCount(0)
150:   {}
151:
152:   PartsList::~PartsList()
153:   {
154:      delete pHead;
155:   }
156:
157:   Part*   PartsList::GetFirst() const
158:   {
159:      if (pHead)
160:         return pHead->GetPart();
161:      else
162:         return NULL;  // error catch here
163:   }
164:
165:   Part *  PartsList::operator[](int offSet) const
166:   {
167:      PartNode* pNode = pHead;
168:
```

LISTING 16.5   continued

16

```
169:     if (!pHead)
170:         return NULL; // error catch here
171:
172:     if (offSet > itsCount)
173:         return NULL; // error
174:
175:     for (int i-0;i<offSet; i++)
176:         pNode = pNode->GetNext();
177:
178:     return   pNode->GetPart();
179: }
180:
181: Part*   PartsList::Find(
182:     int & position,
183:     int PartNumber)  const
184: {
185:     PartNode * pNode = 0;
186:     for (pNode = pHead, position = 0;
187:           pNode!=NULL;
188:           pNode = pNode->GetNext(), position++)
189:     {
190:        if (pNode->GetPart()->GetPartNumber() == PartNumber)
191:           break;
192:     }
193:     if (pNode == NULL)
194:        return NULL;
195:     else
196:        return pNode->GetPart();
197: }
198:
199: void PartsList::Iterate(void (Part::*func)()const) const
200: {
201:     if (!pHead)
202:        return;
203:     PartNode* pNode = pHead;
204:     do
205:        (pNode->GetPart()->*func)();
206:     while (pNode = pNode->GetNext());
207: }
208:
209: void PartsList::Insert(Part* pPart)
210: {
211:     PartNode * pNode = new PartNode(pPart);
212:     PartNode * pCurrent = pHead;
213:     PartNode * pNext = 0;
214:
215:     int New =  pPart->GetPartNumber();
216:     int Next = 0;
```

LISTING 16.5   continued

```
217:        itsCount++;
218:
219:        if (!pHead)
220:        {
221:           pHead = pNode;
222:           return;
223:        }
224:
225:        // if this one is smaller than head
226:        // this one is the new head
227:        if (pHead->GetPart()->GetPartNumber() > New)
228:        {
229:           pNode->SetNext(pHead);
230:           pHead = pNode;
231:           return;
232:        }
233:
234:        for (;;)
235:        {
236:           // if there is no next, append this new one
237:           if (!pCurrent->GetNext())
238:           {
239:              pCurrent->SetNext(pNode);
240:              return;
241:           }
242:
243:           // if this goes after this one and before the next
244:           // then insert it here, otherwise get the next
245:           pNext = pCurrent->GetNext();
246:           Next = pNext->GetPart()->GetPartNumber();
247:           if (Next > New)
248:           {
249:              pCurrent->SetNext(pNode);
250:              pNode->SetNext(pNext);
251:              return;
252:           }
253:           pCurrent = pNext;
254:        }
255:     }
256:
257:
258:
259:  class PartsCatalog
260:  {
261:  public:
262:     void Insert(Part *);
263:     int Exists(int PartNumber);
264:     Part * Get(int PartNumber);
265:     operator+(const PartsCatalog &);
```

LISTING 16.5   continued

```
266:     void ShowAll() { thePartsList.Iterate(Part::Display); }
267:  private:
268:     PartsList thePartsList;
269:  };
270:
271:  void PartsCatalog::Insert(Part * newPart)
272:  {
273:     int partNumber =  newPart->GetPartNumber();
274:     int offset;
275:
276:     if (!thePartsList.Find(offset, partNumber))
277:        thePartsList.Insert(newPart);
278:     else
279:     {
280:        cout << partNumber << " was the ";
281:        switch (offset)
282:        {
283:        case 0:  cout << "first "; break;
284:        case 1:  cout << "second "; break;
285:        case 2:  cout << "third "; break;
286:        default: cout << offset+1 << "th ";
287:        }
288:        cout << "entry. Rejected!\n";
289:     }
290:  }
291:
292:  int PartsCatalog::Exists(int PartNumber)
293:  {
294:     int offset;
295:     thePartsList.Find(offset,PartNumber);
296:     return offset;
297:  }
298:
299:  Part * PartsCatalog::Get(int PartNumber)
300:  {
301:     int offset;
302:     Part * thePart = thePartsList.Find(offset, PartNumber);
303:     return thePart;
304:  }
305:
306:
307:  int main()
308:  {
309:     PartsCatalog pc;
310:     Part * pPart = 0;
311:     int PartNumber;
312:     int value;
313:     int choice;
314:
```

16

LISTING 16.5   continued

```
315:     while (1)
316:     {
317:        cout << "(0)Quit (1)Car (2)Plane: ";
318:        cin >> choice;
319:
320:        if (!choice)
321:        break;
322:
323:        cout << "New PartNumber?: ";
324:        cin >>  PartNumber;
325:
326:        if (choice == 1)
327:        {
328:           cout << "Model Year?: ";
329:           cin >> value;
330:           pPart = new CarPart(value,PartNumber);
331:        }
332:        else
333:        {
334:           cout << "Engine Number?: ";
335:           cin >> value;
336:           pPart = new AirPlanePart(value,PartNumber);
337:        }
338:        pc.Insert(pPart);
339:     }
340:     pc.ShowAll();
341:     return 0;
342: }
```

OUTPUT

```
(0)Quit (1)Car (2)Plane:  1
New PartNumber?: 1234
Model Year?: 94
(0)Quit (1)Car (2)Plane:  1
New PartNumber?: 4434
Model Year?: 93
(0)Quit (1)Car (2)Plane:  1
New PartNumber?: 1234
Model Year?: 94
1234 was the first entry. Rejected!
(0)Quit (1)Car (2)Plane:  1
New PartNumber?: 2345
Model Year?: 93
(0)Quit (1)Car (2)Plane:  0

Part Number: 1234
Model Year: 94
```

```
Part Number: 2345
Model Year: 93

Part Number: 4434
Model Year: 93
```

Note

Some compilers cannot compile line 267, even though it is legal C++. If your compiler complains about this line, change it to

```
267:         void ShowAll() { thePartsList.Iterate(&Part::Display); }
```

(Note the addition of the ampersand in front of Part::Display). If that fixes the problem, immediately call your compiler vendor and complain.

16

ANALYSIS Listing 16.5 reproduces the Part, PartNode, and PartsList classes from Week 2 in Review.

A new class, PartsCatalog, is declared on lines 259–269. PartsCatalog has a PartsList as its data member, to which it delegates list management. Another way to say this is that the PartsCatalog is implemented in terms of this PartsList.

Note that clients of the PartsCatalog do not have access to the PartsList directly. The interface is through the PartsCatalog, and as such, the behavior of the PartsList is dramatically changed. For example, the PartsCatalog::Insert() method does not allow duplicate entries into the PartsList.

The implementation of PartsCatalog::Insert() starts on line 271. The Part that is passed in as a parameter is asked for the value of its itsPartNumber member variable. This value is fed to the PartsList's Find() method, and if no match is found, the number is inserted; otherwise, an informative error message is printed.

Note that PartsCatalog does the actual insert by calling Insert() on its member variable, pl, which is a PartsList. The mechanics of the actual insertion and the maintenance of the linked list, as well as searching and retrieving from the linked list, are maintained in the contained PartsList member of PartsCatalog. No reason exists for PartsCatalog to reproduce this code; it can take full advantage of the well-defined interface.

This is the essence of reusability within C++: PartsCatalog can reuse the PartsList code, and the designer of PartsCatalog is free to ignore the implementation details of PartsList. The interface to PartsList (that is, the class declaration) provides all the information needed by the designer of the PartsCatalog class.

Private Inheritance

If PartsCatalog needed access to the protected members of PartsList (in this case, none exist), or needed to override any of the PartsList methods, then PartsCatalog would be forced to inherit from PartsList.

Because a PartsCatalog is not a PartsList object, and because you don't want to expose the entire set of functionality of PartsList to clients of PartsCatalog, you need to use private inheritance.

The first thing to know about private inheritance is that all the base member variables and functions are treated as if they were declared to be private, regardless of their actual access level in the base. Thus, to any function that is not a member function of PartsCatalog, every function inherited from PartsList is inaccessible. This is critical: Private inheritance does not involve inheriting interface, only implementation.

To clients of the PartsCatalog class, the PartsList class is invisible. None of its interface is available to them: They can't call any of its methods. They can call PartsCatalog methods, however; PartsCatalog methods can then access all of PartsList because PartsCatalog is derived from PartsList. The important thing here is that the PartsCatalog isn't a PartsList, as would have been implied by public inheritance. It is implemented in terms of a PartsList, just as would have been the case with containment. The private inheritance is just a convenience.

Listing 16.6 demonstrates the use of private inheritance by rewriting the PartsCatalog class as privately derived from PartsList.

LISTING **16.6**   Private Inheritance

```
0:   //Listing 16.6 demonstrates private inheritance
1:   #include <iostream>
2:   using namespace std;
3:
4:   // *************** Part ***********
5:
6:   // Abstract base class of parts
7:   class Part
8:   {
9:   public:
10:      Part():itsPartNumber(1) {}
11:      Part(int PartNumber):
12:      itsPartNumber(PartNumber){}
13:      virtual ~Part(){}
14:      int GetPartNumber() const
15:         { return itsPartNumber; }
16:      virtual void Display() const =0;
```

LISTING 16.6   continued

16

```
17:  private:
18:     int itsPartNumber;
19:  };
20:
21:  // implementation of pure virtual function so that
22:  // derived classes can chain up
23:  void Part::Display() const
24:  {
25:     cout << "\nPart Number: " << itsPartNumber << endl;
26:  }
27:
28:  // *************** Car Part ***********
29:
30:  class CarPart : public Part
31:  {
32:  public:
33:     CarPart():itsModelYear(94){}
34:     CarPart(int year, int partNumber);
35:     virtual void Display() const
36:     {
37:        Part::Display();
38:        cout << "Model Year: ";
39:        cout << itsModelYear << endl;
40:     }
41:  private:
42:     int itsModelYear;
43:  };
44:
45:  CarPart::CarPart(int year, int partNumber):
46:     itsModelYear(year),
47:     Part(partNumber)
48:  {}
49:
50:
51:  // *************** AirPlane Part ***********
52:
53:  class AirPlanePart : public Part
54:  {
55:  public:
56:     AirPlanePart():itsEngineNumber(1){};
57:     AirPlanePart(int EngineNumber, int PartNumber);
58:     virtual void Display() const
59:     {
60:        Part::Display();
61:        cout << "Engine No.: ";
62:        cout << itsEngineNumber << endl;
63:     }
64:  private:
65:     int itsEngineNumber;
```

LISTING 16.6   continued

```
66:  };
67:
68:  AirPlanePart::AirPlanePart
69:  (int EngineNumber, int PartNumber):
70:     itsEngineNumber(EngineNumber),
71:     Part(PartNumber)
72:  {}
73:
74:  // *************** Part Node ***********
75:  class PartNode
76:  {
77:  public:
78:     PartNode (Part*);
79:     ~PartNode();
80:     void SetNext(PartNode * node)
81:        { itsNext = node; }
82:     PartNode * GetNext() const;
83:     Part * GetPart() const;
84:  private:
85:     Part *itsPart;
86:     PartNode * itsNext;
87:  };
88:  // PartNode Implementations...
89:
90:  PartNode::PartNode(Part* pPart):
91:     itsPart(pPart),
92:     itsNext(0)
93:  {}
94:
95:  PartNode::~PartNode()
96:  {
97:     delete itsPart;
98:     itsPart = 0;
99:     delete itsNext;
100:     itsNext = 0;
101:  }
102:
103:  // Returns NULL if no next PartNode
104:  PartNode * PartNode::GetNext() const
105:  {
106:     return itsNext;
107:  }
108:
109:  Part * PartNode::GetPart() const
110:  {
111:     if (itsPart)
112:        return itsPart;
113:     else
```

LISTING **16.6**   continued

```
114:           return NULL; //error
115:    }
116:
117:
118:
119:    // *************** Part List ************
120:    class PartsList
121:    {
122:    public:
123:       PartsList();
124:       ~PartsList();
125:       // needs copy constructor and operator equals!
126:       void     Iterate(void (Part::*f)()const) const;
127:       Part*    Find(int & position, int PartNumber)  const;
128:       Part*    GetFirst() const;
129:       void     Insert(Part *);
130:       Part*    operator[](int) const;
131:       int    GetCount() const { return itsCount; }
132:       static    PartsList& GetGlobalPartsList()
133:       {
134:          return  GlobalPartsList;
135:       }
136:    private:
137:       PartNode * pHead;
138:       int itsCount;
139:       static PartsList GlobalPartsList;
140:    };
141:
142:    PartsList PartsList::GlobalPartsList;
143:
144:
145:    PartsList::PartsList():
146:       pHead(0),
147:       itsCount(0)
148:    {}
149:
150:    PartsList::~PartsList()
151:    {
152:       delete pHead;
153:    }
154:
155:    Part*   PartsList::GetFirst() const
156:    {
157:       if (pHead)
158:          return pHead->GetPart();
159:       else
160:          return NULL;  // error catch here
161:    }
162:
```

LISTING 16.6   continued

```
163:  Part *  PartsList::operator[](int offSet) const
164:  {
165:     PartNode* pNode = pHead;
166:
167:     if (!pHead)
168:        return NULL; // error catch here
169:
170:     if (offSet > itsCount)
171:        return NULL; // error
172:
173:     for (int i=0;i<offSet; i++)
174:        pNode = pNode->GetNext();
175:
176:     return   pNode->GetPart();
177:  }
178:
179:  Part*   PartsList::Find(int & position, int PartNumber)   const
180:  {
181:     PartNode * pNode = 0;
182:     for (pNode = pHead, position = 0;
183:        pNode!=NULL;
184:     pNode = pNode->GetNext(), position++)
185:     {
186:        if (pNode->GetPart()->GetPartNumber() == PartNumber)
187:        break;
188:     }
189:     if (pNode == NULL)
190:        return NULL;
191:     else
192:        return pNode->GetPart();
193:  }
194:
195:  void PartsList::Iterate(void (Part::*func)()const) const
196:  {
197:     if (!pHead)
198:        return;
199:     PartNode* pNode = pHead;
200:     do
201:        (pNode->GetPart()->*func)();
202:     while (pNode = pNode->GetNext());
203:  }
204:
205:  void PartsList::Insert(Part* pPart)
206:  {
207:     PartNode * pNode = new PartNode(pPart);
208:     PartNode * pCurrent = pHead;
209:     PartNode * pNext = 0;
210:
211:     int New =  pPart->GetPartNumber();
```

LISTING 16.6   continued

```
212:      int Next = 0;
213:      itsCount++;
214:
215:      if (!pHead)
216:      {
217:         pHead = pNode;
218:         return;
219:      }
220:
221:      // if this one is smaller than head
222:      // this one is the new head
223:      if (pHead->GetPart()->GetPartNumber() > New)
224:      {
225:         pNode->SetNext(pHead);
226:         pHead = pNode;
227:         return;
228:      }
229:
230:      for (;;)
231:      {
232:         // if there is no next, append this new one
233:         if (!pCurrent->GetNext())
234:         {
235:            pCurrent->SetNext(pNode);
236:            return;
237:         }
238:
239:         // if this goes after this one and before the next
240:         // then insert it here, otherwise get the next
241:         pNext = pCurrent->GetNext();
242:         Next = pNext->GetPart()->GetPartNumber();
243:         if (Next > New)
244:         {
245:            pCurrent->SetNext(pNode);
246:            pNode->SetNext(pNext);
247:            return;
248:         }
249:         pCurrent = pNext;
250:      }
251:   }
252:
253:
254:
255:   class PartsCatalog : private PartsList
256:   {
257:   public:
258:      void Insert(Part *);
259:      int Exists(int PartNumber);
260:      Part * Get(int PartNumber);
```

16

LISTING **16.6**   continued

```
261:        operator+(const PartsCatalog &);
262:        void ShowAll() { Iterate(Part::Display); }
263:    private:
264:    };
265:
266:    void PartsCatalog::Insert(Part * newPart)
267:    {
268:        int partNumber =  newPart->GetPartNumber();
269:        int offset;
270:
271:        if (!Find(offset, partNumber))
272:            PartsList::Insert(newPart);
273:        else
274:        {
275:            cout << partNumber << " was the ";
276:            switch (offset)
277:            {
278:            case 0:  cout << "first "; break;
279:            case 1:  cout << "second "; break;
280:            case 2:  cout << "third "; break;
281:            default: cout << offset+1 << "th ";
282:            }
283:            cout << "entry. Rejected!\n";
284:        }
285:    }
286:
287:    int PartsCatalog::Exists(int PartNumber)
288:    {
289:        int offset;
290:        Find(offset,PartNumber);
291:        return offset;
292:    }
293:
294:    Part * PartsCatalog::Get(int PartNumber)
295:    {
296:        int offset;
297:        return (Find(offset, PartNumber));
298:
299:    }
300:
301:    int main()
302:    {
303:        PartsCatalog pc;
304:        Part * pPart = 0;
305:        int PartNumber;
306:        int value;
307:        int choice;
308:
309:        while (1)
```

LISTING 16.6   continued

```
310:    {
311:        cout << "(0)Quit (1)Car (2)Plane: ";
312:        cin >> choice;
313:
314:        if (!choice)
315:        break;
316:
317:        cout << "New PartNumber?: ";
318:        cin >>  PartNumber;
319:
320:        if (choice == 1)
321:        {
322:           cout << "Model Year?: ";
323:           cin >> value;
324:           pPart = new CarPart(value,PartNumber);
325:        }
326:        else
327:        {
328:           cout << "Engine Number?: ";
329:           cin >> value;
330:           pPart = new AirPlanePart(value,PartNumber);
331:        }
332:        pc.Insert(pPart);
333:    }
334:    pc.ShowAll();
335:    return 0;
336: }
```

OUTPUT

```
(0)Quit (1)Car (2)Plane:  1
New PartNumber?: 1234
Model Year?: 94
(0)Quit (1)Car (2)Plane:  1
New PartNumber?: 4434
Model Year?: 93
(0)Quit (1)Car (2)Plane:  1
New PartNumber?: 1234
Model Year?: 94
1234 was the first entry. Rejected!
(0)Quit (1)Car (2)Plane:  1
New PartNumber?: 2345
Model Year?: 93
(0)Quit (1)Car (2)Plane:  0

Part Number: 1234
Model Year: 94

Part Number: 2345
Model Year: 93
```

```
Part Number: 4434
Model Year: 93
```

ANALYSIS Listing 16.6 shows a changed interface to PartsCatalog and the rewritten driver program. The interfaces to the other classes are unchanged from Listing 16.5.

On line 255 of Listing 16.6, PartsCatalog is declared to derive privately from PartsList. The interface to PartsCatalog doesn't change from Listing 16.5, although, of course, it no longer needs an object of type PartsList as member data.

The PartsCatalog ShowAll() function calls PartsList Iterate() with the appropriate pointer to member function of class Part. ShowAll() acts as a public interface to Iterate(), providing the correct information but preventing client classes from calling Iterate() directly. Although PartsList might allow other functions to be passed to Iterate(), PartsCatalog does not.

The Insert() function has changed as well. Note, on line 273, that Find() is now called directly because it is inherited from the base class. The call on line 272 to Insert() must be fully qualified, of course, or it would endlessly recurse into itself.

In short, when methods of PartsCatalog want to call PartsList methods, they may do so directly. The only exception is when PartsCatalog has overridden the method and the PartsList version is needed, in which case the function name must be qualified fully.

Private inheritance enables the PartsCatalog to inherit what it can use, but still provides mediated access to Insert and other methods to which client classes should not have direct access.

Do	Don't
DO inherit publicly when the derived object is a kind of the base class.	**DON'T** use private inheritance when you need to use more than one of the base class. You must use containment. For example, if PartsCatalog needed two PartsLists, you could not have used private inheritance.
DO use containment when you want to delegate functionality to another class, but you don't need access to its protected members.	
DO use private inheritance when you need to implement one class in terms of another, and you need access to the base class's protected members.	**DON'T** use public inheritance when members of the base class should not be available to clients of the derived class.

Friend Classes

Sometimes you will create classes together, as a set. For example, `PartNode` and `PartsList` were tightly coupled, and it would have been convenient if `PartsList` could have read `PartNode`'s `Part` pointer, `itsPart`, directly.

You wouldn't want to make `itsPart` public, or even protected, because this is an implementation detail of `PartNode` and you want to keep it private. You do want to expose it to `PartsList`, however.

If you want to expose your private member data or functions to another class, you must declare that class to be a friend. This extends the interface of your class to include the friend class.

After `PartsNode` declares `PartsList` to be a friend, all `PartsNode`'s member data and functions are public as far as `PartsList` is concerned.

It is important to note that friendship cannot be transferred. Although you are my friend and Joe is your friend, that doesn't mean Joe is my friend. Friendship is not inherited, either. Again, although you are my friend and I'm willing to share my secrets with you, that doesn't mean I'm willing to share my secrets with your children.

Finally, friendship is not commutative. Assigning Class One to be a friend of Class Two does not make Class Two a friend of Class One. You may be willing to tell me your secrets, but that doesn't mean I am willing to tell you mine.

Listing 16.7 illustrates friendship by rewriting the example from Listing 16.6, making `PartsList` a friend of `PartNode`. Note that this does not make `PartNode` a friend of `PartsList`.

LISTING 16.7   Friend Class Illustrated

```
0:   //Listing 16.7 Friend Class Illustrated
1:
2:   #include <iostream>
3:   using namespace std;
4:
5:   // *************** Part ************
6:
7:   // Abstract base class of parts
8:   class Part
9:   {
10:  public:
11:      Part():itsPartNumber(1) {}
12:      Part(int PartNumber):
13:      itsPartNumber(PartNumber){}
14:      virtual ~Part(){}
```

16

LISTING 16.7   continued

```
15:      int GetPartNumber() const
16:          { return itsPartNumber; }
17:      virtual void Display() const =0;
18:  private:
19:      int itsPartNumber;
20:  };
21:
22:  // implementation of pure virtual function so that
23:  // derived classes can chain up
24:  void Part::Display() const
25:  {
26:      cout << "\nPart Number: ";
27:      cout << itsPartNumber << endl;
28:  }
29:
30:  // **************** Car Part ************
31:
32:  class CarPart : public Part
33:  {
34:  public:
35:      CarPart():itsModelYear(94){}
36:      CarPart(int year, int partNumber);
37:      virtual void Display() const
38:      {
39:          Part::Display();
40:          cout << "Model Year: ";
41:          cout << itsModelYear << endl;
42:      }
43:  private:
44:      int itsModelYear;
45:  };
46:
47:  CarPart::CarPart(int year, int partNumber):
48:      itsModelYear(year),
49:      Part(partNumber)
50:  {}
51:
52:
53:  // **************** AirPlane Part ************
54:
55:  class AirPlanePart : public Part
56:  {
57:  public:
58:      AirPlanePart():itsEngineNumber(1){};
59:      AirPlanePart(int EngineNumber, int PartNumber);
60:      virtual void Display() const
61:      {
62:          Part::Display();
63:          cout << "Engine No.: ";
```

LISTING 16.7   continued

```
64:          cout << itsEngineNumber << endl;
65:      }
66:  private:
67:      int itsEngineNumber;
68:  };
69:
70:  AirPlanePart::AirPlanePart(int EngineNumber, int PartNumber):
71:      itsEngineNumber(EngineNumber),
72:      Part(PartNumber)
73:  {}
74:
75:  // *************** Part Node ************
76:  class PartNode
77:  {
78:  public:
79:      friend class PartsList;
80:      PartNode (Part*);
81:      ~PartNode();
82:      void SetNext(PartNode * node)
83:          { itsNext = node; }
84:      PartNode * GetNext() const;
85:      Part * GetPart() const;
86:  private:
87:      Part *itsPart;
88:      PartNode * itsNext;
89:  };
90:
91:
92:  PartNode::PartNode(Part* pPart):
93:      itsPart(pPart),
94:      itsNext(0)
95:  {}
96:
97:  PartNode::~PartNode()
98:  {
99:      delete itsPart;
100:     itsPart = 0;
101:     delete itsNext;
102:     itsNext = 0;
103: }
104:
105: // Returns NULL if no next PartNode
106: PartNode * PartNode::GetNext() const
107: {
108:     return itsNext;
109: }
110:
111: Part * PartNode::GetPart() const
112: {
```

16

LISTING 16.7   continued

```
113:    if (itsPart)
114:        return itsPart;
115:    else
116:        return NULL; //error
117: }
118:
119:
120: // *************** Part List ************
121: class PartsList
122: {
123: public:
124:     PartsList();
125:     ~PartsList();
126:     // needs copy constructor and operator equals!
127:     void     Iterate(void (Part::*f)()const) const;
128:     Part*    Find(int & position, int PartNumber) const;
129:     Part*    GetFirst() const;
130:     void     Insert(Part *);
131:     Part*    operator[](int) const;
132:     int      GetCount() const { return itsCount; }
133:     static   PartsList& GetGlobalPartsList()
134:     {
135:         return  GlobalPartsList;
136:     }
137: private:
138:     PartNode * pHead;
139:     int itsCount;
140:     static PartsList GlobalPartsList;
141: };
142:
143: PartsList PartsList::GlobalPartsList;
144:
145: // Implementations for Lists...
146:
147: PartsList::PartsList():
148:     pHead(0),
149:     itsCount(0)
150: {}
151:
152: PartsList::~PartsList()
153: {
154:     delete pHead;
155: }
156:
157: Part*   PartsList::GetFirst() const
158: {
159:     if (pHead)
160:         return pHead->itsPart;
161:     else
```

LISTING 16.7   continued

```
162:           return NULL;  // error catch here
163:    }
164:
165:    Part * PartsList::operator[](int offSet) const
166:    {
167:       PartNode* pNode = pHead;
168:
169:       if (!pHead)
170:          return NULL; // error catch here
171:
172:       if (offSet > itsCount)
173:          return NULL; // error
174:
175:       for (int i=0;i<offSet; i++)
176:          pNode = pNode->itsNext;
177:
178:       return   pNode->itsPart;
179:    }
180:
181:    Part* PartsList::Find(int & position, int PartNumber) const
182:    {
183:       PartNode * pNode = 0;
184:       for (pNode = pHead, position = 0;
185:          pNode!=NULL;
186:       pNode = pNode->itsNext, position++)
187:       {
188:          if (pNode->itsPart->GetPartNumber() == PartNumber)
189:             break;
190:       }
191:       if (pNode == NULL)
192:          return NULL;
193:       else
194:          return pNode->itsPart;
195:    }
196:
197:    void PartsList::Iterate(void (Part::*func)()const) const
198:    {
199:       if (!pHead)
200:          return;
201:       PartNode* pNode = pHead;
202:       do
203:          (pNode->itsPart->*func)();
204:       while (pNode = pNode->itsNext);
205:    }
206:
207:    void PartsList::Insert(Part* pPart)
208:    {
209:       PartNode * pNode = new PartNode(pPart);
210:       PartNode * pCurrent = pHead;
```

LISTING 16.7 continued

```
211:      PartNode * pNext = 0;
212:
213:      int New =  pPart->GetPartNumber();
214:      int Next = 0;
215:      itsCount++;
216:
217:      if (!pHead)
218:      {
219:         pHead = pNode;
220:         return;
221:      }
222:
223:      // if this one is smaller than head
224:      // this one is the new head
225:      if (pHead->itsPart->GetPartNumber() > New)
226:      {
227:         pNode->itsNext = pHead;
228:         pHead = pNode;
229:         return;
230:      }
231:
232:      for (;;)
233:      {
234:         // if there is no next, append this new one
235:         if (!pCurrent->itsNext)
236:         {
237:            pCurrent->itsNext = pNode;
238:            return;
239:         }
240:
241:         // if this goes after this one and before the next
242:         // then insert it here, otherwise get the next
243:         pNext = pCurrent->itsNext;
244:         Next = pNext->itsPart->GetPartNumber();
245:         if (Next > New)
246:         {
247:            pCurrent->itsNext = pNode;
248:            pNode->itsNext = pNext;
249:            return;
250:         }
251:         pCurrent = pNext;
252:      }
253:   }
254:
255: class PartsCatalog : private PartsList
256: {
257: public:
258:      void Insert(Part *);
259:      int Exists(int PartNumber);
```

LISTING 16.7   continued

```
260:       Part * Get(int PartNumber);
261:       operator+(const PartsCatalog &);
262:       void ShowAll() { Iterate(Part::Display); }
263:  private:
264:  };
265:
266:  void PartsCatalog::Insert(Part * newPart)
267:  {
268:      int partNumber =  newPart->GetPartNumber();
269:      int offset;
270:
271:      if (!Find(offset, partNumber))
272:          PartsList::Insert(newPart);
273:      else
274:      {
275:          cout << partNumber << " was the ";
276:          switch (offset)
277:          {
278:          case 0:  cout << "first "; break;
279:          case 1:  cout << "second "; break;
280:          case 2:  cout << "third "; break;
281:          default: cout << offset+1 << "th ";
282:          }
283:          cout << "entry. Rejected!\n";
284:      }
285:  }
286:
287:  int PartsCatalog::Exists(int PartNumber)
288:  {
289:      int offset;
290:      Find(offset,PartNumber);
291:      return offset;
292:  }
293:
294:  Part * PartsCatalog::Get(int PartNumber)
295:  {
296:      int offset;
297:      return (Find(offset, PartNumber));
298:  }
299:
300:  int main()
301:  {
302:      PartsCatalog pc;
303:      Part * pPart = 0;
304:      int PartNumber;
305:      int value;
306:      int choice;
307:
308:      while (1)
```

LISTING 16.7   continued

```
309:     {
310:        cout << "(0)Quit (1)Car (2)Plane: ";
311:        cin >> choice;
312:
313:        if (!choice)
314:           break;
315:
316:        cout << "New PartNumber?: ";
317:        cin >>  PartNumber;
318:
319:        if (choice == 1)
320:        {
321:           cout << "Model Year?: ";
322:           cin >> value;
323:           pPart = new CarPart(value,PartNumber);
324:        }
325:        else
326:        {
327:           cout << "Engine Number?: ";
328:           cin >> value;
329:           pPart = new AirPlanePart(value,PartNumber);
330:        }
331:        pc.Insert(pPart);
332:     }
333:     pc.ShowAll();
334:     return 0;
335:  }
```

OUTPUT

```
(0)Quit (1)Car (2)Plane:  1
New PartNumber?: 1234
Model Year?: 94
(0)Quit (1)Car (2)Plane:  1
New PartNumber?: 4434
Model Year?: 93
(0)Quit (1)Car (2)Plane:  1
New PartNumber?: 1234
Model Year?: 94
1234 was the first entry. Rejected!
(0)Quit (1)Car (2)Plane:  1
New PartNumber?: 2345
Model Year?: 93
(0)Quit (1)Car (2)Plane:  0

Part Number: 1234
Model Year: 94

Part Number: 2345
Model Year: 93
```

```
Part Number: 4434
Model Year: 93
```

ANALYSIS On line 79, the class `PartsList` is declared to be a friend to the `PartNode` class.

This listing places the friend declaration in the public section, but this is not required; it can be put anywhere in the class declaration without changing the meaning of the statement. Because of this statement, all the private member data and functions are available to any member function of class `PartsList`.

On line 157, the implementation of the member function `GetFirst()` reflects this change. Rather than returning `pHead->GetPart`, this function can now return the otherwise private member data by writing `pHead->itsPart`. Similarly, the `Insert()` function can now write `pNode->itsNext = pHead`, rather than writing `pNode->SetNext(pHead)`.

Admittedly, these are trivial changes, and a good enough reason does not exist to make `PartsList` a friend of `PartNode`, but they do serve to illustrate how the keyword `friend` works.

Declarations of `friend` classes should be used with extreme caution. If two classes are inextricably entwined, and one must frequently access data in the other, good reason may exist to use this declaration. But use it sparingly; it is often just as easy to use the public accessor methods, and doing so enables you to change one class without having to recompile the other.

Note

You will often hear novice C++ programmers complain that friend declarations "undermine" the encapsulation so important to object-oriented programming. This is, frankly, errant nonsense. The friend declaration makes the declared friend part of the class interface and is no more an undermining of encapsulation than is public derivation.

Friend Class

Declare one class to be a friend of another by putting the word `friend` into the class granting the access rights. That is, I can declare you to be my friend, but you can't declare yourself to be my friend.

Example

```
class PartNode{
public:
friend class PartsList;  // declares PartsList to be a friend of
PartNode
};
```

Friend Functions

At times, you will want to grant this level of access not to an entire class, but only to one or two functions of that class. You can do this by declaring the member functions of the other class to be friends, rather than declaring the entire class to be a friend. In fact, you can declare any function, whether or not it is a member function of another class, to be a friend function.

Friend Functions and Operator Overloading

Listing 16.1 provided a String class that overrode the operator+. It also provided a constructor that took a constant character pointer, so that string objects could be created from C-style strings. This enabled you to create a string and add to it with a C-style string.

Note   C-style strings are null-terminated character arrays, such as char myString[] = "Hello World".

What you could not do, however, was create a C-style string (a character string) and add to it using a string object, as shown in this example:

```
char cString[] = {"Hello"};
String sString(" World");
String sStringTwo = cString + sString;   //error!
```

C-style strings don't have an overloaded operator+. As discussed on Day 10, "Advanced Functions," when you say cString + sString; what you are really calling is cString.operator+(sString). Because you can't call operator+() on a C-style string, this causes a compile-time error.

You can solve this problem by declaring a friend function in String, which overloads operator+ but takes two string objects. The C-style string will be converted to a string object by the appropriate constructor, and then operator+ will be called using the two string objects.

LISTING 16.8   Friendly operator+

```
0:  //Listing 16.8 - friendly operators
1:
2:  #include <iostream>
3:  #include <string.h>
4:  using namespace std;
```

LISTING 16.8 continued

```
5:
6:     // Rudimentary string class
7:     class String
8:     {
9:     public:
10:        // constructors
11:        String();
12:        String(const char *const);
13:        String(const String &);
14:        ~String();
15:
16:        // overloaded operators
17:        char & operator[](int offset);
18:        char operator[](int offset) const;
19:        String operator+(const String&);
20:        friend String operator+(const String&, const String&);
21:        void operator+=(const String&);
22:        String & operator= (const String &);
23:
24:        // General accessors
25:        int GetLen()const { return itsLen; }
26:        const char * GetString() const { return itsString; }
27:
28:     private:
29:        String (int);          // private constructor
30:        char * itsString;
31:        unsigned short itsLen;
32:     };
33:
34:     // default constructor creates string of 0 bytes
35:     String::String()
36:     {
37:        itsString = new char[1];
38:        itsString[0] = '\0';
39:        itsLen=0;
40:        // cout << "\tDefault string constructor\n";
41:        // ConstructorCount++;
42:     }
43:
44:     // private (helper) constructor, used only by
45:     // class methods for creating a new string of
46:     // required size.  Null filled.
47:     String::String(int len)
48:     {
49:        itsString = new char[len+1];
50:        for (int i = 0; i<=len; i++)
51:           itsString[i] = '\0';
52:        itsLen=len;
53:        // cout << "\tString(int) constructor\n";
```

LISTING 16.8   continued

```
54:     // ConstructorCount++;
55:  }
56:
57:  // Converts a character array to a String
58:  String::String(const char * const cString)
59:  {
60:     itsLen = strlen(cString);
61:     itsString = new char[itsLen+1];
62:     for (int i = 0; i<itsLen; i++)
63:        itsString[i] = cString[i];
64:     itsString[itsLen]='\0';
65:     // cout << "\tString(char*) constructor\n";
66:     // ConstructorCount++;
67:  }
68:
69:  // copy constructor
70:  String::String (const String & rhs)
71:  {
72:     itsLen=rhs.GetLen();
73:     itsString = new char[itsLen+1];
74:     for (int i = 0; i<itsLen;i++)
75:        itsString[i] = rhs[i];
76:     itsString[itsLen] = '\0';
77:     // cout << "\tString(String&) constructor\n";
78:     // ConstructorCount++;
79:  }
80:
81:  // destructor, frees allocated memory
82:  String::~String ()
83:  {
84:     delete [] itsString;
85:     itsLen = 0;
86:     // cout << "\tString destructor\n";
87:  }
88:
89:  // operator equals, frees existing memory
90:  // then copies string and size
91:  String& String::operator=(const String & rhs)
92:  {
93:     if (this == &rhs)
94:        return *this;
95:     delete [] itsString;
96:     itsLen=rhs.GetLen();
97:     itsString = new char[itsLen+1];
98:     for (int i = 0; i<itsLen;i++)
99:        itsString[i] = rhs[i];
100:    itsString[itsLen] = '\0';
101:    return *this;
102:    // cout << "\tString operator=\n";
```

LISTING 16.8   continued

16

```
103:   }
104:
105:   //non constant offset operator, returns
106:   // reference to character so it can be
107:   // changed!
108:   char & String::operator[](int offset)
109:   {
110:      if (offset > itsLen)
111:         return itsString[itsLen-1];
112:      else
113:         return itsString[offset];
114:   }
115:
116:   // constant offset operator for use
117:   // on const objects (see copy constructor!)
118:   char String::operator[](int offset) const
119:   {
120:      if (offset > itsLen)
121:         return itsString[itsLen-1];
122:      else
123:         return itsString[offset];
124:   }
125:
126:   // creates a new string by adding current
127:   // string to rhs
128:   String String::operator+(const String& rhs)
129:   {
130:      int  totalLen = itsLen + rhs.GetLen();
131:      String temp(totalLen);
132:      int i, j;
133:      for (i = 0; i<itsLen; i++)
134:         temp[i] = itsString[i];
135:      for (j = 0, i = itsLen; j<rhs.GetLen(); j++, i++)
136:         temp[i] = rhs[j];
137:      temp[totalLen]='\0';
138:      return temp;
139:   }
140:
141:   // creates a new string by adding
142:   // one string to another
143:   String operator+(const String& lhs, const String& rhs)
144:   {
145:      int  totalLen = lhs.GetLen() + rhs.GetLen();
146:      String temp(totalLen);
147:      int i, j;
148:      for (i = 0; i<lhs.GetLen(); i++)
149:         temp[i] = lhs[i];
150:      for (j = 0, i = lhs.GetLen(); j<rhs.GetLen(); j++, i++)
151:         temp[i] = rhs[j];
```

LISTING 16.8   continued

```
152:       temp[totalLen]='\0';
153:       return temp;
154:  }
155:
156:  int main()
157:  {
158:       String s1("String One ");
159:       String s2("String Two ");
160:       char *c1 = { "C-String One " } ;
161:       String s3;
162:       String s4;
163:       String s5;
164:
165:       cout << "s1: " << s1.GetString() << endl;
166:       cout << "s2: " << s2.GetString() << endl;
167:       cout << "c1: " << c1 << endl;
168:       s3 = s1 + s2;
169:       cout << "s3: " << s3.GetString() << endl;
170:       s4 = s1 + c1;
171:       cout << "s4: " << s4.GetString() << endl;
172:       s5 = c1 + s2;
173:       cout << "s5: " << s5.GetString() << endl;
174:       return 0;
175:  }
```

OUTPUT

```
s1: String One
s2: String Two
c1: C-String One
s3: String One String Two
s4: String One C-String One
s5: C-String One String Two
```

ANALYSIS   The implementation of all the string methods except operator+ are unchanged from Listing 16.1. On line 21, a new operator+ is overloaded to take two constant string references and to return a string, and this function is declared to be a friend.

Note that this operator+ is not a member function of this or any other class. It is declared within the declaration of the String class only so that it can be made a friend, but because it is declared, no other function prototype is needed.

The implementation of this operator+ is on lines 143–154. Note that it is similar to the earlier operator+, except that it takes two strings and accesses them both through their public accessor methods.

The driver program demonstrates the use of this function on line 172, where operator+ is now called on a C-style string!

> **Friend Functions**
>
> Declare a function to be a friend by using the keyword `friend` and then the full specification of the function. Declaring a function to be a friend does not give the `friend` function access to your `this` pointer, but it does provide full access to all private and protected member data and functions.
>
> **Example**
>
> ```
> class PartNode
> {   // ...
>     // make another class's member function a _friend
>     friend void PartsList::Insert(Part *);
>     // make a global function a friend
>     friend int SomeFunction();
>     // ...
> };
> ```

Overloading the Insertion Operator

You are finally ready to give your `String` class the capability to use `cout` the same as any other type. Until now, when you've wanted to print a string, you've been forced to write the following:

```
cout << theString.GetString();
```

What you would like to do is write this:

```
cout << theString;
```

To accomplish this, you must override `operator<<()`. Day 17, "Streams," presents the ins and outs (`cins` and `couts`?) of working with `iostreams`; for now, Listing 16.9 illustrates how `operator<<` can be overloaded using a friend function.

LISTING 16.9   Overloading `operator<<()`

```
0:  // Listing 16.9 Overloading operator<<()
1:
2:  #include <iostream>
3:  #include <string.h>
4:  using namespace std;
5:
6:  class String
7:  {
8:  public:
9:      // constructors
10:     String();
```

LISTING 16.9   continued

```
11:        String(const char *const);
12:        String(const String &);
13:        ~String();
14:
15:        // overloaded operators
16:        char & operator[](int offset);
17:        char operator[](int offset) const;
18:        String operator+(const String&);
19:        void operator+=(const String&);
20:        String & operator= (const String &);
21:        friend ostream& operator<<
22:           ( ostream& theStream,String& theString);
23:        // General accessors
24:        int GetLen()const { return itsLen; }
25:        const char * GetString() const { return itsString; }
26:
27:    private:
28:        String (int);          // private constructor
29:        char * itsString;
30:        unsigned short itsLen;
31:    };
32:
33:
34:    // default constructor creates string of 0 bytes
35:    String::String()
36:    {
37:        itsString = new char[1];
38:        itsString[0] = '\0';
39:        itsLen=0;
40:        // cout << "\tDefault string constructor\n";
41:        // ConstructorCount++;
42:    }
43:
44:    // private (helper) constructor, used only by
45:    // class methods for creating a new string of
46:    // required size.  Null filled.
47:    String::String(int len)
48:    {
49:        itsString = new char[len+1];
50:        for (int i = 0; i<=len; i++)
51:           itsString[i] = '\0';
52:        itsLen=len;
53:        // cout << "\tString(int) constructor\n";
54:        // ConstructorCount++;
55:    }
56:
57:    // Converts a character array to a String
58:    String::String(const char * const cString)
59:    {
```

LISTING 16.9 continued

```
60:     itsLen = strlen(cString);
61:     itsString = new char[itsLen+1];
62:     for (int i = 0; i<itsLen; i++)
63:         itsString[i] = cString[i];
64:     itsString[itsLen]='\0';
65:     // cout << "\tString(char*) constructor\n";
66:     // ConstructorCount++;
67: }
68:
69: // copy constructor
70: String::String (const String & rhs)
71: {
72:     itsLen=rhs.GetLen();
73:     itsString = new char[itsLen+1];
74:     for (int i = 0; i<itsLen;i++)
75:         itsString[i] = rhs[i];
76:     itsString[itsLen] = '\0';
77:     // cout << "\tString(String&) constructor\n";
78:     // ConstructorCount++;
79: }
80:
81: // destructor, frees allocated memory
82: String::~String ()
83: {
84:     delete [] itsString;
85:     itsLen = 0;
86:     // cout << "\tString destructor\n";
87: }
88:
89: // operator equals, frees existing memory
90: // then copies string and size
91: String& String::operator=(const String & rhs)
92: {
93:     if (this == &rhs)
94:         return *this;
95:     delete [] itsString;
96:     itsLen=rhs.GetLen();
97:     itsString = new char[itsLen+1];
98:     for (int i = 0; i<itsLen;i++)
99:         itsString[i] = rhs[i];
100:     itsString[itsLen] = '\0';
101:     return *this;
102:     // cout << "\tString operator=\n";
103: }
104:
105: //non constant offset operator, returns
106: // reference to character so it can be
107: // changed!
108: char & String::operator[](int offset)
```

LISTING 16.9   continued

```
109:  {
110:      if (offset > itsLen)
111:          return itsString[itsLen-1];
112:      else
113:          return itsString[offset];
114:  }
115:
116:  // constant offset operator for use
117:  // on const objects (see copy constructor!)
118:  char String::operator[](int offset) const
119:  {
120:      if (offset > itsLen)
121:          return itsString[itsLen-1];
122:      else
123:          return itsString[offset];
124:  }
125:
126:  // creates a new string by adding current
127:  // string to rhs
128:  String String::operator+(const String& rhs)
129:  {
130:      int  totalLen = itsLen + rhs.GetLen();
131:      String temp(totalLen);
132:      int i, j;
133:      for (i = 0; i<itsLen; i++)
134:          temp[i] = itsString[i];
135:      for (j = 0; j<rhs.GetLen(); j++, i++)
136:          temp[i] = rhs[j];
137:      temp[totalLen]='\0';
138:      return temp;
139:  }
140:
141:  // changes current string, returns nothing
142:  void String::operator+=(const String& rhs)
143:  {
144:      unsigned short rhsLen = rhs.GetLen();
145:      unsigned short totalLen = itsLen + rhsLen;
146:      String  temp(totalLen);
147:      int i, j;
148:      for (i = 0; i<itsLen; i++)
149:          temp[i] = itsString[i];
150:      for (j = 0, i = 0; j<rhs.GetLen(); j++, i++)
151:          temp[i] = rhs[i-itsLen];
152:      temp[totalLen]='\0';
153:      *this = temp;
154:  }
155:
156:  // int String::ConstructorCount =
157:  ostream& operator<< ( ostream& theStream,String& theString)
```

LISTING 16.9   continued

```
158:  {
159:      theStream << theString.itsString;
160:      return theStream;
161:  }
162:
163:  int main()
164:  {
165:      String theString("Hello world.");
166:      cout << theString;
167:      return 0;
168:  }
```

OUTPUT   Hello world.

ANALYSIS   On line 21, operator<< is declared to be a friend function that takes an ostream
reference and a String reference and then returns an ostream reference. Note
that this is not a member function of String. It returns a reference to an ostream so that
you can concatenate calls to operator<<, such as this:

```
cout << "myAge: " << itsAge << " years.";
```

The implementation of this friend function is on lines 157–161. All this really does is
hide the implementation details of feeding the string to the ostream, and that is just as it
should be. You'll see more about overloading this operator and operator>> on Day 17.

Summary

Today you saw how to delegate functionality to a contained object. You also saw how to
implement one class in terms of another by using either containment or private inheritance. Containment is restricted in that the new class does not have access to the protected members of the contained class, and it cannot override the member functions of the
contained object. Containment is simpler to use than private inheritance, and should be
used when possible.

You also saw how to declare both friend functions and friend classes. Using a friend
function, you saw how to overload the extraction operator, to allow your new classes to
use cout the same as the built-in classes do.

Remember that public inheritance expresses *is-a*, containment expresses *has-a*, and private inheritance expresses *implemented in terms of*. The relationship delegates to can be
expressed using either containment or private inheritance, although containment is more
common.

Q&A

Q Why is it so important to distinguish between *is-a*, *has-a*, and *implemented in terms of*?

A The point of C++ is to implement well-designed, object-oriented programs. Keeping these relationships straight helps to ensure that your design corresponds to the reality of what you are modeling. Furthermore, a well-understood design will more likely be reflected in well-designed code.

Q Why is containment preferred over private inheritance?

A The challenge in modern programming is to cope with complexity. The more you can use objects as black boxes, the fewer details you have to worry about and the more complexity you can manage. Contained classes hide their details; private inheritance exposes the implementation details.

Q Why not make all classes friends of all the classes they use?

A Making one class a friend of another exposes the implementation details and reduces encapsulation. The ideal is to keep as many of the details of each class hidden from all other classes as possible.

Q If a function is overloaded, do you need to declare each form of the function to be a friend?

A Yes, if you overload a function and declare it to be a friend of another class, you must declare friend for each form that you wish to grant this access to.

Workshop

The Workshop contains quiz questions to help solidify your understanding of the material covered and exercises to provide you with experience in using what you've learned. Try to answer the quiz and exercise questions before checking the answers in Appendix D, and make sure you understand the answers before going to the next chapter.

Quiz

1. How do you establish an *is-a* relationship?
2. How do you establish a *has-a* relationship?
3. What is the difference between containment and delegation?
4. What is the difference between delegation and *implemented in terms of*?
5. What is a friend function?
6. What is a friend class?

7. If Dog is a friend of Boy, is Boy a friend of Dog?

8. If Dog is a friend of Boy, and Terrier derives from Dog, is Terrier a friend of Boy?

9. If Dog is a friend of Boy and Boy is a friend of House, is Dog a friend of House?

10. Where must the declaration of a friend function appear?

Exercises

1. Show the declaration of a class, Animal, that contains a data member that is a string object.

2. Show the declaration of a class, BoundedArray, that is an array.

3. Show the declaration of a class, Set, that is declared in terms of an array.

4. Modify Listing 16.1 to provide the String class with an extraction operator (>>).

5. **BUG BUSTERS:** What is wrong with this program?

```
1:     #include <iostream>
2:     using namespace std;
3:     class Animal;
4:
5:     void setValue(Animal& , int);
6:
7:
8:     class Animal
9:     {
10:    public:
11:       int GetWeight()const { return itsWeight; }
12:       int GetAge() const { return itsAge; }
13:    private:
14:       int itsWeight;
15:       int itsAge;
16:    };
17:
18:    void setValue(Animal& theAnimal, int theWeight)
19:    {
20:       friend class Animal;
21:       theAnimal.itsWeight = theWeight;
22:    }
23:
24:    int main()
25:    {
26:       Animal peppy;
27:       setValue(peppy,5);
28:      return 0;
29:    }
```

6. Fix the listing in Exercise 5 so that it compiles.

7. **BUG BUSTERS:** What is wrong with this code?

```
1:      #include <iostream>
2:      using namespace std;
3:      class Animal;
4:
5:      void setValue(Animal& , int);
6:      void setValue(Animal& ,int,int);
7:
8:      class Animal
9:      {
10:     friend void setValue(Animal& ,int); // here's the change!
11:     private:
12:         int itsWeight;
13:         int itsAge;
14:     };
15:
16:     void setValue(Animal& theAnimal, int theWeight)
17:     {
18:          theAnimal.itsWeight = theWeight;
19:     }
20:
21:
22:     void setValue(Animal& theAnimal, int theWeight, int theAge)
23:     {
24:         theAnimal.itsWeight = theWeight;
25:         theAnimal.itsAge = theAge;
26:     }
27:
28:     int main()
29:     {
30:         Animal peppy;
31:         setValue(peppy,5);
32:         setValue(peppy,7,9);
33:       return 0;
34:     }
```

8. Fix Exercise 7 so that it compiles.

Streams

Until now, you've been using `cout` to write to the screen and `cin` to read from the keyboard, without a full understanding of how they work.

Today you will learn

- What streams are and how they are used.
- How to manage input and output using streams.
- How to write to and read from files using streams.

Overview of Streams

C++ does not define how data is written to the screen or to a file, nor how data is read into a program. These are clearly essential parts of working with C++, however, and the standard C++ library includes the `iostream` library, which facilitates input and output (I/O).

The advantage of having the input and output kept apart from the language and handled in libraries is that it is easier to make the language "platform-independent." That is, you can write C++ programs on a PC and then recompile them and run them on a Sun Workstation. The compiler manufacturer supplies the right library, and everything works. At least that's the theory.

Note   A library is a collection of .obj files that can be linked to your program to provide additional functionality. This is the most basic form of code reuse and has been around since ancient programmers chiseled 1s and 0s into the walls of caves.

Encapsulation

The iostream classes view the flow of data from your program to the screen as being a stream of data, one byte following another. If the destination of the stream is a file or the screen, the source is usually some part of your program. If the stream is reversed, the data can come from the keyboard or a disk file and be "poured" into your data variables.

One principal goal of streams is to encapsulate the problems of getting the data to and from the disk or the screen. After a stream is created, your program works with the stream and the stream sweats the details. Figure 17.1 illustrates this fundamental idea.

FIGURE 17.1

Encapsulation through streams.

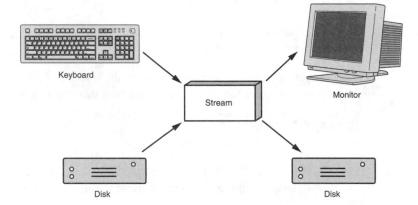

Buffering

Writing to the disk (and to a lesser extent the screen) is very "expensive." It takes a long time (relatively speaking) to write data to the disk or to read data from the disk, and execution of the program is generally blocked by disk writes and reads. To solve this problem, streams provide "buffering." Data is written into the stream, but is not written back out to the disk immediately. Instead, the stream's buffer fills and fills, and when it is full, it writes to the disk all at once.

| Note | While data is technically a plural noun, we will treat it as singular, as do nearly all native speakers of English. |

Picture water trickling into the top of a tank and the tank filling and filling, but no water running out of the bottom. Figure 17.2 illustrates this idea.

FIGURE 17.2

Filling the buffer.

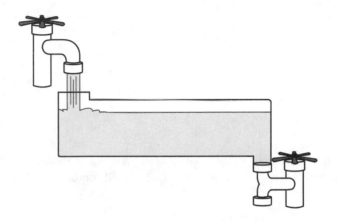

When the water (data) reaches the top, the valve opens and all the water flows out in a rush. Figure 17.3 illustrates this.

FIGURE 17.3

Emptying the buffer.

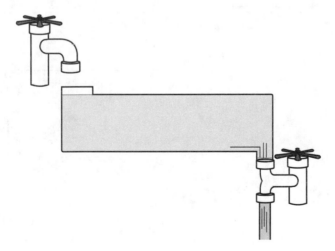

After the buffer is empty, the bottom valve closes, the top valve opens, and more water flows into the buffer tank. Figure 17.4 illustrates this.

FIGURE 17.4

Refilling the buffer.

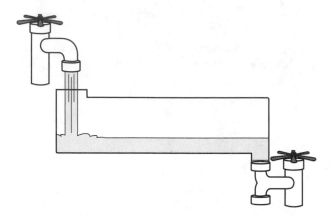

Every once in a while you need to get the water out of the tank even before it is full. This is called "flushing the buffer." Figure 7.5 illustrates this idea.

FIGURE 17.5

Flushing the buffer.

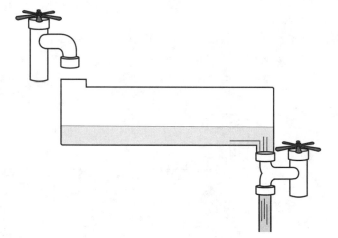

Streams and Buffers

As you might expect, C++ takes an object-oriented view toward implementing streams and buffers.

- The `streambuf` class manages the buffer, and its member functions provide the capability to fill, empty, flush, and otherwise manipulate the buffer.

- The ios class is the base class to the input and output stream classes. The ios class has a streambuf object as a member variable.
- The istream and ostream classes derive from the ios class and specialize input and output stream behavior, respectively.
- The iostream class is derived from both the istream and the ostream classes and provides input and output methods for writing to the screen.
- The fstream classes provide input and output from files.

Standard I/O Objects

When a C++ program that includes the iostream classes starts, four objects are created and initialized:

Note

> The iostream class library is added automatically to your program by the compiler. All you need to do to use these functions is to put the appropriate include statement at the top of your program listing.

- cin (pronounced "see-in") handles input from the standard input, the keyboard.
- cout (pronounced "see-out") handles output to the standard output, the screen.
- cerr (pronounced "see-err") handles unbuffered output to the standard error device, the screen. Because this is unbuffered, everything sent to cerr is written to the standard error device immediately, without waiting for the buffer to fill or for a flush command to be received.
- clog (pronounced "see-log") handles buffered error messages that are output to the standard error device, the screen. It is common for this to be "redirected" to a log file, as described in the following section.

Redirection

Each of the standard devices, input, output, and error, can be redirected to other devices. Standard error is often redirected to a file, and standard input and output can be piped to files using operating system commands.

Redirecting refers to sending output (or input) to a place different than the default. The redirection operators for DOS and UNIX are (<) redirect input and (>) redirect output.

Piping refers to using the output of one program as the input of another.

DOS provides rudimentary redirection commands, such as redirect output (>) and redirect input (<). (redirect output operator)> UNIX provides more advanced redirection capabilities, but the general idea is the same: Take the output intended for the screen and write it to a file, or pipe it into another program. Alternatively, the input for a program can be extracted from a file rather than from the keyboard.

Redirection is more a function of the operating system than of the iostream libraries. C++ just provides access to the four standard devices; it is up to the user to redirect the devices to whatever alternatives are needed.

Input Using `cin`

The global object `cin` is responsible for input and is made available to your program when you include iostream. In previous examples, you used the overloaded extraction operator (>>) to put data into your program's variables. How does this work? The syntax, as you may remember, is the following:

```
int someVariable;
cout << "Enter a number: ";
cin >> someVariable;
```

The global object `cout` is discussed later today; for now, focus on the third line, `cin >> someVariable;`. What can you guess about `cin`?

Clearly, it must be a global object because you didn't define it in your own code. You know from previous operator experience that `cin` has overloaded the extraction operator (>>) and that the effect is to write whatever data `cin` has in its buffer into your local variable, `someVariable`.

What may not be immediately obvious is that `cin` has overloaded the extraction operator for a great variety of parameters, among them `int&`, `short&`, `long&`, `double&`, `float&`, `char&`, `char*`, and so forth. When you write `cin >> someVariable;`, the type of `someVariable` is assessed. In the preceding example, `someVariable` is an integer, so the following function is called:

```
istream & operator>> (int &)
```

Note that because the parameter is passed by reference, the extraction operator is able to act on the original variable. Listing 17.1 illustrates the use of `cin`.

LISTING 17.1   `cin` Handles Different Data Types

```
0:  //Listing 17.1 - character strings and cin
1:
2:  #include <iostream>
```

LISTING 17.1 continued

```
3:   using namespace std;
4:
5:   int main()
6:   {
7:       int myInt;
8:       long myLong;
9:       double myDouble;
10:      float myFloat;
11:      unsigned int myUnsigned;
12:
13:      cout << "Int: ";
14:      cin >> myInt;
15:      cout << "Long: ";
16:      cin >> myLong;
17:      cout << "Double: ";
18:      cin >> myDouble;
19:      cout << "Float: ";
20:      cin >> myFloat;
21:      cout << "Unsigned: ";
22:      cin >> myUnsigned;
23:
24:      cout << "\n\nInt:\t" << myInt << endl;
25:      cout << "Long:\t" << myLong << endl;
26:      cout << "Double:\t" << myDouble << endl;
27:      cout << "Float:\t" << myFloat << endl;
28:      cout << "Unsigned:\t" << myUnsigned << endl;
29:      return 0;
30:  }
```

OUTPUT

```
int: 2
Long: 70000
Double: 987654321
Float: 3.33
Unsigned: 25

Int:     2
Long:    70000
Double: 9.87654e+08
Float:  3.33
Unsigned:        25
```

ANALYSIS On lines 7–11, variables of various types are declared. On lines 13–22, the user is prompted to enter values for these variables, and the results are printed (using cout) on lines 24–28.

The output reflects that the variables were put into the right "kinds" of variables, and the program works as you might expect.

Strings

cin can also handle character pointer (char*) arguments; thus, you can create a character buffer and use cin to fill it. For example, you can write the following:

```
char YourName[50]
cout << "Enter your name: ";
cin >> YourName;
```

If you enter Jesse, the variable YourName will be filled with the characters J, e, s, s, e, \0. The last character is a null; cin automatically ends the string with a null character, and you must have enough room in the buffer to allow for the entire string plus the null. The null signals "end of string" to the standard library functions discussed on Day 21, "What's Next."

String Problems

After all this success with cin, you might be surprised when you try to enter a full name into a string. cin believes that whitespace is a separator. When it sees a space or a newline, it assumes the input for the parameter is complete, and in the case of strings, it adds a null character right then and there. Listing 17.2 illustrates this problem.

LISTING **17.2**   Trying to Write More Than One Word to cin

```
0:   //Listing 17.2 - character strings and cin
1:
2:   #include <iostream>
3:
4:   int main()
5:   {
6:       char YourName[50];
7:       std::cout << "Your first name: ";
8:       std::cin >> YourName;
9:       std::cout << "Here it is: " << YourName << std::endl;
10:      std::cout << "Your entire name: ";
11:      std::cin >> YourName;
12:      std::cout << "Here it is: " << YourName << std::endl;
13:      return 0;
14:  }
```

OUTPUT
```
Your first name: Jesse
Here it is: Jesse
Your entire name: Jesse Liberty
Here it is: Jesse
```

ANALYSIS On line 6, a character array is created to hold the user's input. On line 7, the user is prompted to enter one name, and that name is stored properly, as shown in the output.

On line 10, the user is again prompted, this time for a full name. cin reads the input, and when it sees the space between the names, it puts a null character after the first word and terminates input. This is not exactly what was intended.

To understand why this works this way, examine Listing 17.3, which shows input for several fields.

LISTING 17.3   Multiple Input

```
0:   //Listing 17.3 - character strings and cin
1:
2:   #include <iostream>
3:   using namespace std;
4:
5:   int main()
6:   {
7:       int myInt;
8:       long myLong;
9:       double myDouble;
10:      float myFloat;
11:      unsigned int myUnsigned;
12:      char myWord[50];
13:
14:      cout << "int: ";
15:      cin >> myInt;
16:      cout << "Long: ";
17:      cin >> myLong;
18:      cout << "Double: ";
19:      cin >> myDouble;
20:      cout << "Float: ";
21:      cin >> myFloat;
22:      cout << "Word: ";
23:      cin >> myWord;
24:      cout << "Unsigned: ";
25:      cin >> myUnsigned;
26:
27:      cout << "\n\nInt:\t" << myInt << endl;
28:      cout << "Long:\t" << myLong << endl;
29:      cout << "Double:\t" << myDouble << endl;
30:      cout << "Float:\t" << myFloat << endl;
31:      cout << "Word: \t" << myWord << endl;
32:      cout << "Unsigned:\t" << myUnsigned << endl;
33:
34:      cout << "\n\nInt, Long, Double, Float, Word, Unsigned: ";
35:      cin >> myInt >> myLong >> myDouble;
```

17

LISTING 17.3   continued

```
36:      cin >> myFloat >> myWord >> myUnsigned;
37:      cout << "\n\nInt:\t" << myInt << endl;
38:      cout << "Long:\t" << myLong << endl;
39:      cout << "Double:\t" << myDouble << endl;
40:      cout << "Float:\t" << myFloat << endl;
41:      cout << "Word: \t" << myWord << endl;
42:      cout << "Unsigned:\t" << myUnsigned << endl;
43:
44:
45:      return 0;
46:  }
```

OUTPUT
```
Int: 2
Long: 30303
Double: 393939397834
Float: 3.33
Word: Hello
Unsigned: 85

Int:    2
Long:   30303
Double: 3.93939e+11
Float:  3.33
Word:   Hello
Unsigned:       85

Int, Long, Double, Float, Word, Unsigned: 3 304938 393847473 6.66 bye -2

Int:    3
Long:   304938
Double: 3.93847e+08
Float:  6.66
Word:   bye
Unsigned: 4294967294
```

ANALYSIS   Again, several variables are created, this time including a char array. The user is prompted for input and the output is faithfully printed.

On line 34, the user is prompted for all the input at once, and then each "word" of input is assigned to the appropriate variable. It is to facilitate this kind of multiple assignment that cin must consider each word in the input to be the full input for each variable. If cin was to consider the entire input to be part of one variable's input, this kind of concatenated input would be impossible.

Note that on line 42, the last object requested was an unsigned integer, but the user entered -2. Because cin believes it is writing to an unsigned integer, the bit pattern of -2 was evaluated as an unsigned integer, and when written out by cout, the value 4294967294 was displayed. The unsigned value 4294967294 has the exact bit pattern of the signed value -2.

Later today you will see how to enter an entire string into a buffer, including multiple words. For now, the question arises, "How does the extraction operator manage this trick of concatenation?"

operator>> Returns a Reference to an `istream` Object

The return value of cin is a reference to an istream object. Because cin itself is an istream object, the return value of one extraction operation can be the input to the next extraction.

```
int VarOne, varTwo, varThree;
cout << "Enter three numbers: "
cin >> VarOne >> varTwo >> varThree;
```

When you write cin >> VarOne >> varTwo >> varThree;, the first extraction is evaluated (cin >> VarOne). The return value from this is another istream object, and that object's extraction operator gets the variable varTwo. It is as if you had written this:

```
((cin >> varOne) >> varTwo) >> varThree;
```

You'll see this technique repeated later when cout is discussed.

Other Member Functions of `cin`

In addition to overloading operator>>, cin has a number of other member functions. These are used when finer control over the input is required.

Single Character Input

operator>> taking a character reference can be used to get a single character from the standard input. The member function get() can also be used to obtain a single character, and can do so in two ways: get() can be used with no parameters, in which case the return value is used, or it can be used with a reference to a character.

Using `get()` with No Parameters

The first form of get() is without parameters. This returns the value of the character found and will return EOF (end of file) if the end of the file is reached. get() with no parameters is not often used. It is not possible to concatenate this use of get() for multiple input because the return value is not an iostream object. Thus, the following won't work:

```
cin.get() >>myVarOne >> myVarTwo; //    illegal
```

The return value of `cin.get()` >> `myVarOne` is an integer, not an `iostream` object.

A common use of `get()` with no parameters is illustrated in Listing 17.4.

LISTING 17.4   Using `get()` with No Parameters

```
0:  // Listing 17.4 - Using get() with no parameters
1:
2:  #include <iostream>
3:
4:  int main()
5:  {
6:     char ch;
7:     while ( (ch = std::cin.get()) != EOF)
8:     {
9:        std::cout << "ch: " << ch << std::endl;
10:    }
11:    std::cout << "\nDone!\n";
12:    return 0;
13: }
```

> **Note**   To exit this program, you must send end of file from the keyboard. On DOS computers use Ctrl+Z; on UNIX units use Ctrl+D.

OUTPUT
```
Hello
ch: H
ch: e
ch: l
ch: l
ch: o
ch:

World
ch: W
ch: o
ch: r
ch: l
ch: d
ch:

  (ctrl-z)
Done!
```

ANALYSIS   On line 6, a local character variable is declared. The `while` loop assigns the input received from `cin.get()` to `ch`, and if it is not EOF, the string is printed out.

This output is buffered until an end of line is read, however. When EOF is encountered (by pressing Ctrl+Z on a DOS machine, or Ctrl+D on a UNIX machine), the loop exits.

Note that not every implementation of istream supports this version of get(), although it is now part of the ANSI/ISO standard.

Using get() with a Character Reference Parameter

When a character is passed as input to get(), that character is filled with the next character in the input stream. The return value is an iostream object, and so this form of get() can be concatenated, as illustrated in Listing 17.5.

LISTING 17.5   Using get() with Parameters

```
0:   // Listing 17.5 - Using get() with parameters
1:
2:   #include <iostream>
3:
4:   int main()
5:   {
6:       char a, b, c;
7:
8:       std::cout << "Enter three letters: ";
9:
10:      std::cin.get(a).get(b).get(c);
11:
12:      std::cout << "a: " << a << "\nb: ";
13:      std::cout << b << "\nc: " << c << std::endl;
14:      return 0;
15:  }
```

OUTPUT

```
Enter three letters: one
a: o
b: n
c: e
```

ANALYSIS   On line 6, three character variables are created. On line 10, cin.get() is called three times, concatenated. First cin.get(a) is called. This puts the first letter into a and returns cin so that when it is done, cin.get(b) is called, putting the next letter into b. The end result of this is that cin.get(c) is called and the third letter is put in c.

Because cin.get(a) evaluates to cin, you could have written this:

```
cin.get(a) >> b;
```

In this form, cin.get(a) evaluates to cin, so the second phrase is cin >> b;.

17

Getting Strings from Standard Input

The extraction operator (>>) can be used to fill a character array, as can the member functions get() and getline().

The final form of get() takes three parameters. The first parameter is a pointer to a character array, the second parameter is the maximum number of characters to read plus one, and the third parameter is the termination character.

If you enter 20 as the second parameter, get() will read 19 characters and then will null-terminate the string, which it will store in the first parameter. The third parameter, the termination character, defaults to newline ('\n'). If a termination character is reached before the maximum number of characters is read, a null is written and the termination character is left in the buffer.

Listing 17.6 illustrates the use of this form of get().

LISTING 17.6   Using get() with a Character Array

```
0:   // Listing 17.6 - Using get() with a character array
1:
2:   #include <iostream>
3:   using namespace std;
4:
5:   int main()
6:   {
7:       char stringOne[256];
8:       char stringTwo[256];
9:
10:      cout << "Enter string one: ";
11:      cin.get(stringOne,256);
12:      cout << "stringOne: " << stringOne << endl;
13:
14:      cout << "Enter string two: ";
15:      cin >> stringTwo;
16:      cout << "StringTwo: " << stringTwo << endl;
17:      return 0;
18:   }
```

OUTPUT

```
Enter string one: Now is the time
stringOne: Now is the time
Enter string two: For all good
StringTwo: For
```

ANALYSIS On lines 7 and 8, two character arrays are created. On line 9, the user is prompted to enter a string, and `cin.get()` is called on line 11. The first parameter is the
buffer to fill, and the second is one more than the maximum number for `get()` to accept
(the extra position being given to the null character, (`'\0'`)). The defaulted third parameter is a newline.

The user enters "Now is the time." Because the user ends the phrase with a newline, that
phrase is put into `stringOne`, followed by a terminating null.

The user is prompted for another string on line 14, and this time the extraction operator
is used. Because the extraction operator takes everything up to the first whitespace, the
string `For`, with a terminating null character, is stored in the second string, which, of
course, is not what was intended.

Another way to solve this problem is to use `getline()`, as illustrated in Listing 17.7.

17

LISTING 17.7   Using `getline()`

```
0:  // Listing 17.7 - Using getline()
1:
2:  #include <iostream>
3:  using namespace std;
4:
5:  int main()
6:  {
7:      char stringOne[256];
8:      char stringTwo[256];
9:      char stringThree[256];
10:
11:     cout << "Enter string one: ";
12:     cin.getline(stringOne,256);
13:     cout << "stringOne: " << stringOne << endl;
14:
15:     cout << "Enter string two: ";
16:     cin >> stringTwo;
17:     cout << "stringTwo: " << stringTwo << endl;
18:
19:     cout << "Enter string three: ";
20:     cin.getline(stringThree,256);
21:     cout << "stringThree: " << stringThree << endl;
22:     return 0;
23: }
```

OUTPUT

```
Enter string one: one two three
stringOne: one two three
Enter string two: four five six
stringTwo: four
Enter string three: stringThree: five six
```

ANALYSIS This example warrants careful examination; some potential surprises exist. On lines 7–9, three character arrays are declared.

On line 11, the user is prompted to enter a string, and that string is read by `getline()`. Like `get()`, `getline()` takes a buffer and a maximum number of characters. Unlike `get()`, however, the terminating newline is read and thrown away. With `get()` the terminating newline is not thrown away. It is left in the input buffer.

On line 15, the user is prompted again, and this time the extraction operator is used. The user enters `four five six`, and the first word, `four`, is put in `stringTwo`. The string `Enter string three` is then displayed, and `getline()` is called again. Because `five six` is still in the input buffer, it is immediately read up to the newline; `getline()` terminates and the string in `stringThree` is printed on line 21.

The user has no chance to enter string three because the second `getline()` call is fulfilled by the string remaining in the input buffer after the call to the extraction operator on line 16.

The extraction operator (>>) reads up to the first whitespace and puts the word into the character array.

The member function `get()` is overloaded. In one version, it takes no parameters and returns the value of the character it receives. In the second version, it takes a single character reference and returns the `istream` object by reference.

In the third and final version, `get()` takes a character array, a number of characters to get, and a termination character (which defaults to newline). This version of `get()` reads characters into the array until it gets to one fewer than its maximum number of characters or it encounters the termination character, whichever comes first. If `get()` encounters the termination character, it leaves that character in the input buffer and stops reading characters.

The member function `getline()` also takes three parameters: the buffer to fill, one more than the maximum number of characters to `get`, and the termination character. `getline()` functions the same as `get()` does with these parameters, except `getline()` throws away the terminating character.

Using `cin.ignore()`

At times, you want to ignore the remaining characters on a line until you hit either end of
line (EOL) or end of file (EOF). The member function `ignore()` serves this purpose.
`ignore()` takes two parameters: the maximum number of characters to ignore and the
termination character. If you write `ignore(80,'\n')`, up to 80 characters will be thrown
away until a newline character is found. The newline is then thrown away and the
`ignore()` statement ends. Listing 17.8 illustrates the use of `ignore()`.

LISTING 17.8   Using `ignore()`

```
0:  // Listing 17.8 - Using ignore()
1:  #include <iostream>
2:  using namespace std;
3:
4:  int main()
5:  {
6:      char stringOne[255];
7:      char stringTwo[255];
8:
9:      cout << "Enter string one:";
10:     cin.get(stringOne,255);
11:     cout << "String one: " << stringOne << endl;
12:
13:     cout << "Enter string two: ";
14:     cin.getline(stringTwo,255);
15:     cout << "String two: " << stringTwo << endl;
16:
17:     cout << "\n\nNow try again...\n";
18:
19:     cout << "Fnter string one: ";
20:     cin.get(stringOne,255);
21:     cout << "String one: " << stringOne<< endl;
22:
23:     cin.ignore(255,'\n');
24:
25:     cout << "Enter string two: ";
26:     cin.getline(stringTwo,255);
27:     cout << "String Two: " << stringTwo<< endl;
28:     return 0;
29: }
```

OUTPUT

```
Enter string one:once upon a time
String one: once upon a time
Enter string two: String two:

Now try again...
Enter string one: once upon a time
```

17

```
String one: once upon a time
Enter string two: there was a
String Two: there was a
```

ANALYSIS On lines 6 and 7, two character arrays are created. On line 9, the user is prompted for input and types once upon a time, followed by Enter. On line 10, get() is used to read this string. get() fills stringOne and terminates on the newline, but leaves the newline character in the input buffer.

On line 13, the user is prompted again, but the getline() on line 14 reads the newline that is already in the buffer and terminates immediately, before the user can enter any input.

On line 19, the user is prompted again and puts in the same first line of input. This time, however, on line 23, ignore() is used to "eat" the newline character. Thus, when the getline() call on line 26 is reached, the input buffer is empty, and the user can input the next line of the story.

peek() and putback()

The input object cin has two additional methods that can come in rather handy: peek(), which looks at but does not extract the next character, and putback(), which inserts a character into the input stream. Listing 17.9 illustrates how these might be used.

LISTING 17.9   Using peek() and putback()

```
0:  // Listing 17.9 - Using peek() and putback()
1:  #include <iostream>
2:  using namespace std;
3:
4:  int main()
5:  {
6:      char ch;
7:      cout << "enter a phrase: ";
8:      while ( cin.get(ch) )
9:      {
10:         if (ch == '!')
11:             cin.putback('$');
12:         else
13:             cout << ch;
14:         while (cin.peek() == '#')
15:             cin.ignore(1,'#');
16:     }
17:     return 0;
18: }
```

OUTPUT
```
enter a phrase: Now!is#the!time#for!fun#!
Now$isthe$timefor$fun$
```

ANALYSIS On line 6, a character variable, ch, is declared, and on line 7, the user is prompted to enter a phrase. The purpose of this program is to turn any exclamation marks (!) into dollar signs ($) and to remove any pound symbols (#).

The program loops as long as it is getting characters other than the end of file (Ctrl+C on Windows machines, Ctrl+Z or Ctrl+D on other operating systems). (Remember that cin.get() returns 0 for end of file.) If the current character is an exclamation point, it is thrown away and the $ symbol is put back into the input buffer; it will be read the next time through. If the current item is not an exclamation point, it is printed. The next character is "peeked" at, and when pound symbols are found, they are removed.

This is not the most efficient way to do either of these things (and it won't find a pound symbol if it is the first character), but it does illustrate how these methods work. They are relatively obscure, so don't spend a lot of time worrying about when you might really use them. Put them into your bag of tricks; they'll come in handy eventually.

17

Tip | peek() and putback() are typically used for parsing strings and other data, such as when writing a compiler.

Output with cout

You have used cout along with the overloaded insertion operator (<<) to write strings, integers, and other numeric data to the screen. It is also possible to format the data, aligning columns and writing the numeric data in decimal and hexadecimal. This section will show you how.

Flushing the Output

You've already seen that using endl will flush the output buffer. endl calls cout's member function flush(), which writes all the data it is buffering. You can call the flush() method directly, either by calling the flush() member method or by writing the following:

```
cout << flush
```

This can be convenient when you need to ensure that the output buffer is emptied and that the contents are written to the screen.

Related Functions

Just as the extraction operator can be supplemented with get() and getline(), the insertion operator can be supplemented with put() and write().

The function put() is used to write a single character to the output device. Because put() returns an ostream reference and because cout is an ostream object, you can concatenate put() the same as you do the insertion operator. Listing 17.10 illustrates this idea.

LISTING **17.10**   Using put()

```
0:   // Listing 17.10 - Using put()
1:
2:   #include <iostream>
3:
4:   int main()
5:   {
6:      std::cout.put('H').put('e').put('l').put('l').put('o').put('\n');
7:      return 0;
8:   }
```

OUTPUT   Hello

> **Note**   Some compilers have trouble printing using this code. If your compiler will
> not print the word Hello, you may want to skip this listing.

Line 6 is evaluated like this: std::cout.put('H') writes the letter H to the screen and returns the cout object. This leaves the following:

cout.put('e').put('l').put('l').put('o').put('\n');

The letter e is written, leaving cout.put('l'). This process repeats, each letter being written and the cout object returned until the final character ('\n') is written and the function returns.

The function write() works the same as the insertion operator (<<), except that it takes a parameter that tells the function the maximum number of characters to write. Listing 17.11 illustrates its use.

LISTING 17.11   Using write()

```
0:  // Listing 17.11 - Using write()
1:  #include <iostream>
2:  #include <string.h>
3:  using namespace std;
4:
5:  int main()
6:  {
7:     char One[] = "One if by land";
8:
9:       int fullLength = strlen(One);
10:      int tooShort = fullLength -4;
11:      int tooLong = fullLength + 6;
12:
13:      cout.write(One,fullLength) << "\n";
14:      cout.write(One,tooShort) << "\n";
15:      cout.write(One,tooLong) << "\n";
16:      return 0;
17:  }
```

OUTPUT
```
One if by land
One if by
One if by land i?!
```

Note

> The last line of output may look different on your computer.

ANALYSIS   On line 7, one phrase is created. On line 9, the integer fullLength is set to the length of the phrase, tooShort is set to that length minus four, and tooLong is set to fullLength plus six.

On line 13, the complete phrase is printed using write(). The length is set to the actual length of the phrase, and the correct phrase is printed.

On line 14, the phrase is printed again, but it is four characters shorter than the full phrase, and that is reflected in the output.

On line 15, the phrase is printed again, but this time write() is instructed to write an extra six characters. After the phrase is written, the next six bytes of contiguous memory are written.

Manipulators, Flags, and Formatting Instructions

The output stream maintains a number of state flags, determining which base (decimal or hexadecimal) to use, how wide to make the fields, and what character to use to fill in fields. A state flag is a byte whose individual bits are each assigned a special meaning. Manipulating bits in this way is discussed on Day 21. Each of `ostream`'s flags can be set using member functions and manipulators.

Using `cout.width()`

The default width of your output will be just enough space to print the number, character, or string in the output buffer. You can change this by using `width()`. Because `width()` is a member function, it must be invoked with a `cout` object. It only changes the width of the very next output field and then immediately reverts to the default. Listing 17.12 illustrates its use.

LISTING 17.12   Adjusting the Width of Output

```
0:   // Listing 17.12 - Adjusting the width of output
1:   #include <iostream>
2:   using namespace std;
3:
4:   int main()
5:   {
6:       cout << "Start >";
7:       cout.width(25);
8:       cout << 123 << "< End\n";
9:
10:      cout << "Start >";
11:      cout.width(25);
12:      cout << 123<< "< Next >";
13:      cout << 456 << "< End\n";
14:
15:      cout << "Start >";
16:      cout.width(4);
17:      cout << 123456 << "< End\n";
18:
19:      return 0;
20:  }
```

```
Start >                        123< End
Start >                        123< Next >456< End
Start >123456< End
```

ANALYSIS The first output, on lines 6–8, prints the number 123 within a field whose width is set to 25 on line 7. This is reflected in the first line of output.

The second line of output first prints the value 123 in the same field whose width is set to 25, and then prints the value 456. Note that 456 is printed in a field whose width is reset to just large enough; as stated, the effect of width() lasts only as long as the very next output.

The final output reflects that setting a width that is smaller than the output is the same as setting a width that is just large enough.

Setting the Fill Characters

Normally cout fills the empty field created by a call to width() with spaces, as shown above. At times, you may want to fill the area with other characters, such as asterisks. To do this, you call fill() and pass in as a parameter the character you want used as a fill character. Listing 17.13 illustrates this.

LISTING 17.13 Using fill()

```
0:  // Listing 17.13 - fill()
1:
2:  #include <iostream>
3:  using namespace std;
4:
5:  int main()
6:  {
7:      cout << "Start >";
8:      cout.width(25);
9:      cout << 123 << "< End\n";
10:
11:
12:      cout << "Start >";
13:      cout.width(25);
14:      cout.fill('*');
15:      cout << 123 << "< End\n";
16:      return 0;
17:  }
```

OUTPUT
```
Start >                      123< End
Start >******************123< End
```

ANALYSIS Lines 7–9 repeat the functionality from the previous example. Lines 12–15 repeat this again, but this time, on line 14, the fill character is set to asterisks, as reflected in the output.

Set Flags

The `iostream` objects keep track of their state by using flags. You can set these flags by calling `setf()` and passing in one or another of the predefined enumerated constants.

Objects are said to have state when some or all of their data represents a condition that can change during the course of the program.

For example, you can set whether to show trailing zeros (so that 20.00 does not become truncated to 20). To turn trailing zeros on, call `setf(ios::showpoint)`.

The enumerated constants are scoped to the `iostream` class (`ios`) and thus are called with the full qualification `ios::flagname`, such as `ios::showpoint`.

You can turn on the plus sign (+) before positive numbers by using `ios::showpos`. You can change the alignment of the output by using `ios::left`, `ios::right`, or `ios::internal`.

Finally, you can set the base of the numbers for display by using `ios::dec` (decimal), `ios::oct` (octal—base eight), or `ios::hex` (hexadecimal—base sixteen). These flags can also be concatenated into the insertion operator. Listing 17.14 illustrates these settings. As a bonus, Listing 17.14 also introduces the `setw` manipulator, which sets the width but can also be concatenated with the insertion operator.

LISTING 17.14   Using `setf`

```
0:  // Listing 17.14 - Using setf
1:  #include <iostream>
2:  #include <iomanip>
3:  using namespace std;
4:
5:  int main()
6:  {
7:      const int number = 185;
8:      cout << "The number is " << number << endl;
9:
10:     cout << "The number is " << hex <<  number << endl;
11:
12:     cout.setf(ios::showbase);
13:     cout << "The number is " << hex <<  number << endl;
14:
15:     cout << "The number is " ;
16:     cout.width(10);
17:     cout << hex << number << endl;
18:
19:     cout << "The number is " ;
20:     cout.width(10);
21:     cout.setf(ios::left);
```

LISTING 17.14   continued

```
22:     cout << hex << number << endl;
23:
24:     cout << "The number is " ;
25:     cout.width(10);
26:     cout.setf(ios::internal);
27:     cout << hex << number << endl;
28:
29:     cout << "The number is:" << setw(10) << hex << number << endl;
30:     return 0;
31:  }
```

OUTPUT
```
The number is 185
The number is b9
The number is 0xb9
The number is          0xb9
The number is 0xb9
The number is 0x       b9
The number is:0x       b9
```

ANALYSIS   On line 7, the constant int number is initialized to the value 185. This is displayed on line 8.

The value is displayed again on line 10, but this time the manipulator hex is concatenated, causing the value to be displayed in hexadecimal as b9. (The value b in hexadecimal represents 11. 11 times 16 equals 176; add the 9 for a total of 185.)

On line 12, the flag showbase is set. This causes the prefix 0x to be added to all hexadecimal numbers, as reflected in the output.

On line 16, the width is set to 10, and the value is pushed to the extreme right. On line 20, the width is again set to 10, but this time the alignment is set to the left, and the number is again printed flush left.

On line 25, again the width is set to 10, but this time the alignment is internal. Thus the 0x is printed flush left, but the value, b9, is printed flush right.

Finally, on line 29, the concatenation operator setw() is used to set the width to 10, and the value is printed again.

Streams Versus the `printf()` Function

Most C++ implementations also provide the standard C I/O libraries, including the printf() statement. Although printf() is in some ways easier to use than cout, it is much less desirable.

printf() does not provide type safety, so it is easy to inadvertently tell it to display an integer as if it were a character, and vice versa. printf() also does not support classes, and so it is not possible to teach it how to print your class data; you must feed each class member to printf() one by one.

Because there is a lot of legacy code using printf, this section will briefly review how printf is used. To use printf(), be sure to include the stdio.h header file. In its simplest form, printf() takes a formatting string as its first parameter and then a series of values as its remaining parameters.

The formatting string is a quoted string of text and conversion specifiers. All conversion specifiers must begin with the percent symbol (%). The common conversion specifiers are presented in Table 17.1.

TABLE 17.1   The Common Conversion Specifiers

Specifier	Used For
%s	strings
%d	integers
%l	long integer
%ld	double
%f	float

Each of the conversion specifiers can also provide a width statement and a precision statement, expressed as a float, where the digits to the left of the decimal are used for the total width, and the digits to the right of the decimal provide the precision for floats. Thus, %5d is the specifier for a 5-digit-wide integer, and %15.5f is the specifier for a 15-digit-wide float, of which the final five digits are dedicated to the decimal portion. Listing 17.15 illustrates various uses of printf().

LISTING 17.15   Printing with printf()

```
0:   //17.15 Printing with printf()
1:   #include <stdio.h>
2:
3:   int main()
4:   {
5:       printf("%s","hello world\n");
6:
7:       char *phrase = "Hello again!\n";
8:       printf("%s",phrase);
9:
10:      int x = 5;
```

LISTING 17.15   continued

```
11:     printf("%d\n",x);
12:
13:     char *phraseTwo = "Here's some values: ";
14:     char *phraseThree = " and also these: ";
15:     int y = 7, z = 35;
16:     long longVar = 98456;
17:     float floatVar =  8.8f;
18:
19:     printf("%s %d %d",phraseTwo,y,z);
20:     printf("%s %ld %f\n",phraseThree,longVar,floatVar);
21:
22:     char *phraseFour = "Formatted: ";
23:     printf("%s %5d %10d   %10.5f\n",phraseFour,y,z,floatVar);
24:
25:     return 0;
26:  }
```

OUTPUT

```
hello world
Hello again!
5
Here's some values: 7 35   and also these: 98456 8.800000
Formatted:       7        35      8.800000
```

ANALYSIS The first `printf()` statement, on line 5, uses the standard form: the term `printf`, followed by a quoted string with a conversion specifier (in this case `%s`), followed by a value to insert into the conversion specifier.

The `%s` indicates that this is a string, and the value for the string is, in this case, the quoted string "hello world."

The second `printf()` statement is the same as the first, but this time a `char` pointer is used, rather than quoting the string right in place in the `printf()` statement.

The third `printf()`, on line 11, uses the integer conversion specifier, and for its value the integer variable x. The fourth `printf()` statement, on line 19, is more complex. Here three values are concatenated. Each conversion specifier is supplied, and then the values are provided, separated by commas.

Finally, on line 23, format specifications are used to specify width and precision. As you can see, all this is somewhat easier than using manipulators.

As stated previously, however, the limitation here is that no type checking occurs and `printf()` cannot be declared a friend or member function of a class. So if you want to print the various member data of a class, you must feed each accessor method to the `printf()` statement explicitly.

17

FAQ

Can you summarize how I manipulate output?

Answer: (with special thanks to Robert Francis) To format output in C++, you use a combination of special characters, output manipulators, and flags.

The following special characters are included in an output string being sent to `cout` using the insertion operator:

> \n—Newline
>
> \r—Carriage return
>
> \t—Tab
>
> \\—Backslash
>
> \ddd (octal number)—ASCII character
>
> \a—Alarm (ring bell)

For example

```
cout << "\aAn error occured\t"
```

rings the bell, prints an error message, and moves to the next tab stop. Manipulators are used with the `cout` operator. Those manipulators that take arguments require that you include `iomanip` in your file.

The following is a list of manipulators that do *not* require `iomanip`:

> `flush`—Flushes the output buffer
>
> `endl`—Inserts newline and flushes the output buffer
>
> `oct`—Sets output base to octal
>
> `dec`—Sets output base to decimal
>
> `hex`—Sets output base to hexadecimal

The following is a list of manipulators that *do* require `iomanip`:

> `setbase` (base)—Sets output base (0 = decimal, 8 = octal, 10 = decimal, 16 = hex)
>
> `setw` (width)—Sets minimum output field width
>
> `setfill` (ch)—Fills character to be used when width is defined
>
> `setprecision` (p)—Sets precision for floating point numbers.
>
> `setiosflags` (f)—Sets one or more ios flags
>
> `resetiosflags` (f)—Resets one or more ios flags

For example

```
cout << setw(12) << setfill('#') << hex << x << endl;
```

sets the field width to 12, sets the fill character to '#', specifies hex output, prints the value of 'x', puts a newline in the buffer, and flushes the buffer. All the manipulators except `flush`, `endl`, and `setw` remain in effect until changed or until the end of the program. `setw` returns to the default after the current `cout`.

The following ios flags can be used with the `setiosflags` and `resetiosflags` manipulators:

    `ios::left`—Left justifies output in specified width

    `ios::right`—Right justifies output in specified width

    `ios::internal`—Sign is left justified, value is right justified

    `ios::dec`—Decimal output

    `ios::oct`—Octal output

    `ios::hex`—Hexadecimal output

    `ios::showbase`—Adds 0x to hexadecimal numbers, 0 to octal numbers

    `ios::showpoint`—Adds trailing zeros as required by precision

    `ios::uppercase`—Hex and scientific notation numbers shown in uppercase

    `ios::showpos`—+ sign shown for positive numbers

    `ios::scientific`—Shows floating point in scientific notation

    `ios::fixed`—Shows floating point in decimal notation

Additional information can be obtained from file `ios` and from your compiler's documentation.

File Input and Output

Streams provide a uniform way of dealing with data coming from the keyboard or the hard disk and going out to the screen or hard disk. In either case, you can use the insertion and extraction operators or the other related functions and manipulators. To open and close files, you create `ifstream` and `ofstream` objects as described in the next few sections.

ofstream

The particular objects used to read from or write to files are called `ofstream` objects. These are derived from the `iostream` objects you've been using so far.

To get started with writing to a file, you must first create an `ofstream` object, and then associate that object with a particular file on your disk. To use `ofstream` objects, you must be sure to include `fstream.h` in your program.

Note Because `fstream.h` includes `iostream.h`, you do not need to include `iostream` explicitly.

Condition States

The iostream objects maintain flags that report on the state of your input and output. You can check each of these flags using the Boolean functions eof(), bad(), fail(), and good(). The function eof() returns TRUE if the iostream object has encountered EOF, end of file. The function bad() returns TRUE if you attempt an invalid operation. The function fail() returns TRUE anytime bad() is true or an operation fails. Finally, the function good() returns TRUE anytime all three of the other functions are FALSE.

Opening Files for Input and Output

To open the file myfile.cpp with an ofstream object, declare an instance of an ofstream object and pass in the filename as a parameter:

```
ofstream fout("myfile.cpp");
```

Opening this file for input works the same way, except that it uses an ifstream object:

```
ifstream fin("myfile.cpp");
```

Note that fout and fin are names you assign; here fout has been used to reflect its similarity to cout, and fin has been used to reflect its similarity to cin.

One important file stream function that you will need right away is close(). Every file stream object you create opens a file for either reading or writing (or both). It is important to close() the file after you finish reading or writing; this ensures that the file won't be corrupted and that the data you've written is flushed to the disk.

After the stream objects are associated with files, they can be used the same as any other stream objects. Listing 17.16 illustrates this.

LISTING 17.16   Opening Files for Read and Write

```
0:  //Listing 17.16 Opening Files for Read and Write
1:  #include <fstream>
2:  #include <iostream>
3:  using namespace std;
4:
5:  int main()
6:  {
7:      char fileName[80];
8:      char buffer[255];    // for user input
9:      cout << "File name: ";
10:     cin >> fileName;
11:
12:     ofstream fout(fileName);  // open for writing
13:     fout << "This line written directly to the file...\n";
14:     cout << "Enter text for the file: ";
```

LISTING 17.16   continued

```
15:    cin.ignore(1,'\n');  // eat the newline after the file name
16:    cin.getline(buffer,255);  // get the user's input
17:    fout << buffer << "\n";   // and write it to the file
18:    fout.close();             // close the file, ready for reopen
19:
20:    ifstream fin(fileName);    // reopen for reading
21:    cout << "Here's the contents of the file:\n";
22:    char ch;
23:    while (fin.get(ch))
24:       cout << ch;
25:
26:    cout << "\n***End of file contents.***\n";
27:
28:    fin.close();              // always pays to be tidy
29:    return 0;
30: }
```

OUTPUT
```
File name: test1
Enter text for the file: This text is written to the file!
Here's the contents of the file:
This line written directly to the file...
This text is written to the file!

***End of file contents.***
```

ANALYSIS   On line 7, a buffer is set aside for the filename, and on line 8, another buffer is set aside for user input. The user is prompted to enter a filename on line 9, and this response is written to the `fileName` buffer. On line 12, an `ofstream` object is created, `fout`, which is associated with the new filename. This opens the file; if the file already exists, its contents are thrown away.

On line 13, a string of text is written directly to the file. On line 14, the user is prompted for input. The newline character left over from the user's input of the filename is eaten on line 15, and the user's input is stored into buffer on line 16. That input is written to the file along with a newline character on line 17, and then the file is closed on line 18.

On line 20, the file is reopened, this time in input mode, and the contents are read, one character at a time, on lines 23 and 24.

Changing the Default Behavior of `ofstream` on Open

The default behavior upon opening a file is to create the file if it doesn't yet exist and to truncate the file (that is, delete all its contents) if it does exist. If you don't want this default behavior, you can explicitly provide a second argument to the constructor of your `ofstream` object.

Valid arguments include

- ios::app—Appends to the end of existing files rather than truncating them.
- ios::ate—Places you at the end of the file, but you can write data anywhere in the file.
- ios::trunc—The default. Causes existing files to be truncated.
- ios::nocreate—If the file does not exist, the open fails.
- ios::noreplace—If the file does already exist, the open fails.

Note that app is short for append, ate is short for at end, and trunc is short for truncate. Listing 17.17 illustrates using append by reopening the file from Listing 17.16 and appending to it.

LISTING 17.17   Appending to the End of a File

```
0:   //Listing 17.17 Appending to the End of a File
1:   #include <fstream>
2:   #include <iostream>
3:   using namespace std;
4:
5:   int main()    // returns 1 on error
6:   {
7:       char fileName[80];
8:       char buffer[255];
9:       cout << "Please re-enter the file name: ";
10:      cin >> fileName;
11:
12:      ifstream fin(fileName);
13:      if (fin)                // already exists?
14:      {
15:         cout << "Current file contents:\n";
16:         char ch;
17:         while (fin.get(ch))
18:            cout << ch;
19:         cout << "\n***End of file contents.***\n";
20:      }
21:      fin.close();
22:
23:      cout << "\nOpening " << fileName << " in append mode...\n";
24:
25:      ofstream fout(fileName,ios::app);
26:      if (!fout)
27:      {
28:         cout << "Unable to open " << fileName << " for appending.\n";
29:         return(1);
30:      }
31:
```

LISTING 17.17   continued

```
32:     cout << "\nEnter text for the file: ";
33:     cin.ignore(1,'\n');
34:     cin.getline(buffer,255);
35:     fout << buffer << "\n";
36:     fout.close();
37:
38:     fin.open(fileName);  // reassign existing fin object!
39:     if (!fin)
40:     {
41:        cout << "Unable to open " << fileName << " for reading.\n";
42:        return(1);
43:     }
44:     cout << "\nHere's the contents of the file:\n";
45:     char ch;
46:     while (fin.get(ch))
47:        cout << ch;
48:     cout << "\n***End of file contents.***\n";
49:     fin.close();
50:     return 0;
51:  }
```

17

OUTPUT
```
Please re-enter the file name: test1
Current file contents:
This line written directly to the file...
This text is written to the file!

***End of file contents.***

Opening test1 in append mode...

Enter text for the file: More text for the file!

Here's the contents of the file:
This line written directly to the file...
This text is written to the file!
More text for the file!

***End of file contents.***
```

ANALYSIS   The user is again prompted to enter the filename. This time an input file stream object is created on line 12. That open is tested on line 13, and if the file already exists, its contents are printed on lines 15–19. Note that if(fin) is synonymous with if (fin.good()).

The input file is then closed, and the same file is reopened, this time in append mode, on line 25. After this open (and every open), the file is tested to ensure that the file was opened properly. Note that if(!fout) is the same as testing if (fout.fail()). The user is then prompted to enter text, and the file is closed again on line 36.

Finally, as in Listing 17.16, the file is reopened in read mode; however, this time `fin` does not need to be redeclared. It is just reassigned to the same filename. Again the open is tested, on line 39, and if all is well, the contents of the file are printed to the screen and the file is closed for the final time.

Do	Don't
DO test each open of a file to ensure that it opened successfully.	**DON'T** try to close or reassign `cin` or `cout`.
DO reuse existing `ifstream` and `ofstream` objects.	
DO close all `fstream` objects when you are done using them.	

Binary Versus Text Files

Some operating systems, such as DOS, distinguish between text files and binary files. Text files store everything as text (as you might have guessed), so large numbers such as 54,325 are stored as a string of numerals ('5', '4', ',', '3', '2', '5'). This can be inefficient, but has the advantage that the text can be read using simple programs such as the DOS program `type`.

To help the file system distinguish between text and binary files, C++ provides the `ios::binary` flag. On many systems, this flag is ignored because all data is stored in binary format. On some rather prudish systems, the `ios::binary` flag is illegal and won't compile!

Binary files can store not only integers and strings, but entire data structures. You can write all the data at one time by using the `write()` method of `fstream`.

If you use `write()`, you can recover the data using `read()`. Each of these functions expects a pointer to character, however, so you must cast the address of your class to be a pointer to character.

The second argument to these functions is the number of characters to write, which you can determine using `sizeof()`. Note that what is being written is the data, not the methods. What is recovered is only data. Listing 17.18 illustrates writing the contents of a class to a file.

LISTING 17.18   Writing a Class to a File

```
0:   //Listing 17.18 Writing a Class to a File
1:   #include <fstream>
2:   #include <iostream.h>
3:   using namespace std;
4:
5:   class Animal
6:   {
7:   public:
8:       Animal(int weight,long days):itsWeight(weight),DaysAlive(days){}
9:       ~Animal(){}
10:
11:      int GetWeight()const { return itsWeight; }
12:      void SetWeight(int weight) { itsWeight = weight; }
13:
14:      long GetDaysAlive()const { return DaysAlive; }
15:      void SetDaysAlive(long days) { DaysAlive = days; }
16:
17:  private:
18:      int itsWeight;
19:      long DaysAlive;
20:  };
21:
22:  int main()    // returns 1 on error
23:  {
24:      char fileName[80];
25:
26:
27:      cout << "Please enter the file name: ";
28:      cin >> fileName;
29:      ofstream fout(fileName,ios::binary);
30:      if (!fout)
31:      {
32:         cout << "Unable to open " << fileName << " for writing.\n";
33:         return(1);
34:      }
35:
36:      Animal Bear(50,100);
37:      fout.write((char*) &Bear,sizeof Bear);
38:
39:      fout.close();
40:
41:      ifstream fin(fileName,ios::binary);
42:      if (!fin)
43:      {
44:         cout << "Unable to open " << fileName << " for reading.\n";
45:         return(1);
46:      }
47:
48:      Animal BearTwo(1,1);
```

17

LISTING 17.18   continued

```
49:
50:        cout << "BearTwo weight: " << BearTwo.GetWeight() << endl;
51:        cout << "BearTwo days: " << BearTwo.GetDaysAlive() << endl;
52:
53:        fin.read((char*) &BearTwo, sizeof BearTwo);
54:
55:        cout << "BearTwo weight: " << BearTwo.GetWeight() << endl;
56:        cout << "BearTwo days: " << BearTwo.GetDaysAlive() << endl;
57:        fin.close();
58:        return 0;
59:    }
```

OUTPUT

```
Please enter the file name: Animals
BearTwo weight: 1
BearTwo days: 1
BearTwo weight: 50
BearTwo days: 100
```

ANALYSIS   On lines 5–20, a stripped-down `Animal` class is declared. On lines 24–34, a file is created and opened for output in binary mode. An animal whose weight is 50 and who is 100 days old is created on line 36, and its data is written to the file on line 37.

The file is closed on line 39 and reopened for reading in binary mode on line 41. A second animal is created, on line 48, whose weight is 1 and who is only one day old. The data from the file is read into the new animal object on line 53, wiping out the existing data and replacing it with the data from the file.

Command-Line Processing

Many operating systems, such as DOS and UNIX, enable the user to pass parameters to your program when the program starts. These are called command-line options and are typically separated by spaces on the command line. For example:

```
SomeProgram Param1 Param2 Param3
```

These parameters are not passed to `main()` directly. Instead, every program's `main()` function is passed two parameters. The first is an integer count of the number of arguments on the command line. The program name itself is counted, so every program has at least one parameter. The sample command line shown previously has four. (The name `SomeProgram` plus the three parameters make a total of four command-line arguments.)

The second parameter passed to main() is an array of pointers to character strings. Because an array name is a constant pointer to the first element of the array, you can declare this argument to be a pointer to a pointer to char, a pointer to an array of char, or an array of arrays of char.

Typically, the first argument is called argc (argument count), but you may call it anything you like. The second argument is often called argv (argument vector), but again this is just a convention.

It is common to test argc to ensure you've received the expected number of arguments and to use argv to access the strings themselves. Note that argv[0] is the name of the program, and argv[1] is the first parameter to the program, represented as a string. If your program takes two numbers as arguments, you will need to translate these numbers to strings. On Day 21 you will see how to use the standard library conversions. Listing 17.19 illustrates how to use the command-line arguments.

LISTING 17.19   Using Command-line Arguments

```
0:  //Listing 17.19 Using Command-line Arguments
1:  #include <iostream>
2:  int main(int argc, char **argv)
3:  {
4:     std::cout << "Received " << argc << " arguments...\n";
5:     for (int i=0; i<argc; i++)
6:        std::cout << "argument " << i << ": " << argv[i] << std::endl;
7:     return 0;
8:  }
```

OUTPUT

```
TestProgram  Teach Yourself C++ In 21 Days
Received 7 arguments...
argumnet 0: TestProgram.exe
argument 1: Teach
argument 2: Yourself
argument 3: C++
argument 4: In
argument 5: 21
argument 6: Days
```

Note

You must either run this code from the command line (that is, from a DOS box) or you must set the command line parameters in your compiler (see your compiler documentation).

ANALYSIS The function `main()` declares two arguments: `argc` is an integer that contains the count of command-line arguments, and `argv` is a pointer to the array of strings. Each string in the array pointed to by `argv` is a command-line argument. Note that `argv` could just as easily have been declared as `char *argv[]` or `char argv[][]`. It is a matter of programming style how you declare `argv`; even though this program declared it as a pointer to a pointer, array offsets were still used to access the individual strings.

On line 4, `argc` is used to print the number of command-line arguments: seven in all, counting the program name itself.

On lines 5 and 6, each of the command-line arguments is printed, passing the null-terminated strings to cout by indexing into the array of strings.

A more common use of command-line arguments is illustrated by modifying Listing 17.18 to take the filename as a command-line argument.

LISTING 17.20   Using Command-line Arguments

```
0:  //Listing 17.20 Using Command-line Arguments
1:  #include <fstream>
2:  #include <iostream>
3:  using namespace std;
4:
5:  class Animal
6:  {
7:  public:
8:      Animal(int weight,long days):itsWeight(weight),DaysAlive(days){}
9:      ~Animal(){}
10:
11:     int GetWeight()const { return itsWeight; }
12:     void SetWeight(int weight) { itsWeight = weight; }
13:
14:     long GetDaysAlive()const { return  DaysAlive; }
15:     void SetDaysAlive(long days) { DaysAlive = days; }
16:
17: private:
18:     int itsWeight;
19:     long DaysAlive;
20: };
21:
22: int main(int argc, char *argv[])    // returns 1 on error
23: {
24:    if (argc != 2)
25:    {
26:       cout << "Usage: " << argv[0] << " <filename>" << endl;
27:       return(1);
28:    }
29:
```

LISTING 17.20 continued

```
30:       ofstream fout(argv[1],ios::binary);
31:       if (!fout)
32:       {
33:          cout << "Unable to open " << argv[1] << " for writing.\n";
34:          return(1);
35:       }
36:
37:       Animal Bear(50,100);
38:       fout.write((char*) &Bear,sizeof Bear);
39:
40:       fout.close();
41:
42:       ifstream fin(argv[1],ios::binary);
43:       if (!fin)
44:       {
45:          cout << "Unable to open " << argv[1] << " for reading.\n";
46:          return(1);
47:       }
48:
49:       Animal BearTwo(1,1);
50:
51:       cout << "BearTwo weight: " << BearTwo.GetWeight() << endl;
52:       cout << "BearTwo days: " << BearTwo.GetDaysAlive() << endl;
53:
54:       fin.read((char*) &BearTwo, sizeof BearTwo);
55:
56:       cout << "BearTwo weight: " << BearTwo.GetWeight() << endl;
57:       cout << "BearTwo days: " << BearTwo.GetDaysAlive() << endl;
58:       fin.close();
59:       return 0;
60:  }
```

OUTPUT

```
BearTwo weight: 1
BearTwo days: 1
BearTwo weight: 50
BearTwo days: 100
```

ANALYSIS The declaration of the Animal class is the same as in Listing 17.18. This time, however, rather than prompting the user for the filename, command-line arguments are used. On line 22, main() is declared to take two parameters: the count of the command-line arguments and a pointer to the array of command-line argument strings.

On lines 24–28 the program ensures that the expected number of arguments (exactly two) is received. If the user fails to supply a single filename, an error message is printed:

```
Usage TestProgram <filename>
```

17

Then the program exits. Note that by using `argv[0]` rather than hard-coding a program name, you can compile this program to have any name, and this usage statement will work automatically.

On line 30, the program attempts to open the supplied filename for binary output. No reason exists to copy the filename into a local temporary buffer. It can be used directly by accessing `argv[1]`.

This technique is repeated on line 42 when the same file is reopened for input, and it is used in the error condition statements when the files cannot be opened, on lines 33 and 45.

Summary

Today streams were introduced, and the global objects `cout` and `cin` were described. The goal of the `istream` and `ostream` objects is to encapsulate the work of writing to device drivers and buffering input and output.

Four standard stream objects are created in every program: `cout`, `cin`, `cerr`, and `clog`. Each of these can be "redirected" by many operating systems.

The `istream` object `cin` is used for input, and its most common use is with the overloaded extraction operator (`>>`). The `ostream` object `cout` is used for output, and its most common use is with the overloaded insertion operator (`<<`).

Each of these objects has a number of other member functions, such as `get()` and `put()`. Because the common forms of each of these methods returns a reference to a stream object, it is easy to concatenate each of these operators and functions.

The state of the stream objects can be changed by using manipulators. These can set the formatting and display characteristics and various other attributes of the stream objects.

File I/O can be accomplished by using the `fstream` classes, which derive from the stream classes. In addition to supporting the normal insertion and extraction operators, these objects also support `read()` and `write()` for storing and retrieving large binary objects.

Q&A

Q How do you know when to use the insertion and extraction operators and when to use the other member functions of the stream classes?

A In general, it is easier to use the insertion and extraction operators, and they are preferred when their behavior is what is needed. In those unusual circumstances when these operators don't do the job (such as reading in a string of words), the other functions can be used.

Q What is the difference between `cerr` and `clog`?

A `cerr` is not buffered. Everything written to `cerr` is immediately written out. This is fine for errors to be written to the screen, but may have too high a performance cost for writing logs to disk. `clog` buffers its output, and thus can be more efficient.

Q Why were streams created if `printf()` works well?

A `printf()` does not support the strong type system of C++, and it does not support user-defined classes.

Q When would you ever use `putback()`?

A When one read operation is used to determine whether a character is valid, but a different read operation (perhaps by a different object) needs the character to be in the buffer. This is most often used when parsing a file; for example, the C++ compiler might use `putback()`.

Q When would you use `ignore()`?

A A common use of this is after using `get()`. Because `get()` leaves the terminating character in the buffer, it is not uncommon to immediately follow a call to `get()` with a call to `ignore(1,'\n');`. Again, this is often used in parsing.

Q My friends use `printf()` in their C++ programs. Can I?

A No. At this point `printf()` should properly be considered obsolete.

Workshop

The Workshop contains quiz questions to help solidify your understanding of the material covered and exercises to provide you with experience in using what you've learned. Try to answer the quiz and exercise questions before checking the answers in Appendix D, and make sure you understand the answers before going to the next chapter.

Quiz

1. What is the insertion operator, and what does it do?
2. What is the extraction operator, and what does it do?
3. What are the three forms of `cin.get()`, and what are their differences?
4. What is the difference between `cin.read()` and `cin.getline()`?
5. What is the default width for outputting a `long` integer using the insertion operator?
6. What is the return value of the insertion operator?
7. What parameter does the constructor to an `ofstream` object take?
8. What does the `ios::ate` argument do?

Exercises

1. Write a program that writes to the four standard iostream objects: `cin`, `cout`, `cerr`, and `clog`.

2. Write a program that prompts the user to enter her full name and then displays it on the screen.

3. Rewrite Listing 17.9 to do the same thing, but without using `putback()` or `ignore()`.

4. Write a program that takes a filename as a parameter and opens the file for reading. Read every character of the file and display only the letters and punctuation to the screen. (Ignore all nonprinting characters.) Then close the file and exit.

5. Write a program that displays its command-line arguments in reverse order and does not display the program name.

DAY **18**

Namespaces

Namespaces help programmers avoid name clashes when using more than one library.

Today you will learn

- How functions and classes are resolved by name.
- How to create a namespace.
- How to use a namespace.
- How to use the standard namespace std.

Getting Started

Name conflicts have been a source of aggravation to both C and C++ developers. A name clash happens when a duplicate name with matching scope is found in two parts of your program. The most common occurrence can be found in different library packages. For example, a container class library will almost certainly declare and implement a List class. (You'll learn more about container classes when we discuss templates on Day 19.)

It is not a surprise to find a List class also being used in a windowing library. Suppose that you want to maintain a list of windows for your application. Further assume that you are using the List class found in the container class library. You declare an instance of the window library's List to hold your windows, and you discover that the member functions you want to call are not available. The compiler has matched your List declaration to the List container in the standard library, but what you really wanted is the List found in the vendor-specific window library.

Namespaces are used to partition the global namespace and to eliminate, or at least reduce, name conflicts. Namespaces are similar in some ways to classes, and the syntax is very similar.

Items declared within the namespace are owned by the namespace. All items within a namespace have public visibility. Namespaces can be nested within other namespaces. Functions can be defined within the body of the namespace or defined outside the body of the namespace. If a function is defined outside the body of the namespace, it must be qualified by the namespace's name.

Functions and Classes Are Resolved by Name

As it parses source code and builds a list of function and variable names, the compiler checks for name conflicts. Those conflicts that can't be resolved by the compiler may be resolved by the linker.

The compiler cannot check for name clashes across translation units (for example, object files); that is the purpose of the linker. Thus, the compiler will not even offer a warning.

It is not uncommon for the linker to fail with the message *Identifier* multiply defined (*identifier* is some named type). You see this linker message if you have defined the same name with the same scope in different translation units. You get a compiler error if you redefine a name within a single file having the same scope. The following example, when compiled and linked, will produce an error message by the linker:

```
// file first.cpp
int integerValue = 0 ;
int main( ) {
    int integerValue = 0 ;
    // . . .
    return 0 ;
} ;

// file second.cpp
int integerValue = 0 ;
// end of second.cpp
```

My linker announces the following diagnostic: in second.obj: *integerValue* already defined in first.obj. If these names were in a different scope, the compiler and linker would not complain.

It is also possible to receive a warning from the compiler concerning *identifier hiding*. The compiler should warn, in first.cpp above, that integerValue in main() is *hiding* the global variable with the same name.

To use the integerValue declared outside main(), you must explicitly scope the variable to global scope. Consider this example, which assigns the value 10 to the integerValue outside main() and not to the integerValue declared within main():

```
// file first.cpp
int integerValue = 0 ;
int main( )
{
    int integerValue = 0 ;
    ::integerValue = 10 ; //assign to global "integerValue"
    // . . .
    return 0 ;
} ;

// file second.cpp
int integerValue = 0 ;
// end of second.cpp
```

18

Note Note the use of the scope resolution operator ::, indicating that the integerValue being referred to is global, not local.

The problem with the two global integers defined outside of any functions is that they have the same name and visibility, and thus will cause a linker error.

NEW TERM The term *visibility* is used to designate the scope of a defined object, whether it is a variable, a class, or a function. For example, a variable declared and defined outside any function has *file*, or *global*, scope. The visibility of this variable is from the point of its definition through the end of the file. A variable having a *block*, or *local*, scope is found within a block structure. The most common examples are variables defined within functions. The following example shows the scope of variables:

```
int globalScopeInt = 5 ;
void f( )
{
    int localScopeInt = 10 ;
}
```

```
int main( )
{
    int localScopeInt = 15 ;
    {
        int anotherLocal = 20 ;
        int localScopeInt = 30 ;
    }
    return 0 ;
}
```

The first int definition, globalScopeInt, is visible within the functions f() and main(). The next definition is found within the function f() and is named localScopeInt. This variable has local scope, meaning that it is visible only within the block defining it.

The main() function cannot access f()'s localScopeInt. When the function returns, localScopeInt goes out of scope. The third definition, also named localScopeInt, is found in the main() function. This variable has block scope.

Note that main()'s localScopeInt does not conflict with f()'s localScopeInt. The next two definitions, anotherLocal and localScopeInt, both have block scope. As soon as we reach the closing brace, these two variables lose their visibility.

Notice that that this localScopeInt is hiding the localScopeInt defined just before the opening brace (the second localScopeInt defined in the program). When the program moves past the closing brace, the second localScopeInt defined resumes visibility. Any changes made to the localScopeInt defined within the braces does not affect the contents of the outer localScopeInt.

NEW TERM Names can have *internal* and *external linkage*. These two terms refer to the use or availability of a name across multiple translation units or within a single translation unit. Any name having *internal* linkage can only be referred to within the translation unit in which it is defined. For example, a variable defined to have internal linkage can be shared by functions within the same translation unit. Names having *external* linkage are available to other translation units. The following example demonstrates internal and external linkage:

```
// file: first.cpp
int externalInt = 5 ;
const int j = 10 ;
int main()
{
    return 0 ;
}
```

```
// file: second.cpp
extern int externalInt ;
int anExternalInt = 10 ;
const int j = 10 ;
```

The `externalInt` variable defined in `first.cpp` has external linkage. Although it is defined in `first.cpp`, `second.cpp` can also access it. The two `j`s found in both files are `const`, which, by default, have internal linkage. You can override the `const` default by providing an explicit declaration, as shown here:

```
// file: first.cpp
extern const int j = 10 ;

// file: second.cpp
extern const int j ;
#include <iostream>
int main()
{
    std::cout << "j is " << j << std::endl ;
    return 0 ;
}
```

Note that we call `cout` with the namespace designation of `std`; this allows us to refer to all the "standard" objects in the ANSI Standard Library. When built, this example displays the following:

```
j is 10
```

The standards committee has deprecated the following type of usage:

```
static int staticInt = 10 ;
int main()
{
    //...
}
```

The use of `static` to limit the scope of external variables is no longer recommended and may become illegal in the future. You should now use namespaces instead of `static`.

Do	Don't
DO use namespaces instead.	**DON'T** apply the `static` keyword to a variable defined at file scope.

18

Creating a Namespace

The syntax for a namespace declaration is similar to the syntax for a `struct` or class declaration: First, apply the keyword `namespace` followed by an optional namespace name, and then an opening curly brace. The namespace is concluded with a closing brace but no terminating semicolon.

For example:

```
namespace Window
{
    void move( int x, int y) ;
}
```

The name `Window` uniquely identifies the namespace. You can have many occurrences of a named namespace. These multiple occurrences can occur within a single file or across multiple translation units. The C++ Standard Library namespace, `std`, is a prime example of this feature. This makes sense because the standard library is a logical grouping of functionality.

The main concept behind namespaces is to group related items into a specified (named) area. The following is a brief example of a namespace that spans multiple header files:

```
// header1.h
namespace Window
{
    void move( int x, int y) ;
}

// header2.h
namespace Window
{
    void resize( int x, int y ) ;
}
```

Declaring and Defining Types

You can declare and define types and functions within namespaces. Of course, this is a design and maintenance issue. Good design dictates that you should separate interface from implementation. You should follow this principle not only with classes but also with namespaces. The following example demonstrates a cluttered and poorly defined namespace:

```
namespace Window {
    // . . . other declarations and variable definitions.
    void move( int x, int y) ; // declarations
    void resize( int x, int y ) ;
    // . . . other declarations and variable definitions.
```

```
void move( int x, int y )
{
    if( x < MAX_SCREEN_X  && x > 0 )
        if( y < MAX_SCREEN_Y  && y > 0 )
            platform.move( x, y ) ; // specific routine
}

void resize( int x, int y )
{
    if( x < MAX_SIZE_X  && x > 0 )
        if( y < MAX_SIZE_Y  && y > 0 )
            platform.resize( x, y ) ; // specific routine
}
// . . . definitions continue
}
```

You can see how quickly the namespace becomes cluttered! The previous example is approximately 20 lines in length; imagine if this namespace were four times longer.

Defining Functions Outside a Namespace

You should define namespace functions outside the namespace body. Doing so illustrates a clear separation of the declaration of the function and its definition—and also keeps the namespace body uncluttered. Separating the function definition from the namespace also enables you to put the namespace and its embodied declarations within a header file; the definitions can be placed into an implementation file.

For example:

```
// file header.h
namespace Window {
    void move( int x, int y) ;
    // other declarations ...
}

// file impl.cpp
void Window::move( int x, int y )
{
    // code to move the window
}
```

Adding New Members

New members can be added to a namespace only within its body. You cannot define new members using qualifier syntax. The most you can expect from this style of definition is a complaint from your compiler. The following example demonstrates this error:

```
namespace Window {
    // lots of declarations
}
//...some code
int Window::newIntegerInNamespace ; // sorry, can't do this
```

The preceding line of code is illegal. Your (conforming) compiler will issue a diagnostic reflecting the error. To correct the error—or avoid it altogether—move the declaration within the namespace body.

All members encased within a namespace are public. The following code does not compile:

```
namespace Window {
    private:
        void move( int x, int y ) ;
}
```

Nesting Namespaces

A namespace can be nested within another namespace. The reason they can be nested is because the definition of a namespace is also declaration. As with any other namespace, you must qualify a name using the enclosing namespace. If you have nested namespaces, you must qualify each namespace in turn. For example, the following shows a named namespace nested within another named namespace:

```
namespace Window {
    namespace Pane {
        void size( int x, int y ) ;
    }
}
```

To access the function size() outside of Window, you must qualify the function with both enclosing namespace names. The following demonstrates the qualification:

```
int main( )
{
    Window::Pane::size( 10, 20 ) ;
    return 0 ;
}
```

Using a Namespace

Let's take a look at an example of using a namespace and the associated use of the scope resolution operator. I will first declare all types and functions for use within the namespace Window. After I define everything required, I then define any member functions declared. These member functions are defined outside of the namespace; the names are explicitly identified using the scope resolution operator. Listing 18.1 illustrates using a namespace.

LISTING 18.1 Using a Namespace

```
0: #include <iostream>
1: // Using a Namespace
2:
3: namespace Window
4: {
5:     const int MAX_X = 30 ;
6:     const int MAX_Y = 40 ;
7:     class Pane
8:     {
9:         public:
10:             Pane() ;
11:             ~Pane() ;
12:             void size( int x, int y ) ;
13:             void move( int x, int y ) ;
14:             void show( ) ;
15:         private:
16:             static int cnt ;
17:             int x ;
18:             int y ;
19:     };
20: }
21:
22: int Window::Pane::cnt = 0 ;
23: Window::Pane::Pane() : x(0), y(0) { }
24: Window::Pane::~Pane() { }
25:
26: void Window::Pane::size( int x, int y )
27: {
28:     if( x < Window::MAX_X  &&  x > 0 )
29:         Pane::x = x ;
30:     if( y < Window::MAX_Y  &&  y > 0 )
31:         Pane::y = y ;
32: }
33: void Window::Pane::move( int x, int y )
34: {
35:     if( x < Window::MAX_X  &&  x > 0 )
36:         Pane::x = x ;
37:     if( y < Window::MAX_Y  &&  y > 0 )
38:         Pane::y = y ;
39: }
40: void Window::Pane::show( )
41: {
42:     std::cout << "x " << Pane::x ;
43:     std::cout << " y " << Pane::y << std::endl ;
44: }
```

18

LISTING 18.1   continued

```
45:
46: int main( )
47: {
48:     Window::Pane pane ;
49:
50:     pane.move( 20, 20 ) ;
51:     pane.show( ) ;
52:
53:     return 0 ;
54: }
```

OUTPUT   x 20 y 20

ANALYSIS Note that class Pane is nested inside the namespace Window. This is the reason you have to qualify the name Pane with the Window:: qualifier.

The static variable cnt, which is declared in Pane on line 16, is defined as usual. Within the function Pane::size() on lines 26–32, notice that MAX_X and MAX_Y are fully qualified. This is because Pane is in scope; otherwise, the compiler would issue an error diagnostic. This also holds true for the function Pane::move().

Also interesting is the qualification of Pane::x and Pane::y inside both function definitions. Why is this? Well, if the function Pane::move() were written like this, you would have a problem:

```
void Window::Pane::move( int x, int y )
{
    if( x < Window::MAX_X  &&  x > 0 )
        x = x ;
    if( y < Window::MAX_Y  &&  y > 0 )
        y = y ;
    Platform::move( x, y ) ;
}
```

Can you spot the issue? You probably won't get much of an answer from your compiler; some won't issue any kind of diagnostic message at all.

The source of the problem is the function's arguments. Arguments x and y hide the private x and y instance variables declared within class Pane. Effectively, the statements assign both x and y to itself:

```
x = x ;
y = y ;
```

The using Keyword

The using keyword is used for both the using directive and the using declaration. The syntax of the using keyword determines whether the context is a directive or a declaration.

The using Directive

The using directive effectively exposes all names declared in a namespace to be in the current scope. You can refer to the names without qualifying them with their respective namespace name. The following example shows the using directive:

```
namespace Window {
    int value1 = 20 ;
    int value2 = 40 ;
}
. . .
Window::value1 = 10 ;

using namespace Window ;
value2 = 30 ;
```

The scope of the using directive begins at its declaration and continues on to the end of the current scope. Notice that value1 must be qualified in order to reference it. The variable value2 does not require the qualification because the directive introduces all names in a namespace into the current scope.

The using directive can be used at any level of scope. This enables you to use the directive within block scope; when that block goes out of scope, so do all the names within the namespace. The following sample shows this behavior:

```
namespace Window {
    int value1 = 20 ;
    int value2 = 40 ;
}
//. . .
void f()
{
    {
        using namespace Window ;
        value2 = 30 ;
    }
    value2 = 20 ; //error!
}
```

The last line of code in f(), value2 = 20 ; is an error because value2 is not defined. The name is accessible in the previous block because the directive pulls the name into that block. When that block goes out of scope, so do the names in namespace Window.

18

Variable names declared within a local scope hide any namespace names introduced in that scope. This behavior is similar to how a local variable hides a global variable. Even if you introduce a namespace after a local variable, that local variable will hide the namespace name. The following example shows this:

```
namespace Window {
    int value1 = 20 ;
    int value2 = 40 ;
}
//. . .
void f()
{
    int value2 = 10 ;
    using namespace Window ;
    std::cout << value2 << std::endl  ;
}
```

The output of this function is 10, not 40. This output confirms the fact that the value2 in namespace Window is hidden by the value2 in f(). If you need to use a name within a namespace, you must qualify the name with the namespace name.

An ambiguity can arise using a name that is both globally defined and defined within a namespace. The ambiguity surfaces only if the name is used, not just when a namespace is introduced. This is demonstrated with the following code fragment:

```
namespace Window {
    int value1 = 20 ;
}
//. . .
using namespace Window ;
int value1 = 10 ;
void f( )
{
    value1 = 10 ;
}
```

The ambiguity occurs within function f(). The directive effectively brings Window::value1 into the global namespace; because a value1 is already globally defined, the use of value1 in f() is an error. Note that if the line of code in f() were removed, no error would exist.

The using Declaration

The using declaration is similar to the using directive except that the declaration provides a finer level of control. More specifically, the using declaration is used to declare a specific name (from a namespace) to be in the current scope. You can then refer to the specified object by its name only. The following example demonstrates the use of the using declaration:

```
namespace Window {
    int value1 = 20 ;
    int value2 = 40 ;
    int value3 = 60 ;
}
//. . .
using Window::value2 ; //bring value2 into current scope
Window::value1 = 10 ;   //value1 must be qualified
value2 = 30 ;
Window::value3 = 10 ;   //value3 must be qualified
```

The using declaration adds the specified name to the current scope. The declaration does not affect the other names within the namespace. In the previous example, value2 is referenced without qualification, but value1 and value3 require qualification. The using declaration provides more control over namespace names that you bring into scope. This is in contrast with the directive that brings all names in a namespace into scope.

After a name is brought into a scope, it is visible until the end of that scope. This behavior is the same as any other declaration. A using declaration may be used in the global namespace or within any local scope.

It is an error to introduce a duplicate name into a local scope where a namespace name has been declared. The reverse is also true. The following example shows this:

```
namespace Window {
    int value1 = 20 ;
    int value2 = 40 ;
}
//. . .
void f()
{
    int value2 = 10 ;
    using Window::value2 ; // multiple declaration
    std::cout << value2 << std::endl ;
}
```

The second line in function f() will produce a compiler error because the name value2 is already defined. The same error occurs if the using declaration is introduced before the definition of the local value2.

Any name introduced at local scope with a using declaration hides any name outside that scope. The following code snippet demonstrates this behavior:

```
namespace Window {
    int value1 = 20 ;
    int value2 = 40 ;
}
int value2 = 10 ;
//. . .
```

18

```
void f()
{
    using Window::value2 ;
    std::cout << value2 << std::endl   ;
}
```

The using declaration in f() hides the value2 defined in the global namespace.

As mentioned before, a using *declaration* gives you finer control over the names introduced from a namespace. A using *directive* brings all names from a namespace into the current scope. It is preferable to use a declaration over a directive because a directive effectively defeats the purpose of the namespace mechanism. A declaration is more definitive because you are explicitly identifying the names you want to introduce into a scope. A using declaration will not pollute the global namespace, as is the case with a using directive (unless, of course, you declare all names found in the namespace). Name hiding, global namespace pollution, and ambiguity all are reduced to a more manageable level by using the using declaration.

The Namespace Alias

A namespace *alias* is designed to provide another name for a named namespace. An alias provides a shorthand term for you to use to refer to a namespace. This is especially true if a namespace name is very long; creating an alias can help cut down on lengthy, repetitive typing. Let's look at an example:

```
namespace the_software_company {
    int value ;
    // . . .
}
the_software_company::value = 10 ;
. . .
namespace TSC = the_software_company ;
TSC::value = 20 ;
```

A drawback, of course, is that your alias may collide with an existing name. If this is the case, the compiler will catch the conflict and you can resolve it by renaming the alias.

The Unnamed Namespace

An unnamed namespace is simply that—a namespace that does not have a name. A common use of unnamed spaces is to shield global data from potential name clashes between translation units. Every translation unit has its own unique, unnamed namespace. All names defined within the unnamed namespace (within each translation unit) can be referred to without explicit qualification. The following is an example of two unnamed namespaces found in two separate files:

```
// file: one.cpp
namespace {
    int value ;
    char p( char *p ) ;
    //. . .
}

// file: two.cpp
namespace {
    int value ;
    char p( char *p ) ;
    //. . .
}
int main( )
{
    char c = p( ptr ) ;
}
```

Each of the names, `value` and function `p()`, is distinct to its respective file. To refer to a (unnamed namespace) name within a translation unit, use the name without qualification. This usage is demonstrated in the previous example with the call to function `p()`. This use implies a `using` directive for objects referred to from an unnamed namespace. Because of this, you cannot access members of an unnamed namespace in another translation unit. The behavior of an unnamed namespace is the same as a `static` object having external linkage. Consider this example:

```
static int value = 10 ;
```

Remember that this use of the `static` keyword is deprecated by the standards committee. Namespaces now exist to replace code as previously shown. Another way to think of unnamed namespaces is that they are global variables with internal linkage.

The Standard Namespace `std`

The best example of namespaces is found in the C++ Standard Library. The standard library is completely encased within the namespace named `std`. All functions, classes, objects, and templates are declared within the namespace `std`.

You will, no doubt, see code such as the following:

```
#include <iostream>
using namespace std ;
```

Remember that the `using` directive pulls everything in from the named namespace. It is bad form to employ the `using` directive when using the standard library. Why? Because doing so defeats the purpose of using a namespace; the global namespace will be polluted with all the names found in the header. Keep in mind that all header files use the namespace feature, so if you include multiple standard header files and specify the `using` directive, then everything declared in the headers will be in the global namespace. Please note that most of the examples in this book violate this rule; this action is not an intent to advocate violating the rule, but it is used for brevity of the examples. You should use the `using` declaration instead, as in the following example:

```
#include <iostream>
using std::cin ;
using std::cout ;
using std::endl ;
int main( )
{
    int value = 0 ;
    cout << "So, how many eggs did you say you wanted?" << endl ;
    cin >> value ;
    cout << value << " eggs, sunny-side up!" << endl ;
    return( 0 ) ;
}
```

The following shows a sample run of the program:

```
So, how many eggs did you say you wanted?
4
4 eggs, sunny-side up!
```

As an alternative, you could fully qualify the names that you use, as in the following code sample:

```
#include <iostream>
int main( )
{
    int value = 0 ;
    std::cout << "How many eggs did you want?" << std::endl ;
    std::cin >> value ;
    std::cout << value << " eggs, sunny-side up!" << std::endl ;
    return( 0 ) ;
}
```

Sample output from this program is shown here:

```
How many eggs did you want?
4
4 eggs, sunny-side up!
```

This might be appropriate for shorter programs but can become quite cumbersome for any significant amount of code. Imagine having to prefix `std::` for every name you use that is found in the standard library!

Summary

Creating a namespace is very similar to a class declaration. A couple of differences are worth noting. First, a semicolon does not follow a namespace's closing brace. Second, a namespace is open, whereas a class is closed. This means that you can continue to define the namespace in other files or in separate sections of a single file.

Anything that can be declared can be inserted into a namespace. If you are designing classes for a reusable library, you should be using the namespace feature. Functions declared within a namespace should be defined outside of that namespace's body. This promotes a separation of interface from implementation and also keeps the namespace from becoming cluttered.

Namespaces can be nested. A namespace is a declaration; this fact enables you to nest namespaces. Don't forget that you must fully qualify names that are nested.

The using directive is used to expose all names in a namespace in to the current scope. This effectively pollutes the global namespace with all names found in the named namespace. It is generally bad practice to use the using directive, especially with respect to the standard library. Use using declarations instead.

The using declaration is used to expose a specific namespace name into the current scope. This allows you to refer to the object by its name only.

A namespace alias is similar in nature to a typedef. A namespace alias enables you to create another name for a named namespace. This can be quite useful when you are using a namespace with a long name.

Every file can contain an unnamed namespace. An unnamed namespace, as its name implies, is a namespace without a name. An unnamed namespace allows you to use the names within the namespace without qualification. It keeps the namespace names local to the translation unit. Unnamed namespaces are the same as declaring a global variable with the static keyword.

The C++ Standard Library is enclosed in a namespace named std. Avoid using the using directive when using the standard library; instead, use the using declaration.

Q&A

Q Do I have to use namespaces?

A No, you can write simple programs and ignore namespaces altogether. Be sure to use the old standard libraries (for example, #include <string.h>) rather than the new libraries (for example, #include <cstring>).

Q **What are the two forms of statements with the `using` keyword? What are the differences between those two forms?**

A The `using` keyword can be used for the `using` directives and the `using` declarations. A `using` directive allows all names in a namespace to be used as if they are normal names. A `using` declaration, on the other hand, enables the program to use an individual name from a namespace without qualifying it with the namespace qualifier.

Q **What are the unnamed namespaces? Why do we need unnamed namespaces?**

A Unnamed namespaces are namespaces without names. They are used to wrap a collection of declarations against possible name clashes. Names in an unnamed namespace cannot be used outside of the translation unit where the namespace is declared.

Workshop

The Workshop contains quiz questions to help solidify your understanding of the material covered and exercises to provide you with experience in using what you've learned. Try to answer the quiz and exercise questions before checking the answers in Appendix D, and make sure you understand the answers before going to the next chapter.

Quiz

1. Can I use names defined in a namespace without using the `using` keyword?

2. What are the major differences between normal and unnamed namespaces?

3. What is the standard namespace?

Exercises

1. **BUG BUSTERS:** What is wrong in this program?

```
#include <iostream>
int main()
{
    cout << "Hello world!" << end;
    return 0;
}
```

2. List three ways of fixing the problem found in Exercise 1.

DAY 19

Templates

A powerful new tool for C++ programmers is "parameterized types" or *templates*. Templates are so useful that the Standard Template Library (STL) has been adopted into the definition of the C++ language.

Today you will learn

- What templates are and how to use them.
- How to create class templates.
- How to create function templates.
- What the Standard Template Library is and how to use it.

What Are Templates?

At the end of Week 2, you saw how to build a PartsList object and how to use it to create a PartsCatalog. If you want to build on the PartsList object to make a list of cats, you have a problem: PartsList only knows about parts.

To solve this problem, you can create a List base classs. You could then cut and paste much of the PartsList class into the new CatsList declaration. Next week, when you want to make a list of Car objects, you would then have to make a new class, and again you would cut and paste.

Needless to say, this is not a satisfactory solution. Over time, the List class and its derived classes will have to be extended. Making sure that all the changes are propagated to all the related classes would be a nightmare.

Templates solve this problem, and with the adoption of the ANSI standard, they are an integral part of the language. Like all of C++, they are type-safe and very flexible.

Parameterized Types

Templates enable you to teach the compiler how to make a list of any type of thing, rather than creating a set of type-specific lists—a PartsList is a list of parts, a CatsList is a list of cats. The only way in which they differ is the type of the thing on the list. With templates, the type of the thing on the list becomes a parameter to the definition of the class.

A common component of virtually all C++ libraries is an array class. As you saw with Lists, it is tedious and inefficient to create one array class for integers, another for doubles, and yet another for an array of Animals. Templates let you declare a parameterized array class and then specify what type of object each instance of the array will hold. Note that the Standard Template Library provides a standardized set of *container* classes, including arrays, lists, and so forth. We'll explore what it would take to write your own so that you fully understand how templates work; but in a commercial program, you would almost certainly use the STL classes rather than creating your own.

Instantiating an Instance of a Template

Instantiation is the act of creating a specific type from a template. The individual classes are called instances of the template.

Parameterized templates provide you with the capability to create a general class and pass types as parameters to that class to build specific instances.

Template Definition

You declare a parameterized Array object (a template for an array) by writing

```
1: template <class T>     // declare the template and the parameter
2: class Array            // the class being parameterized
3: {
4:    public:
5:       Array();
6:    // full class declaration here
7: };
```

The keyword `template` is used at the beginning of every declaration and definition of a template class. The parameters of the template are after the keyword `template`. The parameters are the things that will change with each instance. In the array template shown previously, for example, the type of the objects stored in the array will change. One instance might store an array of integers and another might store an array of `Animals`.

In this example, the keyword `class` is used, followed by the identifier `T`. The keyword `class` indicates that this parameter is a type. The identifier `T` is used throughout the rest of the template definition to refer to the parameterized type. One instance of this class will substitute `int` everywhere `T` appears, and another will substitute `Cat`.

To declare an `int` and a `Cat` instance of the parameterized `Array` class, you would write

```
Array<int> anIntArray;
Array<Cat> aCatArray;
```

The object `anIntArray` is of the type *array of integers*; the object `aCatArray` is of the type *array of cats*. You can now use the type `Array<int>` anywhere you would normally use a type—as the return value from a function, as a parameter to a function, and so forth. Listing 19.1 provides the full declaration of this stripped-down `Array` template.

Note

Listing 19.1 is not a complete program!

LISTING 19.1 A Template of an Array Class

19

```
0:  //Listing 19.1 A template of an array class
1:  #include <iostream>
2:  using namespace std;
3:  const int DefaultSize = 10;
4:
5:  template <class T>  // declare the template and the parameter
6:  class Array          // the class being parameterized
7:  {
8:  public:
9:      // constructors
10:     Array(int itsSize = DefaultSize);
11:     Array(const Array &rhs);
12:     ~Array() { delete [] pType; }
13:
14:     // operators
15:     Array& operator=(const Array&);
16:     T& operator[](int offSet) { return pType[offSet]; }
17:
18:     // accessors
```

LISTING 19.1   continued

```
19:        int getSize() { return itsSize; }
20:
21:    private:
22:        T *pType;
23:        int  itsSize;
24:    };
```

OUTPUT   There is no output. This is an incomplete program.

ANALYSIS   The definition of the template begins on line 5 with the keyword `template` followed by the parameter. In this case, the parameter is identified to be a type by the keyword `class`, and the identifier `T` is used to represent the parameterized type.

From line 6 until the end of the template on line 24, the rest of the declaration is like any other class declaration. The only difference is that wherever the type of the object would normally appear, the identifier `T` is used instead. For example, `operator[]` would be expected to return a reference to an object in the array, and in fact, it is declared to return a reference to a `T`.

When an instance of an integer array is declared, the `operator=` that is provided to that array will return a reference to an integer. When an instance of an `Animal` array is declared, the `operator=` provided to the `Animal` array will return a reference to an `Animal`.

Using the Name

Within the class declaration, the word `Array` may be used without further qualification. Elsewhere in the program, this class will be referred to as `Array<T>`. For example, if you do not write the constructor within the class declaration, you must write

```
template <class T>
Array<T>::Array(int size):
itsSize = size
{
    pType = new T[size];
    for (int i = 0; i<size; i++)
    pType[i] = 0;
}
```

The declaration on the first line of this code fragment is required to identify the type (`class T`). The template name is `Array<T>`, and the function name is `Array(int size)`.

The remainder of the function is the same as it would be for a non-template function. It is a common and preferred method to get the class and its functions working as a simple declaration before turning it into a template. This simplifies development, allowing you first to concentrate on the programming objective, and then later to generalize the solution with templates.

Implementing the Template

The full implementation of the `Array` template class requires implementation of the copy constructor, `operator=`, and so forth. Listing 19.2 provides a simple driver program to exercise this template class.

Note

> Some older compilers do not support templates. Templates are, however, part of the ANSI C++ standard. All major compiler vendors support templates in their current versions. If you have a very old compiler, you won't be able to compile and run the exercises in this chapter. It's still a good idea to read through the entire chapter, however, and return to this material when you upgrade your compiler.

LISTING 19.2   The Implementation of the Template Array

```
0:   //Listing 19.2 The Implementation of the Template Array
1:   #include <iostream>
2:
3:   const int DefaultSize = 10;
4:
5:   // declare a simple Animal class so that we can
6:   // create an array of animals
7:
8:   class Animal
9:   {
10:  public:
11:      Animal(int);
12:      Animal();
13:      ~Animal() {}
14:      int GetWeight() const { return itsWeight; }
15:      void Display() const { std::cout << itsWeight; }
16:  private:
17:      int itsWeight;
18:  };
19:
20:  Animal::Animal(int weight):
21:      itsWeight(weight)
22:  {}
23:
```

19

LISTING 19.2   continued

```
24:   Animal::Animal():
25:       itsWeight(0)
26:   {}
27:
28:
29:   template <class T>  // declare the template and the parameter
30:   class Array              // the class being parameterized
31:   {
32:   public:
33:       // constructors
34:       Array(int itsSize = DefaultSize);
35:       Array(const Array &rhs);
36:       ~Array() { delete [] pType; }
37:
38:       // operators
39:       Array& operator=(const Array&);
40:       T& operator[](int offSet) { return pType[offSet]; }
41:       const T& operator[](int offSet) const
42:           { return pType[offSet]; }
43:       // accessors
44:       int GetSize() const { return itsSize; }
45:
46:   private:
47:       T *pType;
48:       int  itsSize;
49:   };
50:
51:   // implementations follow...
52:
53:   // implement the Constructor
54:   template <class T>
55:   Array<T>::Array(int size):
56:   itsSize(size)
57:   {
58:       pType = new T[size];
59:       for (int i = 0; i<size; i++)
60:           pType[i] = 0;
61:   }
62:
63:   // copy constructor
64:   template <class T>
65:   Array<T>::Array(const Array &rhs)
66:   {
67:       itsSize = rhs.GetSize();
68:       pType = new T[itsSize];
69:       for (int i = 0; i<itsSize; i++)
70:           pType[i] = rhs[i];
71:   }
72:
```

LISTING 19.2   continued

```
73:    // operator=
74:    template <class T>
75:    Array<T>& Array<T>::operator=(const Array &rhs)
76:    {
77:       if (this == &rhs)
78:          return *this;
79:       delete [] pType;
80:       itsSize = rhs.GetSize();
81:       pType = new T[itsSize];
82:       for (int i = 0; i<itsSize; i++)
83:          pType[i] = rhs[i];
84:       return *this;
85:    }
86:
87:    // driver program
88:    int main()
89:    {
90:       Array<int> theArray;      // an array of integers
91:       Array<Animal> theZoo;     // an array of Animals
92:       Animal *pAnimal;
93:
94:       // fill the arrays
95:       for (int i = 0; i < theArray.GetSize(); i++)
96:       {
97:          theArray[i] = i*2;
98:          pAnimal = new Animal(i*3);
99:          theZoo[i] = *pAnimal;
100:          delete pAnimal;
101:       }
102:       // print the contents of the arrays
103:       for (int j = 0; j < theArray.GetSize(); j++)
104:       {
105:          std::cout << "theArray[" << j << "]:\t";
106:          std::cout << theArray[j] << "\t\t";
107:          std::cout << "theZoo[" << j << "]:\t";
108:          theZoo[j].Display();
109:          std::cout << std::endl;
110:       }
111:
112:       return 0;
113:    }
```

OUTPUT

```
theArray[0]:    0        theZoo[0]:    0
theArray[1]:    2        theZoo[1]:    3
theArray[2]:    4        theZoo[2]:    6
theArray[3]:    6        theZoo[3]:    9
theArray[4]:    8        theZoo[4]:    12
theArray[5]:    10       theZoo[5]:    15
```

19

```
theArray[6]:    12        theZoo[6]:     18
theArray[7]:    14        theZoo[7]:     21
theArray[8]:    16        theZoo[8]:     24
theArray[9]:    18        theZoo[9]:     27
```

ANALYSIS Lines 8–26 provide a stripped-down Animal class, created here so that objects of a user-defined type are available to add to the array.

Line 29 declares that what follows is a template and that the parameter to the template is a type, designated as T. The Array class has two constructors as shown, the first of which takes a size and defaults to the constant integer DefaultSize.

The assignment and offset operators are declared, with the latter declaring both a const and a non-const variant. The only accessor provided is GetSize(), which returns the size of the array.

One can certainly imagine a fuller interface, and, for any serious Array program, what has been supplied here would be inadequate. At a minimum, operators to remove elements, to expand the array, to pack the array, and so forth would be required. All this is supplied by the STL container classes, as we will discuss toward the end of this chapter.

The private data consists of the size of the array and a pointer to the actual in-memory array of objects.

Template Functions

If you want to pass an array object to a function, you must pass a particular instance of the array, not a template. Therefore, if SomeFunction() takes an integer array as a parameter, you may write

```
void SomeFunction(Array<int>&);    // ok
```

but you may not write

```
void SomeFunction(Array<T>&);    // error!
```

because there is no way to know what a T& is. You also may not write

```
void SomeFunction(Array &);      // error!
```

because there is no class Array—only the template and the instances.

To accomplish the more general approach, you must declare a template function.

```
template <class T>
void MyTemplateFunction(Array<T>&);    // ok
```

Here the function `MyTemplateFunction()` is declared to be a template function by the declaration on the top line. Note that template functions can have any name, the same as other functions can.

Template functions can also take instances of the template in addition to the parameterized form. The following is an example:

```
template <class T>
void MyOtherFunction(Array<T>&, Array<int>&);   // ok
```

Note that this function takes two arrays: a parameterized array and an array of integers. The former can be an array of any object, but the latter is always an array of integers.

Templates and Friends

Template classes can declare three types of friends:

- A non-template friend class or function
- A general template friend class or function
- A type-specific template friend class or function

Non-Template Friend Classes and Functions

It is possible to declare any class or function to be a friend to your template class. Each instance of the class will treat the friend properly, as if the declaration of friendship had been made in that particular instance. Listing 19.3 adds a trivial friend function, `Intrude()`, to the template definition of the `Array` class, and the driver program invokes `Intrude()`. Because it is a friend, `Intrude()` can then access the private data of the `Array`. Because this is not a template function, it can only be called on `Array`s of int.

LISTING 19.3 Non-template Friend Function

```
0:  // Listing 19.3 - Type specific friend functions in templates
1:
2:  #include <iostream>
3:  using namespace std;
4:
5:  const int DefaultSize = 10;
6:
7:  // declare a simple Animal class so that we can
8:  // create an array of animals
9:
10:  class Animal
11:  {
12:  public:
13:      Animal(int);
```

19

LISTING 19.3 continued

```
14:     Animal();
15:     ~Animal() {}
16:     int GetWeight() const { return itsWeight; }
17:     void Display() const { cout << itsWeight; }
18:  private:
19:     int itsWeight;
20:  };
21:
22:  Animal::Animal(int weight):
23:     itsWeight(weight)
24:  {}
25:
26:  Animal::Animal():
27:     itsWeight(0)
28:  {}
29:
30:  template <class T>  // declare the template and the parameter
31:  class Array            // the class being parameterized
32:  {
33:  public:
34:     // constructors
35:     Array(int itsSize = DefaultSize);
36:     Array(const Array &rhs);
37:     ~Array() { delete [] pType; }
38:
39:     // operators
40:     Array& operator=(const Array&);
41:     T& operator[](int offSet) { return pType[offSet]; }
42:     const T& operator[](int offSet) const
43:     { return pType[offSet]; }
44:     // accessors
45:     int GetSize() const { return itsSize; }
46:
47:     // friend function
48:     friend void Intrude(Array<int>);
49:
50:  private:
51:     T *pType;
52:     int  itsSize;
53:  };
54:
55:  // friend function. Not a template, can only be used
56:  // with int arrays! Intrudes into private data.
57:  void Intrude(Array<int> theArray)
58:  {
59:     cout << "\n*** Intrude ***\n";
60:     for (int i = 0; i < theArray.itsSize; i++)
61:        cout << "i: " <<    theArray.pType[i] << endl;
```

LISTING 19.3   continued

```
62:     cout << "\n";
63:  }
64:
65:  // implementations follow...
66:
67:  // implement the Constructor
68:  template <class T>
69:  Array<T>::Array(int size):
70:      itsSize(size)
71:  {
72:     pType = new T[size];
73:     for (int i = 0; i<size; i++)
74:         pType[i] = 0;
75:  }
76:
77:  // copy constructor
78:  template <class T>
79:  Array<T>::Array(const Array &rhs)
80:  {
81:     itsSize = rhs.GetSize();
82:     pType = new T[itsSize];
83:     for (int i = 0; i<itsSize; i++)
84:         pType[i] = rhs[i];
85:  }
86:
87:  // operator=
88:  template <class T>
89:  Array<T>& Array<T>::operator=(const Array &rhs)
90:  {
91:     if (this == &rhs)
92:         return *this;
93:     delete [] pType;
94:     itsSize = rhs.GetSize();
95:     pType = new T[itsSize];
96:     for (int i = 0; i<itsSize; i++)
97:         pType[i] = rhs[i];
98:     return *this;
99:  }
100:
101:  // driver program
102:  int main()
103:  {
104:     Array<int> theArray;        // an array of integers
105:     Array<Animal> theZoo;       // an array of Animals
106:     Animal *pAnimal;
107:
108:     // fill the arrays
109:     for (int i = 0; i < theArray.GetSize(); i++)
110:     {
```

19

LISTING **19.3**   continued

```
111:            theArray[i] = i*2;
112:            pAnimal = new Animal(i*3);
113:            theZoo[i] = *pAnimal;
114:        }
115:
116:        int j;
117:        for (j = 0; j < theArray.GetSize(); j++)
118:        {
119:            cout << "theZoo[" << j << "]:\t";
120:            theZoo[j].Display();
121:            cout << endl;
122:        }
123:        cout << "Now use the friend function to ";
124:        cout << "find the members of Array<int>";
125:        Intrude(theArray);
126:
127:        cout << "\n\nDone.\n";
128:        return 0;
129: }
```

OUTPUT

```
theZoo[0]:       0
theZoo[1]:       3
theZoo[2]:       6
theZoo[3]:       9
theZoo[4]:       12
theZoo[5]:       15
theZoo[6]:       18
theZoo[7]:       21
theZoo[8]:       24
theZoo[9]:       27
Now use the friend function to find the members of Array<int>
*** Intrude ***
i: 0
i: 2
i: 4
i: 6
i: 8
i: 10
i: 12
i: 14
i: 16
i: 18

Done.
```

ANALYSIS   The declaration of the Array template has been extended to include the friend function Intrude(). This declares that every instance of an int array will consider Intrude() to be a friend function; thus, Intrude() will have access to the private member data and functions of the array instance.

On line 60, `Intrude()` accesses `itsSize` directly, and on line 61, it accesses `pType` directly. This trivial use of these members was unnecessary because the `Array` class provides public accessors for this data, but it serves to demonstrate how friend functions can be declared with templates.

General Template Friend Class or Function

It would be helpful to add a display operator to the `Array` class. One approach would be to declare a display operator for each possible type of `Array`, but this would undermine the whole point of having made `Array` a template.

What is needed is an insertion operator that works for any possible type of `Array`:

```
ostream& operator<< (ostream&, Array<T>&);
```

To make this work, we need to declare `operator<<` to be a template function:

```
template <class T> ostream& operator<< (ostream&, Array<T>&)
```

Now that `operator<<` is a template function, you need only to provide an implementation. Listing 19.4 shows the `Array` template extended to include this declaration and provides the implementation for the `operator<<`.

LISTING 19.4 Using Operator `ostream`

```
0:   //Listing 19.4 Using Operator ostream
1:   #include <iostream>
2:   using namespace std;
3:
4:   const int DefaultSize = 10;
5:
6:   class Animal
7:   {
8:   public:
9:       Animal(int);
10:      Animal();
11:      ~Animal() {}
12:      int GetWeight() const { return itsWeight; }
13:      void Display() const { cout << itsWeight; }
14:  private:
15:      int itsWeight;
16:  };
17:
18:  Animal::Animal(int weight):
19:      itsWeight(weight)
20:  {}
21:
22:  Animal::Animal():
23:      itsWeight(0)
```

19

LISTING 19.4   continued

```
24:  {}
25:
26:  template <class T>   // declare the template and the parameter
27:  class Array            // the class being parameterized
28:  {
29:  public:
30:     // constructors
31:     Array(int itsSize = DefaultSize);
32:     Array(const Array &rhs);
33:     ~Array() { delete [] pType; }
34:
35:     // operators
36:     Array& operator=(const Array&);
37:     T& operator[](int offSet) { return pType[offSet]; }
38:     const T& operator[](int offSet) const
39:        { return pType[offSet]; }
40:     // accessors
41:     int GetSize() const { return itsSize; }
42:
43:     friend ostream& operator<< (ostream&, Array<T>&);
44:
45:  private:
46:     T *pType;
47:     int  itsSize;
48:  };
49:
50:  template <class T>
51:  ostream& operator<< (ostream& output, Array<T>& theArray)
52:  {
53:     for (int i = 0; i<theArray.GetSize(); i++)
54:        output << "[" << i << "] " << theArray[i] << endl;
55:     return output;
56:  }
57:
58:  // implementations follow...
59:
60:  // implement the Constructor
61:  template <class T>
62:  Array<T>::Array(int size):
63:     itsSize(size)
64:  {
65:     pType = new T[size];
66:     for (int i = 0; i<size; i++)
67:        pType[i] = 0;
68:  }
69:
70:  // copy constructor
71:  template <class T>
72:  Array<T>::Array(const Array &rhs)
```

LISTING 19.4   continued

```
73:   {
74:     itsSize = rhs.GetSize();
75:     pType = new T[itsSize];
76:     for (int i = 0; i<itsSize; i++)
77:         pType[i] = rhs[i];
78:   }
79:
80:   // operator=
81:   template <class T>
82:   Array<T>& Array<T>::operator=(const Array &rhs)
83:   {
84:     if (this == &rhs)
85:         return *this;
86:     delete [] pType;
87:     itsSize = rhs.GetSize();
88:     pType = new T[itsSize];
89:     for (int i = 0; i<itsSize; i++)
90:         pType[i] = rhs[i];
91:     return *this;
92:   }
93:
94:   int main()
95:   {
96:     bool Stop = false;        // flag for looping
97:     int offset, value;
98:     Array<int> theArray;
99:
100:    while (!Stop)
101:    {
102:       cout << "Enter an offset (0-9) ";
103:       cout << "and a value. (-1 to stop): " ;
104:       cin >> offset >> value;
105:
106:       if (offset < 0)
107:          break;
108:
109:       if (offset > 9)
110:       {
111:          cout << "***Please use values between 0 and 9.***\n";
112:          continue;
113:       }
114:
115:       theArray[offset] = value;
116:    }
117:
118:    cout << "\nHere's the entire array:\n";
119:    cout << theArray << endl;
120:    return 0;
121: }
```

19

OUTPUT
```
Enter an offset (0-9) and a value. (-1 to stop): 1 10
Enter an offset (0-9) and a value. (-1 to stop): 2 20
Enter an offset (0-9) and a value. (-1 to stop): 3 30
Enter an offset (0-9) and a value. (-1 to stop): 4 40
Enter an offset (0-9) and a value. (-1 to stop): 5 50
Enter an offset (0-9) and a value. (-1 to stop): 6 60
Enter an offset (0-9) and a value. (-1 to stop): 7 70
Enter an offset (0-9) and a value. (-1 to stop): 8 80
Enter an offset (0-9) and a value. (-1 to stop): 9 90
Enter an offset (0-9) and a value. (-1 to stop): 10 10
***Please use values between 0 and 9.***
Enter an offset (0-9) and a value. (-1 to stop): -1 -1

Here's the entire array:
[0] 0
[1] 10
[2] 20
[3] 30
[4] 40
[5] 50
[6] 60
[7] 70
[8] 80
[9] 90
```

ANALYSIS   On line 43, the function template operator<<() is declared to be a friend of the Array class template. Because operator<<() is implemented as a template function, every instance of this parameterized array type will automatically have an operator<<(). The implementation for this operator starts on line 50. Every member of an array is called in turn. This only works if an operator<<() is defined for every type of object stored in the array.

Using Template Items

You can treat template items as you would any other type. You can pass them as parameters, either by reference or by value, and you can return them as the return values of functions, also by value or by reference. Listing 19.5 demonstrates how to pass template objects.

LISTING 19.5   Passing Template Objects to and from Functions

```
0:  //Listing 19.5 Passing Template Objects to and from Functions
1:  #include <iostream>
2:  using namespace std;
3:
4:  const int DefaultSize = 10;
5:
```

LISTING 19.5   continued

```
6:   // A trivial class for adding to arrays
7:   class Animal
8:   {
9:   public:
10:      // constructors
11:      Animal(int);
12:      Animal();
13:      ~Animal();
14:
15:      // accessors
16:      int GetWeight() const { return itsWeight; }
17:      void SetWeight(int theWeight) { itsWeight = theWeight; }
18:
19:      // friend operators
20:      friend ostream& operator<< (ostream&, const Animal&);
21:
22:   private:
23:      int itsWeight;
24:   };
25:
26:   // extraction operator for printing animals
27:   ostream& operator<<
28:   (ostream& theStream, const Animal& theAnimal)
29:   {
30:      theStream << theAnimal.GetWeight();
31:      return theStream;
32:   }
33:
34:   Animal::Animal(int weight):
35:   itsWeight(weight)
36:   {
37:      // cout << "Animal(int)\n";
38:   }
39:
40:   Animal::Animal():
41:   itsWeight(0)
42:   {
43:      // cout << "Animal()\n";
44:   }
45:
46:   Animal::~Animal()
47:   {
48:      // cout << "Destroyed an animal...\n";
49:   }
50:
51:   template <class T>  // declare the template and the parameter
52:   class Array                // the class being parameterized
53:   {
54:   public:
```

19

LISTING **19.5**   continued

```
55:        Array(int itsSize = DefaultSize);
56:        Array(const Array &rhs);
57:        ~Array() { delete [] pType; }
58:
59:        Array& operator=(const Array&);
60:        T& operator[](int offSet) { return pType[offSet]; }
61:        const T& operator[](int offSet) const
62:           { return pType[offSet]; }
63:        int GetSize() const { return itsSize; }
64:
65:        // friend function
66:        friend ostream& operator<< (ostream&, const Array<T>&);
67:
68:    private:
69:        T *pType;
70:        int  itsSize;
71:    };
72:
73:    template <class T>
74:    ostream& operator<< (ostream& output, const Array<T>& theArray)
75:    {
76:        for (int i = 0; i<theArray.GetSize(); i++)
77:            output << "[" << i << "] " << theArray[i] << endl;
78:        return output;
79:    }
80:
81:    // implementations follow...
82:
83:    // implement the Constructor
84:    template <class T>
85:    Array<T>::Array(int size):
86:    itsSize(size)
87:    {
88:        pType = new T[size];
89:        for (int i = 0; i<size; i++)
90:            pType[i] = 0;
91:    }
92:
93:    // copy constructor
94:    template <class T>
95:    Array<T>::Array(const Array &rhs)
96:    {
97:        itsSize = rhs.GetSize();
98:        pType = new T[itsSize];
99:        for (int i = 0; i<itsSize; i++)
100:           pType[i] = rhs[i];
101:    }
102:
103:    void IntFillFunction(Array<int>& theArray);
```

LISTING 19.5 continued

```
104:    void AnimalFillFunction(Array<Animal>& theArray);
105:
106:    int main()
107:    {
108:       Array<int> intArray;
109:       Array<Animal> animalArray;
110:       IntFillFunction(intArray);
111:       AnimalFillFunction(animalArray);
112:       cout << "intArray...\n" << intArray;
113:       cout << "\nanimalArray...\n" << animalArray << endl;
114:       return 0;
115:    }
116:
117:    void IntFillFunction(Array<int>& theArray)
118:    {
119:       bool Stop = false;
120:       int offset, value;
121:       while (!Stop)
122:       {
123:          cout << "Enter an offset (0-9) ";
124:          cout << "and a value. (-1 to stop): " ;
125:          cin >> offset >> value;
126:          if (offset < 0)
127:             break;
128:          if (offset > 9)
129:          {
130:             cout << "***Please use values between 0 and 9.***\n";
131:             continue;
132:          }
133:          theArray[offset] = value;
134:       }
135:    }
136:
137:
138:    void AnimalFillFunction(Array<Animal>& theArray)
139:    {
140:       Animal * pAnimal;
141:       for (int i = 0; i<theArray.GetSize(); i++)
142:       {
143:          pAnimal = new Animal;
144:          pAnimal->SetWeight(i*100);
145:          theArray[i] = *pAnimal;
146:          delete pAnimal;   // a copy was put in the array
147:       }
148:    }
```

19

OUTPUT

```
Enter an offset (0-9) and a value. (-1 to stop): 1 10
Enter an offset (0-9) and a value. (-1 to stop): 2 20
Enter an offset (0-9) and a value. (-1 to stop): 3 30
Enter an offset (0-9) and a value. (-1 to stop): 4 40
Enter an offset (0-9) and a value. (-1 to stop): 5 50
Enter an offset (0-9) and a value. (-1 to stop): 6 60
Enter an offset (0-9) and a value. (-1 to stop): 7 70
Enter an offset (0-9) and a value. (-1 to stop): 8 80
Enter an offset (0-9) and a value. (-1 to stop): 9 90
Enter an offset (0-9) and a value. (-1 to stop): 10 10
***Please use values between 0 and 9.***
Enter an offset (0-9) and a value. (-1 to stop): -1 -1

intArray:...
[0] 0
[1] 10
[2] 20
[3] 30
[4] 40
[5] 50
[6] 60
[7] 70
[8] 80
[9] 90

animalArray:...
[0] 0
[1] 100
[2] 200
[3] 300
[4] 400
[5] 500
[6] 600
[7] 700
[8] 800
[9] 900
```

ANALYSIS Most of the Array class implementation is left out to save space. The Animal class is declared on lines 7–24. Although this is a stripped-down and simplified class, it does provide its own insertion operator (<<) to allow the printing of Animals. Printing simply prints the current weight of the Animal.

Note that Animal has a default constructor. This is necessary because, when you add an object to an array, the object's default constructor is used to create the object. This creates some difficulties, as you'll see.

On line 103, the function IntFillFunction() is declared. The prototype indicates that this function takes an integer array. Note that this is not a template function. IntFillFunction() expects only one type of an array—an integer array. Similarly, on line 104, AnimalFillFunction() is declared to take an Array of Animal.

The implementations for these functions are different from one another because filling an array of integers does not have to be accomplished in the same way as filling an array of Animals.

Specialized Functions

If you uncomment the print statements in Animal's constructors and destructor in Listing 19.5, you'll find unanticipated extra constructions and destructions of Animals.

When an object is added to an array, the object's default constructor is called. The Array constructor, however, goes on to assign 0 to the value of each member of the array, as shown on lines 59 and 60 of Listing 19.2.

When you write someAnimal = (Animal) 0;, you call the default operator= for Animal. This causes a temporary Animal object to be created, using the constructor, which takes an integer (zero). That temporary is used as the right-hand side of the operator= and then is destroyed.

This is an unfortunate waste of time because the Animal object was already properly initialized. However, you can't remove this line because integers are not automatically initialized to a value of 0. The solution is to teach the template not to use this constructor for Animals, but to use a special Animal constructor.

You can provide an explicit implementation for the Animal class, as indicated in Listing 19.6.

LISTING 19.6   Specializing Template Implementations

```
0:   #include <iostream>
1:   using namespace std;
2:
3:   const int DefaultSize = 3;
4:
5:   // A trivial class for adding to arrays
6:   class Animal
7:   {
8:   public:
9:       // constructors
10:      Animal(int);
11:      Animal();
12:      ~Animal();
13:
14:      // accessors
15:      int GetWeight() const { return itsWeight; }
16:      void SetWeight(int theWeight) { itsWeight = theWeight; }
17:
18:      // friend operators
```

19

LISTING **19.6**   continued

```
19:     friend ostream& operator<< (ostream&, const Animal&);
20:
21: private:
22:     int itsWeight;
23: };
24:
25: // extraction operator for printing animals
26: ostream& operator<<
27: (ostream& theStream, const Animal& theAnimal)
28: {
29:     theStream << theAnimal.GetWeight();
30:     return theStream;
31: }
32:
33: Animal::Animal(int weight):
34: itsWeight(weight)
35: {
36:     cout << "animal(int) ";
37: }
38:
39: Animal::Animal():
40: itsWeight(0)
41: {
42:     cout << "animal() ";
43: }
44:
45: Animal::~Animal()
46: {
47:     cout << "Destroyed an animal...";
48: }
49:
50: template <class T>  // declare the template and the parameter
51: class Array          // the class being parameterized
52: {
53: public:
54:     Array(int itsSize = DefaultSize);
55:     Array(const Array &rhs);
56:     ~Array() { delete [] pType; }
57:
58:     // operators
59:     Array& operator=(const Array&);
60:     T& operator[](int offSet) { return pType[offSet]; }
61:     const T& operator[](int offSet) const
62:     { return pType[offSet]; }
63:
64:     // accessors
65:     int GetSize() const { return itsSize; }
66:
67:     // friend function
68:     friend ostream& operator<< (ostream&, const Array<T>&);
```

LISTING 19.6   continued

```
69:
70:   private:
71:      T *pType;
72:      int  itsSize;
73:   };
74:
75:   template <class T>
76:   Array<T>::Array(int size = DefaultSize):
77:   itsSize(size)
78:   {
79:      pType = new T[size];
80:      for (int i = 0; i<size; i++)
81:         pType[i] = (T)0;
82:   }
83:
84:   template <class T>
85:   Array<T>& Array<T>::operator=(const Array &rhs)
86:   {
87:      if (this == &rhs)
88:         return *this;
89:      delete [] pType;
90:      itsSize = rhs.GetSize();
91:      pType = new T[itsSize];
92:      for (int i = 0; i<itsSize; i++)
93:         pType[i] = rhs[i];
94:      return *this;
95:   }
96:
97:   template <class T>
98:   Array<T>::Array(const Array &rhs)
99:   {
100:      itsSize = rhs.GetSize();
101:      pType = new T[itsSize];
102:      for (int i = 0; i<itsSize; i++)
103:         pType[i] = rhs[i];
104:   }
105:
106:
107:   template <class T>
108:   ostream& operator<< (ostream& output, const Array<T>& theArray)
109:   {
110:      for (int i = 0; i<theArray.GetSize(); i++)
111:         output << "[" << i << "] " << theArray[i] << endl;
112:      return output;
113:   }
114:
115:
116:   Array<Animal>::Array(int AnimalArraySize):
117:   itsSize(AnimalArraySize)
118:   {
```

19

LISTING 19.6   continued

```
119:      pType = new Animal[AnimalArraySize];
120:  }
121:
122:
123:  void IntFillFunction(Array<int>& theArray);
124:  void AnimalFillFunction(Array<Animal>& theArray);
125:
126:  int main()
127:  {
128:      Array<int> intArray;
129:      Array<Animal> animalArray;
130:      IntFillFunction(intArray);
131:      AnimalFillFunction(animalArray);
132:      cout << "intArray...\n" << intArray;
133:      cout << "\nanimalArray...\n" << animalArray << endl;
134:      return 0;
135:  }
136:
137:  void IntFillFunction(Array<int>& theArray)
138:  {
139:      bool Stop = false;
140:      int offset, value;
141:      while (!Stop)
142:      {
143:         cout << "Enter an offset (0-2) and a value. ";
144:         cout << "(-1 to stop): " ;
145:         cin >> offset >> value;
146:         if (offset < 0)
147:            break;
148:         if (offset > 2)
149:         {
150:            cout << "***Please use values between 0 and 2.***\n";
151:            continue;
152:         }
153:         theArray[offset] = value;
154:      }
155:  }
156:
157:
158:  void AnimalFillFunction(Array<Animal>& theArray)
159:  {
160:      Animal * pAnimal;
161:      for (int i = 0; i<theArray.GetSize(); i++)
162:      {
163:         pAnimal = new Animal(i*10);
164:         theArray[i] = *pAnimal;
165:         delete pAnimal;
166:      }
167:  }
```

Note | Line numbers have been added to the output to make analysis easier. Line numbers will not appear in your output.

```
1:  animal() animal() animal() Enter an offset (0-2) and a value. (-1 to
    ➥stop): 0 0
2:  Enter an offset (0-2) and a value. (-1 to stop): 0 1
3:  Enter an offset (0-2) and a value. (-1 to stop): 1 2
4:  Enter an offset (0-2) and a value. (-1 to stop): 2 3
5:  Enter an offset (0-2) and a value. (-1 to stop): -1 -1
6:  animal(int) Destroyed an animal...animal(int) Destroyed an
    ➥animal...animal(int) Destroyed an animal...initArray...
7: [0] 0
8: [1] 1
9: [2] 2
10:
11: animal array...
12: [0] 0
13: [1] 10
14: [2] 20
15:
16: Destroyed an animal...Destroyed an animal...Destroyed an animal...
17: <<< Second run >>>
18: animal(int)   Destroyed an animal...
19: animal(int)   Destroyed an animal...
20: animal(int)   Destroyed an animal...
21: Enter an offset (0-9) and a value. (-1 to stop): 0 0
22: Enter an offset (0-9) and a value. (-1 to stop): 1 1
23: Enter an offset (0-9) and a value. (-1 to stop): 2 2
24: Enter an offset (0-9) and a value. (-1 to stop): 3 3
25: animal(int)
26: Destroyed an animal...
27: animal(int)
28: Destroyed an animal...
29: animal(int)
30: Destroyed an animal...
31: initArray...
32: [0] 0
33: [1] 1
34: [2] 2
35:
36: animal array...
37: [0] 0
38: [1] 10
39: [2] 20
40:
41: Destroyed an animal...
42: Destroyed an animal...
43: Destroyed an animal...
```

19

OUTPUT

ANALYSIS Listing 19.6 reproduces both classes in their entirety so that you can see the creation and destruction of temporary `Animal` objects. The value of `DefaultSize` has been reduced to 3 to simplify the output.

The `Animal` constructors and destructors on lines 33–48 each print a statement indicating when they are called.

On lines 75–82, the template behavior of an `Array` constructor is declared. On lines 116–120, the specialized constructor for an `Array` of `Animals` is demonstrated. Note that in this special constructor, the default constructor is allowed to set the initial value for each `Animal`, and no explicit assignment is done.

The first time this program is run, the first set of output is shown. Line 1 of the output shows the three default constructors called by creating the array. The user enters four numbers, and these are entered into the integer array.

Execution jumps to `AnimalFillFunction()`. Here a temporary `Animal` object is created on the heap on line 163, and its value is used to modify the `Animal` object in the array on line 164. On line 165, the temporary `Animal` is destroyed. This is repeated for each member of the array and is reflected in the output on line 6.

At the end of the program, the arrays are destroyed, and when their destructors are called, all their objects are destroyed as well. This is reflected in the output on line 16.

For the second set of output (lines 18–43), the special implementation of the array of character constructor, shown on lines 114–118 of the program, is commented out. When the program is run again, the template constructor, shown on lines 74–81 of the program, is run when the `Animal` array is constructed.

This causes temporary `Animal` objects to be called for each member of the array on lines 79 and 80 of the program, and is reflected in the output on lines 18–20 of the output.

In all other respects, the output for the two runs is identical, as you would expect.

Static Members and Templates

A template can declare static data members. Each instantiation of the template then has its own set of static data, one per class type. That is, if you add a static member to the `Array` class (for example, a counter of how many arrays have been created), you will have one such member per type: one for all the arrays of `Animals` and another for all the arrays of integers. Listing 19.7 adds a static member and a static function to the `Array` class.

LISTING 19.7   Using Static Member Data and Functions with Templates

```cpp
0:   #include <iostream>
1:   using namespace std;
2:
3:   const int DefaultSize = 3;
4:
5:   // A trivial class for adding to arrays
6:   class Animal
7:   {
8:   public:
9:       // constructors
10:      Animal(int);
11:      Animal();
12:      ~Animal();
13:
14:      // accessors
15:      int GetWeight() const { return itsWeight; }
16:      void SetWeight(int theWeight) { itsWeight = theWeight; }
17:
18:      // friend operators
19:      friend ostream& operator<< (ostream&, const Animal&);
20:
21:   private:
22:      int itsWeight;
23:   };
24:
25:   // extraction operator for printing animals
26:   ostream& operator<<
27:      (ostream& theStream, const Animal& theAnimal)
28:   {
29:      theStream << theAnimal.GetWeight();
30:      return theStream;
31:   }
32:
33:   Animal::Animal(int weight):
34:      itsWeight(weight)
35:   {
36:      //cout << "animal(int) ";
37:   }
38:
39:   Animal::Animal():
40:      itsWeight(0)
41:   {
42:      //cout << "animal() ";
43:   }
44:
45:   Animal::~Animal()
46:   {
47:      //cout << "Destroyed an animal...";
48:   }
```

19

LISTING **19.7**   continued

```
49:
50:   template <class T>  // declare the template and the parameter
51:   class Array           // the class being parameterized
52:   {
53:   public:
54:      // constructors
55:      Array(int itsSize = DefaultSize);
56:      Array(const Array &rhs);
57:      ~Array() { delete [] pType;   itsNumberArrays--; }
58:
59:      // operators
60:      Array& operator=(const Array&);
61:      T& operator[](int offSet) { return pType[offSet]; }
62:      const T& operator[](int offSet) const
63:      { return pType[offSet]; }
64:      // accessors
65:      int GetSize() const { return itsSize; }
66:      static int GetNumberArrays() { return itsNumberArrays; }
67:
68:      // friend function
69:      friend ostream& operator<< (ostream&, const Array<T>&);
70:
71:   private:
72:      T *pType;
73:      int  itsSize;
74:      static int itsNumberArrays;
75:   };
76:
77:   template <class T>
78:   int Array<T>::itsNumberArrays = 0;
79:
80:   template <class T>
81:   Array<T>::Array(int size = DefaultSize):
82:      itsSize(size)
83:   {
84:      pType = new T[size];
85:      for (int i = 0; i<size; i++)
86:         pType[i] = (T)0;
87:      itsNumberArrays++;
88:   }
89:
90:   template <class T>
91:   Array<T>& Array<T>::operator=(const Array &rhs)
92:   {
93:      if (this == &rhs)
94:         return *this;
95:      delete [] pType;
96:      itsSize = rhs.GetSize();
97:      pType = new T[itsSize];
```

LISTING 19.7 continued

```
98:    for (int i = 0; i<itsSize; i++)
99:        pType[i] = rhs[i];
100: }
101:
102: template <class T>
103: Array<T>::Array(const Array &rhs)
104: {
105:    itsSize = rhs.GetSize();
106:    pType = new T[itsSize];
107:    for (int i = 0; i<itsSize; i++)
108:        pType[i] = rhs[i];
109:    itsNumberArrays++;
110: }
111:
112: template <class T>
113: ostream& operator<< (ostream& output, const Array<T>& theArray)
114: {
115:    for (int i = 0; i<theArray.GetSize(); i++)
116:        output << "[" << i << "] " << theArray[i] << endl;
117:    return output;
118: }
119:
120: int main()
121: {
122:    cout << Array<int>::GetNumberArrays() << " integer arrays\n";
123:    cout << Array<Animal>::GetNumberArrays();
124:    cout << " animal arrays\n\n";
125:    Array<int> intArray;
126:    Array<Animal> animalArray;
127:
128:    cout << intArray.GetNumberArrays() << " integer arrays\n";
129:    cout << animalArray.GetNumberArrays();
130:    cout << " animal arrays\n\n";
131:
132:    Array<int> *pIntArray = new Array<int>;
133:
134:    cout << Array<int>::GetNumberArrays() << " integer arrays\n";
135:    cout << Array<Animal>::GetNumberArrays();
136:    cout << " animal arrays\n\n";
137:
138:    delete pIntArray;
139:
140:    cout << Array<int>::GetNumberArrays() << " integer arrays\n";
141:    cout << Array<Animal>::GetNumberArrays();
142:    cout << " animal arrays\n\n";
143:    return 0;
144: }
```

19

OUTPUT
```
0 integer arrays
0 animal arrays

1 integer arrays
1 animal arrays

2 integer arrays
1 animal arrays

1 integer arrays
1 animal arrays
```

ANALYSIS   The `Array` class has added the static variable `tsNumberArrays` on line 74, and because this data is private, the static public accessor `GetNumberArrays()` was added on line 66.

Initialization of the static data is accomplished with a full template qualification, as shown on lines 77 and 78. The constructors of `Array` and the destructor are each modified to keep track of how many arrays exist at any moment.

Accessing the static members is the same as accessing the static members of any class: You can do so with an existing object, as shown on lines 134 and 135, or by using the full class specification, as shown on lines 128 and 129. Note that you must use a specific type of array when accessing the static data. One variable exists for each type.

Do

DO use statics with templates as needed.

DO specialize template behavior by overriding template functions by type.

DO use the parameters to template functions to narrow their instances to be type-safe.

The Standard Template Library

A new development in C++ is the adoption of the Standard Template Library (STL). All the major compiler vendors now offer the STL as part of their compilers. STL is a library of template-based container classes, including vectors, lists, queues, and stacks. The STL also includes a number of common algorithms, including sorting and searching.

The goal of the STL is to give you an alternative to reinventing the wheel for these common requirements. The STL is tested and debugged, offers high performance, and is free. Most important, the STL is reusable; after you understand how to use an STL container, you can use it in all your programs without reinventing it.

Containers

A *container* is an object that holds other objects. The Standard C++ Library provides a series of container classes that are powerful tools that help C++ developers handle common programming tasks. Two types of Standard Template Library container classes are sequence and associative. *Sequence* containers are designed to provide sequential and random access to their members, or *elements*. *Associative* containers are optimized to access their elements by key values. As with other components of the Standard C++ Library, the STL is portable between various operating systems. All STL container classes are defined in `namespace std`.

Understanding Sequence Containers

The Standard Template Library sequence containers provide efficient sequential access to a list of objects. The Standard C++ Library provides three sequence containers: `vector`, `list`, and `deque`.

The Vector Container

You often use arrays to store and access a number of elements. Elements in an array are of the same type and are accessed with an index. The STL provides a container class `vector` that behaves like an array but that is more powerful and safer to use than the standard C++ array.

A *vector* is a container optimized to provide fast access to its elements by an index. The container class `vector` is defined in the header file `<vector>` in `namespace std` (see Chapter 18, "Namespaces," for more information on the use of namespaces). A vector can grow itself as necessary. Suppose that you have created a vector to contain 10 elements. After you have filled the vector with 10 objects, the vector is full. If you then add another object to the vector, the vector automatically increases its capacity so that it can accommodate the eleventh object. Here is how the `vector` class is defined:

```
template <class T, class A = allocator<T>> class vector
{
    // class members
};
```

The first argument (`class T`) is the type of the elements in the vector. The second argument (`class A`) is an allocator class. *Allocators* are memory managers responsible for memory allocation and deallocation of elements for the containers. The concept and implementation of allocators are advanced topics that are beyond the scope of this book.

19

By default, elements are created using the operator `new()` and are freed using the operator `delete()`. That is, the default constructor of class `T` is called to create a new element. This provides another argument in favor of explicitly defining a default constructor for your own classes. If you do not, you cannot use the standard vector container to hold a set of instances of your class.

You can define vectors that hold integers and floats as follows:

```
vector<int>     vInts;          // vector holding int elements
vector<float>   vFloats;        // vector holding float elements
```

Usually, you would have some idea as to how many elements a vector will contain. For instance, suppose that in your school, the maximum number of students is 50. To create a vector of students in a class, you will want the vector to be large enough to contain 50 elements. The standard vector class provides a constructor that accepts the number of elements as its parameter. So we can define a vector of 50 students as follows:

```
vector<Student> MathClass(50);
```

A compiler will allocate enough memory spaces for 50 students; each element is created using the default constructor `Student::Student()`.

The number of elements in a vector can be retrieved using a member function `size()`. In this example, `vStudent.size()` will return `50`.

Another member function `capacity()` tells us exactly how many elements a vector can accommodate before its size needs to be increased. We will see more on this later.

A vector is said to be empty if no element is in a vector; that is, the vector's size is zero. To make it easier to test whether a vector is empty, the `vector` class provides a member function `empty()` that evaluates to true if the vector is empty.

To assign a `Student` object `Harry` to the `MathClass`, we can use the subscripting operator `[]`:

```
MathClass[5] = Harry;
```

The subscript starts at `0`. As you may have noticed, the overloaded assignment operator of the `Student` class is used here to assign `Harry` to the sixth element in `MathClass`. Similarly, to find out `Harry`'s age, we can access his record using:

```
MathClass[5].GetAge();
```

As mentioned earlier, vectors can grow automatically when you add more elements than they can handle. For instance, suppose one class in your school has become so popular that the number of students exceeds 50. Well, it may not happen to our math class, but who knows, strange things do happen. When the fifty-first student, `Sally`, is added to the `MathClass`, the compiler will expand it to accommodate her.

You can add an element into a vector in several ways; one of them is push_back():

```
MathClass.push_back(Sally);
```

This member function appends the new Student object Sally to the end of the vector MathClass. Now we have 51 elements in MathClass, and Sally is placed at MathClass[50].

For this function to work, our Student class must define a copy constructor. Otherwise this push_back() function will not be able to make a copy of object Sally.

STL does not specify the maximum number of elements in a vector; the compiler vendors are in better positions to make this decision. The vector class provides a member function that tells you what this magic number is in your compiler: max_size().

Listing 19.8 demonstrates the members of the vector class we have discussed so far. You will see that the standard string class is used in this listing to simplify the handling of strings. For more details about the string class, check your compiler's documentation.

LISTING 19.8   Vector Creation and Element Access

```
0:   #include <iostream>
1:   #include <string>
2:   #include <vector>
3:   using namespace std;
4:
5:   class Student
6:   {
7:   public:
8:       Student();
9:       Student(const string& name, const int age);
10:      Student(const Student& rhs);
11:      ~Student();
12:
13:      void    SetName(const string& name);
14:      string  GetName()   const;
15:      void    SetAge(const int age);
16:      int     GetAge()    const;
17:
18:      Student& operator=(const Student& rhs);
19:
20:   private:
21:      string itsName;
22:      int itsAge;
23:   };
24:
25:   Student::Student()
26:   : itsName("New Student"), itsAge(16)
27:   {}
28:
```

19

LISTING **19.8**   continued

```
29:    Student::Student(const string& name, const int age)
30:    : itsName(name), itsAge(age)
31:    {}
32:
33:    Student::Student(const Student& rhs)
34:    : itsName(rhs.GetName()), itsAge(rhs.GetAge())
35:    {}
36:
37:    Student::~Student()
38:    {}
39:
40:    void Student::SetName(const string& name)
41:    {
42:        itsName = name;
43:    }
44:
45:    string Student::GetName() const
46:    {
47:        return itsName;
48:    }
49:
50:    void Student::SetAge(const int age)
51:    {
52:        itsAge = age;
53:    }
54:
55:    int Student::GetAge() const
56:    {
57:        return itsAge;
58:    }
59:
60:    Student& Student::operator=(const Student& rhs)
61:    {
62:        itsName = rhs.GetName();
63:        itsAge = rhs.GetAge();
64:        return *this;
65:    }
66:
67:    ostream& operator<<(ostream& os, const Student& rhs)
68:    {
69:        os << rhs.GetName() << " is " << rhs.GetAge() << " years old";
70:        return os;
71:    }
72:
73:    template<class T>
74:    // display vector properties
75:    void ShowVector(const vector<T>& v);
76:
77:    typedef vector<Student>    SchoolClass;
78:
```

LISTING 19.8   continued

```
79:    int main()
80:    {
81:        Student Harry;
82:        Student Sally("Sally", 15);
83:        Student Bill("Bill", 17);
84:        Student Peter("Peter", 16);
85:
86:        SchoolClass    EmptyClass;
87:        cout << "EmptyClass:\n";
88:        ShowVector(EmptyClass);
89:
90:        SchoolClass GrowingClass(3);
91:        cout << "GrowingClass(3):\n";
92:        ShowVector(GrowingClass);
93:
94:        GrowingClass[0] = Harry;
95:        GrowingClass[1] = Sally;
96:        GrowingClass[2] = Bill;
97:        cout << "GrowingClass(3) after assigning students:\n";
98:        ShowVector(GrowingClass);
99:
100:        GrowingClass.push_back(Peter);
101:        cout << "GrowingClass() after added 4th student:\n";
102:        ShowVector(GrowingClass);
103:
104:        GrowingClass[0].SetName("Harry");
105:        GrowingClass[0].SetAge(18);
106:        cout << "GrowingClass() after Set\n:";
107:        ShowVector(GrowingClass);
108:
109:        return 0;
110:    }
111:
112:    //
113:    // Display vector properties
114:    //
115:    template<class T>
116:    void ShowVector(const vector<T>& v)
117:    {
118:        cout << "max_size() = " << v.max_size();
119:        cout << "\tsize() = " << v.size();
120:        cout << "\tcapacity() = " << v.capacity();
121:        cout << "\t" << (v.empty()? "empty": "not empty");
122:        cout << "\n";
123:
124:        for (int i = 0; i < v.size(); ++i)
125:            cout << v[i] << "\n";
126:
127:        cout << endl;
128:    }
```

19

```
EmptyClass:
max_size() = 214748364  size() = 0        capacity() = 0  empty

GrowingClass(3):
max_size() = 214748364  size() = 3        capacity() = 3  not empty
New Student is 16 years old
New Student is 16 years old
New Student is 16 years old

GrowingClass(3) after assigning students:
max_size() = 214748364  size() = 3        capacity() = 3  not empty
New Student is 16 years old
Sally is 15 years old
Bill is 17 years old

GrowingClass() after added 4th student:
max_size() = 214748364  size() = 4        capacity() = 6  not empty
New Student is 16 years old
Sally is 15 years old
Bill is 17 years old
Peter is 16 years old

GrowingClass() after Set:
max_size() = 214748364 size() = 4         capacity() = 6  not empty
Harry is 18 years old
Sally is 15 years old
Bill is 17 years old
Peter is 16 years old
```

ANALYSIS Our `Student` class is defined on lines 5–23. Its member function implementations are on lines 25–65. It is simple and vector-container friendly. For the reasons discussed earlier, we defined a default constructor, a copy constructor, and an overloaded assignment operator. Note that its member variable `itsName` is defined as an instance of the C++ `string` class. As you can see here, it is much easier to work with a C++ string than with a C-style string `char*`.

The template function `ShowVector()` is declared on lines 73 and 75 and defined on lines 115–128. It demonstrates the usage of some of the vector member functions: `max_size()`, `size()`, `capacity()`, and `empty()`. As we can see from the output, the maximum number of `Student` objects a vector can accommodate is 214,748,364 in Visual C++. This number may be different for other types of elements. For instance, a vector of integers can have up to 1,073,741,823 elements. If you are using other compilers, you may have a different value and maximum number of elements.

On lines 124 and 125, we go through each element in the vector and display its value using the overloaded insertion operator `<<`, which is defined on lines 67–71.

Four students are created on lines 81–84. On line 86, an empty vector, properly named EmptyClass, is defined using the default constructor of the vector class. When a vector is created in this way, no space is allocated for it by the compiler. As we can see in the output produced by ShowVector(EmptyClass), its size and capacity are both zero.

On line 90, a vector of three Student objects is defined. Its size and capacity are both three, as we expect. Elements in the GrowingClass are assigned with the Student objects on lines 94–96 using the subscripting operator [].

The fourth student, Peter is added to the vector on line 100. This increases the size of the vector to four. Interestingly, its capacity is now set to six. This means that the compiler has allocated enough space for up to six Student objects. Because vectors must be allocated to a continuous block of memory, expanding them requires a set of operations. First, a new block of memory large enough for all four Student objects is allocated. Second, the three elements are copied to this newly allocated memory and the fourth element is appended after the third element. And last, the original memory block is returned to the memory. When we have a large number of elements in a vector, this deallocation and reallocation process can be time-consuming. Therefore, a compiler employs an optimization strategy to reduce the possibility of such expensive operations. In this example, if we append one or two more objects to the vector, no need exists to deallocate and reallocate memory.

On lines 104 and 105, we again use the subscripting operator [] to change the member variables for the first object in the GrowingClass.

Do
DO define a default constructor for a class if its instances are likely to be held in a vector.
DO define a copy constructor for such a class.
DO define an overloaded assignment operator for such a class.

19

The vector container class has other member functions. The front() function returns a reference to the first element in a list. The back() function returns a reference to the last element. The at() function works like the subscription operator []. It is safer because it checks whether the subscript passed to it is within the range of available elements. If it is out of range, it throws an out_of_range exception. (Exceptions are covered tomorrow.)

The insert() function inserts one or more nodes into a given position in a vector. The pop_back() function removes the last element from a vector. At last, a remove() function removes one or more elements from a vector.

The List Container

A list is a container designed to provide optimal frequent insertions and deletions of elements.

The list STL container class is defined in the header file `<list>` in the namespace `std`. The list class is implemented as a doubly-linked list, where each node has links to both the previous node and the next node in the list.

The list class has all the member functions provided by the vector class. As you have seen in "Week 2 In Review," you can traverse a list by following the links provided in each node. Typically, the links are implemented using pointers. The standard list container class uses a mechanism called the iterator for the same purpose.

An iterator is a generalization of a pointer. You can dereference an iterator to retrieve the node it points to. Listing 19.9 demonstrates the use of iterators in accessing nodes in a list.

LISTING 19.9   Traverse a List Using an Iterator

```
0:   #include <iostream>
1:   #include <list>
2:   using namespace std;
3:
4:   typedef list<int> IntegerList;
5:
6:   int main()
7:   {
8:       IntegerList   intList;
9:
10:      for (int i = 1; i <= 10; ++i)
11:          intList.push_back(i * 2);
12:
13:      for (IntegerList::const_iterator ci = intList.begin();
14:                      ci != intList.end(); ++ci)
15:          cout << *ci << " ";
16:
17:      return 0;
18:   }
```

OUTPUT   2 4 6 8 10 12 14 16 18 20

ANALYSIS   On line 8, `intList` is defined as a list of integers. The first 10 positive even numbers are added to the list using the `push_back()` function on lines 10 and 11.

On lines 13–15, we access each node in the list using a constant iterator. This indicates that we do not intend to change the nodes with this iterator. If we would like to change a node pointed to be an iterator, we need to use a non-const iterator instead:

```
intList::iterator
```

The begin() member function returns an iterator pointing to the first node of the list. As we can see here, the increment operator ++ can be use to point an iterator to the next node. The end() member function is kind of strange—it returns an iterator pointing to one-pass-last node of a list. So we must be sure that we don't let our iterator reach end().

The iterator is dereferenced the same as a pointer, to return the node pointed to, as shown on line 15.

Although we introduce iterators here with the list class, iterators are also provided by the vector class. In addition to functions introduced in the vector class, the list class also provides the push_front() and pop_front() functions that work just like push_back() and pop_back(). Instead of adding and removing elements at the back of the list, they add and remove elements in the front of the list.

The Deque Container

A deque is like a double-ended vector—it inherits the vector container class's efficiency in sequential read and write operations. But, in addition, the deque container class provides optimized front-end and back-end operations. These operations are implemented similarly to the list container class, where memory allocations are engaged only for new elements. This feature of the deque class eliminates the need to reallocate the whole container to a new memory location, as the vector class has to do. Therefore, deques are ideally suited for applications in which insertions and deletions take place at either one or both ends, and for which sequential access of elements is important. An example of such an application is a train-assembly simulator, in which carriages can join the train at both ends.

19

Stacks

One of the most commonly used data structures in computer programming is the stack. The stack, however, is not implemented as an independent container class. Instead, it is implemented as a wrapper of a container. The template class stack is defined in the header file <stack> in the namespace std.

A *stack* is a continuously allocated block that can grow or shrink at the back end. Elements in a stack can only be accessed or removed from the back. You have seen similar characteristics in the sequence containers, notably vector and deque. In fact, any sequence container that supports the back(), push_back(), and pop_back() operations can be used to implement a stack. Most of the other container methods are not required for the stack and are, therefore, not exposed by the stack.

The STL stack template class is designed to contain any type of objects. The only restriction is that all elements must be of the same type.

A stack is a *LIFO* (*last in, first out*) structure. It's like an overcrowded elevator: The first person who walks in is pushed toward the wall and the last person stands right next to the door. When the elevator reaches the destination floor, the last person in is the first to go out. If someone wants to leave the elevator earlier, all those who stand between her and the door must make way for her, probably by going out of the elevator and then coming back in.

By convention, the open end of a stack is often called the *top* of the stack, and operations carried out to a stack are often called *push* and *pop*. The stack class inherits these conventional terms.

Note   The STL stack class is not the same as the stack mechanism used by compilers and operating systems, in which stacks can contain different types of objects. The underlying functionality, however, is very similar.

Understanding Queues

A *queue* is another commonly used data structure in computer programming. Elements are added to the queue at one end and taken out at the other. The classic analogy is this: A stack is like a stack of dishes at a salad bar. You add to the stack by placing a dish on top (pushing the stack down), and you take from the stack by "popping" the top dish (the one most recently added to the stack) off the top.

A queue is like a line at the theater. You enter the queue at the back, and you leave the queue at the front. This is known as a *FIFO* (first in, first out) structure; a stack is a *LIFO* (last in, first out) structure. Of course, every once in a while, you're second-to-last in a long line at the supermarket when someone opens a new register and grabs the last person in line—turning what should be a FIFO queue into a LIFO stack, and making you grind your teeth in frustration.

Like the stack, the queue is implemented as a wrapper class to a container. The container must support front(), back(), push_back(), and pop_front() operations.

Understanding Associative Containers

Although sequence containers are designed for sequential and random access of elements using the index or an iterator, the associative containers are designed for fast random access of elements using keys. The Standard C++ Library provides four associative containers: map, multimap, set, and multiset.

The Map Container

You have seen that a vector is like an enhanced version of an array. It has all the characteristics of an array and some additional features. Unfortunately, the vector also suffers from one of the significant weaknesses of arrays: It has no provision for the random access of elements using key values other than the index or iterator. Associative containers, on the other hand, provide fast random access based on key values.

The C++ Standard Library provides four associative containers: map, multimap, set, and multiset. In the following example, a map is used to implement the school class example shown in Listing 19.8.

LISTING 19.10   A Map Container Class

```cpp
0:  #include <iostream>
1:  #include <string>
2:  #include <map>
3:  using namespace std;
4:
5:  class Student
6:  {
7:  public:
8:      Student();
9:      Student(const string& name, const int age);
10:     Student(const Student& rhs);
11:     ~Student();
12:
13:     void    SetName(const string& name);
14:     string  GetName()   const;
15:     void    SetAge(const int age);
16:     int     GetAge()    const;
17:
18:     Student& operator=(const Student& rhs);
19:
20:  private:
21:      string itsName;
22:      int itsAge;
23:  };
24:
25:  Student::Student()
```

19

LISTING 19.10   continued

```
26:    : itsName("New Student"), itsAge(16)
27:    {}
28:
29:    Student::Student(const string& name, const int age)
30:    : itsName(name), itsAge(age)
31:    {}
32:
33:    Student::Student(const Student& rhs)
34:    : itsName(rhs.GetName()), itsAge(rhs.GetAge())
35:    {}
36:
37:    Student::~Student()
38:    {}
39:
40:    void Student::SetName(const string& name)
41:    {
42:        itsName = name;
43:    }
44:
45:    string Student::GetName() const
46:    {
47:        return itsName;
48:    }
49:
50:    void Student::SetAge(const int age)
51:    {
52:        itsAge = age;
53:    }
54:
55:    int Student::GetAge() const
56:    {
57:        return itsAge;
58:    }
59:
60:    Student& Student::operator=(const Student& rhs)
61:    {
62:        itsName = rhs.GetName();
63:        itsAge = rhs.GetAge();
64:        return *this;
65:    }
66:
67:    ostream& operator<<(ostream& os, const Student& rhs)
68:    {
69:        os << rhs.GetName() << " is " << rhs.GetAge() << " years old";
70:        return os;
71:    }
72:
73:    template<class T, class A>
74:    void ShowMap(const map<T, A>& v);    // display map properties
```

LISTING 19.10   continued

```
75:
76:   typedef map<string, Student>    SchoolClass;
77:
78:   int main()
79:   {
80:      Student Harry("Harry", 18);
81:      Student Sally("Sally", 15);
82:      Student Bill("Bill", 17);
83:      Student Peter("Peter", 16);
84:
85:      SchoolClass    MathClass;
86:      MathClass[Harry.GetName()] = Harry;
87:      MathClass[Sally.GetName()] = Sally;
88:      MathClass[Bill.GetName()] = Bill;
89:      MathClass[Peter.GetName()] = Peter;
90:
91:      cout << "MathClass:\n";
92:      ShowMap(MathClass);
93:
94:      cout << "We know that " << MathClass["Bill"].GetName()
95:          << " is " << MathClass["Bill"].GetAge() << " years old\n";
96:
97:      return 0;
98:   }
99:
100:  //
101:  // Display map properties
102:  //
103:  template<class T, class A>
104:  void ShowMap(const map<T, A>& v)
105:  {
106:     for (map<T, A>::const_iterator ci = v.begin();
107:              ci != v.end(); ++ci)
108:        cout << ci->first << ": " << ci->second << "\n";
109:
110:     cout << endl;
111:  }
```

OUTPUT

```
MathClass:
Bill: Bill is 17 years old
Harry: Harry is 18 years old
Peter: Peter is 16 years old
Sally: Sally is 15 years old

We know that Bill is 17 years old
```

19

ANALYSIS   On line 2, we include the header file <map> because we will be using the standard map container class. Consequently, we define the ShowMap template function to display the elements in a map. On line 76, the SchoolClass is defined as a map of elements; each consists of a (key, value) pair. The first value in the pair is the key value. In our SchoolClass, we use students' names as their key values, which are of type string. The key value of elements in the map container must be unique; that is, no two elements can have the same key value. The second value in the pair is the actual object, a Student object in the example. The pair data type is implemented in STL as a struct of two members: namely, first and second. We can use these members to access a node's key and value.

We'll skip the main() function and take a look at the ShowMap function first. The ShowMap function uses a constant iterator to access a map object. On line 108, ci->first points to the key, or a student's name. ci->second points to the Student object.

Back on lines 80–83, four Student objects are created. The MathClass is defined as an instance of our SchoolClass on line 85. On lines 86–89, we add the four students to the MathClass using the following syntax:

```
map_object[key_value] = object_value;
```

We could also use the push_back() or insert() functions to add a (key, value) pair to the map; you can look up your compiler's documentation for more details.

After all Student objects have been added to the map, we can access any of them using their key values. On lines 94 and 95, we use MathClass["Bill"] to retrieve Bill's record.

Other Associative Containers

The multimap container class is a map class without the restriction of unique keys. More than one element can have the same key value.

The set container class is also similar to the map class. The only difference is that its elements are not (key, value) pairs. An element is only the key.

Finally, the multiset container class is a set class that allows duplex key values.

Algorithm Classes

A container is a useful place to store a sequence of elements. All standard containers define operations that manipulate the containers and their elements. Implementing all these operations in your own sequences, however, can be laborious and prone to error. Because most of those operations are likely to be the same in most sequences, a set of generic algorithms can reduce the need to write your own operations for each new container. The standard library provides approximately 60 standard algorithms that perform the most basic and commonly used operations of containers.

Standard algorithms are defined in <algorithm> in namespace std.

To understand how the standard algorithms work, we need to learn the concept of function objects. A function object is an instance of a class that defines the overloaded operator (). Therefore, it can be called as a function. Listing 19.11 demonstrates a function object.

LISTING 19.11 A Function Object

```
0:  #include <iostream>
1:  using namespace std;
2:
3:  template<class T>
4:  class Print    {
5:  public:
6:      void operator()(const T& t)
7:      {
8:        cout << t << " ";
9:      }
10: };
11:
12: int main()
13: {
14:     Print<int> DoPrint;
15:     for (int i = 0; i < 5; ++i)
16:        DoPrint(i);
17:     return 0;
18: }
```

19

OUTPUT 0 1 2 3 4

ANALYSIS On lines 3–10, a template class Print is defined. The overloaded operator () on lines 6–9 takes an object and outputs it to the standard output. On line 14, DoPrint is defined as an instance of the Print class. We can then use DoPrint just like a function to print any integer values, as shown on line 16.

Non-Mutating Sequence Operations

Non-mutating sequence operations perform operations that don't change the elements in a sequence. These include operators such as for_each() and find(), search(), count(), and so forth. Listing 19.12 shows how to use a function object and the for_each algorithm to print elements in a vector.

LISTING 19.12   Using the `for_each()` algorithm

```
0:   #include <iostream>
1:   #include <vector>
2:   #include <algorithm>
3:   using namespace std;
4:
5:   template<class T>
6:   class Print
7:   {
8:   public:
9:       void operator()(const T& t)
10:      {
11:          cout << t << " ";
12:      }
13:  };
14:
15:  int main()
16:  {
17:      Print<int>   DoPrint;
18:      vector<int>   vInt(5);
19:
20:      for (int i = 0; i < 5; ++i)
21:          vInt[i] = i * 3;
22:
23:      cout << "for_each()\n";
24:      for_each(vInt.begin(), vInt.end(), DoPrint);
25:      cout << "\n";
26:
27:      return 0;
28:  }
```

OUTPUT

```
for_each()
0 3 6 9 12
```

ANALYSIS   Note that all C++ standard algorithms are defined in `<algorithm>`, so we must include it here. Most of the program should be easy for you. On line 24, the `for_each()` function is called to go through each element in the vector `vInt`. For each element, it invokes the `DoPrint` function object and passes the element to `DoPrint.operator()`. This results in the value of the element to be printed on the screen.

Mutating Sequence Algorithms

Mutating sequence operations perform operations that change the elements in a sequence, including operations which fill or reorder collections. Listing 19.13 shows the `fill()` algorithm.

LISTING 19.13 A Mutating Sequence Algorithm

```
0:  #include <iostream>
1:  #include <vector>
2:  #include <algorithm>
3:  using namespace std;
4:
5:  template<class T>
6:  class Print
7:  {
8:  public:
9:      void operator()(const T& t)
10:     {
11:         cout << t << " ";
12:     }
13: };
14:
15: int main()
16: {
17:     Print<int>   DoPrint;
18:     vector<int>   vInt(10);
19:
20:     fill(vInt.begin(), vInt.begin() + 5, 1);
21:     fill(vInt.begin() + 5, vInt.end(), 2);
22:
23:     for_each(vInt.begin(), vInt.end(), DoPrint);
24:     cout << "\n\n";
25:
26:     return 0;
27: }
```

OUTPUT

1 1 1 1 1 2 2 2 2 2

ANALYSIS The only new content in this listing is on lines 20 and 21, where the `fill()` algorithm is used. The fill algorithm fills the elements in a sequence with a given value. On line 20, it assigns an integer value 1 to the first five elements in vInt. The last five elements of vInt are assigned with integer 2 on line 21.

Summary

Today you learned how to create and use templates. Templates are a built-in facility of C++, used to create parameterized types—types that change their behavior based on parameters passed in at creation. They are a way to reuse code safely and effectively.

The definition of the template determines the parameterized type. Each instance of the template is an actual object, which can be used like any other object—as a parameter to a function, as a return value, and so forth.

19

Template classes can declare three types of friend functions: non-template, general template, and type-specific template. A template can declare static data members, in which case each instance of the template has its own set of static data.

If you need to specialize behavior for some template functions based on the actual type, you can override a template function with a particular type. This works for member functions as well.

Q&A

Q Why use templates when macros will do?

A Templates are type-safe and built into the language.

Q What is the difference between the parameterized type of a template function and the parameters to a normal function?

A A regular function (non-template) takes parameters on which it may take action. A template function enables you to parameterize the type of a particular parameter to the function. That is, you can pass an `Array` of `Type` to a function and then have the `Type` determined by the template instance.

Q When do you use templates and when do you use inheritance?

A Use templates when all the behavior, or virtually all the behavior, is unchanged, except in regard to the type of the item on which your class acts. If you find yourself copying a class and changing only the type of one or more of its members, it may be time to consider using a template.

Q When do you use general template friend classes?

A When every instance, regardless of type, should be a friend to this class or function.

Q When do you use type-specific template friend classes or functions?

A When you want to establish a one-to-one relationship between two classes. For example, `array<int>` should match `iterator<int>`, but not `iterator<Animal>`.

Q What are the two types of standard containers?

A Sequence containers and associative containers. Sequence containers provides optimized sequential and random access to their elements. Associative containers provide optimized element access using key values.

Q What attributes must your class have to be used with the standard containers?

A The class must define a default constructor, a copy constructor, and an overloaded assignment operator.

Workshop

The Workshop provides quiz questions to help you solidify your understanding of the material covered and exercises to provide you with experience in using what you've learned. Try to answer the quiz and exercise questions before checking the answers in Appendix D, and make sure you understand the answers before continuing to the next chapter.

Quiz

1. What is the difference between a template and a macro?

2. What is the difference between the parameter in a template and the parameter in a function?

3. What is the difference between a type-specific template friend class and a general template friend class?

4. Is it possible to provide special behavior for one instance of a template but not for other instances?

5. How many static variables are created if you put one static member into a template class definition?

Exercises

1. Create a template based on this List class:

```
class List
{
private:

public:
    List():head(0),tail(0),theCount(0) {}
    virtual ~List();
    void insert( int value );
    void append( int value );
    int is_present( int value ) const;
    int is_empty() const { return head == 0; }
    int count() const { return theCount; }
private:
    class ListCell
    {
    public:
        ListCell(int value, ListCell *cell = 0):val(value),next(cell){}
        int val;
        ListCell *next;
    };
    ListCell *head;
```

19

```
        ListCell *tail;
        int theCount;
};
```

2. Write the implementation for the `List` class (non-template) version.

3. Write the template version of the implementations.

4. Declare three list objects: a list of `Strings`, a list of `Cats`, and a list of `ints`.

5. **BUG BUSTERS:** What is wrong with the following code? (Assume the `List` template is defined and `Cat` is the class defined earlier in the book.)

```
List<Cat> Cat_List;
Cat Felix;
CatList.append( Felix );
cout << "Felix is " <<
    ( Cat_List.is_present( Felix ) ) ? "" : "not " << "present\n";
```

HINT (this is tough): What makes `Cat` different from `int`?

6. Declare friend `operator==` for `List`.

7. Implement friend `operator==` for `List`.

8. Does `operator==` have the same problem as in Exercise 5?

9. Implement a template function for `swap`, which exchanges two variables.

DAY 20

Exceptions and Error Handling

The code you've seen in this book has been created for illustration purposes. It has not dealt with errors so that you would not be distracted from the central issues being presented. Real-world programs must take error conditions into consideration.

Today you will learn

- What exceptions are.
- How exceptions are used, and what issues they raise.
- How to build exception hierarchies.
- How exceptions fit into an overall error-handling approach.
- What a debugger is.

Bugs, Errors, Mistakes, and Code Rot

All programs have bugs. The bigger the program, the more bugs, and many of those bugs actually "get out the door" and into final, released software. That this is true does not make it okay, and making robust, bug-free programs is the number-one priority of anyone serious about programming.

The single biggest problem in the software industry is buggy, unstable code. The biggest expense in many major programming efforts is testing and fixing. The person who solves the problem of producing good, solid, bulletproof programs at low cost and on time will revolutionize the software industry.

A number of discrete kinds of bugs can trouble a program. The first is poor logic: The program does just what you asked, but you haven't thought through the algorithms properly. The second is syntactic: You used the wrong idiom, function, or structure. These two are the most common, and they are the ones most programmers are on the lookout for.

Research and real-world experience have shown beyond a doubt that the later in the development process you find a problem, the more it costs to fix it. The least expensive problems or bugs to fix are the ones you manage to avoid creating. The next cheapest are those the compiler spots. The C++ standards force compilers to put a lot of energy into making more and more bugs show up at compile time.

Bugs that get compiled in but are caught at the first test—those that crash every time— are less expensive to find and fix than those that are flaky and only crash once in a while.

A more common runtime problem than logic or syntactic bugs is fragility: Your program works just fine if the user enters a number when you ask for one, but it crashes if the user enters letters. Other programs crash if they run out of memory, if the floppy disk is left out of the drive, or if the modem drops the line.

To combat this kind of fragility, programmers strive to make their programs bulletproof. A *bulletproof* program is one that can handle anything that comes up at runtime, from bizarre user input to running out of memory.

It is important to distinguish between bugs, which arise because the programmer made a mistake; logic errors, which arise because the programmer misunderstood the problem or how to solve it; and exceptions, which arise because of unusual but predictable problems such as running out of resources (memory or disk space).

Exceptions

You can't eliminate exceptional circumstances; you can only prepare for them. Your users will run out of memory from time to time, and the only question is what your program will do in response. Your choices include

- Crash.
- Inform the user and exit gracefully.
- Inform the user and allow the user to try to recover and continue.
- Take corrective action and continue without disturbing the user.

Although it is not always necessary (or even desirable) to automatically and silently recover from all exceptional circumstances, it is clear that you must do better than crashing.

C++ exception handling provides a type-safe, integrated method for coping with the predictable but unusual conditions that arise while running a program.

Exceptions

In C++, an exception is an object that is passed from the area of code where a problem occurs to the part of the code that is going to handle the problem. The type of the exception determines which area of code will handle the problem, and the contents of the object thrown, if any, may be used to provide feedback to the user.

The basic idea behind exceptions is fairly straightforward:

- The actual allocation of resources (for example, the allocation of memory or the locking of a file) is usually done at a very low level in the program.
- The logic of what to do when an operation fails, memory cannot be allocated, or a file cannot be locked is usually high in the program, with the code for interacting with the user.
- Exceptions provide an express path from the code that allocates resources to the code that can handle the error condition. If intervening layers of functions exist, they are given an opportunity to clean up memory allocations but are not required to include code whose only purpose is to pass along the error condition.

20

How Exceptions Are Used

try blocks are created to surround areas of code that may have a problem. For example:

```
try
{
    SomeDangerousFunction();
}
```

catch blocks handle the exceptions thrown in the try block. For example:

```
try
{
    SomeDangerousFunction();
}
catch(OutOfMemory)
{
    // take some actions
}
catch(FileNotFound)
{
    // take other action
}
```

The basic steps in using exceptions are

1. Identify those areas of the program in which you begin an operation that might raise an exception, and put them in try blocks.

2. Create catch blocks to catch the exceptions if they are thrown, to clean up allocated memory, and to inform the user as appropriate. Listing 20.1 illustrates the use of both try blocks and catch blocks.

Exceptions are objects used to transmit information about a problem.

A try block is a block surrounded by braces in which an exception may be thrown.

A catch block is the block immediately following a try block, in which exceptions are handled.

When an exception is thrown (or raised), control transfers to the appropriate catch block following the current try block.

Note

Some very old compilers do not support exceptions. Exceptions are part of the ANSI C++ standard, however, and every compiler vendor's latest edition fully supports native exceptions. If you have an older compiler, you won't be able to compile and run the exercises in this chapter. It's still a good idea to read through the entire chapter, however, and return to this material when you upgrade your compiler.

LISTING 20.1   Raising an Exception

```
0:   #include <iostream>
1:   using namespace std;
2:
3:   const int DefaultSize = 10;
4:
5:   class Array
6:   {
7:   public:
8:       // constructors
9:       Array(int itsSize = DefaultSize);
10:      Array(const Array &rhs);
11:      ~Array() { delete [] pType;}
12:
13:      // operators
14:      Array& operator=(const Array&);
15:      int& operator[](int offSet);
16:      const int& operator[](int offSet) const;
17:
18:      // accessors
19:      int GetitsSize() const { return itsSize; }
20:
21:      // friend function
22:      friend ostream& operator<< (ostream&, const Array&);
23:
24:      class xBoundary {};   // define the exception class
25:
26:   private:
27:      int *pType;
28:      int  itsSize;
29:   };
30:
31:
32:   Array::Array(int size):
33:      itsSize(size)
34:   {
35:      pType = new int[size];
36:      for (int i = 0; i<size; i++)
37:         pType[i] = 0;
38:   }
39:
40:
41:   Array& Array::operator=(const Array &rhs)
42:   {
43:      if (this == &rhs)
44:         return *this;
45:      delete [] pType;
46:      itsSize = rhs.GetitsSize();
47:      pType = new int[itsSize];
48:      for (int i = 0; i<itsSize; i++)
```

20

LISTING 20.1   continued

```
49:            pType[i] = rhs[i];
50:        return *this;
51:    }
52:
53:    Array::Array(const Array &rhs)
54:    {
55:        itsSize = rhs.GetitsSize();
56:        pType = new int[itsSize];
57:        for (int i = 0; i<itsSize; i++)
58:            pType[i] = rhs[i];
59:    }
60:
61:
62:    int& Array::operator[](int offSet)
63:    {
64:        int size = GetitsSize();
65:        if (offSet >= 0 && offSet < GetitsSize())
66:            return pType[offSet];
67:        throw xBoundary();
68:        return pType[0]; // appease MSC
69:    }
70:
71:
72:    const int& Array::operator[](int offSet) const
73:    {
74:        int mysize = GetitsSize();
75:        if (offSet >= 0 && offSet < GetitsSize())
76:            return pType[offSet];
77:        throw xBoundary();
78:        return pType[0]; // appease MSC
79:    }
80:
81:    ostream& operator<< (ostream& output, const Array& theArray)
82:    {
83:        for (int i = 0; i<theArray.GetitsSize(); i++)
84:            output << "[" << i << "] " << theArray[i] << endl;
85:        return output;
86:    }
87:
88:    int main()
89:    {
90:        Array intArray(20);
91:        try
92:        {
93:            for (int j = 0; j< 100; j++)
94:            {
95:                intArray[j] = j;
96:                cout << "intArray[" << j << "] okay..." << endl;
97:            }
```

LISTING 20.1 continued

```
98:      }
99:      catch (Array::xBoundary)
100:     {
101:         cout << "Unable to process your input!\n";
102:     }
103:     cout << "Done.\n";
104:     return 0;
105: }
```

OUTPUT

```
intArray[0] okay...
intArray[1] okay...
intArray[2] okay...
intArray[3] okay...
intArray[4] okay...
intArray[5] okay...
intArray[6] okay...
intArray[7] okay...
intArray[8] okay...
intArray[9] okay...
intArray[10] okay...
intArray[11] okay...
intArray[12] okay...
intArray[13] okay...
intArray[14] okay...
intArray[15] okay...
intArray[16] okay...
intArray[17] okay...
intArray[18] okay...
intArray[19] okay...
Unable to process your input!
Done.
```

ANALYSIS Listing 20.1 presents a somewhat stripped-down Array class, based on the template developed on Day 19, "Templates."

On line 24, a new class, xBoundary, is declared within the declaration of the outer class Array.

This new class is not in any way distinguished as an exception class. It is just a class the same as any other. This particular class is incredibly simple; it has no data and no methods. Nonetheless, it is a valid class in every way.

In fact, it is incorrect to say it has no methods, because the compiler automatically assigns it a default constructor, destructor, copy constructor, and the assignment operator (operator equals); so it actually has four class functions, but no data.

20

Note that declaring it from within Array serves only to couple the two classes together. As discussed on Day 16, "Advanced Inheritance," Array has no special access to xBoundary, nor does xBoundary have preferential access to the members of Array.

On lines 62–69 and 72–79, the offset operators are modified to examine the offset requested, and if it is out of range, to throw the xBoundary class as an exception. The parentheses are required to distinguish between this call to the xBoundary constructor and the use of an enumerated constant. Note that some Microsoft compilers require that you provide a return statement to match the declaration (in this case, returning an integer reference), even though if an exception is thrown on line 67, the code will never reach line 68. This is a compiler bug, proving only that even Microsoft finds this stuff difficult and confusing!

On line 91, the keyword try begins a try block that ends on line 98. Within that try block, 101 integers are added to the array that was declared on line 90.

On line 99, the catch block to catch xBoundary exceptions is declared.

In the driver program on lines 88–105, a try block is created in which each member of the array is initialized. When j (line 93) is incremented to 20, the member at offset 20 is accessed. This causes the test on line 66 to fail, and operator[] raises an xBoundary exception on line 67.

Program control switches to the catch block on line 99, and the exception is caught or handled by the catch on the same line, which prints an error message. Program flow drops through to the end of the catch block on line 102.

---

try Blocks

A try block is a series of statements that begins with the keyword try; it is followed by an opening brace and ends with a closing brace.

Example

```
try
{
Function();
};
```

---

catch Blocks

A catch block is a series of statements, each of which begins with the keyword catch, followed by an exception type in parentheses, followed by an opening brace, and ending with a closing brace.

Example
```
try
{
Function();
};
catch (OutOfMemory)
{
// take action
}
```

Using try Blocks and catch Blocks

Figuring out where to put your try blocks is nontrivial: It is not always obvious which actions might raise an exception. The next question is where to catch the exception. It may be that you'll want to throw all memory exceptions where the memory is allocated, but you'll want to catch the exceptions high in the program where you deal with the user interface.

When trying to determine try block locations, look to where you allocate memory or use resources. Other things to look for are out-of-bounds errors, illegal input, and so forth.

Catching Exceptions

Here's how it works: When an exception is thrown, the call stack is examined. The call stack is the list of function calls created when one part of the program invokes another function.

The call stack tracks the execution path. If main() calls the function Animal::GetFavoriteFood(), and GetFavoriteFood() calls Animal::LookupPreferences(), which in turn calls fstream::operator>>(), all these are on the call stack. A recursive function might be on the call stack many times.

The exception is passed up the call stack to each enclosing block. This is called "unwinding the stack." As the stack is unwound, the destructors for local objects on the stack are invoked, and the objects are destroyed.

One or more catch statements follow each try block. If the exception matches one of the catch statements, it is considered to be handled by having that statement execute. If it doesn't match any, the unwinding of the stack continues.

If the exception reaches all the way to the beginning of the program (main()) and is still not caught, a built-in handler is called that terminates the program.

20

It is important to note that the exception unwinding of the stack is a one-way street. As it progresses, the stack is unwound and objects on the stack are destroyed. There is no going back: Once the exception is handled, the program continues after the try block of the catch statement that handled the exception.

Thus, in Listing 20.1, execution will continue on line 101, the first line after the try block of the catch statement that handled the xBoundary exception. Remember that when an exception is raised, program flow continues after the catch block, not after the point where the exception was thrown.

More Than One catch Specification

It is possible for more than one condition to cause an exception. In this case, the catch statements can be lined up one after another, much like the conditions in a switch statement. The equivalent to the default statement is the "catch everything" statement, indicated by catch(...). Listing 20.2 illustrates multiple exception conditions.

LISTING 20.2   Multiple Exceptions

```
0:   #include <iostream>
1:   using namespace std;
2:
3:   const int DefaultSize = 10;
4:
5:   class Array
6:   {
7:   public:
8:       // constructors
9:       Array(int itsSize = DefaultSize);
10:      Array(const Array &rhs);
11:      ~Array() { delete [] pType;}
12:
13:      // operators
14:      Array& operator=(const Array&);
15:      int& operator[](int offSet);
16:      const int& operator[](int offSet) const;
17:
18:      // accessors
19:      int GetitsSize() const { return itsSize; }
20:
21:      // friend function
22:      friend ostream& operator<< (ostream&, const Array&);
23:
24:      // define the exception classes
25:      class xBoundary {};
26:      class xTooBig {};
27:      class xTooSmall{};
```

LISTING 20.2   continued

```
28:     class xZero {};
29:     class xNegative {};
30:  private:
31:     int *pType;
32:     int  itsSize;
33:  };
34:
35:  int& Array::operator[](int offSet)
36:  {
37:     int size = GetitsSize();
38:     if (offSet >= 0 && offSet < GetitsSize())
39:        return pType[offSet];
40:     throw xBoundary();
41:     return pType[0];   // appease MFC
42:  }
43:
44:
45:  const int& Array::operator[](int offSet) const
46:  {
47:     int mysize = GetitsSize();
48:     if (offSet >= 0 && offSet < GetitsSize())
49:        return pType[offSet];
50:     throw xBoundary();
51:
52:     return pType[0];   // appease MFC
53:  }
54:
55:
56:  Array::Array(int size):
57:     itsSize(size)
58:  {
59:     if (size == 0)
60:        throw xZero();
61:     if (size < 10)
62:        throw xTooSmall();
63:     if (size > 30000)
64:        throw xTooBig();
65:     if (size < 1)
66:        throw xNegative();
67:
68:     pType = new int[size];
69:     for (int i = 0; i<size; i++)
70:        pType[i] = 0;
71:  }
72:
73:  int main()
74:  {
75:     try
76:     {
```

20

LISTING 20.2 continued

```
77:        Array intArray(0);
78:        for (int j = 0; j< 100; j++)
79:        {
80:            intArray[j] = j;
81:            cout << "intArray[" << j << "] okay...\n";
82:        }
83:    }
84:    catch (Array::xBoundary)
85:    {
86:        cout << "Unable to process your input!\n";
87:    }
88:    catch (Array::xTooBig)
89:    {
90:        cout << "This array is too big...\n";
91:    }
92:    catch (Array::xTooSmall)
93:    {
94:        cout << "This array is too small...\n";
95:    }
96:    catch (Array::xZero)
97:    {
98:        cout << "You asked for an array";
99:        cout << " of zero objects!\n";
100:   }
101:   catch (...)
102:   {
103:        cout << "Something went wrong!\n";
104:   }
105:   cout << "Done.\n";
106:   return 0;
107: }
```

OUTPUT
```
You asked for an array of zero objects!
Done.
```

ANALYSIS Four new classes are created in lines 25–29: xTooBig, xTooSmall, xZero, and xNegative. In the constructor, on lines 56–71, the size passed to the constructor is examined. If it's too big, too small, negative, or zero, an exception is thrown.

The try block is changed to include catch statements for each condition other than negative, which is caught by the "catch everything" statement catch(...), shown on line 101.

Try this with a number of values for the size of the array. Then try putting in –5. You might have expected xNegative to be called, but the order of the tests in the constructor prevented this: size < 10 was evaluated before size < 1. To fix this, swap lines 61 and 62 with lines 65 and 66 and recompile.

Exception Hierarchies

Exceptions are classes, and as such, they can be derived from. It may be advantageous to create a class xSize, and to derive from it xZero, xTooSmall, xTooBig, and xNegative. Thus, some functions might just catch xSize errors, and other functions might catch the specific type of xSize error. Listing 20.3 illustrates this idea.

LISTING 20.3   Class Hierarchies and Exceptions

```
0:   #include <iostream>
1:   using namespace std;
2:
3:   const int DefaultSize = 10;
4:
5:   class Array
6:   {
7:   public:
8:       // constructors
9:       Array(int itsSize = DefaultSize);
10:      Array(const Array &rhs);
11:      ~Array() { delete [] pType;}
12:
13:      // operators
14:      Array& operator=(const Array&);
15:      int& operator[](int offSet);
16:      const int& operator[](int offSet) const;
17:
18:      // accessors
19:      int GetitsSize() const { return itsSize; }
20:
21:      // friend function
22:      friend ostream& operator<< (ostream&, const Array&);
23:
24:      // define the exception classes
25:      class xBoundary {};
26:      class xSize {};
27:      class xTooBig : public xSize {};
28:      class xTooSmall : public xSize {};
29:      class xZero  : public xTooSmall {};
30:      class xNegative  : public xSize {};
31:  private:
32:      int *pType;
33:      int  itsSize;
34:  };
35:
36:
37:  Array::Array(int size):
38:      itsSize(size)
39:  {
```

20

LISTING 20.3   continued

```
40:        if (size == 0)
41:            throw xZero();
42:        if (size > 30000)
43:            throw xTooBig();
44:        if (size <1)
45:            throw xNegative();
46:        if (size < 10)
47:            throw xTooSmall();
48:
49:        pType = new int[size];
50:        for (int i = 0; i<size; i++)
51:            pType[i] = 0;
52:    }
53:
54:    int& Array::operator[](int offSet)
55:    {
56:        int size = GetitsSize();
57:        if (offSet >= 0 && offSet < GetitsSize())
58:            return pType[offSet];
59:        throw xBoundary();
60:        return pType[0];   // appease MFC
61:    }
62:
63:
64:    const int& Array::operator[](int offSet) const
65:    {
66:        int mysize = GetitsSize();
67:        if (offSet >= 0 && offSet < GetitsSize())
68:            return pType[offSet];
69:        throw xBoundary();
70:
71:        return pType[0];   // appease MFC
72:    }
73:
74:    int main()
75:    {
76:        try
77:        {
78:            Array intArray(0);
79:            for (int j = 0; j< 100; j++)
80:            {
81:                intArray[j] = j;
82:                cout << "intArray[" << j << "] okay...\n";
83:            }
84:        }
85:        catch (Array::xBoundary)
86:        {
87:            cout << "Unable to process your input!\n";
88:        }
```

LISTING 20.3   continued

```
89:     catch (Array::xTooBig)
90:     {
91:        cout << "This array is too big...\n";
92:     }
93:
94:     catch (Array::xTooSmall)
95:     {
96:        cout << "This array is too small...\n";
97:     }
98:     catch (Array::xZero)
99:     {
100:       cout << "You asked for an array";
101:       cout << " of zero objects!\n";
102:    }
103:    catch (...)
104:    {
105:       cout << "Something went wrong!\n";
106:    }
107:    cout << "Done.\n";
108:    return 0;
109: }
```

OUTPUT

```
This array is too small...
Done.
```

ANALYSIS The significant change is on lines 27–30, where the class hierarchy is established. Classes xTooBig, xTooSmall, and xNegative are derived from xSize, and xZero is derived from xTooSmall.

The Array is created with size zero, but what's this? The wrong exception appears to be caught! Examine the catch block carefully, however, and you will find that it looks for an exception of type xTooSmall before it looks for an exception of type xZero. Because an xZero object is thrown and an xZero object is an xTooSmall object, it is caught by the handler for xTooSmall. Once handled, the exception is not passed on to the other handlers, so the handler for xZero is never called.

The solution to this problem is to carefully order the handlers so that the most specific handlers come first and the less specific handlers come later. In this particular example, switching the placement of the two handlers xZero and xTooSmall will fix the problem.

20

Data in Exceptions and Naming Exception Objects

Often you will want to know more than just what type of exception was thrown so you can respond properly to the error. Exception classes are the same as any other class. You are free to provide data, initialize that data in the constructor, and read that data at any time. Listing 20.4 illustrates how to do this.

LISTING 20.4　Getting Data Out of an Exception Object

```
0:  #include <iostream>
1:  using namespace std;
2:
3:  const int DefaultSize = 10;
4:
5:  class Array
6:  {
7:  public:
8:      // constructors
9:      Array(int itsSize = DefaultSize);
10:     Array(const Array &rhs);
11:     ~Array() { delete [] pType;}
12:
13:     // operators
14:     Array& operator=(const Array&);
15:     int& operator[](int offSet);
16:     const int& operator[](int offSet) const;
17:
18:     // accessors
19:     int GetitsSize() const { return itsSize; }
20:
21:     // friend function
22:     friend ostream& operator<< (ostream&, const Array&);
23:
24:     // define the exception classes
25:     class xBoundary {};
26:     class xSize
27:     {
28:     public:
29:         xSize(int size):itsSize(size) {}
30:         ~xSize(){}
31:         int GetSize() { return itsSize; }
32:     private:
33:         int itsSize;
34:     };
35:
36:     class xTooBig : public xSize
37:     {
```

LISTING 20.4   continued

```
38:     public:
39:        xTooBig(int size):xSize(size){}
40:     };
41:
42:     class xTooSmall : public xSize
43:     {
44:     public:
45:        xTooSmall(int size):xSize(size){}
46:     };
47:
48:     class xZero   : public xTooSmall
49:     {
50:     public:
51:        xZero(int size):xTooSmall(size){}
52:     };
53:
54:     class xNegative : public xSize
55:     {
56:     public:
57:        xNegative(int size):xSize(size){}
58:     };
59:
60:  private:
61:     int *pType;
62:     int  itsSize;
63:  };
64:
65:
66:  Array::Array(int size):
67:  itsSize(size)
68:  {
69:     if (size == 0)
70:        throw xZero(size);
71:     if (size > 30000)
72:        throw xTooBig(size);
73:     if (size <1)
74:        throw xNegative(size);
75:     if (size < 10)
76:        throw xTooSmall(size);
77:
78:     pType = new int[size];
79:     for (int i = 0; i<size; i++)
80:        pType[i] = 0;
81:  }
82:
83:
84:  int& Array::operator[] (int offSet)
85:  {
86:     int size = GetitsSize();
```

20

LISTING 20.4   continued

```
87:      if (offSet >= 0 && offSet < GetitsSize())
88:          return pType[offSet];
89:      throw xBoundary();
90:      return pType[0];
91:  }
92:
93:  const int& Array::operator[] (int offSet) const
94:  {
95:     int size = GetitsSize();
96:     if (offSet >= 0 && offSet < GetitsSize())
97:          return pType[offSet];
98:      throw xBoundary();
99:      return pType[0];
100: }
101:
102:  int main()
103:  {
104:     try
105:     {
106:        Array intArray(9);
107:        for (int j = 0; j< 100; j++)
108:        {
109:           intArray[j] = j;
110:           cout << "intArray[" << j << "] okay..." << endl;
111:        }
112:     }
113:     catch (Array::xBoundary)
114:     {
115:        cout << "Unable to process your input!\n";
116:     }
117:     catch (Array::xZero theException)
118:     {
119:        cout << "You asked for an Array of zero objects!" << endl;
120:        cout << "Received " << theException.GetSize() << endl;
121:     }
122:     catch (Array::xTooBig theException)
123:     {
124:        cout << "This Array is too big..." << endl;
125:        cout << "Received " << theException.GetSize() << endl;
126:     }
127:     catch (Array::xTooSmall theException)
128:     {
129:        cout << "This Array is too small..." << endl;
130:        cout << "Received " << theException.GetSize() << endl;
131:     }
132:     catch (...)
133:     {
134:        cout << "Something went wrong, but I've no idea what!\n";
135:     }
```

LISTING 20.4   continued

```
136:      cout << "Done.\n";
137:      return 0;
138:  }
```

OUTPUT
```
This array is too small...
Received 9
Done.
```

ANALYSIS   The declaration of xSize has been modified to include a member variable, itsSize, on line 33 and a member function, GetSize(), on line 31. Additionally, a constructor has been added that takes an integer and initializes the member variable, as shown on line 29.

The derived classes declare a constructor that does nothing but initialize the base class. No other functions were declared, in part to save space in the listing.

The catch statements on lines 113–135 are modified to name the exception they catch, theException, and to use this object to access the data stored in itsSize.

Note

> Keep in mind that if you are constructing an exception, it is because an exception has been raised: Something has gone wrong, and your exception should be careful not to kick off the same problem. Therefore, if you are creating an OutOfMemory exception, you probably don't want to allocate memory in its constructor.

It is tedious and error-prone to have each of these catch statements individually print the appropriate message. This job belongs to the object, which knows what type of object it is and what value it received. Listing 20.5 takes a more object-oriented approach to this problem, using virtual functions so that each exception "does the right thing."

20

LISTING 20.5   Passing by Reference and Using Virtual Functions in Exceptions

```
0:  #include <iostream>
1:  using namespace std;
2:
3:  const int DefaultSize = 10;
4:
5:  class Array
6:  {
7:  public:
8:  // constructors
```

LISTING 20.5   continued

```
9:        Array(int itsSize = DefaultSize);
10:       Array(const Array &rhs);
11:       ~Array() { delete [] pType;}
12:
13:       // operators
14:       Array& operator=(const Array&);
15:       int& operator[](int offSet);
16:       const int& operator[](int offSet) const;
17:
18:       // accessors
19:       int GetitsSize() const { return itsSize; }
20:
21:       // friend function
22:       friend ostream& operator<<
23:       (ostream&, const Array&);
24:
25:       // define the exception classes
26:       class xBoundary {};
27:       class xSize
28:       {
29:       public:
30:          xSize(int size):itsSize(size) {}
31:          ~xSize(){}
32:          virtual int GetSize() { return itsSize; }
33:          virtual void PrintError()
34:          {
35:             cout << "Size error. Received: ";
36:             cout << itsSize << endl;
37:          }
38:       protected:
39:          int itsSize;
40:       };
41:
42:       class xTooBig : public xSize
43:       {
44:       public:
45:          xTooBig(int size):xSize(size){}
46:          virtual void PrintError()
47:          {
48:             cout << "Too big! Received: ";
49:             cout << xSize::itsSize << endl;
50:          }
51:       };
52:
53:       class xTooSmall : public xSize
54:       {
55:       public:
56:          xTooSmall(int size):xSize(size){}
57:          virtual void PrintError()
```

LISTING 20.5   continued

```
58:         {
59:             cout << "Too small! Received: ";
60:             cout << xSize::itsSize << endl;
61:         }
62:     };
63:
64:     class xZero  : public xTooSmall
65:     {
66:     public:
67:         xZero(int size):xTooSmall(size){}
68:         virtual void PrintError()
69:         {
70:             cout << "Zero!!. Received: " ;
71:             cout << xSize::itsSize << endl;
72:         }
73:     };
74:
75:     class xNegative : public xSize
76:     {
77:     public:
78:         xNegative(int size):xSize(size){}
79:         virtual void PrintError()
80:         {
81:             cout << "Negative! Received: ";
82:             cout << xSize::itsSize << endl;
83:         }
84:     };
85:
86:  private:
87:      int *pType;
88:      int  itsSize;
89:  };
90:
91:  Array::Array(int size):
92:      itsSize(size)
93:  {
94:      if (size == 0)
95:          throw xZero(size);
96:      if (size > 30000)
97:          throw xTooBig(size);
98:      if (size <1)
99:          throw xNegative(size);
100:     if (size < 10)
101:         throw xTooSmall(size);
102:
103:     pType = new int[size];
104:     for (int i = 0; i<size; i++)
105:         pType[i] = 0;
106: }
```

20

LISTING 20.5 continued

```
107:
108:    int& Array::operator[] (int offSet)
109:    {
110:       int size = GetitsSize();
111:       if (offSet >= 0 && offSet < GetitsSize())
112:          return pType[offSet];
113:       throw xBoundary();
114:       return pType[0];
115:    }
116:
117:    const int& Array::operator[] (int offSet) const
118:    {
119:       int size = GetitsSize();
120:       if (offSet >= 0 && offSet < GetitsSize())
121:          return pType[offSet];
122:       throw xBoundary();
123:       return pType[0];
124:    }
125:
126:    int main()
127:    {
128:       try
129:       {
130:          Array intArray(9);
131:          for (int j = 0; j< 100; j++)
132:          {
133:             intArray[j] = j;
134:             cout << "intArray[" << j << "] okay...\n";
135:          }
136:       }
137:       catch (Array::xBoundary)
138:       {
139:          cout << "Unable to process your input!\n";
140:       }
141:       catch (Array::xSize& theException)
142:       {
143:          theException.PrintError();
144:       }
145:       catch (...)
146:       {
147:          cout << "Something went wrong!\n";
148:       }
149:       cout << "Done.\n";
150:       return 0;
151:    }
```

OUTPUT

```
Too small! Received: 9
Done.
```

ANALYSIS Listing 20.5 declares a virtual method in the xSize class, PrintError(), that prints an error message and the actual size of the class. This is overridden in each of the derived classes.

On line 141, the exception object is declared to be a reference. When PrintError() is called with a reference to an object, polymorphism causes the correct version of PrintError() to be invoked. The code is cleaner, easier to understand, and easier to maintain.

Exceptions and Templates

When creating exceptions to work with templates, you have a choice: You can create an exception for each instance of the template, or you can use exception classes declared outside the template declaration. Listing 20.6 illustrates both approaches.

LISTING 20.6   Using Exceptions with Templates

```
0:  #include <iostream>
1:  using namespace std;
2:
3:  const int DefaultSize = 10;
4:  class xBoundary {};
5:
6:  template <class T>
7:  class Array
8:  {
9:  public:
10:     // constructors
11:     Array(int itsSize = DefaultSize);
12:     Array(const Array &rhs);
13:     ~Array() { delete [] pType;}
14:
15:     // operators
16:     Array& operator=(const Array<T>&);
17:     T& operator[](int offSet);
18:     const T& operator[](int offSet) const;
19:
20:     // accessors
21:     int GetitsSize() const { return itsSize; }
22:
23:     // friend function
24:     friend ostream& operator<< (ostream&, const Array<T>&);
25:
26:     // define the exception classes
27:
28:     class xSize {};
29:
```

LISTING 20.6   continued

```
30:  private:
31:     int *pType;
32:     int  itsSize;
33:  };
34:
35:  template <class T>
36:  Array<T>::Array(int size):
37:     itsSize(size)
38:  {
39:     if (size <10 || size > 30000)
40:        throw xSize();
41:     pType = new T[size];
42:     for (int i = 0; i<size; i++)
43:        pType[i] = 0;
44:  }
45:
46:  template <class T>
47:  Array<T>& Array<T>::operator=(const Array<T> &rhs)
48:  {
49:     if (this == &rhs)
50:        return *this;
51:     delete [] pType;
52:     itsSize = rhs.GetitsSize();
53:     pType = new T[itsSize];
54:     for (int i = 0; i<itsSize; i++)
55:        pType[i] = rhs[i];
56:  }
57:  template <class T>
58:  Array<T>::Array(const Array<T> &rhs)
59:  {
60:     itsSize = rhs.GetitsSize();
61:     pType = new T[itsSize];
62:     for (int i = 0; i<itsSize; i++)
63:        pType[i] = rhs[i];
64:  }
65:
66:  template <class T>
67:  T& Array<T>::operator[](int offSet)
68:  {
69:     int size = GetitsSize();
70:     if (offSet >= 0 && offSet < GetitsSize())
71:        return pType[offSet];
72:     throw xBoundary();
73:     return pType[0];
74:  }
75:
76:  template <class T>
77:  const T& Array<T>::operator[](int offSet) const
78:  {
```

LISTING 20.6 continued

```
79:       int mysize = GetitsSize();
80:       if (offSet >= 0 && offSet < GetitsSize())
81:           return pType[offSet];
82:       throw xBoundary();
83:   }
84:
85:   template <class T>
86:   ostream& operator<< (ostream& output, const Array<T>& theArray)
87:   {
88:       for (int i = 0; i<theArray.GetitsSize(); i++)
89:           output << "[" << i << "] " << theArray[i] << endl;
90:       return output;
91:   }
92:
93:
94:   int main()
95:   {
96:       try
97:       {
98:           Array<int> intArray(9);
99:           for (int j = 0; j< 100; j++)
100:          {
101:              intArray[j] = j;
102:              cout << "intArray[" << j << "] okay..." << endl;
103:          }
104:      }
105:      catch (xBoundary)
106:      {
107:          cout << "Unable to process your input!\n";
108:      }
109:      catch (Array<int>::xSize)
110:      {
111:          cout << "Bad Size!\n";
112:      }
113:
114:      cout << "Done.\n";
115:      return 0;
116:  }
```

20

OUTPUT
```
Bad Size!
Done.
```

ANALYSIS The first exception, xBoundary, is declared outside the template definition on line 4. The second exception, xSize, is declared from within the definition of the template on line 28.

The exception xBoundary is not tied to the template class, but it can be used the same as any other class. xSize is tied to the template and must be called based on the instantiated Array. You can see the difference in the syntax for the two catch statements. Line 105 shows catch (xBoundary), but line 109 shows catch (Array<int>::xSize). The latter is tied to the instantiation of an integer Array.

Exceptions Without Errors

When C++ programmers get together for a virtual beer in the cyberspace bar after work, talk often turns to whether exceptions should be used for routine conditions. Some maintain that by their nature, exceptions should be reserved for those predictable but exceptional circumstances (hence the name!) that a programmer must anticipate, but that are not part of the routine processing of the code.

Others point out that exceptions offer a powerful and clean way to return through many layers of function calls without danger of memory leaks. A frequent example is this: The user requests an action in a GUI environment. The part of the code that catches the request must call a member function on a dialog manager, which, in turn, calls code that processes the request, which calls code that decides which dialog box to use, which in turn calls code to put up the dialog box, which finally calls code that processes the user's input. If the user clicks Cancel, the code must return to the very first calling method where the original request was handled.

One approach to this problem is to put a try block around the original call and catch CancelDialog as an exception, which can be raised by the handler for the Cancel button. This is safe and effective, but clicking Cancel is a routine circumstance, not an exceptional one.

This frequently becomes something of a religious argument, but a reasonable way to decide the question is to ask the following: Does use of exceptions in this way make the code easier or harder to understand? Are there fewer risks of errors and memory leaks, or more? Will it be harder or easier to maintain this code? These decisions, like so many others, will require an analysis of the trade-offs; no single, obvious right answer exists.

A Word About Code Rot

Code rot is a well-known phenomenon in which software deteriorates due to being neglected. A perfectly well-written, fully debugged program will turn bad on your customer's shelf just weeks after you deliver it. After a few months, your customer will notice that a green mold has covered your logic, and many of your objects have begun to flake apart.

Besides shipping your source code in air-tight containers, your only protection is to write your programs so that when you go back to fix the spoilage, you can quickly and easily identify where the problems are.

Note Code rot is a programmer's joke which teaches an important lesson. Programs are enormously complex, and bugs, errors, and mistakes can hide for a long time before turning up. Protect yourself by writing easy-to-maintain code.

This means that your code must be written to be understood, and commented where tricky. Six months after you deliver your code, you will read it with the eyes of a total stranger, bewildered by how anyone could ever have written such convoluted and twisty syntax.

Bugs and Debugging

Nearly all modern development environments include one or more high-powered debuggers. The essential idea of using a debugger is this: You run the debugger, which loads your source code, and then you run your program from within the debugger. This enables you to see each instruction in your program as it executes and to examine your variables as they change during the life of your program.

All compilers will let you compile with or without symbols. Compiling with symbols tells the compiler to create the necessary mapping between your source code and the generated program; the debugger uses this to point to the line of source code that corresponds to the next action in the program.

Full-screen symbolic debuggers make this chore a delight. When you load your debugger, it will read through all your source code and show the code in a window. You can step over function calls or direct the debugger to step into the function, line by line.

With most debuggers, you can switch between the source code and the output to see the results of each executed statement. More powerfully, you can examine the current state of each variable, look at complex data structures, examine the value of member data within classes, and look at the actual values in memory of various pointers and other memory locations. You can execute several types of control within a debugger that include setting breakpoints, setting watch points, examining memory, and looking at the assembler code.

20

Breakpoints

Breakpoints are instructions to the debugger that when a particular line of code is ready to be executed, the program should stop. This allows you to run your program unimpeded until the line in question is reached. Breakpoints help you analyze the current condition of variables just before and after a critical line of code.

Watch Points

It is possible to tell the debugger to show you the value of a particular variable or to break when a particular variable is read or written to. Watch points enable you to set these conditions, and at times even to modify the value of a variable while the program is running.

Examining Memory

At times it is important to see the actual values held in memory. Modern debuggers can show values in the form of the actual variable; that is, strings can be shown as characters, longs as numbers rather than as four bytes, and so forth. Sophisticated C++ debuggers can even show complete classes and provide the current value of all the member variables, including the `this` pointer.

Assembler

Although reading through the source can be all that is required to find a bug, when all else fails, it is possible to instruct the debugger to show you the actual assembly code generated for each line of your source code. You can examine the memory registers and flags, and generally delve as deep into the inner workings of your program as required.

Learn to use your debugger. It can be the most powerful weapon in your holy war against bugs. Runtime bugs are the hardest to find and squash, and a powerful debugger can make it possible, if not easy, to find nearly all of them.

Summary

Today you learned how to create and use exceptions. Exceptions are objects that can be created and thrown at points in the program where the executing code cannot handle the error or other exceptional condition that has arisen. Other parts of the program, higher in the call stack, implement `catch` blocks that catch the exception and take appropriate action.

Exceptions are normal, user-created objects, and as such may be passed by value or by reference. They may contain data and methods, and the `catch` block may use that data to decide how to deal with the exception.

It is possible to create multiple catch blocks, but once an exception matches a catch block's signature, it is considered to be handled and is not given to the subsequent catch blocks. It is important to order the catch blocks appropriately so that more specific catch blocks have first chance, and more general catch blocks handle those not otherwise handled.

This chapter also examined some of the fundamentals of symbolic debuggers, including using watch points, breakpoints, and so forth. These tools can help you zero in on the part of your program that is causing the error and let you see the value of variables as they change during the course of the execution of the program.

Q&A

Q Why bother with raising exceptions? Why not handle the error right where it happens?

A Often, the same error can be generated in different parts of the code. Exceptions let you centralize the handling of errors. Additionally, the part of the code that generates the error may not be the best place to determine how to handle the error.

Q Why generate an object? Why not just pass an error code?

A Objects are more flexible and powerful than error codes. They can convey more information, and the constructor/destructor mechanisms can be used for the creation and removal of resources that may be required to properly handle the exceptional condition.

Q Why not use exceptions for non-error conditions? Isn't it convenient to be able to express-train back to previous areas of the code, even when non-exceptional conditions exist?

A Yes, some C++ programmers use exceptions for just that purpose. The danger is that exceptions might create memory leaks as the stack is unwound and some objects are inadvertently left in the free store. With careful programming techniques and a good compiler, this can usually be avoided. Otherwise, it is a matter of personal aesthetic; some programmers feel that by their nature exceptions should not be used for routine conditions.

Q Does an exception have to be caught in the same place where the try block created the exception?

A No, it is possible to catch an exception anywhere in the call stack. As the stack is unwound, the exception is passed up the stack until it is handled.

20

Q **Why use a debugger when you can use `cout` with conditional (`#ifdef debug`) compiling?**

A The debugger provides a much more powerful mechanism for stepping through your code and watching values change without having to clutter your code with thousands of debugging statements.

Workshop

The Workshop contains quiz questions to help solidify your understanding of the material covered and exercises to provide you with experience in using what you've learned. Try to answer the quiz and exercise questions before checking the answers in Appendix D, and make sure you understand the answers before going to the next chapter.

Quiz

1. What is an exception?
2. What is a `try` block?
3. What is a `catch` statement?
4. What information can an exception contain?
5. When are exception objects created?
6. Should you pass exceptions by value or by reference?
7. Will a `catch` statement catch a derived exception if it is looking for the base class?
8. If two `catch` statements are used, one for base and one for derived, which should come first?
9. What does `catch(...)` mean?
10. What is a breakpoint?

Exercises

1. Create a `try` block, a `catch` statement, and a simple exception.
2. Modify the answer from Exercise 1, put data into the exception along with an accessor function, and use it in the `catch` block.
3. Modify the class from Exercise 2 to be a hierarchy of exceptions. Modify the `catch` block to use the derived objects and the base objects.
4. Modify the program from Exercise 3 to have three levels of function calls.

5. **BUG BUSTERS:** What is wrong with the following code?

```
#include "stringc.h"              // our string class

class xOutOfMemory
{
public:
    xOutOfMemory( const String& where ) : location( where ){}
    ~xOutOfMemory(){}
    virtual String where(){ return location };
private:
    String location;
}

main()
{
    try {
        char *var = new char;
        if ( var == 0 )
            throw xOutOfMemory();
    }
    catch( xOutOfMemory& theException )
    {
        cout << "Out of memory at " << theException.location() << "\n";
    }
}
```

This exercise shows the intended bug, which is that we are allocating memory to present the error message, but we are doing so precisely when no memory is available to allocate (after all, that is what this exception manages!). You can test this program by changing the line if (var == 0) to if (1), which will force the exception to be thrown.

20

DAY **21**

What's Next

Congratulations! You are nearly done with a full three-week intensive introduction to C++. By now you should have a solid understanding of C++, but in modern programming there is always more to learn. This chapter will fill in some missing details and then set the course for continued study.

Most of what you write in your source code files is C++. This is interpreted by the compiler and turned into your program. Before the compiler runs, however, the preprocessor runs, and this provides an opportunity for conditional compilation.

Today you will learn

- What conditional compilation is and how to manage it.
- How to write macros using the preprocessor.
- How to use the preprocessor in finding bugs.
- How to manipulate individual bits and use them as flags.
- What the next steps are in learning to use C++ effectively.

The Preprocessor and the Compiler

Every time you run your compiler, your preprocessor runs first. The preprocessor looks for preprocessor instructions, each of which begins with a pound symbol (#). The effect of each of these instructions is a change to the text of the source code. The result is a new source code file—a temporary file that you normally don't see, but that you can instruct the compiler to save so you can examine it if you want to.

The compiler does not read your original source code file; it reads the output of the preprocessor and compiles that file. You've seen the effect of this already with the #include directive. This instructs the preprocessor to find the file whose name follows the #include directive and to write it into the intermediate file at that location. It is as if you had typed that entire file right into your source code, and by the time the compiler sees the source code, the included file is there.

Seeing the Intermediate Form

Nearly every compiler has a switch that you can set either in the integrated development environment (IDE) or at the command line, which instructs the compiler to save the intermediate file. Check your compiler manual for the right switches to set for your compiler if you'd like to examine this file.

Using #define

The #define command defines a string substitution. If you write

```
#define BIG 512
```

you have instructed the precompiler to substitute the string 512 wherever it sees the string BIG. This is not a string in the C++ sense. The characters 512 are substituted in your source code wherever the token BIG is seen. A token is a string of characters that can be used wherever a string or constant or other set of letters might be used. Thus, if you write

```
#define BIG 512
int myArray[BIG];
```

the intermediate file produced by the precompiler will look like this:

```
int myArray[512];
```

Note that the #define statement is gone. Precompiler statements are all removed from the intermediate file; they do not appear in the final source code at all.

Using #define for Constants

One way to use #define is as a substitute for constants. This is almost never a good idea, however, because #define merely makes a string substitution and does no type checking. As explained in the section on constants, tremendous advantages exist in using the const keyword rather than #define.

Using #define for Tests

A second way to use #define, however, is simply to declare that a particular character string is defined. Therefore, you could write

```
#define BIG
```

Later, you can test whether BIG has been defined and take action accordingly. The precompiler commands to test whether a string has been defined are #ifdef (if defined) and #ifndef (if not defined). Both must be followed by the command #endif before the block ends (before the next closing brace).

#ifdef evaluates to true if the string it tests has been defined already. So, you can write

```
#ifdef DEBUG
cout << "Debug defined";
#endif
```

When the precompiler reads the #ifdef, it checks a table it has built to see if you've defined DEBUG. If you have, the #ifdef evaluates to true, and everything to the next #else or #endif is written into the intermediate file for compiling. If it evaluates to false, nothing between #ifdef DEBUG and #endif will be written into the intermediate file; it will be as if it were never in the source code in the first place.

Note that #ifndef is the logical reverse of #ifdef. #ifndef evaluates to true if the string has not been defined up to that point in the file.

The #else Precompiler Command

As you might imagine, the term #else can be inserted between either #ifdef or #ifndef and the closing #endif. Listing 21.1 illustrates how these terms are used.

LISTING 21.1   Using #define

```
0:   #define DemoVersion
1:   #define NT_VERSION 5
2:   #include <iostream>
3:
4:
5:   int main()
```

21

LISTING 21.1   continued

```
6:  {
7:      std::cout << "Checking on the definitions of DemoVersion,";
8:      std::cout << "NT_VERSION and WINDOWS_VERSION...\n";
9:
10:     #ifdef DemoVersion
11:         std::cout << "DemoVersion defined.\n";
12:     #else
13:         std::cout << "DemoVersion not defined.\n";
14:     #endif
15:
16:     #ifndef NT_VERSION
17:         std::cout << "NT_VERSION not defined!\n";
18:     #else
19:         std::cout<<"NT_VERSION defined as: "<<NT_VERSION<<std::endl;
20:     #endif
21:
22:     #ifdef WINDOWS_VERSION
23:         std::cout << "WINDOWS_VERSION defined!\n";
24:     #else
25:         std::cout << "WINDOWS_VERSION was not defined.\n";
26:     #endif
27:
28:     std::cout << "Done.\n";
29:     return 0;
30: }
```

OUTPUT

```
Checking on the definitions of DemoVersion, NT_VERSION_and
WINDOWS_VERSION...
DemoVersion defined.
NT_VERSION defined as: 5
WINDOWS_VERSION was not defined.
Done.
```

ANALYSIS   On lines 0 and 1, DemoVersion and NT_VERSION are defined, with NT_VERSION defined with the string 5. On line 10, the definition of DemoVersion is tested, and because DemoVersion is defined (albeit with no value), the test is true and the string on line 11 is printed.

On line 16 is the test that NT_VERSION is not defined. Because NT_VERSION is defined, this test fails and execution jumps to line 19. Here the string 5 is substituted for the word NT_VERSION; this is seen by the compiler as

```
cout << "NT_VERSION defined as: " << 5 << endl;
```

Note that the first word NT_VERSION is not substituted because it is in a quoted string. The second NT_VERSION is substituted, however, and thus the compiler sees 5 as if you had typed 5 there.

Finally, on line 22, the program tests for WINDOWS_VERSION. Because you did not define WINDOWS_VERSION, the test fails and the message on line 25 is printed.

Inclusion and Inclusion Guards

You will create projects with many different files. You will probably organize your directories so that each class has its own header file (for example, .hpp) with the class declaration and its own implementation file (for example, .cpp) with the source code for the class methods.

Your main() function will be in its own .cpp file, and all the .cpp files will be compiled into .obj files, which will then be linked into a single program by the linker.

Because your programs will use methods from many classes, many header files will be included in each file. Also, header files often need to include one another. For example, the header file for a derived class's declaration must include the header file for its base class.

Imagine that the Animal class is declared in the file ANIMAL.hpp. The Dog class (which derives from Animal) must include the file ANIMAL.hpp in DOG.hpp, or Dog will not be able to derive from Animal. The Cat header also includes ANIMAL.hpp for the same reason.

If you create a method that uses both a Cat and a Dog, you will be in danger of including ANIMAL.hpp twice. This will generate a compile-time error because it is not legal to declare a class (Animal) twice, even though the declarations are identical. You can solve this problem with inclusion guards. At the top of your ANIMAL header file, you write these lines:

```
#ifndef ANIMAL_HPP
#define ANIMAL_HPP
...                          // the whole file goes here
#endif
```

This says, if you haven't defined the term ANIMAL_HPP, go ahead and define it now. Between the #define statement and the closing #endif are the entire contents of the file.

The first time your program includes this file, it reads the first line and the test evaluates to true; that is, you have not yet defined ANIMAL_HPP. So, it defines it and then includes the entire file.

The second time your program includes the ANIMAL.hpp file, it reads the first line and the test evaluates to FALSE; ANIMAL.hpp has been defined. It therefore skips to the next #else (in this case there isn't one) or the next #endif (at the end of the file). Thus, it skips the entire contents of the file, and the class is not declared twice.

21

The actual name of the defined symbol (ANIMAL_HPP) is not important, although it is customary to use the filename in all uppercase with the dot (.) changed to an underscore. This is purely convention, however.

 Note It never hurts to use inclusion guards. Often they will save you hours of debugging time.

Macro Functions

The #define directive can also be used to create macro functions. A macro function is a symbol created using #define; it takes an argument, much like a function does. The preprocessor will substitute the substitution string for whatever argument it is given. For example, you can define the macro TWICE as

```
#define TWICE(x) ( (x) * 2 )
```

and then in your code you write

```
TWICE(4)
```

The entire string TWICE(4) will be removed, and the value 8 will be substituted! When the precompiler sees the 4, it will substitute ((4) * 2), which will then evaluate to 4 * 2, or 8.

A macro can have more than one parameter, and each parameter can be used repeatedly in the replacement text. Two common macros are MAX and MIN:

```
#define MAX(x,y) ( (x) > (y) ? (x) : (y) )
#define MIN(x,y) ( (x) < (y) ? (x) : (y) )
```

Note that in a macro function definition, the opening parenthesis for the parameter list must immediately follow the macro name, with no spaces. The preprocessor is not as forgiving of whitespace as is the compiler.

If you were to write

```
#define MAX (x,y) ( (x) > (y) ? (x) : (y) )
```

and then tried to use MAX like this:

```
int x = 5, y = 7, z;
z = MAX(x,y);
```

the intermediate code would be

```
int x = 5, y = 7, z;
z = (x,y) ( (x) > (y) ? (x) : (y) )(x,y)
```

A simple text substitution would be done, rather than invoking the macro function. Thus, the token MAX would have substituted for it (x,y) ((x) > (y) ? (x) : (y)), and then that would be followed by the (x,y), which followed MAX.

By removing the space between MAX and (x,y), however, the intermediate code becomes

```
int x = 5, y = 7, z;
z =7;
```

Why All the Parentheses?

You may be wondering why so many parentheses are in many of the macros presented so far. The preprocessor does not demand that parentheses be placed around the arguments in the substitution string, but the parentheses help you to avoid unwanted side effects when you pass complicated values to a macro. For example, if you define MAX as

```
#define MAX(x,y) x > y ? x : y
```

and pass in the values 5 and 7, the macro works as intended. But if you pass in a more complicated expression, you'll get unintended results, as shown in Listing 21.2.

LISTING 21.2   Using Parentheses in Macros

```
0:  // Listing 21.2 Macro Expansion
1:  #include <iostream>
2:  using namespace std;
3:
4:  #define CUBE(a) ( (a) * (a) * (a) )
5:  #define THREE(a) a * a * a
6:
7:  int main()
8:  {
9:      long x = 5;
10:     long y = CUBE(x);
11:     long z = THREE(x);
12:
13:     cout << "y: " << y << endl;
14:     cout << "z: " << z << endl;
15:
16:     long a = 5, b = 7;
17:     y = CUBE(a+b);
18:     z = THREE(a+b);
19:
20:     cout << "y: " << y << endl;
21:     cout << "z: " << z << endl;
22:     return 0;
23: }
```

21

OUTPUT
```
y: 125
z: 125
y: 1728
z: 82
```

ANALYSIS On line 4, the macro CUBE is defined, with the argument x put into parentheses each time it is used. On line 5, the macro THREE is defined, without the parentheses.

In the first use of these macros, the value 5 is given as the parameter, and both macros work fine. CUBE(5) expands to ((5) * (5) * (5)), which evaluates to 125, and THREE(5) expands to 5 * 5 * 5, which also evaluates to 125.

In the second use, on lines 16–18, the parameter is 5 + 7. In this case, CUBE(5+7) evaluates to

((5+7) * (5+7) * (5+7))

which evaluates to

((12) * (12) * (12))

which, in turn, evaluates to 1728. THREE(5+7), however, evaluates to

5 + 7 * 5 + 7 * 5 + 7

Because multiplication has a higher precedence than addition, this becomes

5 + (7 * 5) + (7 * 5) + 7

which evaluates to

5 + (35) + (35) + 7

which finally evaluates to 82.

Macros Versus Functions and Templates

Macros suffer from four problems in C++. The first is that they can be confusing if they get large, because all macros must be defined on one line. You can extend that line by using the backslash character (\), but large macros quickly become difficult to manage.

The second problem is that macros are expanded inline each time they are used. This means that if a macro is used a dozen times, the substitution will appear 12 times in your program, rather than appearing once as a function call will. On the other hand, they are usually quicker than a function call because the overhead of a function call is avoided.

The fact that they are expanded inline leads to the third problem, which is that the macro does not appear in the intermediate source code used by the compiler; therefore, it is unavailable in most debuggers. This makes debugging macros tricky.

The final problem, however, is the biggest: Macros are not type-safe. Although it is convenient that absolutely any argument may be used with a macro, this completely undermines the strong typing of C++ and so is an anathema to C++ programmers. Of course, the right way to solve this is with templates, as you saw on Day 19.

Inline Functions

It is often possible to declare an inline function rather than a macro. For example, Listing 21.3 creates a CUBE function, which accomplishes the same thing as the CUBE macro in Listing 21.2, but it does so in a type-safe way.

LISTING 21.3   Using Inline Rather than a Macro

```
0:   #include <iostream>
1:   using namespace std;
2:
3:   inline unsigned long Square(unsigned long a) { return a * a; }
4:   inline unsigned long Cube(unsigned long a)
5:       { return a * a * a; }
6:   int main()
7:   {
8:       unsigned long x=1 ;
9:       for (;;)
10:        {
11:            cout << "Enter a number (0 to quit): ";
12:            cin >> x;
13:            if (x == 0)
14:                break;
15:            cout << "You entered: " << x;
16:            cout << ".  Square(" << x << "): ";
17:            cout  << Square(x);
18:            cout<< ". Cube(" << x << "): ";
19:            cout << Cube(x) << "." << endl;
20:        }
21:        return 0;
22:   }
```

OUTPUT

```
Enter a number (0 to quit): 1
You entered: 1.  Square(1): 1. Cube(1): 1.
Enter a number (0 to quit): 2
You entered: 2.  Square(2): 4. Cube(2): 8.
Enter a number (0 to quit): 3
You entered: 3.  Square(3): 9. Cube(3): 27.
Enter a number (0 to quit): 4
You entered: 4.  Square(4): 16. Cube(4): 64.
Enter a number (0 to quit): 5
```

21

```
You entered: 5.  Square(5): 25. Cube(5): 125.
Enter a number (0 to quit): 6
You entered: 6.  Square(6): 36. Cube(6): 216.
Enter a number (0 to quit): 0
```

ANALYSIS On lines 3 and 4, two inline functions are defined: Square() and Cube(). Each is declared to be inline, so like a macro function, these will be expanded in place for each call, and no function call overhead will occur.

As a reminder, expanded inline means that the content of the function will be placed into the code wherever the function call would be made (for example, on line 17). Because the function call is never made, there is no overhead of putting the return address and the parameters on the stack.

On line 17, the function Square is called, as is the function Cube on line 19. Again, because these are inline functions, it is exactly as if this line had been written like this:

```
16:          cout << ".  Square(" << x << "): "  << x * x << ". Cube(" << x <<
      ➥"): " << x * x * x <<
      ➥"." << endl;
```

String Manipulation

The preprocessor provides two special operators for manipulating strings in macros. The stringizing operator (#) substitutes a quoted string for whatever follows the stringizing operator. The concatenation operator bonds two strings into one.

Stringizing

The stringizing operator puts quotes around any characters following the operator, up to the next white space. Thus, if you write

```
#define WRITESTRING(x) cout << #x
```

and then call

```
WRITESTRING(This is a string);
```

the precompiler will turn it into

```
cout << "This is a string";
```

Note that the string This is a string is put into quotes, as required by cout.

Concatenation

The concatenation operator allows you to bond more than one term into a new word. The new word is actually a token that can be used as a class name, a variable name, an offset into an array, or anywhere else a series of letters might appear.

Assume for a moment that you have five functions named fOnePrint, fTwoPrint, fThreePrint, fFourPrint, and fFivePrint. You can then declare

```
#define fPRINT(x) f ## x ## Print
```

and then use it with fPRINT(Two) to generate fTwoPrint and with fPRINT(Three) to generate fThreePrint.

At the conclusion of Week 2, a PartsList class was developed. This list could only handle objects of type List. Suppose that this list works well, and you'd like to be able to make lists of animals, cars, computers, and so forth.

One approach would be to create AnimalList, CarList, ComputerList, and so on, cutting and pasting the code in place. This will quickly become a nightmare because every change to one list must be written to all the others.

An alternative is to use macros and the concatenation operator. For example, you could define

```
#define Listof(Type)  class Type##List \
{ \
public: \
Type##List(){} \
private:          \
int itsLength; \
};
```

This example is overly sparse, but the idea would be to put in all the necessary methods and data. When you were ready to create an AnimalList, you would write

```
Listof(Animal)
```

and this would be turned into the declaration of the AnimalList class. Some problems occur with this approach, all of which are discussed in detail on Day 19, "Templates."

Predefined Macros

Many compilers predefine a number of useful macros, including __DATE__, __TIME__, __LINE__, and __FILE__. Each of these names is surrounded by two underscore characters to reduce the likelihood that the names will conflict with names you've used in your program.

When the precompiler sees one of these macros, it makes the appropriate substitutes. For __DATE__, the current date is substituted. For __TIME__, the current time is substituted. __LINE__ and __FILE__ are replaced with the source code line number and filename, respectively. You should note that this substitution is made when the source is precompiled, not when the program is run. If you ask the program to print __DATE__, you will not get the current date; instead, you will get the date the program was compiled. These defined macros are very useful in debugging.

assert()

Many compilers offer an assert() macro. The assert() macro returns TRUE if its parameter evaluates TRUE and takes some kind of action if it evaluates FALSE. Many compilers will abort the program on an assert() that fails; others will throw an exception (see Day 20, "Exceptions and Error Handling").

One powerful feature of the assert() macro is that the preprocessor collapses it into no code at all if DEBUG is not defined. It is a great help during development, and when the final product ships, there is no performance penalty or increase in the size of the executable version of the program.

Rather than depending on the compiler-provided assert(), you are free to write your own assert() macro. Listing 21.4 provides a simple assert() macro and shows its use.

LISTING 21.4   A Simple assert() Macro

```
0:  // Listing 21.4 ASSERTS
1:  #define DEBUG
2:  #include <iostream>
3:  using namespace std;
4:
5:  #ifndef DEBUG
6:      #define ASSERT(x)
7:  #else
8:      #define ASSERT(x) \
9:              if (! (x)) \
10:            { \
11:                cout << "ERROR!! Assert " << #x << " failed\n"; \
12:                cout << " on line " << __LINE__ << "\n"; \
13:                cout << " in file " << __FILE__ << "\n"; \
14:            }
15:  #endif
16:
17:  int main()
18:  {
19:     int x = 5;
20:     cout << "First assert: \n";
21:     ASSERT(x==5);
22:     cout << "\nSecond assert: \n";
23:     ASSERT(x != 5);
24:     cout << "\nDone.\n";
25:     return 0;
26:  }
```

OUTPUT

```
First assert:

Second assert:
ERROR!! Assert x !=5 failed
 on line 24
 in file test1704.cpp
Done.
```

ANALYSIS On line 1, the term DEBUG is defined. Typically, this would be done from the command line (or the IDE) at compile time, so you can turn this on and off at will. On lines 8–14, the assert() macro is defined. Typically, this would be done in a header file, and that header (ASSERT.hpp) would be included in all your implementation files.

On line 5, the term DEBUG is tested. If it is not defined, assert() is defined to create no code at all. If DEBUG is defined, the functionality defined on lines 8–14 is applied.

The assert() itself is one long statement split across seven source code lines as far as the precompiler is concerned. On line 9, the value passed in as a parameter is tested; if it evaluates FALSE, the statements on lines 11–13 are invoked, printing an error message. If the value passed in evaluates TRUE, no action is taken.

Debugging with assert()

When writing your program, you will often know deep down in your soul that something is true: A function has a certain value, a pointer is valid, and so forth. It is the nature of bugs that what you know to be true might not be so under some conditions. For example, you know that a pointer is valid, yet the program crashes. assert() can help you find this type of bug, but only if you make it a regular practice to use assert() liberally in your code. Every time you assign or are passed a pointer as a parameter or function return value, be sure to assert that the pointer is valid. Any time your code depends on a particular value being in a variable, assert() that that is true.

No penalty is assessed for frequent use of assert(); it is removed from the code when you undefine debugging. It also provides good internal documentation, reminding the reader of what you believe is true at any given moment in the flow of the code.

assert() Versus Exceptions

Yesterday, you saw how to work with exceptions to handle error conditions. It is important to note that assert() is not intended to handle runtime error conditions such as bad data, out-of-memory conditions, unable to open file, and so forth. assert() is created to catch programming errors only. That is, if an assert() "fires," you know you have a bug in your code.

21

This is critical because when you ship your code to your customers, instances of assert() will be removed. You can't depend on an assert() to handle a runtime problem because the assert() won't be there.

It is a common mistake to use assert() to test the return value from a memory assignment:

```
Animal *pCat = new Cat;
Assert(pCat);    // bad use of assert
pCat->SomeFunction();
```

This is a classic programming error; every time the programmer runs the program, enough memory is available and the assert() never fires. After all, the programmer is running with lots of extra RAM to speed up the compiler, debugger, and so forth. The programmer then ships the executable, and the poor user, who has less memory, reaches this part of the program and the call to new fails and returns NULL. The assert(), however, is no longer in the code and nothing indicates that the pointer points to NULL. As soon as the statement pCat->SomeFunction() is reached, the program crashes.

Getting NULL back from a memory assignment is not a programming error, although it is an exceptional situation. Your program must be able to recover from this condition, if only by throwing an exception. Remember: The entire assert() statement is gone when DEBUG is undefined. Exceptions are covered in detail on Day 20.

Side Effects

It is not uncommon to find that a bug appears only after the instances of assert() are removed. This is almost always due to the program unintentionally depending on side effects of things done in assert() and other debug-only code. For example, if you write

```
ASSERT (x = 5)
```

when you mean to test whether x == 5, you will create a particularly nasty bug.

Suppose that just prior to this assert(), you called a function that set x equal to 0. With this assert(), you think you are testing whether x is equal to 5; in fact, you are setting x equal to 5. The test returns TRUE because x = 5 not only sets x to 5, but returns the value 5, and because 5 is non-zero, it evaluates as TRUE.

When you pass the assert() statement, x really is equal to 5 (you just set it!). Your program runs just fine. You're ready to ship it, so you turn off debugging. Now the assert() disappears, and you are no longer setting x to 5. Because x was set to 0 just before this, it remains at 0 and your program breaks.

In frustration, you turn debugging back on, but hey! Presto! The bug is gone. Again, this is rather funny to watch, but not to live through, so be very careful about side effects in debugging code. If you see a bug that only appears when debugging is turned off, take a look at your debugging code with an eye out for nasty side effects.

Class Invariants

Most classes have some conditions that should always be true whenever you are finished with a class member function. These class invariants are the sine qua non of your class. For example, it may be true that your CIRCLE object should never have a radius of zero or that your ANIMAL should always have an age greater than zero and less than 100.

It can be very helpful to declare an Invariants() method that returns TRUE only if each of these conditions is still true. You can then ASSERT(Invariants()) at the start and at the completion of every class method. The exception would be that your Invariants() would not expect to return TRUE before your constructor runs or after your destructor ends. Listing 21.5 demonstrates the use of the Invariants() method in a trivial class.

LISTING 21.5 Using Invariants()

```
0:   #define DEBUG
1:   #define SHOW_INVARIANTS
2:   #include <iostream>
3:   #include <string.h>
4:   using namespace std;
5:
6:   #ifndef DEBUG
7:       #define ASSERT(x)
8:   #else
9:       #define ASSERT(x) \
10:            if (! (x)) \
11:           { \
12:                cout << "ERROR!! Assert " << #x << " failed\n"; \
13:                cout << " on line " << __LINE__  << "\n"; \
14:                cout << " in file " << __FILE__ << "\n";  \
15:           }
16:   #endif
17:
18:
19:   const int FALSE = 0;
20:   const int TRUE = 1;
21:   typedef int BOOL;
22:
23:
24:   class String
25:   {
26:   public:
```

21

LISTING 21.5   continued

```
27:        // constructors
28:        String();
29:        String(const char *const);
30:        String(const String &);
31:        ~String();
32:
33:        char & operator[](int offset);
34:        char operator[](int offset) const;
35:
36:        String & operator= (const String &);
37:        int GetLen()const { return itsLen; }
38:        const char * GetString() const { return itsString; }
39:        BOOL Invariants() const;
40:
41:   private:
42:        String (int);          // private constructor
43:        char * itsString;
44:        // unsigned short itsLen;
45:        int itsLen;
46:   };
47:
48:   // default constructor creates string of 0 bytes
49:   String::String()
50:   {
51:        itsString = new char[1];
52:        itsString[0] = '\0';
53:        itsLen=0;
54:        ASSERT(Invariants());
55:   }
56:
57:   // private (helper) constructor, used only by
58:   // class methods for creating a new string of
59:   // required size.  Null filled.
60:   String::String(int len)
61:   {
62:        itsString = new char[len+1];
63:        for (int i = 0; i<=len; i++)
64:            itsString[i] = '\0';
65:        itsLen=len;
66:        ASSERT(Invariants());
67:   }
68:
69:   // Converts a character array to a String
70:   String::String(const char * const cString)
71:   {
72:        itsLen = strlen(cString);
73:        itsString = new char[itsLen+1];
74:        for (int i = 0; i<itsLen; i++)
75:            itsString[i] = cString[i];
```

LISTING 21.5 continued

```
76:      itsString[itsLen]='\0';
77:      ASSERT(Invariants());
78:   }
79:
80:   // copy constructor
81:   String::String (const String & rhs)
82:   {
83:      itsLen=rhs.GetLen();
84:      itsString = new char[itsLen+1];
85:      for (int i = 0; i<itsLen;i++)
86:         itsString[i] = rhs[i];
87:      itsString[itsLen] = '\0';
88:      ASSERT(Invariants());
89:   }
90:
91:   // destructor, frees allocated memory
92:   String::~String ()
93:   {
94:      ASSERT(Invariants());
95:      delete [] itsString;
96:      itsLen = 0;
97:   }
98:
99:   // operator equals, frees existing memory
100:  // then copies string and size
101:  String& String::operator=(const String & rhs)
102:  {
103:     ASSERT(Invariants());
104:     if (this == &rhs)
105:        return *this;
106:     delete [] itsString;
107:     itsLen=rhs.GetLen();
108:     itsString = new char[itsLen+1];
109:     for (int i = 0; i<itsLen;i++)
110:        itsString[i] = rhs[i];
111:     itsString[itsLen] = '\0';
112:     ASSERT(Invariants());
113:     return *this;
114:  }
115:
116:  //non constant offset operator
117:  char & String::operator[](int offset)
118:  {
119:     ASSERT(Invariants());
120:     if (offset > itsLen)
121:     {
122:        ASSERT(Invariants());
123:        return itsString[itsLen-1];
124:     }
```

21

LISTING 21.5   continued

```
125:    else
126:    {
127:        ASSERT(Invariants());
128:        return itsString[offset];
129:    }
130: }
131:
132: // constant offset operator
133: char String::operator[](int offset) const
134: {
135:    ASSERT(Invariants());
136:    char retVal;
137:    if (offset > itsLen)
138:        retVal = itsString[itsLen-1];
139:    else
140:        retVal = itsString[offset];
141:    ASSERT(Invariants());
142:    return retVal;
143: }
144:
145: BOOL String::Invariants() const
146: {
147:    #ifdef SHOW_INVARIANTS
148:        cout << "Invariants Tested";
149:    #endif
150:    return ( (itsLen && itsString) || (!itsLen && !itsString) );
151: }
152:
153: class Animal
154: {
155: public:
156:    Animal():itsAge(1),itsName("John Q. Animal")
157:        {ASSERT(Invariants());}
158:    Animal(int, const String&);
159:    ~Animal(){}
160:    int GetAge() {  ASSERT(Invariants()); return itsAge;}
161:    void SetAge(int Age)
162:    {
163:        ASSERT(Invariants());
164:        itsAge = Age;
165:        ASSERT(Invariants());
166:    }
167:    String& GetName()
168:    {
169:        ASSERT(Invariants());
170:        return itsName;
171:    }
172:    void SetName(const String& name)
173:    {
```

LISTING 21.5   continued

```
174:            ASSERT(Invariants());
175:            itsName = name;
176:            ASSERT(Invariants());
177:        }
178:        BOOL Invariants();
179:    private:
180:        int itsAge;
181:        String itsName;
182:    };
183:
184:    Animal::Animal(int age, const String& name):
185:        itsAge(age),
186:        itsName(name)
187:    {
188:        ASSERT(Invariants());
189:    }
190:
191:    BOOL Animal::Invariants()
192:    {
193:        #ifdef SHOW_INVARIANTS
194:            cout << "Invariants Tested";
195:        #endif
196:            return (itsAge > 0 && itsName.GetLen());
197:    }
198:
199:    int main()
200:    {
201:        Animal sparky(5,"Sparky");
202:        cout << "\n" << sparky.GetName().GetString() << " is ";
203:        cout << sparky.GetAge() << " years old.";
204:        sparky.SetAge(8);
205:        cout << "\n" << sparky.GetName().GetString() << " is ";
206:        cout << sparky.GetAge() << " years old.";
207:        return 0;
208:    }
```

OUTPUT

```
String OK  String OK  String OK  String OK  String OK String OK String
OK
String OK  String OK  Animal OK  String OK  Animal OK
Sparky is  Animal OK 5 years old. Animal OK  Animal OK
Animal OK  Sparky is  Animal OK 8 years old. String OK
```

ANALYSIS On lines 9–15, the assert() macro is defined. If DEBUG is defined, this will write out an error message when the assert() macro evaluates FALSE.

On line 39, the String class member function Invariants() is declared; it is defined on lines 143–150. The constructor is declared on lines 49–55; on line 54, after the object is fully constructed, Invariants() is called to confirm proper construction.

21

This pattern is repeated for the other constructors, and the destructor calls `Invariants()` only before it sets out to destroy the object. The remaining class functions call `Invariants()` before taking any action and then again before returning. This both affirms and validates a fundamental principle of C++: Member functions other than constructors and destructors should work on valid objects and should leave them in a valid state.

On line 176, class `Animal` declares its own `Invariants()` method, implemented on lines 189–195. Note on lines 155, 158, 161, and 163 that inline functions can call the `Invariants()` method.

Printing Interim Values

In addition to asserting that something is true using the `assert()` macro, you may want to print the current value of pointers, variables, and strings. This can be very helpful in checking your assumptions about the progress of your program and in locating off-by-one bugs in loops. Listing 21.6 illustrates this idea.

LISTING 21.6   Printing Values in DEBUG Mode

```
0:   // Listing 21.6 - Printing values in DEBUG mode
1:   #include <iostream>
2:   using namespace std;
3:   #define DEBUG
4:
5:   #ifndef DEBUG
6:      #define PRINT(x)
7:   #else
8:      #define PRINT(x) \
9:            cout << #x << ":\t" << x << endl;
10:  #endif
11:
12:  enum BOOL { FALSE, TRUE } ;
13:
14:  int main()
15:  {
16:     int x = 5;
17:     long y = 738981;
18:     PRINT(x);
19:     for (int i = 0; i < x; i++)
20:     {
21:        PRINT(i);
22:     }
23:
24:     PRINT (y);
25:     PRINT("Hi.");
26:     int *px = &x;
```

LISTING 21.6 continued

```
27:    PRINT(px);
28:    PRINT (*px);
29:    return 0;
30: }
```

OUTPUT
```
x:      5
i:      0
i:      1
i:      2
i:      3
i:      4
y:      73898
"Hi.":  Hi.
px:         0x2100
*px:    5
```

ANALYSIS The macro on lines 5–10 provides printing of the current value of the supplied parameter. Note that the first thing fed to cout is the stringized version of the parameter; that is, if you pass in x, cout receives "x".

Next, cout receives the quoted string ":\t", which prints a colon and then a tab. Third, cout receives the value of the parameter (x), and then finally, endl, which writes a new line and flushes the buffer.

Note that you may receive a value other than 0x2100.

Debugging Levels

In large, complex projects, you may want more control than simply turning DEBUG on and off. You can define debug levels and test for these levels when deciding which macros to use and which to strip out.

To define a level, simply follow the #define DEBUG statement with a number. Although you can have any number of levels, a common system is to have four levels: HIGH, MEDIUM, LOW, and NONE. Listing 21.7 illustrates how this might be done, using the String and Animal classes from Listing 21.5.

LISTING 21.7 Levels of Debugging

```
0:  enum LEVEL { NONE, LOW, MEDIUM, HIGH };
1:  const int FALSE = 0;
2:  const int TRUE = 1;
3:  typedef int BOOL;
4:
5:  #define DEBUGLEVEL HIGH
```

21

LISTING 21.7   continued

```
6:
7:   #include <iostream.h>
8:   #include <string.h>
9:
10:  #if DEBUGLEVEL < LOW   // must be medium or high
11:      #define ASSERT(x)
12:  #else
13:      #define ASSERT(x) \
14:          if (! (x)) \
15:          { \
16:          cout << "ERROR!! Assert " << #x << " failed\n"; \
17:          cout << " on line " << __LINE__  << "\n"; \
18:          cout << " in file " << __FILE__ << "\n";  \
19:          }
20:  #endif
21:
22:  #if DEBUGLEVEL < MEDIUM
23:      #define EVAL(x)
24:  #else
25:      #define EVAL(x) \
26:          cout << #x << ":\t" << x << endl;
27:  #endif
28:
29:  #if DEBUGLEVEL < HIGH
30:      #define PRINT(x)
31:  #else
32:      #define PRINT(x) \
33:          cout << x << endl;
34:  #endif
35:
36:
37:  class String
38:  {
39:  public:
40:      // constructors
41:      String();
42:      String(const char *const);
43:      String(const String &);
44:      ~String();
45:
46:      char & operator[](int offset);
47:      char operator[](int offset) const;
48:
49:      String & operator= (const String &);
50:      int GetLen()const { return itsLen; }
51:      const char * GetString() const
52:          { return itsString; }
53:      BOOL Invariants() const;
54:
```

LISTING 21.7 continued

```
55:   private:
56:      String (int);          // private constructor
57:      char * itsString;
58:      unsigned short itsLen;
59:   };
60:
61:   // default constructor creates string of 0 bytes
62:   String::String()
63:   {
64:      itsString = new char[1];
65:      itsString[0] = '\0';
66:      itsLen=0;
67:      ASSERT(Invariants());
68:   }
69:
70:   // private (helper) constructor, used only by
71:   // class methods for creating a new string of
72:   // required size.  Null filled.
73:   String::String(int len)
74:   {
75:      itsString = new char[len+1];
76:      for (int i = 0; i<=len; i++)
77:         itsString[i] = '\0';
78:      itsLen=len;
79:      ASSERT(Invariants());
80:   }
81:
82:   // Converts a character array to a String
83:   String::String(const char * const cString)
84:   {
85:      itsLen = strlen(cString);
86:      itsString = new char[itsLen+1];
87:      for (int i = 0; i<itsLen; i++)
88:         itsString[i] = cString[i];
89:      itsString[itsLen]='\0';
90:      ASSERT(Invariants());
91:   }
92:
93:   // copy constructor
94:   String::String (const String & rhs)
95:   {
96:      itsLen=rhs.GetLen();
97:      itsString = new char[itsLen+1];
98:      for (int i = 0; i<itsLen;i++)
99:         itsString[i] = rhs[i];
100:     itsString[itsLen] = '\0';
101:     ASSERT(Invariants());
102:  }
103:
```

21

LISTING **21.7** continued

```
104:   // destructor, frees allocated memory
105:   String::~String ()
106:   {
107:       ASSERT(Invariants());
108:       delete [] itsString;
109:       itsLen = 0;
110:   }
111:
112:   // operator equals, frees existing memory
113:   // then copies string and size
114:   String& String::operator=(const String & rhs)
115:   {
116:       ASSERT(Invariants());
117:       if (this == &rhs)
118:           return *this;
119:       delete [] itsString;
120:       itsLen=rhs.GetLen();
121:       itsString = new char[itsLen+1];
122:       for (int i = 0; i<itsLen;i++)
123:           itsString[i] = rhs[i];
124:       itsString[itsLen] = '\0';
125:       ASSERT(Invariants());
126:       return *this;
127:   }
128:
129:   //non constant offset operator
130:   char & String::operator[](int offset)
131:   {
132:       ASSERT(Invariants());
133:       if (offset > itsLen)
134:       {
135:           ASSERT(Invariants());
136:           return itsString[itsLen-1];
137:       }
138:       else
139:       {
140:           ASSERT(Invariants());
141:           return itsString[offset];
142:       }
143:   }
144:
145:   // constant offset operator
146:   char String::operator[](int offset) const
147:   {
148:       ASSERT(Invariants());
149:       char retVal;
150:       if (offset > itsLen)
151:           retVal = itsString[itsLen-1];
152:       else
```

LISTING 21.7 continued

```
153:        retVal = itsString[offset];
154:     ASSERT(Invariants());
155:     return retVal;
156:  }
157:
158:  BOOL String::Invariants() const
159:  {
160:     PRINT("(String Invariants Checked)");
161:     return ((BOOL)(itsLen&&itsString)||(!itsLen&&!itsString));
162:  }
163:
164:  class Animal
165:  {
166:  public:
167:     Animal():itsAge(1),itsName("John Q. Animal")
168:        {ASSERT(Invariants());}
169:
170:     Animal(int, const String&);
171:     ~Animal(){}
172:
173:     int GetAge()
174:     {
175:        ASSERT(Invariants());
176:        return itsAge;
177:     }
178:
179:     void SetAge(int Age)
180:     {
181:        ASSERT(Invariants());
182:        itsAge = Age;
183:        ASSERT(Invariants());
184:     }
185:     String& GetName()
186:     {
187:        ASSERT(Invariants());
188:        return itsName;
189:     }
190:
191:     void SetName(const String& name)
192:     {
193:        ASSERT(Invariants());
194:        itsName = name;
195:        ASSERT(Invariants());
196:     }
197:
198:     BOOL Invariants();
199:  private:
200:     int itsAge;
201:     String itsName;
```

21

LISTING 21.7   continued

```
202:  };
203:
204:  Animal::Animal(int age, const String& name):
205:      itsAge(age),
206:      itsName(name)
207:  {
208:      ASSERT(Invariants());
209:  }
210:
211:  BOOL Animal::Invariants()
212:  {
213:      PRINT("(Animal Invariants Checked)");
214:      return (itsAge > 0 && itsName.GetLen());
215:  }
216:
217:  int main()
218:  {
219:      const int AGE = 5;
220:      EVAL(AGE);
221:      Animal sparky(AGE,"Sparky");
222:      cout << "\n" << sparky.GetName().GetString();
223:      cout << " is ";
224:      cout << sparky.GetAge() << " years old.";
225:      sparky.SetAge(8);
226:      cout << "\n" << sparky.GetName().GetString();
227:      cout << " is ";
228:      cout << sparky.GetAge() << " years old.";
229:      return 0;
230:  }
```

OUTPUT

```
AGE:      5
 (String Invariants Checked)
 (String Invariants Checked)
 (String Invariants Checked)
 (String Invariants Checked)
 (String Invariants Checked)
 (String Invariants Checked)
 (String Invariants Checked)
 (String Invariants Checked)
 (String Invariants Checked)
 (String Invariants Checked)

Sparky is (Animal Invariants Checked)
5 Years old. (Animal Invariants Checked)
 (Animal Invariants Checked)
 (Animal Invariants Checked)

Sparky is (Animal Invariants Checked)
```

```
8 years old. (String Invariants Checked)
 (String Invariants Checked)

// run again with DEBUG = MEDIUM

AGE:     5
Sparky is 5 years old.
Sparky is 8 years old.
```

ANALYSIS On lines 11–21, the assert() macro is defined to be stripped if DEBUGLEVEL is less than LOW (that is, DEBUGLEVEL is NONE). If any debugging is enabled, the assert() macro will work. On line 22, EVAL is declared to be stripped if DEBUG is less than MEDIUM; if DEBUGLEVEL is NONE or LOW, EVAL is stripped.

Finally, on lines 30–35, the PRINT macro is declared to be stripped if DEBUGLEVEL is less than HIGH. PRINT is used only when DEBUGLEVEL is HIGH; you can eliminate this macro by setting DEBUGLEVEL to MEDIUM and still maintain your use of EVAL and assert().

PRINT is used within the Invariants() methods to print an informative message. EVAL is used on line 220 to evaluate the current value of the constant integer AGE.

Do	**Don't**
DO use CAPITALS for your macro names. This is a pervasive convention, and other programmers will be confused if you don't. **DO** surround all arguments with parentheses in macro functions.	**DON'T** allow your macros to have side effects. Don't increment variables or assign values from within a macro.

Bit Twiddling

Often you will want to set flags in your objects to keep track of the state of your object. (Is it in AlarmState? Has this been initialized yet? Are you coming or going?)

You can do this with user-defined Booleans, but when you have many flags, and when storage size is an issue, it is convenient to be able to use the individual bits as flags.

Each byte has eight bits, so in a 4-byte long you can hold 32 separate flags. A bit is said to be "set" if its value is 1 and clear if its value is 0. When you set a bit, you make its value 1, and when you clear it, you make its value 0. (Set and clear are both adjectives and verbs.) You can set and clear bits by changing the value of the long, but that can be tedious and confusing.

21

Note | Appendix A, "Binary and Hexadecimal," provides valuable additional information about binary and hexadecimal manipulation.

C++ provides bitwise operators that act upon the individual bits. These look like, but are different from, the logical operators, so many novice programmers confuse them. The bitwise operators are presented in Table 21.1.

TABLE 21.1   The Bitwise Operators

Symbol	Operator
&	AND
|	OR
^	exclusive OR
~	complement

Operator AND

The AND operator (&) is a single ampersand, in contrast to the logical AND, which is two ampersands. When you AND two bits, the result is 1 if both bits are 1, but 0 if either or both bits are 0. The way to think of this is the following: The result is 1 if bit 1 is set and if bit 2 is set.

Operator OR

The second bitwise operator is OR (|). Again, this is a single vertical bar, in contrast to the logical OR, which is two vertical bars. When you OR two bits, the result is 1 if either bit is set or if both are.

Operator Exclusive OR

The third bitwise operator is exclusive OR (^). When you exclusive OR two bits, the result is 1 if the two bits are different.

The Complement Operator

The complement operator (~) clears every bit in a number that is set and sets every bit that is clear. If the current value of the number is 1010 0011, the complement of that number is 0101 1100.

Setting Bits

When you want to set or clear a particular bit, you use masking operations. If you have a 4-byte flag and you want to sct bit 8 TRUE, you need to OR the flag with the value 128. Why? 128 is 1000 0000 in binary; thus the value of the eighth bit is 128. Whatever the current value of that bit (set or clear), if you OR it with the value 128, you will set that bit and not change any of the other bits. Assume that the current value of the 8 bits is 1010 0110 0010 0110. ORing 128 to it looks like this:

```
9 8765 4321
1010 0110 0010 0110   // bit 8 is clear
|    0000 0000 1000 0000   // 128

_ _ _ _ _ _ _ _ _ _ _
1010 0110 1010 0110   // bit 8 is set
```

There are a few things to note. First, as usual, bits are counted from right to left. Second, the value 128 is all zeros except for bit 8, the bit you want to set. Third, the starting number 1010 0110 0010 0110 is left unchanged by the OR operation, except that bit 8 was set. Had bit 8 already been set, it would have remained set, which is what you want.

Clearing Bits

If you want to clear bit 8, you can AND the bit with the complement of 128. The complement of 128 is the number you get when you take the bit pattern of 128 (1000 0000), set every bit that is clear, and clear every bit that is set (0111 1111). When you AND these numbers, the original number is unchanged, except for the eighth bit, which is forced to zero.

```
1010 0110 1010 0110  // bit 8 is set
& 1111 1111 0111 1111  // ~128

_ _ _ _ _ _ _ _ _ _ _
1010 0110 0010 0110  // bit 8 cleared
```

To fully understand this solution, do the math yourself. Each time both bits are 1, write 1 in the answer. If either bit is 0, write 0 in the answer. Compare the answer with the original number. It should be the same except that bit 8 was cleared.

Flipping Bits

Finally, if you want to flip bit 8, no matter what its state, you exclusive OR the number with 128. Thus:

```
1010 0110 1010 0110  // number
^ 0000 0000 1000 0000  // 128

_ _ _ _ _ _ _ _ _ _ _
1010 0110 0010 0110  // bit flipped
^ 0000 0000 1000 0000  // 128

_ _ _ _ _ _ _ _ _ _ _
1010 0110 1010 0110  // flipped back
```

21

Do
DO set bits by using masks and the OR operator.
DO clear bits by using masks and the AND operator.
DO flip bits using masks and the exclusive OR operator.

Bit Fields

Under some circumstances, every byte counts, and saving six or eight bytes in a class can make all the difference. If your class or structure has a series of Boolean variables or variables that can have only a very small number of possible values, you may save some room using bit fields.

Using the standard C++ data types, the smallest type you can use in your class is a type `char`, which is one byte. You will usually end up using an `int`, which is two, or more often four, bytes. By using bit fields, you can store eight binary values in a `char` and 32 such values in a `long`.

Here's how bit fields work: Bit fields are named and accessed the same as any class member. Their type is always declared to be `unsigned int`. After the bit field name, write a colon followed by a number. The number is an instruction to the compiler as to how many bits to assign to this variable. If you write 1, the bit will represent either the value 0 or 1. If you write 2, the bit can represent 0, 1, 2, or 3, a total of four values. A three-bit field can represent eight values, and so forth. Appendix A reviews binary numbers. Listing 21.8 illustrates the use of bit fields.

LISTING 21.8   Using Bit Fields

```
0:   #include <iostream>
1:   using namespace std;
2:   #include <string.h>
3:
4:   enum STATUS { FullTime, PartTime } ;
5:   enum GRADLEVEL { UnderGrad, Grad } ;
6:   enum HOUSING { Dorm, OffCampus };
7:   enum FOODPLAN { OneMeal, AllMeals, WeekEnds, NoMeals };
8:
9:   class student
10:  {
11:  public:
12:     student():
13:        myStatus(FullTime),
14:        myGradLevel(UnderGrad),
15:        myHousing(Dorm),
```

LISTING 21.8   continued

```
16:         myFoodPlan(NoMeals)
17:      {}
18:      ~student(){}
19:      STATUS GetStatus();
20:      void SetStatus(STATUS);
21:      unsigned GetPlan() { return myFoodPlan; }
22:
23:  private:
24:      unsigned myStatus : 1;
25:      unsigned myGradLevel: 1;
26:      unsigned myHousing : 1;
27:      unsigned myFoodPlan : 2;
28:  };
29:
30:  STATUS student::GetStatus()
31:  {
32:      if (myStatus)
33:          return FullTime;
34:      else
35:          return PartTime;
36:  }
37:
38:  void student::SetStatus(STATUS theStatus)
39:  {
40:      myStatus = theStatus;
41:  }
42:
43:  int main()
44:  {
45:      student Jim;
46:
47:      if (Jim.GetStatus()== PartTime)
48:          cout << "Jim is part time" << endl;
49:      else
50:          cout << "Jim is full time" << endl;
51:
52:      Jim.SetStatus(PartTime);
53:
54:      if (Jim.GetStatus())
55:          cout << "Jim is part time" << endl;
56:      else
57:          cout << "Jim is full time" << endl;
58:
59:      cout << "Jim is on the " ;
60:
61:      char Plan[80];
62:      switch (Jim.GetPlan())
63:          {
64:      case OneMeal: strcpy(Plan,"One meal"); break;
```

LISTING 21.8   continued

```
65:     case AllMeals: strcpy(Plan,"All meals"); break;
66:     case WeekEnds: strcpy(Plan,"Weekend meals"); break;
67:     case NoMeals: strcpy(Plan,"No Meals");break;
68:     default : cout << "Something bad went wrong!\n"; break;
69:     }
70:     cout << Plan << " food plan." << endl;
71:     return 0;
72: }
```

OUTPUT

```
Jim is part time
Jim is full time
Jim is on the No Meals food plan.
```

ANALYSIS   On lines 4–7, several enumerated types are defined. These serve to define the possible values for the bit fields within the student class.

student is declared in lines 9–28. Although this is a trivial class, it is interesting because all the data is packed into five bits. The first bit represents the student's status, full-time or part-time. The second bit represents whether this is an undergraduate. The third bit represents whether the student lives in a dorm. The final two bits represent the four possible food plans.

The class methods are written as for any other class and are in no way affected by the fact that these are bit fields and not integers or enumerated types.

The member function GetStatus() reads the Boolean bit and returns an enumerated type, but this is not necessary. It could just as easily have been written to return the value of the bit field directly. The compiler would have done the translation.

To prove that to yourself, replace the GetStatus() implementation with this code:

```
STATUS student::GetStatus()
{
return myStatus;
}
```

No change whatsoever should occur in the functioning of the program. It is a matter of clarity when reading the code; the compiler isn't particular.

Note that the code on line 47 must check the status and then print the meaningful message. It is tempting to write this:

```
cout << "Jim is " << Jim.GetStatus() << endl;
```

That will simply print this:

```
Jim is 0
```

The compiler has no way to translate the enumerated constant `PartTime` into meaningful text.

On line 62, the program switches on the food plan, and for each possible value, it puts a reasonable message into the buffer, which is then printed on line 70. Note again that the `switch` statement could have been written as follows:

```
case  0: strcpy(Plan,"One meal"); break;
case  1: strcpy(Plan,"All meals"); break;
case  2: strcpy(Plan,"Weekend meals"); break;
case  3: strcpy(Plan,"No Meals");break;
```

The most important thing about using bit fields is that the client of the class need not worry about the data storage implementation. Because the bit fields are private, you can feel free to change them later and the interface will not need to change.

Style

As stated elsewhere in this book, it is important to adopt a consistent coding style, although in many ways it doesn't matter which style you adopt. A consistent style makes it easier to guess what you meant by a particular part of the code, and you avoid having to look up whether you spelled the function with an initial cap the last time you invoked it.

The following guidelines are arbitrary; they are based on the guidelines used in projects I've worked on in the past, and they've worked well. You can just as easily make up your own, but these will get you started.

As Emerson said, "Foolish consistency is the hobgoblin of small minds," but having some consistency in your code is a good thing. Make up your own, but then treat it as if it were dispensed by the programming gods.

Indenting

Tab size should be four spaces. Make sure your editor converts each tab to four spaces.

Braces

How to align braces can be the most controversial topic between C and C++ programmers. Here are the tips I suggest:

- Matching braces should be aligned vertically.
- The outermost set of braces in a definition or declaration should be at the left margin. Statements within should be indented. All other sets of braces should be in line with their leading statements.

21

- No code should appear on the same line as a brace. For example:

```
if (condition==true)
{
    j = k;
    SomeFunction();
}
m++;
```

Long Lines

Keep lines to the width displayable on a single screen. Code that is off to the right is easily overlooked, and scrolling horizontally is annoying. When a line is broken, indent the following lines. Try to break the line at a reasonable place, and try to leave the intervening operator at the end of the previous line (instead of at the beginning of the following line) so that it is clear that the line does not stand alone and that more is coming.

In C++, functions tend to be much shorter than they were in C, but the old, sound advice still applies. Try to keep your functions short enough to print the entire function on one page.

`switch` Statements

Indent switches as follows to conserve horizontal space:

```
switch(variable)
{
    case ValueOne:
        ActionOne();
        break;
    case ValueTwo:
        ActionTwo();
        break;
    default:
        assert("bad Action");
        break;
}
```

Program Text

You can use several tips to create code that is easy to read. Code that is easy to read is easy to maintain.

- Use whitespace to help readability.
- Objects and arrays are really referring to one thing. Don't use spaces within object references (., ->, []).

- Unary operators are associated with their operands, so don't put a space between them. Do put a space on the side away from the operand. Unary operators include !, ~, ++, --, -, * (for pointers), & (casts), `sizeof`.

- Binary operators should have spaces on both sides: +, =, *, /, %, >>, <<, <, >, ==, !=, &, |, &&, ||, ?:, =, +=, and so on.

- Don't use lack of spaces to indicate precedence (4+ 3*2).

- Put a space after commas and semicolons, not before.

- Parentheses should not have spaces on either side.

- Keywords, such as `if`, should be set off by a space: `if (a == b)`.

- The body of a comment should be set off from the // with a space.

- Place the pointer or reference indicator next to the type name, not the variable name:

```
char* foo;
int& theInt;
```

rather than

```
char *foo;
int &theInt;
```

- Do not declare more than one variable on the same line.

Identifier Names

The following are guidelines for working with identifiers:

- Identifier names should be long enough to be descriptive.

- Avoid cryptic abbreviations.

- Take the time and energy to spell things out.

- Do not use Hungarian notation. C++ is strongly typed and there is no reason to put the type into the variable name. With user-defined types (classes), Hungarian notation quickly breaks down. The exceptions to this may be to use a prefix for pointers (p) and references (r), as well as for class member variables (its).

- Short names (i, p, x, and so on) should be used only where their brevity makes the code more readable and where the usage is so obvious that a descriptive name is not needed.

- The length of a variable's name should be proportional to its scope.

- Make sure identifiers look and sound different from one another to minimize confusion.

21

- Function (or method) names are usually verbs or verb-noun phrases: `Search()`, `Reset()`, `FindParagraph()`, `ShowCursor()`. Variable names are usually abstract nouns, possibly with an additional noun: `count`, `state`, `windSpeed`, `windowHeight`. Boolean variables should be named appropriately: `windowIconized`, `fileIsOpen`.(d)Spelling and Capitalization of Names

Spelling and capitalization should not be overlooked when creating your own style. Some tips for these areas include the following:

- Use all uppercase and underscore to separate the logical words of `#defined` names, such as `SOURCE_FILE_TEMPLATE`. Note, however, that these are rare in C++. Consider using constants and templates in most cases.

- All other identifiers should use mixed case—no underscores. Function names, methods, class, typedef, and struct names should begin with a capitalized letter. Elements such as data members or locals should begin with a lowercase letter.

- Enumerated constants should begin with a few lowercase letters as an abbreviation for the enum. For example:

```
enum TextStyle
{
    tsPlain,
    tsBold,
    tsItalic,
    tsUnderscore,
};
```

Comments

Comments can make it much easier to understand a program. Sometimes you will not work on a program for several days or even months. In that time you can forget what certain code does or why it has been included. Problems in understanding code can also occur when someone else reads your code. Comments that are applied in a consistent, well thought out style can be well worth the effort. Several tips to remember concerning comments include the following:

- Wherever possible, use C++ `//` comments rather than the `/* */` style. Reserve the C-style (`/* */`) for commenting out blocks of code that might include C++ comments.

- Higher-level comments are infinitely more important than process details. Add value; do not merely restate the code.

  `n++; // n is incremented by one`

This comment isn't worth the time it takes to type it in. Concentrate on the semantics of functions and blocks of code. Say what a function does. Indicate side effects, types of parameters, and return values. Describe all assumptions that are made (or not made), such as "assumes n is non-negative" or "will return –1 if x is invalid." Within complex logic, use comments to indicate the conditions that exist at that point in the code.

- Use complete English sentences with appropriate punctuation and capitalization. The extra typing is worth it. Don't be overly cryptic and don't abbreviate. What seems exceedingly clear to you as you write code will be amazingly obtuse in a few months.

- Use blank lines freely to help the reader understand what is going on. Separate statements into logical groups.

Access

The way you access portions of your program should also be consistent. Some tips for access include the following:

- Always use `public:`, `private:`, and `protected:` labels; don't rely on the defaults.

- List the public members first, then protected, then private. List the data members in a group after the methods.

- Put the constructor(s) first in the appropriate section, followed by the destructor. List overloaded methods with the same name adjacent to each other. Group accessor functions together whenever possible.

- Consider alphabetizing the method names within each group and alphabetizing the member variables. Be sure to alphabetize the filenames in include statements.

- Even though the use of the `virtual` keyword is optional when overriding, use it anyway; it helps to remind you that it is virtual, and it also keeps the declaration consistent.

Class Definitions

Try to keep the definitions of methods in the same order as the declarations. It makes things easier to find.

When defining a function, place the return type and all other modifiers on a previous line so that the class name and function name begin at the left margin. This makes it much easier to find functions.

21

include Files

Try as hard as you can to keep from including files into header files. The ideal minimum is the header file for the class this one derives from. Other mandatory includes will be those for objects that are members of the class being declared. Classes that are merely pointed to or referenced only need forward references of the form.

Don't leave out an include file in a header just because you assume that whatever .cpp file includes this one will also have the needed include.

Tip	All header files should use inclusion guards.

assert()

Use assert() freely. It helps find errors, but it also greatly helps a reader by making it clear what the assumptions are. It also helps to focus the writer's thoughts around what is valid and what isn't.

const

Use const wherever appropriate: for parameters, variables, and methods. Often there is a need for both a const and a non-const version of a method; don't use this as an excuse to leave one out. Be very careful when explicitly casting from const to non-const and vice versa (at times, this is the only way to do something), but be certain that it makes sense, and include a comment.

Next Steps

You've spent three long, hard weeks working at C++, and you are now a competent C++ programmer, but you are by no means finished. There is much more to learn and many more places you can get valuable information as you move from novice C++ programmer to expert.

The following sections recommend a number of specific sources of information, and these recommendations reflect only my personal experience and opinions. Dozens of books are available on each of these topics, however, so be sure to get other opinions before purchasing.

Where to Get Help and Advice

The very first thing you will want to do as a C++ programmer will be to tap into one of the C++ conferences on an online service. These groups supply immediate contact with hundreds or thousands of C++ programmers who can answer your questions, offer advice, and provide a sounding board for your ideas.

I participate in the C++ Internet newsgroups (comp.lang.c++ and comp.lang.c++.moderated), and I recommend them as excellent sources of information and support.

Also, you may want to look for local user groups. Many cities have C++ interest groups where you can meet other programmers and exchange ideas.

On to C#?

Microsoft's new .Net platform is radically changing the way many of us develop for the Internet. A key component of .Net is the new language: C#.

C# is a natural extension of C++, and is an easy bridge to .Net for C++ programmers. There are a number of good books on C#, and I hope you'll take a look at my newest: *Programming C#* (O'Reilly press).

Staying in Touch

If you have comments, suggestions, or ideas about this book or other books, I'd love to hear them. Please contact me through my Web site: `www.libertyassociates.com`. I look forward to hearing from you.

Do	Don't
DO look at other books. There's plenty to learn and no single book can teach you everything you need to know.	DON'T just read code! The best way to learn C++ is to write C++ programs.
DO join a good C++ user group.	

Summary

Today you learned more details about working with the preprocessor. Each time you run the compiler, the preprocessor runs first and translates your preprocessor directives such as #define and #ifdef.

The preprocessor does text substitution, although with the use of macros these can be somewhat complex. By using #ifdef, #else, and #ifndef, you can accomplish conditional compilation, compiling in some statements under one set of conditions and in

21

another set of statements under other conditions. This can assist in writing programs for more than one platform and is often used to conditionally include debugging information.

Macro functions provide complex text substitution based on arguments passed at compile time to the macro. It is important to put parentheses around every argument in the macro to ensure the correct substitution takes place.

Macro functions, and the preprocessor in general, are less important in C++ than they were in C. C++ provides a number of language features, such as const variables and templates, that offer superior alternatives to use of the preprocessor.

You also learned how to set and test individual bits and how to allocate a limited number of bits to class members.

Finally, C++ style issues were addressed, and resources were provided for further study.

Q&A

Q If C++ offers better alternatives than the preprocessor, why is this option still available?

A First, C++ is backward-compatible with C, and all significant parts of C must be supported in C++. Second, some uses of the preprocessor are still used frequently in C++, such as inclusion guards.

Q Why use macro functions when you can use a regular function?

A Macro functions are expanded inline and are used as a substitute for repeatedly typing the same commands with minor variations. Again, however, templates offer a better alternative.

Q How do you know when to use a macro versus an inline function?

A Use inline functions whenever possible. While macros offer character substitution, stringizing, and concatenation, they are not type-safe and make for code that is more difficult to maintain.

Q What is the alternative to using the preprocessor to print interim values during debugging?

A The best alternative is to use watch statements within a debugger. For information on watch statements, consult your compiler or debugger documentation.

Q How do you decide when to use an assert() and when to throw an exception?

A If the situation you're testing can be true without your having committed a programming error, use an exception. If the only reason for this situation to ever be true is a bug in your program, use an assert().

Q **When would you use bit structures rather than simply using integers?**

A When the size of the object is crucial. If you are working with limited memory or with communications software, you may find that the savings offered by these structures is essential to the success of your product.

Q **Why do style wars generate so much emotion?**

A Programmers become very attached to their habits. If you are used to the following indentation:

```
if (SomeCondition){
    // statements
}    // closing brace
```

it is a difficult transition to give it up. New styles look wrong and create confusion. If you get bored, try logging on to a popular online service and asking which indentation style works best, which editor is best for C++, or which product is the best word processor. Then sit back and watch as ten thousand messages are generated, all contradicting one another.

Q **What is the very next thing to read?**

A Here are some books I've written to provide a course of study, although there are many others of great value. *C++ Unleashed* (Sams Publishing, 1998) offers white papers on advanced topics in C++. *Beginning Object-Oriented Analysis and Design* (Wrox Press, 1997) offers an in-depth primer in object-oriented software development. *Career Change C++* (Sams Publishing, 1999) offers insight into the business of professional software development.

Q **Is that it?**

A Yes! You've learned C++, but...no. Ten years ago it was possible for one person to learn all there was to know about microcomputers, or at least to feel pretty confident that he was close. Today it is out of the question. You can't possibly catch up, and even as you try, the industry is changing. Be sure to keep reading, and stay in touch with the resources—magazines and online services—that will keep you current with the latest changes.

Workshop

The Workshop provides quiz questions to help you solidify your understanding of the material covered and exercises to provide you with experience in using what you've learned. Try to answer the quiz and exercise questions before checking the answers in Appendix D, and make sure you understand the answers before continuing to the next chapter.

21

Quiz

1. What is an inclusion guard?

2. How do you instruct your compiler to print the contents of the intermediate file showing the effects of the preprocessor?

3. What is the difference between #define debug 0 and #undef debug?

Exercises

1. Write the inclusion guard statements for the header file STRING.H.

2. Write an assert() macro that prints an error message and the file and line number if debug level is 2, that prints a message (without file and line number) if the level is 1, and that does nothing if the level is 0.

3. Write a macro DPrint that tests if DEBUG is defined and, if it is, prints the value passed in as a parameter.

WEEK 3

In Review

The following program brings together many of the advanced techniques you've learned during the past three weeks of hard work. Week 3 in Review provides a template-based linked list with exception handling. Examine it in detail; if you understand it fully, you are a C++ programmer.

Warning   If your compiler does not support templates, or if your compiler does not support try and catch, you will not be able to compile or run this listing.

LISTING R3.1   Week 3 in Review Listing

```
0:  // **************************************************
1:  //
2:  // Title:      Week 3 in Review
3:  //
4:  // File:       Week3
5:  //
6:  // Description:  Provide a template-based linked list
7:  //                 demonstration program with exception handling
8:  //
9:  // Classes:    PART - holds part numbers and potentially other
10: //                    information about parts. This will be the
11: //                    example class for the list to hold
12: //                    Note use of operator<< to print the
13: //                    information about a part based on its
14: //                    runtime type.
15: //
16: //                 Node - acts as a node in a List
17: //
18: //                 List - template-based list which provides the
19: //                    mechanisms for a linked list
20: //
21: //
22: // Author:     Jesse Liberty (jl)
23: //
24: // Developed:  Pentium 200 Pro. 128MB RAM MVC 5.0
25: //
26: // Target:     Platform independent
27: //
28: // Rev History:  9/94 - First release (jl)
29: //               4/97 - Updated (jl)
30: // **************************************************
31:
32: #include <iostream>
33: using namespace std;
34:
35: // exception classes
36: class Exception {};
37: class OutOfMemory :   public Exception{};
38: class NullNode :      public Exception{};
39: class EmptyList :     public Exception {};
40: class BoundsError :   public Exception {};
41:
42:
```

LISTING R3.1   continued

```
43:   // *************** Part ************
44:   // Abstract base class of parts
45:   class Part
46:   {
47:   public:
48:       Part():itsObjectNumber(1) {}
49:       Part(int ObjectNumber):itsObjectNumber(ObjectNumber){}
50:       virtual ~Part(){};
51:       int GetObjectNumber() const { return itsObjectNumber; }
52:       virtual void Display() const =0;   // must be overridden
53:
54:   private:
55:       int itsObjectNumber;
56:   };
57:
58:   // implementation of pure virtual function so that
59:   // derived classes can chain up
60:   void Part::Display() const
61:   {
62:       cout << "\nPart Number: " << itsObjectNumber << endl;
63:   }
64:
65:   // this one operator<< will be called for all part objects.
66:   // It need not be a friend as it does not access private data
67:   // It calls Display() which uses the required polymorphism
68:   // We'd like to be able to override this based on the real type
69:   // of thePart, but C++ does not support contravariance
70:   ostream& operator<<( ostream& theStream,Part& thePart)
71:   {
72:       thePart.Display();   // virtual contravariance!
73:       return theStream;
74:   }
75:
76:   // *************** Car Part ************
77:   class CarPart : public Part
78:   {
79:   public:
80:       CarPart():itsModelYear(94){}
81:       CarPart(int year, int partNumber);
82:       int GetModelYear() const { return itsModelYear; }
83:       virtual void Display() const;
84:   private:
85:       int itsModelYear;
86:   };
87:
88:   CarPart::CarPart(int year, int partNumber):
89:       itsModelYear(year),
90:       Part(partNumber)
91:   {}
```

LISTING R3.1   continued

```
92:
93:  void CarPart::Display() const
94:  {
95:    Part::Display();
96:    cout << "Model Year: " << itsModelYear << endl;
97:  }
98:
99:  // *************** AirPlane Part ************
100: class AirPlanePart : public Part
101: {
102: public:
103:    AirPlanePart():itsEngineNumber(1){};
104:    AirPlanePart(int EngineNumber, int PartNumber);
105:    virtual void Display() const;
106:    int GetEngineNumber()const { return itsEngineNumber; }
107: private:
108:    int itsEngineNumber;
109: };
110:
111: AirPlanePart::AirPlanePart(int EngineNumber, int PartNumber):
112:    itsEngineNumber(EngineNumber),
113:    Part(PartNumber)
114: {}
115:
116: void AirPlanePart::Display() const
117: {
118:    Part::Display();
119:    cout << "Engine No.: " << itsEngineNumber << endl;
120: }
121:
122: // forward declaration of class List
123: template <class T>
124: class List;
125:
126: // *************** Node ************
127: // Generic node, can be added to a list
128: // **********************************
129:
130: template <class T>
131: class Node
132: {
133: public:
134:    friend class List<T>;
135:    Node (T*);
136:    ~Node();
137:    void SetNext(Node * node) { itsNext = node; }
138:    Node * GetNext() const;
139:    T * GetObject() const;
140: private:
```

LISTING R3.1   continued

```
141:        T* itsObject;
142:        Node * itsNext;
143:    };
144:
145:    // Node Implementations...
146:
147:    template <class T>
148:    Node<T>::Node(T* pOjbect):
149:        itsObject(pOjbect),
150:        itsNext(0)
151:    {}
152:
153:    template <class T>
154:    Node<T>::~Node()
155:    {
156:        delete itsObject;
157:        itsObject = 0;
158:        delete itsNext;
159:        itsNext = 0;
160:    }
161:
162:    // Returns NULL if no next Node
163:    template <class T>
164:    Node<T> * Node<T>::GetNext() const
165:    {
166:        return itsNext;
167:    }
168:
169:    template <class T>
170:    T * Node<T>::GetObject() const
171:    {
172:        if (itsObject)
173:            return itsObject;
174:        else
175:            throw NullNode();
176:    }
177:
178:    // **************** List ***********
179:    // Generic list template
180:    // Works with any numbered object
181:    // ********************************
182:    template <class T>
183:    class List
184:    {
185:    public:
186:        List();
187:        ~List();
188:
189:        T*          Find(int & position, int ObjectNumber)  const;
```

LISTING R3.1   continued

```
190:     T*        GetFirst() const;
191:     void        Insert(T *);
192:     T*        operator[](int) const;
193:     int       GetCount() const { return itsCount; }
194:  private:
195:     Node<T> * pHead;
196:     int      itsCount;
197:  };
198:
199:  // Implementations for Lists...
200:  template <class T>
201:  List<T>::List():
202:     pHead(0),
203:     itsCount(0)
204:  {}
205:
206:  template <class T>
207:  List<T>::~List()
208:  {
209:     delete pHead;
210:  }
211:
212:  template <class T>
213:  T*   List<T>::GetFirst() const
214:  {
215:     if (pHead)
216:         return pHead->itsObject;
217:     else
218:         throw EmptyList();
219:  }
220:
221:  template <class T>
222:  T *  List<T>::operator[](int offSet) const
223:  {
224:     Node<T>* pNode = pHead;
225:
226:     if (!pHead)
227:         throw EmptyList();
228:
229:     if (offSet > itsCount)
230:         throw BoundsError();
231:
232:     for (int i=0;i<offSet; i++)
233:         pNode = pNode->itsNext;
234:
235:     return   pNode->itsObject;
236:  }
237:
238:  // find a given object in list based on its unique number (id)
```

LISTING R3.1 continued

```
239:    template <class T>
240:    T*   List<T>::Find(int & position, int ObjectNumber)   const
241:    {
242:        Node<T> * pNode = 0;
243:        for (pNode = pHead, position = 0;
244:                pNode!=NULL;
245:                pNode = pNode->itsNext, position++)
246:        {
247:            if (pNode->itsObject->GetObjectNumber() == ObjectNumber)
248:                break;
249:        }
250:        if (pNode == NULL)
251:            return NULL;
252:        else
253:            return pNode->itsObject;
254:    }
255:
256:    // insert if the number of the object is unique
257:    template <class T>
258:    void List<T>::Insert(T* pObject)
259:    {
260:        Node<T> * pNode = new Node<T>(pObject);
261:        Node<T> * pCurrent = pHead;
262:        Node<T> * pNext = 0;
263:
264:        int New =  pObject->GetObjectNumber();
265:        int Next = 0;
266:        itsCount++;
267:
268:        if (!pHead)
269:        {
270:            pHead = pNode;
271:            return;
272:        }
273:
274:        // if this one is smaller than head
275:        // this one is the new head
276:        if (pHead->itsObject->GetObjectNumber() > New)
277:        {
278:            pNode->itsNext = pHead;
279:            pHead = pNode;
280:            return;
281:        }
282:
283:        for (;;)
284:        {
285:            // if there is no next, append this new one
286:            if (!pCurrent->itsNext)
287:            {
```

LISTING R3.1   continued

```
288:            pCurrent->itsNext = pNode;
289:            return;
290:        }
291:
292:        // if this goes after this one and before the next
293:        // then insert it here, otherwise get the next
294:        pNext = pCurrent->itsNext;
295:        Next = pNext->itsObject->GetObjectNumber();
296:        if (Next > New)
297:        {
298:            pCurrent->itsNext = pNode;
299:            pNode->itsNext = pNext;
300:            return;
301:        }
302:        pCurrent = pNext;
303:    }
304: }
305:
306:
307: int main()
308: {
309:    List<Part> theList;
310:    int choice;
311:    int ObjectNumber;
312:    int value;
313:    Part * pPart;
314:    while (1)
315:    {
316:        cout << "(0)Quit (1)Car (2)Plane: ";
317:        cin >> choice;
318:
319:        if (!choice)
320:            break;
321:
322:        cout << "New PartNumber?: ";
323:        cin >>  ObjectNumber;
324:
325:        if (choice == 1)
326:        {
327:            cout << "Model Year?: ";
328:            cin >> value;
329:            try
330:            {
331:                pPart = new CarPart(value,ObjectNumber);
332:            }
333:            catch (OutOfMemory)
334:            {
335:                cout << "Not enough memory; Exiting..." << endl;
336:                return 1;
```

LISTING R3.1   continued

```
337:                 }
338:             }
339:         else
340:         {
341:             cout << "Engine Number?: ";
342:             cin >> value;
343:             try
344:             {
345:                 pPart = new AirPlanePart(value,ObjectNumber);
346:             }
347:             catch (OutOfMemory)
348:             {
349:                 cout << "Not enough memory; Exiting..." << endl;
350:                 return 1;
351:             }
352:         }
353:         try
354:         {
355:             theList.Insert(pPart);
356:         }
357:         catch (NullNode)
358:         {
359:             cout << "The list is broken, and the node is null!" <<
                    ➥endl;
360:             return 1;
361:         }
362:         catch (EmptyList)
363:         {
364:             cout << "The list is empty!" << endl;
365:             return 1;
366:         }
367:     }
368:     try
369:     {
370:         for (int i = 0; i < theList.GetCount(); i++ )
371:             cout << *(theList[i]);
372:     }
373:     catch (NullNode)
374:     {
375:         cout << "The list is broken, and the node is null!" <<
                ➥endl;
376:         return 1;
377:     }
378:     catch (EmptyList)
379:     {
380:         cout << "The list is empty!" << endl;
381:         return 1;
382:     }
383:     catch (BoundsError)
```

LISTING R3.1 continued

```
384:             {
385:               cout << "Tried to read beyond the end of the list!" <<
endl;
386:               return 1;
387:           }
388:       return 0;
389:   }

(0)Quit (1)Car (2)Plane: 1
New PartNumber?: 2837
Model Year? 90

 (0)Quit (1)Car (2)Plane: 2
New PartNumber?: 378
Engine Number?: 4938

 (0)Quit (1)Car (2)Plane: 1
New PartNumber?: 4499
Model Year? 94

 (0)Quit (1)Car (2)Plane: 1
New PartNumber?: 3000
Model Year? 93

 (0)Quit (1)Car (2)Plane: 0

Part Number: 378
Engine No. 4938

Part Number: 2837
Model Year: 90

Part Number: 3000
Model Year: 93

Part Number 4499
Model Year: 94
```

The Week 3 in Review listing modifies the program provided in Week 2 to add templates, ostream processing, and exception handling. The output is identical.

On lines 36–40, a number of exception classes are declared. In the somewhat primitive exception handling provided by this program, no data or methods are required of these exceptions; they serve as flags to the catch statements, which print out a very simple warning and then exit. A more robust program might pass these exceptions by reference and then extract context or other data from the exception objects in an attempt to recover from the problem.

On line 45, the abstract base class `Part` is declared exactly as it was in Week 2. The only interesting change here is in the non-class member `operator<<()`, which is declared on lines 70–74. Note that this is neither a member of `Part` nor a friend of `Part`, it simply takes a `Part` reference as one of its arguments.

You might want to have `operator<<` take a `CarPart` and an `AirPlanePart` in the hopes that the correct `operator<<` would be called, based on whether a car part or an airplane part is passed. Since the program passes a pointer to a part, however, and not a pointer to a car part or an airplane part, C++ would have to call the right function based on the real type of one of the arguments to the function. This is called contravariance and is not supported in C++.

There are only two ways to achieve polymorphism in C++: function polymorphism and virtual functions. Function polymorphism won't work here because in every case you are matching the same signature: the one taking a reference to a `Part`.

Virtual functions won't work here because `operator<<` is not a member function of `Part`. You can't make `operator<<` a member function of `Part` because you want to invoke

```
cout << thePart
```

and that means that the actual call would be to `cout.operator<<(Part&)`, and `cout` does not have a version of `operator<<` that takes a `Part` reference!

To get around this limitation, the Week 3 program uses just one `operator<<`, taking a reference to a `Part`. This then calls `Display()`, which is a virtual member function, and thus the right version is called.

On lines 130–143, `Node` is defined as a template. It serves the same function as `Node` did in the Week 2 Review program, but this version of `Node` is not tied to a `Part` object. It can, in fact, be the node for any type of object.

Note that if you try to get the object from `Node`, and there is no object, this is considered an exception, and the exception is thrown on line 175.

On lines 182 and 183, a generic `List` class template is defined. This `List` class can hold nodes of any objects that have unique identification numbers, and it keeps them sorted in ascending order. Each of the list functions checks for exceptional circumstances and throws the appropriate exceptions as required.

On lines 307 and 308, the driver program creates a list of two types of `Part` objects and then prints out the values of the objects in the list by using the standard streams mechanism.

If C++ did support contravariance, we could override the function based on the real type of the object at runtime. Listing R3.2 won't compile in C++, but if it supported contravariance, it would…

Warning: This listing will not compile!

LISTING R3.2

```
#include<iostream.h>
class Animal
{
public:
    virtual void Speak() { cout << "Animal
                    Speaks\n"; }
};

class Dog : public Animal
{
public:
    void Speak() { cout << "Dog Speaks\n"; }
};


class Cat : public Animal
{
public:
    void Speak() { cout << "Cat Speaks\n"; }
};

void DoIt(Cat*);
void DoIt(Dog*);
```

LISTING R3.2

```
int main()
{

    Animal * pA = new Dog;
    DoIt(pA);
    return 0;
}

void DoIt(Cat * c)
{
    cout << "They passed a cat!\n" << endl;
    c->Speak();
}

void DoIt(Dog * d)
{
    cout << "They passed a dog!\n" << endl;
    d->Speak();
}
```

What you can do, of course, is to use a virtual function, which partially solves the problem.

```
#include<iostream.h>

class Animal
{
public:
    virtual void Speak() { cout << "Animal Speaks\n"; }
};

class Dog : public Animal
{
public:
    void Speak() { cout << "Dog Speaks\n"; }
};


class Cat : public Animal
{
public:
    void Speak() { cout << "Cat Speaks\n"; }
};

void DoIt(Animal*);

int main()
{
```

LISTING R3.2

```
    Animal * pA = new Dog;
    DoIt(pA);
    return 0;
}

void DoIt(Animal * c)
{
    cout << "They passed some kind of
                    animal\n" << endl;
    c->Speak();
}
```

APPENDIX A

Binary and Hexadecimal

You learned the fundamentals of arithmetic so long ago, it is hard to imagine what it would be like without that knowledge. When you look at the number 145, you instantly see "one hundred forty-five" without much reflection.

Understanding binary and hexadecimal requires that you re-examine the number 145 and see it not as a number, but as a code for a number.

Start small: Examine the relationship between the number three and "3." The numeral "3" is a squiggle on a piece of paper; the number three is an idea. The numeral is used to represent the number.

The distinction can be made clear by realizing that three, 3, |||, III, and *** all can be used to represent the same idea of three.

In base 10 (decimal) math you use the numerals 0, 1, 2, 3, 4, 5, 6, 7, 8, 9 to represent all numbers. How is the number ten represented?

One can imagine that we would have evolved a strategy of using the letter A to represent ten; or we might have used IIIIIIIII to represent that idea. The Romans used X. The Arabic system, which we use, makes use of position in conjunction with numerals to represent values. The first (right-most) column is used for ones, and the next column (to the left) is used for tens. Thus, the number fifteen is represented as 15 (read "one, five"); that is, 1 ten and 5 ones.

Certain rules emerge, from which some generalizations can be made:

1. Base 10 uses the digits 0–9.
2. The columns are powers of ten: 1s, 10s, 100s, and so on.
3. If the third column is 100, the largest number you can make with two columns is 99. More generally, with n columns you can represent 0 to (10^n-1). Thus, with 3 columns you can represent 0 to (10^3-1) or 0-999.

Other Bases

It is not a coincidence that we use base 10; we have 10 fingers. One can imagine a different base, however. Using the rules found in base 10, you can describe base 8:

1. The digits used in base 8 are 0–7.
2. The columns are powers of 8: 1s, 8s, 64s, and so on.
3. With n columns you can represent 0 to 8^n-1.

To distinguish numbers written in each base, write the base as a subscript next to the number. The number fifteen in base 10 would be written as 15_{10} and read as "one, five, base ten."

Thus, to represent the number 15_{10} in base 8 you would write 17_8. This is read "one, seven, base eight." Note that it can also be read "fifteen" as that is the number it continues to represent.

Why 17? The 1 means 1 eight, and the 7 means 7 ones. One eight plus seven ones equals fifteen. Consider fifteen asterisks:

```
*****      *****
*****
```

The natural tendency is to make two groups, a group of ten asterisks and another of five. This would be represented in decimal as 15 (1 ten and 5 ones). You can also group the asterisks as

```
****            *******
****
```

That is, eight asterisks and seven. That would be represented in base 8 as 17_8. That is, one eight and seven ones.

Around the Bases

You can represent the number fifteen in base 10 as 15, in base 9 as 16_9, in base 8 as 17_8, in base 7 as 21_7. Why 21_7? In base 7 there is no numeral 8. In order to represent fifteen, you will need two sevens and one 1.

How do you generalize the process? To convert a base 10 number to base 7, think about the columns: in base 7 they are ones, sevens, forty-nines, three-hundred forty-threes, and so on. Why these columns? They represent 7^0, 7^1, 7^2, 7^4, and so forth.

Remember, any number to the zeroth power (for example, 7^0) is 1, any number to the first power (for example, 7^1) is the number itself, any number to the 2nd power is that number times itself ($7^2 = 7*7 = 49$) and any number to the 3rd power is that number times itself and then times itself again ($7^3 = 7*7*7 = 343$).

Create a table for yourself:

Column	4	3	2	1
Power	7^3	7^2	7^1	7^0
Value	343	49	7	1

The first row represents the column number. The second row represents the power of 7. The third row represents the decimal value of each number in that row.

To convert from a decimal value to base 7, here is the procedure: Examine the number and decide which column to use first. If the number is 200, for example, you know that column 4 (343) is 0, and you don't have to worry about it.

To find out how many 49s there are, divide 200 by 49. The answer is 4, so put 4 in column 3 and examine the remainder: 4. There are no 7s in 4, so put a zero in the 7s column. There are 4 ones in 4, so put a 4 in the 1s column. The answer is 404_7.

Column	4	3	2	1
Power	7^3	7^2	7^1	7^0
Value	343	49	7	1
200 in base 7	0	4	0	4
Decimal value	0	$4*49 = 196$	0	$4*1 = 4$

In this example, the 4 in the third column represents the decimal value 196, and the 4 in the first column represents the value 4. 196+4 = 200. Thus $404_7 = 200_{10}$.

Let's try another example.

To convert the number 968 to base 6:

Column	5	4	3	2	1
Power	6^4	6^3	6^2	6^1	6^0
Value	1296	216	36	6	1

Make sure you are comfortable with why these are the column values. Remember that 6^3 = 6*6*6 = 216.

To determine the base 6 representation of 968 we start at column 5. How many 1296s are there in 968? There are none, so column 5 has 0. Dividing 968 by 216 yields 4 with a remainder of 104. Column 4 is 4. That is, column 4 will represent 4*216 (864).

We must now represent the remaining value (968–864 = 104). Dividing 104 by 36 yields 2 with a remainder of 32. Column 3 is 2. Dividing 32 by 6 yields 5 with a remainder of 2. The answer therefore is 4252_6.

Column	5	4	3	2	1
Power	6^4	6^3	6^2	6^1	6^0
Value	1296	216	36	6	1
968 in base 6	0	4	2	5	2
Decimal value	0	4*216=864	2*36=72	5*6=30	2*1=2

864+72+30+2 = 968.

Binary

Base 2 is the ultimate extension of this idea. There are only two digits: 0 and 1. The columns are

Column	8	7	6	5	4	3	2	1
Power	2^7	2^6	2^5	2^4	2^3	2^2	2^1	2^0
Value	128	64	32	16	8	4	2	1

To convert the number 88 to base 2, you follow the same procedure: There are no 128s, so column 8 is 0.

There is one 64 in 88, so column 7 is 1 and 24 is the remainder. There are no 32s in 24 so column 6 is 0.

There is one 16 in 24 so column 5 is 1. The remainder is 8. There is one 8 in 8, and so column 4 is 1. There is no remainder, so the rest of the columns are 0.

Column	8	7	6	5	4	3	2	1
Power	2^7	2^6	2^5	2^4	2^3	2^2	2^1	2^0
Value	128	64	32	16	8	4	2	1
88_2	0	1	0	1	1	0	0	0
Value	0	64	0	16	8	0	0	0

To test this answer, convert it back:

```
1 * 64 =  64
0 * 32 =   0
1 * 16 =  16
1 *  8 =   8
0 *  4 =   0
0 *  2 =   0
0 *  1 =   0
          88
```

Why Base 2?

Base 2 is important in programming because it corresponds so cleanly to what a computer needs to represent. Computers do not really know anything at all about letters, numerals, instructions, or programs. At their core they are just circuitry, and at a given juncture there either is a lot of power or there is very little.

To keep the logic clean, engineers do not treat this as a relative scale (a little power, some power, more power, lots of power, tons of power), but rather as a binary scale ("enough power" or "not enough power"). Rather than saying "enough" or "not enough," they simplify it to "yes" or "no." Yes or no, or true or false, can be represented as 1 or 0. By convention, 1 means true or Yes, but that is just a convention; it could just as easily have meant false or no.

Once you make this great leap of intuition, the power of binary becomes clear: With 1s and 0s you can represent the fundamental truth of every circuit (there is power or there isn't). All a computer ever knows is, "Is you is, or is you ain't?" Is you is = 1; is you ain't = 0.

Bits, Bytes, and Nybbles

Once the decision is made to represent truth and falsehood with 1s and 0s, *bi*nary dig*its* (or bits) become very important. Since early computers could send 8 bits at a time, it was natural to start writing code using 8-bit numbers—called bytes.

> **Note**
>
> Half a byte (4 bits) is called a nybble!

With eight binary digits you can represent up to 256 different values. Why? Examine the columns: If all 8 bits are set (1), the value is 255. (128+64+32+16+8+4+2+1) If none is set (all the bits are clear or zero) the value is 0. 0–255 is 256 possible states.

What's a KB?

It turns out that 2^{10} (1,024) is roughly equal to 10^3 (1,000). This coincidence was too good to miss, so computer scientists started referring to 2^{10} bytes as 1K or 1 kilobyte, based on the scientific prefix of kilo for thousand.

Similarly, 1024*1024 (1,048,576) is close enough to one million to receive the designation 1MB or 1 megabyte, and 1,024 megabytes is called 1 gigabyte (giga implies thousand-million or billion).

Binary Numbers

Computers use patterns of 1s and 0s to encode everything they do. Machine instructions are encoded as a series of 1s and 0s and interpreted by the fundamental circuitry. Arbitrary sets of 1s and 0s can be translated back into numbers by computer scientists, but it would be a mistake to think that these numbers have intrinsic meaning.

For example, the Intel 8086 chip set interprets the bit pattern 1001 0101 as an instruction. You certainly can translate this into decimal (149), but that number per se has no meaning.

Sometimes the numbers are instructions, sometimes they are values, and sometimes they are codes. One important standardized code set is ASCII. In ASCII every letter and punctuation is given a 7-digit binary representation. For example, the lowercase letter "a" is represented by 0110 0001. This is not a number, although you can translate it to the number 97 in base 10 (64+32+1). It is in this sense that people say that the letter "a" is represented by 97 in ASCII; but the truth is that the binary representation of 97, 01100001, is the encoding of the letter "a," and the decimal value 97 is a human convenience.

Hexadecimal

Because binary numbers are difficult to read, a simpler way to represent the same values is sought. Translating from binary to base 10 involves a fair bit of manipulation of numbers; but it turns out that translating from base 2 to base 16 is very simple, because there is a very good shortcut.

To understand this, you must first understand base 16, which is known as hexadecimal. In base 16 there are sixteen numerals: 0, 1, 2, 3, 4, 5, 6, 7, 8, 9, A, B, C, D, E, and F. The last six are arbitrary; the letters A–F were chosen because they are easy to represent on a keyboard. The columns in hexadecimal are

Column	4	3	2	1
Power	16^3	16^2	16^1	16^0
Value	4096	256	16	1

To translate from hexadecimal to decimal, you can multiply. Thus, the number F8C represents:

```
F * 256 = 15 * 256 = 3840
8 * 16 =            128
C * 1 = 12 * 1 =     12
3980
```

(Remember that F in Hexadecimal is equal to 15_{10})

Translating the number FC to binary is best done by translating first to base 10, and then to binary:

```
F * 16 = 15 * 16 =  240
C * 1 = 12 * 1 =     12
252
```

Converting 252_{10} to binary requires the chart:

Column	9	8	7	6	5	4	3	2	1
Power	2^8	2^7	2^6	2^5	2^4	2^3	2^2	2^1	2^0
Value	256	128	64	32	16	8	4	2	1

There are no 256s.

1*128 = 128. 252–128 = 124

1*64 = 64. 124–64 = 60

1*32 = 32. 60–32 = 28

1*16 = 16. 28–16 = 12

1*8 = 8. 12–8 = 4

1*4 = 4. 4–4 = 0

0*2 = 0

0*1 = 0

124+60+28+12+4 = 252.

Thus, the answer in binary is 11111100.

Now, it turns out that if you treat this binary number as two sets of 4 digits (1111 1100), you can do a magical transformation.

The right set is 1100. In decimal that is 12, or in hexadecimal it is C. (1*8 + 1*4 + 0*2 + 0*1)

The left set is 1111, which in base 10 is 15, or in hex is F.

Thus, you have:

```
1111 1100
F    C
```

Putting the two hex numbers together is FC, which is the real value of 1111 1100. This shortcut always works! You can take any binary number of any length, and reduce it to sets of 4, translate each set of four to hex, and put the hex numbers together to get the result in hex. Here's a much larger number:

```
1011 0001 1101 0111
```

To check our assumption, let's first convert this number to decimal.

We can find the value of the columns by doubling. The right-most column is 1, the next is 2, then 4, 8, 16 and so forth.

We start with the right-most column, which is worth 1 in decimal. We have a 1 there so that column is worth 1. The next column to the left is 2. Again, we have a 1 in that column, so we add 2 and we get a total of 3.

The next column to the left is worth 4 (we double for each column). Thus we have 4+2+1 = 7).

We continue this for each column:

1×1	1
1×2	2
1×4	4
0×8	0
1×16	16

A

0×32	0
1×64	64
1×128	128
1×256	256
0×512	0
0×1024	0
0×2048	0
1×4096	4,096
1×8192	8,192
0×16384	0
1×32768	32,768
Total	**45,527**

Converting this to hexadecimal requires a chart with the hexadecimal values.

Column	4	3	2	1
Power	16^3	16^2	16^1	16^0
Value	4096	256	16	1

There are 11 4096s (45,056), with a remainder of 471. There is one 256 in 471 with a remainder of 215. There are 13 16s (208) in 215 with a remainder of 7. Thus, the hexadecimal number is B1D7.

Checking the math:

```
B (11) * 4096 =    45,056
1 * 256 =             256
D (13) * 16 =         208
7 * 1 =                 7
Total              45,527
```

The shortcut version would be to take the original binary number, 1011000111010111, and break it into groups of four: 1011 0001 1101 0111. Each of the four then is evaluated as a hexadecimal number:

```
1011 =
1 x 1 =    1
1 x 2 =    2
0 x 4 =    0
1 x 8 =    8
Total     11
Hex:       B
```

```
0001 =
1 x 1 =    1
0 x 2 =    0
0 x 4 =    0
0 x 8 =    0
Total   1
Hex:    1

1101 =
1 x 1 =    1
0 x 2 =    0
1 x 4 =    4
1 x 8 =    8
Total   13
Hex =    D

0111 =
1 x 1 =    1
1 x 2 =    2
1 x 4 =    4
0 x 8 =    0
Total   7
Hex:    7

Total Hex:  B1D7
```

Hey! Presto! The shortcut conversion from binary to hexadecimal gives us the same answer as the longer version.

You will find that programmers use hexadecimal fairly frequently in advanced programming; buy you'll also find that you can work quite effectively in programming for a long time without ever using any of this!

APPENDIX B

C++ Keywords

Keywords are reserved to the compiler for use by the language. You cannot define classes, variables, or functions that have these keywords as their names.

```
asm
auto
bool
break
case
catch
char
class
const
const_cast
continue
default
delete
do
double
dynamic_cast
else
enum
explicit
extern
false
```

```
float
for
friend
goto
if
inline
int
long
mutable
namespace
new
operator
private
protected
public
register
reinterpret_cast
return
short
signed
sizeof
static
static_cast
struct
switch
template
this
throw
true
try
typedef
typeid
typename
union
unsigned
using
virtual
void
volatile
wchar_t
while
```

APPENDIX C

Operator Precedence

It is important to understand that operators have a precedence, but it is not essential to memorize the precedence.

Precedence is the order in which a program performs the operations in a formula. If one operator has precedence over another operator, it is evaluated first.

Higher precedence operators "bind tighter" than lower precedence operators; thus, higher precedence operators are evaluated first. The lower the rank in Table C.1, the higher the precedence.

TABLE C.1   Operator Precedence

Rank	Name	Operator
1	scope resolution	::
2	member selection, subscripting, function calls, postfix increment and decrement	. -> () ++ --
3	sizeof, prefix increment and decrement, complement, and, not, unary minus and plus, address of and dereference, new, new[], delete, delete[], casting, sizeof()	++ -- ^ ! - + & * ()

TABLE C.1 continued

Rank	Name	Operator
4	member selection for pointer	.* ->*
5	multiply, divide, modulo	* / %
6	add, subtract	+ -
7	shift (shift left, shift right)	<< >>
8	inequality relational	< <= > >=
9	equality, inequality	== !=
10	bitwise AND	&
11	bitwise exclusive OR	^
12	bitwise OR	|
13	logical AND	&&
14	logical OR	||
15	conditional	?:
16	assignment operators	= *= /= %= += -= <<= >>= &= |= ^=
17	throw operator	throw
18	comma	,

APPENDIX D

Answers

Day 1

Quiz

1. What is the difference between an interpreter and a compiler?

   Interpreters read through source code and translate a program, turning the programmer's "code," or program instructions, directly into actions. Compilers translate source code into an executable program that can be run at a later time.

2. How do you compile the source code with your compiler?

   Every compiler is different. Be sure to check the documentation that came with your compiler.

3. What does the linker do?

   The linker's job is to tie together your compiled code with the libraries supplied by your compiler vendor and other sources. The linker lets you build your program in "pieces" and then link together the pieces into one big program.

4. What are the steps in the normal development cycle?

   Edit source code, compile, link, test, repeat.

Exercises

1. Look at the following program and try to guess what it does without running it.

```
1: #include <iostream>
2: int main()
3: {
4:   int x = 5;
5:   int y = 7;
6:   std::cout << "\n";
7:   std::cout << x + y << " " << x * y;
8:   std::cout << "\n";
9:   return 0;
10:}
```

This program initializes two integer variables and then prints out their sum and their product.

2. Type in the program from Exercise 1, and then compile and link it. What does it do? Does it do what you guessed?

See your compiler manual.

3. Type in the following program and compile it. What error do you receive?

```
1: include <iostream>
2: int main()
3: {
4:     std::cout << "Hello World\n";
5:     return 0;
6: }
```

You must put a # symbol before the word include on the first line.

4. Fix the error in the program in Exercise 3 and recompile, link, and run it. What does it do?

This program prints the words Hello World to the screen, followed by a new line (carriage return).

Day 2

Quiz

1. What is the difference between the compiler and the preprocessor?

Each time you run your compiler, the preprocessor runs first. It reads through your source code and includes the files you've asked for, and performs other housekeeping chores.

2. Why is the function main() special?

main() is called automatically, each time your program is executed. It may not be called by any other function and it must exist in your program.

3. What are the two types of comments, and how do they differ?

C++-style comments are two slashes (//) and they comment out any text until the end of the line. C-style comments come in pairs (/* */) and everything between the matching pairs is commented out. You must be careful to ensure you have matched pairs.

4. Can comments be nested?

Yes, C++-style comments can be nested within C-style comments. You can, in fact, nest C-style comments within C++-style comments, as long as you remember that the C++-style comments end at the end of the line.

5. Can comments be longer than one line?

C-style comments can. If you want to extend C++-style comments to a second line, you must put another set of double slashes (//).

Exercises

1. Write a program that writes "I love C++" to the screen.

```
1: #include <iostream>
2: using namespace std;
3: int main()
4: {
5:    cout << "I love C++\n";
6:    return 0;
7: }
```

2. Write the smallest program that can be compiled, linked, and run.

```
int main(){}
```

3. **BUG BUSTERS:** Enter this program and compile it. Why does it fail? How can you fix it?

```
1: #include <iostream>
2: main()
3: {
4:      std::cout << Is there a bug here?";
5: }
```

Line 4 is missing an opening quote for the string.

4. Fix the bug in Exercise 3 and recompile, link, and run it.

```
1: #include <iostream>
2: main()
3: {
4:      std::cout << "Is there a bug here?";
5: }
```

D

Day 3

Quiz

1. What is the difference between an integer variable and a floating-point variable?

   Integer variables are whole numbers; floating-point variables are "reals" and have a "floating" decimal point. Floating-point numbers can be represented using a mantissa and exponent.

2. What are the differences between an `unsigned short int` and a `long int`?

   The keyword `unsigned` means that the integer will hold only positive numbers. On most computers, short integers are 2 bytes and long integers are 4.

3. What are the advantages of using a symbolic constant rather than a literal constant?

   A symbolic constant explains itself; the name of the constant tells what it is for. Also, symbolic constants can be redefined at one location in the source code, rather than the programmer having to edit the code everywhere the literal is used.

4. What are the advantages of using the `const` keyword rather than `#define`?

   `const` variables are "typed," and thus the compiler can check for errors in how they are used. Also, they survive the preprocessor, and thus the name is available in the debugger.

5. What makes for a good or bad variable name?

   A good variable name tells you what the variable is for; a bad variable name has no information. `myAge` and `PeopleOnTheBus` are good variable names, but `xjk` and `prndl` are probably less useful.

6. Given this `enum`, what is the value of `BLUE`?

   ```
   enum COLOR { WHITE, BLACK = 100, RED, BLUE, GREEN = 300 };
   ```

   BLUE = 102

7. Which of the following variable names are good, which are bad, and which are invalid?

   a. `Age`

      Good

   b. `!ex`

      Not legal

   c. `R79J`

      Legal, but a bad choice

   d. `TotalIncome`

Good

e. __Invalid

Legal, but a bad choice

Exercises

1. What would be the correct variable type in which to store the following information?

    a. Your age.

    Unsigned short integer.

    b. The area of your backyard.

    Unsigned long integer or unsigned float.

    c. The number of stars in the galaxy.

    Unsigned double.

    d. The average rainfall for the month of January.

    Unsigned short integer.

2. Create good variable names for this information.

    a. myAge

    b. backYardArea

    c. StarsInGalaxy

    d. averageRainFall

3. Declare a constant for pi as 3.14159.

    const float PI = 3.14159;

4. Declare a float variable and initialize it using your pi constant.

    float myPi = PI;

Day 4

Quiz

1. What is an expression?

    Any statement that returns a value.

2. Is x = 5 + 7 an expression? What is its value?

    Yes, 12.

3. What is the value of 201 / 4?

    50.

D

4. What is the value of 201 % 4?

   1.

5. If myAge, a, and b are all int variables, what are their values after

   ```
   myAge = 39;
   a = myAge++;
   b = ++myAge;
   ```

   myAge: 41, a: 39, b: 41.

6. What is the value of 8+2*3?

   14.

7. What is the difference between if (x = 3) and if (x == 3)?

   The first one assigns 3 to x and returns the value 3 which is interpreted as true. The second one tests whether x is equal to 3; it returns true if the value of x is equal to 3 and false if it is not.

8. Do the following values evaluate to True or False?

a. 0 False

b. 1 True

c. -1 True

d. x = 0 False

e. x == 0 // assume that x has the value of 0 True

Exercises

1. Write a single if statement that examines two integer variables and changes the larger to the smaller, using only one else clause.

   ```
   if (x > y)
        x = y;
   else              // y > x || y == x
        y = x;
   ```

2. Examine the following program. Imagine entering three numbers, and write what output you expect.

   ```
   1:    #include <iostream>
   2:    using namespace std;
   3:    int main()
   4:    {
   5:        int a, b, c;
   6:        cout << "Please enter three numbers\n";
   7:        cout << "a: ";
   8:        cin >> a;
   9:        cout << "\nb: ";
   ```

```
10:        cin >> b;
11:        cout << "\nc: ";
12:        cin >> c;
13:
14:        if (c = (a-b))
15:            cout << "a: " << a << " minus b: " << b << "
                            _equals c: " << c;
16:        else
17:            cout << "a-b does not equal c: ";
18:     return 0;
19:  }
```

3. Enter the program from Exercise 2; compile, link, and run it. Enter the numbers 20, 10, and 50. Did you get the output you expected? Why not?

   Enter **20, 10, 50**.

   Get back a: 20, b: 30, c: 10.

   Line 14 is assigning, not testing for equality.

4. Examine this program and anticipate the output:

```
1:   #include <iostream>
2:   using namespace std;
3:    int main()
4:     {
5:         int a = 2, b = 2, c;
6:         if (c = (a-b))
7:             cout << "The value of c is: " << c;
8:     return 0;
9:      }
```

5. Enter, compile, link, and run the program from Exercise 4. What was the output? Why?

   Because line 5 is assigning the value of a-b to c, the value of the assignment is a (1) minus b (1), or 0. Because 0 is evaluated as false, the if fails and nothing is printed.

Day 5

Quiz

1. What are the differences between the function prototype and the function definition?

   The function prototype declares the function; the definition defines it. The prototype ends with a semicolon; the definition need not. The declaration can include the keyword inline and default values for the parameters; the definition cannot. The declaration need not include names for the parameters; the definition must.

2. Do the names of parameters have to agree in the prototype, definition, and call to the function?

No. All parameters are identified by position, not name.

3. If a function doesn't return a value, how do you declare the function?

Declare the function to return void.

4. If you don't declare a return value, what type of return value is assumed?

Any function that does not explicitly declare a return type returns int. You should always declare the return type as a matter of good programming practice.

5. What is a local variable?

A local variable is a variable passed into or declared within a block, typically a function. It is visible only within the block.

6. What is scope?

Scope refers to the visibility and lifetime of local and global variables. Scope is usually established by a set of braces.

7. What is recursion?

Recursion generally refers to the ability of a function to call itself.

8. When should you use global variables?

Global variables are typically used when many functions need access to the same data. Global variables are very rare in C++; once you know how to create static class variables, you will almost never create global variables.

9. What is function overloading?

Function overloading is the ability to write more than one function with the same name, distinguished by the number or type of the parameters.

10. What is polymorphism?

Polymorphism is the ability to treat many objects of differing but related types without regard to their differences. In C++, polymorphism is accomplished by using class derivation and virtual functions.

Exercises

1. Write the prototype for a function named `Perimeter()`, which returns an unsigned long int and which takes two parameters, both unsigned short ints.

```
unsigned long int Perimeter(unsigned short int, unsigned short int);
```

2. Write the definition of the function `Perimeter()` as described in Exercise 1. The two parameters represent the length and width of a rectangle and have the function return the perimeter (twice the length plus twice the width).

```cpp
unsigned long int Perimeter(unsigned short int length, unsigned short
int width)
{
  return 2*length + 2*width;
}
```

3. **BUG BUSTERS:** What is wrong with the function in the following code?

```cpp
#include <iostream>
void myFunc(unsigned short int x);
int main()
{
    unsigned short int x, y;
    y = myFunc(int);
    std::cout << "x: " << x << " y: " << y << "\n";
return 0;
}

void myFunc(unsigned short int x)
{
    return (4*x);
}
```

The function is declared to return `void` and it cannot return a value.

4. **BUG BUSTERS:** What is wrong with the function in the following code?

```cpp
#include <iostream>
int myFunc(unsigned short int x);
int main()
{
    unsigned short int x, y;
    x = 7;
    y = myFunc(x);
    std::cout << "x: " << x << " y: " << y << "\n";
return 0;
}

int myFunc(unsigned short int x);
{
    return (4*x);
}
```

This function would be fine, but there is a semicolon at the end of the function definition's header.

5. Write a function that takes two `unsigned short` integer arguments and returns the result of dividing the first by the second. Do not do the division if the second number is 0, but do return –1.

```
short int Divider(unsigned short int valOne, unsigned short int
valTwo)
{
    if (valTwo == 0)
            return -1;
    else
            return valOne / valTwo;
}
```

6. Write a program that asks the user for two numbers and calls the function you
   wrote in Exercise 5. Print the answer, or print an error message if you get −1.

```
#include <iostream>
using namespace std;
typedef unsigned short int USHORT;
typedef unsigned long int ULONG;
short int Divider(
unsigned short int valone,
unsigned short int valtwo);
int main()
{
    USHORT one, two;
    short int answer;
    cout << "Enter two numbers.\n Number one: ";
    cin >> one;
    cout << "Number two: ";
    cin >> two;
    answer = Divider(one, two);
    if (answer > -1)
        cout << "Answer: " << answer;
    else
        cout << "Error, can't divide by zero!";
return 0;
}
```

7. Write a program that asks for a number and a power. Write a recursive function
   that takes the number to the power. Thus, if the number is 2 and the power is 4, the
   function will return 16.

```
#include <iostream>
using namespace std;
typedef unsigned short USHORT;
typedef unsigned long ULONG;
ULONG GetPower(USHORT n, USHORT power);
int main()
{
    USHORT number, power;
    ULONG answer;
    cout << "Enter a number: ";
    cin >> number;
    cout << "To what power? ";
```

```
    cin >> power;
    answer = GetPower(number,power);
    cout << number << " to the " << power << "th power is " <<
answer << endl;
return 0;
}

ULONG GetPower(USHORT n, USHORT power)
{
    if(power == 1)
     return n;
    else
        return (n * GetPower(n,power-1));
}
```

Day 6

Quiz

1. What is the dot operator, and what is it used for?

   The dot operator is the period (.). It is used to access the members of the class.

2. Which sets aside memory—declaration or definition?

   Definitions of variables set aside memory. Declarations of classes don't set aside memory.

3. Is the declaration of a class its interface or its implementation?

   The declaration of a class is its interface; it tells clients of the class how to interact with the class. The implementation of the class is the set of member functions—usually in a related CPP file.

4. What is the difference between public and private data members?

   Public data members can be accessed by clients of the class. Private data members can be accessed only by member functions of the class.

5. Can member functions be private?

   Yes. Both member functions and member data can be private.

6. Can member data be public?

   Although member data can be public, it is good programming practice to make it private and to provide public accessor functions to the data.

7. If you declare two Cat objects, can they have different values in their itsAge member data?

   Yes. Each object of a class has its own data members.

D

8. Do class declarations end with a semicolon? Do class method definitions?

Declarations end with a semicolon after the closing brace; function definitions do not.

9. What would the header be for a Cat function, Meow(), that takes no parameters and returns void?

The header for a Cat function, Meow(), that takes no parameters and returns void looks like this:

```
void Cat::Meow()
```

10. What function is called to initialize a class?

The constructor is called to initialize a class.

Exercises

1. Write the code that declares a class called Employee with these data members: age, yearsOfService, and Salary.

```
class Employee
{
    int Age;
    int YearsOfService;
    int Salary;
};
```

2. Rewrite the Employee class to make the data members private, and provide public accessor methods to get and set each of the data members.

```
class Employee
{
public:
    int GetAge() const;
    void SetAge(int age);
    int GetYearsOfService()const;
    void SetYearsOfService(int years);
    int GetSalary()const;
    void SetSalary(int salary);

private:
    int Age;
    int YearsOfService;
    int Salary;
};
```

3. Write a program with the Employee class that makes two employees; sets their age, YearsOfService, and Salary; and prints their values.

```
#include <iostream>
using namespace std;
```

```
main()
{
    Employee John;
    Employee Sally;
    John.SetAge(30);
    John.SetYearsOfService(5);
    John.SetSalary(50000);

    Sally.SetAge(32);
    Sally.SetYearsOfService(8);
    Sally.SetSalary(40000);

    cout << "At AcmeSexist company, John and Sally have the same
job.\n";
    cout << "John is " << John.GetAge() << " years old and he has
been with";
    cout << "the firm for " << John.GetYearsOfService << "
years.\n";
    cout << "John earns $" << John.GetSalary << " dollars per
year.\n\n";
    cout << "Sally, on the other hand is " << Sally.GetAge() << "
years old and has";
    cout << "been with the company " << Sally.GetYearsOfService;
    cout << " years. Yet Sally only makes $" << Sally.GetSalary();
    cout << " dollars per year!  Something here is unfair.";

}
```

4. Continuing from Exercise 3, provide a method of `Employee` that reports how many thousands of dollars the employee earns, rounded to the nearest 1,000.

```
float Employee:GetRoundedThousands()const
{
    return Salary / 1000;
}
```

5. Change the `Employee` class so that you can initialize age, `YearsOfService`, and `Salary` when you create the employee.

```
class Employee
{
public:

    Employee(int age, int yearsOfService, int salary);
    int GetAge()const;
    void SetAge(int age);
    int GetYearsOfService()const;
    void SetYearsOfService(int years);
    int GetSalary()const;
    void SetSalary(int salary);
```

D

```
private:
    int Age;
    int YearsOfService;
    int Salary;
};
```

6. **BUG BUSTERS:** What is wrong with the following declaration?

```
class Square
{
public:
    int Side;
}
```

Class declarations must end with a semicolon.

7. **BUG BUSTERS:** Why isn't the following class declaration very useful?

```
class Cat
{
    int GetAge()const;
private:
    int itsAge;
};
```

The accessor GetAge() is private. Remember: All class members are private unless you say otherwise.

8. **BUG BUSTERS:** What three bugs in this code will the compiler find?

```
class  TV
{
public:
    void SetStation(int Station);
    int GetStation() const;
private:
    int itsStation;
};

main()
{
    TV myTV;
    myTV.itsStation = 9;
    TV.SetStation(10);
    TV myOtherTv(2);
}
```

You can't access itsStation directly. It is private.

You can't call SetStation() on the class. You can call SetStation() only on objects.

You can't initialize myOtherTV because there is no matching constructor.

Day 7

Quiz

1. How do I initialize more than one variable in a `for` loop?

   Separate the initializations with commas, such as

   `for (x = 0, y = 10; x < 100; x++, y++).`

2. Why is `goto` avoided?

   `goto` jumps in any direction to any arbitrary line of code. This makes for source code that is difficult to understand and therefore difficult to maintain.

3. Is it possible to write a `for` loop with a body that is never executed?

   Yes, if the condition is false after the initialization, the body of the `for` loop will never execute. Here's an example:

   `for (int x = 100; x < 100; x++)`

4. Is it possible to nest `while` loops within `for` loops?

   Yes. Any loop may be nested within any other loop.

5. Is it possible to create a loop that never ends? Give an example.

   Yes. Following are examples for both a `for` loop and a `while` loop:

   ```
   for(;;)
   {
       // This for loop never ends!
   }
   while(1)
   {
       // This while loop never ends!
   }
   ```

6. What happens if you create a loop that never ends?

   Your program "hangs" and you usually must reboot the computer.

Exercises

1. What is the value of x when the `for` loop completes?

   `for (int x = 0; x < 100; x++)`

   The variable x is out of scope; has no value.

2. Write a nested `for` loop that prints a 10×10 pattern of 0s.

   ```
   for (int i = 0; i< 10; i++)
   {
       for ( int j = 0; j< 10; j++)
          cout << "0";
       cout << "\n";
   }
   ```

3. Write a `for` statement to count from 100 to 200 by 2s.

```
for (int x = 100; x<=200; x+=2)
```

4. Write a `while` loop to count from 100 to 200 by 2s.

```
int x = 100;
while (x <= 200)
    x+= 2;
```

5. Write a do...while loop to count from 100 to 200 by 2s.

```
int x = 100;
do
{
    x+=2;
} while (x <= 200);
```

6. **BUG BUSTERS:** What is wrong with this code?

```
int counter = 0
while (counter < 10)
{
    cout << "counter: " << counter;
}
```

counter is never incremented and the `while` loop will never terminate.

7. **BUG BUSTERS:** What is wrong with this code?

```
for (int counter = 0; counter < 10; counter++);
    cout << counter << "\n";
```

There is a semicolon after the loop and the loop does nothing. The programmer may have intended this, but if counter was supposed to print each value, it won't.

8. **BUG BUSTERS:** What is wrong with this code?

```
int counter = 100;
while (counter < 10)
{
    cout << "counter now: " << counter;
    counter--;
}
```

counter is initialized to 100, but the test condition is that if it is less than 10, the test will fail and the body will never be executed. If line 1 were changed to `int counter = 5;`, the loop would not terminate until it had counted down past the smallest possible int. Since int is `signed` by default, this would not be what was intended.

9. **BUG BUSTERS:** What is wrong with this code?

```
cout << "Enter a number between 0 and 5: ";
cin >> theNumber;
switch (theNumber)
```

```
{
   case 0:
         doZero();
   case 1:                    // fall through
   case 2:                    // fall through
   case 3:                    // fall through
   case 4:                    // fall through
   case 5:
         doOneToFive();
         break;
   default:
         doDefault();
         break;
}
```

Case 0 probably needs a break statement. If not, it should be documented with a comment.

Day 8

Quiz

1. What operator is used to determine the address of a variable?

   The address of operator (&) is used to determine the address of any variable.

2. What operator is used to find the value stored at an address held in a pointer?

   The dereference operator (*) is used to access the value at an address in a pointer.

3. What is a pointer?

   A pointer is a variable that holds the address of another variable.

4. What is the difference between the address stored in a pointer and the value at that address?

   The address stored in the pointer is the address of another variable. The value stored at that address is any value stored in any variable. The indirection operator (*) returns the value stored at the address, which itself is stored in the pointer.

5. What is the difference between the indirection operator and the address of operator?

   The indirection operator returns the value at the address stored in a pointer. The address of operator (&) returns the memory address of the variable.

6. What is the difference between const int * ptrOne and int * const ptrTwo?

   The const int * ptrOne declares that ptrOne is a pointer to a constant integer. The integer itself cannot be changed using this pointer.

The `int * const ptrTwo` declares that `ptrTwo` is a constant pointer to integer. Once it is initialized, this pointer cannot be reassigned.

Exercises

1. What do these declarations do?

    a. `int * pOne;`

    b. `int vTwo;`

    c. `int * pThree = &vTwo;`

a. `int * pOne;` declares a pointer to an integer.

b. `int vTwo;` declares an integer variable.

c. `int * pThree = &vTwo;` declares a pointer to an integer and initializes it with the address of another variable.

2. If you have an `unsigned short` variable named `yourAge`, how would you declare a pointer to manipulate `yourAge`?

   `unsigned short *pAge = &yourAge;`

3. Assign the value `50` to the variable `yourAge` by using the pointer that you declared in Exercise 2.

   `*pAge = 50;`

4. Write a small program that declares an integer and a pointer to integer. Assign the address of the integer to the pointer. Use the pointer to set a value in the integer variable.

   ```
   int theInteger;
   int *pInteger = &theInteger;
   *pInteger = 5;
   ```

5. **BUG BUSTERS:** What is wrong with this code?

   ```
   #include <iostream>
   using namespace std;
   int main()
   {
       int *pInt;
       *pInt = 9;
       cout << "The value at pInt: " << *pInt;
   return 0;
   }
   ```

   `pInt` should have been initialized. More importantly, because it was not initialized and was not assigned the address of any memory, it points to a random place in memory. Assigning `9` to that random place is a dangerous bug.

6. **BUG BUSTERS:** What is wrong with this code?

```
int main()
{
    int SomeVariable = 5;
    cout << "SomeVariable: " << SomeVariable << "\n";
    int *pVar = & SomeVariable;
    pVar = 9;
    cout << "SomeVariable: " << *pVar << "\n";
return 0;
}
```

Presumably, the programmer meant to assign 9 to the value at pVar. Unfortunately, 9 was assigned to be the value of pVar because the indirection operator (*) was left off. This will lead to disaster if pVar is used to assign a value.

Day 9

Quiz

1. What is the difference between a reference and a pointer?

   A reference is an alias, and a pointer is a variable that holds an address. References cannot be null and cannot be assigned to.

2. When must you use a pointer rather than a reference?

   When you may need to reassign what is pointed to, or when the pointer may be null.

3. What does new return if there is insufficient memory to make your new object?

   A null pointer (0).

4. What is a constant reference?

   This is a shorthand way of saying a reference to a constant object.

5. What is the difference between passing by reference and passing a reference?

   Passing *by* reference means not making a local copy. It can be accomplished by passing a reference or by passing a pointer.

Exercises

1. Write a program that declares an int, a reference to an int, and a pointer to an int. Use the pointer and the reference to manipulate the value in the int.

```
int main()
{
int varOne;
int& rVar = varOne;
```

D

```
int* pVar = &varOne;
rVar = 5;
*pVar = 7;
return 0;
}
```

2. Write a program that declares a constant pointer to a constant integer. Initialize the pointer to an integer variable, varOne. Assign 6 to varOne. Use the pointer to assign 7 to varOne. Create a second integer variable, varTwo. Reassign the pointer to varTwo. Do not compile this exercise yet.

```
int main()
{
    int varOne;
    const int * const pVar = &varOne;
    *pVar = 7;
    int varTwo;
    pVar = &varTwo;
return 0;
}
```

3. Compile the program in Exercise 2. What produces errors? What produces warnings?

You can't assign a value to a constant object, and you can't reassign a constant pointer.

4. Write a program that produces a stray pointer.

```
int main()
{
int * pVar;
*pVar = 9;
return 0;
}
```

5. Fix the program from Exercise 4.

```
int main()
{
int VarOne;
int * pVar = &varOne;
*pVar = 9;
return 0;
}
```

6. Write a program that produces a memory leak.

```
int FuncOne();
int main()
{
    int localVar = FunOne();
    cout << "the value of localVar is: " << localVar;
return 0;
}
```

```
int FuncOne()
{
   int * pVar = new int (5);
   return *pVar;
}
```

7. Fix the program from Exercise 6.

```
void FuncOne();
int main()
{
   FuncOne();
return 0;
}

void FuncOne()
{
   int * pVar = new int (5);
   cout << "the value of *pVar is: " << *pVar ;
}
```

8. **BUG BUSTERS:** What is wrong with this program?

```
1:    #include <iostream>
2:    using namespace std;
3:    class CAT
4:    {
5:       public:
6:          CAT(int age) { itsAge = age; }
7:          ~CAT(){}
8:          int GetAge() const { return itsAge;}
9:       private:
10:          int itsAge;
11:    };
12:
13:    CAT & MakeCat(int age);
14:    int main()
15:    {
16:       int age = 7;
17:       CAT Boots = MakeCat(age);
18:       cout << "Boots is " << Boots.GetAge() << " years old\n";
19:     return 0;
20:    }
21:
22:    CAT & MakeCat(int age)
23:    {
24:       CAT * pCat = new CAT(age);
25:       return *pCat;
26:    }
```

MakeCat returns a reference to the CAT created on the free store. There is no way to free that memory, and this produces a memory leak.

9. Fix the program from Exercise 8.

```
1:      #include <iostream>
2:      using namespace std;
3:      class CAT
4:      {
5:         public:
6:            CAT(int age) { itsAge = age; }
7:            ~CAT(){}
8:            int GetAge() const { return itsAge;}
9:         private:
10:           int itsAge;
11:     };
12:
13:     CAT * MakeCat(int age);
14:     int main()
15:     {
16:        int age = 7;
17:        CAT * Boots = MakeCat(age);
18:        cout << "Boots is " << Boots->GetAge() << " years old\n";
19:        delete Boots;
20:      return 0;
21:     }
22:
23:     CAT * MakeCat(int age)
24:     {
25:        return new CAT(age);
26:     }
```

Day 10

Quiz

1. When you overload member functions, in what ways must they differ?

   Overloaded member functions are functions in a class that share a name but differ in the number or type of their parameters.

2. What is the difference between a declaration and a definition?

   A definition sets aside memory, but a declaration does not. Almost all declarations are definitions; the major exceptions are class declarations, function prototypes, and typedef statements.

3. When is the copy constructor called?

   Whenever a temporary copy of an object is created. This happens every time an object is passed by value.

4. When is the destructor called?

   The destructor is called each time an object is destroyed, either because it goes out of scope or because you call delete on a pointer pointing to it.

5. How does the copy constructor differ from the assignment operator (=)?

   The assignment operator acts on an existing object; the copy constructor creates a new one.

6. What is the this pointer?

   The this pointer is a hidden parameter in every member function that points to the object itself.

7. How do you differentiate between overloading the prefix and postfix increments?

   The prefix operator takes no parameters. The postfix operator takes a single int parameter, which is used as a signal to the compiler that this is the postfix variant.

8. Can you overload the operator+ for short integers?

   No, you cannot overload any operator for built-in types.

9. Is it legal in C++ to overload operator++ so that it decrements a value in your class?

   It is legal, but it is a bad idea. Operators should be overloaded in a way that is likely to be readily understood by anyone reading your code.

10. What return value must conversion operators have in their declarations?

    None. Like constructors and destructors, they have no return values.

D

Exercises

1. Write a SimpleCircle class declaration (only) with one member variable: itsRadius. Include a default constructor, a destructor, and accessor methods for radius.

```
class SimpleCircle
{
public:
     SimpleCircle();
     ~SimpleCircle();
     void SetRadius(int);
     int GetRadius();
private:
     int itsRadius;
};
```

2. Using the class you created in Exercise 1, write the implementation of the default constructor, initializing itsRadius with the value 5.

```
SimpleCircle::SimpleCircle():
itsRadius(5)
{}
```

3. Using the same class, add a second constructor that takes a value as its parameter and assigns that value to `itsRadius`.

```
SimpleCircle::SimpleCircle(int radius):
itsRadius(radius)
{}
```

4. Create a prefix and postfix increment operator for your `SimpleCircle` class that increments `itsRadius`.

```
const SimpleCircle& SimpleCircle::operator++()
{
    ++(itsRadius);
    return *this;
}


// Operator ++(int) postfix.
// Fetch then increment
const SimpleCircle SimpleCircle::operator++ (int)
{
// declare local SimpleCircle and initialize to value of *this
    SimpleCircle temp(*this);
    ++(itsRadius);
    return temp;
}
```

5. Change `SimpleCircle` to store `itsRadius` on the free store, and fix the existing methods.

```
class SimpleCircle
{
public:
    SimpleCircle();
    SimpleCircle(int);
    ~SimpleCircle();
    void SetRadius(int);
    int GetRadius();
    const SimpleCircle& operator++();
    const SimpleCircle operator++(int);
private:
    int *itsRadius;
};


SimpleCircle::SimpleCircle()
{itsRadius = new int(5);}

SimpleCircle::SimpleCircle(int radius)
{itsRadius = new int(radius);}
```

```cpp
const SimpleCircle& SimpleCircle::operator++()
{
    ++(itsRadius);
    return *this;
}

// Operator ++(int) postfix.
// Fetch then increment
const SimpleCircle SimpleCircle::operator++ (int)
{
// declare local SimpleCircle and initialize to value of *this
    SimpleCircle temp(*this);
    ++(itsRadius);
    return temp;
}
```

6. Provide a copy constructor for `SimpleCircle`.

```cpp
SimpleCircle::SimpleCircle(const SimpleCircle & rhs)
{
    int val = rhs.GetRadius();
    itsRadius = new int(val);
}
```

7. Provide an assignment operator for `SimpleCircle`.

```cpp
SimpleCircle& SimpleCircle::operator=(const SimpleCircle & rhs)
{
    if (this == &rhs)
        return *this;
    delete itsRadius;
    itsRadius = new int;
    *itsRadius = rhs.GetRadius();
    return *this;
}
```

8. Write a program that creates two `SimpleCircle` objects. Use the default constructor on one and instantiate the other with the value 9. Call the increment operator on cach and then print their values. Finally, assign the second to the first and print its values.

```cpp
#include <iostream>
using namespace std;

class SimpleCircle
{
public:
    // constructors
    SimpleCircle();
    SimpleCircle(int);
    SimpleCircle(const SimpleCircle &);
    ~SimpleCircle() {}
```

```
// accessor functions
    void SetRadius(int);
    int GetRadius()const;

// operators
    const SimpleCircle& operator++();
    const SimpleCircle operator++(int);
    SimpleCircle& operator=(const SimpleCircle &);

private:
    int *itsRadius;
};


SimpleCircle::SimpleCircle()
{itsRadius = new int(5);}

SimpleCircle::SimpleCircle(int radius)
{itsRadius = new int(radius);}

SimpleCircle::SimpleCircle(const SimpleCircle & rhs)
{
    int val = rhs.GetRadius();
    itsRadius = new int(val);
}
SimpleCircle& SimpleCircle::operator=(const SimpleCircle & rhs)
{
    if (this == &rhs)
        return *this;
    *itsRadius = rhs.GetRadius();
    return *this;
}

const SimpleCircle& SimpleCircle::operator++()
{
    ++(itsRadius);
    return *this;
}

// Operator ++(int) postfix.
// Fetch then increment
const SimpleCircle SimpleCircle::operator++ (int)
{
// declare local SimpleCircle and initialize to value of *this
    SimpleCircle temp(*this);
    ++(itsRadius);
    return temp;
}
int SimpleCircle::GetRadius() const
{
    return *itsRadius;
}
```

```
int main()
{
    SimpleCircle CircleOne, CircleTwo(9);
    CircleOne++;
    ++CircleTwo;
    cout << "CircleOne: " << CircleOne.GetRadius() << endl;
    cout << "CircleTwo: " << CircleTwo.GetRadius() << endl;
    CircleOne = CircleTwo;
    cout << "CircleOne: " << CircleOne.GetRadius() << endl;
    cout << "CircleTwo: " << CircleTwo.GetRadius() << endl;
return 0;
}
```

9. **BUG BUSTERS:** What is wrong with this implementation of the assignment operator?

```
SQUARE SQUARE ::operator=(const SQUARE & rhs)
{
    itsSide = new int;
    *itsSide = rhs.GetSide();
    return *this;
}
```

You must check to see whether rhs equals this, or the call to a = a will crash your program.

10. **BUG BUSTERS:** What is wrong with this implementation of the addition operator?

```
VeryShort  VeryShort::operator+ (const VeryShort& rhs)
{
    itsVal += rhs.GetItsVal();
    return *this;
}
```

This operator+ is changing the value in one of the operands, rather than creating a new VeryShort object with the sum. The right way to do this is as follows:

```
VeryShort  VeryShort::operator+ (const VeryShort& rhs)
{
    return VeryShort(itsVal + rhs.GetItsVal());
}
```

Day 11

Quiz

1. What is the difference between object-oriented programming and procedural programming?

Procedural programming focuses on functions separate from data. Object-oriented programming ties data and functionality together into objects, and focuses on the interaction among the objects.

2. What are the phases of object-oriented analysis and design?

The phases of object-oriented analysis and design include conceptualization, which is the single sentence that describes the great idea; analysis, which is the process of understanding the requirements; and design, which is the process of creating the model of your classes, from which you will generate your code.

3. What is encapsulation?

Encapsulation refers to the (desirable) trait of bringing together in one class all the data and functionality of one discreet entity.

Exercises

1. Suppose you had to simulate the intersection of Massachusetts Avenue and Vassar Street—two typical two-lane roads with traffic lights and crosswalks. The purpose of the simulation is to determine whether the timing of the traffic signal allows for a smooth flow of traffic.

   What kinds of objects should be modeled in the simulation? What would the classes be for the simulation?

   Cars, motorcycles, trucks, bicycles, pedestrians, and emergency vehicles all use the intersection. In addition, there is a traffic signal with Walk/Don't Walk lights.

   Should the road surface be included in the simulation? Certainly, road quality can have an effect on the traffic, but for a first design, it may be simpler to leave this consideration aside.

   The first object is probably the intersection itself. Perhaps the intersection object maintains lists of cars waiting to pass through the signal in each direction, as well as lists of people waiting to cross at the crosswalks. It will need methods to choose which and how many cars and people go through the intersection.

   There will only be one intersection, so you may want to consider how you will ensure that only one object is instantiated (hint: Think about static methods and protected access).

   People and cars are both clients of the intersection. They share a number of characteristics: They can appear at any time, there can be any number of them, and they both wait at the signal (although in different lines). This suggests that you will want to consider a common base class for pedestrians and cars.

The classes would therefore include:

```
class Entity;              // a client of the
➥intersection
class Vehicle : Entity ...;          // the root of
➥all cars, trucks, bicycles and emergency vehicles.
class Pedestrian : Entity...;     // the root of all
➥People
class Car : public Vehicle...;
class Truck : public Vehicle...;
class Motorcycle : public Vehicle...;
class Bicycle : public Vehicle...;
class Emergency_Vehicle : public Vehicle...;
class Intersection;          // contains lists of
➥cars and people waiting to pass
```

2. Suppose the intersections from Exercise 1 were in a suburb of Boston, which has arguably the least friendly streets in the United States. At any time, three kinds of Boston drivers exist:

Locals, who continue to drive through intersections after the light turns red; tourists, who drive slowly and cautiously (in a rental car, typically); and taxis, which have a wide variation of driving patterns, depending on the kinds of passengers in the cabs.

Also, Boston has two kinds of pedestrians: locals, who cross the street whenever they feel like it, and seldom use the crosswalk buttons; and tourists, who always use the crosswalk buttons and only cross when the Walk/Don't Walk light permits. Finally, Boston has bicyclists who never pay attention to stoplights.

How do these considerations change the model?

A reasonable start on this would be to create derived objects that model the refinements suggested by the problem:

```
class Local_Car : public Car...;
        class Tourist_Car : public Car...;
        class Taxi : public Car...;
        class Local_Pedestrian : public
Pedestrian...;
        class Tourist_Pedestrian : public
Pedestrian...;
        class Boston_Bicycle : public Bicycle...;
```

By using virtual methods, each class can modify the generic behavior to meet its own specifications. For example, the Boston driver can react to a red light differently than a tourist does, while still inheriting the generic behaviors that continue to apply.

3. You are asked to design a group scheduler. The software enables you to arrange meetings among individuals or groups and to reserve a limited number of conference rooms. Identify the principal subsystems.

Two discrete programs need to be written for this project: the client, which the users run; and the server, which would run on a separate machine. In addition, the client machine would have an administrative component to enable a system administrator to add new people and rooms.

If you decide to implement this as a client/server model, the client would accept input from users and generate a request to the server. The server would service the request and send back the results to the client. With this model, many people can schedule meetings at the same time.

On the client's side, there are two major subsystems in addition to the administrative module: the user interface and the communications subsystem. The server's side consists of three main subsystems: communications, scheduling, and a mail interface, which would announce to the user when changes have occurred in the schedule.

4. Design and show the interfaces to the classes in the room reservation portion of the program discussed in Exercise 3.

A meeting is defined as a group of people reserving a room for a certain amount of time. The person making the schedule may wish for a specific room, or a specified time; but the scheduler must always be told how long the meeting will last and who is required.

The objects will probably include the users of the system as well as the conference rooms. Don't forget to include classes for the calendar, and perhaps a class Meeting that encapsulates all that is known about a particular event.

The prototypes for the classes might include

```
class Calendar_Class;          // forward reference
class Meeting;                 // forward reference
class Configuration
{
public:
    Configuration();
    ~Configuration();
    Meeting Schedule( ListOfPerson&, Delta Time
duration );
    Meeting Schedule( ListOfPerson&, Delta Time
duration, Time );
    Meeting Schedule( ListOfPerson&, Delta Time
duration, Room );
    ListOfPerson&     People();     // public
accessors
    ListOfRoom&       Rooms();      // public accessors
protected:
    ListOfRoom      rooms;
    ListOfPerson     people;
};
```

```
typedef long       Room_ID;
class Room
{
public:
    Room( String name, Room_ID id, int capacity,
String directions = "", String description = "" );
    ~Room();
    Calendar_Class Calendar();

protected:
    Calendar_Class     calendar;
    int            capacity;
    Room_ID     id;
    String          name;
    String          directions;        // where is this room?
    String          description;
};
typedef long Person_ID;
class Person
{
public:
    Person( String name, Person_ID id );
    ~Person();
    Calendar_Class Calendar();            // the access point to add
➥meetings
protected:
    Calendar_Class     calendar;
    Person_ID     id;
    String          name;
};
class Calendar_Class
{
public:
    Calendar_Class();
    ~Calendar_Class();

    void Add( const Meeting& );        // add a meeting to the calendar
    void Delete( const Meeting& );
    Meeting* Lookup( Time );            // see if there is a meeting at
➥the
                                    // given time

    Block( Time, Duration, String reason = "" );
// allocate time to yourself...

protected:
    OrderedListOfMeeting meetings;
};
class Meeting
{
```

```
public:
    Meeting( ListOfPerson&, Room room,
         Time when, Duration duration, String purpose
= "" );
    ~Meeting();
protected:
    ListOfPerson     people;
    Room             room;
    Time             when;
    Duration         duration;
    String           purpose;
};
```

Day 12

Quiz

1. What is a v-table?

A v-table, or virtual function table, is a common way for compilers to manage virtual functions in C++. The table keeps a list of the addresses of all the virtual functions, and depending on the runtime type of the object pointed to, invokes the right function.

2. What is a virtual destructor?

A destructor of any class can be declared to be virtual. When the pointer is deleted, the runtime type of the object will be assessed and the right derived destructor invoked.

3. How do you show the declaration of a virtual constructor?

There are no virtual constructors.

4. How can you create a virtual copy constructor?

By creating a virtual method in your class, which itself calls the copy constructor.

5. How do you invoke a base member function from a derived class in which you've overridden that function?

`Base::FunctionName();`

6. How do you invoke a base member function from a derived class in which you have not overridden that function?

`FunctionName();`

7. If a base class declares a function to be virtual, and a derived class does not use the term `virtual` when overriding that class, is it still virtual when inherited by a third-generation class?

Yes, the virtuality is inherited and *cannot* be turned off.

8. What is the `protected` keyword used for?

   `protected` members are accessible to the member functions of derived objects.

Exercises

1. Show the declaration of a virtual function that takes an integer parameter and returns void.

```
virtual void SomeFunction(int);
```

2. Show the declaration of a class `Square`, which derives from `Rectangle`, which in turn derives from `Shape`.

```
class Square : public Rectangle
{};
```

3. If, in Example 2, `Shape` takes no parameters, `Rectangle` takes two (length and width), but `Square` takes only one (length), show the constructor initialization for `Square`.

```
Square::Square(int length):
    Rectangle(length, length){}
```

4. Write a virtual copy constructor for the class `Square` (in Exercise 3).

```
class Square
    {
        public:
        // ...
        virtual Square * clone() const { return new Square(*this); }
    // ...
    };
```

5. **BUG BUSTERS:** What is wrong with this code snippet?

```
void SomeFunction (Shape);
Shape * pRect = new Rectangle;
SomeFunction(*pRect);
```

Perhaps nothing. `SomeFunction` expects a `Shape` object. You've passed it a `Rectangle` "sliced" down to a `Shape`. As long as you don't need any of the `Rectangle` parts, this will be fine. If you do need the `Rectangle` parts, you'll need to change `SomeFunction` to take a pointer or a reference to a `Shape`.

6. **BUG BUSTERS:** What is wrong with this code snippet?

```
class Shape()
{
public:
    Shape();
    virtual ~Shape();
    virtual Shape(const Shape&);
};
```

You can't declare a copy constructor to be virtual.

Day 13

Quiz

1. What are the first and last elements in `SomeArray[25]`?

   `SomeArray[0]`, `SomeArray[24]`

2. How do you declare a multidimensional array?

   Write a set of subscripts for each dimension. For example, `SomeArray[2][3][2]` is a three-dimensional array. The first dimension has two elements, the second has three, and the third has two.

3. Initialize the members of the array in Question 2.

   `SomeArray[2][3][2] = { { {1,2},{3,4},{5,6} } , { {7,8},{9,10},{11,12} } };`

4. How many elements are in the array `SomeArray[10][5][20]`?

   10*5*20=1,000

5. What is the maximum number of elements that you can add to a linked list?

   There is no fixed maximum. It depends on how much memory you have available.

6. Can you use subscript notation on a linked list?

   You can use subscript notation on a linked list only by writing your own class to contain the linked list and overloading the subscript operator.

7. What is the last character in the string "Brad is a nice guy"?

   The null character.

Exercises

1. Declare a two-dimensional array that represents a tic-tac-toe game board.

   `int GameBoard[3][3];`

2. Write the code that initializes all the elements in the array you created in Exercise 1 to the value 0.

   `int GameBoard[3][3] = { {0,0,0},{0,0,0},{0,0,0} }`

3. Write the declaration for a `Node` class that holds integers.

   ```
   class Node
    {
    public:
       Node ();
       Node (int);
       ~Node();
       void SetNext(Node * node) { itsNext = node; }
       Node * GetNext() const { return itsNext; }
       int GetVal() const { return itsVal; }
   ```

```
      void Insert(Node *);
      void Display();
   private:
      int itsVal;
      Node * itsNext;
   };
```

4. **BUG BUSTERS:** What is wrong with this code fragment?

```
unsigned short SomeArray[5][4];
for (int i = 0; i<4; i++)
    for (int j = 0; j<5; j++)
        SomeArray[i][j] = i+j;
```

The array is 5 elements by 4 elements, but the code initializes 4×5.

5. **BUG BUSTERS:** What is wrong with this code fragment?

```
unsigned short SomeArray[5][4];
for (int i = 0; i<=5; i++)
    for (int j = 0; j<=4; j++)
        SomeArray[i][j] = 0;
```

You wanted to write i<5, but you wrote i<=5 instead. The code will run when i ==
5 and j == 4, but there is no such element as SomeArray[5][4].

Day 14

Quiz

1. What is a down cast?

   A down cast (also called "casting down") is a declaration that a pointer to a base
   class is to be treated as a pointer to a derived class.

2. What is the v-ptr?

   The v-ptr, or virtual-function pointer, is an implementation detail of virtual functions. Each object in a class with virtual functions has a v-ptr, which points to the
   virtual function table for that class.

3. If a round-rectangle has straight edges and rounded corners, and your RoundRect
   class inherits both from Rectangle and from Circle, and they in turn both inherit
   from Shape, how many Shapes are created when you create a RoundRect?

   If neither class inherits using the keyword virtual, two Shapes are created, one
   for Rectangle and one for Shape. If the keyword virtual is used for both classes,
   only one shared Shape is created.

4. If Horse and Bird inherit from Animal using virtual inheritance, do their constructors initialize the Animal constructor? If Pegasus inherits from both Horse and
   Bird, how does it initialize Animal's constructor?

Both Horse and Bird initialize their base class, Animal, in their constructors. Pegasus does as well, and when a Pegasus is created, the Horse and Bird initializations of Animal are ignored.

5. Declare a class vehicle and make it an abstract data type.

```
class Vehicle
{
    virtual void Move() = 0;
}
```

6. If a base class is an ADT, and it has three pure virtual functions, how many of these functions must be overridden in its derived classes?

None must be overridden unless you want to make the class non-abstract, in which case all three must be overridden.

Exercises

1. Show the declaration for a class JetPlane, which inherits from Rocket and Airplane.

```
class JetPlane : public Rocket, public Airplane
```

2. Show the declaration for Seven47, which inherits from the JetPlane class described in Exercise 1.

```
class Seven47: public JetPlane
```

3. Write a program that derives Car and Bus from the class Vehicle. Make Vehicle an ADT with two pure virtual functions. Make Car and Bus not be ADTs.

```
class Vehicle
{
    virtual void Move() = 0;
    virtual void Haul() = 0;
};

class Car : public Vehicle
{
    virtual void Move();
    virtual void Haul();
};

class Bus : public Vehicle
{
    virtual void Move();
    virtual void Haul();
};
```

4. Modify the program in Exercise 3 so that `Car` is an ADT, and derive `SportsCar` and `Coupe` from `Car`. In the `Car` class, provide an implementation for one of the pure virtual functions in `Vehicle` and make it non-pure.

```
class Vehicle
{
    virtual void Move() = 0;
    virtual void Haul() = 0;
};

class Car : public Vehicle
{
    virtual void Move();
};

class Bus : public Vehicle
{
    virtual void Move();
    virtual void Haul();
};

class SportsCar : public Car
{
    virtual void Haul();
};

class Coupe : public Car
{
    virtual void Haul();
};
```

Day 15

Quiz

1. Can static member variables be private?

   Yes. They are member variables and their access can be controlled like any other. If they are private, they can be accessed only by using member functions or, more commonly, static member functions.

2. Show the declaration for a static member variable.

   ```
   static int itsStatic;
   ```

3. Show the declaration for a static function.

   ```
   static int SomeFunction();
   ```

4. Show the declaration for a pointer to function returning `long` and taking an integer parameter.

   ```
   long (* function)(int);
   ```

5. Modify the pointer in Question 4 so it's a pointer to member function of class Car.

```
long ( Car::*function)(int);
```

6. Show the declaration for an array of 10 pointers as defined in Question 5.

```
long ( Car::*function)(int) theArray [10];
```

Exercises

1. Write a short program declaring a class with one member variable and one static member variable. Have the constructor initialize the member variable and increment the static member variable. Have the destructor decrement the member variable.

```
1:      class myClass
2:      {
3:      public:
4:          myClass();
5:          ~myClass();
6:      private:
7:          int itsMember;
8:          static int itsStatic;
9:      };
10:
11:     myClass::myClass():
12:      itsMember(1)
13:     {
14:         itsStatic++;
15:     }
16:
17:     myClass::~myClass()
18:     {
19:         itsStatic--;
20:     }
21:
22:     int myClass::itsStatic = 0;
23:
24:     int main()
25:     {}
```

2. Using the program from Exercise 1, write a short driver program that makes three objects and then displays their member variables and the static member variable. Then destroy each object and show the effect on the static member variable.

```
1:      #include <iostream>
2:      using namespace std;
3:      class myClass
4:      {
5:      public:
6:          myClass();
7:          ~myClass();
```

```
8:          void ShowMember();
9:          void ShowStatic();
10:    private:
11:        int itsMember;
12:        static int itsStatic;
13:    };
14:
15:    myClass::myClass():
16:     itsMember(1)
17:    {
18:        itsStatic++;
19:    }
20:
21:    myClass::~myClass()
22:    {
23:        itsStatic--;
24:        cout << "In destructor. ItsStatic: " << itsStatic << endl;
25:    }
26:
27:    void myClass::ShowMember()
28:    {
29:        cout << "itsMember: " << itsMember << endl;
30:    }
31:
32:    void myClass::ShowStatic()
33:    {
34:        cout << "itsStatic: " << itsStatic << endl;
35:    }
36:    int myClass::itsStatic = 0;
37:
38:    int main()
39:    {
40:        myClass obj1;
41:        obj1.ShowMember();
42:        obj1.ShowStatic();
43:
44:        myClass obj2;
45:        obj2.ShowMember();
46:        obj2.ShowStatic();
47:
48:        myClass obj3;
49:        obj3.ShowMember();
50:        obj3.ShowStatic();
51:     return 0;
52:    }
```

3. Modify the program from Exercise 2 to use a static member function to access the static member variable. Make the static member variable private.

```
1:      #include <iostream>
2:      using namespace std;
```

```
3:      class myClass
4:      {
5:      public:
6:         myClass();
7:         ~myClass();
8:         void ShowMember();
9:         static int GetStatic();
10:     private:
11:        int itsMember;
12:        static int itsStatic;
13:     };
14:
15:     myClass::myClass():
16:      itsMember(1)
17:     {
18:        itsStatic++;
19:     }
20:
21:     myClass::~myClass()
22:     {
23:        itsStatic--;
24:        cout << "In destructor. ItsStatic: " << itsStatic << endl;
25:     }
26:
27:     void myClass::ShowMember()
28:     {
29:        cout << "itsMember: " << itsMember << endl;
30:     }
31:
32:     int myClass::itsStatic = 0;
33:
34:     void myClass::GetStatic()
35:     {
36:        return itsStatic;
37:     }
38:
39:     int main()
40:     {
41:        myClass obj1;
42:        obj1.ShowMember();
43:        cout << "Static: " << myClass::GetStatic() << endl;
44:
45:        myClass obj2;
46:        obj2.ShowMember();
47:        cout << "Static: " << myClass::GetStatic() << endl;
48:
49:        myClass obj3;
50:        obj3.ShowMember();
51:        cout << "Static: " << myClass::GetStatic() << endl;
52:      return 0;
53:     }
```

4. Write a pointer to member function to access the non-static member data in the program in Exercise 3, and use that pointer to print the value of that data.

```
1:      #include <iostream>
2:      using namespace std;
3:      class myClass
4:      {
5:      public:
6:          myClass();
7:          ~myClass();
8:          void ShowMember();
9:          static int GetStatic();
10:     private:
11:         int itsMember;
12:         static int itsStatic;
13:     };
14:
15:     myClass::myClass():
16:      itsMember(1)
17:     {
18:         itsStatic++;
19:     }
20:
21:     myClass::~myClass()
22:     {
23:         itsStatic--;
24:         cout << "In destructor. ItsStatic: " << itsStatic << endl;
25:     }
26:
27:     void myClass::ShowMember()
28:     {
29:         cout << "itsMember: " << itsMember << endl;
30:     }
31:
32:     int myClass::itsStatic = 0;
33:
34:     int myClass::GetStatic()
35:     {
36:         return itsStatic;
37:     }
38:
39:     int main()
40:     {
41:         void (myClass::*PMF) ();
42:
43:         PMF=myClass::ShowMember;
44:
45:         myClass obj1;
46:         (obj1.*PMF)();
47:         cout << "Static: " << myClass::GetStatic() << endl;
48:
```

```
49:        myClass obj2;
50:        (obj2.*PMF)();
51:        cout << "Static: " << myClass::GetStatic() << endl;
52:
53:        myClass obj3;
54:        (obj3.*PMF)();
55:        cout << "Static: " << myClass::GetStatic() << endl;
56:     return 0;
57:     }
```

5. Add two more member variables to the class from the previous exercises. Add accessor functions that get the value of these data and give all the member functions the same return values and signatures. Use the pointer to member function to access these functions.

```
1:      #include <iostream>
2:      using namespace std;
3:      class myClass
4:      {
5:      public:
6:          myClass();
7:          ~myClass();
8:          void ShowMember();
9:          void ShowSecond();
10:         void ShowThird();
11:         static int GetStatic();
12:     private:
13:         int itsMember;
14:         int itsSecond;
15:         int itsThird;
16:         static int itsStatic;
17:     };
18:
19:     myClass::myClass():
20:      itsMember(1),
21:      itsSecond(2),
22:      itsThird(3)
23:     {
24:         itsStatic++;
25:     }
26:
27:     myClass::~myClass()
28:     {
29:         itsStatic--;
30:         cout << "In destructor. ItsStatic: " << itsStatic << endl;
31:     }
32:
33:     void myClass::ShowMember()
34:     {
35:         cout << "itsMember: " << itsMember << endl;
```

```
36:     }
37:
38:     void myClass::ShowSecond()
39:     {
40:         cout << "itsSecond: " << itsSecond << endl;
41:     }
42:
43:     void myClass::ShowThird()
44:     {
45:         cout << "itsThird: " << itsThird << endl;
46:     }
47:     int myClass::itsStatic = 0;
48:
49:     int myClass::GetStatic()
50:     {
51:         return itsStatic;
52:     }
53:
54:     int main()
55:     {
56:         void (myClass::*PMF) ();
57:
58:         myClass obj1;
59:         PMF=myClass::ShowMember;
60:         (obj1.*PMF)();
61:         PMF=myClass::ShowSecond;
62:         (obj1.*PMF)();
63:         PMF=myClass::ShowThird;
64:         (obj1.*PMF)();
65:         cout << "Static: " << myClass::GetStatic() << endl;
66:
67:         myClass obj2;
68:         PMF=myClass::ShowMember;
69:         (obj2.*PMF)();
70:         PMF=myClass::ShowSecond;
71:         (obj2.*PMF)();
72:         PMF=myClass::ShowThird;
73:         (obj2.*PMF)();
74:         cout << "Static: " << myClass::GetStatic() << endl;
75:
76:         myClass obj3;
77:         PMF=myClass::ShowMember;
78:         (obj3.*PMF)();
79:         PMF=myClass::ShowSecond;
80:         (obj3.*PMF)();
81:         PMF=myClass::ShowThird;
82:         (obj3.*PMF)();
83:         cout << "Static: " << myClass::GetStatic() << endl;
84:     return 0;
85:     }
```

D

Day 16

Quiz

1. How do you establish an *is-a* relationship?

    With public inheritance.

2. How do you establish a *has-a* relationship?

    With containment; that is, one class has a member that is an object of another type.

3. What is the difference between containment and delegation?

    Containment describes the idea of one class having a data member that is an object of another type. Delegation expresses the idea that one class uses another class to accomplish a task or goal. Delegation is usually accomplished by containment.

4. What is the difference between delegation and *implemented in terms of*?

    Delegation expresses the idea that one class uses another class to accomplish a task or goal. *Implemented in terms of* expresses the idea of inheriting implementation from another class.

5. What is a friend function?

    A friend function is a function declared to have access to the protected and private members of your class.

6. What is a friend class?

    A friend class is a class declared so that all of its member functions are friend functions of your class.

7. If Dog is a friend of Boy, is Boy a friend of Dog?

    No, friendship is not commutative.

8. If Dog is a friend of Boy, and Terrier derives from Dog, is Terrier a friend of Boy?

    No, friendship is not inherited.

9. If Dog is a friend of Boy and Boy is a friend of House, is Dog a friend of House?

    No, friendship is not associative.

10. Where must the declaration of a friend function appear?

    Anywhere within the class declaration. It makes no difference whether you put the declaration within the public:, protected:, or private: access areas.

Exercises

1. Show the declaration of a class, Animal, that contains a data member that is a string object.

```
class Animal:
{
private:
   String itsName;
};
```

2. Show the declaration of a class, `BoundedArray`, that is an array.

```
class boundedArray : public Array
{
//...
}
```

3. Show the declaration of a class, `Set`, that is declared in terms of an array.

```
class Set : private Array
{
// ...
}
```

4. Modify Listing 16.1 to provide the `String` class with an extraction operator (>>).

```
1:          #include <iostream.h>
2:          #include <string.h>
3:
4:          class String
5:          {
6:              public:
7:                  // constructors
8:                  String();
9:                  String(const char *const);
10:                 String(const String &);
11:                 ~String();
12:
13:                 // overloaded operators
14:                 char & operator[](int offset);
15:                 char operator[](int offset) const;
16:                 String operator+(const String&);
17:                 void operator+=(const String&);
18:                 String & operator= (const String &);
19:                 friend ostream& operator<<( ostream&
                                        _theStream,String& theString);
20:                 friend istream& operator>>( istream&
        _theStream,String& theString);
21:                 // General accessors
22:                 int GetLen()const { return itsLen; }
23:                 const char * GetString() const { return itsString; }
24:                 // static int ConstructorCount;
25:
26:             private:
27:                 String (int);          // private constructor
28:                 char * itsString;
29:                 unsigned short itsLen;
```

```
30:
31:         };
32:
33:         ostream& operator<<( ostream& theStream,String& theString)
34:         {
35:             theStream << theString.GetString();
36:             return theStream;
37:         }
38:
39:         istream& operator>>( istream& theStream,String& theString)
40:         {
41:             theStream >> theString.GetString();
42:             return theStream;
43:         }
44:
45:         int main()
46:         {
47:             String theString("Hello world.");
48:             cout << theString;
49:       return 0;
50:         }
```

5. **BUG BUSTERS:** What is wrong with this program?

```
1:      #include <iostream>
2:      using namespace std;
3:      class Animal;
4:
5:      void setValue(Animal& , int);
6:
7:
8:      class Animal
9:      {
10:     public:
11:         int GetWeight()const { return itsWeight; }
12:         int GetAge() const { return itsAge; }
13:     private:
14:         int itsWeight;
15:         int itsAge;
16:     };
17:
18:     void setValue(Animal& theAnimal, int theWeight)
19:     {
20:         friend class Animal;
21:         theAnimal.itsWeight = theWeight;
22:     }
23:
24:     int main()
25:     {
26:        Animal peppy;
27:        setValue(peppy,5);
28:      return 0;
29:     }
```

You can't put the `friend` declaration into the function. You must declare the function to be a friend in the class.

6. Fix the listing in Exercise 5 so that it will compile.

```
1:      #include <iostream>
2:      using namespace std;
3:      class Animal;
4:
5:      void setValue(Animal& , int);
6:
7:
8:      class Animal
9:      {
10:     public:
11:         friend void setValue(Animal&, int);
12:         int GetWeight()const { return itsWeight; }
13:         int GetAge() const { return itsAge; }
14:     private:
15:         int itsWeight;
16:         int itsAge;
17:     };
18:
19:     void setValue(Animal& theAnimal, int theWeight)
20:     {
21:         theAnimal.itsWeight = theWeight;
22:     }
23:
24:     int main()
25:     {
26:         Animal peppy;
27:         setValue(peppy,5);
28:       return 0;
29:     }
```

7. **BUG BUSTERS:** What is wrong with this code?

```
1:      #include <iostream>
2:      using namespace std;
3:      class Animal;
4:
5:      void setValue(Animal& , int);
6:      void setValue(Animal& ,int,int);
7:
8:      class Animal
9:      {
10:     friend void setValue(Animal& ,int); // here's the change!
11:     private:
12:         int itsWeight;
13:         int itsAge;
14:     };
15:
16:     void setValue(Animal& theAnimal, int theWeight)
17:     {
```

```
18:           theAnimal.itsWeight = theWeight;
19:       }
20:
21:
22:       void setValue(Animal& theAnimal, int theWeight, int theAge)
23:       {
24:          theAnimal.itsWeight = theWeight;
25:          theAnimal.itsAge = theAge;
26:       }
27:
28:       int main()
29:       {
30:          Animal peppy;
31:          setValue(peppy,5);
32:          setValue(peppy,7,9);
33:        return 0;
34:       }
```

The function setValue(Animal&,int) was declared to be a friend, but the over-loaded function setValue(Animal&,int,int) was not declared to be a friend.

8. Fix Exercise 7 so that it compiles.

```
1:       #include <iostream>
2:       using namespace std;
3:       class Animal;
4:
5:       void setValue(Animal& , int);
6:       void setValue(Animal& ,int,int); // here's the change!
7:
8:       class Animal
9:       {
10:      friend void setValue(Animal& ,int);
11:      friend void setValue(Animal& ,int,int);
12:      private:
13:         int itsWeight;
14:         int itsAge;
15:      };
16:
17:      void setValue(Animal& theAnimal, int theWeight)
18:      {
19:          theAnimal.itsWeight = theWeight;
20:      }
21:
22:
23:      void setValue(Animal& theAnimal, int theWeight, int _theAge)
24:      {
25:         theAnimal.itsWeight = theWeight;
26:         theAnimal.itsAge = theAge;
27:      }
```

```
28:
29:    int main()
30:    {
31:       Animal peppy;
32:       setValue(peppy,5);
33:       setValue(peppy,7,9);
34:     return 0;
35:    }
```

Day 17

Quiz

1. What is the insertion operator, and what does it do?

   The insertion operator (<<) is a member operator of the ostream object and is used for writing to the output device.

2. What is the extraction operator, and what does it do?

   The extraction operator (>>) is a member operator of the istream object and is used for writing to your program's variables.

3. What are the three forms of cin.get(), and what are their differences?

   The first form of get() is without parameters. This returns the value of the character found, and will return EOF (end of file) if the end of the file is reached.

   The second form of get() takes a character reference as its parameter; that character is filled with the next character in the input stream. The return value is an iostream object.

   The third form of get() takes an array, a maximum number of characters to get, and a terminating character. This form of get() fills the array with up to one fewer characters than the maximum (appending null) unless it reads the terminating character, in which case it immediately writes a null and leaves the terminating character in the buffer.

4. What is the difference between cin.read() and cin.getline()?

   cin.read() is used for reading binary data structures.

   getline() is used to read from the istream's buffer.

5. What is the default width for ouputting a long integer using the insertion operator?

   Wide enough to display the entire number.

6. What is the return value of the insertion operator?

   A reference to an istream object.

D

7. What parameter does the constructor to an `ofstream` object take?

The filename to be opened.

8. What does the `ios::ate` argument do?

`ios::ate` places you at the end of the file, but you can write data anywhere in the file.

Exercises

1. Write a program that writes to the four standard `iostream` objects: `cin`, `cout`, `cerr`, and `clog`.

```
1:      #include <iostream>
2:      int main()
3:      {
4:          int x;
5:          std::cout << "Enter a number: ";
6:          std::cin >> x;
7:          std::cout << "You entered: " << x << std::endl;
8:          std::cerr << "Uh oh, this to cerr!" << std::endl;
9:          std::clog << "Uh oh, this to clog!" << std::endl;
10:     return 0;
11:     }
```

2. Write a program that prompts the user to enter her full name and then displays it on the screen.

```
1:      #include <iostream>
2:      int main()
3:      {
4:          char name[80];
5:          std::cout << "Enter your full name: ";
6:          std::cin.getline(name,80);
7:          std::cout << "\nYou entered: " << name << std::endl;
8:      return 0;
9:      }
```

3. Rewrite Listing 17.9 to do the same thing, but without using `putback()` or `ignore()`.

```
1:      // Listing
2:      #include <iostream>
3:      using namespace std;
4:      int main()
5:      {
6:          char ch;
7:          cout << "enter a phrase: ";
8:          while ( cin.get(ch) )
9:          {
10:             switch (ch)
11:             {
12:                 case '!':
```

```
13:                    cout << '$';
14:                    break;
15:                case '#':
16:                    break;
17:                default:
18:                    cout << ch;
19:                    break;
20:            }
21:        }
22:    return 0;
23:    }
```

4. Write a program that takes a filename as a parameter and opens the file for reading. Read every character of the file and display only the letters and punctuation to the screen. (Ignore all non-printing characters.) Then close the file and exit.

```
1:     #include <fstream.h>
2:     enum BOOL { FALSE, TRUE };
3:
4:     int main(int argc, char**argv)    // returns 1 on error
5:     {
6:
7:         if (argc != 2)
8:         {
9:             cout << "Usage: argv[0] <infile>\n";
10:            return(1);
11:        }
12:
13:    // open the input stream
14:        ifstream fin (argv[1],ios::binary);
15:        if (!fin)
16:        {
17:            cout << "Unable to open " << argv[1] <<" for reading.\n";
18:            return(1);
19:        }
20:
21:        char ch;
22:        while ( fin.get(ch))
23:            if ((ch > 32 && ch < 127) || ch == '\n'|| ch == '\t')
24:                cout << ch;
25:        fin.close();
26:    }
```

5. Write a program that displays its command-line arguments in reverse order and does not display the program name.

```
1:     #include <fstream.h>
2:
3:     int main(int argc, char**argv)    // returns 1 on error
4:     {
5:         for (int ctr = argc; ctr ; ctr--)
6:             cout << argv[ctr] << " ";
7:     }
```

Day 18

Quiz

1. Can I use names defined in a namespace without using the `using` keyword?

   Yes you can use names defined in a namespace by prefixing them with the namespace qualifier.

2. What are the major differences between normal and unnamed namespaces?

   Names in a normal namespace can be used outside of the translation unit where the namespace is declared. Names in an unnamed namespace can only be used within the translation unit where the namespace is declared.

3. What is the standard namespace?

   The standard namespace `std` is defined by the C++ Standard Library. It includes declarations of all names in the Standard Library.

Exercises

1. **BUG BUSTERS:** What is wrong in this program?

   ```
   #include <iostream>
   int main()
   {
       cout << "Hello world!" << end;
       return 0;
   }
   ```

   The C++ standard `iostream` header file declares `cout` and `endl` in namespace `std`. They cannot be used outside of the standard namespace `std` without a namespace qualifier.

2. List 3 ways of fixing the problem found in Exercise 1.

   ```
   1.    using namespace std;
   2.    using std::cout;
         using std::endl;
   3.    std::cout << "Hello world!" << std::endl;
   ```

Day 19

Quiz

1. What is the difference between a template and a macro?

   Templates are built into the C++ language and are type-safe. Macros are implemented by the preprocessor and are not type-safe.

2. What is the difference between the parameter in a template and the parameter in a function?

The parameter to the template creates an instance of the template for each type. If you create six template instances, six different classes or functions are created. The parameters to the function change the behavior or data of the function, but only one function is created.

3. What is the difference between a type-specific template friend class and a general template friend class?

The general template friend function creates one function for every type of the parameterized class; the type-specific function creates a type-specific instance for each instance of the parameterized class.

4. Is it possible to provide special behavior for one instance of a template but not for other instances?

Yes, create a specialized function for the particular instance. In addition to creating `Array<t>::SomeFunction()`, also create `Array<int>::SomeFunction()` to change the behavior for integer arrays.

5. How many static variables are created if you put one static member into a template class definition?

One for each instance of the class.

Exercises

1. Create a template based on this `List` class:

```
class List
{
private:

public:
    List():head(0),tail(0),theCount(0) {}
    virtual ~List();

    void insert( int value );
    void append( int value );
    int is_present( int value ) const;
    int is_empty() const { return head == 0; }
    int count() const { return theCount; }
private:
    class ListCell
    {
    public:
        ListCell(int value, ListCell *cell = 0):val(value),next(cell){}
        int val;
        ListCell *next;
    };
```

```
        ListCell *head;
        ListCell *tail;
        int theCount;
};
```

One way to implement this template:

```
template <class Type>
class List
{

public:
        List():head(0),tail(0),theCount(0) { }
        virtual ~List();

        void insert( Type value );
        void append( Type value );
        int is_present( Type value ) const;
        int is_empty() const { return head == 0; }
        int count() const { return theCount; }

private:
        class ListCell
        {
        public:
                ListCell(Type value, ListCell *cell = 0):val(value),next(cell){}
                Type val;
                ListCell *next;
        };

        ListCell *head;
        ListCell *tail;
        int theCount;
};
```

2. Write the implementation for the List class (non-template) version.

```
void List::insert(int value)
{
        ListCell *pt = new ListCell( value, head );

        // this line added to handle tail
        if ( head == 0 ) tail = pt;

        head = pt;
        theCount++;
}

void List::append( int value )
{
        ListCell *pt = new ListCell( value );
        if ( head == 0 )
                head = pt;
```

```
    else
        tail->next = pt;

    tail = pt;
    theCount++;
}

int List::is_present( int value ) const
{
    if ( head == 0 ) return 0;
    if ( head->val == value || tail->val == value )
        return 1;

    ListCell *pt = head->next;
    for (; pt != tail; pt = pt->next)
        if ( pt->val == value )
            return 1;

    return 0;
}
```

3. Write the template version of the implementations.

```
template <class Type>
List<Type>::~List()
{
    ListCell *pt = head;

    while ( pt )
    {
        ListCell *tmp = pt;
        pt = pt->next;
        delete tmp;
    }
    head = tail = 0;
}

template <class Type>
void List<Type>::insert(Type value)
{
    ListCell *pt = new ListCell( value, head );
    assert (pt != 0);

    // this line added to handle tail
    if ( head == 0 ) tail = pt;

    head = pt;
    theCount++;
}

template <class Type>
```

D

```
void List<Type>::append( Type value )
{
    ListCell *pt = new ListCell( value );
    if ( head == 0 )
          head = pt;
    else
          tail->next = pt;

    tail = pt;
    theCount++;
}

template <class Type>
int List<Type>::is_present( Type value ) const
{
    if ( head == 0 ) return 0;
    if ( head->val == value || tail->val == value )
         return 1;

    ListCell *pt = head->next;
    for (; pt != tail; pt = pt->next)
         if ( pt->val == value )
              return 1;

    return 0;
}
```

4. Declare three list objects: a list of strings, a list of Cats and a list of ints.

   ```
   List<String> string_list;
   List<Cat> Cat_List;
   List<int> int_List;
   ```

5. **BUG BUSTERS:** What is wrong with the following code? (Assume the List template is defined and Cat is the class defined earlier in the book.)

   ```
   List<Cat> Cat_List;
   Cat Felix;
   CatList.append( Felix );
   cout << "Felix is " <<
        ( Cat_List.is_present( Felix ) ) ? "" : "not " << "present\n";
   ```

   HINT: (this is tough) What makes Cat different from int?

   Cat doesn't have operator == defined; all operations that compare the values in the List cells, such as is_present, will result in compiler errors. To reduce the chance of this, put copious comments before the template definition stating what operations must be defined for the instantiation to compile.

6. Declare friend operator== for List.

   ```
   friend int operator==( const Type& lhs, const Type& rhs );
   ```

7. Implement friend operator== for List.

```
template <class Type>
int List<Type>::operator==( const Type& lhs, const Type& rhs )
{
    // compare lengths first
    if ( lhs.theCount != rhs.theCount )
        return 0;       // lengths differ

    ListCell *lh = lhs.head;
    ListCell *rh = rhs.head;

    for(; lh != 0; lh = lh.next, rh = rh.next )
        if ( lh.value != rh.value )
            return 0;

    return 1;              // if they don't differ, they must match
}
```

8. Does operator== have the same problem as in Exercise 5?

Yes, because comparing the array involves comparing the elements, operator!= must be defined for the elements as well.

9. Implement a template function for swap, which exchanges two variables.

```
// template swap:
// must have assignment and the copy constructor defined for the Type.
template <class Type>
void swap( Type& lhs, Type& rhs)
{
    Type temp( lhs );
    lhs = rhs;
    rhs = temp;
}
```

Day 20

Quiz

1. What is an exception?

An exception is an object that is created as a result of invoking the keyword throw. It is used to signal an exceptional condition, and is passed up the call stack to the first catch statement that handles its type.

2. What is a try block?

A try block is a set of statements that might generate an exception.

3. What is a catch statement?

A catch statement has a signature of the type of exception it handles. It follows a try block and acts as the receiver of exceptions raised within the try block.

4. What information can an exception contain?

An exception is an object and can contain any information that can be defined within a user-created class.

5. When are exception objects created?

Exception objects are created when you invoke the keyword throw.

6. Should you pass exceptions by value or by reference?

In general, exceptions should be passed by reference. If you don't intend to modify the contents of the exception object, you should pass a const reference.

7. Will a catch statement catch a derived exception if it is looking for the base class?

Yes, if you pass the exception by reference.

8. If two catch statements are used, one for base and one for derived, which should come first?

catch statements are examined in the order they appear in the source code. The first catch statement whose signature matches the exception is used.

9. What does catch(...) mean?

catch(...) will catch any exception of any type.

10. What is a breakpoint?

A breakpoint is a place in the code where the debugger will stop execution.

Exercises

1. Create a try block, a catch statement, and a simple exception.

```cpp
#include <iostream>
using namespace std;
class OutOfMemory {};
int main()
{

    try
    {
        int *myInt = new int;
        if (myInt == 0)
            throw OutOfMemory();
    }
    catch (OutOfMemory)
    {
        cout << "Unable to allocate memory!\n";
    }
return 0;
 }
```

2. Modify the answer from Exercise 1, put data into the exception along with an accessor function, and use it in the `catch` block.

```
#include <iostream>
#include <stdio.h>
#include <string.h>
using namespace std;
class OutOfMemory
{
public:
      OutOfMemory(char *);
      char* GetString() { return itsString; }
private:
      char* itsString;
};

OutOfMemory::OutOfMemory(char * theType)
{
      itsString = new char[80];
      char warning[] = "Out Of Memory! Can't allocate room for: ";
      strncpy(itsString,warning,60);
      strncat(itsString,theType,19);
}

int main()
{

      try
      {
            int *myInt = new int;
            if (myInt == 0)
                  throw OutOfMemory("int");
      }
      catch (OutOfMemory& theException)
      {
            cout << theException.GetString();
      }
return 0;
 }
```

3. Modify the class from Exercise 2 to be a hierarchy of exceptions. Modify the `catch` block to use the derived objects and the base objects.

```
1:    #include <iostream>
2:    using namespace std;
3:    // Abstract exception data type
4:    class Exception
5:    {
6:    public:
7:       Exception(){}
8:       virtual ~Exception(){}
9:       virtual void PrintError() = 0;
```

```
10:     };
11:
12:     // Derived class to handle memory problems.
13:     // Note no allocation of memory in this class!
14:     class OutOfMemory : public Exception
15:     {
16:     public:
17:         OutOfMemory(){}
18:         ~OutOfMemory(){}
19:         virtual void PrintError();
20:     private:
21:     };
22:
23:     void OutOfMemory::PrintError()
24:     {
25:         cout << "Out of Memory!!\n";
26:     }
27:
28:     // Derived class to handle bad numbers
29:     class RangeError : public Exception
30:     {
31:     public:
32:         RangeError(unsigned long number){badNumber = number;}
33:         ~RangeError(){}
34:         virtual void PrintError();
35:         virtual unsigned long GetNumber() { return badNumber; }
36:         virtual void SetNumber(unsigned long number) {badNumber =
➥number;}
37:     private:
38:         unsigned long badNumber;
39:     };
40:
41:     void RangeError::PrintError()
42:     {
43:         cout << "Number out of range. You used " << GetNumber() <<
➥"!!\n";
44:     }
45:
46:     void MyFunction();   // func. prototype
47:
48:     int main()
49:     {
50:         try
51:         {
52:             MyFunction();
53:         }
54:         // Only one catch required, use virtual functions to do the
55:         // right thing.
56:         catch (Exception& theException)
57:         {
58:             theException.PrintError();
```

```
59:        }
60:        return 0;
61:    }
62:
63:    void MyFunction()
64:    {
65:        unsigned int *myInt = new unsigned int;
66:        long testNumber;
67:        if (myInt == 0)
68:            throw OutOfMemory();
69:        cout << "Enter an int: ";
70:        cin >> testNumber;
71:        // this weird test should be replaced by a series
72:        // of tests to complain about bad user input
73:        if (testNumber > 3768 || testNumber < 0)
74:            throw RangeError(testNumber);
75:
76:        *myInt = testNumber;
77:        cout << "Ok. myInt: " << *myInt;
78:        delete myInt;
79:    }
```

4. Modify the program from Exercise 3 to have three levels of function calls.

```
1:     #include <iostream.h>
2:     using namespace std;
3:     // Abstract exception data type
4:     class Exception
5:     {
6:     public:
7:         Exception(){}
8:         virtual ~Exception(){}
9:         virtual void PrintError() = 0;
10:    };
11:
12:    // Derived class to handle memory problems.
13:    // Note no allocation of memory in this class!
14:    class OutOfMemory : public Exception
15:    {
16:    public:
17:        OutOfMemory(){}
18:        ~OutOfMemory(){}
19:        virtual void PrintError();
20:    private:
21:    };
22:
23:    void OutOfMemory::PrintError()
24:    {
25:        cout << "Out of Memory!!\n";
26:    }
27:
28:    // Derived class to handle bad numbers
```

D

```
29:    class RangeError : public Exception
30:    {
31:    public:
32:       RangeError(unsigned long number){badNumber = number;}
33:       ~RangeError(){}
34:       virtual void PrintError();
35:       virtual unsigned long GetNumber() { return badNumber; }
36:       virtual void SetNumber(unsigned long number) {badNumber =
➥number;}
37:    private:
38:       unsigned long badNumber;
39:    };
40:
41:    void RangeError::PrintError()
42:    {
43:       cout << "Number out of range. You used " << GetNumber() <<
➥"!!\n";
44:    }
45:
46:    // func. prototypes
47:    void MyFunction();
48:    unsigned int * FunctionTwo();
49:    void FunctionThree(unsigned int *);
50:
51:    int main()
52:    {
53:       try
54:       {
55:          MyFunction();
56:       }
57:       // Only one catch required, use virtual functions to do the
58:       // right thing.
59:       catch (Exception& theException)
60:       {
61:          theException.PrintError();
62:       }
63:       return 0;
64:    }
65:
66:    unsigned int * FunctionTwo()
67:    {
68:       unsigned int *myInt = new unsigned int;
69:      if (myInt == 0)
70:        throw OutOfMemory();
71:      return myInt;
72:    }
73:
74:    void MyFunction()
75:    {
76:        unsigned int *myInt = FunctionTwo();
77:
```

```
78:          FunctionThree(myInt);
79:          cout << "Ok. myInt: " << *myInt;
80:          delete myInt;
81:     }
82:
83:     void FunctionThree(unsigned int *ptr)
84:     {
85:          long testNumber;
86:          cout << "Enter an int: ";
87:          cin >> testNumber;
88:          // this weird test should be replaced by a series
89:          // of tests to complain about bad user input
90:          if (testNumber > 3768 || testNumber < 0)
91:              throw RangeError(testNumber);
92:          *ptr = testNumber;
93:     }
```

5. **BUG BUSTERS:** What is wrong with the following code?

```
#include "stringc.h"         // our string class

class xOutOfMemory
{
public:
    xOutOfMemory( const String& where ) : location( where ){}
    ~xOutOfMemory(){}
    virtual String where(){ return location };
private:
    String location;
}

main()
{
    try {
        char *var = new char;
        if ( var == 0 )
            throw xOutOfMemory();
    }
    catch( xOutOfMemory& theException )
    {
        cout << "Out of memory at " << theException.location() << "\n";
    }
}
```

In the process of handling an "out of memory" condition, a string object is created by the constructor of xOutOfMemory. This exception can only be raised when the program is out of memory, and so this allocation must fail.

It is possible that trying to create this string will raise the same exception, creating an infinite loop until the program crashes. If this string is really required, you can allocate the space in a static buffer before beginning the program, and then use it as needed when the exception is thrown.

Day 21

Quiz

1. What is an inclusion guard?

   Inclusion guards are used to protect a header file from being included into a program more than once.

2. How do you instruct your compiler to print the contents of the intermediate file showing the effects of the preprocessor?

   This quiz question must be answered by you, depending on the compiler you are using.

3. What is the difference between `#define debug 0` and `#undef debug`?

   `#define debug 0` defines the term debug to equal 0 (zero). Everywhere the word debug is found, the character 0 will be substituted. `#undef debug` removes any definition of `debug`; when the word `debug` is found in the file, it will be left unchanged.

Exercises

1. Write the inclusion guard statements for the header file `STRING.H`.
   ```
   #ifndef STRING_H
   #define STRING_H
   ...
   #endif
   ```

2. Write an `assert()` macro that prints an error message and the file and line number if debug level is 2, that prints a message (without file and line number) if the level is 1, and that does nothing if the level is 0.
   ```
   1:      #include <iostream.h>
   2:      using namespace std;
   3:      #ifndef DEBUG
   4:      #define ASSERT(x)
   5:      #elif DEBUG == 1
   6:      #define ASSERT(x) \
   7:              if (! (x)) \
   8:              { \
   9:                  cout << "ERROR!! Assert " << #x << " failed\n"; \
   10:             }
   11:     #elif DEBUG == 2
   12:     #define ASSERT(x) \
   13:             if (! (x) ) \
   14:             { \
   15:                 cout << "ERROR!! Assert " << #x << " failed\n"; \
   16:                 cout << " on line " << __LINE__  << "\n"; \
   ```

```
17:                         cout << " in file " << __FILE__ << "\n";  \
18:                    }
19:     #endif
```

3. Write a macro DPrint that tests whether DEBUG is defined, and if it is, prints the value passed in as a parameter.

```
#ifndef DEBUG
#define DPRINT(string)
#else
#define DPRINT(STRING) cout << #STRING ;
#endif
```

D

INDEX

Symbols

Other Related Titles

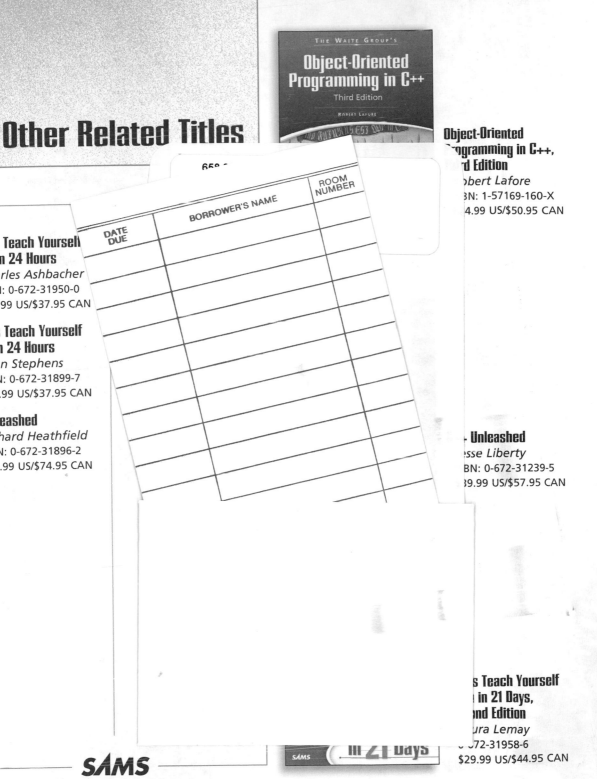

The Waite Group's

Object-Oriented Programming in C++
Third Edition
Robert Lafore

**Object-Oriented
Programming in C++,
Third Edition**
Robert Lafore
ISBN: 1-57169-160-X
$34.99 US/$50.95 CAN

**Sams Teach Yourself
XML in 24 Hours**
Charles Ashbacher
ISBN: 0-672-31950-0
$24.99 US/$37.95 CAN

**Sams Teach Yourself
SQL in 24 Hours**
Ryan Stephens
ISBN: 0-672-31899-7
$24.99 US/$37.95 CAN

C Unleashed
Richard Heathfield
ISBN: 0-672-31896-2
$49.99 US/$74.95 CAN

C++ Unleashed
Jesse Liberty
ISBN: 0-672-31239-5
$39.99 US/$57.95 CAN

**Sams Teach Yourself
C++ in 21 Days,
Second Edition**
Laura Lemay
ISBN: 0-672-31958-6
$29.99 US/$44.95 CAN

DATE DUE	BORROWER'S NAME	ROOM NUMBER

SAMS
www.samspublishing.com

All prices are subject to change.

Operator precedence and associativity

Level	Operators	Evaluation Order
1 (high)	( ) . [ ] -> ::	left-to-right
2	* & ! ~ ++ -- + - sizeof new delete	right-to-left
3	.* -> *	left-to-right
4	* / %	left-to-right
5	+ -	left-to-right
6	<< >>	left-to-right
7	< <= > >=	left-to-right
8	== !=	left-to-right
9	&	left-to-right
10	^	left-to-right
11	|	left-to-right
12	&&	left-to-right
13	||	left-to-right
14	?:	right-to-left
15	= *= /= += -= %= <<= >>= &= ^= |=	right-to-left
16 (low)	,	left-to-right

Operators at the top of the table have higher precedence than operators below. In expressions beginning with arguments in the innermost set of parentheses (if any), programs evaluate operators of higher precedence before evaluating operators of lower precedence.

Unary plus (+) and unary minus (–) are at level 2, and have precedence over arithmetic plus and minus at level 5. The & symbol at level 2 is the address-of operator; the & symbol at level 9 is the bitwise AND operator. The * symbol at level 2 is the pointer-dereference operator; the * symbol at level 4 is the multiplication operator. In the absence of clarifying parentheses, operators on the same level are evaluated according to their left-to-right or right-to-left evaluation order.

Operators that may be overloaded

*	/	+	-	%	^	&	|	~	!	,	=	<	>
<=	>=	++	--	<<	>>	==	!=	&&	||	*=	/=	%=	^=
&=	|=	+=	-=	<<=	>>=	->	->*	[]	()	new	delete		

Operators +, -, *, and & may be overloaded for binary and unary expressions. Operators ., .*, ::, ?:, and sizeof may not be overloaded. In addition, =, (), [], and -> must be implemented as nonstatic member functions.

Visual database components

TDBCheckBox — A data-aware TCheckBox component.

TDBComboBox — A data-aware TComboBox component.

TDBEdit — A data-aware TEdit single-line text entry component.

SSView — A data-aware text-only TGrid component.

TDBImage — A data-aware graphical TImage component.

TDBListBox — A data-aware TListBox component.

TDBLookupCombo — A data-aware TComboBox component with the capability to search a lookup table.

TDBLookupList — A data-aware TListBox component with the capability to search a lookup table.

TDBMemo — A data-aware TMemo multiple-line text-entry component.

TDBNavigator — A sophisticated database browsing and editing tool. This component is to database programming what a remote control is to a video recorder. Users click the control's buttons to move through database records, insert new records, delete records, and perform other navigational operations.

TDBRadioGroup — A data-aware TRadioGroup component.

TDBText — A data-aware read-only text component for displaying database information that you don't want users to be able to edit.

Nonvisual database components

TBatchMove — Performs operations on records and tables, such as updating all records that match a specified argument.

TBlobField — A field of indefinite size of a record in a dataset that consists of an arbitrary set of bytes—typically a graphical image such as a bitmap.

TDatabase — Provides additional database services such as server log-ins and local aliases.

TDataSet — The immediate ancestor of TDBDataSet.

TDataSource — Connects dataset components such as TTable and TQuery with data-aware components such as TDBEdit and TDBMenu. Every database application needs at least one TDataSource object.

TDBDataSet — The direct ancestor of TTable, TQuery, and TStoredProc. Most applications use the derived classes TTable, TQuery, and TStoredProc for dataset access rather than TDBDataSet. However, functions may pass parameters of this type to operate on all types of datasets and the results of queries.

TField — Provides access to fields in a record.

TFieldDef — Defines the structure of physical fields in records. All TField objects do not necessarily have corresponding TFieldDef objects. For example, calculated TField objects have no physical record fields and, therefore, no TFieldDef objects.

TFieldDefs — Holds the TFieldDef objects that define the physical fields in a data set.

TIndexDef — Describes the index of a table.

TIndexDefs — Holds the set of all TIndexDef objects for a table.

TParam — Defines parameters for TQuery and TStoredProc objects.

TParams — Holds all parameters for TQuery and TStoredProc objects.